JOHN W. KENNEDY

    Professor of Economics
    The University of North Carolina at Greensboro

ARTHUR R. OLSEN

    Emeritus Professor of Economics
    Western Illinois University
    Macomb, Illinois

Published by

SOUTH-WESTERN PUBLISHING CO.

Cincinnati   West Chicago, Ill.   Dallas   New Rochelle, N.Y.
Burlingame, Calif.   Brighton, England

EIGHTH EDITION

ECONOMICS
PRINCIPLES AND APPLICATIONS

Copyright © 1972

Philippine Copyright, 1972

by SOUTH-WESTERN PUBLISHING CO.

Cincinnati, Ohio

All Rights Reserved

The text of this publication, or any part thereof, may not be reproduced or transmitted in any form or by any means, electronic or mechanical, including photocopying, recording, storage in an information retrieval system, or otherwise, without the prior written permission of the publisher.

Library of Congress Catalog Card Number: 74-175900

ISBN: 0-538-08420-0

3 4 5 6 7 8 K 7 6 5 4

Printed in the United States of America

Preface

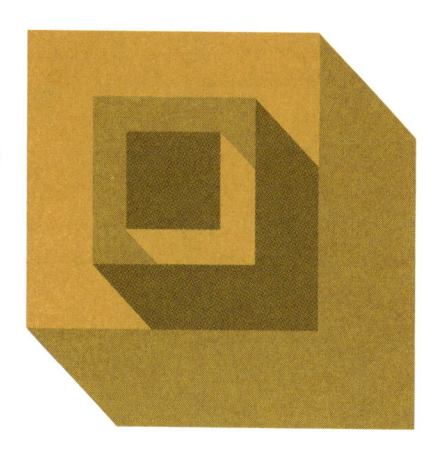

An economic education program that challenges students of the 1970's underlies the design of ECONOMICS — *Principles and Applications*, Eighth Edition, and its supplementary materials. Students of this decade have not only been better taught, but they are also better prepared than their counterparts of a preceding decade. Students of the present day are eager for a viable education and the acquisition of knowledge. Their possession of a greater social sensitivity and awareness has increased their indifference to fragmented, static, and sterile knowledge. Their greater social consciousness seeks challenge in acquiring knowledge that is unified, alive, and dynamic. Consequently, students are searching for an ever-increasing knowledge that is relevant and applicable to the socioeconomic problems that have been created by a seemingly uncontrolled scientific and technological revolution.

The authors have been responsive to providing a program that not only challenges students but also accommodates those with varying degrees of maturity, experience, and interests. The most suitable approach — analytical, descriptive, historical, or institutional — has been used for teaching each economic concept. Effective communication of economic concepts and analytical structure has been simplified without underrating student ability or capacity to learn. Reinforcement of economic understanding has been achieved through the inclusion of innovative repetitive procedures. Relevancy has been continuously recognized; numerous activities have been provided which challenge students to apply their knowledge of economic principles and analytical skills to contemporary socioeconomic problems and issues.

Since economics is a disparate discipline, a knowledge of its structure is basic to economic understanding. Additionally, economics is an integral part of the unity of the social sciences. An integration of these two factors has been achieved in the textbook; the economic discipline's facts, content, and structure have been related to current social phenomena. Topical discussions provide for further integration and relevancy; the components of man's economic activities have been presented as interrelated aspects of his historical, political, and social development.

Features of this eighth edition of *ECONOMICS — Principles and Applications* include:

1. The text emphasizes the basic economic problem faced by all economic societies. The chronological evolution of the American economy and the role that the economic discipline played in shaping the American economic system are presented as a basis for economic understanding. Consequently, the previously acquired knowledge concerning the economic freedom and overall efficiency of the American system provides a requisite basis for the comparative study of other economic systems and international economic interrelationships that ensues in Unit 8.

2. Economic problems have their origin in an existing economic system; moreover, a knowledge of the economic discipline and its analytical tools must precede their use in solving economic problems. Thus, the personal and domestic economic problem discussions have been logically placed in the final unit.

3. As new inclusions, production possibility theory, the economic aspects of ecology, the technological revolution, the effects of population change, and the domestic problems of farm flight and city blight have been added. These are contemporary concerns which have a special appeal to students.

4. The basic economic concepts that are recommended by the National Task Force on Economic Education are introduced in appropriate chapters. Revised treatment, utilizing recent statistical data and content, is reflected throughout the subject matter in its entirety.

5. The basic discussions of economic institutions, policies, and practices are retained.

    An overview of our economic system emphasizes the roles of freedom and specialization in resource utilization.
    The chapters on production discuss the role of the business organization, the revised structure of cooperatives, the importance of capital formation, and the nature of contemporary production problems.

The discussions on marginal productivity, cost push inflation, the governmental guideposts, and price determination provide depth in the analysis of income distribution.

The chapters on money and credit indicate the recent changes in money issuance and credit regulations.

The increased and rapid expansion of governmental involvement in health, education, and welfare is highlighted as a factor affecting individual welfare.

6. To whet the student's curiosity and interest, a few questions are raised at the beginning of each chapter.

7. Illustrative materials are used to stimulate interest. Graphic and photographic illustrations add impact and meaning to factual data and discussion of principles.

8. The essence and significance of the topics in each chapter are presented in summary form at the end of each chapter. A list of new terms reemphasizes the significant economic concepts.

9. Appropriate end-of-chapter questions and exercises provide for an evaluation and a reinforcement of student learning.

10. At the end of the book there is a list of suggested student readings for each of the units in the book and a comprehensive glossary of terms.

Supplementary materials for use with the textbook include a study guide, a series of tests, a game series, a kit of transparencies, and a teacher's manual. The use of these materials provides additional possibilities for learning and teaching.

The authors believe that the design and features of this program will provide the challenges and promote the realization of the aims of economic education.

We take this opportunity to thank the many students, teachers, reviewers, and businessmen whose criticisms and suggestions have contributed to this edition. A number of business firms, government agencies, and nonprofit institutions provided photographic or graphic materials. To all these we express our thanks.

JOHN W. KENNEDY
ARTHUR R. OLSEN

Contents

Unit 1   OUR ECONOMIC SYSTEM

Chapter 1 The Meaning and Importance of Economics	3
Chapter 2 Our Economic System and Its Evolution	21
Chapter 3 Freedom and Specialization in Our Economy	41

Unit 2   PRODUCTION OF GOODS AND SERVICES

Chapter 4 Goods, Income, and Production	61
Chapter 5 Marketing: From Producers to Consumers	79
Chapter 6 Organizing and Managing Business	95
Chapter 7 Corporations and Cooperatives	109
Chapter 8 Some Problems of Modern Production	131

Unit 3   PRICE DETERMINATION

Chapter 9 Competition and Prices	151
Chapter 10 Monopoly and Prices	169
Chapter 11 Government Control of Prices	181
Chapter 12 Prices and the Value of Money	197

Unit 4   DISTRIBUTION OF NATIONAL INCOME

Chapter 13 Sharing the National Income	213
Chapter 14 Wages for Labor	223
Chapter 15 Rent for Land	241
Chapter 16 Interest for Capital	253
Chapter 17 Profits for Enterprisers	265
Chapter 18 Labor Unions and Employers	274

Unit 5 — MONEY, CREDIT, AND BANKING

Chapter 19 Money and Its Use — 297
Chapter 20 Credit and Its Use — 315
Chapter 21 Money, Credit, and Banking — 327

Unit 6 — NATIONAL INCOME — GROWTH AND STABILITY

Chapter 22 Measures of Our National Production and Income — 349
Chapter 23 Business Cycles and Economic Growth — 365

Unit 7 — GOVERNMENT FINANCE AND TAXATION

Chapter 24 Government, Taxes, and the Public Debt — 385
Chapter 25 Our Tax System — 404

Unit 8 — INTERNATIONAL ECONOMIC PROBLEMS

Chapter 26 Buying and Selling Between Nations — 419
Chapter 27 Making Payments Between Nations — 437
Chapter 28 Nations With Other Economic Systems — 453
Chapter 29 Our Interest in the Underdeveloped Nations — 473

Unit 9 — PERSONAL AND DOMESTIC ECONOMIC PROBLEMS

Chapter 30 Your Work — 491
Chapter 31 Planning and Spending — 507
Chapter 32 Private Insurance and Social Security — 525
Chapter 33 Saving and Investing — 543
Chapter 34 Domestic Economic Problems — 555

APPENDIXES

Part A Bibliography: Text and Other References for Advanced Reading and Study — 575
Part B Glossary — 583

INDEX — 601

To the Student

The pony express rider in 1860 found his challenge in confronting a series of unusual and different experiences. His preparation involved acquiring new knowledge, performing new skills, and changing his attitude toward the new and unknown environment of a western wilderness. In a similar way, numerous socioeconomic issues confront today's students and offer you the challenge of their resolution. Preparation is also necessary for success in meeting this challenge.

The resolution of socioeconomic problems will involve you in the making of economic decisions. Intelligent decision making requires that you learn new facts, develop new skills, and reevaluate your attitudes prior to making choices among economic alternatives. Just as communication can be achieved by a pony express, telegraph lines, or space relay satellites, economic performance can be achieved by use of capitalism, socialism, or communism. Yet the speed and distance of their performance will differ, depending upon the choice of the system that is used. What system will enable one to reach the ultimate goal of greater economic satisfactions for all? What economic system preserves the greatest amount of freedom for the individual? What economic skills can one acquire which will prove useful for analysis and application? The answers to these questions can be determined more accurately through your own systematic study of economics and through your application of what you have learned to current conditions and problems. Here are some suggestions that can be of great help to you.

At the beginning of each chapter are a few questions designed to alert you to the basic principles, issues, and problems presented in the chapter. Read the entire chapter and then the summary for the overall idea of what is included. Make a special effort to understand the definitions of new terms.

Different styles of type and headings are used to make it simpler for you to outline each chapter. Review the outline of the chapter to see the relationship of each part to the central idea of the chapter. For the more difficult parts, reread them and study them more intensively.

As special aids for learning, the textbook discussion and summary in each chapter are followed by four types of activities:

New Terms. Define each term in the list in your own words. Check your definitions with the glossary of terms or with the definition given in the chapter.

Questions on the Chapter. These questions are based directly on the textbook discussion. Try to answer each question and then compare your answer with the textbook presentation to make sure that you accurately expressed its economic meaning.

Applying Your Economic Understanding. These questions and problems use life situations to which you should apply economic principles and facts to arrive at your answer or to take the action required.

Challenges to Economic Competence. These activities are related to economic ideas and principles emphasized in the chapter. Your instructor will probably assign them for presentation as special reports to the class or will perhaps suggest them for students wishing extra credit.

In the appendix helpful readings are suggested to increase your understanding of each unit. These books, magazines, and pamphlets supplement the discussion in the text. Read as many of these references as your time permits.

If you are using the study guide that correlates with this textbook, you will find for each chapter (1) a set of questions and exercises that are based on the textbook discussion, and (2) one or more problems or exercises that give you additional opportunities to apply what you have learned.

You are now ready to begin your journey toward the goal of fuller economic understanding. Your textbook and its supplementary materials serve as guides for reaching that destination. But ultimate success in reaching that objective can be achieved only through use of your own efforts, skills, and good judgment.

Unit 1

Our Economic System

Chapter 1 The Meaning and Importance of Economics
Chapter 2 Our Economic System and Its Evolution
Chapter 3 Freedom and Specialization in Our Economy

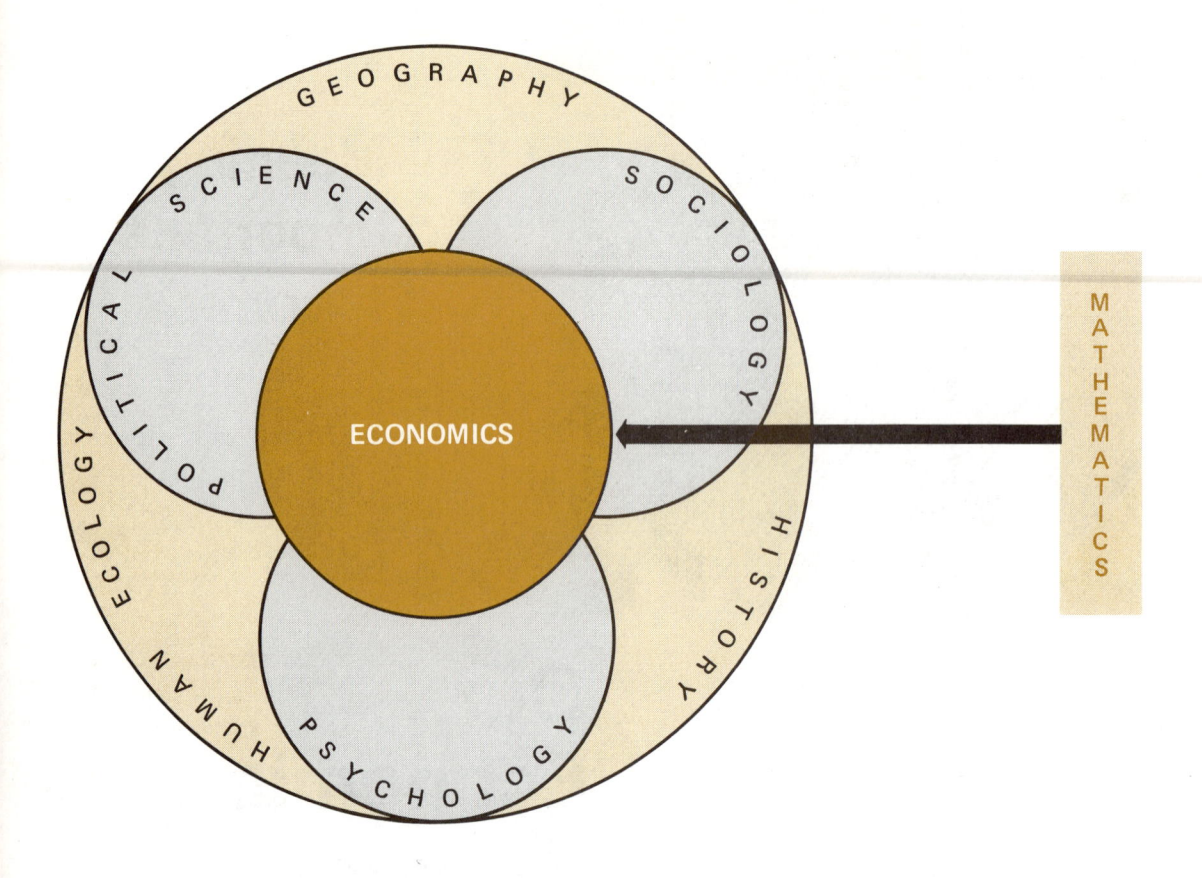

Economics is the social science that deals with matters related to the efforts of human beings to make use of resources for the production and the consumption of want-satisfying goods and services. Economics is sometimes classified with psychology, sociology, and political science as a behavioral science. As a science, it uses mathematics — the science of figures and forms with their sizes and relationships — as a tool for analysis. The other social sciences of geography, history, and human ecology are also interrelated with economics.

Chapter 1

The Meaning and Importance of Economics

What is economics?
Why should I study economics?
Is the study of economics interesting?

These questions probably occur to most students as they begin the study of economics. Therefore, you, too, are likely to be wondering what the subject is about, why it is important, and whether you are going to find the study of economics interesting.

One of the major national objectives of the founding fathers of the United States was to provide for the protection and promotion of the economic rights of the American people. This concern for the well-being of citizens in their efforts to make a living was stated in the Preamble to the Constitution by the words "secure the blessings of liberty to ourselves and our posterity." Many of the attempts to reach this goal are largely of an economic nature. In the years that have elapsed since the Constitution was adopted, the American people have made vast strides toward the attainment of that goal. And the "American way of life" became a slogan to indicate that free men could prove to be effective producers.

Other peoples, impressed by our example, have sought a change in their mode of living. Some of these peoples, eager for immediate results, have substituted more direct processes for our democratic procedures and — at the loss of individual freedom — have purchased a rapid expansion of technological and military power.

Now, in this decade, our leadership is being challenged. Will the American way of living and making a living survive? The answer will depend upon our unity as we apply ourselves to the solution of the basic economic problem.

THE MEANING OF ECONOMICS

Economics is the social science that deals with matters related to the efforts of human beings to make use of resources for the production and the consumption of want-satisfying goods and services. It is a social science since it involves interactions among members in a society. Because economics deals largely with problems created by man's activities, it is sometimes classified with psychology, sociology, and political science as a behavioral science. Economic behavior may be personal, such as in individual consumer activity, or impersonal, such as in international trade activity.

As a science, economics is concerned with the cause-and-effect relations of factors that produce economic conditions and problems. Understanding these cause-and-effect relations enables us to do something about solving such problems. The knowledge of economic facts and theories may enable us to propose logical solutions to economic problems. The use of economic knowledge to solve problems may be referred to as *applied economics*. As we shall see, economics is a field of study that is concerned with man's efforts to live and improve his way of life.

THE BASIC ECONOMIC PROBLEM AFFECTS OUR LIVES

All of us are involved in our own efforts and the efforts of others for survival. Moreover, the basic economic problem affects directly or indirectly every human interest. To understand the scope and nature of the basic economic problem, it is helpful to begin with a recognition of two simple facts. These facts are:

1. We have many needs and wants, and the number of our wants is almost unlimited.

2. The supply of most of the things we want is limited because of the relative scarcity of economic resources. The basic *economic problem* can be defined as the selection of the process by which society can best satisfy its unlimited wants within the limits of relatively scarce productive resources.

OUR ECONOMIC WANTS AND THE ECONOMIC PROBLEM

The basis for our many and almost unlimited wants are needs. A *need* is a state of tension or stress within ourselves. Such a state of tension arises because the normal condition of the body has been disturbed. For example, it is normal for the cells in the body to be undergoing a continuous process of metabolism, breaking down and rebuilding. When the supply of nourishing elements is insufficient, a state of tension results that we call "hunger." Early in life we learned that by eating food the feeling of hunger can be relieved, and in this way we experience pleasure and satisfaction.

Practically speaking, we may say that our needs are of two kinds: (a) organic, or physical needs, and (b) personality, or psychological needs.

Organic or physical needs. Our basic *organic needs* are those that relate to our physical health and well-being. These include the need for food, fresh air, water, rest, sleep, proper body temperature, and others.

Personality or psychological needs. It has been said that "man does not live by bread alone." Although food, shelter, and clothing may be necessary for survival, living is more than mere existence. We have needs, known as *personality needs*, that cannot be relieved or satisfied merely by the use or consumption of material goods. Sometimes these needs are called "social needs," or needs that lead to wants or wishes for (1) affection, (2) recognition or social approval, (3) a feeling of achievement, (4) independence or freedom to make choices, (5) a feeling of security, and (6) a variety of experiences. The satisfaction of such needs is often as necessary to our happiness as is the satisfaction of our organic needs.

Organic and personality needs exert great influence on our lives and determine our wants. A *want* is a desire for something that we feel will give us pleasure or satisfaction. For example, if one is thirsty, he wants a

Illus. 1-1. A want is a desire for something that we feel will give us pleasure or satisfaction.

U.S.D.A. Photograph by Purdy

drink of water; if he is hungry, he wants food; if he is bored, he wants a variety of experiences. Our wants are of two kinds: (a) noneconomic wants, and (b) economic wants.

Noneconomic wants. These wants might be illustrated by the desire for attention satisfied by the mother's kiss on the bruised knee of her child; the wish for approval satisfied by a word of praise from a father to his son who had achieved scholastic honors; or one's own craving for achievement satisfied by the successful completion of a job. *Noneconomic wants* are those that are satisfied without monetary or economic expenditure.

Economic wants. In contrast to the wants given above are wants only too familiar to all of us — wants for material goods and services that require the expenditure of money or effort if they are to be satisfied. Examples are the desire for an automobile, for one's own telephone, for a new suit, and for color TV. Most of us have an endless list of economic wants.

In the study of economics, we shall be especially concerned with *economic wants* because they are measurable in money value, there is no limit to the number of things wanted by all the people, and these wants can be satisfied by the use of scarce resources.

OUR ECONOMIC RESOURCES AND THE ECONOMIC PROBLEM

Ordinarily — but not always — there is enough sunshine and fresh air for all of us. Therefore, in most cases, getting all we need of these things does not present a problem. However, most of the things we need to satisfy our individual wants are scarce relative to the wants of all the people. These things, economic goods and services, are produced by the utilization of resources. Resources are of three types: (a) natural resources or land, (b) labor resources, and (c) capital resources.

Natural resources or land. The gifts of nature, materials not made by man, are termed *natural resources*. These resources are not equally distributed by nature throughout the world. The United States and some other nations may have great quantities of natural resources in the form of fertile land and a climate suitable for the production of wheat, corn, and other agricultural products. However, these same nations may lack suitable land and climate for producing cacao, natural rubber, or coffee. The amounts of minerals, metals, forests, fresh water, and other forms of natural resources are gifts of nature and are not always in proportion to the population of the area. Thus, for all natural resources for any given society there is a scarcity problem.

Illus. 1-2. These things, economic goods and services, are produced by the utilization of resources. Resources are of three types: (a) natural resources or land, (b) labor resources, and (c) capital resources.

Labor resources. The production of all economic goods and services requires the application of either physical or mental labor or both. *Labor resources* are the quantity and quality of human effort available for use in production in a society. The scarcity of labor resources may arise because of an insufficient number of workers, or because of a lack of workers with the kinds of skills and abilities necessary to perform specific kinds of work. Although a nation may have a part of its labor force unemployed, it may also encourage the immigration of persons to fill certain kinds of jobs for which its own labor force cannot or will not compete. Your daily newspaper may show help-wanted advertisements for kinds of jobs that your local unemployed are not qualified to perform.

As an example of labor scarcity, industries and educational institutions may bid for the services of the same mathematician, scientist, or artist. The unsuccessful bidders are then limited in their production of specific economic goods and services for society. Thus, for any single society, labor resources required to satisfy all wants are usually scarce.

Capital resources. *Capital resources* are goods which are used to produce other economic goods. The production of an automobile requires buildings, machinery, office equipment, materials, and other resources.

The production of railroad transportation requires rails, railroad cars, engines or locomotives, switching towers, depots, as well as other capital resources. All these tools, machines, and other equipment for use in production are called *capital*.

Illus. 1-3. The production of railroad transportation requires rails, railroad cars, engines or locomotives, switching towers, depots, as well as other capital resources.

Southern Railway System

Capital formation means the saving of funds or goods in the present for use in producing goods in the future. Capital formation provides the investment in the present economy that makes possible future production and the growth thereof. As an example, when the American Indians harvested corn, they knew that, regardless of their appetites, some of the corn had to be saved for next year's planting. Unless this saving was made and invested as seed corn, there could be no corn the next year. An increase in current-year saving of seed corn — successfully planted, cultivated, and harvested the next year — would result in a greater corn crop, a typical form of economic growth.

The value of invested capital is often expressed in money amounts, or as *capital funds*. Citizens of countries where incomes are higher — such as the United States — are able to save more for direct investment in their own businesses or for use as capital funds by other businesses. In economically developing countries, lower incomes tend to limit the savings of citizens; this results in less availability of capital funds for production and economic growth. The immensity of capital funds invested in the

United States is a major contributing factor in the achievement of a high level of living.

It is also necessary to understand that through taxation and borrowing part of our capital resources has originated through governmental action in the form of "forced saving" or investment. Our public school facilities, our courthouses, our defense sites, our post offices, our fire and police stations, and similar governmental forms of capital compete with each other and with nongovernmental capital users for the savings and the investments of our people. Thus, capital to provide all of society's wants is scarce.

Since most of the economic goods and services which we desire to satisfy our wants are produced through various combinations of scarce land, scarce labor, and scarce capital, choices must be made as to what goods and services will be produced for society's use. The varied possibilities for alternative uses of scarce resources raise some major economic questions.

THE ECONOMIC PROBLEM RAISES SOME MAJOR ECONOMIC QUESTIONS

The American society, as well as each society of the past, the present, and the future, has answered or must respond to some major economic questions. Although the answers may differ, depending upon a group's size, its location, its membership, and its basic beliefs, the major economic questions are the same for each society. These universal and fundamental questions are:

1. What economic goods and services shall be produced and how many shall be produced?
2. How shall the economic goods and services be produced?
3. How shall the economic goods and services be distributed?

(1) The what and the how many of production. In a free-enterprise system, such as ours, people using spending power express their desires for the kinds and quantities of goods that they want. This consumer demand influences private producers, individuals and groups who have hopes of making a profit from production activity. These free-enterprise producers supply most of the goods that consumers demand. Therefore, market prices which are influenced by both consumer demand and producer supply help to provide the signals as to the kinds and quantities of goods to be produced and consumed.

Not all demand is for individual use. There is also demand for economic goods and services that are public in nature; this demand is for

Illus. 1-4. There is also demand for economic goods and services that are public in nature; this demand is for public or social services.

U.S. Post Office Department

public or social services. These economic goods and services, such as national defense, police protection, and public education, are produced by group action through legislation enacted by the elected representatives of the people or through direct referendums, such as bond issue elections.

(2) The how of production. Here in the United States there are geographical areas with certain natural resources that are favorable to the production of goods of one kind or another, including agricultural, mining, and manufactured products. There are several hundred thousand factories of one kind or another and millions of farms in the United States which use varied combinations of resources and technology to produce goods. The production of marketing services to get these goods to consumers is equally vital.

The labor force available to accomplish production now exceeds 85 million persons. Some people work on farms, some in factories, some in stores, others in banks; some practice law, medicine, or other professions; and so on. Through specialization in work, production is a form of cooperative endeavor.

As a rule, enterprisers own some or all of the money or capital needed to initiate and to carry on production. In some cases, however, it might be possible for one to borrow most of the money needed, hire the labor, and rent the land needed without putting much of his funds into the business at all. In such a case he would have to repay the borrowed money, pay his employees from the income of the business, and pay his rent. If the income from the business was more than the amounts needed for these purposes, he would have a profit. If not, he would just break even, or he would suffer a loss.

In the area of governmental production, the how of production may vary depending on the service to be provided. Much of the capital equipment, such as weapons for defense or trucks for a postal department, is produced by private industry. However, defense personnel or postal personnel may be directly employed by the governmental agency involved in the production process.

Basic to the "how" question of production is modern technology. Business will seek out the most economically efficient means of production in order to reduce costs and increase profits. This determines how production is carried out.

(3) Production for whom. In a free economy, persons with spendable incomes, either in the form of money or credit, decide to whom most economic goods will go. Their offers to buy or refusals to buy in the free market decide who will get what. In times of emergency, group decisions limit or deprive the individual of certain items he wishes or can afford so that resources — for total defense, as an example — can be used for the protection of all. Where persons are not in possession of spendable income — certain elderly persons or kinless orphans — government may either transfer income to them directly or bid for goods and services in the free market and supply these to such persons through public and charitable institutions.

THE ECONOMIC PROBLEM INVOLVES ECONOMIC ACTIVITIES

Attempting to solve the economic problem in the modern world, especially in advanced industrial nations, is a highly complex process. To attempt to provide for the satisfactions of the wants of a population exceeding 200 million persons in this country is a tremendous undertaking. In one way or another the following activities must be performed:

1. Production, or producing goods and services.
2. Distribution, or distributing incomes to individuals and families.
3. Exchange, or exchanging what is produced.
4. Consumption, or using goods and services.

(1) Production. *Production* is the creation of utility, or want-satisfying power in goods or services. The vast size and the complexity of our economic system, the changes in the population's wants, the methods of merchandising, and other factors constantly present problems of production that tax the ingenuity of producers. The inputs of land, labor, and capital are relatively scarce and are constantly changing as their use is coordinated to meet ever-changing demand. As one example, when new freeways are constructed, new businesses develop along these routes; older businesses on the abandoned routes are affected and may also be abandoned. As another example, the enterpriser opening a pizza hut requires kitchen help and equipment that differ from the requisites of a business that will sell hamburgers, or chili, or chitlins.

Those who undertake production for the market assume a number of responsibilities. They must provide the funds needed to buy, build, or rent quarters for a factory or other productive establishment; set up a working organization; adopt policies; and manage the business. After goods have been produced, they must be placed in the right marketing channels so that they will find their way to those who want them. If those who have to make these decisions have good judgment and luck is with them, they will be able to make a profit as a reward for the risks they have assumed. Otherwise, they suffer financial loss.

(2) Distribution. The economic activity of *distribution* helps to determine the ownership of wealth and how the income of a society is shared among its people. Since the production of practically all the goods in the nation is the result of a vast cooperative undertaking, the problem of sharing these goods is very important. We do not undertake to divide these goods on a per capita basis. Rather, the money income that arises in connection with the production of goods and services is distributed among all those who take part in production.

Illus. 1-5. Those who undertake production for the market assume a number of responsibilities.

Bureau of the Census

Not all of those engaged in production contribute labor. Some furnish capital in the form of money, machines, and tools; others furnish land; and still others operate businesses with the hope of getting a profit after payments have been made for the use of labor, capital, and land.

How shall money incomes be allotted? As we shall see later, the incomes of individuals are determined for the most part by the market prices for the services of labor, land, and capital used in production. As we have said, those who own business establishments hope to get profits as a reward for assuming business risks.

Are incomes distributed fairly? This question often results in arguments. Some disagreements between workers and employers over the wages of the workers result in lengthy disputes and strikes. In addition, we have tax laws that redistribute part of the wealth and the incomes of individuals as well as the incomes of corporations. This is done by levying a higher tax rate on large incomes than on small incomes or by tax levies on the wealth of estates. Thus, problems arise because of varying opinions as to how incomes are — or should be — distributed among those who help to produce the goods and services needed for the satisfaction of wants.

(3) Exchange. The giving up of a good or service for something else of value is an *exchange*. In a few circumstances, the exchange function may be performed in the direct acquisition of a good or service. Some tenant farmers work for a share of the crop; some persons swap or barter one article for another. The President of the United States has the use of an official house as part payment for his services while he serves as the chief executive. In most circumstances, however, people exchange their own resources of land, labor, and capital for money or credit. The money or credit received in exchange can be spent in the marketplace to satisfy personal wants. In other words, money and credit are vital elements in exchange activity.

Among the problems of exchange are a few predominant ones such as: the availability of money and credit to meet our economic needs, the velocity of money and credit, the roles of government and the banking system in the area of exchange activity, and the fluctuations in the value of money or in its purchasing power. Each of these can expand or curtail our exchange actions. Conditions of inflation, deflation, "good times," and depression relate to the exchange activity.

(4) Consumption. Although all individuals do not necessarily participate in the three previously stated economic activities, everyone participates in the consumption function from the "cradle to the grave." Sheer basic

Illus. 1-6. It has become necessary for the federal government to impose penalties for misbranding and other forms of misrepresentation of merchandise.

survival requires the consumption of necessities. *Consumption* is the use of economic goods and services to satisfy personal wants.

Some consumption problems are self-solved, like the making of wise choices when buying goods with present or anticipated income. By and large, our competitive system provides the consumers with protection against the sale of goods that do not measure up to the quality represented by the sellers. But experience has shown that some manufacturers and merchants will misrepresent their goods and cheat buyers if they can. For this reason it has become necessary for the federal government, as well as the state governments, to enact laws to control business in some ways and to impose penalties for misbranding and other forms of misrepresentation.

SATISFYING WANTS IN DIFFERENT SOCIETIES

All societies engage in the four areas of economic activities. In the world today, however, there are major differences between "planned" and "unplanned" economic societies in the activities of economic living. In some countries — Russia, for example — most basic decisions concerning the economic problem are made by representatives of the central government. The central government is controlled by the Communist Party which is a small minority of the total Russian population. In an unplanned or a free-enterprise society, the majority of economic decisions is made by the majority of the population — free citizens who make free choices.

HOW TO STUDY ECONOMICS

The field of economics is broad and complex. In order to get the most benefit from your study of the subject, you must (1) learn certain facts, (2) understand certain economic principles, or "laws," and (3) practice solving economic problems by logical reasoning. For example, if we undertake to find the solution to the economic problem in a society, our method should be to look for certain facts about the matter, and then try to discover the cause-and-effect relationships between these facts. By this method we may be able to see why a problem exists and perhaps to devise a correct solution to it.

This study method can be illustrated by means of the accompanying figure. It is called a *production possibility curve* since it shows possible units of product depending upon how resources are used. Sometimes it is also called a transformation curve; it shows resources transformed into product. With full employment of resources, production of one product or a combination of both products is possible at any point along the diagonal (GA) or the curve (GA).

The figure is based upon certain facts about a primitive tribe. This tribe has no tools or capital. It lives in an area where food can be gathered

PRODUCTION POSSIBILITIES FOR A PRIMITIVE TRIBE

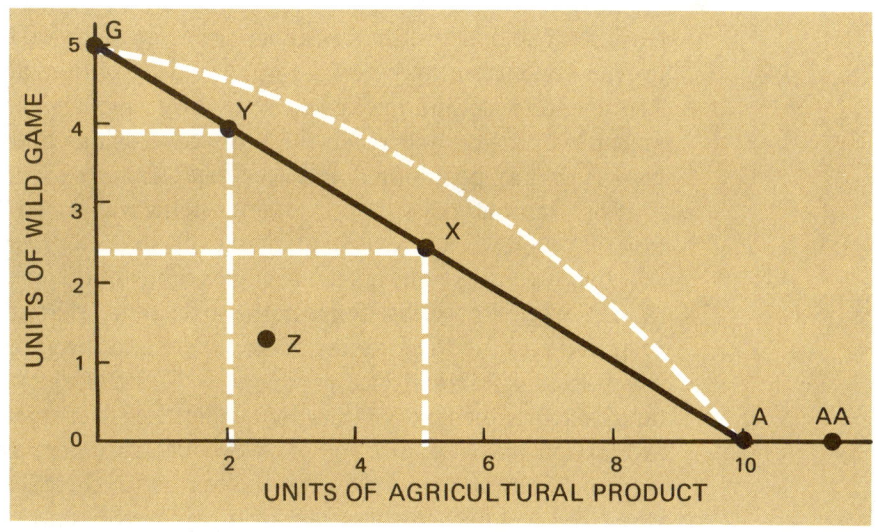

Figure 1-1.

and where wild game is available through hunting. It is assumed that each tribal worker is equal to each other worker in his skills of both gathering and hunting. The tribal economic problem involves its limited resources for the satisfaction of its unlimited wants. The scarcity necessitates the making of economic choices.

If all the workers use the day for gathering, they can produce 10 units (point A) of agricultural product; but they would not be hunting and the wild game production would be zero (0) units. If all the workers use the day for hunting, they can produce 5 units (point G) of wild game; but they would not be gathering, and the agricultural product would be zero units. If half of the workers hunt and the other half gather, the tribe can produce daily 2½ units of wild game and 5 units (point X) of agricultural product. Can you explain the result if the tribe chooses to produce at point Y? Would the tribe at point Y be showing a stronger preference for wild game at the cost of having less agricultural product?

Let us assume that half of the tribe's workers rebel; they refuse to work. Would point Z illustrate a possibility of the tribal production under this condition? Does less than full employment of resources result in less tribal product than would be possible under full employment?

The method or process which an economist uses to formulate a theory is known as the *scientific method*, which is important to the economist as a tool with which to apply theory to economic situations. The economist makes a statement about an economic idea which he believes is valid or true. Then he gathers all the information, called "data," that he can find about his idea. He checks and rechecks the validity of this data. He organizes the valid data in order to reach a reasoned and accurate conclusion. The conclusion may either prove or disprove his statement. His proven conclusion may now be published by him as an *economic theory*. The scientific method may give rise to economic law. If other economists repeat his method and reach the same conclusions about the theory, this new truth may be adopted and accepted as an *economic law*.

For example, the tribal production data was based upon the assumption that each worker was equal in all skills to each other worker. Suppose that the dissenting workers made some claims that workers were not equal to each other in all skills. Some gatherers claimed that other gatherers, who preferred hunting to gathering, teased them and the gatherers argued back, which lessened agricultural production. Some workers, who preferred to hunt, daydreamed about hunting while they were gathering; gathering production was reduced. Some workers, who were good at gathering, were not able to keep up during the hunt with the pace of some workers who liked to hunt; this lessened wild game production.

Would a new economic labor employment arrangement increase production? Suppose we let those hunt who prefer to hunt and seem best suited for hunting. We will let those gather who prefer to gather and seem best suited for that type of work. If by using this new arrangement the production possibility changes and becomes the dotted sloping curve rather than the straight diagonal line, has production possibility increased? Can an economic theory be worded based on our logic? Thinking as an economist, we have just worked out a theory; specialization of labor leads to increased productivity.

Our discussion of scarcity was at one time a theory about scarcity; however scarcity has become so universal, as a theory, that it has been restated as the law of scarcity.

IS ECONOMICS IMPORTANT?

There are those who assert that "the best things in life are free." At the same time, in the pursuit of our noneconomic interests and goals, we frequently encounter problems of an economic nature. Our spiritual life is furthered by organized church activities which require the expenditure of large sums of money. The getting of a liberal education which helps an individual to develop his potentialities requires an educational system with annual national expenditures of billions of dollars. The establishment of a home with all that it means to the members of a family is determined in large measure by economic considerations. Likewise, the extent to which we can enjoy freedom is affected by the conditions that relate to the ways by which we make a living.

Most of the political questions in our state and nation are primarily economic in origin. The communist and the noncommunist worlds result from differences of opinion as to matters relating to the processes of economic problem solving. Our well-being in the United States today is in large measure determined by economic conditions in the rest of the world. As was stated before, our very way of life is being challenged at present, and our survival depends largely upon our ability to solve economic problems at home and upon our help abroad.

WILL THE STUDY PROVE INTERESTING?

Everyone who wishes to be an informed and effective citizen must recognize that social and political issues usually arise from or are closely related to economic problems. Such issues as federal aid to education, changes in many laws, government spending, and aid to certain nations are good examples. Personal progress and success in life involve, to a great extent, dealing successfully with personal economic problems.

It is logical to conclude, then, that if you want to be an effective citizen and a successful person, you will be interested in understanding the economic facts and principles with which you will have to deal. The study of economics opens up new and fascinating frontiers for investigation.

SUMMARY

Economics is the social science that deals with man's efforts to make use of relatively limited resources to satisfy, through production and consumption, his unlimited wants for goods and services. The basic economic problem is caused by the conflict of: (1) demand for the satisfaction of unlimited wants, and (2) limits to a society's resources for fulfilling all the demands.

Our wants arise from both organic and personality or psychological needs. Wants are of two kinds, noneconomic wants and economic wants; the latter type involves monetary or economic costs. Economic wants are satisfied through the production of economic goods which require the use of resources.

Nature supplies us with natural resources from which material goods can be made, but the making of such goods requires effort. Human effort to produce goods is the labor resource. Capital, or man-made goods used to produce other goods, is also a resource. The saving of capital for capital formation and the investment of capital funds affect a society's economic growth. The amount of capital resources in a society determines, in a large measure, its level of living, and vice versa. The relative scarcity of all these resources is a part of the economic problem.

The economic problem raises three universal questions. These are concerned with the what and how much, the how, and the for whom of production. In response to these questions, people engage in four kinds of economic activities: (1) production concerns creating goods and services; (2) distribution concerns the ownership of wealth and how incomes are allocated or shared; (3) exchange, or exchanging what is produced, concerns the money and credit factors of economics; and (4) consumption concerns the use of goods and services to satisfy our personal wants. Satisfying wants requires different methods in a planned economy from those applied in the unplanned economies.

The economist develops economic theory, in large part, by using the scientific method. The application of economic theory is the basis for much of our economic activity today.

A glance at the table of contents of this book will give you a more detailed idea of the scope of economics. The study of economics broadens one's understanding and helps one to be a more effective citizen because it explains the origin of many of the social and personal problems that arise from our efforts to make a living.

NEW TERMS

applied economics
capital
capital formation

capital funds
capital resources
consumption

Ch. 1 THE MEANING AND IMPORTANCE OF ECONOMICS

distribution
economic law
economic problem
economics
economic theory
economic wants
exchange
labor resources
natural resources

need
noneconomic wants
organic needs
personality needs
production
production possibility curve
scientific method
want

QUESTIONS ON THE CHAPTER

1. How was the plan of the founding fathers of the United States related to economic goals?
2. What is "economics"? Is economics a science? Why is it called a "social" science? A "behavioral" science?
3. What two simple facts explain why making a living requires effort?
4. What is the "basic economic problem"?
5. What are the meanings of the terms "needs" and "wants"?
6. What do the terms "organic" and "personality" needs imply? Give an example to illustrate each term.
7. What is the distinction between "noneconomic" and "economic" wants?
8. Why is work or effort by someone required to obtain most of the things that we want? Would we be happier if this were not true?
9. What are three types of resources? What do they have in common?
10. What is capital formation, and why is it important?
11. What is the function of saving in an economic system?
12. How is society forced to save?
13. What are the major economic questions for any society?
14. What four basic economic activities are involved in attempting to solve the economic problem? Define each activity.
15. What difference is there in the way planned and unplanned societies go about attempting to solve the economic problem?
16. What is a production possibility curve?

APPLYING YOUR ECONOMIC UNDERSTANDING

1. Locate a copy of the Constitution of the United States. Review Article 1, Section 8. How does this relate to the authors' statement that an objective of the founding fathers was to protect and promote the economic rights of the American people?
2. Refer to the table of contents and state which unit discusses personal or individual consumer economics. List the major areas of personal economics that the unit covers.

3. Turn to the table of contents and examine Unit 6. Is this unit a good example of impersonal or national economics? Why or why not?
4. Check the figures on the economic classes of imports to the United States in the latest edition of the *World Almanac*. How do the data relate to the idea that the satisfaction of our wants is limited because of scarcity?
5. Is it possible for certain economic wants to relate to both organic and personality needs? Illustrate your answer.
6. How would a bottle of catsup illustrate the economic concept that a combination of resources may be necessary for the production of a good?
7. List some of the major types of communication media and discuss how each type is related to economic affairs.
8. In the area of exchange activity, what might the following persons have in common: a state governor, a prison warden, an ocean liner captain, an ambassador to a foreign nation?
9. Using the chapter's graph of production possibilities for a primitive tribe, can you answer the following questions? (a) What quantities of production are available at point (Y)? (b) What quantities of production are available at point (Z)? (c) With specialization of labor, fully employed, and the choice of 2½ units of wild game, how many units of agricultural product would be available? (d) If the tribe were able to purchase bushel baskets somewhere and used them as capital for gathering, how would this action relate to point (AA)? (e) If a worker skilled in gathering migrated to this tribe and joined it, how would this action relate to point (AA)?

CHALLENGES TO ECONOMIC COMPETENCE

1. Refer to Unit 1 in your textbook and arrange a bulletin board display of recent news clippings that pertain to the chapter headings in the unit.
2. Arrange a conference with your science teacher and with your mathematics teacher to discuss with them the meaning of scientific method in their fields. Report to the class about the similarities and differences between scientific method in those fields and the use of scientific method in economics.
3. Write a special report on one of the following: (a) Changing Pattern of Economic Distribution in the United States, (b) A Comparison of Consumption Changes from 1900 to the Present, (c) Education Affects Our Economic Life, (d) My Personal Economic Needs and Wants.
4. Prepare an oral report to present to the class to show how economic life was affected by the economic theory of one of the following persons: (a) Thomas R. Malthus on Population, (b) John Stuart Mill on International Trade, (c) David Ricardo on Land Rent, (d) Thorstein Veblen on the Leisure Class, (e) Karl Marx on Communism, (f) John Maynard Keynes on Saving and Investment.

Chapter 2

Our Economic System and Its Evolution

Does environment affect the ways of making a living?
What is the nature of our economic system?
Is our economic system evolutionary and dynamic?
What is the nature of capitalism?

One's material and social environment largely determines what he can do to get the things he wants. In these matters we Americans have been most fortunate. The land that became the territory of the United States was rich in natural wealth. The form of society that was established here was such that it stimulated industry and the mental development of the people. It imbued them with optimism and hope for an increasingly better future. These are the reasons why our technology — industrial science — and our production have become the wonder of the world.

Today in America's high schools and colleges, a concern about man's environment centers on *ecology*. Ecology is a branch of biology that studies organisms — forms of life — and their environment. Man as a form of life is dependent upon other forms of life. Man is also dependent upon his inorganic — nonliving — environmental resources. Man's misuse of his environment thus becomes a serious threat to his continued existence. Since man's misuse of his environment may result from certain kinds of economic activity, conservation is a way of achieving certain positive ecological goals.

Let us turn our attention, then, to a study of our natural resources and their conservation, the nature of our economic society, the nature of its evolution, the era of mercantilism, and the nature of capitalism.

OUR NATURAL RESOURCES

All the materials in the goods that people use come originally from nature's storehouse. The food we eat is composed of the elements of

Illus. 2-1. All the materials in the goods that people use come originally from nature's storehouse. Our houses are built from the timber of trees, and from sand, clay, and lime in the form of plaster and brick.

Union Electric Company

plant food taken from the soil and the air. Our houses are built from the timber of trees, and from sand, clay, and lime in the form of plaster and brick. The fuel we use to heat our homes, schools, and offices and to generate power for factories comes from coal, oil, or falling water. And so it is with all the material goods we use. Nature provides the crude materials, and we change them into things that we can use.

The American people have had an abundance of most of the natural resources they have needed. Thousands of square miles of land are suitable for the production of many different kinds of crops. In several regions there are rich deposits of resources needed for industrial production.

THE CONSERVATION OF OUR NATURAL RESOURCES

For too long a time our people took our natural wealth for granted. Probably this wealth seemed inexhaustible, and little attempt was made to economize in its use. Since 1900, the pressures of the United States' population increases have created new problems concerning *conservation*. The demand on resources to supply 76 million people in 1900 has intensified to a demand on resources to meet the requirements of over 225 million people in the early 1970's. These pressures shown in the graphs are more serious than the national three-fold population increase indicates. In some states, such as California, the population increase will exceed 1,000 percent in that period; in some urban communities the population rate of

Ch. 2   OUR ECONOMIC SYSTEM AND ITS EVOLUTION

THE GREAT MIGRATION

from rural to urban . . .

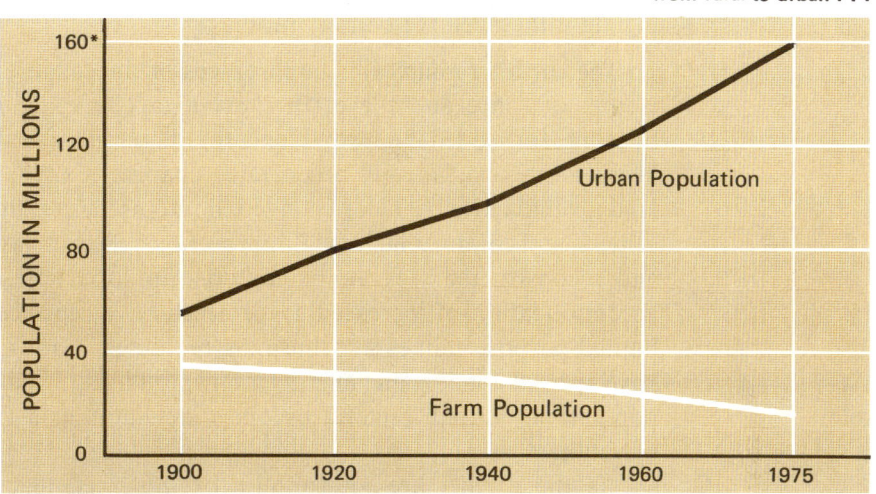

*This figure excludes the estimated 70 million who will be living in rural, nonfarm areas.

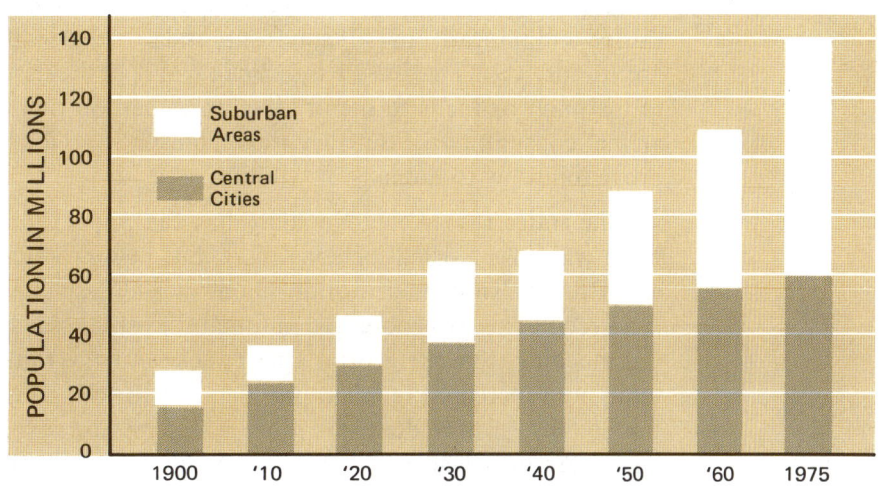

from city to suburb . . .

Figure 2-1.

E. I. du Pont de Nemours & Co.

It is estimated that in 1975 there will be 230 million people in the United States. About 140 million will live in urban areas, fewer than 20 million on farms, and 70 million in rural, non-farm areas. Suburban areas will have a much greater population than the central cities.

gain has already exceeded the projected rate of gain in California. The pressures on the earth, water, and air resources throughout the country highlight the need for conservation.

The earth's resources. The resources of the earth, or land, involve the factors of space and the earth elements. The space required for more housing, for added highways, and for larger numbers of industrial and business sites has already necessitated change. Farms, orchards, and idle land around cities have been converted into homesites, highways, shopping centers, and commercial lots. Entire sections of cities have been demolished and reconstructed. Towering high-rise multipurpose structures for the accommodation of increased space needs have replaced the old single or limited-purpose homes and business buildings. However, these changes have proved inadequate in meeting the building needs of an expanding population. Urban renewal becomes inevitable as a form of space conservation.

As the earth's present supplies of minerals, metals, and gases are depleted, new sources must be located and more efficient methods of extracting and using these elements become essential tasks of conservation. The prevention of the destruction of land by erosion, fire, and flood demands continuous control. As land space is taken over for human purposes, the wildlife and game that formerly used it as a habitat must be shifted and relocated in parks, refuges, and sanctuaries if these forms of life are to survive. The use of insecticides and pesticides may be necessary to maintain or increase the production of certain products for human or animal consumption. But they must be utilized in a manner that will not prove injurious to humans or wildlife.

The water resources. Not only has the population increase required more water for normal personal uses, but new products and new uses of water have also caused a drain upon, or the destruction of, some water resources. The bathroom, the automatic washing machine and dishwashing machine, the refrigerator's icemaker, and the family outdoor swimming pool increase the per capita demand for the consumption of water. Family leisure time demands more water resources for recreation at the lake, river, or seashore. Additional billions of gallons of water are required daily for use in the production of paper, steel, chemicals, and other products for which demand has increased. Our total water wants create an insatiable demand upon our water resources.

At the same time, society has been negligent in the conservation of the supplies of water that exist. The dripping faucet wastes water that others may need. The detergents, the human and the industrial misuses, the

Illus. 2-2. Family leisure time demands more water resources for recreation at the lake, river, or seashore.

Starcraft Boat Division

dumped sewage, and the oil seepages that flow into our present water sources pollute water that humans as well as nature's other living creatures need for their survival. The shortages of fresh water supplies force the economy to resort to costly processes of water collection and purification. In some areas, processes of desalting or distilling seawater at high costs are mandatory. The conservation of our water resources becomes more urgent every day. It demands personal individual action as well as action on every level of government — local, state, and federal.

The air resources. Of mounting concern to the people of this nation is the increasing contamination of the air. On the national scene, we face the pollution of the air through uncontrolled nuclear testing and fallout. In certain areas, dangerous pollution of the air results from the use of sprays or dusts regarded as necessary for maximum agricultural or forestry production. Millions of homes and other buildings spew forth wastes from their heating systems. To this is added the gas and wastes from various forms of industrial production and the burning refuse piles of city government dumps. Fewer than 5,000 automotive vehicles were manufactured in 1900 to give off carbon monoxide and other gases. Today there is a rising stream of destruction of air from an approaching 109,000,000 registered automotive vehicles. The heaviest pollution tends to be in the major cities and suburbs that also have the highest concentration of population. In many communities buildings and outdoor works of art reveal the dirt and grime present in the air. All these forms of air pollution take their toll in human lives.

Resource conservation programs. In many varied ways, and at all levels of community living, programs for conservation are under way. Droughts in many parts of the country call for a stringent regulation in the use of water which suddenly becomes a most precious commodity. Local temporary ordinances are passed to restrict the washing of cars or the watering of lawns. Even the daily bath may be frowned upon.

Citizens have approved state bond referendums calling for expenditures of billions of dollars in efforts to provide, cleanup, and conserve an adequate water supply. The federal government has funded programs to research and develop huge desalting plants in strategic areas; other funds have been made available for preserving an improved ecological balance. The major federal law setting water standards is the Water Quality Act of 1965; this act is administered by the Department of the Interior.

Communities, such as Los Angeles, are desperately trying to solve the problem of smog; some communities are attempting to lessen the amount of air pollution resulting from the use of diesel engines or the exhaust from millions of automobiles; others may be combatting the problem of dust that results from the operation of cement plants. On the federal level, the

Illus. 2-3. The attempts of the State Department to secure international control agreements to prevent the contamination of the air by nuclear testing are of greatest importance.

U.S. Arms Control and Disarmament Agency

attempts of the State Department to secure international control agreements to prevent the contamination of the air by nuclear testing are of greatest importance. Federal control of domestic air pollution is the responsibility of the Department of Health, Education, and Welfare which administers the Air Quality Act of 1967.

Now we recognize that our natural resources are being rapidly consumed, and for that reason the conservation of these resources has become an important social and economic problem.

Essentially the problem of conservation is this: how to utilize our air, soils, minerals and metals, forests, water and waterpower, and wildlife resources in such a way that they will serve our needs but will not be wasted. Certainly we have no moral right to use the natural wealth to gratify our own wants and for personal enrichment today without thought for tomorrow and the generations that will come after us.

THE NATURE OF OUR ECONOMIC SOCIETY

An *economy* is a system of institutions and practices under which people in society undertake to make a living. In America we have always emphasized the importance of the individual. That is to say, we look upon social, political, and economic organizations and institutions as means for promoting the welfare of individuals, and not as ends in themselves. Because we do recognize the dignity and importance of the individual, our form of political government and our economic system are designed to permit a great deal of personal freedom. Basic in the American society

Illus. 2-4. Because we do recognize the dignity and importance of the individual, our form of political government and our economic system are designed to permit a great deal of personal freedom.

P & O — Orient Lines Inc.

is the idea that individuals should be self-reliant, honorable in their relations with others, and willing to play fair in their efforts to make a living. Of course, there have always been those who have not observed this basic idea. But the conduct of such persons does not receive public approval.

The economy or economic system in the United States is the outgrowth of changes in the methods of producing goods and services and of the longing of individuals for personal freedom. We can understand what this means by considering how the fundamental factors in our economy have evolved during the long period of man's economic progress.

Economic evolution, a process of slow or gradual development, is associated with economic dynamics. By *dynamics* we mean the forces that bring about change. In societies with a high level of living, one such force is education. Education advances science and thus promotes improved technology. Education also tends to improve the effectiveness and the productivity of the labor force. Another example of dynamics is freedom of capital investment; this has enabled capital to be used for applied research in the creation and production of new and diverse products.

Illus. 2-5. By dynamics we mean the forces that bring about change. In societies with a high level of living, one such force is education. Education advances science and thus promotes improved technology.

The Columbia Gas System

Conversely, there are economic statics. *Statics* are forces that tend toward equilibrium, that is, to resist change or to hold down growth. The land area of most nations is static since the amount of land itself cannot be greatly increased. Population is static if it does not increase either in quantity or quality. The nature or culture of a society is static if it prevents the change of customs and thus hinders economic growth. In some societies, the class system or caste has prevented the economic improvement of the labor force and thus retarded economic development in those nations.

As we study man and his economic activities through the passage of time, the dynamics and statics which contributed to his making a living are evident.

ECONOMIC EVOLUTION AND DEVELOPMENT

Modern industry and ways of making a living in the economically advanced nations are the consequence of a long evolutionary process. The process has not been the same in all parts of the world. But in a broad outline we can sketch the economic development of western economic societies.

(1) The early stages of rural development. In the age of appropriation, our ancestors were directly dependent upon nature for the goods they needed. Earliest man obtained his living by hunting, by fishing, and by gathering wild fruits, nuts, berries, and other things that could be eaten mostly in their raw state. His clothing was simple, and he had little shelter from the weather.

Eventually, man's intelligence and increasing wants caused him to consider other ways of getting a living. He came to see that it would be more desirable to catch and keep a number of animals in captivity. Some of the animals became adapted to living near human beings and as a result become domesticated. This stage of domestication of animals provided man with a more constant food supply. In order to furnish an additional labor resource, slavery became a common practice.

Moving was occasionally required to find better grazing for the animals. People, however, began to live a more settled type of existence. Tents were made for shelter, simple weaving provided cloth for dress, and time became available for creating simple household articles and tools. Some trading was carried on, but not much. Since little or no money was available for exchange, "swapping" or *barter* was a common method of exchange.

As time moved on, the stage of agriculture or the cultivation of grains, fruits, and vegetables naturally followed the domestication of animals.

Illus. 2-6. Moving was occasionally required to find better grazing for the animals.

World Bank

The necessity for supplying the herd with food led to the raising of hay and other foodstuffs for animals. By cultivating wild grains and vegetables, the people increased the certainty of their food supply. Agriculture was the major way of life for many societal groups. A more permanent way of life developed as houses were built and villages were established in agricultural communities.

With the expansion of economic agricultural development in Western Europe, both land and property ownership became more complex. Questions concerning the legality of property rights and the best means of protecting wealth and property rights became more important. Answers required the adoption of new economic, political, and social relationships.

In the feudal period, people sought the answers by granting controlling power to certain strong leaders and decision makers. The leaders assuming these roles came from both the church and the general public. As feudal lords, these spiritual and secular leaders demanded obedience, loyalty, and economic support from the ruled.

(2) The evolution of urban economic life. In the latter part of the Middle Ages, on the continent of Europe and in England, towns increased in number and size. This change to urban living gave rise to: (a) the development of handicrafts, (b) craft guilds, (c) merchant guilds, and (d) the domestic system.

(a) The development of handicrafts. The increased, concentrated population provided an opportunity for persons of ability to develop a high degree of skill in making and selling various kinds of articles. Some specialized in the making of shoes, others in furniture, others in weaving cloth, and so on. Thus, began such occupations as those of the cobbler, the carpenter, the weaver, the baker, the tailor, the candlemaker, and others. At first the products were sold to the townspeople, but later they were sold to those living in other communities. During the handicraft stage, manufacturing was done by hand. ("Manufacturing" comes from two Latin words, *manus*, meaning "hand," and *facere*, meaning "to make.")

(b) Craft guilds. As time went on, the number of shoemakers, cabinetmakers, and other specialized craftsmen increased. The increase in the number of workers and in production gave rise to new problems relating to production. Therefore, the craftsmen in each branch of production formed organizations for the regulation of the training of new workers, standards of quality for their products, methods of assisting unfortunate members, and other matters. These organizations were called *craft guilds*.

Each guild had an apprenticeship system. To learn a trade, a youth was required to serve as an *apprentice* under a *master workman* for a number of years. At the end of the required period of training, which was sometimes as long as seven years, the apprentice was supposed to be a skilled worker and was called a *journeyman*.

(c) Merchant guilds. As the number of manufactured articles increased, trade grew in importance. The craftsmen became traders also. They formed organizations called *merchant guilds*. At first, one of the main purposes of the merchant guild was to provide mutual protection against robbers. Later these organizations undertook to monopolize trade and to control competition. Thus, the attention of the merchant guilds centered on the problems of marketing goods. These guilds regulated all kinds of trade.

(d) The domestic system. About the fifteenth century the strength of the craft guilds began to decline. The craft rules were rigid, and the number of boys accepted as apprentices became restricted. As a result, many workers other than master workmen set up shops of their own.

Illus. 2-7. As the number of manufactured articles increased, trade grew in importance. The craftsmen became traders also.

A number of capitalists, men having money to invest, bought goods wherever they could obtain them, whether the goods were made by members of guilds or not. Then they sold the goods at a profit. Often they contracted with workmen for quantities of goods, an arrangement that solved the workman's marketing problem. Sometimes workers were paid wages. Frequently the capitalists supplied the workers with raw materials, and later on it was not unusual for them to rent to the workmen the tools they needed. Work was often done in the workmen's homes or shops, and for that reason the practice is sometimes referred to as the *domestic system*.

With these changes, urban production for trade and trade between towns increased. This expansion required better transportation, improved protection, a unified money system, and standards for weights and measures. Wealth from economic activity increased. These economic changes influenced the more powerful feudal lords to extend their control over the weaker lords. Thus, the previously separated feudal holdings were consolidated into kingdoms and nations. As this political and economic power was centralized, the system of mercantilism was adopted to support national self-interests.

(3) **The era of mercantilism.** Before the Industrial Revolution, the prevailing political and economic thought in Europe was that of *mercantilism*. Since merchants and their trade were believed to be the major force behind a strong and growing economy, the word "mercantilism" was

adopted to describe the economic system of that era. The aim of mercantilism was to build a strong nation. To achieve this goal, it was the policy of each nation to (1) get as much gold as possible by discovery or by trade with other nations; (2) encourage the exportation of goods and discourage imports; (3) encourage manufacturing; and (4) encourage the growth of population in order to provide a supply of workers and soldiers.

From your studies of history, you may recall that governments pursued a number of interesting practices to carry out the policies of mercantilism. As applied economic practice, each mercantilistic nation (1) levied taxes on goods imported from other countries; (2) made treaties to crush competing nations; (3) gave bonuses to certain favored manufacturers or producers; (4) gave exclusive privileges to certain individuals and business concerns; (5) discouraged some industries; (6) established colonies; (7) controlled the use of some goods and required the use of other goods; and (8) encouraged shipbuilding.

Mercantilism encouraged the discovery of the New World as well as its exploration for the exploitation of its gold and silver resources. Later, the American colonies provided sources of raw materials for use by European producers. The colonies also provided markets for the exports of Europe. From the colonists' viewpoint, British mercantilism curbed their economic and political freedom through its practices of taxation and its restrictions on colonial manufacturing and trade. In part, the American Revolution was as much a revolt against British mercantilism as it was a rebellion against the political power and rule of the crown.

As people revolted against the absolute kings and monarchs, political and economic power was restored to the people. Legislative control was placed in the hands of elected representatives. The system of courts also was made independent; this provided greater justice for the people. One further economic advance was necessary to usher in capitalism with its ideas of economic freedom. This advance began with a surge of new inventions that introduced the age of modern industry.

(4) The age of modern industry. After about the middle of the eighteenth century inventions revolutionized manufacturing and resulted in the creation of the *industrial* or *factory stage.*

(a) Inventors and inventions. Power-driven machinery has been in use for only about two hundred years. As early as 1733 John Kay, an Englishman, invented a "flying shuttle," which enabled weavers to weave cloth faster than the thread could be spun on the single-spindle wheels. Then in 1769 Richard Arkwright, a barber, patented his spinning frame. This machine, together with the spinning jenny, patented about the same time

by James Hargreaves, a carpenter, made it possible to spin many threads with no more effort than had been required to spin one.

In 1763 James Watt, an engineer, devised a steam engine that actually worked, crude as it was. In 1785 Edmund Cartwright, a clergyman, constructed a loom that was driven by waterpower. All these inventions took place in England.

(b) The Industrial Revolution. The rapid transition from the use of muscle power and tools to that of steam power and waterpower and machines created a revolution in production methods and in ways of making a living. Prior to the middle of the eighteenth century methods of producing goods changed very slowly. Then — largely as a result of the use of machines and steam power in production — changes in economic thinking and organization began to take place. This was especially true in England. Home production for the market rapidly gave way to production in factories. Markets expanded, and businessmen became more important in community and national affairs.

These changes which began in England were so great and so rapid that the last half of the eighteenth and the first half of the nineteenth centuries are often referred to as the period of the *Industrial Revolution.* In order to prevent the rise of competition abroad, England tried to prevent the export of machinery and the emigration of engineers and skilled workmen who might be able to build duplicates of the English machines in America. Thus, England gained a head start over us of nearly fifty years. But eventually we acquired machines and developed "know-how" for our own industrial development.

THE NATURE OF CAPITALISM

The introduction of powered machinery, tools, and factories as capital was made by profit-seeking private businessmen. As owners of capital, they became capitalists who promoted mass industrialization. Thus, *capitalism* is an economic system in which the profit motive induces private capital owners to produce economic goods. Capitalism is based on the doctrine of *individualism*; each person should rely on his own economic efforts to gain his greatest economic satisfactions. It implies that men who are free to act in their economic self-interest will be more effective in promoting the society's economic interests than economic action that is directed or operated by government.

The system of capitalism is composed of certain economic institutions. *Institutions* are the well established and accepted relationships which are essential to support an economic system. Some of the more important economic institutions are: (1) private property, (2) freedom of enterprise, (3) competition, and (4) the profit motive.

(1) Private property. *Private property* is an owner's right, protected by government, that gives the owner control over the uses of the things owned. This right of control includes the acquiring, keeping, using, and disposing of things in any form. One important form of private property used in business is a *contract*, an agreement dealing with property rights. A private property owner, while living, may extend the control over the use or distribution of his property even after his death.

Where another attempts to deprive an owner of his private property, government will protect the right by forcing its return or by a reimbursement of its value to the owner. Similarly, the government may restrict the use of any private property against its misuse. For example, one may own and use an automobile. However, existing ordinances and traffic codes can restrict the automobile's use to protect others from harmful misuse.

As an institution of capitalism, private property gives the owners decision-making power to employ their resources in economic activity. It also encourages owners to increase their property through saving and investment; this increases total investment and promotes society's total economic growth.

(2) Freedom of enterprise. *Freedom of enterprise* enables an individual, or groups of individuals, to gather and coordinate productive resources

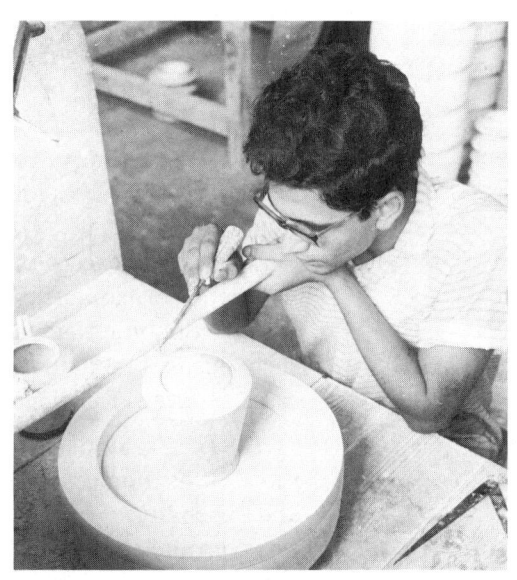

Illus. 2-8. Freedom of enterprise enables an individual, or groups of individuals, to gather and coordinate productive resources for use in creating specific economic goods.

World Bank

for use in creating specific economic goods. It is not an unrestricted institution. Government may set limits on its exercise. For example, equipment used by a barber may come in contact with the skin of a customer. To prevent the spread of skin diseases, government may require barbers to be licensed; codes may demand the maintaining of certain barbershop health standards. Usually, the freedom is otherwise unrestricted by government; the restrictions require compliance with any general laws.

Enterprises are influenced by market prices. Enterprisers are guided by those prices in their decisions to start, operate, enlarge, or shut down an enterprise. Freedom of enterprise allows one to make decisions that will permit the fullest employment of resources that are under one's control. It permits the adoption of new inventions, technology, product changes, or any reorganization of the enterprise to stimulate production development.

(3) Competition. As an economic institution, *competition* refers to economic rivalry. Consumers are free to bid for products against other consumers. One member of the labor force bids against other members of the labor force for a job. A producer bids against other producers for the factors of production. A product is offered in the market in opposition to another product each seeking the consumer's favor and his spendable dollars.

The "so-called" market or free market of capitalism which determines prices and the efficiency of production requires competition for its operation. Briefly, competition forces lower pricing, or prices that approximate the costs of production. A more complete discussion about the role of competition in pricing is presented in Chapter 9.

Competition causes producers to maintain the quality of their goods and to strive to improve them. It also results in the discovery of new and better ways of making goods, and it leads to the production of new kinds of products.

With some exceptions — as in the cases of patents and copyrights — the theory of capitalism does not approve of monopolies. It holds that where monopolies actually exist, so that there is little or no competition, such business should be regulated by government. This is true in the cases of electric power companies and transportation companies.

(4) The profit motive. Each enterprise has costs which require expenditures. It also takes in receipts or income. The difference between income and expenditures results in profit. When income is greater than expenditures, profit is positive. If the difference is negative, it is called a loss. The *profit motive* means that enterprisers are moved to engage in production in

Ch. 2   OUR ECONOMIC SYSTEM AND ITS EVOLUTION

Illus. 2-9. Competition causes producers to maintain the quality of their goods and to strive to improve them. It also results in the discovery of new and better ways of making goods, and it leads to the production of new kinds of products.

anticipation of a difference between expected income and expected expenditures.

In capitalism, the profit motive performs like a water faucet. Market demand with positive profit possibility opens the production faucet. An increase in the positive profit demand opens the faucet wider; or it may call for an increase in the size of the line and the faucet. Conversely, decreased demand expressed by decreased or negative profit may turn down the flow of production or shut it off completely.

Since the profit motive is a key institution of capitalism, a broader presentation of profit will be presented in Chapter 17. The preceding brief general overview of the nature of capitalism and its institutions provides a background for use in the next chapter, which proposes a question. How are freedom and capitalism interrelated?

SUMMARY

The United States has become a rich and powerful nation partly because it has possessed an abundance of most of the important natural resources for the production of the goods that the people have wanted. Population increases and technological changes have created pressures on our resources. This requires that an understanding of ecology and practices for the conservation of our earth, water, and air resources be given greater attention.

Our nation also has an extensive home market and a form of society that has constantly stimulated the initiative, industry, and optimism of the people.

Our economic evolution can be traced through the ages or stages of: (1) The early stages of rural development, (2) the evolution of urban economic life, (3) the era of mercantilism, and (4) the age of modern industry. During the first three stages, growth was evolutionary due to economic statics, forces that resisted change and held down economic growth.

Mercantilism was concerned with the national group as a whole, and not so much with the welfare of individuals. It pursued certain policies that, it was believed, would make the nation strong — economically, politically, and militarily. Consequently, the American colonists objected to British mercantilism since it curbed their internal economic development.

During the fourth stage, dynamic forces brought about rapid economic change through the Industrial Revolution and the adoption of capitalism. The theory and practices of capitalism supplanted those of mercantilism. Roughly speaking, the change from mercantilism to capitalism occurred about two hundred years ago. Capitalism is characterized by the institutions of (1) private property, (2) freedom of enterprise, (3) competition, and (4) the profit motive. Capitalism is based on the doctrine of individualism and relies chiefly on the profit motive as the incentive for production.

NEW TERMS

apprentice
barter
capitalism
competition
conservation
contract
craft guilds
domestic system
dynamics
ecology
economy
freedom of enterprise
individualism
Industrial Revolution
industrial *or* factory stage
institutions
journeyman
master workman
mercantilism
merchant guilds
private property
profit motive
statics

QUESTIONS ON THE CHAPTER

1. What determines how people make a living? Explain.
2. What is ecology? How are conservation and ecology related?
3. Why should you be interested in conservation of resources?
4. What effects has the nature of our society had on the people?
5. What is the meaning of economic dynamics? Economic statics?
6. How was a solution to the economic problem sought under the feudal system?
7. What were the purposes of the craft guilds? Of the merchant guilds?
8. What caused the domestic system to disappear?

9. What were the economic policies of mercantilism? What practices were followed in carrying out these policies?
10. What caused the Industrial Revolution?
11. What do we mean by capitalism? Does capitalism mean the same thing as individualism? Explain.
12. What place does the right of private property have in the system of capitalism? Explain.
13. What are contracts, and how important are they in a capitalistic system?
14. What is meant by freedom of enterprise?
15. Does freedom of enterprise lead to competition? If so, why?
16. Does capitalism advocate monopoly? Should government permit monopoly to exist?
17. What is meant by profit motive in production? Is everyone motivated by it?

APPLYING YOUR ECONOMIC UNDERSTANDING

1. Has the Constitution of the United States influenced the form of our society to stimulate the industry and the mental development of our people? Explain your answer in detail with reference to specific sections in the Constitution.
2. Explain how "teach-ins" on environment relate to ecology. Cite some economic activities which contribute to a misuse of man's environment. How do these activities create ecological imbalance?
3. In what ways has the natural environment of your community affected its economic evolution? Has conservation been a factor?
4. Would the nature of your own state's economy indicate that it is dynamic or static? Give reasons to support your answer.
5. The decline of craft guilds was in part due to restrictions on admitting apprentices, and the long period of apprenticeship. Discuss whether a similarity exists in certain craft union practices of the present.
6. Mercantilism was achieved by pursuing four policies. Show which of these policies may be present in the United States today.
7. How do Articles IV and V of the amendments to the United States Constitution relate to capitalism and political rights?
8. Is there a relationship between the nationalist movement in Africa and mercantilism? Why or why not?
9. Give some examples of forms of contracts which we are free to enter into in the United States.

CHALLENGES TO ECONOMIC COMPETENCE

1. Make a collection of contract forms secured from a lawyer, a bank, an automobile dealer, a real estate agent, or other sources. Use these forms to prepare a bulletin board display on "Capitalism and Freedom of Contract."

2. Invite some retired persons to tell your class about working conditions, food, clothing, transportation, and communication when they were teen-agers. Then lead a class discussion to show comparisons and contrasts with economic life of today.
3. Prepare a tape recording by a refugee from communism in which he or she contrasts economic freedom as it prevailed under communism and as it functions in the United States. Play the recording in the classroom.
4. Ask your English teacher or librarian to recommend a novel or a biography that reflects living conditions under a system of capitalism. Read it and prepare a class report using short excerpts from the book to illustrate various concepts of capitalism.
5. Prepare a written report as an article for your school newspaper which might "sell" the student body on the need for conservation. Suggested headlines are: (a) Water, Water, Everywhere? (b) Land's End — Man's End, (c) Into the Wild Grey Yonder.
6. Prepare and present to the class an oral report that discusses the relationship of estates, estate trusts, and inheritance to the institutions of private property.

Chapter 3

Freedom and Specialization in Our Economy

How are freedom and capitalism interrelated?
Does specialization in production result in cooperation?
What are some of the problems that arise because of specialization?
How will automation and atomic energy affect ways of making a living?

At the present time we hear a great deal of discussion about the rights of man. Television and radio programs as well as newspaper and magazine articles are devoted to this topic. Yet we seldom consider how these rights came to be recognized. What is the importance of the statement in the Declaration of Independence that men "are endowed by their Creator with certain unalienable rights"?

A citizen of the United States has a rich heritage of freedom resulting from the struggle of others to gain and protect what have been called "the rights of man." These rights or freedoms may be religious — the right to worship as one chooses; or political — the right to vote for one's choice of candidate for office; or economic — the right to choose one's way of making a living.

These freedoms continue to exist, however, because they are protected by the type of government we established. And citizens, through government, reserve the right to decide upon the proper course of action when an individual's rights conflict with the rights of others.

In a complex society such as ours a close interrelationship exists between the political and the economic orders. As the nation entered the 1970's, our gross national product exceeded $930 billion. Government at all levels was purchasing over $214 billion of the economy's goods and services; half of this purchasing was made by the federal government alone. Before the end of this decade the term billion will be inadequate to describe American productivity; the term trillion will become common in our language. It takes an extraordinarily active economy to produce in this gigantic way to satisfy private and public demands.

Private or free enterprise has a dominant role in the American economy. But free enterprise could not exist without a form of government which supports and protects a system of capitalism. This protection of economic rights by the exercise of political rights and vice versa is important in safeguarding the security of the individual and society.

Although individual freedom has a high priority in the American society, the complex nature of its economy demands a high degree of cooperation among individuals. Americans, as individuals, are not independently self-sufficient but are specialized in their economic activity. Consequently, this specialization makes them highly dependent upon other specialized individuals in the total economy.

Illus. 3-1. Americans, as individuals, are not independently self-sufficient but are specialized in their economic activity. Consequently, this specialization makes them highly dependent upon other specialized individuals in the economy.

National Bureau of Standards

In the following pages, we shall consider the interrelationship of freedom and capitalism, the nature of specialization, and the advantages and disadvantages of specialization that concern the future growth of our country.

POLITICAL FREEDOM IS ESSENTIAL TO CAPITALISM OR FREE ENTERPRISE

Political freedom means the right to be equal to others before the law; to run for public office; to vote in the election of public officers; to speak and write our opinions as to what is needed in government, as well as on other matters; to criticize government and public officials; and so on.

According to the American idea, you have *economic freedom* if you have the right to go into business for yourself, to own property, and to enter into binding agreements to buy or sell goods and services, to choose an occupation, and to compete for the sale or purchase of goods and services. Your right to do these things should be limited by law only when the things you do take away similar rights from others. One of the responsibilities of our government is to preserve economic freedom.

The people must have a great deal of political freedom if the ideas of capitalism are to be practiced. For example, your right to make contracts, to enter a line of business, and to vote for candidates who advocate certain laws that would affect ways of making a living is protected by political government. Capitalism simply cannot work if the people do not have a great amount of political freedom.

Does not a great deal of individual political freedom sometimes result in selfish "dog-eat-dog" practices? Unfortunately this sometimes happens. As the division of labor increases and ways of making a living become more specialized, new laws to prevent certain groups from taking advantage of others have become necessary. For example, there are laws for the regulation of both big labor unions and big business concerns.

Illus. 3-2. As the division of labor increases and ways of living become more specialized, new laws to prevent certain groups from taking advantage of others have become necessary.

POLITICAL FREEDOM WAS INCREASED BY THE ACCEPTANCE OF CAPITALISM

It is an interesting fact that there is more political freedom in those countries that have adopted capitalism than in those that have not. As you know from your study of history, the countries in which all the people have achieved the greatest degree of political freedom include the United States, England, the English-speaking dominions of the British Commonwealth, France, and the Scandinavian countries. And these are the countries that have had modified forms of capitalism longer than the others which have had less political freedom. Of course, these peoples are not free to do just as they please — that would be an impossible situation; and there are instances where influential individuals and groups get laws enacted for their own benefit. But in comparison with those elsewhere, individuals in these countries have long enjoyed great political freedom.

IS MERCANTILISM BEING REVIVED?

Occasionally, someone in public life expresses the fear that we are going back to the ways of mercantilism. Such expressions are always a proposal for new laws to regulate business. Is such a fear justified?

America has never practiced pure capitalism. It is a mistake to imagine that there was ever a time when the American people accepted the theory of pure *laissez-faire* (let alone) capitalism. For example, capitalism formerly held that trade between nations should be free and not discouraged by taxes or tariffs; that railroads, if they were to be privately owned, should be built, financed, and regulated entirely by the owners; and that banks should be financed and regulated by the owners, and not subsidized by government.

But from the early days of the nation the federal government has furnished certain manufacturers with protection from foreign competition by means of tariffs. It has helped to finance banks and railroads. At the present time it is spending billions of dollars to help to stimulate business, including lending money and credit to business concerns and farmers.

Government regulates business. Chapters that follow will discuss some of the many ways by which government attempts to regulate business and to control prices. Does this mean that the nation has abandoned capitalism and is going back to mercantilism? Unfortunately one cannot get the answer by asking the American people, for some of them say that such controls by government are necessary in order to make capitalism and democ-

Illus. 3-3. The federal government is spending billions of dollars to help to stimulate business, including lending money and credit to business concerns and farmers.

racy work. Others insist that the economy is going back to mercantilism so rapidly that before long free enterprise will be a thing of the past.

DOES CAPITALISM DESCRIBE THE AMERICAN ECONOMIC SYSTEM?

It is difficult to find a term generally acceptable to describe our economic system. Our system is not *laissez-faire* capitalism. Neither is it socialism, which would mean that government owned all productive wealth and controlled all production. At the same time, we do use government to promote our economic welfare in many ways.

Some of the terms that have been suggested to designate our economic system include *mixed economic system*, capitalism, *American capitalism*, free-enterprise system, and the private-profit system. But whatever term is used, the system is based on a belief in the institutions of private property, free enterprise, competition, and the profit motive. Although government — especially the federal government — plays a more important part than formerly, it is still general practice to refer to our system as capitalism, American capitalism, or the free-enterprise system.

THE NATURE OF SPECIALIZATION

Whatever we may call our economic system, its operation as an economic system requires a high degree of specialization in performing its many varied functions.

Each of us wants many of the modern products and services produced in our complex society. Yet as individuals we are unable to produce a good such as an automobile. We lack the combined talents of the inventor, the designer, the engineer, the toolmaker, the upholsterer, the metal worker, and the assembler — not to mention the resources of the capitalist — which are necessary for its production. What is true in the case of the automobile can be repeated in the case of most other goods and services. We recognize, then, that most of us are dependent upon the diverse labors of others. Each of us contributes his skill, highly specialized though it may be, and the resulting cooperation enables all of us to secure some of the economic satisfactions of modern life.

Thus, the business of making a living in the United States and other nations with economic systems similar to ours is a vast undertaking that is both competitive and cooperative. This seemingly antithetic situation is easily understood. In order to meet our numerous wants, some workers are engaged in the production of food; some are engaged in the manufacture of shoes, clothes, or furniture; some, in the construction of houses and roads; some, in transportation by rail, highway, water, or air; and some, in professional work such as law, medicine, or teaching. Most of the things produced are not intended to be used by the workers themselves but to be sold on the market and thus made available to others who need them. Thus, by means of a *division of labor* or *specialization* we cooperate in producing the things we want.

Illus. 3-4. Each of us wants many of the modern products and services produced in our complex society. Yet as individuals we are unable to produce a good such as an automobile.

Swift & Co.

One evidence of this specialization is to be found in the labor resources of society as we analyze its occupational groups. How many tens of thousands of ways are there by which people earn a living in the United States? It is difficult to answer this question because there are so many ways by which workers may be classified. The U.S. Employment Service has made studies of over 30,000 occupations in industry, business, and government. One frequently used classification of workers is shown in the accompanying illustration.

MAJOR OCCUPATION GROUPS

Professional, technical, and kindred workers
Farmers and farm managers
Managers, officials, and proprietors, except farm
Clerical and kindred workers
Sales workers
Craftsmen, foremen, and kindred workers
Operatives and kindred workers
Private household workers
Service workers, except private household
Farm laborers and foremen
Laborers, except farm and mine

SOURCE: Bureau of Labor Statistics.

These occupational titles are convenient to use. But they do not give very much information as to the nature of the work done by the individuals in the different groups. For example, professional workers include physicians, lawyers, professors, dentists, artists, and actors, among others.

WHAT ARE THE FORMS OF SPECIALIZATION?

Usually we think of the specialization of labor in one of four ways.

(1) Specialization by trade or profession. This is the simplest form of specialization or division of labor. It takes place when each individual worker devotes his time to a particular trade. Bricklayers, carpenters, physicians, and ministers illustrate this form of specialization.

(2) Specialization by stages of production. When more than one step is necessary to change raw materials — such as iron ore, timber, or wheat — into finished articles, specialization by stages of production occurs. If furniture made of wood is to be produced, trees must be felled and cut into logs, which are taken to a sawmill; the sawmill turns the logs into various shapes of lumber; and the manufacturer uses the lumber to build radio and television cabinets, chairs, and other kinds of household furniture and equipment. The production of the completed article involves a series of operations, each of which is performed by special groups of workers.

(3) Specialization by geographic regions. Still another form of specialization in production results from climatic conditions and the location of natural resources, such as particular kinds of soil, minerals, and timber. Illustrations of this form of specialization are the growing of wheat in Kansas, cotton in Mississippi, corn in Iowa; or the manufacturing of steel in Pennsylvania, automobiles in Michigan; or mining in West Virginia and fishing in the Great Northwest.

(4) Specialization according to tasks. Specialization takes place when certain workers perform only a comparatively small and simple part of the work in the production of an article. For example, in a shoe factory some workers prepare the leather; other workers cut the leather into the different shapes required; others fasten the uppers to the soles; others attach the heels; and so on. So specialized is the production of shoes that scores of distinct operations performed by different workers are necessary before a pair of shoes is finished. Where goods of any kind are produced in factories in great quantities, the same thing is true: the total production is carried on by workers whose individual tasks are relatively simple. Such specialization speeds production and usually improves the quality of workmanship.

WHAT ARE THE ADVANTAGES OF SPECIALIZATION?

"The Jack-of-all-trades is the master of none" is an old saying. Specialization tends to make of each worker an expert in one line of work and to reduce the cost of producing goods in various ways. There are many advantages that result from specialization in production.

(1) Specialization makes the best use of individual ability. Each of us possesses certain aptitudes or abilities. Where work is highly specialized, an individual has a chance of finding the work that is best suited to his particular ability and liking. For example, in the production of automobiles, there are hundreds of different tasks. Some of these tasks require men of considerable strength; other tasks may require less physical strength but accurate manipulation. In fact, men who have suffered the loss of both legs, or of an arm, or who are blind are able to find employment in the making of an automobile.

Illus. 3-5. Where work is highly specialized, an individual has a chance of finding the work that is best suited to his particular ability and liking.

General Dynamics

(2) Specialization develops skill. If we perform a simple act or task over and over again, we may soon learn to do it with precision and with less effort than at first. The machinist and other workers in a factory learn to do their work accurately and with ease. As a result they perform their tasks with little loss of time and a minimum waste of materials.

(3) Specialization simplifies the training of workers. To refer to the shoe industry again, shoes were formerly made by individuals who spent years perfecting their skill. In those days the shoemaker made the entire shoe to fit his customer. Now no single worker performs all the operations necessary in the making of shoes. The whole process is broken down into simple tasks. Therefore, most workers in a shoe factory can be quickly trained. The same thing is generally true in all types of manufacturing.

(4) Specialization economizes the worker's time. When an individual completes an article himself, much time is lost in changing from one task or phase of the work to another. But when each worker does only one simple task, time is saved, and machines may be kept in constant use, thus economizing on time.

(5) Specialization enables workers to change employers. More and more the tasks in making most products are becoming standardized. The skills acquired by painters, bricklayers, and machine operators enable workers to work for any employer who may need their services. Most of the workers in any automobile factory could easily and quickly take a job in another automobile factory because the operation of many of the machines in factories of this kind is very similar.

(6) Specialization simplifies inspection. It is comparatively easy for foremen and other supervisors to oversee the work of a group of specialized workers. The jobs of inspectors of the finished product are made easier since they, too, are specialists who make use of definite standards in passing or rejecting the articles at the different stages of production.

Illus. 3-6. Specialists make use of definite standards in passing or rejecting the articles at the different stages of production.

U.S. Department of Agriculture

(7) Specialization encourages inventions. As tasks have become standardized and simplified, inventors have devised machines to do much of the work formerly done by hand. For example, in the making of a book such as this, the steps in the making of the covers, cutting the paper, and setting of the type are largely performed by machines. When machines are used, the worker's burden becomes much lighter, and work is performed more speedily and with greater precision.

WHAT ARE THE DISADVANTAGES OF SPECIALIZATION?

On the other hand, there are several disadvantages of specialization in production.

(1) Work may tend to become monotonous. Probably you have heard it said, "Variety is the spice of life." As we saw in Chapter 1, all of us have a craving for variety. But much of the work in modern industry calls for almost endless repetition of a simple act, over and over, sometimes thousands of times a day. As a result workers may become bored with their jobs.

Progressive managers are making efforts to do something about this matter, such as allowing short rest periods or providing music in shops and offices where the work does not call for a great deal of concentration of thought.

(2) The interests and skills of workers may tend to become narrow. After a few years the specialized worker may tend to lose interest in other kinds of work, and in activities and problems not related to his job. As a rule he develops only one particular skill. If he loses his job and cannot find similar work elsewhere, he may remain unemployed for a long time. Both government and private employers have initiated a variety of vocational education programs to train youthful workers. Projects for retraining workers to meet currently demanded skills have also been adopted using direct or indirect federal financial support.

Illus. 3-7. Both government and private employers have initiated a variety of vocational education programs to train youthful workers.

American Oil Company

Prospective workers should, therefore, try to keep a broad interest in various kinds of work and, if possible, learn how to do more than one job. As someone has said, "You can't prepare for tomorrow's jobs if you depend upon the skills of yesterday."

(3) Workers are interdependent. The job of every worker is directly or indirectly related to the jobs of other workers. For example, it sometimes happens that a few key workers, who are usually highly skilled, go on a

RATES OF GROWTH AND DECLINE IN JOB OPPORTUNITIES BY INDUSTRY GROUPS

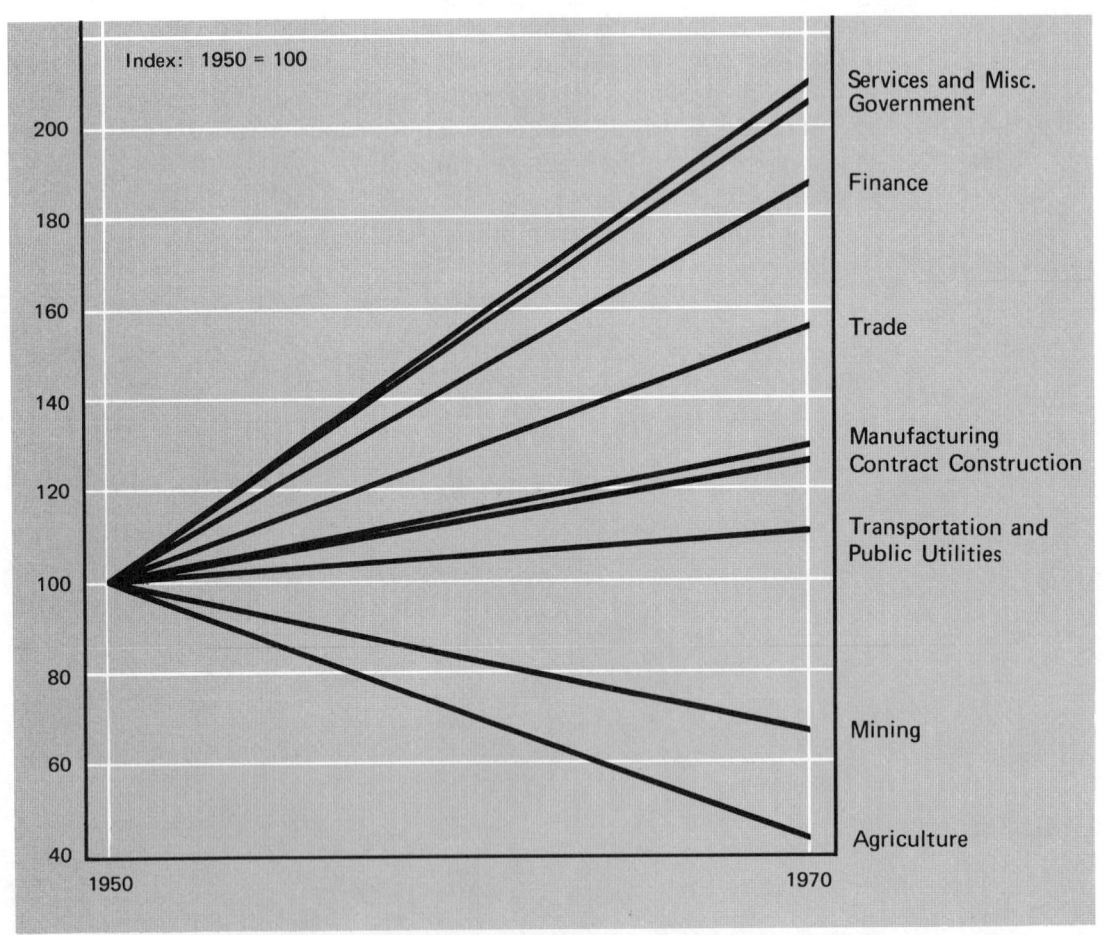

Index: 1950 = 100

- Services and Misc. Government
- Finance
- Trade
- Manufacturing
- Contract Construction
- Transportation and Public Utilities
- Mining
- Agriculture

SOURCES: *Federal Reserve Bulletin* and *Statistical Abstract of the United States — 1970*

Figure 3-1.
Prospective workers should try to keep a broad interest in various kinds of work and, if possible, learn how to do more than one job.

strike; as a result thousands of other workers cannot continue their work. Think of the effects that a long-continued strike of airline pilots would have on other jobs. Moreover, a decrease in the demand for the product of certain workers or in the supply of the materials they need may cause widespread unemployment. If a strike among steelworkers lessens the nation's output of this basic material, workers in an automobile plant may become unemployed.

(4) Workers may be careless with tools and equipment. Most workers use the tools and equipment furnished by employers. As a result they cannot feel pride of ownership of the tools and machines they use. In some cases they may be careless with the employer's property. If so, needless breakage and waste increase production costs.

THE ROLE OF SPECIALIZATION IN OUR ECONOMY

During the War of 1812 and thereafter manufacturing in this nation made considerable progress. But because of the small population and an abundance of fine land that could be had for the taking, for a long time we remained for the most part an agricultural people. From the time of the Civil War to the present, however, the change to industrial ways of making a living has been rapid. The free land is now gone; population has greatly increased; inventions have emerged with breathtaking rapidity; machinery has accumulated in almost unbelievable amounts; the

| YEAR | ENERGY SUPPLIED BY— | | | TOTAL TOOL INVESTMENT | AVERAGE WEEKLY HOURS OF EMPLOYMENT | OUTPUT PER MAN-HOUR |
	MEN	ANIMALS	MECHANICAL POWER			
1850	23%	51%	26%		70 hrs. weekly	GOODS AND SERVICES 27¢ WORTH PER HOUR
1900	15%	33%	52%	7 BILLION DOLLARS	60 hrs. weekly	GOODS AND SERVICES 56¢ WORTH PER HOUR
1950	4%	2%	94%	33 BILLION DOLLARS	40 hrs. weekly	GOODS AND SERVICES $1.21 WORTH PER HOUR
2000	?	?	?	?	?	?

AS THIS INVESTMENT INCREASES → THIS GOES DOWN → AND THIS GOES UP

Wilke Brothers Foundation (by adaptation)

Figure 3-2.

people are industrious and ambitious; many workers are skilled; and business leadership is capable. All these factors, combined in a nation rich in many natural resources and providing freedom and opportunity for individual initiative, account for the enviable position of economic leadership that the United States occupies.

The industrialization of the nation has resulted in many new jobs and in an increased amount of specialization in occupations and tasks. But it has also created new economic problems, such as unemployment and the equitable distribution of incomes, which we are trying to solve within the framework of our democratic principles.

Illus. 3-8. The industrialization of the nation has resulted in many new jobs and in an increased amount of specialization in occupations and tasks.

The Hobart Manufacturing Company

CHANGES IN THE WAYS OF MAKING A LIVING ARE STILL GOING ON

To people born 60 or 70 years ago the changes in production seem revolutionary. These people have witnessed many changes in the ways of making a living in our country. For example, when they were young children, nearly 50 out of every 100 employed persons were farmers or farmhands. But present estimates by the Bureau of the Census indicate that only about 4 out of every 100 employed persons are working on farms or are farm owners and managers.

In the past century many entirely new industries have come into existence. The telephone, radio, television, electric lights, electric power, busses, trucks, automobiles, sound pictures, airplanes, X-ray machines, plastics of many kinds, diesel engines, farm tractors, milking machines, and many other things that we now take for granted were unknown or regarded as impractical gadgets only a relatively short time ago. The use of these new kinds of goods has changed the lives of the American people in many ways.

ENTERING THE AGE OF TECHNOLOGICAL REVOLUTION

The perfection of the steam engine and the invention of machines ushered in the Industrial Revolution. Now we are told that technology with its automation and the use of atomic energy will, in the next few decades, bring about an even more startling revolution in the ways of making a living.

Technology arises from (1) new inventions and new discovery, (2) improvements or combinations of old inventions, and (3) new sources of energy.

(1) New inventions and new discovery. One example of this source of technology is space exploration. Space exploration has added to our knowledge of weather conditions, expanded our communications industries, developed new materials, such as heat- and cold-resistant ceramics, and increased the science of propulsion power. All such developments will have far-reaching effects on our occupational activities.

(2) Improvements or combinations of old inventions. Color television is an example of an improvement of an older invention, black and white television. *Automation* results from the combination of known inventions which makes possible the automatic control of a production process. The modern electric washing machine is a familiar application of automation. A housewife puts in the detergent, the laundry, and then sets the controls to start the machine's operation. From that point on circuits and switches take over adding and subtracting water, starting and stopping the agitator, or starting and stopping the spin cycles; in the final stage it may turn on a heating mechanism and then through a sensor mechanism feel the dryness of the wash to shut the machine off.

Automation has been adopted by many types of industries and producers. Colleges have automated registration and fee collection processes. Telephone companies through the adoption of the dial or the touch tone phones have automated the transmission of calls and billing customers for the calls. Other examples of the adoption of automation are to be found in the canned and packaged food industries, newspaper publishing, and steel making.

(3) New sources of energy. Atomic energy is typical of one of the newer sources of energy. One report from the Atomic Energy Commission has given us this information: (1) When the atoms in a handful of uranium are split, the energy released is equal to that which is generated by burning three thousand tons of coal. In terms of heat, this would be enough to heat a small house for five hundred years! (2) Isotopes (in substances like salt, for instance, that have been made radioactive and that give off rays) can be used to reveal how plants grow and to indicate what fertilizers are needed. As a result agricultural production may be enormously increased. (3) Experiments suggest that cancer and other diseases may be controlled or even cured by the use of atomic materials. (4) A number of great atomic energy plants have been constructed to produce electricity in abundance. (5) Machines, called "reactors," are being built to increase greatly the possibilities of generating atomic energy. It has been predicted that the next few years may add as much to health, longevity, and food production as did a century of the past.

In past years, literature that described man living in space or underwater was called fantasy. Today, in an age of spaceships and nuclear powered submarines, this has become a reality. As the technological revolution progresses, man must be prepared to face new forms of economic change.

SUMMARY

Economic freedom relates to the rights of making a living. Political freedom involves our rights as they are protected through law. Many people feel that capitalism has expanded our political freedom over the years; moreover, political freedom is essential to the continuance of capitalism and to the protection of our economic freedom.

In making a living we cooperate with each other by means of a division of labor; that is, each one specializes in some kind of work.

There are many occupational groups in the United States. The Bureau of the Census classifies all workers in eleven occupational groups. One way of listing types of specialization is as follows: (1) by trade or profession; (2) by stages of production; (3) by geographic regions; and (4) by tasks.

The advantages of specialization are that it: (1) makes use of natural ability; (2) develops skill; (3) simplifies training of workers; (4) economizes the worker's time; (5) facilitates change of employers; (6) simplifies inspection of products; and (7) encourages inventions.

The disadvantages of specialization include: (1) monotony; (2) narrowing of interests; (3) greater interdependence; and (4) possibly less careful use of tools and machinery by employees.

Specialization and cooperation through specialization have helped to make the United States a great industrial nation. Over the years, the changes in occupations and the rise of new industries with their new products have changed and enriched the lives of the American people. New technological developments, automation, the use of atomic energy, and space exploration are likely to bring about many more changes in our economic way of life.

Ch. 3   FREEDOM AND SPECIALIZATION IN OUR ECONOMY   57

NEW TERMS

American capitalism
automation
division of labor *or* specialization
economic freedom

laissez faire
mixed economic system
political freedom
technology

QUESTIONS ON THE CHAPTER

1. Does it make sense to say that ours is both an individualistic and a cooperative economic system? Explain.
2. Which comes first, economic freedom or political freedom? Can they exist separately?
3. Should our economic freedoms be limited by law?
4. Have we ever practiced pure capitalism? Would you want to practice it?
5. What is meant by the doctrine of *laissez faire*?
6. What are the institutions on which our economic system is based?
7. What eleven occupational groups are mentioned in the chapter?
8. What is the meaning of specialization of labor?
9. How would you explain the meaning of the following: (a) specialization by trade or profession; (b) specialization by stages of production; (c) specialization by geographic regions; and (d) specialization in production?
10. What are the advantages of specialization in production?
11. Does specialization in production tend to result in the production of more goods at lower cost? Explain.
12. What are the disadvantages of specialization in the production of goods?
13. Why do some people say that we are entering another Industrial Revolution?
14. What are some technical and economic changes that have resulted from space exploration?
15. What benefits are expected from the development of atomic energy?

APPLYING YOUR ECONOMIC UNDERSTANDING

1. What examples from history would support the statement ". . . there has been more political freedom in those countries that adopted capitalism than in those that did not"?
2. How can one illustrate the assertion that "Capitalism simply cannot work if the people do not have a great amount of political freedom"?
3. For a natural resource, such as oil, explain how the theory of pure *laissez-faire* capitalism is not operative.
4. Using the classification of major occupational groups given in the chapter as chalkboard headings, poll the class as to their parents' occupations and

their own part-time occupations. Enter the results under the chalkboard headings. Which classification predominates? Does your community have a particular specialization?
5. Using Bureau of Labor statistics from an almanac, *Statistical Abstract*, or other source for the decades since 1900, check the percentage distribution of the major occupation groups. Which groups are increasing and why? Which are decreasing and why?
6. Present a sociodrama concerning the advantages and disadvantages of specialization in labor in one industry. Have persons in the class represent management, union laborers, and the general public.
7. Why do many other nations look to the United States as a leader in economic wealth and power? What factors best explain this leadership?
8. Discuss the reasons for the trend of private power utilities toward adopting nuclear energy as a power source. Why has the public in the areas of such proposed plants disapproved of the construction of such plants?
9. How will specialization in industry be affected by the trend toward the use of nuclear energy as a source of power?
10. The electric household can opener is a form of applied technology. What evidence can be cited to prove the validity of the preceding statement?

CHALLENGES TO ECONOMIC COMPETENCE

1. Choose a biography or autobiography concerning a person, such as Benvenuto Cellini, who lived during the days of the craft guilds. Select some descriptive portions that relate to the craft guild and read them to the class.
2. Write to the Atomic Energy Commission at Oak Ridge, Tennessee, to secure pamphlets describing the use of atomic energy for peaceful purposes. Prepare a five-minute talk or a paper on "Living in an Age of Atomic Energy."
3. Take a series of photographs which depict different types of specialization of workers in your community. Use this with appropriate headings and captions for a bulletin board display.
4. Make a collection of clippings from recently discarded magazines and newspapers which supplement the material presented in the chapter. Add to this a selection of pamphlets and brochures from the federal, state, and local government agencies which discusses freedom and specialization. Compile them into a vertical file folder to be used by the class as resource materials on the topic "Freedom and Specialization in Our Economic Evolution."
5. Prepare an oral report for a class presentation. The report should indicate the advantages and disadvantages of living on a telecommunication space station.
6. Organize a debate to be presented at a school assembly on the theme: The Technological Revolution Should be Controlled By the Congress of the United States.

Unit 2

Production of Goods and Services

Chapter 4 Goods, Income, and Production
Chapter 5 Marketing: From Producers to Consumers
Chapter 6 Organizing and Managing a Business
Chapter 7 Business Corporations
Chapter 8 Some Problems of Modern Production

THE CIRCULAR FLOW OF INCOME

PAYMENTS FOR WAGES, RENT, INTEREST, PROFITS   (INCOME)

SERVICES OF FACTORS OF PRODUCTION

BUSINESS FIRMS

CONSUMERS

GOODS AND SERVICES

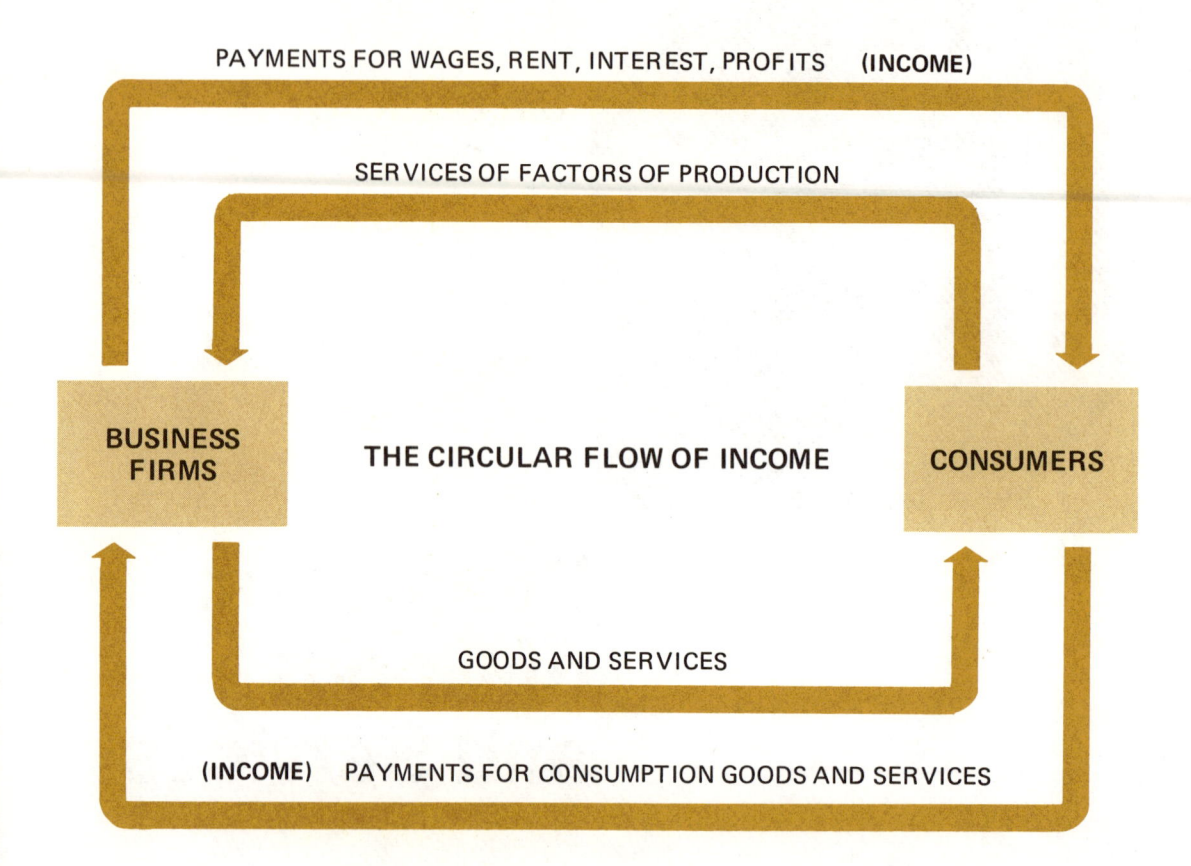

(INCOME)   PAYMENTS FOR CONSUMPTION GOODS AND SERVICES

America at work is a population of more than 80 million people engaged in diverse tasks and undertakings. But all of them have this in common: (1) they constitute a factor of production and help to produce goods and services for the satisfaction of human wants, and (2) they earn incomes with which to buy goods and services that are produced. How well they and their dependents can live depends largely upon what and how much all of them together produce. The sum total of all the goods and services produced is the measure of the nation's productivity, which is the highest in the world.

Chapter 4

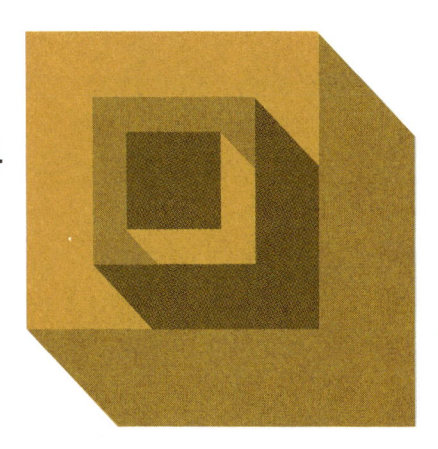

Goods, Income, and Production

What is an "economic good"?
What factors usually contribute to the production of any good?
How is production related to income?
Is government a producer?
What are some of the problems that result from changes in methods of production?

The world at work is a fascinating scene. Try to visualize some of the many activities that one might observe were he able to see the people of the United States at their various jobs. On the wide plains, in the river valleys, and on many a sloping hillside the farmers of the nation are busy producing food. Some of them are driving tractors, operating combines, cultivating corn, or picking peaches, depending on the season and the locality.

Here and there in some mountain regions miners are digging coal and bringing it to the surface so that homes may be heated and great plants kept in operation. In and around cities and in small towns are thousands of factory buildings where men and women are producing millions of articles of various kinds. Stretching in long, curving lines are the railroads over which passenger and freight trains are moving. And along the highways, tens of thousands of trucks of different sizes are moving goods from one locality to another. In the stores merchants and salespersons are selling goods. In the banks loans are being made, deposits are being received, and checks are being cashed. Professional workers, doctors, lawyers, dentists, and others are rendering their services. In the harbors are great ocean-going vessels — mute reminders that trade does not stop at shorelines.

PRODUCTION OF GOODS AND SERVICES — Unit 2

U.S. Department of Agriculture

State of Illinois: Department of Business and Economic Development

Illus. 4-1. On the wide plains, in the river valleys, and on many a sloping hillside the farmers of the nation are busy producing food.

Illus. 4-2. In the harbors are great ocean-going vessels — mute reminders that trade does not stop at shorelines.

America at work is a population of more than 80 million people engaged in diverse tasks and undertakings. But all of them have this in common: (1) they constitute a factor of production and help to produce goods and services for the satisfaction of human wants, and (2) they earn incomes with which to buy goods and services that are produced. How well they and their dependents can live depends largely upon what and how much all of them together produce. The sum total of all the goods and services produced is the measure of the nation's productivity, which is the highest in the world. Each year this productivity continues to increase, which means that the average person will have available a greater amount of goods and services. Men and women work to produce goods and services for which they receive income with which to buy what others produce.

To understand the world of work and the nature of goods, income, and production, in the next few sections we shall study the nature of goods, wealth, income, utility and production, the major factors of production, and technological unemployment.

WHAT ARE GOODS?

As the term is used in economics, a *good* is anything that has the capacity to satisfy a want. Usually a good is something material, as a loaf of bread, a pair of shoes, or a house. But sometimes the term is used to include services as well, such as the services of surgeons, teachers, and entertainers. According to our definition of a good, however, it is logical to say that such services are goods, although they are nonmaterial in nature. Goods may be classified as free and economic goods.

Free goods. Some of the needed and wanted things are supplied by nature in quantities sufficient for all who want them and in such a condition that they can be used just as they are. The supplies of air and of sunshine, for example, are sufficient in most places for everyone. Such things need not be changed in any way before they are used, nor do they cost any effort or money to obtain. For these reasons they are called *free goods*.

Economic goods. On the other hand, many things (like coal or water) must be changed in one or more ways before they can be used for most purposes. Furthermore, most goods, including services, are scarce compared to the wants of all the people. The supply of nearly all the things wanted is so limited that effort or money must be used to obtain them. For this reason we must economize in their use. There are great deposits of coal in the United States, enough to last for hundreds of years at the rate at which coal is being used at the present time. But the coal has to be dug from the mine and transported to the place where it is wanted. Consequently, factories, families, and other users of coal have to pay for it. One might consider water a free good — a gift of Nature — yet for large cities, water must be collected in reservoirs, filtration plants must be constructed, pipes must be run, and meters must be installed in homes and industrial plants. Therefore, in order to distinguish them from free goods, those goods that are scarce relative to demand and that cost effort or money to obtain are called *economic goods*.

THERE ARE THREE CLASSES OF MATERIAL ECONOMIC GOODS

In discussing business and economic problems it is often desirable to classify material economic goods as: (1) land, (2) capital goods, and (3) consumers' goods.

(1) What is land? As the economist uses the term, *land* refers to all natural resources that have been created without man's labor. These resources include the soil in its natural condition, rivers, forests, wildlife, minerals, ores, and climatic conditions.

(2) What are capital goods? *Capital goods* or *producers' goods* mean economic goods that may be used to produce other goods, such as a machine in a textile plant. Capital goods may be classified or grouped in two ways: (a) according to durability, that is the length of time the goods

KINDS OF GOODS

I. Free goods: Those goods that are present in quantities sufficient for all who want them and that may be had without money or effort. (Examples: air and sunshine, and sometimes land.)

II. Economic goods: Commodities and services that are not present in quantities sufficient for all who desire them and that can be obtained only by money or effort.

  A. *Intangible (nonmaterial) goods:* Services. (Examples: services of physicians, teachers, lawyers, and actors.)

  B. *Tangible (material) goods:*
    1. *Land:* All natural resources created without man's labor. (Examples: soil, forests, wildlife, minerals, etc.)
    2. *Capital (producers') goods:* Man-made economic goods used to produce other goods.
      a. Classification according to durability:
        (1) *Fixed capital:* Goods that may be used repeatedly in the production of other goods. (Examples: factory buildings, tools, machinery, office equipment, and farm equipment.)
        (2) *Circulating capital:* Goods that are used up immediately in the process of production. (Examples: coal, gas, electric power used in a factory.)
      b. Classification according to use:
        (1) *Free capital:* Goods that may be used for a great many purposes. (Examples: coal and electricity.)
        (2) *Specialized capital:* Goods that may be used for one purpose or only a limited number of purposes. (Examples: a steam shovel, a furnace stoker.)
    3. *Consumers' goods:* Goods intended to be used directly in the satisfaction of wants.
      a. *Durable consumers' goods:* Goods that do not wear out quickly when used by consumers. (Examples: automobiles and furniture.)
      b. *Nondurable consumers' goods:* Goods that are used up at once or at least rather quickly by consumers. (Examples: milk, bread, and pencils.)

may be used before wearing out, and (b) according to the ways in which the goods may be used.

(a) Capital classified according to durability. *Fixed capital* consists of producers' goods that may be used repeatedly in the production of other goods. Examples of fixed capital are a factory building, factory equipment, a steamship, a tractor, a derrick, and a typewriter. *Circulating capital* consists of producers' goods that are used up immediately in the process of production, as, for example, coal, fuel oil, electric current, and paper used in printing a newspaper.

(b) Capital classified according to use. The same goods that are classified as fixed capital and as circulating capital may also be classified according to use as free capital or as specialized capital. *Free capital* refers to those producers' goods which may be used for a number of purposes, such as electric current, which may be used to light our streets or to run a train. Coal may be used to operate a steel mill or to heat a home. *Specialized capital* applies to producers' goods that have only one use or a very limited number of uses. Both a steam shovel and a cash register are highly specialized forms of capital.

(3) What are consumers' goods? *Consumers' goods* are those economic goods that, in a finished state or condition, are to be used directly by persons for enjoyment, or to satisfy a need. They include both material goods and services.

Illus. 4-3. Examples of fixed capital are a factory building and factory equipment.

Commonwealth Edison Company

If you read books, news items, and magazine articles dealing with business conditions, you will frequently run across the terms "durable consumers' goods" and "nondurable consumers' goods." *Durable consumers' goods* are those material goods that do not wear out quickly when used by consumers. Refrigerators, automobiles, and television sets belong in this category. *Nondurable consumers' goods* are those goods that are used up rather quickly by consumers, such as milk, eggs, bread, and clothing.

INDUSTRIAL PRODUCTION BY MAJOR DIVISIONS

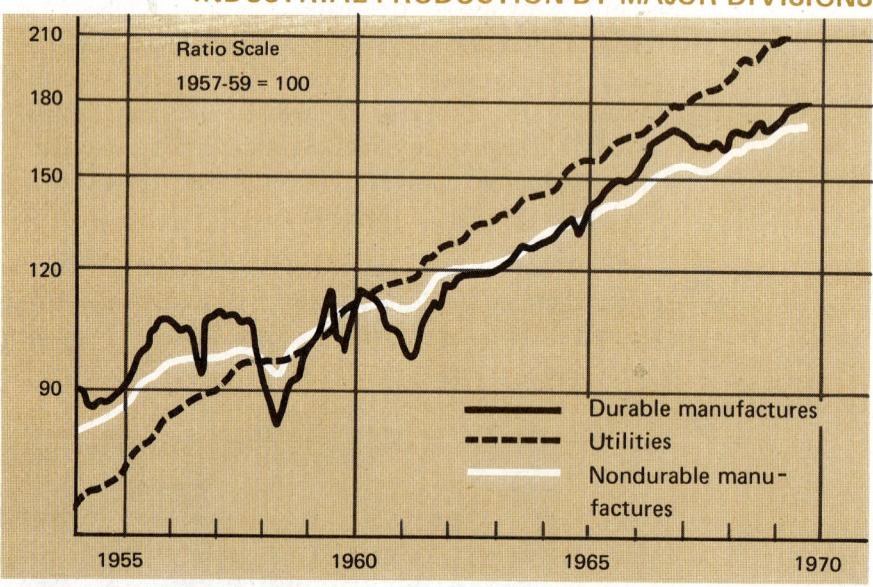

Figure 4-1

ADAPTED FROM: *Historical Chart Book, 1969*, Board of Governors of the Federal Reserve System.

THE ECONOMIC MEANING OF "WEALTH"

Like many other terms used every day, the word "wealth" is often used in various ways. But in the study of economics we limit the meaning of *wealth* to those material economic goods the ownership of which may be transferred from one person to another.

If you doubt whether a thing is wealth in the economic sense, ask yourself the following three questions: Is it material? Is it an economic good? Is ownership transferable? If the answers to these questions are "Yes," the article is a form of wealth.

(1) Who owns the wealth in a nation? Material economic goods that are owned by individuals and private business concerns are *private wealth*.

Ch. 4 GOODS, INCOME, AND PRODUCTION

Illus. 4-4. Material economic goods that are owned by individuals and private business concerns are private wealth.

When owned by government, material economic goods are referred to as *public wealth*. The *national wealth* is the sum of all the valuable material things owned by private individuals and concerns and by government.

(2) Is money wealth? Metal money is wealth. Its value as wealth is based upon the intrinsic value of the metal — not the face value of the coins. But paper money, although material, has little or no value except for the power it gives its owner to purchase material and nonmaterial things. Therefore, paper money and money in the bank are not wealth, although they give the owner the power to obtain wealth.

A share of stock in a corporation represents a fractional part of the ownership of the business; it is not a part of the buildings and equipment of the concern. Consequently, a share of stock of a corporation is not wealth. Nor is a check or a promissory note wealth. Such things have value since they give the owner the power to acquire wealth.

WHAT IS INCOME?

The term "income" implies that something "comes in." When used in economics, *income* refers to money, material goods, and services received or earned during a given period of time, as a month or a year. Individual income is usually received in the form of money payments of wages, salaries, rents, dividends, interest, profits, annuities, or pensions, which enable the recipient to obtain goods. The original source of the real income in the nation is the production of goods and services.

(1) The difference between money income and real income. *Money income* is the amount of money that one receives during a given period of time, as $400 a month, or $4,800 a year. *Real income* refers to the amount of goods that can be bought with the money received during a period of time. Thus, if one's annual income during two successive years is $4,800, and if the prices of all goods double during the second year, the amount of real income decreases 50 percent, even though the money income remains the same.

The real incomes of individuals and families are often greatly affected by changes in the prices of the goods that people buy. The cause of these changes is a subject in which all of us should be interested. We shall discuss this matter from time to time as we proceed with our study of economics.

(2) The nature of our national income. In the course of a year all the people working together in their various occupations produce a great quantity of goods and services of different kinds. Those who supply the land, labor, or capital, or who take certain risks receive incomes in the form of money. Such incomes are customarily referred to as rent, wages, salaries, fees, interest, and profits. The total of all such incomes derived from services contributed to production is the *national income*.

(3) The two ways for studying income. Imagine that you could observe the United States by orbiting over it in a space capsule. You would see that it is broken up into smaller parts by natural boundaries. You would also see its smallest parts as represented by cities, villages, and crossroads. The economist views the nation's economy in the same way. He can see the whole of an economic area, such as national income, national product, or national investment. This view, a study of aggregates or the total picture, is called *macroeconomics*. In Chapter 22, we shall discuss more fully the importance of total income and other examples of macroeconomics.

When the economist views the parts which make up the total economic area of income, such as the incomes of all real estate owners, or the detailed study of a single real estate owner, it is a study in *microeconomics*. Microeconomics involves a study of a small area of the economy's income, or product, or investment. In Chapter 15 we shall discuss how supply and demand for land affects rental income; that discussion is an example of a study in microeconomics.

UTILITY AND PRODUCTION

A good has the power to satisfy a human want; or it has *utility*, a term that means the same thing. How does this want-satisfying power, or utility, of a good arise? It arises because an article has certain physical characteristics, is where it is needed when it is needed, and because the person wanting it has it in his possession and can use it. This means that the actual utility of a good is really the sum of several kinds of utility.

Form utility. Iron ore and coal as they exist in the earth are of little value because in that condition they cannot be used to satisfy our wants. Before it can be made into articles of commerce, the iron ore must be smelted by placing it in a blast furnace in order to remove the impurities. Coal must be broken into pieces before it can be used. These are examples that illustrate the need for changing natural resources into forms that make it possible for them to satisfy our needs. Changes in the shape or composition of materials that make the materials more usable result in the creation of *form utility*.

Illus. 4-5. Changes in the shape or composition of materials that make the materials more usable result in the creation of form utility.

The International Nickel Company, Inc.

Place utility. After a good has acquired the desired form, it must be at the place where it is needed if it is to satisfy a want. For example, after automobiles have been manufactured, they must be delivered to the dealers and finally to the purchasers or consumers. Automobiles may be perfect and complete so far as form utility is concerned, but they cannot be used until they are at the place where they are wanted. The capacity of a good to satisfy a want by being at the place where it is wanted is called *place utility*.

Time utility. In addition to being at the place where it is needed, a good must be there at the time it is needed. Thus, an automobile that exists now in a distant city but which cannot be delivered to you until next month cannot serve your present need for transportation.

The power of a good to satisfy a want because it is available when it is wanted is called *time utility*. One of the main functions of transportation companies and merchants is to create place and time utilities.

Possession utility. If a box of fine chocolates is on your desk but you are not permitted to taste them, the candy can give you little satisfaction. Therefore, as you see, if a good possesses only form, place, and time utilities, something is lacking. It must be possible for one to use a good before it can satisfy a want.

The utility that a good possesses because it is possible to use the good is called *possession* or *ownership utility*. Possession utility is usually created by purchase and sale. In this way one ordinarily acquires the possession and right to use articles. Occasionally one gains permission to borrow an article, in which case the article has possession or ownership utility for the possessor.

The final selling price usually includes all the expenses incurred in giving a good all the forms of utility it possesses at the time.

Illus. 4-6. Possession utility is usually created by purchase and sale. The final selling price usually includes all the expenses incurred in giving a good all the forms of utility it possesses at the time.

Crown Zellerbach

PRODUCTION IS THE CREATION OF UTILITY

Anyone who creates utility or who indirectly aids in the creation of any one of the utilities is a producer. Farmers, miners, lumbermen, manufacturers, factory workers, and bricklayers are engaged primarily in the creation of form utility, although they may also create time and place utilities. Railroad employees and truckers are evidently engaged in the creation of time and place utilities, and so are merchants. And it is the business of merchants to create possession utility by buying and selling goods.

But how about such business workers as bookkeepers and stenographers? Are they producers? Yes, because industrial and business establishments make use of various kinds of records and communication. To keep such records and to help carry on communication with customers and other business concerns calls for the services of many clerical workers. Therefore, accounting and clerical workers are producers.

ENTERPRISE: THE COORDINATOR FOR PRODUCTION

Nothing ever "just happens." There is a cause for everything. This general truth applies to the production or the creation of utilities. Under our private-enterprise system, three major factors or agents of production are: land, labor, and capital. It was noted in Chapter 1 that these resource factors are scarce and must be used wisely or economically.

To produce a good usually requires the use of some combination of the three production factors. To harvest a corn crop on farmland, one could use many laborers to handpick the crop. To harvest a corn crop one could use a mechanical corn picker powered by fuel together with a single laborer as the machine operator. Costs of production would differ, however, depending upon which of the methods was used. If capital were scarce relative to labor, capital costs would be higher. If labor were scarce relative to capital, labor costs would be higher. Whose mental labor should make the decision as to which combination of factors is more economical?

Some economists call this decision making *enterprise*; they consider it a fourth factor of production. Other economists call enterprise the coordinator of production rather than a factor of production; they consider enterprisers as a part of the mental labor force engaged in organizing, managing, and operating businesses.

Enterprise is responsible for the initiation, organization, and operation of productive establishments and for the assumptions of risks of failure. Individuals who assume these responsibilities are called enterprisers, or to use the French expression, *entrepreneurs*. If the enterpriser succeeds, his reward is profit; if he fails, he must expect to bear the loss. The enterpriser either manages his business himself or appoints someone else to manage it. It is his responsibility as the manager to combine the other factors of production and to sell the product.

The factors of production, however, are scarce. Therefore, given amounts of a factor may be used in one of several possible kinds of production. Because of this fact, opportunity cost is a decisive factor in determining how the enterpriser will combine the use of resources. *Opportunity cost* is the payment necessary to attract a given amount of a factor or agent of production — land, labor, or capital — from an alternative use. The amount of the payment needed to attract the factor of production is considered to be the amount that the resource owner would be able to get in the next best opportunity for its employment. Consequently, opportunity costs influence the enterprisers in determining what will be produced.

Under a system of free enterprise or capitalism, the enterpriser is the key man in deciding what, when, where, and how much shall be produced. When the government engages in production, the taxpayers are the risk takers. The funds needed may be obtained by taxation or by borrowing. If the funds are borrowed, the lenders are repaid in money collected as taxes. Thus, the taxpayers supply the capital and assume the risks of failure of government enterprise.

GOVERNMENT AIDS PRODUCTION

The production of goods is not generally regarded as the function of government in this country. Yet the importance of government as a producer of services for private individuals and business concerns engaged in production must not be overlooked. Besides preserving law and order, protecting property, and enforcing contracts, the local, state, and national governments aid business and industry in other ways. For example, the national government collects statistics relating to the number and size, location, and output of business establishments. It also collects information from all parts of the world that aids in the sale of our goods to foreign countries. The Bureau of Standards performs experiments on manufacturing and building materials, helps to set up standards of performance, many of which are useful to manufacturers, and performs other services that help producers. The Weather Bureau observes and reports on weather conditions — a service that is valuable to farmers and to those engaged in shipping goods. The Department of Agriculture maintains experimental centers for research in animal and plant breeding and for the discovery of methods for the prevention and the cure of animal and plant diseases. To these we might add many other services that are furnished by government for the purposes of aiding production.

Ch. 4 GOODS, INCOME, AND PRODUCTION

Government also engages directly in the production of goods and other services, as in the case of the building of public roads, the maintenance of streets, the postal system, and the telecommunication services furnished by such agencies as the National Aeronautics and Space Administration.

Illus. 4-7. Government also engages directly in the production of goods and other services, as in the case of the postal system.

U.S. Post Office Department

RESULTS OF CHANGE IN PRODUCTION METHODS

A few years ago in a certain small shoe factory more than three hundred workers were employed. Then new laborsaving machinery was installed, and nearly one third of the working force was discharged. In spite of this decrease in the laboring force, the factory turned out more pairs of shoes. The discharged workers were compelled to find employment elsewhere or to go without work. For some of them it was difficult to secure employment, even at lower wages than they had received in the shoe factory.

Unemployment caused by the introduction of laborsaving machinery — called *technological unemployment* — is an important problem in economic and social life. How it can be solved is a question. Some people have opposed the use of laborsaving devices. But if the use of laborsaving tools and machinery is prevented, the most economical way of producing goods will not be used. From the standpoint of the people as a whole, it is desirable that all goods be produced at the lowest possible cost, which is to say, with the least amount of effort.

Perhaps all of us have a responsibility to those workers who are thrown out of work when new kinds of machinery are put to use. If employers install laborsaving machinery, they do so because they wish to reduce the cost of production and thus to make more profit. It would seem, therefore, that they owe something to any workers who are displaced from their jobs. Furthermore, since the use of machinery often means that all of us are able to obtain goods at lower costs, many feel that the public also should help those employees who are displaced from work to find new jobs or to train for a new kind of work. Ordinarily, workers who lose their jobs because of their displacement by machines receive some unemployment benefits.

Of course, when a worker is displaced because of the installation of a new machine in a factory, he is not always discharged. In many cases he is given another place in the same factory, although the work may be different from that to which he has been accustomed. Some firms and also the federal government have retraining programs for displaced workers as we saw in the preceding chapter.

Illus. 4-8. In the long run the use of more efficient machinery creates jobs.

American Iron and Steel Institute

In the long run the use of more efficient machinery creates jobs. In the transportation industry the coming of the railroad caused a great decrease in the numbers of persons engaged in river and canal transportation. And the production of automobiles has done away with the need for nearly all wagon and carriage factories. On the other hand, there are a great many more persons employed in railroad transportation than were needed to operate riverboats and canalboats when the railroad came. There are likewise a great many more workers in the automobile factories than were employed in the wagon and carriage factories forty or fifty years ago. Of course, part of this increase in the number of employees is due to an increase in population, but economic growth spurred by automation contributes to increased employment opportunities.

SUMMARY

A good, in an economic sense, is anything that has the power or capacity to satisfy a want. As to form or nature, a good is either material or nonmaterial. Free goods are those that are so abundant that our wants for them may be satisfied without effort or money. There are three kinds of material economic goods; land, capital, and consumers' goods. Land consists of natural resources. Capital goods are man-made goods that may be used to produce other goods. Capital goods or producers' goods may be classified as fixed or circulating and as free or specialized. Consumers' goods are those that are used for the direct satisfaction of wants. Consumers' goods are durable or nondurable.

Wealth consists of material economic goods, the ownership of which is transferable. Money — except metal money — is not wealth.

Income refers to money or goods that are received during a given period of time. Personal income is income that is received by individuals. Real income refers to goods received or to the amount of goods that may be purchased with a given amount of money income. The national income is the total amount of earnings belonging to all the owners of the factors of production. Its calculation involves macroeconomics or the study of aggregate income. Income received by one individual or a select group of individuals, such as apartment-house landlords, involves microeconomics.

Production is the creation of utility. Utility is the power or capacity of a good to satisfy a want. There are four kinds of utility: form, time, place, and possession.

Enterprise is the activity or decision making that is required to initiate, organize, and operate a business. The enterpriser is a key individual in production. Motivated by opportunity costs, he coordinates the factors of production and assumes the involved business risks. Government also produces goods and services for its citizens and offers many aids to private business concerns.

Production methods keep changing due to technology. New production methods provide more goods and new varieties of goods. In the long run, technology may create employment for more workers than the number of workers it previously displaced.

NEW TERMS

capital *or* producers' goods
circulating capital
consumers' goods
durable consumers' goods
economic goods
enterprise
entrepreneurs
fixed capital
form utility
free capital
free goods
good
income
land
macroeconomics
microeconomics
money income
national income
national wealth
nondurable consumers' goods
opportunity cost
place utility
possession *or* ownership utility
private wealth
public wealth
real income
specialized capital
technological unemployment
time utility
utility
wealth

QUESTIONS ON THE CHAPTER

1. What is the definition of a good?
2. Can goods be "nonmaterial"? Explain.
3. Is land a capital good? Explain.
4. What are some examples of fixed capital and circulating capital?
5. What are the two classes of consumers' goods? Give examples of each.
6. May some goods be classified as either consumers' or producers' goods?
7. How can you judge whether a certain thing is wealth? Give examples of wealth.
8. If paper money and money in the bank are not wealth, why is metal money wealth?
9. What is income? How is income related to wealth?
10. What is the difference between money income and real income?
11. What is national income?
12. What is the difference between macroeconomics and microeconomics as they relate to the study of income?
13. What examples can you cite for each of the four kinds of utility?
14. What is production? Is schoolteaching a form of production?
15. What role does enterprise play in the production process?
16. What is meant by "opportunity cost"? How are production decisions influenced by it?

Ch. 4 GOODS, INCOME, AND PRODUCTION

17. In what ways does the government aid production? Give examples.
18. How does technological change both destroy and create jobs?

APPLYING YOUR ECONOMIC UNDERSTANDING

1. Prepare a list of free goods which you use. Are these free goods available to everyone? What conditions would change them to economic goods?
2. How many types of land resources are available in your local community? How does their value compare with the land resources of some other community in your state?
3. How would free goods and economic goods in the pre-colonial period compare with free goods and economic goods in the United States today?
4. Visit a shoe repair shop and make a list of the major types of capital goods used in it. Classify them as "free capital" or as "specialized capital" goods. Classify them as "durable" and as "nondurable" goods.
5. Recall a school dance which you attended. How many kinds of consumer goods can you recall from the experience? Which were "durable" consumer goods? Which were "nondurable" consumer goods?
6. Use an unabridged dictionary to find five meanings of the term "wealth." Which meaning best describes wealth as an economic concept? Why?
7. You are pulling away from a drive-in after purchasing some refreshments. What four forms of utility did the refreshments have, and why were these utility forms important to you?
8. Using the automobile industry as an example, outline the three major production factors that it requires, and show how each factor is used in the creation of utility. What is the function of enterprise in the industry?
9. What services does the federal government directly provide in your community? What services does the federal government indirectly contribute to your community?
10. Make a classified list of service workers in your community. Are they producers? Why or why not?
11. David needs a scholarship to be able to go on to college. To secure the scholarship a very high score on the social studies section of the College Entrance Board Examination is required. He has one hour each night which he can spend on bowling which he enjoys, or he can use the hour for extra study. How does this relate to "opportunity cost"?

CHALLENGES TO ECONOMIC COMPETENCE

1. Use the library to locate several pictures concerning the life of the American Indians. Show these to your classmates and discuss the types of free goods and the types of economic goods that the pictures illustrate.

2. Prepare a bulletin board display with materials and captions which distinguish macroeconomic data from microeconomic data related to income.
3. Prepare a written report on one of the following topics: (a) The Relationship of Wealth to Income, (b) How Income Payments Differ, (c) Technology Is In — Some Jobs Are Out, (d) From Field Fodder to Frankfurter.
4. Through cooperation with your teacher and your audiovisual center, arrange with your state film library, or other source, to secure a copy of the 16mm color film, *The Marvelous Mousetrap*, produced by: Bureau of National Affairs, Inc., Rockville, Maryland. Preview it, present it in class, and lead a discussion which summarizes how the film relates to production and enterprise.
5. Prepare a pair of collages for classroom display. One collage should be made from materials that illustrate durable consumer economic goods; the other representative of nondurable consumer goods.
6. Make the arrangements for an enterpriser from your community to visit with and discuss with your class how the factors of production are coordinated in his business.

Chapter 5

Marketing: From Producers to Consumers

Why is marketing a form of production?
What are the functions of marketing?
What does each class of marketing middlemen do?
Of what importance are commodity exchanges?

"Have a candy bar?" Both young and old are likely to respond willingly to such an invitation. For a candy bar may meet one's need for energy or fulfill his craving for a sweet. It is highly improbable, though, that the person who accepts the candy so casually has given much thought as to how this good has been made available.

Consider briefly the gathering together of the necessary ingredients. From Tafo in Ghana comes the basis of the chocolate — the cacao bean — which furnishes the "nib" that, when ground and mixed with sugar and cacao butter, is sold as cocoa. Plantation workers in Southeastern Mexico gather the vanilla pods which must be fermented and dried to produce the delicate flavoring we enjoy. The sugar was probably grown in Louisiana and had to undergo many processes before it became available in the form it was offered to the candy manufacturer. Milk and butter may have been local products, but the corn syrup was probably produced in Illinois or Missouri. The almonds which made the candy such a special treat were grown in California.

By ship, train, and highway trucks the ingredients were conveyed to the manufacturer who produced the candy bar. It was wrapped in waxed paper to preserve its freshness, and again in an outside wrapper to assure its cleanliness. Packed in boxes it is now offered for sale in grocery stores in Vermont, in gas stations in Texas, in automatic dispensers in subway stations in New York and Philadelphia, on newsstands in Oregon, and on trains in all parts of the country. What is true of the candy bar is true

Illus. 5-1. From Tafo in Ghana comes the basis of the chocolate — the cacao bean — which furnishes the "nib" that, when ground and mixed with sugar and cacao butter, is sold as cocoa.

United Nations

of most of the articles we use: materials from various sources must be shipped to a factory, made into a finished product, and made available to buyers or to consumers.

The process of making goods available to final users or consumers involves the performance of a number of essential functions. What are these functions or activities? Who performs them? How are they performed? These are the questions that we shall attempt to answer in this chapter.

WHAT IS MARKETING?

Marketing includes all the business activities involved in the physical movements of goods and the transfers of ownership that are necessary to make goods available to those who want to use them.

Therefore, in the marketing of most goods, not only are the services of merchants necessary, but also the services of transportation systems, banks, advertising agencies, newspapers and magazines, radio and television, government bureaus, storage concerns, insurance companies, and other agencies and individuals. Hence, the goods on the retailer's shelves are almost at the end of a long series of business activities of one kind or another. But the marketing of a good is not complete until the good has been purchased by the final consumer.

INCOME OF UNINCORPORATED MARKETING ENTERPRISES, BY INDUSTRY: 1940 TO 1967

[In millions of dollars. Prior to 1960, excludes Alaska and Hawaii. Income equals business receipts (exclusive of capital gains and expenses) less business expenses (exclusive of capital losses and depletion allowances)]

Industry	1940	1945	1950	1955	1960	1965	1967
Transportation....................	286	432	655	754	794	1,194	1,242
Wholesale and retail trade..........	3,904	9,683	10,076	11,143	11,503	12,548	13,198
Finance, insurance, and real estate...	433	899	1,831	2,915	3,163	3,965	4,085
Services	2,642	4,532	6,683	9,617	12,829	17,833	20,321

Preliminary total for 1968 is $62,863 million; detail not available.

SOURCE: Dept. of Commerce, Office of Business Economics; *The National Income and Product Accounts of the United States, 1929-1965* and *Survey of Current Business*, July 1968.

The preceding table reports the incomes of unincorporated marketing enterprises. Since unincorporated businesses are usually small enterprises, opportunities for making a living in marketing have rapidly multiplied since 1940. The rate of growth, particularly in the services, indicates the extent to which affluence has been achieved by many American families. Only after basic needs are met can one begin to indulge in the additional spending that is required if others are to perform services for us.

MARKETING IS A PHASE OF PRODUCTION

Chapter 4 reported that several kinds of utilities must be created before goods can be used to satisfy our wants. The business of some producers is to create form utility. For example, the cacao bean mentioned must be gathered, cleaned, roasted, broken, and the shell removed before the "nib" which is to be used in cocoa is available.

However, form utility alone is not sufficient. Goods must also possess time, place, and possession utilities. Therefore, after certain producers have created form utility, it is necessary to make goods available at the time and at the place where they are wanted and to enable those who will use the goods to acquire possession of them. As you can see, it is the business of retailers, wholesalers, elevator companies, transportation firms, and others to supply various types of productive services. They are often referred to as *middlemen*, which implies that they operate between the producers of form utility and those who finally use the goods.

MARKETING INVOLVES A TWOFOLD FLOW OF PRODUCTS

Two movements of goods are involved in marketing: (1) concentration and (2) dispersion.

(1) Concentration. This term can be illustrated by describing the processes in the marketing of wheat and flour. To begin with, the farmers grow the wheat. Although there are several ways in which the farmers may dispose of their wheat, we may assume that they sell it to an elevator company. The elevator company is a concern organized for the purpose of buying grain from farmers; or it may be operated by a farmers' marketing cooperative. The latter organization is an association of farmers that sells farm products in the large central markets.

Up to this point it is apparent that the wheat has been undergoing the process of *concentration*. That is, after having been grown by many thousands of farmers, the wheat is sold to a comparatively small number of local elevator companies, which then sell it to a still smaller number of buyers.

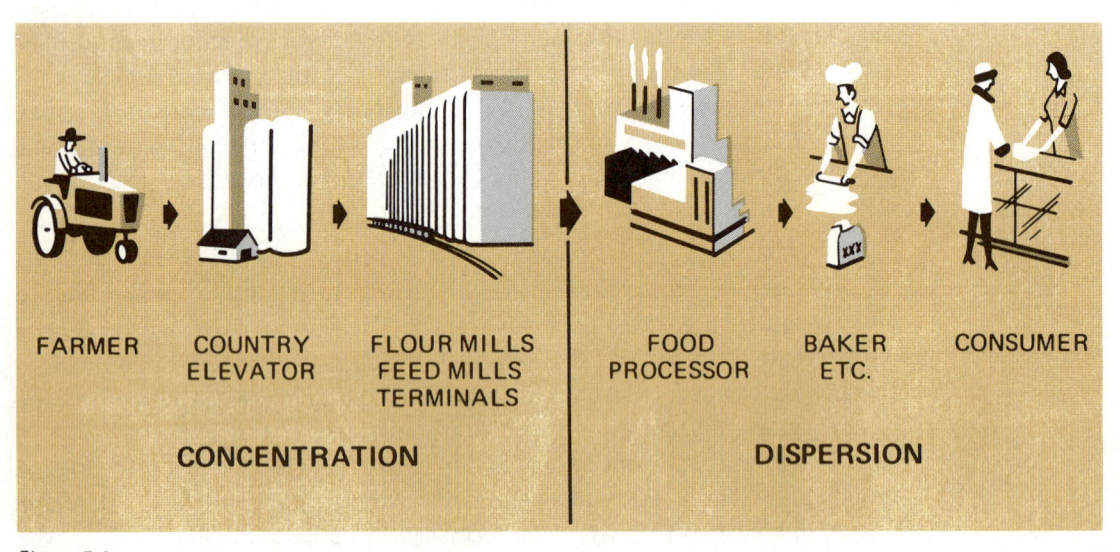

Figure 5-1.

FARMER → COUNTRY ELEVATOR → FLOUR MILLS FEED MILLS TERMINALS → FOOD PROCESSOR → BAKER ETC. → CONSUMER

CONCENTRATION | DISPERSION

Two movements of goods are involved in marketing: (1) concentration and (2) dispersion. Concentration is the movement of goods toward a common center. In the illustration this common center is the mill. Dispersion is the movement of the goods from the common center to the millions of consumers.

(2) Dispersion. A relatively small number of flour mills buy the wheat and convert it into flour. The flour is sold to a larger number of wholesalers, who sell it to many local retailers, from whom it is purchased by millions of consumers. Thus, the flour goes through the process of *dispersion* in a series of steps from the mills to the consumers. Figure 5-1 above illustrates the process of concentration and dispersion.

Ch. 5   MARKETING: FROM PRODUCERS TO CONSUMERS

WHAT ARE THE FUNCTIONS OF MARKETING?

A *marketing function* is one of the activities that is performed in the marketing process. Every one of these activities must be performed by someone before merchandise can be purchased by the consumer. Usually each of them is performed several times before an article is ready for use by the consumer. Often one individual undertakes to perform more than one marketing activity. In many instances, however, specialists undertake the performance of only one of the functions. Most of these functions of marketing may be classified under the following headings: (1) selling, (2) buying, (3) standardizing and grading, (4) financing, (5) transporting, (6) storing, and (7) risk bearing.

(1) Selling. The example of the marketing process given in the diagram below shows that selling first takes place when the farmer sells his wheat to

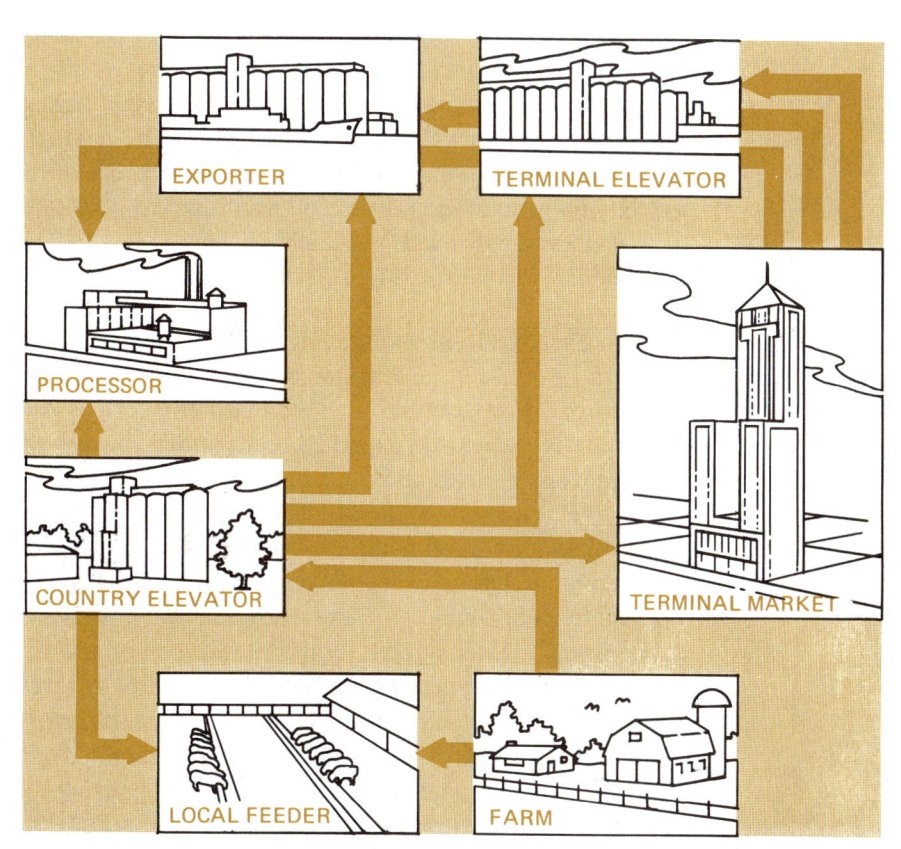

Figure 5-2. Selling may occur several times before the product finally reaches the consumer.

Chicago Board of Trade

the country elevator. Selling may occur several times before the product finally reaches the consumer.

Selling often involves the use of salesmanship and advertising. The flour manufacturer, for example, may employ a great deal of salesmanship and advertising. Moreover, the salesmen who represent a flour mill or a wholesaler have an opportunity to present the merits of their flour in comparison with that of other brands. Finally, the bakers and the retailers undertake to popularize their individual products through the medium of advertising.

(2) Buying. Every time the product is sold, it is also bought; there must be a purchase when there is a sale. But the acts of selling and buying are performed by different parties, and the procedures are different. The buyer of goods seldom advertises. His object is to seek out the source from which he can obtain the desired commodity at the lowest possible price consistent with the quality wanted. Buying for the purpose of resale, however, involves some problems that are different from those of consumer buying. The object, of course, in both cases is to obtain goods at the lowest price consistent with the quality desired. Buying raw materials for a factory or buying manufactured goods for a large store necessitates buying in large volume and according to the needs of the business, instead of buying in small quantities and according to personal wants. The buyer for a manufacturing or a merchandising concern is often a highly paid individual because the duties of the position call for ability of a high order.

(3) Standardizing and grading. When marketing of certain products is undertaken on a large scale, some form of standardization and grading is necessary. For example, if a standard for corn is established as No. 2 yellow, then when the corn has been graded, buyers can make their purchases from samples and according to description with the assurance that what they buy will be the kind and the quality they want. Finally, after cereal has been manufactured, it must be put into standardized packages and containers for the convenience of the retailer and the consumer.

Many goods undergo standardization and grading several times before they reach the consumer. When the farmer or the fruit grower sells his produce, for instance, he makes some attempt to grade it according to certain standards. You are familiar with the cartons of eggs, which might be graded A-large or B-medium size. Vegetables, fruits, and other farm products are frequently subjected to further grading in the local markets and also in the central markets located in the cities. Lumber must also be graded according to recognized specifications; otherwise purchasers would

Ch. 5 MARKETING: FROM PRODUCERS TO CONSUMERS   85

Illus. 5-2. When marketing of certain products is undertaken on a large scale, some form of standardization and grading is necessary.

Chicago Board of Trade

be unable to obtain the quality of lumber they needed unless they examined every piece to be bought.

(4) Financing. Someone must be willing to put money into production before goods can be made ready for use. This fact is true of every type of production and of every stage of production, whether it is in the manufacturing, storage, or transportation of commodities. Someone must, therefore, make provision for financing the marketing as well as the manufacturing of goods. Individual business concerns, commercial banks, and finance companies supply the money or the credit necessary.

(5) Transporting. Transportation is usually performed by organized transportation systems. Since the costs of transportation must be borne by someone, the person who assumes the job of getting the goods to consumers should choose the most economical mode of transportation available. In order to make use of the most suitable means, the buyer or the seller, as the case may be, must be familiar with the various kinds of transportation at his disposal.

(6) Storing. Goods do not move in a continuous stream to the consumer. At various points, periods of waiting are necessary. While the supply is being assembled (as in the case of wheat being collected at the elevator), it is always necessary to utilize storage facilities. Then, too, the factory or mill must keep a supply of raw materials on hand. After

Illus. 5-3. Transportation is usually performed by organized transportation systems.

Farmers Union Grain Terminal Association

a product is manufactured, it must be stored by the manufacturer until wholesalers buy it; it must be stored by each wholesaler until retailers buy it; and it must be stored by each retailer until his customers buy it.

Different kinds of goods require different kinds of storage facilities. For example, conditions suitable for the storage of wheat would hardly do for eggs, animal products, or fruits. Storage facilities adapted to the nature of the product must, therefore, be provided.

So important is storage in the marketing process that specialized agencies for the performance of this function have developed. In addition to grain elevators for the storage of grain, such agencies provide warehouses, cold storage plants, stockyards, and poultry yards.

In many instances the specialization of storage agencies tends to result in lower prices of goods. It also tends to stabilize the prices of commodities because perishable and seasonal goods can be kept available until they are needed. Still another result is that retailers do not, as a rule, try to keep a large supply of goods on hand, but depend upon central suppliers. This practice is more economical than keeping large quantities in stock.

(7) Risk bearing. The greater the risk involved in the marketing of goods, the greater the cost to the consumer. This result naturally follows because no one will undertake the purchase of goods for resale at any point in the marketing process unless he has reason to believe that he will make a profit. If he experiences high losses, he will need to charge enough

Illus. 5-4. So important is storage in the marketing process that specialized agencies for the performance of this function have developed.

for his goods to enable him to cover his possible losses and to leave him a profit besides. The grocery retailer on the eastern seaboard who sells strawberries from California and cantaloupes from Arizona, for example, must undertake the risk of under- or over-ripeness of fruit he purchases for resale.

There are several ways in which individual marketing risks may be minimized. First, modern marketing methods may be used. For example, the development of cold storage has in many instances practically eliminated risks due to spoilage. Second, individual risks may be reduced by the exercise of judgment. A miller, through his knowledge of the supply of wheat and of the prospects of growing crops, may save himself from loss by buying at the right time. Third, insurance may be used to lessen risk in some instances.

THE ROLES OF MIDDLEMEN IN MARKETING

The middlemen who perform marketing services are (1) merchants, (2) agents, and (3) miscellaneous marketing agencies.

(1) Merchants. A *merchant* buys and sells on his own account. He takes title to goods and assumes the risk of their ownership. Merchants include both wholesalers and retailers.

(a) Wholesalers. Wholesalers are merchants who buy in large quantities for the purpose of selling smaller quantities of goods to others, who, in turn, will resell the goods. The wholesaler usually sells to retailers, although he may sometimes sell to other wholesalers. Wholesalers buy from manufacturers, farmers, and other producers, and from importers. They are engaged in the marketing of nearly all kinds of goods.

The wholesaler performs many necessary functions in the marketing process. He usually specializes in a limited line of merchandise, such as clothing of one or more kinds. He buys in large quantities to secure lower unit cost prices and to lower his unit transportation costs. He can pass on some of his mass purchase savings and transportation savings to the retailer in the form of lower prices. His service makes it possible for the retailer to obtain a small quantity of goods from him and generally at a lower cost than the retailer would pay for a direct purchase from the factory.

The wholesaler keeps a supply of goods available for the retailers in his territory. He often extends credit to retailers. Through his services the manufacturer is relieved of a great deal of record keeping, correspondence, and investigation as to the reliability of the retailers, all of which would be necessary before sales could be made on account if the manufacturer undertook to sell directly to retailers.

(b) Retailers. The *retailer* is the kind of merchant with whom we are most familiar. The position of the retailer is indeed one of great importance. In reality, the retailer is the self-appointed purchasing agent

IMPORTANT KINDS OF RETAIL STORES

Accessory-tire-battery shops	Grocery and meat stores
Animal and pet shops	Hardware and implement stores
Bakeries	Hobby and craft shops
Beer and liquor (packaged) stores	Household supply and appliance stores
Camera and photography shops	Jewelry stores
Cigar stores and stands	Lumber and building materials stores
Cosmetic and wig shops	Men's clothing stores
Department stores	Motor vehicle dealers
Drugstores	Radio, stereo, and television shops
Family clothing stores	Restaurants and eating places
Farm and garden supply stores	Sporting goods and toy stores
Fuel and ice stations	Variety stores
Furniture stores	Women's apparel shops

for the consumers whom he serves. The people rely upon retailers to buy for them and to keep on hand the goods that they will want.

Altogether there are about 2 million retail stores and about ½ million wholesalers in the United States. In addition to these firms there are about 3 million firms in the service industries, including hotels, laundries, barbershops, automobile repair shops, amusement enterprises, and others. All these perform certain retailing functions.

(2) Agents. *Agents* buy and sell for others. Brokers and commission men are agents who perform important functions in certain phases of the marketing process.

A *broker* is an individual who brings the buyer and the seller together. He does not buy or sell goods for himself. It often happens that a seller does not know where the best market for his goods is located or that a buyer does not know the best source of the goods that he desires. These conditions enable the broker to perform a valuable service in marketing.

The broker is a specialist. He makes it his business to keep informed as to the location of possible buyers and sellers of particular kinds of goods. When a broker has brought a buyer and a seller together and has effected a sale between them, he receives a commission for his services. *Commission merchants* are similar to brokers except that they actually have the goods in their possession and make sales.

(3) Miscellaneous marketing agencies. In a large measure the marketing process involves all the agencies and the activities of business. Besides merchants and agents, there are many other agencies that aid in the buying and the selling of goods. These agencies include banks, which lend money to merchants; railroads and trucking companies, which transport goods from one place to another; advertising agencies; and insurance companies.

ECONOMIES IN MARKETING BENEFIT CONSUMERS

Whatever reduces the cost of the marketing functions tends to reduce the cost of the goods to the consumer. If storage or transportation expenses can be reduced, the saving may be passed along to the consumer in the form of lower prices. For example, ocean freight formerly was stored and shipped as hundreds of separate cartons. Today this type of freight is increasingly being carried in sealed metal containers that resemble the trailers used in trucking. These containers reduce the costs of storage handling and losses by theft. Trailer vans are now carried "piggyback" on railroad flat cars to reduce the freight rate on the long haul of the distance to be covered. The trucking industry has also reduced costs by lessening the need for drivers and cab equipment through the use of tandem trailers.

If competition among sellers exists all along the line, such competition may also encourage economy in marketing. An illustration of competition can be found in the operation of an organized commodity exchange.

WHAT IS AN ORGANIZED COMMODITY EXCHANGE?

If you will look on the financial pages of a daily newspaper of a large city, you will find price quotations for wheat, cotton, corn, oats, and other commodities. You will notice that the prices are often given for a future month. These prices, however, are not the retail prices of the various products. They are the prices on the organized commodity exchanges, which are located in many of our large cities. An *organized commodity exchange* is simply a place where members of the exchange may meet to buy and sell commodities such as wheat, cotton, and many other commodities, most of which come from farms, for immediate or for future delivery.

A sale of goods on the exchange for immediate delivery is called a *cash sale*. A sale for delivery at some time in the future is called a *future sale*, or merely a *future*. For example, a sale may be made in January for the delivery, or the transfer of ownership, of wheat in March. All transactions completed on the organized exchanges are made on the basis of standardized grades of commodities.

Illus. 5-5. An organized commodity exchange is simply a place where members may meet to buy and sell commodities for immediate or for future delivery.

Chicago Board of Trade

The Chicago Board of Trade is an exchange organized for the purpose of trading in grains. A member may sell wheat in January at, for example, $2 a bushel and agree to make delivery in March. If the seller does not already own the wheat, he will, before the date of delivery, buy it from someone else. If he can obtain it, for example, at $1.90 a bushel, he will make a profit of 10 cents on each bushel. But if he has to pay more for the wheat than his selling price, he will suffer a loss. The possibility of making a profit is one of the chief reasons for trading on organized commodity exchanges.

THE CASE FOR AND AGAINST MARKET SPECULATION

Wheat and other agricultural products are seasonal. At harvest time more wheat is available than the millers can use at that time. If there were no speculators who were willing to buy the wheat and hold it for awhile, the prices that the farmers would receive would be those that the millers were willing to pay. Since the supply at that time would be great, the price at harvest time would be lower than it would be later. Hence, individuals who are willing to assume the risk of ownership by buying and holding wheat create a larger demand for it than there would be if the millers were the only buyers. The increased demand results in higher prices for the farmers at harvest time.

On the other hand, the fact that the speculators have supplies of wheat on hand that can be delivered during the seasons when wheat is not being harvested keeps prices from going as high as they might if less wheat were available.

(1) Speculators hope to make a profit. Naturally the speculators are in business for the purpose of making a profit. They can make a profit, however, only if the market fluctuates as they expect it to. A decrease in price is advantageous to those members of the exchanges who wish to buy, while a rise in price benefits those who wish to sell. In financial circles those who believe that prices will decline in the future are known as "bears"; those who believe that prices will rise are known as "bulls."

(2) Commodity exchanges are regulated by government. The Commodity Exchange Authority is a federal agency the function of which is to regulate future trading in wheat, rice, corn, barley, rye, flaxseed, sorghum, mill feeds, cotton, butter, eggs, Irish potatoes, and wool tops. Only licensed exchanges and brokers are permitted to operate. Prices are allowed to fluctuate only within the limits fixed by the Authority. False reports as to the demand and supply of a commodity are forbidden. The amount of trading by one person may be limited. If, in the opinion of the Authority, one person buys too much of a commodity — tries to "corner the market" — he may be ordered to sell part of it. Dealers are required to maintain correct records.

SUMMARY

Marketing includes all the business activities involved in the physical movements of goods and the transfers of ownership that are necessary to make goods available to people.

Marketing activities are a part of the total productive process because these activities help to create time, place, and ownership utility. In the marketing of most commodities two characteristic movements take place: concentration and dispersion.

There are a number of marketing functions which can be classified under the following heads: (1) selling, (2) buying, (3) standardizing and grading, (4) financing, (5) transporting, (6) storing, and (7) risk bearing.

Broadly speaking, there are three classes of middlemen: (1) merchants, (2) agents, and (3) miscellaneous marketing agencies. Merchants own the goods they sell; agents buy and sell for the accounts of others; and miscellaneous marketing agencies may render various kinds of services that aid in the performance of one of the marketing functions.

Organized commodity exchanges are places where buying and selling, mostly of a speculative nature, are carried on. When properly operated — as they usually are — such exchanges perform socially desirable functions.

NEW TERMS

agents
broker
cash sale
commission merchants
Commodity Exchange Authority
concentration
dispersion
future *or* future sale

marketing
marketing function
merchant
middlemen
organized commodity exchange
retailer
wholesalers

QUESTIONS ON THE CHAPTER

1. What is the definition of marketing?
2. Why is marketing classified as a phase of production?

3. In the production process, who are the middlemen?
4. What is the meaning of the statement "Marketing involves a twofold flow of products"?
5. What is a farmers' marketing cooperative?
6. How would you define and illustrate the following: (a) selling; (b) buying; (c) standardizing and grading; (d) financing; (e) transporting; (f) storing; (g) risk bearing? Is each of these functions essential to modern marketing? Explain.
7. What examples can you give of each of the three classes of middlemen?
8. Does the wholesaler perform any important functions in the marketing process?
9. What is the difference between a broker and a commission merchant?
10. What are some of the miscellaneous marketing agencies?
11. How does economy in marketing affect each one of us?
12. How does an organized commodity exchange operate?
13. Can you explain how a "bear" can profit by a decrease in the price of the commodity he is selling? Discuss.

APPLYING YOUR ECONOMIC UNDERSTANDING

1. Does advertising as a form of marketing have any relationship to the earlier discussion of man's psychological or personality needs? Cite examples.
2. In what ways may a bank serve as a middleman in the marketing process?
3. Is marketing the predominant economic activity in your community? Why or why not?
4. Would a key railroad terminal, such as Chicago or St. Louis, be associated with concentration in marketing? Explain the reason for your answer.
5. How does risk taking under ownership differ from risk bearing in marketing? Illustrate your answer.
6. Using a local newspaper as a reference, determine the percentage of the total newspaper space which serves the marketing function of selling.
7. Despite the number and size of large chain stores, many small retail stores exist and are competitors in the same communities. What accounts for this fact?
8. In writings about the westward movement in the United States, a number of authors have used the term "land speculation." Would this be a correct term to use? Defend your answer.
9. Is the lumber sold in your local lumberyard graded? What effect does grading have on the prices of lumber of the same dimensions?
10. Books can be bought locally or through a "Book-of-the-Month Club" plan. What are the major advantages and disadvantages of each type of purchase?

CHALLENGES TO ECONOMIC COMPETENCE

1. Prepare a bulletin board display of colorful advertising clipped from discarded newspapers and magazines. Have the display arranged to contrast advertising that appeals to psychological needs with that which is directed toward organic needs.
2. Ask your English or history teacher or your librarian to recommend some novel, biography, or other reading which describes the land speculation eras in American history. Prepare an oral report which elaborates on land booms to present to the class.
3. Prepare a vertical file folder for future class use. In it include samples of the many different forms of insurance contracts which show the kinds of risk bearing that the insurance companies assume.
4. Secure the loan of a film from the Chicago Board of Trade which depicts the operation of a commodity market. Preview the film. Prepare some discussion questions about it. Show the film and lead a class discussion on it.
5. Investigate and then prepare a written report on one of the following: (a) Prospective Sales of Lunar Plots, (b) The Pros and Cons of Chain Stores, (c) The Mail-Order House and Our History, (d) Marketing in My Community, (e) The Postal System and Marketing.
6. Prepare and present an illustrated oral report on recent trends in transportation. Include in your report the innovations of containerization, tandem hauling, and "piggyback" shipments.
7. As a photography project, make a series of shots which will illustrate the seven functions of marketing as they are found in your community. Identify the function which each photograph portrays. Present the project to the teacher to be used as a resource in future class discussions about the marketing functions.

Chapter 6

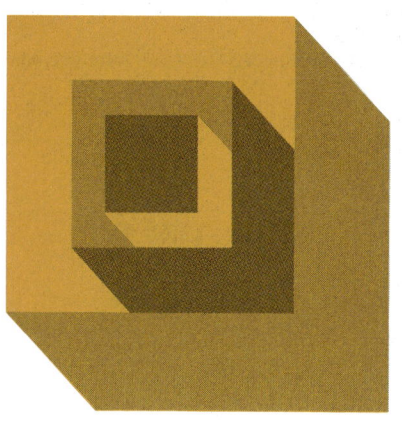

Organizing and Managing Business

What decisions must be made before production can take place?
In our economy who makes these decisions?
What are the advantages and disadvantages of a sole proprietorship?
What are the advantages and disadvantages of a partnership?
Does a problem of survival confront small business?

Before production can take place, the necessary factors of production must be assembled, organized, and managed. This is true whether production is to be undertaken by private individuals or by government. In a free-enterprise economy the functions of organizing and managing industrial and business firms are usually performed by enterprisers, or entrepreneurs.

As indicated in Chapter 1, the hope of making a profit leads the entrepreneur into organizing and continuing the operation of a private business enterprise. The hope of gaining profit income also encourages the enterpriser to assume certain business risks.

THERE ARE MANY KINDS OF BUSINESS RISKS

Many things may cause a business to fail. A list of the causes of business failures includes: (1) lack of capital, (2) lack of judgment and business ability on the part of the managers, (3) lack of demand for the goods, (4) poor location, (5) changes in prices, and (6) physical disasters — such as fires, floods, and wars. As you can see, some of the risks of business are related to personal qualifications of the managers, while some are related to matters over which the manager may have no control. That the risks are ever present is indicated by the number of business failures, which in recent years have averaged more than 11,500 annually. The reduction of some types of risk, such as lack of capital or lack of ability, can be made by choosing wisely the size and the kind of business concern.

COMMERCIAL AND INDUSTRIAL NONBANK FAILURES AND LIABILITIES IN THE UNITED STATES

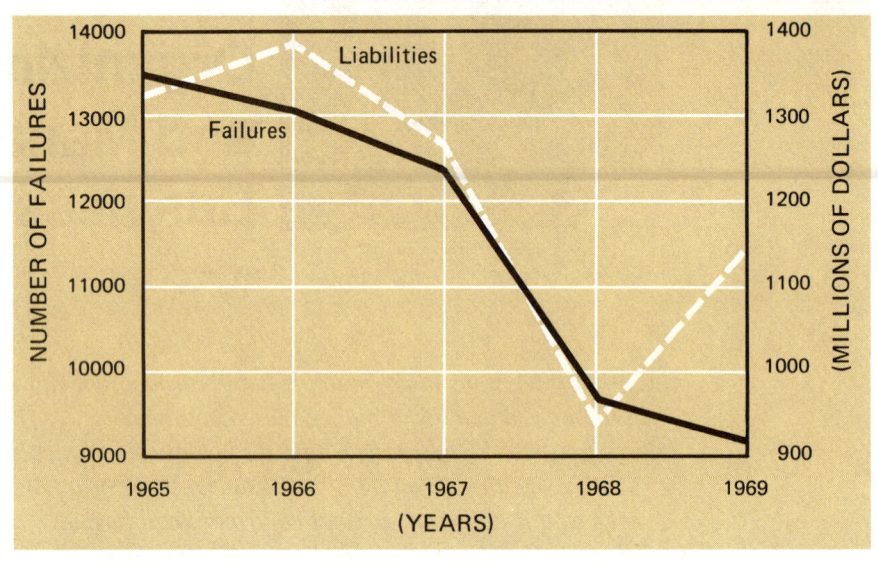

Figure 6-1.

ADAPTED FROM: *1970 Economic Report of the President*

That the risks are ever present is indicated by the number of business failures which in recent years have averaged more than 11,500 annually.

THERE IS ROOM FOR ALL

In a free-enterprise economy there is a place for business concerns of all sizes — small, medium, and large. In some lines of business the smaller firms — sole proprietorships, partnerships, and locally owned corporations — can carry on business as efficiently as can the big corporations. In many cases they are more efficient.

On the other hand, in some industries efficient and economical production can result only if there is mass production. Moreover, the improvement of the quality of certain kinds of articles and the discovery of less expensive methods of production call for scientific research. This means that costly experimental laboratories and high-salaried scientists must be employed.

Viewing American business as a whole, we can say that there is not only room for all sizes and forms of business but also there is need for all.

THERE ARE SEVERAL KINDS OF BUSINESS OWNERSHIP

When the factors of production are brought together, the result is a *business unit* or *firm*. The forms of ownership of business units most commonly found are: (1) the sole proprietorship, (2) the partnership, (3) the corporation, (4) the cooperative, and (5) the government enterprise.

An unincorporated business that is owned by one individual is a sole or individual proprietorship. In a partnership, two or more persons pool or combine their capital or services for the purpose of carrying on a business undertaking. A corporation is a business unit that is authorized by a charter from a state or the national government, and that is controlled by private individuals. A cooperative business or association resembles both a partnership and a corporation in certain respects. A government enterprise is a business unit that is owned by government.

SOLE PROPRIETORSHIPS

An unincorporated business that is owned by one individual is a *sole* or *individual proprietorship*. It is the oldest form of business organization. It is also the most numerous with almost 10 million separate firms.

THERE ARE MANY SOLE PROPRIETORSHIPS

This type of organization seems well adapted to certain kinds of business. This is noticeably true in farming. It is also largely true in the case of newsstands, fruit stands, candy stores, barbershops, beauty parlors, ice cream parlors, and other businesses that do not require large investments of capital. Many doctors, lawyers, and other professional workers operate their businesses as sole proprietorships. In most lines of manufacturing the sole proprietor plays a relatively small part.

Although sole proprietorships are numerous and vary as to what they produce, they have certain similar and distinctive features. Several of the features give advantages to the owners; other features may prove to be disadvantages.

ADVANTAGES OF SOLE PROPRIETORSHIPS

Whether the sole proprietorship possesses advantages or disadvantages as compared with other forms of business enterprise depends on circumstances. For example, one might think that being one's own boss and receiving all the profits of the business would be two advantages as compared with being a partner in a partnership or a stockholder in a corporation. But if one did not have enough money with which to operate on a sufficiently large scale to enable the business to be profitable, these matters would be relatively less important.

Individual owners believe that there are six advantages for the sole proprietorship type of business.

(1) Ease of beginning business. It is comparatively easy to start a one-man or one-woman business. As a rule the owner does not have to comply with many laws or legal restrictions, nor need he consult with other persons as to how the business should be run.

(2) Pride of ownership. The desire for success seems natural. When a person owns his own business, he can see the results of his labor, he can watch the business grow as he succeeds, and he is "his own boss." These are matters of great importance to many owners of small business units. There are some persons who would rather be the sole owner of an enterprise than a member of a partnership or the owner of stock in a corporation, even though their income might be greater if their money were invested in one of the other kinds of business enterprise.

(3) Receipt of all profits. When profits are made, the sole owner of a business receives all of them because he has taken all the risks in the enterprise.

Illus. 6-1. When a person owns his own business, he can see the results of his labor, he can watch the business grow as he succeeds, and he is "his own boss."

Production Credit Association

(4) Personal relations of employer and employees. In millions of sole proprietorships the owner and the members of his family do all the work. If employees are hired, they are usually few in number. For that reason the relations between the employer and his employees are personal and nearly always friendly. Therefore, strikes and other labor problems are infrequent in establishments that are owned by one person.

(5) Freedom from special property and income taxes. No special income or property taxes are imposed on the sole proprietorship. Of course, the owner must pay personal income tax on income received from the business and property tax on the property used in the business. But these taxes are not levied on the business because of its form. In many cases corporations have to pay an income tax simply because they are corporations. In many incorporated communities, boroughs, towns, and cities, certain classes of business must obtain a license or a permit to operate a business. The fees charged may run into several hundreds of dollars; the amount depends on the type of business.

Illus. 6-2. Certain classes of business must obtain a license or a permit to operate a business.

American Iron and Steel Institute

(6) Ease of dissolution. The owner is free to sell his business if he can find a buyer, or to quit without having to consult others, as would be the case in a partnership.

DISADVANTAGES OF SOLE PROPRIETORSHIPS

Individual owners may be faced with five types of disadvantages of the sole proprietorship form of business organization.

(1) Limited capital. The amount of funds or capital that may be used by the sole proprietorship is limited by the amount possessed by the owner and the amount that he can borrow on his personal credit. Since few individuals own enough capital to enable them to carry on business on a large scale, there are not many very large business enterprises that are organized as sole proprietorships.

(2) **Limited managerial ability.** As a rule the sole owner must rely on his own judgment as to the policies and methods he follows. Of course, if he is financially able, he may employ experts to advise and help him. But ordinarily the size of the business does not justify the employment of specialists and experts.

Illus. 6-3. As a rule the sole owner must rely on his own judgment as to the policies and methods he follows.

(3) **Burden of losses.** As the sole owner the sole proprietor must bear the burden of all losses of the business. This prospect is presumably offset by the prospect of receipt of all profits.

(4) **Liability for debts of the business.** The sole owner of a business has unlimited liability for the debts of the concern. This means that any property he may own may be taken through legal action by the creditors of the concern in case the owner does not pay what he owes and the property used in the business is not sufficient to pay the debts that have accumulated.

(5) Length of existence. The sole proprietorship has no definite period of existence. The original ownership of the business comes to an end when the owner dies, decides to quit, or sells the business to another. This fact is sometimes important, especially when the owner wishes to buy goods on account or to borrow money for a long period of time.

The only way by which we can say that the sole proprietorship is preferable to other forms of business organizations is by comparing the features of all the various kinds of business organization with reference to a given situation. For example, if you wanted to open a grocery store, or a dress shop, you might find that the sole proprietorship would be exactly suitable for your purposes. But if you dreamed of manufacturing a new sport car, it is not likely that this form of business organization would meet your needs. It is because the needs and circumstances of business differ that we use several other forms of business organization.

PARTNERSHIPS

A *partnership* exists when two or more persons combine their labor, capital, or land and undertake a business venture for profit. Frequently, small retail stores are operated as partnerships. Larger stores are usually operated by corporations. Often professional men, such as lawyers, doctors, and dentists, form partnerships.

PARTNERSHIP AGREEMENTS SHOULD BE WRITTEN

All partnership agreements should be written. The dangers of misunderstandings and disagreements are so many and so great that the agreement should be drawn up in writing, signed by each partner, and witnessed by responsible individuals. A partnership agreement is referred to as *articles of copartnership*.

THERE ARE DIFFERENT KINDS OF PARTNERSHIPS AND PARTNERS

Most partnerships are *general partnerships*. In such an organization each partner is liable for the debts of the firm, and the partners share the profits and the losses equally or according to some fixed ratio. For example, Messrs. A, B, and C, as members of a partnership, might agree to divide profits and to share losses in the business as follows: A, 40 percent; B, 35 percent; and C, 25 percent.

The laws of some states permit the formation of *limited partnerships*. In a limited partnership there are two classes of partners: *general partners*, whose liability is unlimited; and *limited partners*, whose liability is limited.

In case the business does fail, the partner whose liability is limited loses only the amount of his investment in the enterprise; the creditors of the concern cannot take his other property. The members of a limited partnership must file a certificate with the proper public officer and give notice in a newspaper. Several states have laws permitting the formation of *limited partnership associations* in which the liability of all partners is limited.

Sometimes a person contributes capital to a partnership but does not take an active part in the management of the affairs of the firm. Such a person is a *silent partner*. He shares in the division of the profits or the losses, and he is liable for the debts of the concern.

In some cases an individual is willing to enter a partnership but for some reason does not wish his identity to become known. Such a partner is called a *secret partner*. He becomes liable for the debts of the partnership if his identity becomes known to the creditors.

PARTNERSHIPS MAY HAVE ADVANTAGES

The partnership overcomes two of the disadvantages that are sometimes found in the sole proprietorship. There is a third possible advantage that may characterize the partnership.

(1) Greater capital. By combining their assets, two or more individuals can raise more capital than one of them could by acting alone. If the credit of each is good, two or more partners can borrow more funds from a bank than could any one of the partners if he were the sole owner. Sometimes the ability of a business to obtain a bank loan is very important.

(2) Greater efficiency. By combining their skill and judgment, two or more partners may be able to carry on a business more efficiently than either of them could alone. Thus, if one of them is a good salesman, he may give his time to the selling of goods, while each of the other partners may attend to those duties for which he is best adapted.

(3) Lower income tax liability. There is no special income tax levied on a partnership as there is on a corporation. Thus, the partnership profits, if any, are taxed only as reported personal income on the partners' individual income tax returns.

PARTNERSHIPS MAY HAVE DISADVANTAGES

Most of the disadvantages found in the sole proprietorship are present in the partnership, and there may be additional disadvantages.

(1) Unlimited liability. In the case of a general partnership each partner is individually liable for the debts of the firm. Ordinarily, any partner may contract debts in connection with the business. Each of the partners is liable for the debts incurred by the others, as well as for those contracted by himself. To this extent, then, a partnership may result in a greater liability to a partner than would a sole proprietorship.

(2) The danger of disagreement. In a partnership, disagreements may arise as to the conduct of the business. Besides creating an unpleasant situation, disagreements may lead to the termination of the partnership.

(3) The difficulty of transferring a partnership interest. No partner can sell his interest in the firm without the consent of all the other partners. Nor can another person succeed a partner upon the latter's death, except by the agreement of all concerned. The reason for these rules is that a partnership is an agreement between individuals and must be entered into willingly by each partner.

(4) The division of profits. It is sometimes said that the division of profits is a disadvantage of a partnership. This is a disadvantage, however, only in those cases in which one individual alone could supply the capital and the ability needed to carry on the business. If his share of the partnership profits would be larger than the amount he makes as a sole proprietor, it would be to his advantage to enter into a partnership business.

PARTNERSHIPS HAVE LIMITED POSSIBILITIES

Where large investments are needed, the partnership form of business organization is inadequate and unsatisfactory. The disadvantages listed above are often regarded as serious handicaps. It is in order to escape these handicaps that businesses are frequently organized as corporations or cooperative businesses, which we shall discuss in the next chapter.

A PROBLEM OF SMALL BUSINESS: SURVIVAL

Although there are exceptions, the sole proprietorship and partnership enterprises can be classified as small businesses. A frequently used measure to classify small business is the dollar amount of its liabilities. Enterprises with liabilities under $100,000 are considered to be small businesses. Some 82 percent of the businesses that failed during a recent four-year period were small businesses. However, it would be a mistake to think that small businesses are decreasing in number. On the contrary, seventeen new enterprises, on an average basis, become active each year as replacements for each business that fails to survive.

The problem of small business survival includes three features. These are: (1) the competitive threat to survival, (2) small business opportunity areas, and (3) some requisites for survival.

(1) The competitive threat to survival. In some lines of production there is not much opportunity for the small business concern to compete with the giants of the industry. Society's choice of a free-market system implies that society wants economy; economy demands production that results from the most efficient use of resources. Small business is inadequate and cannot function either competitively or economically in the production of steel, automobiles, petrochemicals, and similar types of goods. The inadequacy of size prevents the small business from acquiring the necessities of know-how, research facilities, and capital. Thus, small business cannot successfully compete against the giants in certain production areas.

The competitive threat is not necessarily competition which uses unfair tactics. The favor of customers is obtained by offering low-priced products. Low-priced products require low-cost production. The chain corporation can frequently hold costs down through large-quantity purchases, greater business efficiency, savings through large-scale advertising, and avoidance of debt by requiring cash sales. Thus, large corporate chain stores that engage in marketing and merchandising may survive and prosper in a locality where the small business competitors failed. If the small business cannot achieve similar economies, its chances for survival are minimal.

(2) Small business opportunity areas. Manufacturing of certain items may be more efficient in a small enterprise than in a larger one. Giant electrical industries, as one example, find it cheaper to purchase transistors from small companies than to produce them in their own plants. The production of trout flies for sportsmen, violins for musicians, and small instruments for surgeons are other examples of opportunity areas where small businesses have been highly successful. Similarly, other opportunities have been found in the following fields: retailing, wholesaling, service industries (barbershops, beauty shops, cleaning establishments, and repair shops of several kinds), transportation (trucking and taxicabs), insurance and real estate, as well as others.

The failure of small business to survive is not necessarily the lack of business opportunity. Rather, the failure may be a result of the selection of an opportunity area that was too competitive an undertaking for any small business.

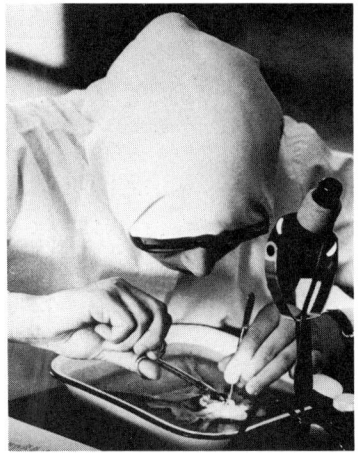

Illus. 6-4. Small instruments for surgeons are other examples of opportunity areas where small businesses have been highly successful.

Arabian American Oil Company

(3) Some requisites for survival. Various studies indicate that some of the conditions for the survival of a strong, healthy population of small business owners are the following:

(a) Better economic and business education of those who expect to go into business for themselves.

(b) Enforcement of laws to prevent unfair treatment of small business concerns by great corporations.

(c) Possibly changes in banking laws so that banks may make loans for longer periods of time to local businessmen.

(d) A cooperative and understanding attitude between employers and employees.

(e) Membership by small business owners in trade associations that carry on research in production and business methods and that provide information which will make the managers more efficient.

(f) More interest on the part of small business owners in all local and national affairs that affect business.

In order to assist small business firms, the Small Business Act of 1953 was passed by Congress. Under this law the agency known as the Small Business Administration was set up by the government. The purposes of the agency are to counsel, aid, assist, and protect the interests of small business firms; to see that small business concerns get a fair proportion of government contracts; and to make loans to small businesses and to the victims of floods and other disasters. Currently the agency expends $240 million annually to carry out its functions.

SUMMARY

As the primary business risk taker, in a free-enterprise economy, the enterpriser has the right to initiate, organize, and manage the business he undertakes. The risks assumed by enterprisers include those that relate to (1) the adequacy of capital, (2) business judgment, (3) demand for goods, (4) location of the business, (5) changes in market prices, and (6) physical disaster.

The principal kinds of private business ownership and organization are the (1) sole proprietorship, (2) partnership, (3) corporation, and (4) cooperative. Also, some businesses are owned and operated by government.

Advantages of the sole proprietorship include: (1) ease of entry, (2) pride of ownership, (3) receipt of all profits, (4) usually pleasant relations between employer and employees, (5) freedom from certain taxes and laws, and (6) ease of dissolution. Disadvantages are: (1) limited capital, (2) limited managerial ability, (3) bearing of all losses, (4) unlimited liability, and (5) uncertain length of existence.

In a partnership, two or more persons agree to pool or combine their capital or services to carry on a business. As a protective measure, all partnership agreements should be in writing. There are two kinds of partnerships: general and limited. A limited partnership is one in which the liability of one partner is limited. A secret partner is one who is unknown to the public. A silent partner takes no part in the management of the business.

As compared with a sole proprietorship, a partnership may have greater capital and greater managerial ability. On the other hand, there may be disadvantages, such as unlimited liability, danger of disagreements between the partners, difficulty of transferring partnership interest, and disputes over the sharing of profits and losses.

Large-scale business, including merchandising, often makes it difficult for certain kinds of small firms to compete. But this does not mean that small firms are decreasing in number or in importance. Survival, a problem of small business, can be achieved if the enterprisers make a wise selection from the many available business opportunities. The Small Business Administration has encouraged small business survival by providing some of the conditions that are requisites for success.

NEW TERMS

articles of copartnership
business unit *or* firm
general partners
general partnerships
limited partners
limited partnership associations
limited partnerships
partnership
secret partner
silent partner
sole *or* individual proprietorship

Ch. 6   ORGANIZING AND MANAGING BUSINESS

QUESTIONS ON THE CHAPTER

1. What functions are performed by enterprisers?
2. Why is our economic system sometimes called the "profit and loss" system?
3. What are some risks that owners of business must assume?
4. To what two sources are these business risks related?
5. What effect has the need for more capital had on the types of business ownership?
6. What are the advantages and disadvantages of the sole proprietorship?
7. Why are partnerships formed?
8. Why should the partnership agreement be written?
9. What are the different kinds of partnerships? Explain each.
10. What are some of the possible advantages of the partnership? Explain.
11. What are some of the possible disadvantages of the partnership? Explain.
12. In what way may a partnership result in greater liability to a partner than he would bear as a sole proprietor?
13. Why are the possibilities of the partnership limited?
14. In deciding between the sole proprietorship and the partnership as a form of business organization, what are some of the factors that should be considered?
15. What are some of the urgent needs of small business?
16. What are the purposes of the Small Business Administration?

APPLYING YOUR ECONOMIC UNDERSTANDING

1. Your father buys $5,000 worth of bonds that were issued by an out-of-state school district. Is he an enterpriser? Why or why not? Your father used another $5,000 and pooled it with the same amount from a friend to operate jointly a drive-in food stand. Is Dad an enterpriser? Why or why not?
2. Use the five common forms of business ownership as headings on the chalkboard. List under the appropriate headings the names of the various business firms that your classmates patronized during the past week. Which form seems to predominate?
3. Prepare a tally sheet listing the six causes of business failures and the six advantages of the sole proprietorship. Conduct a poll of the sole proprietors in your community. Have them vote on which one they think is the main cause of failure and which is the major characteristic of importance. Tally the results and report them to the class.
4. Visit a real estate agency that is either a sole proprietorship or a partnership to learn what the agency believes are the dynamics affecting the growth of small businesses in the community. Discuss the findings in class.

5. How important are sole proprietorships in the United States? Substantiate your answer.
6. Toland and Axton are partners. Axton dies and his widow, the only heir, visits Toland and says that she is now his partner. Is her viewpoint correct? Support your answer.
7. John's father owns a very large ranch. The father orally agrees with John that he will consider John as a half-partner provided that John stays on the ranch and works there. John's mother and several of his brothers and sisters are living, but they do not know the details of the arrangement between John and his dad. Is this a wise business arrangement? Why or why not? Is John a "secret" partner?

CHALLENGES TO ECONOMIC COMPETENCE

1. Invite an attorney to speak to the class on the importance of written partnership contracts. Summarize his remarks. Do they agree or disagree with the viewpoints expressed in your textbook?
2. Select one of the series of the United States Department of Commerce booklets on how to start and operate a small business. Prepare a written summary report on it.
3. Take a series of photographs of sole proprietorships and of partnerships in your community. Classify them with captions according to their production function for use as a bulletin board display.
4. Prepare a bar graph comparing the number of business failures and the number of new entrants into business as reported for the latest ten-year period. (Use Dun and Bradstreet's *Dun's Review and Modern Industry*, *The Statistical Abstract of the United States*, or the latest almanac as data sources.)
5. Secure the federal income tax tables and income form reports for individuals and corporations from your nearest Director of Internal Revenue. Prepare an original research report which supports the view that sole proprietorships and partnerships have certain tax advantages.

Chapter 7

Corporations and Cooperatives

Why are corporations important to an economy?
What is a business corporation?
How is the corporation controlled?
What is a cooperative?

In the United States, there are more than 11 million business firms. Although only about 11 percent are corporations, these corporations collect over 75 percent of the total receipts of all business firms. Corporations also control most manufacturing, electric light and power facilities, transportation and communications systems, mining operations, financial services, merchandising, and trade. The corporate form of business organization has made large-scale business possible. And large-scale production is one of the main reasons for the remarkable economic progress that America has achieved.

In this chapter, we shall define the business corporation, explain how a corporation is organized, and indicate the ways in which it differs from cooperatives and other ownership forms.

WHAT IS A CORPORATION?

We may say that a *corporation* is an association of individuals, known as stockholders, which is empowered by government to engage in business as a single individual. In the famous Dartmouth College case in 1819, Chief Justice Marshall formulated a definition that has often been quoted. This definition began as follows: "A corporation is an artificial being, invisible, intangible, and existing only in contemplation of law . . . ."

A corporation is a legal person. Its life can be terminated only by law or by the expiration of the charter under which it was formed. It has existence separate and distinct from the natural persons who control it.

It also enjoys many of the legal powers of natural persons, including the right to buy, sell, or otherwise dispose of property; to enter into contracts; and to sue and to be sued in the courts. When a corporation is authorized by the state or the federal government, it is given these specific legal powers and privileges.

THE CORPORATION IS CHARTERED BY GOVERNMENT

Each of the states and the federal government have laws governing the formation of corporations. Although these laws vary somewhat, the typical procedure in the formation of a corporation is about as follows:

A preliminary meeting is held by those who propose to form the corporation. The laws specify the minimum number of persons (usually three to five) required to organize a corporation.

A document called the *articles of incorporation* is drawn up. These articles include: (1) the corporation's name, purposes, and home office location; (2) the number of its directors; (3) the names and addresses of the first board of directors; (4) the amount and the kinds of its capital stock; and (5) any other necessary information required by the governmental chartering agency.

The articles of incorporation, together with an application for a *charter* (or *certificate of incorporation*, as it is frequently called) are sent to the state or federal agency which processes the requested charter. If the articles of incorporation comply with the laws, a charter is granted, which brings the corporation into being.

A CORPORATION IS CONTROLLED BY A BOARD OF DIRECTORS

The corporation belongs to those who share in the ownership of the business. These persons are called *stockholders*. The charter gives the stockholders the right to elect a *board of directors*, who operate the corporation as they see fit, as long as their acts conform to law. The procedures to be followed in conducting the affairs of the corporation are set forth in a formal list of rules, called *bylaws*, which are adopted by the stockholders. The bylaws prescribe the time and the place of each meeting of the stockholders, outline the powers and the duties of the directors, and set forth rules of action in regard to other matters.

The board of directors has the responsibility of supervising and controlling the affairs of the corporation. The management of the concern is in its hands. No stockholder, regardless of how much capital stock he may own, has the right to enter into any contract that will bind the corpora-

Illus. 7-1. The corporation belongs to those who share in the ownership of the business. These persons are called stockholders.

tion unless he has been empowered to do so by the board of directors. The number of directors ranges from three to fifteen or twenty, and in a few cases it may be even more.

The responsibilities of the directors are great. If they exceed their authority, the state may cancel the charter. And if they cause the corporation to contract debts that are not authorized by the charter, they themselves become liable for payment.

The directors do not personally attend to the operation of the business. They elect *officers* to whom they delegate the responsibility for carrying on the affairs of the corporation. These officers usually include a president, a vice-president, a secretary, a treasurer, and others. The directors are often also officers.

Figure 7-1 at the top of the next page illustrates a typical organization of a manufacturing corporation. Other types of corporate organization would include differences in the titles and the number of officers or administrators.

STOCKHOLDERS SHARE IN THE PROFITS OF THE CORPORATION

At stated times the board of directors meets in formal session and decides what to do with any profits that may have been earned. Usually the directors feel that some of the profits should be retained in the business and not paid out to the stockholders. Any amount of profit so retained

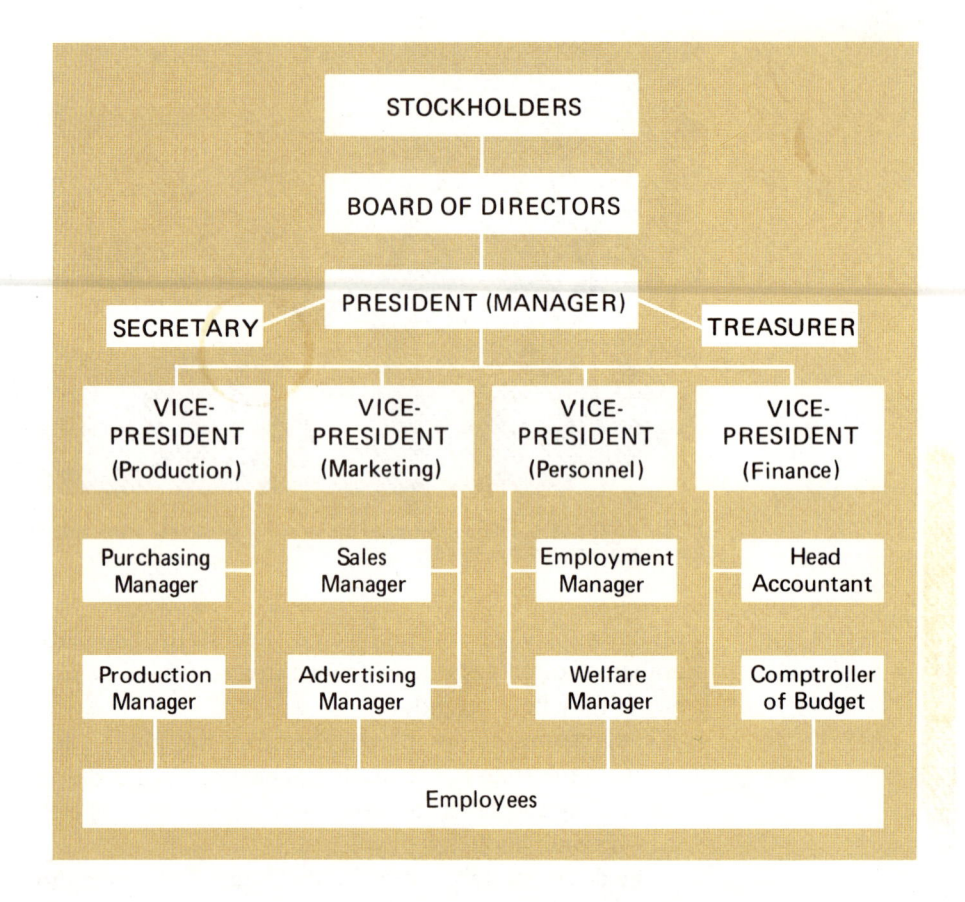

Figure 7-1.

Typical Organization of a Manufacturing Corporation

becomes a part of the *surplus* of the corporation. Although surplus is made up of profits not paid out to the stockholders, it belongs to them.

The profits distributed to the stockholders are called *dividends*. If dividends are paid in the form of cash, they are *cash dividends*. If the stockholders are given additional shares of stock instead of cash, the dividends are called *stock dividends*.

In case of a loss, the stockholders share the loss in proportion to the number of shares of stock they hold. This is done by subtracting the amount of the loss from the surplus which is the accumulated earnings from past operations. In case there is no surplus, the loss results in a *deficit*, which causes the value of the shares of ownership in the business to decrease.

Ch. 7   CORPORATIONS AND COOPERATIVES   113

THE ASSETS OF A CORPORATION ARE OWNED BY THE CORPORATION

Money and capital contributed to the business become the property of the corporation. In exchange for the capital contributed, the individual receives a *stock certificate*, which is a piece of paper certifying that the holder owns a certain number of shares of stock. The holder may sell or otherwise dispose of this certificate without consulting the corporation. A stockholder, however, cannot sell the property of the corporation; he can sell only the stock shares that he owns.

Capital funds become assets and are available to the corporation when it sells its stock; the sale of stock ownership by one stockholder to another person does not add any new capital funds to the corporation.

CAPITAL FORMATION IN CORPORATIONS

The four common sources of capital for corporations are: (1) sale of *capital stock*, (2) *borrowing*, (3) *reinvestment*, and (4) gifts and *subsidies*.

Figure 7-2.

Capital funds become assets and are available to the corporation when it sells its stock; the sale of stock ownership by one stockholder to another person does not add any new capital funds to the corporation.

(1) Capital stock. The corporation sells shares of its ownership to persons or groups that desire to be owners or investors in the corporation. These investment funds are derived from the savings of the investors or from institutional funds which were made available by past savings. As examples, a person may use his personal savings for the direct purchase of stock which a company is offering for sale, or persons may put their savings into banks, insurance companies, or similar institutions which may use these savings to buy the shares offered by the corporation. The latter is an indirect investment by the original savers.

(2) Borrowing. In many cases the stockholders of a corporation do not supply all the capital needed by the concern. Some of it is furnished by those who sell goods to the corporation on credit. The obligations due such creditors are usually paid by the corporation within a few months. Corporations also borrow funds from commercial banks or other sources for short periods of time.

For short-term borrowing, the corporation issues notes or promises to repay. These notes state the interest rate to be paid and the date for repayment of the debt.

Often, however, corporations need funds for a longer period of time. Certificates, known as *bonds*, which are essentially long-term promissory notes are issued. Bonds secured by only a general claim against the corporation's assets are called *debenture bonds*. Bonds that are secured by a lien or mortgage on part or all of a corporation's property are called *mortgage bonds*. Bonds bear interest at a fixed rate; the rate of interest varies. Bond interest, unlike preferred stock dividends, must be paid regardless of whether any profits are earned. If the corporation fails to pay the interest, the bondholders have the right to sell or to take control of the business. The bondholder is a creditor of the business. Like other creditors, his claims for repayment have preference over those of the stockholders or owners.

(3) Reinvestment. When a corporation makes a profit, the directors may decide not to pay out the profit in the form of cash to the stockholders. Instead, this profit may be held as additional capital funds to be used by the corporation for business purposes. In such a case, although the stockholders do not receive cash, they do have an increased money value interest in the corporation.

(4) Gifts and subsidies. Gifts are free contributions made to a corporation. These are usually made to charitable or nonprofit corporations, such as the American Red Cross or colleges. A subsidy is a sum of money given

Ch. 7 CORPORATIONS AND COOPERATIVES 115

Illus. 7-2. In an earlier period of history, governments subsidized stagecoach projects.

Wells Fargo Bank History Room

by government to a corporation so that it can have the necessary capital to operate in the public interest or as a matter of public policy. In an earlier period of history, governments subsidized stagecoach, infant railroad, and internal canal projects. Today, government might make subsidies available, for example, to private corporations for the building of ocean vessels, air transports, other types of transportation, and for communication equipment.

CAPITAL STOCK MAY BE PAR-VALUE OR NO-PAR-VALUE STOCK

When a corporation is chartered, it is given the right to issue a definite number of shares of ownership called *stock*. All of this stock of a corporation is known as its capital stock. Formerly most stock was par-value stock.

Par-value stock is capital stock that has a stated value per share. When par-value stock is issued, an amount in dollars, such as $5 or $100, is printed or written on the face of the stock certificate. The par value does not indicate what the stock is worth at any time. The worth or the *book value* of a share of stock can be found by subtracting the amount of debts owed by the corporation from the total value of its cash and other assets and dividing what is left by the number of shares held by the stockholders.

In recent years, however, the tendency has been to issue stock with no-par value. Each stock certificate specifies that the holder owns a certain number of shares, but it does not give the stated value of each share. Such stock is called *no-par-value stock*.

One of the reasons for issuing no-par-value stock is that investors are less likely to be misled in the case of such stock than if the stock certificate has a stated value printed on it. If a stock certificate states, for example, that the par value is $100, a person may feel that each share will always be worth about $100. In reality, the value of the stock may be very much above or below that amount. Everyone who buys stock should know that the value of stock is determined by the present or estimated future earning power of the corporation, and not by the amount printed on the certificate.

Another reason for issuing no-par-value stock is that, if par-value stock is sold by the corporation at a price below its par value, in case of bankruptcy the buyer may have to pay the difference to the creditors. But no-par-value stock may be sold at any price without making the buyer liable for any additional payment.

Illus. 7-3. The holder of a share of common stock is entitled to vote in the election of the directors.

Amsted Industries

STOCK IS ALSO CLASSIFIED AS COMMON OR PREFERRED

In order to appeal to different kinds of investors, corporations sometimes issue two kinds of stock, common and preferred. The classes of stock are provided for in the charter.

(1) Common stock. If only one kind of stock is issued, it is known as *common stock*. The holder of a share of common stock is entitled to the following rights and privileges: (a) to vote in the election of the directors; (b) to receive a share of the profits, provided a dividend has been declared by the board of directors; (c) to share in the division of the assets if the corporation goes out of business; and (d) to sell or otherwise dispose of his stock. When a corporation has only common stock, all profits belong to the common stockholders, but the power to declare dividends is vested in the board of directors.

(2) Preferred stock. When corporations issue two classes of capital stock, one of these is common stock and the other is *preferred stock*, which entitles the holder to some kind of preference. As a rule the charter of a corporation specifies that the preferred stock does not give the holder the right to vote in the meetings of stockholders, but this may be modified by the charter provisions. The preference usually relates to the division of the profits or to the distribution of the money received from the sale of the assets in case of *liquidation*, that is, in case the corporation goes out of business and the assets are sold.

The holder of preferred stock is entitled to an amount of profit equal to a certain percentage of the par value of the stock. The percentage rate varies among corporations. If the stock has no par value, the rate of dividend is stated as a certain number of cents or dollars on each share.

(a) Participating and nonparticipating preferred stock. In some cases the preferred stock may share equally with the common stock in the profits remaining after both types of stockholders have received equal dividends.

Preferred stock that may share with the common stock in the division of the profits, after each has received dividends, is called *participating preferred stock*. For example, if the profits to be divided in the case of the Williams Milling Company were $16,000, the preferred stockholders might receive $7,000; and then the common stockholders, $7,000. The remaining $2,000 would be divided equally between the two classes of stockholders.

In most instances, however, the charter provides that the preferred stock will not participate in the division of the profits after it has received a stipulated amount. If the stock cannot so participate, it is known as *nonparticipating preferred stock*.

(b) Cumulative and noncumulative preferred stock. Preferred stock is also classified as cumulative and noncumulative. If the preferred stock is *cumulative*, all unpaid dividends on that type of stock must be paid before the common stock is entitled to any share of the profits. If the preferred stock is entitled to dividends only in the event that profits are earned during the year in which they are to be distributed, the stock is *noncumulative*.

(c) Convertible preferred stock. A corporation may issue preferred stock which can be exchanged at the owner's choice for the corporation's common stock using a fixed ratio for the exchange. Since this type of stock can be converted or exchanged it is known as *convertible preferred stock*.

CORPORATIONS HAVE ADVANTAGES

The advantages that the corporate form has over the partnership and sole proprietorship are: (1) limited liability; (2) continuous existence; (3) greater capital; and (4) easy transfer of investment.

(1) Limited liability. As a rule, the liability of the stockholder in a corporation is limited to the amount of his investment. This is one of the main advantages of the corporate form of ownership. In the event of the bankruptcy of the business, the creditors may ordinarily take all the stockholders' investment in property belonging to the corporation; but they cannot, in most cases, take other property belonging personally to the stockholders.

(2) Continuous existence. It may be said that the life of a sole proprietorship or a partnership is limited by the life of the person or persons who own it. The corporation, on the other hand, continues to exist until the expiration of its charter, independent of the individuals or concerns that hold its stock. Usually a charter can be renewed when it expires. If a stockholder dies, his shares of stock become the property of his heirs or his estate.

(3) Greater capital. The investment made by the owner in a sole proprietorship is limited to his personal finances and to what he can borrow. Likewise, the investment of the relatively few owners of a partnership is limited to the personal finances of the partners and their borrowing ability. In a corporation, however, a share of stock usually does not cost a great deal, so that many persons with small savings can become part owners. Of course, those who wish to make large investments in the corporation simply buy a larger number of shares of stock. Furthermore, a person who is not interested in taking an active part in the management of the business can invest his money in shares of stock of a corporation and leave to others the details of management. For these reasons a business organized as a corporation can often secure a large capital investment.

(4) Easy transfer of investment. In general, it is easy for an owner to sell his corporation shares. This *liquidity*, the ease of converting an investment into cash, gives an advantage to the stockholder. It is usually more difficult for a sole proprietor to find a buyer for his business. To dispose of one's partnership investment requires not only finding a buyer but also securing partnership consent.

Illus. 7-4. In general, it is easy for an owner to sell his corporation shares. This liquidity, the ease of converting an investment into cash, gives an advantage to the stockholder.

American Stock Exchange

CORPORATIONS MAY HAVE DISADVANTAGES

On the other hand, the corporation has certain disadvantages. Not all corporations, however, are handicapped by the same kinds or number of disadvantages. The disadvantages most frequently encountered are (1) limitation of credit, (2) amount of government control, and (3) federal and state taxes.

(1) Limitations of credit. A small business operated as a corporation may find it more difficult to obtain a loan from a bank than it would if it were a sole proprietorship or a partnership. This difficulty is due to the limitation of the liability of the stockholders for the debts of the concern.

(2) Amount of governmental control. Corporations are chartered by governmental agencies. Therefore, government assumes great responsibility concerning corporation activities. Consequently, numerous laws and enforcement procedures are specifically designed to control corporations in various ways.

(3) Federal and state taxes. The federal government obtains much of its revenue by taxing corporations. A federal tax is levied on the profit of a corporation. At various times the government has also imposed income, capital-stock, excess-profits, and undistributed-profits taxes on business corporations. There is, however, a tendency to limit federal taxes on corporations to taxes on corporate income. In addition to property taxes, most states require corporations to pay a franchise tax, that is, a tax for the right to carry on business in the state. States having income taxes also levy a tax on the income of corporations. Sometimes special taxes are levied on certain kinds of corporations, such as public utilities and insurance companies.

CORPORATIONS ARE CLASSIFIED AS PUBLIC AND PRIVATE

Corporations designed to carry on business operations may be classified as: (1) *public* or *government-owned corporations*, and (2) *private corporations*.

(1) Public corporations. Sometimes government sets up corporations whose functions are mainly business rather than governmental in nature. An example of such a public or government-owned corporation is the Tennessee Valley Authority, which built many hydroelectric dams in the Tennessee River system, and which now operates these dams and carries on a number of other activities. Public corporations are financed by government through public taxation, bond issues, or revenues.

(2) Private corporations. These may be classified as (a) *nonprofit corporations*, those designed for social, charitable, and educational purposes; (b) *business corporations*, those organized for the purpose of making

Ch. 7 CORPORATIONS AND COOPERATIVES 121

Illus. 7-5. Sometimes government sets up corporations whose functions are mainly business rather than governmental in nature. Public corporations are financed by government through public taxation, bond issues, or revenues.

Tennessee Valley Authority

profits; and (c) *cooperatives*, those formed for the purpose of providing owner-member services.

Since special laws apply to the cooperative form of business, a discussion of the cooperatives will conclude this chapter.

COOPERATIVES

The basic purpose of some business organizations is to provide services for their members, and not to make a profit. Such concerns are usually referred to as *cooperative societies* or *cooperatives*. They are owned by the members whom they are mainly intended to serve. The growth of cooperatives has been sufficient to cause many people to refer to it as the "cooperative movement."

The cooperative movement has been endorsed by the Federal Council of Churches of Christ in America, the National Catholic Rural Life Conference, the Central Conference of American Rabbis, the American Federation of Labor and Congress of Industrial Organizations, the Railroad Brotherhoods, the Grange, the Farm Bureau Federation, the National Farmers Union, and the National Education Association. Many cooperatives are to be found in the United States, Canada, Mexico, Great Britain, Sweden, and in other countries throughout the world. It is estimated that

Illus. 7-6. The growth of cooperatives has been sufficient to cause many people to refer to it as the "cooperative movement."

more than 15 million American families own shares in one or more of 47,000 cooperatives.

COOPERATIVES ARE USUALLY BASED ON THE ROCHDALE PRINCIPLES

People have engaged in cooperative undertakings for a long time. But it is generally recognized that the idea of the cooperative society, as we are using the term, had its origin in Rochdale, England, in 1844. A small group of poor, unemployed weavers met and discussed the possibilities of improving their condition. These "Rochdale Pioneers," as they came to be known, decided to form a consumer buying society. The principles adopted by that group are usually followed by cooperative societies in the United States. However, many cooperatives in the United States operate as corporations rather than as societies; consequently, they are subject to the federal and state laws which apply to all corporations. Therefore, the principles of the "Rochdale pioneers" are not strictly followed when the

A COMPARISON OF A BUSINESS CORPORATION AND A COOPERATIVE ASSOCIATION

	Point of Comparison	The Business Corporation	The Cooperative
1.	Purpose	To earn profits for the corporation through production activities	To perform a service for the members that may save money for them
2.	Source of capital	Supplied by stockholders and creditors	Supplied by member stockholders and creditors
3.	Control	Number of votes depends on number of shares held	A member usually has one vote
4.	Ownership of profits or savings	Profits belong to the corporation	Savings belong to member stockholders
5.	Sharing of profits or savings	Profits shared according to number of shares held	Savings shared according to amount of business done with cooperative, after dividends are paid on capital invested
6.	Freedom to transfer shares	No restrictions	Frequently limited to certain classes of persons (such as farmers)

corporation laws differ from cooperative principles. The principles and exceptions (in parentheses) may be summarized as follows:

(1) Democratic control by members; each member has one vote. (In certain states, such as Illinois, members are permitted to vote by proxy. Voting is on the basis of the number of shares rather than on the one-man, one-vote principle.)

(2) Returns on investment limited to a conservative amount based on the average interest rate. (Prevailing-rate interest is paid on borrowed capital funds, including funds advanced by members. Dividends are paid on all invested funds.)

(3) Savings to be distributed to members in proportion to their patronage. If one member bought twice as much as another through the association, he would receive twice as much savings, or *patronage refunds*, as the other.

(4) The sale of goods at average market prices. (Price determination is not based on average market prices but is generally based on the interaction of many economic factors which apply to all business firms.)

(5) Membership open to men and women without regard to political or religious affiliations. (Because of a common interest some cooperatives often confine membership to a particular group. As an example, members must be Rochdale weavers, or California almond growers, and so forth. Cooperatives, like other enterprises, are regulated by laws which forbid discrimination.)

TYPES OF COOPERATIVES IN THE UNITED STATES

A simple classification of cooperatives is difficult because these organizations vary so much in size, area covered, type of membership, and so forth. Here we shall discuss cooperatives according to two broad classifications: (1) farmers' cooperatives and (2) consumers' cooperatives.

(1) Farmers' cooperatives. A *farmers' cooperative* is a business undertaking that is owned and controlled by a common interest group of farmers for the purpose of carrying on one of several kinds of activities. The nation's 500 largest industrial corporations in 1970 included five agricultural cooperatives. These were Agway, Inc., Farmland Industries, Land O' Lakes Creameries, Cotton Producers Association, and Farmers Union Central Exchange.

Illus. 7-7. A farmers' cooperative is a business undertaking that is owned and controlled by a common interest group of farmers for the purpose of carrying on one of several kinds of activities.

(a) Production cooperatives. Some farm cooperatives are organized for the purpose of carrying on production of one kind or another for the direct benefit of the members. Cooperatives of this type are organized for the purpose of carrying on irrigation projects, the improvement of cattle, and the manufacture of goods.

(b) Business-service cooperatives. These cooperatives are intended to supply farmers with electricity; frozen-food lockers; transportation; telephone; medical, surgical, dental care, and hospitalization; auditing; and burial services.

(c) Marketing cooperatives. This type of cooperative markets grain, cotton, or other products for its members. It may serve as the farmer's selling agent; it may "pool" or lump the production of all members together and sell it; or it may buy each member's farm product and resell it in a central market. The larger marketing cooperatives endeavor to promote "orderly marketing" by sending products to markets where prices are highest and to sell products gradually instead of "glutting" the market.

(d) Purchasing cooperatives. Farmers' purchasing cooperatives are organizations that are owned and operated according to cooperative principles primarily for the purpose of purchasing farm supplies for its members. Much of the purchasing of this kind is carried on by cooperative regional wholesale associations. Most of the commodities purchased consist of feed, seed, fertilizer, petroleum products, and other farm production supplies.

(2) Consumer cooperatives. As a rule the term *consumers' cooperatives* refers to cooperatives other than those that are made up of farmers. They are often organized by the employees in one or more business establishments, church members, teachers' associations, labor unions, and other groups. A typical consumers' cooperative is a retail store that buys commodities directly from manufacturers and wholesalers and sells them at about the average price for similar goods in local "co-op" stores. In some cases consumers' cooperatives have extended their activities into the fields of manufacturing, oil refining, and electric power distribution. A part of the total savings — net receipts — may be retained in the business for educational purposes or for expansion of the activities of the cooperative, and the rest is returned to the members in proportion to their purchases.

A *credit union* is a cooperatively owned savings and loan organization. Interest is paid on savings, and loans are made to members at comparatively low interest rates. There are about 30,000 credit unions in the United States. This type of cooperative is growing rapidly in this country.

CREDIT UNIONS ARE GROWING AND GROWING FAST

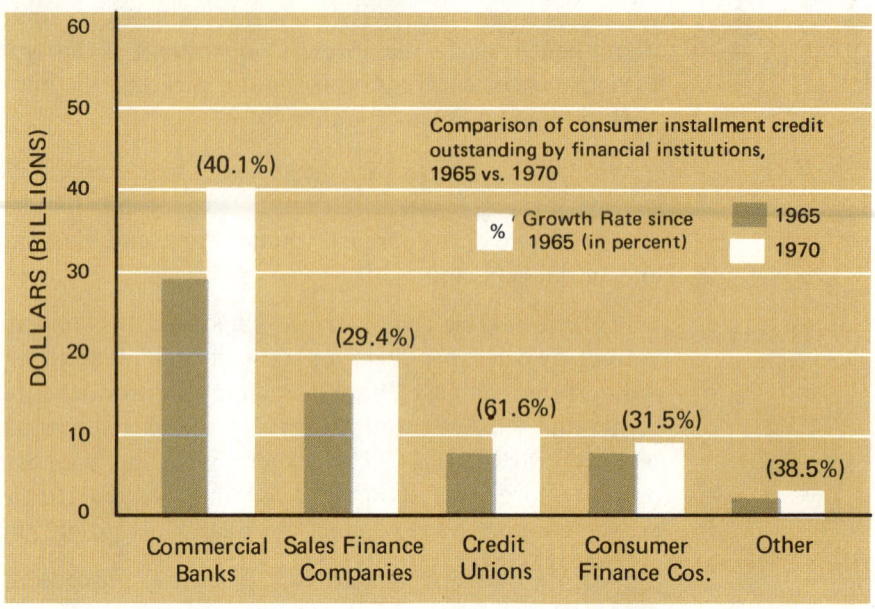

Figure 7-3.

Comparison of consumer installment credit outstanding by financial institutions, 1965 vs. 1970

% Growth Rate since 1965 (in percent)

1965
1970

Commercial Banks (40.1%)
Sales Finance Companies (29.4%)
Credit Unions (61.6%)
Consumer Finance Cos. (31.5%)
Other (38.5%)

SOURCE: Adapted from *Federal Reserve Bulletin, July, 1970.*

SUMMARY

From the standpoint of the volume and type of production in many fields, corporations are very important.

A corporation is a legal entity or legal person created by an act of government. It has the power to own, buy, and sell property and to engage in business according to the provisions of its charter. Public, or government-owned corporations, are financed by government. Private corporations are owned and financed by private individuals or business concerns.

Corporations are not managed directly by the stockholders but by a board of directors elected by the stockholders. The officers who conduct the affairs of the corporation are appointed by the board of directors. The stockholders share in the distribution of the profits of the company when dividends are declared by the board of directors. Cash dividends are paid in money or by check; stock dividends are paid in shares of stock.

The assets or property of a business operated as a corporation are owned by the corporation, not by the stockholders. Four major sources of capital formation are: (1) the sales of stocks or ownership rights, (2) borrowing, (3) reinvestment, and (4) subsidies or gifts.

The capital contributed by the owners of the business is represented by shares of capital stock. A certificate of stock indicates the number of shares owned by a stockholder. Par-value stock has a value of so many cents or dollars per share, which is printed on the stock certificate; no-par-value stock has no stated value. Common stock gives the holder the right to vote for members of the board of directors, to share in profits, to sell his stock, and to share in the division of the property of the business in case of the dissolution of the corporation. Preferred stock gives the holder first claim on profits when dividends are declared and is either participating or nonparticipating.

Liability of both common and preferred stockholders is limited. Other advantages of the corporation are its continuous existence, its possibilities for greater capital formation, and its share liquidity. Disadvantages include credit limitations, governmental control, and greater tax liability.

Cooperatives are businesses organized to provide member-owner services, and not to make a profit. These businesses are operated under the Rochdale (cooperative) principles. The farmers' cooperatives are grouped as producer, business-service, marketing, and purchasing cooperatives. Consumer cooperatives are the nonfarmer cooperatives. The credit union, a savings and loan type of business, is a rapidly growing form of consumer cooperative.

NEW TERMS

- articles of incorporation
- board of directors
- bonds
- book value
- borrowing
- business corporations
- business-service cooperatives
- bylaws
- capital stock
- cash dividends
- charter *or* certificate of incorporation
- common stock
- consumers' cooperatives
- convertible preferred stock
- cooperatives
- cooperative societies
- corporation
- credit union
- cumulative preferred stock
- debenture bonds
- deficit
- dividends
- farmers' cooperatives
- liquidation
- liquidity
- marketing cooperatives
- mortgage bonds
- noncumulative preferred stock
- nonparticipating preferred stock
- nonprofit corporations
- no-par-value stock
- officers
- participating preferred stock
- par-value stock
- patronage refunds
- preferred stock
- private corporations
- production cooperatives
- public *or* government-owned corporations
- purchasing cooperatives
- reinvestment
- stock
- stock certificate
- stock dividends
- stockholders
- subsidies
- surplus

QUESTIONS ON THE CHAPTER

1. Why should we know something about corporations?
2. What is a corporation?
3. Why is a corporation said to be a legal person?
4. What are some examples of nonprofit and business corporations?
5. What are the general steps in organizing and chartering a corporation?
6. What are some of the items included in the articles of incorporation?
7. How are corporations controlled?
8. Can the owner of a large number of shares of stock enter into a contract binding the corporation?
9. What is the usual source of corporation surplus?
10. How do stockholders bear the losses of the corporation?
11. Do the interest payments on a bond depend on the profits of the business?
12. Is a bondholder a creditor of the corporation whose bonds he holds?
13. Is no-par-value stock worth anything? Is par-value stock worth more than no-par-value stock? Explain.
14. What is meant by the book value of a share of stock?
15. Is preferred stock more desirable than common stock? Explain.
16. Do stockholders vote at stockholders' meetings?
17. What are the possible advantages and disadvantages of the corporation compared with other forms of business organizations?
18. What is the basic purpose of cooperatives?
19. When and where did the cooperative movement originate?
20. What are the Rochdale principles?
21. What two broad classifications of cooperatives are given in the chapter?
22. If a consumers' cooperative has net receipts or savings from its operations at the end of the year, how may these be used?

APPLYING YOUR ECONOMIC UNDERSTANDING

1. What are some of the major corporations which function in your community? Classify them as to whether they are public or private corporations. For the private corporations, subdivide their classification as to nonprofit and business corporations.
2. Review the financial pages of a large city newspaper for advertisements of proposed stock sales. Are both the par value and the offer price stated for each stock? What relationship exists between the two? Explain how the advertisements are related to capital formation.

Ch. 7   CORPORATIONS AND COOPERATIVES

3. Discuss with your bank whether it can invest its deposits in stocks and bonds. Report your findings to the class.

4. One student claims that it is better to invest in bonds than it is to invest in stocks. Do you agree or disagree? Support your viewpoint.

5. On his 21st birthday, John received a sum of money. He is considering buying stock in a new small company. His grandfather believes that the stocks of older and larger companies are a safer investment. Which is the safer? Explain.

6. Look up the statistics on the number of stockholders in several companies. Does the trend seem to indicate that more people wish to become owners? Why or why not?

7. A local cooperative had the following expenses in one year:

   Supplies.............................. $635,816.60
   Taxes.................................   211,179.23
   Salaries..............................   99,963.03
   Miscellaneous.........................   31,525.87

   What percent of the expenses were taxes? What form of taxes was probably included in the tax payments made by the cooperative?

8. Organize a panel discussion with a student moderator and a student representing each of three different types of cooperatives. Have them discuss such topics as:
   a. Can you trace the history of your type of business?
   b. What service does each perform for the community?
   c. Who makes the decisions?
   d. Who manages the enterprise?
   e. How is voting done?
   f. Who owns the business?
   g. How is capital raised?
   h. What returns are received on invested money?
   i. How are surplus earnings used?
   j. What taxes does each pay?
   k. What is the liability of the members?

9. Secure data from your nearest local power cooperative relative to the history of money which it borrowed from government sources. What interest rates were paid? What amounts were repaid to the government?

10. In what ways do the Independent Grocers' Association (I.G.A.), the Federal Reserve System, and United Press International (U.P.I.) use cooperative principles?

11. Interview an officer of a local cooperative to learn why and how it was formed. Interview some of its older patrons to learn how it has affected them economically. Share your findings with the class.

CHALLENGES TO ECONOMIC COMPETENCE

1. Secure from your Secretary of State a copy of the laws pertaining to and the regulations regarding the incorporation of a business in *your* state. Prepare a digest of the major points and present it orally to the class.

2. Interview a number of adults whom you know to determine their attitudes toward corporations. Analyze your findings and prepare a report on their reasons for such attitudes.

3. Prepare a bulletin board display of various types of stock certificates and bond forms. Use as a theme: Some Forms of Capital Formation. Stock certificates and bond forms can be secured from corporations and banks by writing to them and explaining the purpose for which you wish to use the forms.

4. As a report, write a theme on one of the following subjects: (a) The New Look: Corporations Woo Their Stockholders, (b) Are Stockholders Forgotten People? (c) Corporations, Government Regulation, and Economic Growth, (d) How the (name) Corporation Grew and Grew.

5. Investigate the development of cooperative apartments in one of the major cities. Prepare a report for oral presentation in class.

6. Organize a bulletin board display depicting the part cooperatives play in the nation's economic life.

7. Prepare an article for the school newspaper on one of the following topics: (a) How Federal and State Cooperatives Differ, (b) Are Cooperatives Taxpayers? (c) The Story of New Harmony (or The Amana Colony), (d) The Cooperatives Share in the Nation's Production.

8. Have your local farm adviser or a representative of the Department of Agriculture talk to the class on the services that government makes available to cooperatives.

Chapter 8

Some Problems of Modern Production

Does population change create production problems?
How do consumption changes cause production problems?
Are producers' motives related to production decisions?
What resource problems confront modern production?

The basic economic problem is like a coin; it has two sides or presentations. A study of the first side will show how population change affects both the quantity and variety of unlimited wants. This change relates to consumer demand which creates some problems for modern business. A study of the second side will show how modern business faces problems caused by the scarcity of resources. The latter will indicate how business may change its organizational form and change resource employment as problem solutions.

Babies may be a boon to their joyful American parents; more babies may also make it possible for more parents to be joyful. But a baby boom creates some of the problems of modern production. These problems concern not only production in the present, but also for the future. Modern production is confronted with the problem of: creating more goods for more people; increasing per capita product for an increased total population; and changing the product mix to satisfy changed tastes and wants as the age distribution of population changes. The demand for rattles by babies shifts to talking toys at age five, portable transistor radios at ten, personal telephones at fifteen, and cassette tape recorders in surging, exhaust-type automobiles by the late teens.

POPULATION CHANGE AND PRODUCTION PROBLEMS

A knowledge of population change within various age groups is helpful for an understanding of one of the basic causes of production problems.

Illus. 8-1. Modern production is confronted with the problem of creating more goods for more people.

The West Bend Company

If you were born in the middle of the 50's, Figure 8-1 at the top of the next page indicates that you were in the under 5 age group numbering less than 20½ million persons. In 1970, this same age group had increased in size by over 3½ million persons. What pressures would this growth place on business now required to supply the additional demands for baby foods, toddler's walking shoes, and crayon picture books?

In 1960, the 15–19 year-old teen-agers numbered about 13½ million. By 1970, this group increased by almost 5½ million persons who were of secondary school and college age. This quantitative increase in demand for the production of school services was further added to qualitatively inasmuch as many in the age group were also demanding more years of improved educational services. In the shorter period of 1960 to 1967, data indicates that public school expenditures increased from $16 billion to $32 billion. What pressures would this change exert on production which would be required to supply the additional staff, building facilities, school equipment, textbooks, and supplies?

Similarly, the continuous baby boom was largely responsible for a shift in size of the total group from 69½ million in 1960 to 84½ million in 1970. What problems would face producers in their attempts to meet the specific needs of an additional 15 million persons aged 19 and under?

Ch. 8   SOME PROBLEMS OF MODERN PRODUCTION

THE POPULATION BOOM! BABIES THROUGH THE TEEN'S

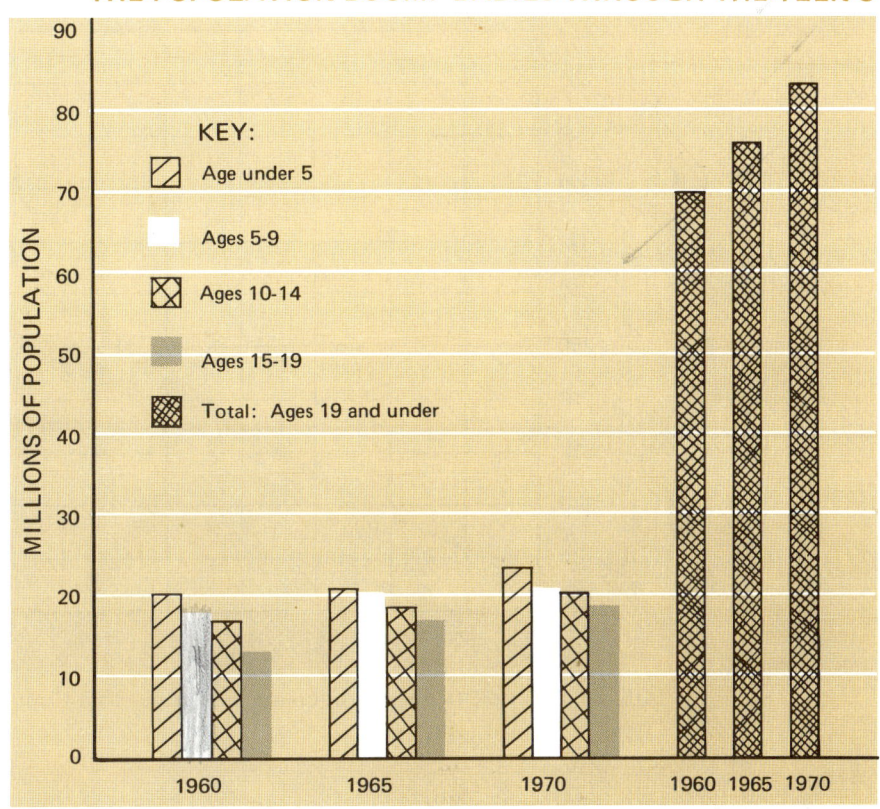

KEY:
- Age under 5
- Ages 5-9
- Ages 10-14
- Ages 15-19
- Total: Ages 19 and under

Figure 8-1.

SOURCE: Actual and tentative data from U.S. Dept. of Commerce, Bureau of the Census.

Total United States population is also rising. Figure 8-2 on the next page shows population projections to the year 2000. Roman numerals I through IV represent various projections of possible increases. Projection I is based on the highest birthrate expectancy; projection IV is based on the lowest birthrate expectancy. These projected trends were estimated in 1960 when total population was about 180 million persons. Point X projects a population of 205 million persons in 1970. By 1970, the population had actually reached 203 million and continued to climb. Projection trends III and IV were fairly accurate in their estimates for 1970. If these trends prove to be accurate in projecting total population increases, how will the increases contribute to present problems of production as well as to problems for the future?

PRODUCTION OF GOODS AND SERVICES   Unit 2

POPULATION PROJECTIONS TO 2000

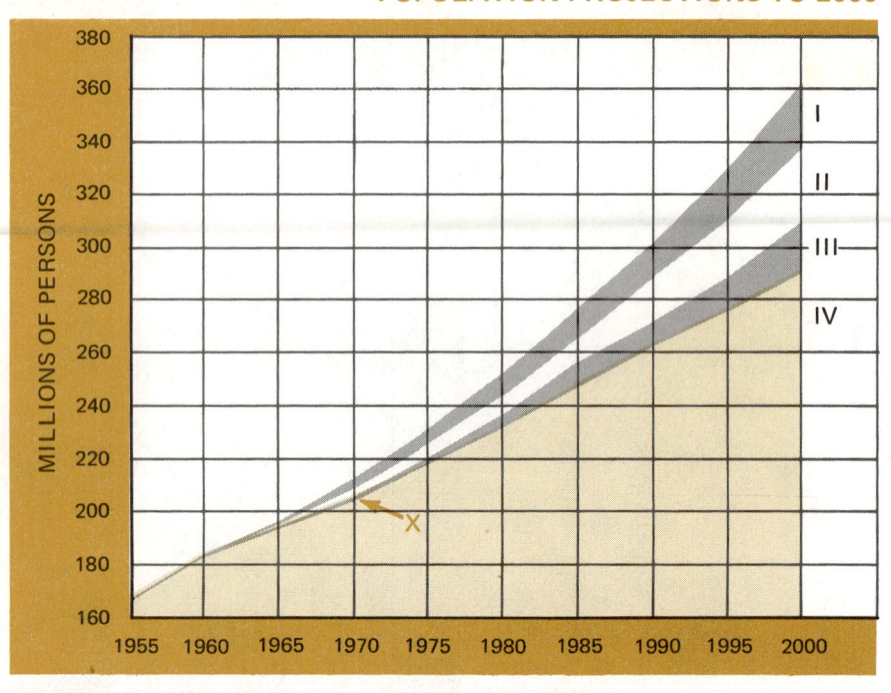

Figure 8-2.

ADAPTED FROM: the Department of Commerce, Bureau of the Census.

PERSONAL CONSUMPTION CHANGE AND PRODUCTION PROBLEMS

In early 1950, American households numbered less than 43 million. Personal consumption was limited. Production provided only one television set in black and white for every four households. Production provided no color television sets at all. Each household averaged two home radio receivers, none of which used transistors and modern circuitry. By 1970, the number of American households exceeded 60 million. Each household, on the average, had the use of more than one black and white television set and the use of four home radios, many of which were transistorized. Moreover, one household in every five was enjoying the use of a color television receiver.

Countless other forms of economic goods were also consumed in greater quantity during this period. Each individual was enjoying not only new types of goods but also increased quantities of improved familiar items. The problems of production became more evident as is shown in the accompanying chart of personal consumption expenditures.

PERSONAL CONSUMPTION EXPENDITURES

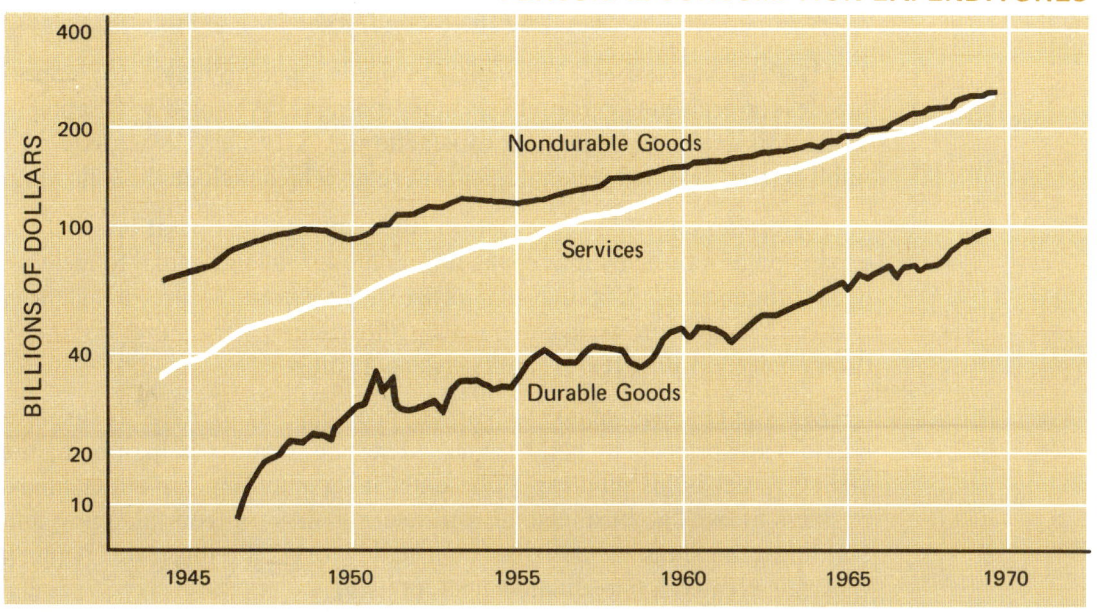

Figure 8-3. ADAPTED FROM: *Historical Chart Book 1969*, Board of Governors of the Federal Reserve System.

During the years from 1950 to 1970, the size of the population increased by one-third; but production was faced with a much higher growth rate in consumer demand. Expenditures had increased over 150 percent for nondurables, almost 300 percent for services, and almost 200 percent for durable goods. Total personal consumer expenditures had increased over 200 percent. In 1950 some 153 million consumers were spending $193 billion, a per capita spending of $1,253. By 1970, some 205 million consumers were spending about $600 billion, a per capita spending of about $2,927. Despite the rise in prices which accounted for part of the higher dollar spending, the most important gain was in the per capita increase in products.

Increases in consumer demand create production expansion problems. What would motivate producers to make the necessary decisions? How would business react as it attempted to solve the problems of production expansion?

PRODUCER MOTIVES AND PROBLEM DECISIONS

Business decisions are made by people either individually or as groups. Depending upon the motivation, business personnel will react in certain ways. Broadly speaking, there are two classes of motives. The first group refers to personal motives, and the second, to economic motives.

(1) Personal motives. Through a business a person may enjoy opportunities for gratifying certain basic human desires. As noted in Chapter 1, each of us seeks psychological satisfactions. A business enterprise may fulfill certain personal psychological cravings, which include the following:

(a) Ambition. The organization, the control, the operation, and the expansion of a business may make it possible for the individual to feel that he is "somebody." Through this outlet the individual secures his identity and his recognition as a person. To illustrate, Henry Ford became a "somebody" in the area of family transportation.

(b) The creative impulse. Normal people seem to have an urge to create, to construct, to build things. The poet's outlet is his poem; the artist's outlet is his painting. The enterpriser may find his outlet in the business firm. The businessman's pleasure is derived from planning and building a business which is his own handiwork. To illustrate, Andrew Carnegie created a coordinated steel industry.

(c) The spirit of adventure. The new, the unknown, and the risks involved are part of adventure. Each business is a venture. It offers the entrepreneur a challenge to cope with the unknown experiences and

Illus. 8-2. Normal people seem to have an urge to create, to build things.

the problems that may arise in its operation. To illustrate, Charles A. Lindbergh made a solo transatlantic flight as a pioneer in overseas air transportation.

(2) Economic motives. A business provides an outlet for the attainment of personal economic satisfactions. Increased wealth or income is obtainable through economic transactions in which income exceeds expenditures. The enterpriser is motivated to secure economic gain or profit. Two sources of gain or profit follow.

(a) Promoters' profits. Promoters and investment bankers in many cases have made large profits, not by producing goods, but merely by bringing about the consolidation of two or more businesses. The concerns may be engaged in the same kind of business, or they may operate different kinds of businesses.

When two or more concerns engaged in the same kind or stage of production form a business combination, the organization is a *horizontal combination.* For example, if two or more grocery stores come under one management, the result is a horizontal combination.

A company engaged in the production of a finished article may control other companies or plants, each of which completes certain stages in the production of the article. For example, a company engaged in the production of steel may acquire coal and iron mines, blast furnaces, rolling mills, steamship lines, railroads, and a number of selling agencies. The company would then control concerns engaged in the successive stages of the production and sale of steel. This organization constitutes a *vertical combination.* Some of our largest business concerns are both horizontal and vertical combinations.

When the combination includes firms that were unrelated in kinds of production, it is called a *conglomerate.* For example, bringing under single management a credit card corporation, a travel service agency, a food processing company, and an insurance corporation creates a conglomerate combination. As a result of the combination, the identity of some or all of the original firms may disappear.

A *merger* takes place when the stockholders vote to dissolve their corporation and to sell the assets to another corporation. The company that purchases the assets pays for the assets by issuing its stock to the stockholders of the dissolved corporation. Thus, the stockholders in the dissolved corporation become stockholders in the merged corporations. Or the stockholders in the dissolved company may be paid in money or in the bonds of the purchasing company.

Sometimes the assets of two or more corporations are combined by *consolidation*, or *amalgamation*, which involves the formation of an entirely new corporation. In this case each of the corporations to be combined is dissolved; and the assets of each concern are turned over to the new company, each stockholder receiving a certain number of shares of stock in the new company. The business owner who promotes the consolidation of his business with another may receive a profit because of the transfer. Investment bankers and brokers who assist in the formation of the new combination may also profit from their services. If the new combination does not increase production at lower cost, the profits of the promoters may not be equalled by a socially beneficial gain to the public.

(b) *Profits from increased production.* Increasing the volume of production often results in a decrease of the cost of each unit of a good produced. In many cases production on a larger scale may enable the producer to turn out more goods at less cost, which he may sell at lower prices, and yet make more profit than when production was less and selling prices higher. Several ways by which increased production can increase profits are:

(1) the employment of specialists, which reduces labor costs.

(2) the use of more efficient machinery and equipment, which reduces capital costs.

Illus. 8-3. Increasing the volume of production often results in a decrease of the cost of each unit.

(3) the employment of experts who seek out inefficiency and introduce more efficient profit-making operations.

(4) the utilization of by-products, which creates additional products from waste materials and increases total income.

(5) the application of research and development, which lowers operational costs or provides added income from new products.

(6) the use of quantity purchasing, which generally lowers unit costs.

(7) the use of large-scale marketing and transportation, which provides unit savings on storage, advertising, shipping, and other similar costs.

The economist's major interest is in economic motives, economic decisions, and economic action all of which relate directly to economic production problems. One type of problem arising from promoters' profit motivation is the problem of centralized control. A different type of problem arising from production expansion profit is the resource problem.

THE PROBLEM OF CENTRALIZED CONTROL

Single or monopoly control over the supply of a product in a marketing area enables the supplier to fix the quantity supplied and its price. The quantity offered can be controlled so that sales income will return the greatest profit. This relationship of monopoly to price will be discussed more fully in Chapter 10.

Certain types of action by the producer may be used to secure a monopoly type of control. Motivated by his desire to make monopoly profit, the producer decides to aid his efforts by adopting a business arrangement that will permit centralized control. Some examples of past and present arrangements used to centralize control are: (1) pools, (2) trusts, (3) holding companies, and (4) communities of interest.

(1) Pools. A *pool* is an agreement between competing concerns to cooperate in fixing prices and in establishing trade practices. It may be a "gentlemen's agreement," a verbal understanding between the managers of the companies involved. Each concern remains independent of the others, except in complying with the agreement's terms. The terms may include (a) the restriction of production to prevent a fall in prices of the goods or services the concerns produce and (b) the division of production among the concerns in some profitable way.

(2) Trusts. The *trust* is an arrangement whereby the stockholders in competing corporations engaged in the same kind of business give over their stock to a group of trustees and receive in exchange "trust certificates." The trustees can then run the corporations as they see fit. The holders of the trust certificates are entitled to part of the profits. If the trust is large enough, competition can be prevented and prices can be fixed as the managers of the trust desire.

(3) Holding companies. A *holding company* is a corporation that has been organized primarily for the purpose of buying and holding stock in other corporations. The companies whose stock is held by the holding company are called *subsidiary companies*. The object of the holding company is to control the policies and the operations of the corporations in which it holds stock. Pure holding companies do no manufacturing or trading in goods; their only function is to hold the stock and control the affairs of operating concerns that actually manufacture or sell goods or services. Operating companies that hold a controlling interest in other corporations are sometimes referred to as holding companies.

Sometimes one holding company is superimposed upon other holding companies in such a way that the control of large amounts of capital is placed in the hands of a few wealthy individuals. The practice of exercising control over producing companies by means of holding companies is sometimes referred to as *pyramiding control*.

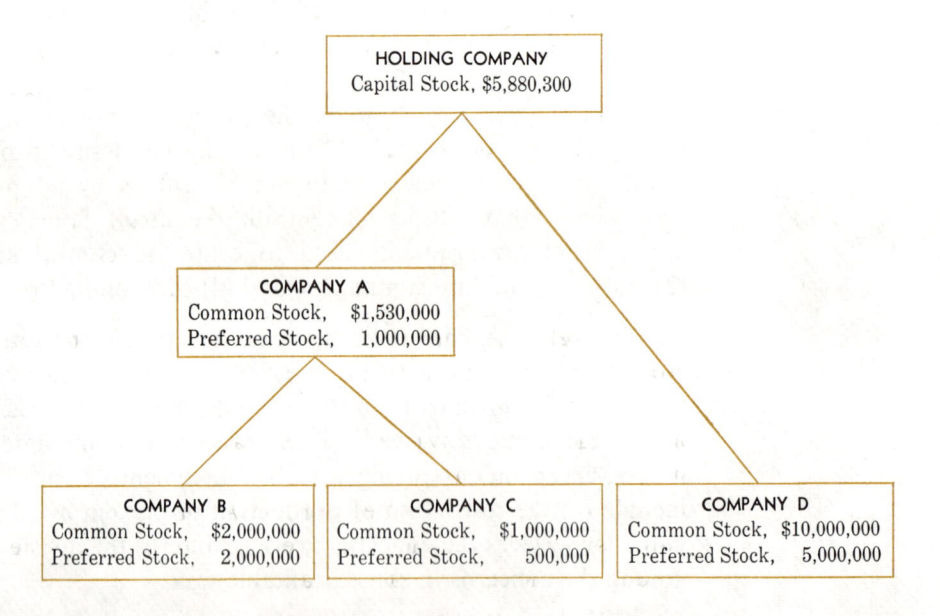

```
                    HOLDING COMPANY
                  Capital Stock, $5,880,300

                          |
                ┌─────────┴─────────┐
                          |
                      COMPANY A
              Common Stock,    $1,530,000
              Preferred Stock,  1,000,000

                          |
        ┌─────────────────┼─────────────────┐
    COMPANY B          COMPANY C          COMPANY D
Common Stock, $2,000,000   Common Stock, $1,000,000   Common Stock, $10,000,000
Preferred Stock, 2,000,000 Preferred Stock, 500,000   Preferred Stock, 5,000,000
```

This is how pyramiding control in a holding company operates: By means of stock ownership a holding company may control the policies and the activities of several companies. With a capital of **$5,880,300**, or 51 percent of the common stock of Companies **A** and **D**, the holding company can control capital amounting to **$23,030,000**.

(4) Communities of interest. When two or more concerns refrain from competing with each other and adopt policies intended to increase the profits of each other, a *community of interest* is said to exist. It is often charged that there are many communities of interest among big business firms, and that cartels have been formed by certain big American, English, and German companies to divide up world trade in some products. (*Cartel* is a term used in Europe to mean "community of interest.") In the United States, communities of interest possibly influence the policies of some groups of business corporations.

Also, a community of interest may exist when the same persons are members of the boards of directors for competing corporations. Such a situation is sometimes referred to as an "interlocking directorate." As a result, competition may be controlled, similar wage and labor policies may be adopted by different companies, and prices may be fixed for each of the companies.

Centralized control may solve the problem of increasing profits for certain individuals and groups. At the same time, it has frequently created other problems. In some cases, it has caused decreased profits for competing producers as a result of unfair or "cut throat" competition. In other cases, it has led to gross overvaluation of some corporations' par value stock; this *watered stock* has resulted in losses to shareholders who purchased it. It has sometimes led to the problem of decreased incomes for small shareholders. The surrender of a stockholder's voting rights by a written agreement, known as a *proxy*, gives control power to corporate directors and officers. When corporate officers abuse their control by voting themselves excessive salaries, pensions, and bonuses, they divert funds that could be paid to shareholders as dividends.

Business has taken some action to improve its public image. Many abuses of centralized business power have been self-corrected. In other instances, government has been responsive to the public's plea for preventive action against abused business power. Through the enactment of various laws, and the establishment of regulatory governmental agencies, other abuses of centralized control have been eliminated or moderated. Such response is found in historical readings which relate to the Interstate Commerce Act of 1887, the Sherman Antitrust Act of 1890, the Clayton Antitrust Act, the Federal Trade Commission Act, the Public Utility Holding Company Act, and to agencies such as the Securities Exchange Commission.

Centralized control has also had a positive side. It has in numerous instances been able to effect economies and to stabilize certain branches of industry and business. For example, control in a holding company —

used by certain public utilities producing light and power — has been able to increase supply in an industry where prices have remained relatively low. The trust arrangement — used by some banking firms — has provided needed large-scale capital funds for an ever-expanding economy. Similar business combinations have been able to make larger profits for all the stockholders while solving consumer demand for an increased supply of lower priced goods.

RESOURCE PROBLEMS OF MODERN PRODUCTION

Production as indicated in Chapter 1, creates the society's total product. Inputs of land, labor, and capital resources affect the quantity and quality of total product. Increased total product requires that the inputs of resources be increased or be used more efficiently. To increase product, modern production is faced with problems of three types:

1. Labor resource employment.
2. Land resource employment.
3. Capital resource employment.

(1) Labor resource employment. In 1950 the civilian employed labor resource was reaching 60 million persons. Reference to the figure indicates that by 1970 some 19 million persons were added to the civilian employed

CIVILIAN EMPLOYMENT

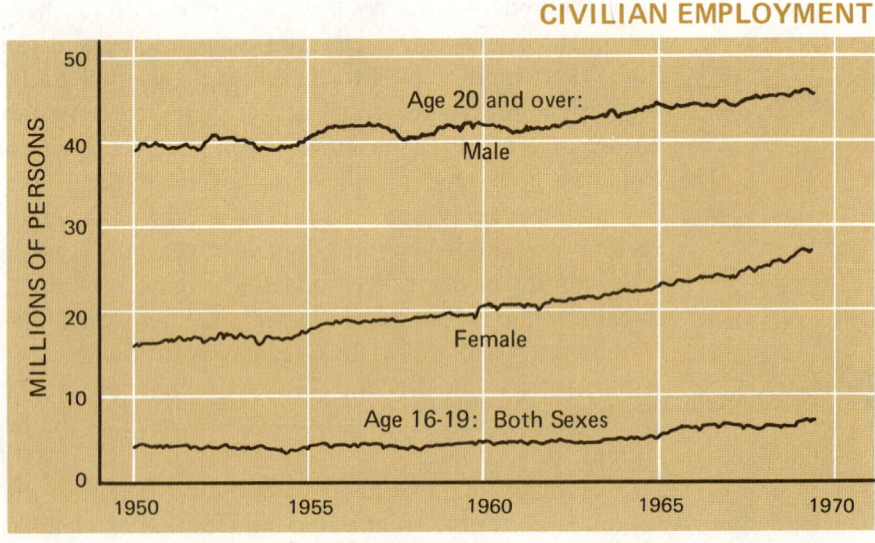

Figure 8-4.

SOURCE: *Historical Chart Book 1969*, Board of Governors of the Federal Reserve System.

labor force. About 10 million women aged 20 and over were added to the labor resource input; this was about a 60 percent increase in the female working force. Males aged 20 and over added about 5 million workers, an increase of less than 13 percent for that group of workers. Teens of both sexes between the ages of 16–19 contributed about 4 million new workers.

Between 1950 and 1970, about 3½ million fewer persons were used as agricultural labor inputs; part of this group became available as a nonagricultural labor input. Because of the downward trend in agricultural employment, additional labor inputs were available for increased production in manufacturing and mining, trade, finance and service, and government. Labor resource inputs showed less gains in meeting transportation and public utilities and construction production needs.

Figure 8-5 on the next page shows that between 1950–1970 the civilian employed labor force contributed 19 million additional workers as labor inputs. Part of this increase was gained by the more efficient use of labor; the rate of unemployment was decreased from 5.3 percent in 1950 to 3.5 percent by 1970. In numbers of persons, the total labor input rate of gain was 33 percent. This was an average yearly increase of less than 1.7 percent, which was inadequate to sustain the demand of an ever-increasing population. Nor could it provide for economic growth, interpreted as an increase in the level of living. Real economic growth would require a growth rate closer to 3 percent as an annual average.

This labor scarcity demanded emphasis on production of certain products at the expense of shortages in other product areas. Part of these shortages were offset as land resource and capital resource inputs were expanded to substitute for the labor scarcity.

(2) Land resource employment. Land or natural resources are not readily increased. However, land or natural resources can be shifted from one use to another. Resources can also be employed more efficiently.

An example of a shift in land use can be found by studying data of recent agricultural production. In 1950, the nation's 5.6 million farms averaged 213 acres each; they used 1.2 billion acres of land. By 1970, there were less than 3 million farms that averaged 377 acres each; these fewer farms reduced the land use to 1.12 billion acres. Thus, some 80 million acres of farmland were released to other production uses. Certain California orchards and vineyards became residential subdivisions. Numerous truck garden farms in New Jersey were transformed into industrial research and development centers. Other thousands of farm acreage were

LABOR FORCE, EMPLOYMENT, AND UNEMPLOYMENT

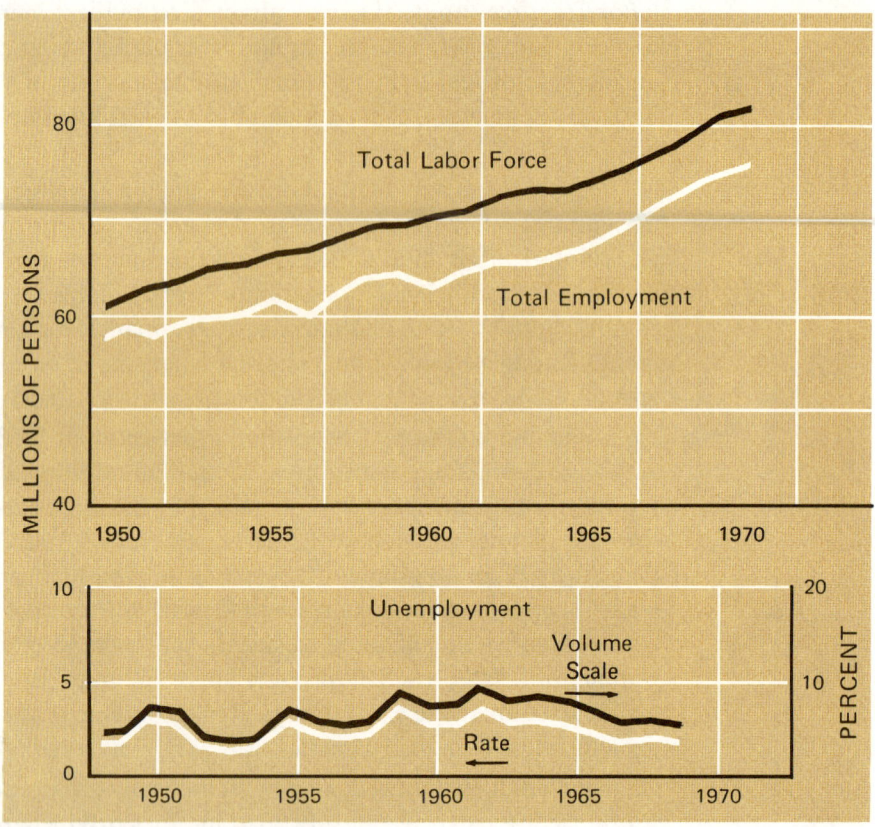

Figure 8-5.

SOURCE: *Historical Chart Book 1969*, Board of Governors of the Federal Reserve System.

released to serve as right-of-ways for interstate highways, as airports, and as multiplex motel and shopping centers.

Similarly, idle lands have been put into efficient uses. Swamplands of Florida, desert lands of Arizona and New Mexico, former Arctic wastes of Alaska, and tidewater lands off the coasts of the Gulf of Mexico have been reclaimed by drainage projects, by irrigation programs, or by new technological exploitation. These and other more efficient uses of land resources have yielded additional landsites and have added to the output of minerals, metals, chemicals, and gases for increased product.

Although use of farmland and farm labor decreased, total product from agriculture was increasing. Although the nonagricultural labor force rate was not increasing as rapidly as the population rate, nonagricultural production was also increasing. To what extent were the scarcity problems of labor and land resources offset by the expansion of the inputs of capital resources?

(3) Capital resource employment. Capital, or man-made goods needed for the production of other goods, requires funds for its purchase and use. Savings are a source for such funds. In 1950, personal savings were $13 billion. By 1970, the annual personal savings had reached $38 billion. Unfortunately in 1950 business investment expenditures for new plant and equipment required $20 billion; by 1970, business fixed investment required $100 billion.

Obviously, the annual personal savings were insufficient to provide the required capital funds. Therefore, in 1950 businesses reinvested some $16 billion of their profits; by 1970, this reinvestment from profits had increased to $26 billion. Through the two decades, the total of savings and reinvestment were short of the required capital investment funds. Some producers raised capital through increased ownership by the sale of additional corporate stock. Many producers secured the balance of their capital funds by borrowing. Long-term bond issues became more important as sources of capital funds. Other funds were obtained by borrowing from banks or by pledging short-term notes.

The substitution of capital resources for the decreased inputs of farm labor and land was made by increasing investment in farm implements and machinery from $12 billion in 1950 to over $30 billion by 1970. This partially accounted for tripling farm output per man-hour during those years and maintained continued agricultural product increases.

Problems of modern production are also influenced by prices and income distribution. The discussion of these influences will follow with a presentation of Price Determination in Unit 3 and of Distribution of National Income in Unit 4.

SUMMARY

Problems of modern production are related to the basic economic problem. Consumer demand creates problems as population increases, as per capita demand grows, and as tastes change. Changes within the various age groups in the population also create additional production problems.

Personal consumption expanded rapidly between 1950 and 1970 as per capita incomes increased from $1,253 to $2,927; the rise in incomes added to the problems of producers. Production demands of consumers increased by 300 percent for services, by 200 percent for durable goods, and by 150 percent for nondurables.

Both personal motives and economic motives influence producers' decisions as they seek to solve production problems. Through business enterprises, producers may seek fulfillment of psychological cravings which include: (a) ambition, (b) the creative impulse, and (c) the spirit of adventure. Economic motives are related to economic gain or profit.

Profit from increased large-scale production may result from certain types of economies. Economies or cost reductions may be achieved by the use of specialists and experts, more and better machinery, by-products, research and development, more economical purchasing practices, and improvements in marketing and transportation.

Centralized control through the use of pools, trusts, holding companies, and communities of interest may create unfair competition, watering of stock, and abuses of corporate power. On the positive side, centralized control may effect economies, reduce or stabilize product prices, and increase stockholders' earnings.

Production problems in recent years have necessitated the more efficient use of and the increased employment of labor, land, and capital resources. Greatest economic growth has been achieved by means of substituting capital resources as replacements for the scarcities of labor and land resources.

NEW TERMS

cartel
community of interest
conglomerate
consolidation *or* amalgamation
holding company
horizontal combination
merger

pool
proxy
pyramiding control
subsidiary companies
trust
vertical combination
watered stock

QUESTIONS ON THE CHAPTER

1. What have been some of the sources of production problems in recent decades?
2. In what ways are the following related to decision making in business: (a) the ambition of business managers, (b) the creative impulse, and (c) the spirit of adventure?
3. What is the distinction between a horizontal combination, a vertical combination, and a conglomerate?
4. How may large-scale production lower production costs? Consider (a) research and development, (b) use of machinery, (c) employment of specialists and experts, (d) utilization of by-products, (e) purchasing, and (f) marketing and transportation.

5. What is the definition of each of the following: (a) pools, (b) trusts, (c) holding companies, (d) communities of interest, (e) cartels?
6. What is unfair competition?
7. How may watered stock be created?
8. How may directors of a corporation abuse their power?
9. How are the Interstate Commerce Act and the Sherman Antitrust Act related to business combinations?
10. What positive results have come from centralization in business?
11. What have been some trends in the use of labor resources in recent decades?
12. What changes in the use of land resources have occurred in recent years?
13. How has business solved the problem of securing adequate capital resources?

APPLYING YOUR ECONOMIC UNDERSTANDING

1. Statistics show that the per capita consumption of coffee is decreasing while the per capita consumption of soft drinks is increasing. Does population change provide any clues regarding these shifts in consumption? Explain the reasons for your answer.
2. Recent trends in automobile sales indicate increased production and purchases of "sports" model cars. What evidence from population changes might explain this trend?
3. Many leaders in industry are concerned about the corporate image of the firm that they work for. When cyclamates (artificial sweetners) were being discussed as to their possible harmful health effects, many products containing cyclamates were voluntarily withdrawn from the market. Explain how this relates to problems of modern production.
4. Name five major corporations and classify each as horizontally or vertically combined.
5. Large city newspapers advertise job offerings with wide ranges in salaries. Refer to one of these newspapers and indicate with your reasons whether the higher salaries have a relationship to large-scale production and lowering of costs.
6. National research and development expenditures have increased rapidly during the past twenty years. How does this trend relate to large-scale production? How does it relate to the level of living?
7. The People's Electric System has investments in the common shares of nine subsidiary light and power companies. Is The People's Electric System a holding company? Is this necessarily harmful? Why or why not?
8. Check advertisements in the financial section of a large city newspaper that reports offerings of new stock issues. Is there a difference in the offered price and the par value? Does a difference imply that it is watered stock? Discuss the reasons for your answers.

9. A leading producer of gas shows a stockholders' equity (ownership) of $698 million in shares. It also has a long-term bonded indebtedness of $857 million, and $97 million of short-term notes and bank debts. Are these facts more specifically related to labor, land, or capital resources? Discuss the relationship.
10. Frequently industries are represented at legislative hearings for presentation of their views on proposed bills. Explain why you accept or reject such representation as politically or morally permissible.

CHALLENGES TO ECONOMIC COMPETENCE

1. Prepare a written report on one of the following topics: (a) The New Corporate Image, (b) The Role of Corporations in Education and Philanthrophy, (c) The Role of Capital in a Growing America, (d) A Case for Large-Scale Enterprise.
2. Prepare a bibliography for student use in your library. The bibliography should contain references of readings and materials that concern LAND RESOURCE EMPLOYMENT.
3. Prepare a graph for a bulletin board display depicting the figures of the United States Department of Commerce as to the number and size of business corporations for the past ten years.
4. Prepare and present a panel discussion on the role and responsibilities of large corporations in the American economy.
5. Make a collection of clippings concerning large corporations and their activities. Organize the clippings under suitable headings for use as a bulletin board display.

Unit 3

Price Determination

Chapter 9 Competition and Prices
Chapter 10 Monopoly and Prices
Chapter 11 Government Control of Prices
Chapter 12 Prices and the Value of Money

American Oil Company

Humble Oil & Refining Company

National Cash Register Company

Armstrong Cork Company

In a free society, land, labor, capital, and enterprise are devoted to the production of those goods which the owners think will be the most profitable.

Chapter 9

Competition and Prices

How do goods and services acquire money value?
What is meant by demand and supply?
How can demand and supply determine price?
How are prices determined under communism?

One of the characters in Oscar Wilde's play *Lady Windemere's Fan* says that a cynic is "a man who knows the price of everything and the value of nothing."

This quotation implies that there is a difference between the meanings of "price" and "value." What is the difference? Which comes first, price or value? Let us examine the meaning of "value," "price," and some other related terms.

VALUE, UTILITY, AND PRICE

The term "value" may be used in a number of ways. For example, we may think of the value of a hat, the value of an education, or the value of a good reputation. In each of these connections the term value implies "worth" or "usefulness." The term does not necessarily suggest value or worth in terms of money.

Utility, as we know, is the power or capacity of a good to satisfy a want. It is not the same thing as value. For anything — a loaf of bread, for instance — must have utility before it can have value. Now, if an object or a service has utility, is relatively scarce, and its worth can be measured in some way, it has *economic value*.

The economic value of one unit of a good compared to that of a unit of another good is called *exchange value*. Or one may say that exchange value is "power in exchange." For example, the exchange value of apples and oranges may be 2 apples for 1 orange, or 1 orange for 2 apples.

Price is exchange value stated in terms of money, which is the common measure — or denominator — of exchange value. By using money as a medium of exchange, the exchange value of a unit of one good compared to units of other goods may be noted. For example, the exchange value of a bushel of wheat may be $1.60; that of a gallon of gasoline, 40 cents; or that of a day's labor, $24. Therefore, a unit of wheat is worth 4 units of gasoline, and a day's labor is worth 15 bushels of wheat.

Thus, we see the relations between value, utility, economic value, economic goods, exchange value, and prices.

PRICES AFFECT US IN MANY WAYS

From the standpoint of our general welfare, prices are important for three reasons: (1) prices determine production, (2) prices influence the use of the factors of production, and (3) prices apportion consumers' goods.

(1) Prices determine production. Under a system of free enterprise, prices determine the production of the kinds and quantities of goods that the people want. For example, when prices are free to move up or down, a rise in the price of wheat results in the production of more wheat. Or if the price of television sets is significantly above the cost of production, an increasing number of sets will be turned out by manufacturers. After a while, if the market for television sets declines and their prices fall, fewer sets will be produced.

(2) Prices influence the use of the factors of production. In a free society, land, labor, capital, and enterprise are devoted to the production of those goods which the owners think will be the most profitable. For example, if the price of wheat is high, owners of land will tend to use more land for growing wheat. Or if the salaries (prices) paid schoolteachers are low in comparison with the salaries paid other white-collar workers, fewer capable men and women will elect teaching as a career. Likewise, the prices for the products of different industries will determine how much of the nation's savings and capital will be available to each industry.

(3) Prices apportion consumers' goods. Ordinarily, prices ration or apportion consumers' goods among the users. This rationing process is carried on by two sets of prices.

In the first place, the income of the consumer is determined largely by the price of what he sells in order to obtain an income. For example, if he sells unskilled labor, the price of his labor is likely to be low, and hence his income will be small. If he is a noted artist, the price of his services will be high, and his income will be large. Thus, the amount of money one has to spend is determined largely by the price of what he sells.

In the second place, the amount of goods of any kind that one can buy depends to a considerable extent on the prices of the goods desired. With a given amount of money, for example, one can buy a certain quantity of meat if the price is $1 a pound. But he can buy less meat if the price is $2 a pound unless his income increases in proportion to prices.

PRICES ARE DETERMINED IN VARIOUS WAYS

In any economic system there is no question more important than that of how market prices are to be determined, for whatever or whoever controls these prices controls the economy. In the case of a one-man dictatorship, the prices of almost all economic goods are fixed by a governmental agency under the direct or indirect control of one individual. But in a free economy the control of prices by individuals is limited. In fact, in many cases no one seller or buyer can have a great influence on the market prices of goods and services.

In this country it is usually assumed that prices are determined by demand and supply under a condition of competition. And it is true that these factors do play an important part in the determination of many prices. At the same time, however, most prices are not fixed by pure competition. Factors other than demand and supply and free competition frequently operate to fix the prices of many of the things we buy.

Illus. 9-1. Most prices are not fixed by pure competition. Factors other than demand and supply and free competition frequently operate to fix the prices of many of the things we buy.

National Cash Register Company

In the case of most commodities, price is determined under one or more of the following conditions: (1) competition, (2) monopoly, (3) monopolistic (imperfect) competition, and (4) direct or indirect regulation by government. In the remainder of this chapter we shall discuss demand, supply, and competition.

WHAT IS PURE COMPETITION?

Pure competition results when there are so many sellers and buyers of an article that no one seller or buyer can influence the price. In such a market each seller is offering a good that is identical or virtually identical with that offered by all other sellers. Buyers, therefore, have no preference for the goods of one seller over another; and no seller is able to charge more than the other sellers and expect to make any sales.

Many agricultural prices are determined by conditions that more nearly conform to the concept of pure competition than is true of most other prices; however, few if any of the prices of the goods we buy are determined under such precise market conditions. It is useful, nevertheless, to see how price is determined when such a condition of pure competition does exist.

WHAT DO WE MEAN BY DEMAND?

By the *demand* for an article we mean the number of units of the article that buyers stand ready to buy in a market at a particular time at different prices. We must not confuse demand with the mere need for or desire for a good. One may need or desire a loaf of bread or a suit of clothes; but if he has no money, he cannot buy either. His needs and desires do not constitute a demand unless he has at least some money with which to pay some price for what he wants. In fact, for demand to be effective in the market, three conditions must exist: (1) desire for the good, (2) willingness to buy it, and (3) ability to pay for it. Given these three conditions, we can then say that there is demand.

Demand schedule. A *demand schedule* is a tabular representation of demand indicating the amounts that buyers would buy at various prices in a given market at a given time. For example, the following is a hypothetical demand or demand schedule for a good:

Price	Quantity
$5	50
4	100
3	150
2	200
1	250

The prices and corresponding quantities are alternative situations. That is, in the purely competitive market, one price would prevail at a given time, and not a series of prices. For this reason the table is read as follows: If the price is $5, then the quantity bought will be 50; if the price is $4, then the quantity bought will be 100; and so on.

You will note a certain relationship between price and quantity, which is expressed in the *law of demand*. This law states that the quantity of a good that people will buy tends to vary inversely with the price of the good; that is, the higher the price, the less they will buy; and the lower the price, the more they will buy.

This law applies to a given market and a given time, and it is extremely difficult to cite valid exceptions to it. Try mink coats for example. One might say that these are purchased partially because they are expensive and, therefore, would not be purchased by present buyers if the price were low. The answer, of course, is that the present owners might lose interest in mink coats because so many other persons have bought them at the lower prices. But this would only bear out the law of demand, would it not? Or as another example, consider the advertisements in your newspaper. Have you ever seen one that read "SALE — ALL PRICES DRASTICALLY INCREASED"? If the law of demand is not true, you will have a difficult time proving this to any businessman.

Demand curve. The demand schedule can also be presented graphically as a *demand curve* as shown in Figure 9-1 on the next page. Note that the curve (often drawn hypothetically as a straight line for convenience) slopes downward to the right as you would expect from the law of demand. But we must now ask why the law of demand is valid.

Explanation for the downward slope of the demand curve. As we have already seen, businessmen generally conduct their businesses on the basis of a belief that they can sell more at any given time by cutting prices, not raising them. Buyers normally are pleased to be able to purchase a good at a low price rather than at a high price, and they will be expected to do so. For example, if the prices of fresh vegetables decrease, more fresh vegetables will be purchased in preference to canned or frozen vegetables. This is the *substitution effect*. Another explanation for the buyer's behavior is that when the price of a good decreases, the buyer feels that he has more purchasing power from his income and reacts by buying more. This is known as the *income effect*. For example, if the price of beef decreases, we can not only buy more beef, but we will also have the choice of using some of the remaining purchasing power to buy other goods.

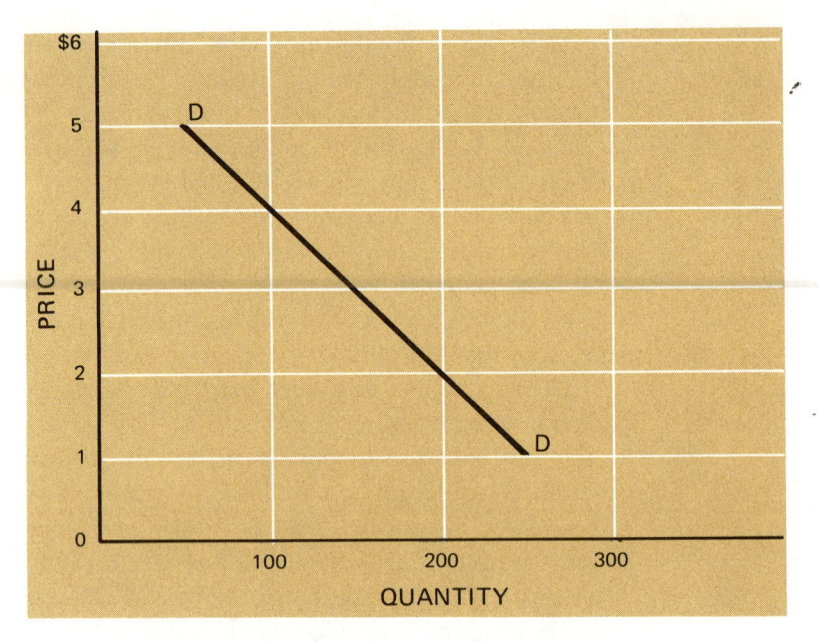

Figure 9-1.

Hypothetical Demand Curve

A final explanation of the downward sloping demand curve is one of which most students will already have at least some knowledge. As you know, it is the utility of a good that causes it to be wanted. The utility — the want-satisfying power of a unit of a good — varies with circumstances. Suppose that you have only one bottle of Coke. If you should spill the contents of the bottle, you would feel a distinct loss. Now suppose that you have a case of Coke. Each bottle is like the others. If you should spill the contents of a bottle, you would not feel the loss nearly so much as you would if you had only one bottle, would you?

To an individual the utility of a unit of a good — in the illustration above, a bottle of Coke — at a given time is the *marginal utility* of the good. It is the utility of one more unit or of one less unit at the time.

As a rule, the marginal utility of a good decreases as the number of units of the good one has, or has consumed, increases. Thus, the utility of a Coke is high if a person has only one bottle. If he has a whole case of 24 bottles, the utility of a bottle is less than if he had only one bottle. The tendency for the marginal utility of a good to decrease as one's supply of units of the good increases is called the *law of diminishing marginal utility*. The operation of this law explains why it is that, while one may be willing to give, say, 20 cents for a bottle of Coke under certain circumstances, he would buy a second bottle only if the price were reduced. In other words, since the second unit of the good will possess less marginal utility for the owner, he will purchase it only if this condition is offset by a lower price.

Perhaps if you find it difficult to accept the law of demand, you might find it of interest to assume that the opposite situation were true, that is, that more will be demanded as prices increase.

Elastic and inelastic demand. A little thought about the way you respond to price changes will cause you to conclude that people have different types of demands for different goods. In some cases a slight change in price will result in a marked change in the number of units of a good that will be purchased. In other cases even a considerable change in price will have little effect on the amount that the public will buy. For example, a relatively small increase in the price of oranges may result in a substantial decrease in the quantity of this fruit that people will buy. In this case people are quite responsive to the price change as shown by their resistance in the form of reduced purchases. On the other hand, a substantial increase in the price of salt would probably not have much effect on the amount of salt that people would buy.

The way a change in price affects the amount of an article that people will buy is referred to as the *elasticity of demand*. When a decrease in price (say 5 percent) results in a relatively greater increase in quantity sold (say 10 percent), the total receipts from sales will increase; and demand is *elastic* (relatively responsive). Receipts increase because the increase in quantity sold at the lower price is relatively large, and this is more than enough to offset the price reduction. Since "receipts equal quantity sold times price," with elastic demand the receipts are influenced more by changes in quantity sold than by the price changes. (In this case, how would receipts react to a price increase?)

But we have seen that people are not always so responsive to price changes. When a decrease in price (say 15 percent) results in a relatively smaller increase in the quantity that people will buy (say 10 percent), and the total receipts from sales decrease, demand is *inelastic* (relatively unresponsive). For an illustration, see the table on page 158.

In general, the demand for a good is more likely to be inelastic if it is a necessity, if there are no good substitutes for it, and if it amounts to only a small portion of one's budget. Our example of salt fits all three conditions. Jewelry, on the other hand, would probably represent just the opposite situation for most people. It is a luxury, and not a necessity; it is often priced high; and there are many other want-satisfying goods that can be substituted for it as an outlet for expenditures. The most important factor

SCHEDULES THAT ILLUSTRATE ELASTIC AND INELASTIC DEMAND

Price	Commodity A (Elastic demand) Number of units that will be bought	Commodity A Total amount of receipts from sales*	Commodity B (Inelastic demand) Number of units that will be bought	Commodity B Total amount of receipts from sales*
$10	1,000	$10,000	1,000	$10,000
9	1,233	11,097	1,099	9,891
8	1,557	12,456	1,200	9,600
7	2,025	14,175	1,300	9,100
6	2,738	16,428	1,500	9,000

*Approximate

Note that in the case of elastic demand the proportionate or percentage decrease (or increase) in price is less than that for the quantity sold. This results in an increase in total receipts when the price falls and a decrease in total receipts when the price rises. In the case of inelastic demand the percentage change in price is greater than the percentage change in the quantity sold. Therefore, the total amount of receipts decreases with a decrease in price even though the quantity sold increases slightly.

separating elastic from inelastic demand is availability or unavailability of good substitutes. For this reason the demand for a particular class of a good, gasoline for example, is less elastic than is the demand for a particular brand of the good. Or, to cite another example, although people must have salt, they find it quite satisfactory to substitute brands.

Is the concept of elasticity of demand useful? Not only is it useful, but knowledge of it is essential for the businessman and the lawmaker. If the demand for his goods is elastic and the businessman thinks of raising prices as the only means of increasing his revenues, he will be disappointed by the results. For he will take in less money than at the lower price. Or if the lawmaker wishes to raise substantial tax revenue by means of a commodity tax, this can be accomplished most readily by taxing goods for which the demand is inelastic. Does this help explain the substantial tax on gasoline?

Changes in demand. Before turning to the supply side of the market, we must consider one other situation for demand, namely, *changes in demand*. These changes may be either increases or decreases. When an increase in demand occurs, a greater number of units of the good will be bought at a given price than was previously the case. A decrease in demand means that a smaller number of units will be bought at a given price. For example, if in a certain community consumers purchased an average of 1,000 dozen eggs per day at a price of $.50 per dozen in 1971, and 1,200 dozen at the same price in 1972, demand has increased. More eggs are bought even without a price reduction. Or if we find that in our local stores 3,000 bathing suits are sold per week for $15 each in June and only 100 in August at the same price, we know that demand has decreased.

As you will understand, there are many things that determine the level of demand, and it is changes in these things that bring about changes in demand. In the first of the examples above, the increased demand for eggs might result from a rise in personal income, an increase in population, or changes in tastes. In the second example, the decrease in the demand for bathing suits is naturally explained by the time of the season. Other changes in demand are caused by changes in habits, styles, customs, or advertising; by discovery of new uses for the good; by changes in the prices of other goods; and by expectations of future prices or of world conditions. For example, fear of impending war may cause a sudden rush to buy goods that are considered likely to become less available. Our concern for the availability of goods requires that we now turn to the supply side of the market.

WHAT DO WE MEAN BY SUPPLY?

The *supply* of a good is a series of quantities of the good that sellers stand ready to offer for sale at a corresponding set of prices at a given time in a particular market. A *supply schedule* is a tabular representation of supply. For example, the following is a hypothetical supply or supply schedule for a good:

Price	Quantity
$5	250
4	200
3	150
2	100
1	50

As with demand, the prices and corresponding quantities are alternative situations. Only one price would prevail at a given time in a purely competitive market, but our sellers would stand ready to offer a different quantity if this price should change. Therefore, we read the table in the same way as we did for demand: If the price is $5, sellers will offer 250 units; if the price is $4, sellers will offer 200 units, and so on.

You will note that with supply the relationship between price and quantity is exactly opposite that of demand. As price increases, quantity increases and vice versa. When plotted, the supply schedule becomes a curve that slopes upward to the right as shown in the graph on the next page. This price-quantity relationship is expressed in the *law of supply* which states that the quantity of a good that will be offered for sale tends to vary

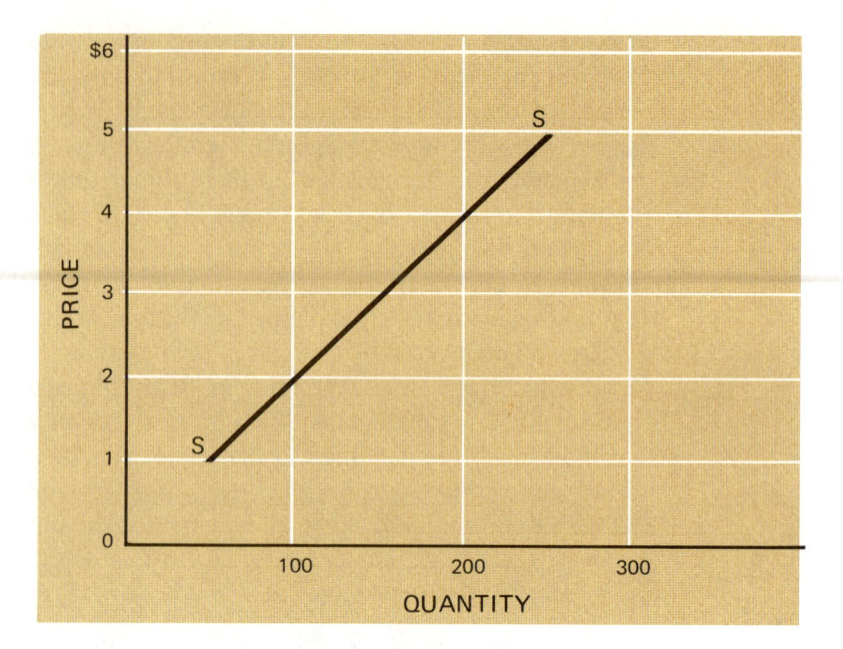

Figure 9-2.

Hypothetical Supply Curve

directly with the price of a good. That is, the higher the price, the greater the quantity offered for sale; and the lower the price, the smaller the quantity offered. This law, like the law of demand, applies to a given market and a given time.

The present quantity of any good that is supplied is largely the result of past estimates as to what the present price would be. Hence, quantities of wheat, cotton, or shoes that will be offered for sale at certain prices next year depend, in a large measure, upon what producers now think prices will be at that time. For example, manufacturers enlarge their plants and buy new equipment and more materials when they feel reasonably sure that the demand for their products will increase. On the other hand, when lower prices are in prospect, they are inclined to curtail production.

Cost of producing a supply of a commodity. Production cost largely determines the supply of a good in the long run. If the price of cotton is 25 cents a pound, but for next year it is estimated that it will be 30 cents, producers will tend to invest more in labor and capital for the production of cotton as long as it seems that it will be profitable for them to do so. Many, perhaps, will invest so heavily in labor and capital that their cost of production will exceed the amount that they will receive for their cotton, even if the price should be 35 cents. In practically every line of production there are those whose costs of production or expenses of carrying on their businesses are more than the income they receive from what they sell. This is true of many farmers, manufacturers, merchants, and others engaged in business and industry.

Producers whose cost of production exceeds the amount that they get for their product are *submarginal producers*. Those whose cost of production exactly equals the amount that they receive for their product are called *marginal producers*. Those whose cost of production is less than they receive from the sale of their products are *supramarginal producers*.

The lowering of the cost of production may cause a luxury to become an article of everyday use. For example, less than one hundred years ago bathtubs were so unusual and expensive that they were considered a luxury. Less than half a century ago an automobile was a luxury for most people. Costs of production decreased — and people have more money — so that now each of these goods is considered a necessity by most American families. Increased efficiency in production, when followed by lower prices, results in the use of a greater variety of goods by more people. After people have become accustomed to using the goods, things that were once looked upon as luxuries may be regarded as necessities.

Do changes in demand affect the supply immediately? Often a considerable time is required for a change in demand to have any effect on the total supply of a commodity. This is due to the fact that much production is a roundabout process or that it is seasonal. In the case of a shortage of color television sets or potatoes, for example, usually some months must elapse before an increased supply can be offered. However, when factories have been built or farms increased in number and size to produce an average supply of an article, and the demand falls, it is often difficult to adjust the supply to the demand without lowering the price.

For example, during World Wars I and II, when the price of wheat was high, more land was brought into cultivation and more farmers went into the business of growing wheat. When the wars ended, and many soldiers went back to farming in the various wheat-growing nations of the world, and as improved methods of production were introduced, the price of wheat fell. Our wheat farmers found it difficult, however, to reduce the amount of wheat produced because they had invested in machinery, and many had built houses and barns with the idea of producing this crop.

We should point out that after World War II wheat prices did not decline as much as they did after World War I because (1) the government had practically guaranteed minimum farm prices and (2) under foreign-aid plans a great deal of wheat was shipped to Europe.

HOW DO DEMAND AND SUPPLY RESULT IN COMPETITIVE PRICE?

We have now seen that buyers and sellers react oppositely to price changes. Buyers prefer low prices, and sellers want high prices. The separate laws of supply and demand can be combined into the *law of supply and demand* which states that in a competitive market, given sufficient time for adjustments to take place, the quantity of a good that buyers want and the quantity that sellers will offer for sale are brought into balance at some price that will just clear the market. This price is the *equilibrium price*.

By way of illustration let us say that the following table shows (1) the amounts of potatoes that people would buy at a given time in a given market at the prices indicated and (2) the amounts of potatoes that sellers would sell at the same prices.

Now suppose that there are many would-be buyers and a great many would-be sellers, so many, in fact, that none of them can by himself have any appreciable influence on price. Each of the would-be buyers is trying to buy at as low a price as possible, and each seller is eager to sell at as high a price as possible. What would be the result? The answer: A market

DEMAND AND SUPPLY SCHEDULES FOR POTATOES

Price per Pound (in cents)	Number of Pounds Buyers Would Purchase	Number of Pounds Sellers Would Sell
14	1,050	10,500
13	1,500	10,020
12	2,100	9,425
11	2,700	8,750
10	3,450	7,825
9	4,400	6,800
8	5,500	5,500
7	6,700	4,200
6	8,600	2,400
5	11,000	0

price would be established at 8 cents a pound, which would not change until either the demand or the supply — or both — changed. Let us see why this is true.

Look at the schedules for demand and supply. You will see that at only one price — 8 cents — are the demand for and the supply of potatoes equal. This means that at 8 cents anyone wishing to buy potatoes may do so. And anyone desiring to sell may do so. None would sell for less. And none could sell for more.

Ch. 9 COMPETITION AND PRICES

A graphic illustration of competitive price. Perhaps a graph will help us to see more clearly how price is determined by competition.

Let us take a piece of graph paper and say that the vertical scale represents prices, going upward from 1 cent to 14 cents. The horizontal scale represents quantities in thousands of pounds, measuring from left to right.

Now let us find a point on the paper that is on a level with a given price and directly above the quantity that would be bought at that price. As we see, at 14 cents the quantity that would be bought is 1,050 pounds; at 13 cents, 1,500 pounds; and so on. Thus, the location of all the points indicating the demand for potatoes at different prices tends to describe a line or curve that falls downward to the right.

In a similar way let us locate points on the graph that indicate the amount of supply, or the number of pounds of potatoes that sellers would sell at different prices. Thus, at 5 cents the amount would be zero pounds; at 6 cents, 2,400 pounds; and so on. The points for supply indicate a line that rises upward to the right.

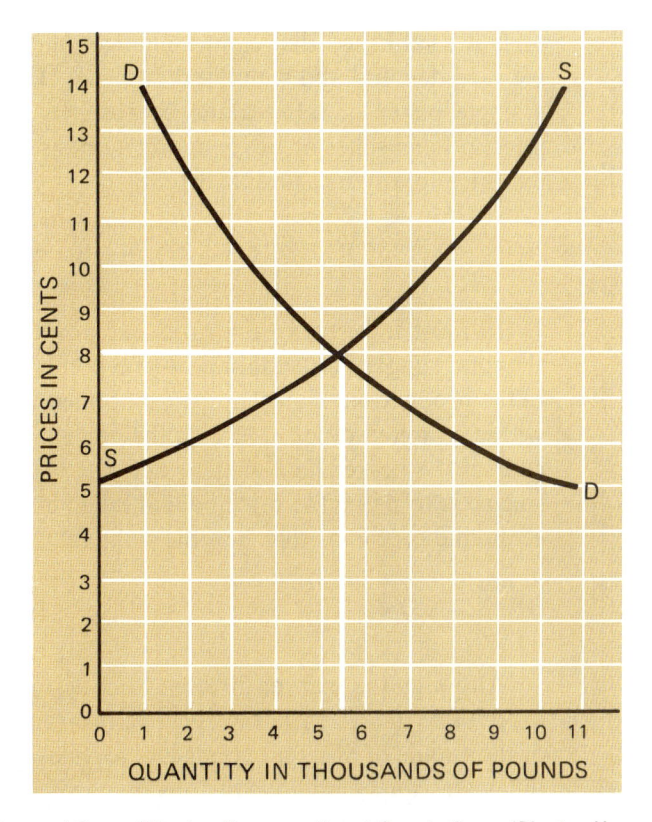

Figure 9-3.

Demand Curve (Sloping Downward) and Supply Curve (Sloping Upward)

At what point do the demand and supply curves cross? At 8 cents. This indicates that at 8 cents the quantity of potatoes demanded, 5,500 pounds, is equal to the quantity supplied. At no other point is this true. This point of intersection of the two curves shows that at 8 cents 5,500 pounds will be bought and sold, thus clearing the market. The price of 8 cents is the equilibrium price.

If the price is above 8 cents, there will be a *surplus* of the good on the market because sellers would be willing to offer more than buyers will buy at such a price. Sellers would then have to lower their prices to get rid of the surplus, and this adjustment would tend to continue until an equilibrium price was reached. If, however, the price is below 8 cents, there will be a *shortage* of the good, for buyers will be attempting to buy more than sellers are offering. Thus, buyers will compete for the limited quantity available and bid the price up to the point of equilibrium. These forces are at work each day in the highly competitive commodity markets such as the Chicago Board of Trade and, to some degree, in other markets.

Thus, we conclude: Under a condition of pure competition, a market price is established that cannot change unless some change in the relation between demand and supply takes place. The price cannot be changed by a single buyer or seller alone because, by our definition of competitive price, no one seller or buyer acting alone is important enough to influence the price to any measurable extent.

MOST PRICES ARE NOT DETERMINED BY PURE COMPETITION

In most industries each producer produces a considerable amount of the total supply of a certain type of a good. This is very true, for example, in the production of steel and automobiles. In such a case the seller can — within a limited range — decide the price at which he will sell his good. Of course, the nearer he comes to being the only producer, the more nearly free he is to name the price he will take. This fact sometimes gives rise to economic problems that become political issues, as we shall see later.

THE MARKET-DIRECTED PRICE SYSTEM HELPS TO PRESERVE FREEDOM

Although the market-directed price system is not perfect in all respects, it performs in a remarkably effective fashion. Seemingly endless quantities of thousands of different goods and services flow through the economy into the possession of millions of consumers. The usual orderliness of the price system causes thoughtful citizens to recognize in it a worthy institution of a free society. Thus, economic decisions that are basic to the welfare of all of us are made through a mechanism that is largely decentralized, that, in fact, enables all of us as buyers and sellers to play a role in influencing economic activity.

Under a system of communism, prices would not be fixed by the free market. On the contrary, prices would be set by a governmental agency. For example, prices would not be primarily relied on to induce producers to supply goods of certain kinds and qualities. Rather, a governmental planning board would say whether the goods should be produced and, if so, how much. Likewise, the allocation of land, labor, and capital to certain firms and industries would be determined by a governmental agency. Thus, communism does not allow demand and supply to influence production decisions in the manner they do in our system. This is one important way in which a communistic economy is less responsive than a market system is to the wishes of the people.

SUMMARY

The term "value" refers to the worth of a thing. Exchange value relates to the value of one unit of a good in terms of a unit of another good. Price is exchange value stated in terms of money.

Prices help to determine (1) what and how much goods of particular kinds will be produced, (2) how the factors of production shall be used in production, and (3) how consumers' goods shall be apportioned among the people.

In the United States prices are determined in several ways. The factors that operate to cause prices to be what they are at any given time are: (1) competition, (2) monopoly, (3) monopolistic competition, and (4) direct or indirect regulation of production by government. Only the first of these factors is considered in this chapter.

Pure competition exists when there are so many buyers and sellers of a good that no one transaction can affect the price. Competitive price results from the relations of demand and supply. A demand schedule refers to a series of quantities of a good that buyers will be willing to buy at a corresponding series of prices in a given market at a given time. It can be represented in a table or as a demand curve. The law of demand expresses an inverse relationship between price and quantity, which is explained by the substitution and income effects of price changes and by the law of diminishing marginal utility.

Elasticity of demand refers to the relative change in the quantity of a good that will be bought as the result of a change in price. If a slight change in price results in more than a proportional change in the quantity that will be bought, the demand is relatively elastic. If such a change in price results in less than a proportional change in the quantity that will be bought, the demand is relatively inelastic.

Changes in demand occur when there is either an increased or a decreased willingness and ability to buy at a price that remains the same.

A supply schedule refers to a series of quantities of a good that sellers are willing to offer for sale at a corresponding series of prices at a given time in a given market.

The law of supply states a direct relationship between price and quantity offered for sale.

Marginal producers are those whose cost of production equals the selling price. Submarginal producers' costs are more than the selling price. Supramarginal producers' costs are less than selling price.

Under pure competition, the forces of the market will tend to bring the quantity supplied and the quantity demanded into equality at the same price. This is a statement of the law of supply and demand, and the price toward which actual price tends to move is called the equilibrium price. Prices above this level cause surpluses, and prices below it result in shortages. Few, if any, goods are sold under the conditions of pure competition, but the analysis is useful in understanding the capitalistic economy. Under communism and some forms of socialism, all important markets are controlled by government.

NEW TERMS

changes in demand
demand
demand curve
demand schedule
economic value
elastic (demand)
elasticity of demand
equilibrium price
exchange value
income effect
inelastic (demand)
law of demand
law of diminishing marginal utility
law of supply
law of supply and demand
marginal producers
marginal utility
price
pure competition
shortage
submarginal producers
substitution effect
supply
supply schedule
supramarginal producers
surplus

QUESTIONS ON THE CHAPTER

1. What is the distinction between value and price? Explain.
2. Under a system of free enterprise, how do prices determine production? Explain (a) how prices influence production; (b) how prices influence the use of the factors of production; and (c) how consumers' goods are apportioned by means of prices.
3. Why should you be concerned with questions involving market pricing?
4. In the United States is price always determined by competition? Explain.
5. What is the definition of pure competition?
6. How do the terms "want" and "demand" differ? Explain.
7. How is the slope of the demand curve explained?

Ch. 9   COMPETITION AND PRICES

8. What is the distinction between elastic and inelastic demand? Why is an understanding of these terms important?
9. Is the demand for a luxury good elastic? Explain.
10. How does the availability of a substitute affect the demand for a good?
11. What is the difference between an increase and a decrease in demand?
12. How does the supply schedule illustrate the law of supply?
13. How do estimates as to future prices of goods affect the supply?
14. How do marginal, submarginal, and supramarginal producers differ?
15. When the market price is at the point where quantities demanded and supplied are equal, can the price change without a change in (a) demand, (b) supply, or (c) both demand and supply? Explain.
16. What is a surplus? A shortage?
17. To what extent would you say that prices in the United States are determined by pure competition?
18. How are the price system and freedom related?
19. Under communism, what use does government make of prices?

APPLYING YOUR ECONOMIC UNDERSTANDING

1. The average worker's wage is $24.00 a day. Check the prices in your community of white dress shirts, sirloin steaks, and evening admissions to a movie theater to determine their money value. What is the exchange value of each compared to the worker's daily wage? What is their exchange value in relation to each other?
2. Mr. Woodward has an apple tree in his yard. Each year he picks apples for the use of his family. Some are eaten fresh and others are canned. He gives the remaining apples away to his neighbors. How does his economic behavior relate to utility?
3. Recently, the railroad lines were permitted to discontinue many of their passenger services that were operated between cities in the United States. How does this relate to the concept that prices determine production?
4. During 1965 to 1970 the high interest rate on home mortgages caused a slump in home building. However, production and sales of mobile homes increased rapidly. In what way would pricing be involved in this situation?
5. Among some retired families eating hamburgers is an economic necessity. Other retired families usually eat steaks and roasts. How do the differing actions of these families relate to prices and the apportionment of consumer goods?
6. A store offered cartons of table salt at a very special price, but at the end of the day found that very few boxes were sold. How did customer reaction demonstrate elasticity or inelasticity of demand?
7. A veteran used his bonus and mustering-out pay to open a small repair shop. At the end of the year he balanced his books and found that his business

income was $12,416.34 and his expenditures $12,724.96. On the basis of cost and income how would you classify him as a producer?

8. Each Thursday a local paper carries advertisements of a number of food stores. Generally, the prices for similar articles are about the same in each of the stores. Explain this relationship with reference to competition as a determiner of price.

9. Plot the data of the following schedules on a sheet of graph paper.

DEMAND AND SUPPLY SCHEDULES FOR FRESH PEACHES

Price Per Pound	Quantity Demanded (in pounds)	Quantity Supplied (in pounds)
90¢	1,500	10,250
80¢	2,000	9,750
70¢	2,750	9,000
60¢	3,750	8,000
50¢	5,000	6,750
40¢	6,500	5,250
30¢	8,250	3,500
20¢	10,250	1,500

(a) What is the market price of peaches according to the graph?

(b) Assume that the demand at each price dropped by one half. What would the price become? Prove your answer by plotting a new demand curve on the same graph.

(c) Assume that the supply at each price dropped by one half. What should the price become under the original demand? Prove your answer by plotting a new supply curve on the same graph.

(d) Given the change in both supply and demand, what would the price be? How does it relate to the price set by the original demand and supply?

CHALLENGES TO ECONOMIC COMPETENCE

1. Make a two-column listing, heading the one *Luxuries*, the other *Necessities*. List five examples of each. Write a definition for the term *luxury*. Check your listings to see whether the listed items conform to your definition.

2. Interview a gas station owner as to what a "price war" is. Report your findings to the class.

3. Prepare a booklet on one of the following topics: (a) Competition, the Lifeblood of Capitalism, (b) Advertising, the Demand Persuader, (c) Are One-Cent Sales Bargains?

4. Secure a current catalog and a previous year's catalog issued by a major mail order firm such as Sears Roebuck. Prepare a report for class presentation which depicts the price changes for drugs and medical items during the time period.

Chapter 10

Monopoly and Prices

What is a business monopoly?
How do monopolies arise?
What factors may affect monopoly price?
What legislation has been passed to control monopolies?

When you visit The Metropolitan Museum of Art in New York City, you will find exhibited among its many world-famous works of art one painting that has a guard assigned to it alone. This painting is Diego Velazquez' "Portrait of Juan de Pareja." But why is it so carefully guarded? The price paid for this extraordinary work was $4,250,000. To the uninitiated in art, it seems extraordinary that a museum would pay this much for a painting! What could make a painted canvas worth four and a quarter million dollars? Is it sufficient to say it is the matchless work of a great artist?

In our daily lives we frequently question the price of an article. A woman may not notice a very great difference between two simple black dresses, yet one is marked $19.98 and the other, three or four times that amount. A man cannot understand why his wife's wisp of a hat costs four times as much as his own sturdy headgear. You may read in the newspaper an announcement of a general price increase by the manufacturers of some leading product, and you may wonder why prices of some other goods never change in this particular fashion. Do some sellers have more ability to control prices than others do? This important question deserves more study.

As we saw in the preceding chapter, pure competition — as economists define the term — means that no one seller or buyer is able to fix the market price at which a good or service is bought and sold. The reason why no one seller or buyer can control the market price is that each seller or buyer contributes only a very small part of the total supply of or demand for the good or service.

But suppose there is only one seller. Then we have *pure monopoly* — one seller — which is the opposite of the situation under pure competition. The word "monopoly" is derived from two Greek words which together mean "one seller." The term *monopsony* is sometimes used to indicate a situation in which there is only one buyer.

In studying competition and monopoly a number of questions may occur to us. For example, what are the results of competition in the long run? How do monopolies originate? What are the aims of the monopolist? Are monopoly prices higher than competitive prices?

PURE COMPETITION RESULTS IN NORMAL PRICE

By *normal price* we mean the price of an article that tends to prevail in the long run under pure competition. The *long run* is a production period long enough for an industry to make the adjustments which result in normal price. It varies in calendar length from industry to industry.

Normal price is a level just high enough to cover the cost of production, including a competitive rate of profit. At any given time the actual market price may be higher or lower than normal price. A rise in price may be due to a temporary decrease in supply or a temporary increase in demand. But an increase in price is very likely to tempt additional producers to undertake production. When they do so, the supply increases, and the price falls, unless there is a corresponding increase in demand. A decline in price will eventually result in a decrease in supply, which will tend to cause the price to rise again. As long as there is *free competition* — where there are a great number of both producers and consumers of a product, and where it is easy for producers to enter or to leave a field of production — the market price does not actually come to rest at a certain level.

The fluctuation in the day-to-day competitive market prices with reference to the long-run tendency of prices may be compared to the waves of the ocean with reference to the normal level of the water. At times the crest of a wave rises above the normal level or surface of the ocean and is followed by a depression, the trough of which is below the surface. But the force of gravity causes the wave to subside, and the pressure of the water causes the depression to fill up. If the disturbances produced by the wind and the attraction of the moon should subside, the water would come to rest at its normal level. Similarly, the forces of changing demand and supply cause market prices to fluctuate around — above or below — the normal price level.

MONOPOLY PROVIDES A MEANS OF SETTING PRICES

Monopoly gives the seller more or less power over price, depending upon his control of the supply of a good or service. It exists where there is but one seller of an article for which there is no satisfactory substitute. But just as there are few examples of pure competition, there are also few cases of pure monopoly. Most prices are determined in markets that have characteristics of both monopoly and competition. Before we study these situations, however, we must know more about monopoly and monopoly price as they differ from purely competitive conditions.

In general, monopolies are (1) public or (2) private. *Public monopolies* include certain economic undertakings carried on by governments, such as building and maintaining streets and roads, and operating gas and electric facilities owned by a city. *Private monopolies* are those held by private concerns and individuals. Public utilities, which are a form of private monopoly, are regulated and controlled by government agencies.

HOW DO PRIVATE MONOPOLIES ORIGINATE?

Monopoly may originate in one or more ways. It may be due to (1) the possession of superior skill or talent, (2) the granting of a privilege, or (3) the ownership of capital.

(1) Monopoly due to superior skill or talent. In the theatrical field those who possess great ability are few. But the few fortunate individuals who do possess outstanding talent are able to command large sums of money for their performances. In other fields, such as music, art, or sports, the possessors of unusual skill or ability often receive great rewards. Absence of competition creates a monopoly for those who are especially endowed. Competition is almost as effectively forestalled as if others were prevented by law from entering the field.

(2) Monopoly due to a privilege. Many private monopolies originate in the granting of a privilege by a government. Such a privilege may be in the form of a franchise, a copyright, or a patent. A *franchise* confers the right to engage in a particular enterprise, such as the operation of an airline, an electric-light system, or a water system. A franchise is granted because, from the point of view of society, it is better to restrict the production of a particular service to one producer or, at the most, to a limited number of producers. For example, it is evident that in most instances there should be only one public transportation system of one type in a community, and it is usually considered best for only one telephone system to be operated in a city.

Illus. 10-1. A franchise confers the right to engage in a particular enterprise, such as the operation of an airline.

American Airlines

A *copyright* gives an author the exclusive right to publish his literary production for a period of 28 years, with the privilege of renewing the copyright for a similar period. Materials written by an American author may be copyrighted in many foreign nations as well as in the United States. An inventor may obtain from the United States Patent Office a *patent*, which will give him the right to make, use, and sell his invention for a period of 17 years. A patent is not renewable. Monopolies in the forms of copyrights and patents are granted because it is thought that they will tend to stimulate the production of literature and the development of inventions and thus benefit society in general.

(3) Monopoly due to the ownership of capital. Under our system of free enterprise individuals have a great deal of freedom to initiate business undertakings. But comparatively few people can embark upon any business enterprise that they might desire to undertake. In some lines of production the "little man" is finding it increasingly difficult to compete with large-scale enterprises. Not all business is being taken over by large corporations, but in certain fields the tendency is toward large-scale methods in production and distribution.

Sometimes the necessity for a great deal of capital makes it practically impossible for more than a few producers to compete in a given field. For example, in the steel industry four concerns produce approximately half of all the steel produced in the United States. In the automobile industry only a few companies manufacture automobiles. Concerns with a small amount of capital could not carry on such businesses.

It is evident that the possession of capital may, in a very real sense, give one company a partial, if not a total, monopoly. Although other individuals or concerns may not be restricted by law from entering the field, they are prevented from doing so by their lack of capital.

THE MONOPOLIST AIMS TO MAKE A PROFIT

From a business point of view, the primary aim of the monopolist is to make a profit. In this respect he is like the purely competitive seller, but the difference is found in the advantage that the monopolist has in achieving this end. This advantage stems from the ability of the monopolist to influence, or to "administer," price by regulating the supply of the product. A price that is set by the producer and maintained for a time at the desired level by adjusting supply is known as an *administered price*. Thus, this price, which reflects monopoly power, is not an automatic result of the free play of competitive demand and supply. This does not mean, however, that a monopolist will sell only that quantity that will bring the highest unit price.

COST OF PRODUCTION IS RELATED TO MONOPOLY PRICE

Like other producers, the monopolist is concerned primarily with the total net profit that he can derive from his business. Therefore, whether he restricts or increases his output depends upon which policy will likely increase his profits. In all cases his profits are determined by the difference between the total cost of production and the total income from sales. His expected total net profit will determine to a large extent whether he will produce fewer units for sale at a high price or more units for sale at a lower price.

Whether he is a monopolist or not, the producer's costs of production usually may be divided into two classes: (1) fixed costs and (2) variable costs. The *fixed costs* of a business are those that do not change in total amount with changes in the volume of production. They include depreciation of buildings and equipment, rent, bond interest, and certain other charges. These costs do not vary proportionately with changes in production. For example, if a shoe factory can turn out 20,000 pairs of shoes monthly and has fixed costs amounting to $50,000, the total amount of fixed cost will not decrease if only 10,000 pairs are produced.

Variable costs are those that vary in total amount with the number of units of the commodity produced. These costs include the wages paid for direct labor (labor used directly in making the product); the cost of raw materials; and any other expenses that are larger when a greater quantity of goods is made and lower when a smaller quantity is produced. Hence, these costs vary with production. For example, the cost of the leather in 100 pairs of shoes is approximately 100 times as much as the cost of leather in one pair.

Up to a certain point producers are able to lower unit costs by increasing the number of units produced. Under some circumstances increased production results in higher unit cost. It all depends upon how well balanced are the amounts of labor and capital that are used by the employer at the time.

(1) Price per Machine	(2) Number of Machines Sold	(3) Income from Number Sold	(4) Variable Cost per Unit	(5) Total Variable Cost	(6) Total Fixed Cost	(7) Total Cost	(8) Profit
$4.00	10,000	$40,000	$1.50	$15,000	$20,000	$35,000	$5,000
3.50	12,500	43,750	1.50	18,750	20,000	38,750	5,000
3.00	17,500	52,500	1.50	26,250	20,000	46,250	6,250
2.50	27,500	68,750	1.50	41,250	20,000	61,250	7,500
2.25	35,000	78,750	1.50	52,500	20,000	72,500	6,250
2.00	40,000	80,000	1.50	60,000	20,000	80,000	0

NOTES: Column 3. The income in each case is the product of the price per machine (Column 1) and the number of machines sold (Column 2).
Column 7. The total cost in each case is the sum of the total variable cost (Column 5) and the total fixed costs (Column 6).
Column 8. The profit is the difference between the income from the number of units sold (Column 3) and the total cost (Column 7).

The table above illustrates how the factor of costs may help to determine the quantity produced and the price charged by a monopolist. Let us assume that the figures are those of the Exclusive Company, which has a monopoly in the production and the sale of a machine for which there is no substitute.

Under the assumed conditions the price of $2.50 a machine would yield the greatest amount of net profit. The monopolist would, therefore, naturally desire to fix the price at that figure.

Under the conditions of competition, however, the supply would probably be larger and the price lower. If conditions were competitive, the Exclusive Company would not be free to limit its supply and set its price, for it would have to lower its prices if its competitors lowered their prices below $2.50. Otherwise it could not sell its product.

Thus, in the competitive market, the presence of many alternative suppliers of a good prevents any one seller from gaining control over price. It is primarily for this reason that many economists believe that, given similar cost structures, competition tends to keep prices nearer the cost of production than monopoly does.

WHAT OTHER FACTORS AFFECT MONOPOLY PRICE?

If only the cost of production were involved, the monopolist would in most cases limit the supply and charge the price for his commodity that would bring him the greatest amount of net profit at the time. But other considerations may prevent him from exercising his power to control supply and price. These include (1) the uncertainty of demand, (2) the possibilities of substitutes, (3) possible competition, and (4) the fear of public control.

(1) The uncertainty of demand. The monopolist cannot predict exactly what the demand would be if the price were changed. Of course, he can raise and lower the price and thus, by a trial-and-error method, ascertain approximately the price that is most profitable. But in any case it is very difficult to fix the supply at exactly the most profitable price.

(2) The possibilities of substitutes. Fear that the public will choose a substitute for his commodity may keep the monopolist from fixing the price as high as he might. For most goods there are usually substitutes — or possible substitutes — to which people will turn if the price is too high.

(3) Possible competition. If the monopoly is not protected by law, and if the fixed price is high, there is always the danger of arousing competition. If a concern is making large profits, others will be encouraged to enter the same kind of business.

(4) The fear of public control. The fear of interference by government may be sufficient to prevent a monopolist from fixing his price too high. Not only may the government bring legal action against the price fixer, but it may also (a) bring the weight of public opinion to bear upon the monopolists, (b) cancel governmental contracts with the alleged offenders, or (c) enter into competition with the suppliers of the good.

MOST PRICES ARE DETERMINED BY OLIGOPOLY AND MONOPOLISTIC COMPETITION

From the standpoint of the supply of a good, we see that there are two extreme possibilities. On the one hand, there may be so many producers that what one produces has no measurable effect on the market price. On the other hand, there may be only one producer; in this case he is free, within certain limits, to fix the supply — and hence the price — as he pleases unless he is forbidden to do so by government.

In most cases, however, goods are not produced under conditions of either pure competition or of pure monopoly, although on the buying side of the market there is usually a large number of buyers, especially in consumer goods markets. The sellers are usually either oligopolists or monopolistically competitive firms. *Oligopoly* consists of a few relatively large producers of products that are essentially identical or that are very close substitutes. For example, only a few large companies produce nearly all of the automobiles, cement, tractors, chewing gum, packinghouse products, typewriters, adding machines, electric equipment, and a large number of other goods that are commonly used. None of the companies produces the entire market supply; but each one produces an important part of the total supply so that, if any one should stop production, the others could raise their prices because of the reduction in the total supply. Likewise, any one of the producers could force the price of the product down by substantially increasing the total supply. In this type of market each producer must be alert to any changes in pricing policies of the other oligopolists.

Monopolistic competition exists where there is a large number of sellers of products that are not identical but that are close substitutes. Purely competitive firms sell identical goods or goods that are essentially identical, but the monopolistically competitive firm attempts to differentiate its product.

PRODUCT DIFFERENTIATION TENDS TO REDUCE COMPETITION

The practice of giving the article that is sold a distinct name, appearance, or slightly unique quality is called *product differentiation*. Mrs. Reese uses a certain brand of soap that has a distinct color and odor. Mr. Wilson prefers a particular brand of aspirin. Why do they use these particular brands? The answer is partly that they think that the article in question is better than others of the same general kind and partly because of habit. They probably became interested in the product in the first place as a result of a television program, a persuasive advertisement, or the style of the container of the article. Then after having become accustomed to the brand, they continued to use it more or less from habit.

Of course, there are variations in the quality and the values of many kinds of consumers' and producers' goods. But, price considered, there may not be as much difference in the quality of different brands of the same kind of goods as most people imagine. If one brand were as much superior as its maker may claim that it is, it would not be long before all the other producers would have to go out of business.

But producers know that certain people like certain qualities in the articles they use. And they believe that many people can be persuaded that their products are different from the others. Therefore, each maker of breakfast food, soap, toothpaste, shaving soap, cosmetics, and other manufactured products endeavors to persuade the public that what he sells is different from and better than the products of his competitors. To do this, he makes use of various devices. If the product is a soap powder, he will manufacture it in such a way as to give it a distinct appearance and package it so that it can be easily recognized. He may sponsor a radio or television program that will appeal to housewives while they work. At frequent intervals during the program, the announcer will, by means of song or verse or eloquent appeal, seek to convince those who may be listening that the sponsor's soap powder is the "only" soap powder.

What is the basic purpose of product differentiation? Product differentiation is used by sellers because they know they will escape competition to the extent that they can convince the public that their product is distinctly better than that of others who sell similar products. Their purpose, therefore, is to acquire a degree of monopoly. And the reason they wish to enjoy at least a certain degree of monopoly is that they will be in a position to exercise some control over the price of what they sell. In other words, they do not wish to have the prices of their products fixed under conditions that approach pure competition.

LAWS ARE NECESSARY TO CONTROL MONOPOLIES

We have never had a society in which all prices — or even a majority — were fixed by pure competition. Competition has always been imperfect, and always some business concerns have enjoyed advantages over others. Furthermore, it is not socially desirable for some businesses to operate as uncontrolled enterprises. For example, it is not socially desirable or practicable to rely on competition to fix fair prices for the use of electricity and telephones. The prices of these things are controlled in part by government.

Imagine the situation if we had pure competition in the production of automobiles, tractors, and any number of other kinds of commodities we could mention. Such a situation would require the productive facilities of thousands, or at least hundreds, of different firms. It is immediately apparent that it is both impossible and undesirable to have such a degree of competition in the production of most of the kinds of articles we use.

The question, therefore, is not whether we shall have pure competition or pure monopoly as a method of determining the prices of the things we buy. Rather it is a question of achieving the benefits of effective competition under conditions where competition will usually be imperfect. If monopoly, or even a high degree of monopoly, is necessary or desirable, then the question of the proper role of government arises. Can government regulate prices in such a situation so that they will be fair to both producers and consumers? The answer to this question is very important to all.

Years ago the federal government began to pass laws to protect the public against exploitation by monopolistic prices and practices. The first important law of this kind was the Interstate Commerce Act (1887), which gave the government the power to regulate railroad rates. The second important federal law to regulate monopolies was the Sherman Antitrust Act (1890), which declared that any contract, combination, or conspiracy in restraint of trade was illegal. Since the passage of these laws, many others have been enacted by Congress and state legislatures to protect the public from monopolistic prices and business practices, as we shall see in the next chapter.

SUMMARY

Neither pure competition nor pure monopoly is often found in practice. Nearly all prices result from imperfect competition. That is, in the determination of most prices, there are elements of both competition and monopoly. Sometimes there appears to be more competition than monopoly; sometimes more monopoly than competition; and sometimes the two appear to be about evenly balanced.

Theoretically, prices are lower under pure competition than under pure monopoly. But it is both impracticable and undesirable to have pure competition in the production of most kinds of articles.

There are two classes of monopoly: public and private. As to origin, monopoly may be the result of: (1) the possession of superior skill or talent, (2) privilege, or (3) ownership of capital.

Monopolists may be deterred from charging the highest possible price because of: (1) uncertainty of demand, (2) possibilities of substitutes for their products, (3) possible competition, and (4) fear of public control.

Oligopoly and monopolistic competition are the market situations in which most goods and services are sold.

Product differentiation results when a producer gives his product a characteristic that distinguishes it from competing brands or makes. Such differentiation is intended to give the producer a certain degree of monopolistic advantage over his competitors.

To the extent that excessive monopoly displaces competition, the government must stand ready to provide the necessary protection of the consumer's interest.

Ch. 10   MONOPOLY AND PRICES   179

NEW TERMS

administered price
copyright
fixed costs
franchise
free competition
long run
monopolistic competition
monopoly
monopsony

normal price
oligopoly
patent
private monopolies
product differentiation
public monopolies
pure monopoly
variable costs

QUESTIONS ON THE CHAPTER

1. What is "normal price"? Is it an actual market price? Explain.
2. Of what value is the concept of a normal price?
3. What is the essence of monopoly power? What is the basic source of this power?
4. How do private monopolies originate?
5. What are some examples that illustrate the various origins of monopoly?
6. What are some examples of fixed cost and variable cost?
7. How would you explain the way a monopolist attempts to fix his price?
8. Why would you expect competitive price to be lower than monopoly price?
9. What factors other than costs may influence the monopolist in fixing his price? Explain each.
10. What is the difference between oligopoly and monopolistic competition?
11. How is product differentiation related to monopoly price?
12. Is product differentiation aimed at establishing a more competitive market?
13. How are democracy and monopoly in business related?
14. What were the first laws to regulate monopolistic practices and what did they do?

APPLYING YOUR ECONOMIC UNDERSTANDING

1. Examine several household appliances or electrical shop tools which you use to determine whether or not they enjoy monopoly privilege. How can you determine this fact?
2. (a) Cite an example of monopoly in a governmental enterprise. (b) Cite an example which demonstrates monopsony in a governmental enterprise. What evidence proves the validity of your answers?

3. Name five persons in different fields who have at least a partial monopoly based upon superior skill or talent. What is the effect of their monopoly advantage?
4. What are some industries, other than steel and automobile, which appear to have an ownership based on capital monopoly?
5. Check on the price of a highly advertised toothpaste in a local store. Check to see if there are other brands of the same product and note their prices. Show how this relates to the statement "Competitive prices are usually lower than monopolistic prices."
6. In 1971 the motion picture, *Love Story*, was introduced to the public and became a financial success for the producers. How is monopoly involved in this situation?
7. Compare the advertisements of several makes of automobiles within the same price range. How are the distinct names of each brand-named car related to differentiation? How are the descriptive terms and phrases related to differentiation?
8. Cite some examples of public and private monopolies in your community. How does price determination in these two types of monopolies differ?
9. Would you agree that farming today is the most competitive of all industries? Why or why not?
10. Some management groups believe that labor unions have created labor monopolies. What arguments do they advance to support their views? What arguments do unions use to refute the belief that unions are monopolies?

CHALLENGES TO ECONOMIC COMPETENCE

1. Prepare and present a debate on the issue "American Business Is Becoming Increasingly More Monopolistic."
2. Using the *Reader's Guide to Periodical Literature* as a reference, find an article and read about a recent example of private monopoly practice and its outcome. Report your findings to the class.
3. Organize a bulletin board display about governmental agencies that regulate or control monopolies and the forms of regulation or control used by each agency.
4. Write a biographical sketch to include the economic contributions made by one of the founders of a business in a key industry. (For example, Astor, Carnegie, du Pont, Ford, Gould, among others.)

Chapter 11

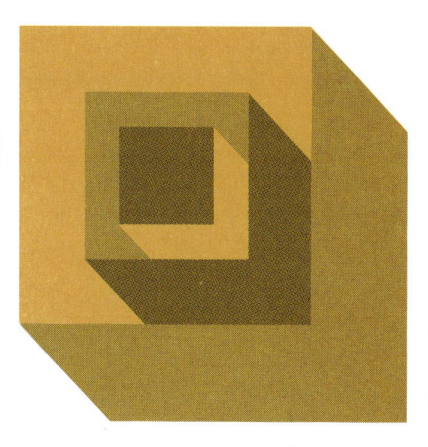

Government Control of Prices

Why does the government control or fix some prices?
Why are some businesses called public utilities?
What factors are considered when government fixes prices?
How does government attempt to control farm prices?

Before the rise of modern industry and business, people in Western countries generally accepted the idea of a "just price." According to this doctrine, prices of articles should be sufficient to cover production costs and enable producers to live at their accustomed levels. Failure to observe the practice of this idea was punishable as an offense against society.

The idea of just price grew out of the moral and religious teachings of the Middle Ages. But with the coming of the Industrial Revolution, increasing production, and the rise of modern business practices, the idea was replaced by the notion that prices should be determined by the relations of demand and supply under conditions of competition.

INCREASING CONTROL OF PRICES BY GOVERNMENT

Until comparatively recently in the United States it was generally believed that, with some exceptions, government should not undertake to fix prices. Of course, from an early date, many of the people — perhaps a majority — did endorse protective tariff laws that at least partially relieved certain manufacturers from competition by foreign producers. Thus, the government indirectly influenced prices by enabling manufacturers to charge more for protected goods than would have been possible without such laws.

During World War II the federal government undertook rigid regulation of prices. Many kinds of goods were rationed by limiting the amount that could be purchased by individuals and families. Merchants who tried to sell at more than maximum prices were subject to arrest and trial. If convicted, they were liable to fine and imprisonment. These severe emergency measures were enacted by Congress to cope with economic conditions that were generally felt to justify their imposition, but following the war they were eventually repealed. With the decade of the 1960's came an intensification of the Viet Nam conflict and increasing threats to price stability in the economy. The power of the Presidency was brought to bear to influence wage negotiations and to discourage price increases in basic industries, such as steel and aluminum. Exercise of executive power in these situations caused many persons, including some economists, to raise the question as to the future of the price-making process in certain important sectors of the economy.

At the present time government is taking a far more active part in price fixing. On the federal level, to mention only a few examples, there are minimum wage laws, government support of minimum farm prices, and the use of certain methods by government to influence interest rates, as well as a continuation of a modified protective tariff policy.

In addition to federal action, state governments regulate the prices charged by intrastate public utilities — telephone and telegraph companies, electric light and power companies, airlines, railroads, highway transportation companies, and others. There are also some state laws that regulate or influence certain other prices either directly or indirectly. For example, some states have statutory regulations that provide for the fixing of minimum prices of milk.

All of these efforts of government to regulate or to fix prices indicate that the people are not always willing to leave the matter of price determination solely to the operation of market forces. The tendency for government to attempt to regulate prices seems more pronounced than it was a few decades ago.

GOVERNMENT REGULATES THE PRICES OF SOME NATURAL MONOPOLIES

In some instances it is easily understandable why the government should attempt price regulation, especially when the public interest is involved, as in some cases of natural monopolies. A *natural monopoly* is: (1) a business concern that has the exclusive possession of the natural source of a commodity or service, as in the case of a diamond field or a famous painting; or (2) a business that controls the production of an article or service requiring a very large amount of capital in comparison with the number of people to be served, as in the case of a railroad; or (3) any busi-

Ch. 11 GOVERNMENT CONTROL OF PRICES 183

ness that may be privately owned but that, for social reasons, cannot be permitted to compete with others or to operate as an unregulated monopoly, as in the case of a power company or telephone company.

For example, a railroad is a natural monopoly. It requires a large amount of capital in order to provide a unit of service, as hauling a ton of coal or a passenger. In most places it is not desirable to have two or more competing railroads built along the same routes because the amount of transportation needed would not justify the building of two railroads. Again, in the case of telephone service it is not desirable to have two or more competing systems in a given city or community; obviously, the needs of a community could be adequately served by one company.

The services supplied by some natural monopolies are essential to the welfare and the convenience of the public. Since it is not feasible for the public to rely on competition to fix fair prices for such services, government must regulate the prices of goods and services provided by natural monopolies. In most cases businesses of this kind are referred to as *public utilities*.

PUBLIC UTILITIES ARE REGULATED BY STATE AND FEDERAL COMMISSIONS

Public-utility companies that operate entirely within a state are subject to control only by the state government. Those whose activities extend

Illus. 11-1. It requires a large amount of capital in order to provide a unit of service, as hauling a ton of coal or a passenger. In most places it is not desirable to have two or more competing railroads built along the same routes.

Santa Fe Railway

across a state boundary are subject to control by the federal government. Both the state legislatures and Congress attempt to control public utilities by means of commissions.

Several *federal utility commissions* control the public utilities engaged in interstate business. These commissions, together with the services over which they have control, are:

    Interstate Commerce Commission — rail and motor-carrier industries

    Federal Communications Commission — telephone, telegraph, radio, and television industries

    Federal Power Commission — navigation, water power, electric power and light, and natural gas

    United States Maritime Commission — interstate, foreign, and intercoastal commerce by water

    Civil Aeronautics Board — air carriers

In addition, the following departments and agencies of the federal government exercise a certain amount of influence over public utilities engaged in interstate business: the Department of Agriculture; the Department of Justice; the Securities and Exchange Commission; the National Labor Relations Board; the Federal Trade Commission; the National Mediation Board; and the Wages and Hours Administration.

Principles in regulating public utilities. The three principles observed in the regulation of public utilities are:

(1) The public is entitled to adequate service. By this we mean as much service as everyone wants and is willing to pay for at a price that is fair in relation to the cost of producing the service.

(2) Persons and concerns who own the public utilities are entitled to a reasonable return on their investments. In practice this amounts to saying that utilities should charge only enough to pay the owners of stocks or bonds of the companies a reasonable rate of profit or interest.

(3) Public utilities should not discriminate between persons in rendering service or in making charges for services. For example, no railroad should charge one person more than it charges another for a coach ticket for a certain number of miles.

Transportation companies may discriminate as to charges for hauling different kinds of products. To illustrate what is sometimes meant by *rate discrimination*, suppose that a railroad carries both silk and coal between the same two cities. In order to encourage both the production and the use of coal, it might haul the coal for about the actual cost of transportation but charge much more than the cost of transportation for hauling the silk. In this way the lack of profit in transporting coal would be offset by the gains in transporting silk.

Two principles in public-utility rate regulation. How much should a railroad, an electric power and light, or other public-utility company charge for its service?

In fixing rates, commissions may be guided by one or both of two principles: (1) the cost of the service and (2) the value of the service. According to the *cost-of-service principle*, rates should be fixed slightly above the cost of rendering the service. According to the *value-of-service principle*, rates should be fixed in proportion to the value of the service to the customer.

Thus, for example, railroad freight rates fixed according to the cost-of-service principle would be high enough to allow the railroad company to make some profit on each item of freight handled. On the other hand, rates fixed according to the value-of-service principle would be determined by what the public is willing to pay for the services of the railroad. The acceptance of either of these principles, however, does not end the problem that confronts the utility commission.

In order to bring out more clearly some of the major problems of the regulation of public utilities, let us consider in greater detail the problem of rate making for railroads.

WHAT RATES SHOULD RAILROADS CHARGE?

In order to try to answer this question, it is necessary to consider (1) the kinds of service to be offered, (2) the kinds of costs to be met, and (3) the valuation of the property owned. Although problems of rate regulation on railroads are emphasized in the following discussion, the principles involved are also applicable to other kinds of public utilities.

(1) Kinds of service. Railroads supply two kinds of transportation, that for passengers and that for goods. We know, too, that there are different classes for each of these kinds of transportation. For example, there are day-coach and Pullman services for passengers. Freight is classified according to the nature of the goods, as first-class, second-class, and so on, depending upon the kind of hauling services required in shipping the goods.

(2) Kinds of costs. As in the case of other large industries, costs of production for a public utility may be classified as fixed and variable.

As we have seen, fixed costs, which usually make up the major portion of total costs for public utilities, include those indirect costs that do not vary in total amount with changes in the amount of goods or service produced. Variable costs are those direct costs that vary in total amount with changes in the output of goods or services. Finally, the production of goods and services may involve *joint costs*. These are costs that are incurred in the simultaneous production of two or more goods or services. For example, in the case of a train made up of day coaches and Pullman cars, the cost of fuel used in generating engine power is a joint cost. The rate-making problem in this case is to determine the relative portions of the joint costs that should be allocated to each separate class of service.

Illus. 11-2. Fixed costs, which usually make up the major portion of total costs for public utilities, include those indirect costs that do not vary in total amount with changes in the amount of goods or services produced.

Jersey Central Power and Light Company

The variable costs in railroad transportation include oil, coal, water, labor, and materials. A fairly accurate record of these is usually kept, and for that reason total variable costs can be known.

Fixed costs include the salaries of executive officers, office expenses, interest on borrowed money, and depreciation. Although it is comparatively easy to find out from the accounting records just how much the total of some of these expenses amounts to, it is very difficult to estimate the amount of depreciation of railroad property. For example, a railroad engine loses part of its value each time it makes a run. Likewise, the rails decrease in value with use and eventually have to be replaced.

Depreciation as a cost of production is just as real and as important as any other cost. It should always be included as part of expenses. The problem is to determine just how much should be allowed to cover the expense due to depreciation. The passenger or freight rate must be high enough to include all direct and indirect expenses, including the decreases in the value of property.

(3) Valuation of property. The importance of the valuation of public-utility property in fixing rates can be seen if we assume that the value of the property owned by a railroad company is $100,000,000. Suppose we say that each year the stockholders are entitled to a 5 percent return on this value. The rates charged should be high enough to cover the amount of fixed and variable costs and $5,000,000 as profit after corporate profit taxes for the stockholders. If the same property is valued at $200,000,000, and a profit of 5 percent is to be allowed, it will be necessary to fix rates high enough to leave a profit of $10,000,000 after all expenses and corporate profit taxes are paid.

Failure to fix rates high enough to allow for a reasonable return on the investment results in the use of private property by the public without due compensation to the owners. Rates that are too high, however, cause the public to pay more than is reasonable for essential transportation services, and they also enrich stockholders at public expense. Both situations are undesirable from society's standpoint, and this problem of public utility rate regulation points up the advantages of the market-directed price system in industries where it can be relied on to function satisfactorily.

HOW ARE RAILROAD RATES FIXED?

As we have seen, much of the cost in railroad transportation is joint cost. It is impossible to say exactly what part of the costs of depreciation, fuel, water, or any other item of overhead or direct expense should be charged to any one shipment or class of shipments. Because of the difficulties of assigning to any shipment its share of the total cost of maintaining and operating the railroad, it is necessary for the Interstate Commerce Commission to rely largely on the value-of-service principle in determining rates.

The value-of-service principle has been referred to as "charging what the traffic will bear." When this principle is used, the purpose is to charge enough to cover variable expenses, but no attempt is made to set rates so as to apportion or distribute fixed costs equally or proportionally among the different kinds of freight.

For example, we can see that over a period of time a railroad company must have enough income to cover its total expenses, both fixed and variable; otherwise it will become bankrupt. But suppose the charge for hauling coal covers the variable expenses but less than a proportional part of the fixed costs, while the charge for hauling silk is high enough to cover the variable expenses and more than the proportional amount of fixed costs belonging to this classification of freight. Under the circumstances we would say that the rate on coal is low and that the rate on silk is high. Because of the low value of coal in comparison with its bulk, it could not stand as high rates as could silk; that is, many consumers of coal could not afford to use the same amount of coal if the price were increased due to an increase in freight rates. An increase of 10 or 15 percent a ton in the freight charge on coal might result in a great decrease in the amount shipped, while a considerably larger increase in the rate on silk might have little effect on the quantity of silk carried by the railroads. Therefore, coal and silk are, to a certain extent, "charged what the traffic will bear."

AMTRAK—INNOVATION IN THE REGULATION OF PASSENGER TRAIN SERVICE

Over and above the difficulties that railroads and the Interstate Commerce Commission faced in rate fixing was the problem of recurrent financial losses from passenger service. Whereas there were some 20,000 intercity trains operating in 1929, losses from passenger service reduced the number to fewer than 370 in 1970. During this period of a generation and a half, people steadily abandoned the train in favor of the more convenient private car, bus, and airlines.

In an effort to place the nation's passenger train service on a sound financial base and to insure the continuation of this service where the need is greatest, Congress established the National Rail Passenger Corporation in 1970, known as Railpax. The corporation adopted the trade name AMTRAK and laid out a system of intercity routes connecting more than 100 major cities which are served by fewer than 200 trains. Thus, 85 percent of the population living in urban areas is served by the network. Passenger fares under the new system are set by Railpax rather than the Interstate Commerce Commission.

THE FEDERAL GOVERNMENT INFLUENCES FARM PRICES

Before World War I few, if any, farmers ever thought of asking the government to guarantee the prices of their products. But during World War I agricultural production was greatly increased by the use of additional acreage, tractor power, and machines. During the war farm prices were high. After the war farm prices declined, but production rose due to the increasing use of farm tractors and scientific methods. By 1930 the prices of farm products were relatively much lower than were the prices of the things farmers had to buy, which made it increasingly harder for the farmers to make a living.

Illus. 11-3. After the war farm prices declined, but production rose due to the increasing use of farm tractors and scientific methods.

Caterpillar Tractor Co.

The Federal Farm Board and the AAA of 1933. In 1929 Congress passed the Agricultural Marketing Act providing for the creation of the Federal Farm Board, which was given half a billion dollars with which to buy up farm products of certain kinds. It was hoped that the purchase of farm products by the government would raise farm prices. But after losing most of the money appropriated for its use because of the decline in the prices of products which it had purchased, the Farm Board was considered a failure.

In 1933 Congress passed the Agricultural Adjustment Act, which was designed to make it possible for farmers to sell their products at parity prices. *Parity prices* for farm commodities means prices for these commodities that are calculated so as to help the farmer to get a proportionate share of the national income equal to the proportionate share received during a former base period. The base period chosen was the period 1909–1914 for all farm commodities except tobacco. The period for tobacco was 1919–1926. It was assumed that in these periods the prices of

PERSONAL INCOME OF THE FARM POPULATION, AND FARM POPULATION AS A PERCENTAGE OF TOTAL POPULATION, 1934-69

Year	Personal income of farm population — From farm sources[1]	Personal income of farm population — Total from all sources[2]	As a percentage of total personal income[3] — From farm sources	As a percentage of total personal income[3] — From all sources	Farm population as a percentage of total population[4]
	Millions	Millions	Percent	Percent	Percent
1934	$3,188	$5,374	5.9	10.0	25.6
1935	5,423	7,730	9.0	12.8	25.3
1936	4,592	7,232	6.7	10.5	24.8
1937	6,228	8,976	8.4	12.1	24.2
1938	4,702	7,177	6.9	10.5	23.8
1939	4,751	7,361	6.5	10.1	23.5
1940	4,838	7,597	6.2	9.7	23.1
1941	6,823	10,080	7.1	10.5	22.6
1942	10,149	14,090	8.3	11.5	21.4
1943	12,120	16,481	8.0	10.9	19.2
1944	12,201	16,636	7.4	10.1	17.9
1945	12,807	17,212	7.5	10.1	17.5
1946	15,475	20,026	8.7	11.2	18.0
1947	15,836	21,133	8.3	11.0	17.9
1948	17,977	23,792	8.6	11.3	16.0
1949	13,284	19,476	6.4	9.4	16.2
1950	14,103	20,366	6.2	8.9	15.2
1951	16,190	22,701	6.3	8.9	14.2
1952	15,352	19,790	5.6	8.1	13.8
1953	13,353	19,790	4.6	6.9	12.4
1954	12,509	18,443	4.3	6.4	11.7
1955	11,382	17,579	3.7	5.7	11.5
1956	11,219	17,803	3.4	5.3	11.1
1957	11,041	17,657	3.1	5.0	10.3
1958	12,800	19,481	3.5	5.4	9.8
1959	11,009	18,059	2.9	4.7	9.4
1960	11,526	18,679	2.9	4.7	8.7
1961	12,195	19,738	2.9	4.7	8.1
1962	12,254	20,449	2.8	4.6	7.7
1963	12,109	20,619	2.6	4.4	7.1
1964	11,334	20,639	2.3	4.1	6.7
1965	13,546	23,591	2.5	4.4	6.4
1966	14,414	24,878	2.4	4.2	5.9
1967	13,010	23,895	2.1	3.8	5.5
1968	13,103	24,877	1.9	3.6	5.2
1969	14,498	27,098	1.9	3.6	5.1

[1]Total net income of farm resident operators, including government payments; and wages, salaries, and other labor income of farm resident workers from farm sources.

[2]Includes, in addition to income of farm population from farming, wages and salaries from nonfarm employment, nonfarm business and professional income, rents from nonfarm real estate, interest, dividends, etc.

[3]Of the farm and nonfarm population.

[4]Farm population as of April 1 and total population as of July 1 are taken as the closest readily available approximations of their respective annual averages.

SOURCE: Economic Research Service, USDA. Published in *Food Costs — Farm Prices, A Compilation of Information Relating to Agriculture*, by the Committee on Agriculture, House of Representatives, Ninety-First Congress, Second Session, June 30, 1970.

farm products and of manufactured products were at a par. Under the AAA of 1933, the government undertook by means of payments to farmers to keep farm prices at parity with other prices. Thus, if the parity price of wheat was announced as being $1 a bushel but the market price was only 75 cents, the government would give the farmer 25 cents for each bushel he sold at the market price. In order to be eligible to receive payments from the government, farmers were required to reduce the acreage of their crops. The purpose of this reduction was to raise the market prices of farm products by decreasing their supply.

To obtain the money with which to pay farmers, the law levied a tax on the processors or manufacturers of farm commodities. But because of this feature, the law was found unconstitutional by the Supreme Court.

The Soil Conservation Act of 1936 and the AAA of 1938. These two acts were intended to give farmers the same kind of aid as did the AAA of 1933. But in order to prevent the laws from being declared unconstitutional, the methods provided were somewhat different.

These laws provide for (1) soil conservation, (2) parity payments, (3) commodity loans, and (4) marketing quotas. Farmers were encouraged to withdraw part of their land from the production of cotton, wheat, corn, tobacco, and other crops customarily grown, and to plant more soil-building crops, including legumes. Parity prices were established for certain farm products, and farmers who agreed to limit production were entitled to the guarantee of these prices by the government. If the market price of a farm product was less than the parity price, the farmer could store his wheat or other products and the government would lend him an amount equal to the amount of the value of the product at parity price. Later if the price of the product rose above parity, the farmer could sell his product and repay his loan. If the price did not rise, the government kept the commodity and the farmer did not have to repay the loan. In order to qualify for this guarantee of a minimum price for his product, it was necessary for the farmer to agree not to produce and market more than a maximum amount, which was set as his quota for that certain product.

When we entered World War II, the government promised farmers that for at least two years after the war was officially ended the price of farm products would be at least 90 percent of parity. For example, if parity price for wheat was calculated to be $2 per bushel, the farmer was, in effect, guaranteed a price of $1.80. Thus, under governmental encouragement, productive capacity in agriculture increased greatly; and large postwar farm commodity surpluses accumulated.

PERSONS SUPPLIED PER FARM WORKER

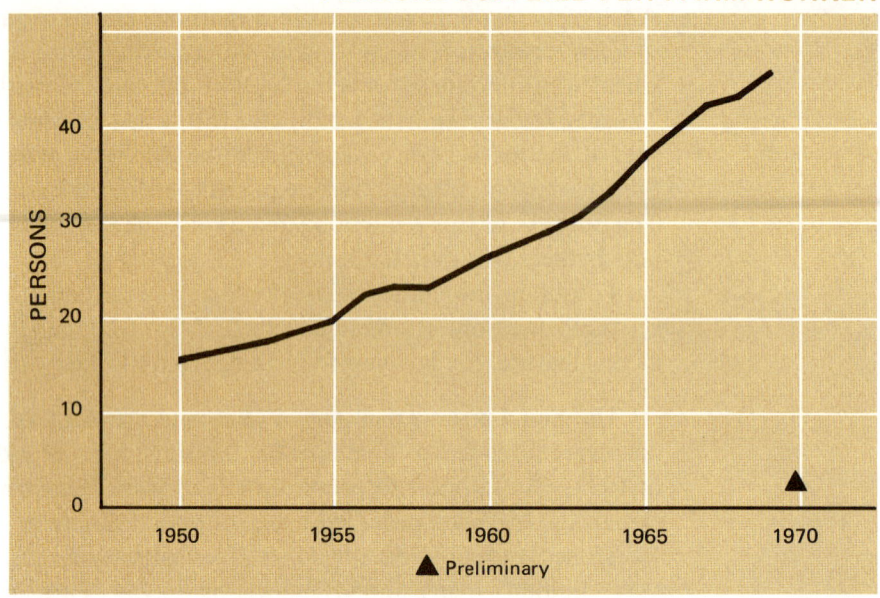

Figure 11-1.

▲ Preliminary

SOURCE: USDA, *1970 Handbook of Agricultural Charts.*

Subsequent legislation. By the passage of the Agricultural Act in 1954, Congress made an attempt to reduce farm subsidies from 90 percent of parity prices by adopting a flexible price-support program for 5 basic commodities — wheat, corn, rice, cotton, and peanuts. The price range for some of these commodities was fixed at from 70 to 90 percent of parity, the exact percent being fixed by the government.

In 1956 the *soil bank* program was inaugurated by the government; that is, the government agreed to pay farmers to withdraw part of their land from production. Nevertheless, because of increased use of mechanical power and scientific methods in farming, production continued to increase.

The Tobacco Acreage-Poundage Act and the Food and Agriculture Act were passed in 1965. Continued accumulations of surplus flue-cured tobacco led to the enactment of the first of these acts. To cope with this problem, poundage limitations were placed on the marketing of tobacco, and restrictions were placed on the acreage planted. The Food and Agriculture Act of 1965 offered special inducements to cotton farmers to reduce production of this crop and also modified the government's program for feed grains, wheat, wool, and dairy products. Under this act, the Soil Bank Act of 1956 was repealed, and the Cropland Adjustment Program was established to encourage farmers to divert approximately 40 million acres of cropland to use for conservation and recreation.

The Food and Agriculture Act offers some hope of ultimate success in achieving a more satisfactory balance between demand for and supply of basic farm commodities. Unlike previous acts that limited authority to only one or two years, the 1965 program provides a means for developing coordinated and sustained efforts over a period of several years.

IS THERE A SOLUTION TO THE FARM PROBLEM?

Essentially, the farm problem arises from the fact that production — supply — increases faster than demand, and that the demand for farm products is rather inelastic. Efforts of the government to "help" the farmer by guaranteeing high farm prices tend to increase production. At the same time, much of the benefit from farm aid has gone to less than 50 percent of the total number of farmers. Those whose farms are large and whose costs of production are lower have benefited more than the small farmers have. Most of the funds needed to aid farmers must be supplied by the government by means of taxation or borrowing. It is true that many nations need our farm surpluses, but they do not have the funds with which to buy them. These are some of the important facts about the farm problem. Evidently, past efforts to solve the problem have not been successful. What, then, should be done?

The Committee for Economic Development (CED), a nonpolitical organization of businessmen and scholars, has proposed the following: (1) restoration of free marketing of farm products, and the gradual elimination of price and income supports; (2) a continuation of the land retirement (soil bank) program, aimed at the retirement of the least productive land and the smaller farms; (3) an agricultural board to work with the Secretary of Agriculture in providing assistance to agriculture; (4) the use of price supports by government to aid farmers during short-run decreases in farm prices due to unexpected changes in production; and (5) extension of financial aid to farmers who cannot make reasonable incomes, to enable them to find work in other occupations. If the fifth proposal is adopted, it is clear that the nonfarm sector of the economy must remain strong to be able to absorb the surplus farm labor. This is one of the main economic challenges of the decade of the 1970's.

It is evident that the farm problem is a problem of prices, or, in other words, a problem of the relation between demand for and supply of farm products. And when the problem is solved, farm prices will be satisfactory and equitable to farmers and to all others in the economy.

FARM OUTPUT PER MAN-HOUR: INDEX NUMBERS, BY FARMING REGIONS, 1960-69[1]
[1957-59 = 100]

Year	Northeast	Lake States	Corn Belt	Northern Plains	Appalachian	Southeast	Delta States	Southern Plains	Mountain	Pacific	United States
1960....	114	112	118	127	114	112	118	121	111	107	115
1961....	120	122	125	121	120	123	130	130	115	110	122
1962....	121	125	134	135	126	127	147	134	121	118	129
1963....	130	135	148	137	132	138	162	145	129	123	138
1964....	137	138	151	143	142	146	181	156	131	130	144
1965....	147	144	169	158	148	160	199	177	139	134	156
1966....	148	157	177	168	146	161	206	182	145	135	164
1967....	166	164	192	174	162	179	220	179	151	137	174
1968....	167	176	203	190	163	176	253	203	159	142	182
1969[2]..	178	180	211	207	174	186	249	192	161	146	189

[1] Index of farm output divided by index of man-hours of labor used on farms.
[2] Preliminary.

SOURCE: USDA, *Agricultural Statistics, 1970*, Table 658, p. 456.

THE ACTIONS OF THE GOVERNMENT AFFECT ALL PRICES

The prices of all goods and services are interrelated. Anything that affects the prices of a number of important commodities affects all prices. Just how much the actions of the federal government influence the prices of many particular items is not known. But it is certain that in many cases the influence of the government on prices is as important a factor as is competition or monopoly by private individuals and concerns.

SUMMARY

On the whole, we do not subscribe to the medieval idea of "just price." But frequently we are willing to use government to control prices. Sometimes the means employed by government to regulate prices is direct; sometimes it is indirect.

There is a strong tendency for government to regulate or fix the prices of products and services provided by natural monopolies. A natural monopoly is: (1) an industry or business that depends on the exclusive possession of a natural resource, (2) an industry or business that requires so much capital that there is little chance for competition to develop, or (3) a business in which competition is not socially desirable.

Public utilities are natural monopolies and are regulated by government. There are three aims in the fixing of utility rates: (1) adequate services, (2) fair return to investors, and (3) prevention of undesirable discrimination.

Ch. 11 GOVERNMENT CONTROL OF PRICES

There are two recognized principles for public-utility rate regulation: (1) cost of service, and (2) value of service. The costs of public utilities may be classified as: (1) fixed, (2) variable, and (3) joint. A fair rate of return on public-utility capital depends on the amount of income in relation to the total amount of capital. Use of the value-of-service principle may result in charging more proportionately for one service than for another.

Since 1929, a number of federal laws to aid farmers have been passed. These include: the Agricultural Marketing Act, 1929; the Agricultural Adjustment Act, 1933; Soil Conservation Act, 1936; Agricultural Adjustment Act, 1938; the Agricultural Act of 1954; the "soil bank" program, 1956; and others, including the Food and Agriculture Act of 1965. The fundamental aim of each of these measures was to raise or stabilize the prices of farm products.

NEW TERMS

cost-of-service principle
federal utility commissions
joint costs
natural monopoly
parity prices

public utilities
rate discrimination
soil bank
value-of-service principle

QUESTIONS ON THE CHAPTER

1. As the term was formerly used, what was meant by a "just price"? By what was this concept replaced?
2. What evidence is there that all matters of price determination are not left to the forces of the marketplace?
3. Why is a railroad a natural monopoly?
4. How are public utilities regulated? Why is regulation necessary?
5. Can the federal government regulate all public utilities? Why or why not?
6. What are some of the federal agencies for the regulation of public utilities?
7. What are the three aims of public-utility commissions in establishing utility rates?
8. What are the two principles that are considered by public-utility commissions in setting rates? Explain.
9. What are the two general classes of service furnished by railroads?
10. What rates should railroads charge? Discuss.
11. How would you evaluate the market-directed price system relative to the problem of rate regulation for public utilities? Is the system effective?
12. How are railroad rates fixed?
13. How does the federal government provide minimum prices for farm products?
14. What is the essence of the farm problem?

15. How is a solution to the farm problem partly dependent on the strength of the nonfarm economy?
16. Has the government been successful in its attempt to fix minimum prices for farm products?

APPLYING YOUR ECONOMIC UNDERSTANDING

1. In recent years, several large corporations announced price increases, and they were reprimanded by the President of the United States. Do such reprimands relate to the idea of "just price"?
2. Using the latest figures from the United States Budget Report, estimate the percentage of federal government expenditure in the agricultural sector of the economy relative to total federal expenditure.
3. A night guard patrols for a corporation. On his duty tour he visits the factory building, the office building, and the warehouses. Would joint costs be involved in the services that he renders? Explain your answer.
4. When Railpax became operative in 1971, the mayor of a city visited Washington D.C., to complain that his city would now be deprived of all rail passenger service. What principle for the regulation of public utilities was involved in his complaint?
5. List some of the natural monopolies in your community. Classify them as to whether they are under federal or state control. What determines which governmental unit exercises the right of control?
6. Secure a copy of a recent annual report of a petroleum company. Present in class the differences between fixed and variable costs as they are reflected in the report you selected.
7. Interview an officer of a public utility company which serves your community to learn how prices are set for the utility's services. Report your findings to the class.
8. The TVA has been used as a yardstick for determining fair electric power rates. Is it a valid measurement? Why or why not?

CHALLENGES TO ECONOMIC COMPETENCE

1. Make a bulletin board display depicting government's role in price control.
2. Prepare a panel discussion on the topic "Are Airline Regulations and Taxes Outmoded?"
3. Prepare a chart to display the major areas in which government supports or controls farm prices and the relative costs of each program.
4. Select one of the major laws that have influenced prices. Prepare a digest of it, and then show how it has been applied in the American economy.

Chapter 12

Prices and the Value of Money

How can we measure changes in the cost of living?
How do changes in the cost of consumer goods and services result from changes in the value of money?
Why do changes in the cost of living affect individuals differently?
How may inflation be prevented?

In 1971 it took about $120 to buy the same amount of goods and services that could be bought by the average American family for $100 in 1967. Why? Prices, of course, had gone up. Or, to say the same thing in a different way, the value of money had gone down.

However we look at it — whether as a change in prices or in the value of money — the fact that one may not be able to buy the same amount of goods for the same amount of money as he did before is a matter of great importance to everyone.

How can we measure changes in prices and the value of money? How do changes in prices affect people? What causes such changes? What, if anything, can be done about it?

PRICE CHANGES ARE MEASURED BY INDEX NUMBERS

When we consider a particular commodity, as wheat or sugar, we can easily compare the price at one date with that at another date. And so far as one commodity is concerned, we can say without any difficulty whether the value of money in terms of that commodity has changed. But when we wish to know whether the purchasing power, or value, of money in terms of many commodities has changed, we encounter a more difficult problem. The prices of some commodities may be lower than they were previously, while those of others may be higher.

Statisticians have devised different methods for calculating changes in the *price level*, that is, the average price of a number of commodities. Each of these methods, however, is intended to show the average price at one date as compared with the average price at another. In figuring a *price index number*, the average price for the *base date* (or period) is considered 100. Then if the average price at a later date has increased 10 percent, the price index number for that date is 110. If it has fallen 10 percent, the price index number is 90.

How are price index numbers calculated? A short example will demonstrate the underlying aim in all methods of calculating price index numbers. Let us take five commodities the prices of which in 1950 and 1971 are assumed to have been as shown in the table below. Assume we wish to calculate the price index for 1971, based on 1950 prices. We therefore treat the price of each commodity in 1950 as 100, or 100 percent. By adding the percentages for all the commodities we get 500, which divided by 5, the number of commodities, gives 100, the average for the total number of commodities.

We then calculate the price percentages for 1971 for each of the commodities. For example, the price of eggs was 120 percent of what it was in 1950; meat, 250 percent; and so on. The average price of all the commodities, in terms of a percentage based on 1950 price, is 200.

Thus, we find that the same amount of money would purchase a smaller total quantity of all the commodities on January 1, 1971, than it would

CALCULATION OF A SIMPLE INDEX NUMBER

Commodity	January 1, 1950 Base Unit Price	January 1, 1950 Base Index Number	January 1, 1971 Price	January 1, 1971 Percentage to Base Index Number*
Eggs	$ 0.50	100	$ 0.60	120
Meat	.40	100	1.00	250
Suits	25.00	100	45.00	180
Rent	50.00	100	75.00	150
Bread	.10	100	.30	300
		5)500		5)1000
	Average index number	100	Average index number	200

*NOTE: Calculate percentage to base index numbers as follows, using meat as an example: ($1.00 ÷ .40) × 100 = 250.

Ch. 12　PRICES AND THE VALUE OF MONEY

CONSUMER PRICES

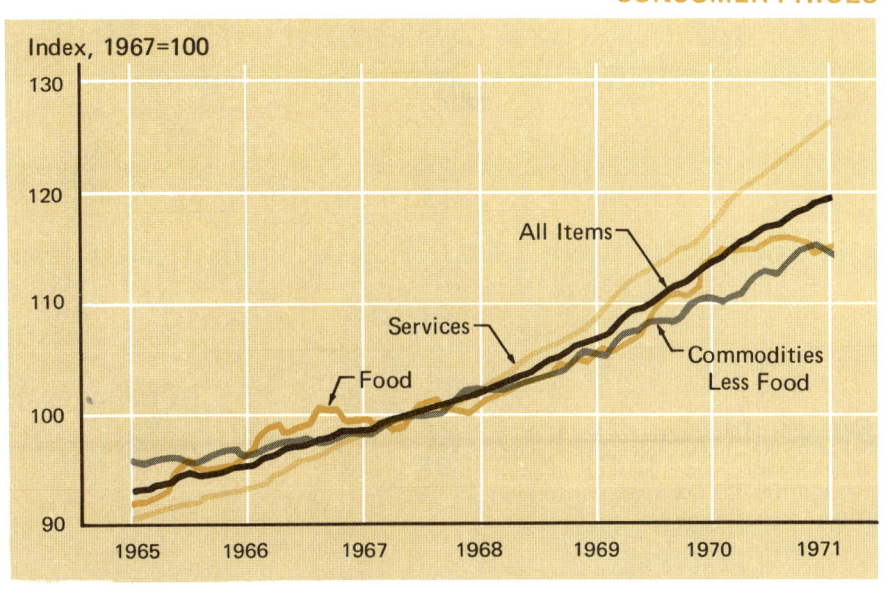

Figure 12-1.

SOURCE: *Economic Indicators,* February, 1971.

In the construction of this chart, the prices for any and all consumer commodities and services are considered as 100 for the year 1967. On this basis the price of all items in January, 1971, was 119.2. In other words, it required $119.20 in that month to buy as much as $100 would buy in 1967.

have purchased on January 1, 1950. That is to say, it took $2 in 1971 to buy as much of these five commodities as $1 would have bought in 1950.

Looking at the matter in another way, we can say that in 1971 (according to figures in the illustration) the dollar was worth only 50 cents (100 ÷ 200 = .50) as compared with its value of 100 cents in 1950.

Weighted index numbers. Of course, a change in the prices of some goods and services is more important than are changes in the prices of others. Therefore, the classes of expenditures should be weighted. If the price of bread is considered as the base for comparison and the expenditures for meat are 10 times as great as those for bread, then the relative price of meat is counted 10 times, while that of bread is counted but once. All other commodities included are weighted in a similar fashion, and a simple weighted arithmetical average, or *weighted index number*, is found.

The Consumer Price Index. The Bureau of Labor Statistics of the United States Department of Labor issues a monthly index of consumer prices, the *Consumer Price Index*. It is an index of changes in the prices of about 400 kinds of goods and services purchased by city wage-earner and

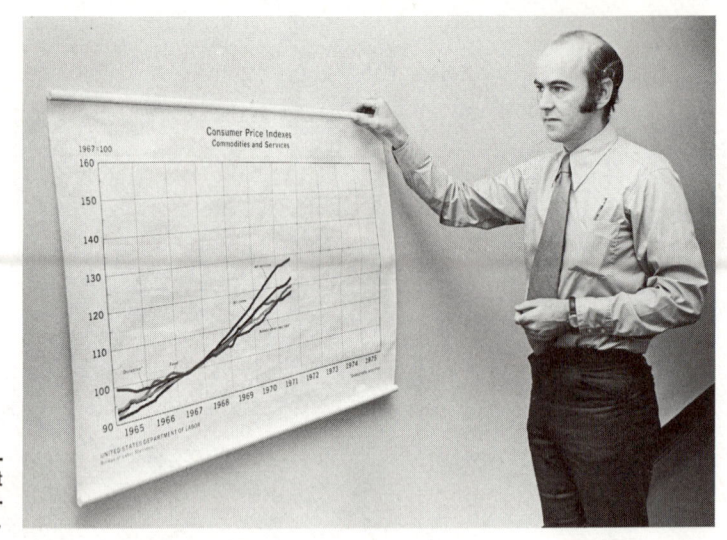

Illus. 12-1. The Bureau of Labor Statistics of the United States Department of Labor issues a monthly index of consumer prices, the *Consumer Price Index.*

Bureau of Labor Statistics

clerical-worker families in order to maintain their customary levels of living. In compiling the index, prices are collected in 39 representative metropolitan areas and 17 smaller cities. Foods, fuels, rents, and a few other items are priced each month. Some other prices are obtained every month in the largest metropolitan areas and every three months in the remaining areas and cities.

This index includes five broad classes of items, namely, food, housing, apparel and upkeep, transportation, and health and recreation.

In 1970 it was estimated by the Department of Commerce that consumers in this country used their personal incomes (a total of over $801 billion) approximately as follows: expenditures for durable goods, 11 percent; for nondurable goods (food, etc.), 33 percent; services, 33 percent; personal taxes, 15 percent; and savings, 6 percent.

SOME ARE HURT AND SOME ARE HELPED BY CHANGES IN THE COST OF LIVING

If the prices of all goods and services changed at the same time, in the same direction, and in the same proportion, changes in the cost of living would not be a matter of much importance, except to those on fixed incomes. For example, if the price of everything your family is accustomed to buying increased 50 percent, and the family income also increased by the same percentage, your family could live as well as it had previously.

The prices of commodities and services do not change equally or at the same time. Therefore, changes in prices affect different people in different ways. Let us consider the effects of price changes with respect to (1) the value of debt payments, (2) the value of fixed incomes, (3) the amount of investment, (4) governmental expenditures, (5) the value of wages, (6) profits, and (7) the value of investments.

(1) The effects of price changes on the value of debt payments. Changes in prices cause debtors to repay a different amount of purchasing power than they borrowed. For example, suppose that in 1971 the consumer price index was 120 as compared with that of 100 for 1967 when John Moore borrowed $100. If Mr. Moore repaid the loan in 1971, he actually repaid $83.33 ($\frac{100}{120} \times \$100 = \$83.33$) in purchasing power as compared with the $100 he had borrowed.

(2) The effects of price changes on the value of fixed incomes. Many people live on fixed incomes, that is, their incomes do not vary. Examples of such incomes are interest payments on bonds; rent from long-term rental contracts, or leases; pensions; and annuities.

Suppose that a widow received $50,000 in insurance money when her husband died and that she invested the money in 3 percent bonds in 1967. The annual income from the investment would be $1,500. But by 1971 the dollar was worth about 83.33 cents as compared with the 1967 dollar. If we multiply $1,500 by .8333, we get $1,249.95, which was the purchasing power value in 1971 of the income from the investment.

All persons with fixed incomes — whatever the sources of such incomes may be — suffer a loss in purchasing power when prices rise. On the other hand, they benefit from a fall in general prices.

(3) The effects of price changes on the amount of investment. The effects of changes in commodity prices are usually reflected in the amounts invested in capital goods. When prices are rising, producers tend to become optimistic and invest increasing amounts in buildings, machinery, and other equipment. If prices are declining, less may be invested in capital goods. When this is true, unemployment will increase.

(4) The effects of price changes on governmental expenditures. Price changes also affect the activities of the various divisions of government. The budget, containing estimates of income and expenditures of government, is prepared in advance of the period to which it applies. The appropriations to be made by the legislative body are estimated on the basis

EFFECTS OF CHANGES IN THE PRICE LEVEL

When Prices Increase —

A debtor repays a *smaller* amount of purchasing power.
Those with fixed incomes *suffer a loss* in purchasing power.
Investments in capital goods *increase*.
Appropriations for government expenditures *buy less;* but government revenues are *greater* than anticipated in the government budget.
Wages tend to *increase* but *less rapidly* than prices.
Profits tend to *increase more rapidly* than prices.
Common stock prices tend to *increase;* most bonds and preferred stock prices *do not increase* much.

When Prices Decrease —

A debtor repays a *greater* amount of purchasing power.
Those with fixed incomes have *increased* purchasing power.
Investments in capital goods *decrease*.
Appropriations for government expenditures *buy more;* but government revenues are *less* than anticipated in the government budget.
Wages tend to *decrease* but *less rapidly* than prices.
Profits tend to *decrease more rapidly* than prices.
Common stock prices tend to *decrease;* most bond and preferred stock prices tend to *increase*.

of the income expected. If prices increase, the amount of money available from taxes will not go as far as it would have if prices had not risen. But if prices decrease, the money will purchase more.

Since the government relies for part of its revenue upon a certain rate of taxation on personal and corporate incomes, the amount collected will vary as such incomes increase or decrease. As the incomes of individuals and corporations are determined largely by the degree of prosperity in business, the amount of revenue collected may be much larger or much smaller than was anticipated, depending upon whether business is good or bad.

(5) The effects of price changes on the value of wages. As prices in general increase, earnings from wages tend to increase. But wages almost always lag behind changes in the prices of commodities. A hardship is therefore imposed upon wage earners when prices are rising because the earnings from wages do not keep pace with the increase in the cost of living. On the other hand, when prices start declining, wages do not immediately decrease. For that reason, a decrease in prices often means an increase in real wages. (See Chapter 14 for a discussion of cost-of-living wage contracts.)

(6) The effects of price changes on profits. Businessmen sometimes favor rising prices. As prices increase, larger profits are made on goods that were bought when prices were lower. On the other hand, a decline in prices is looked upon with disfavor because selling prices are lower than they were expected to be at the time that the goods were purchased for stock.

But unless employment and total wages increase as prices rise, business will not continue to prosper. Eventually, prices will have to fall because consumers cannot buy as much as they could when prices were lower unless total wage payments also increase.

Of course, rising prices affect the purchasing power of the money received as profit by business individuals and concerns. But until increases in wages and the other elements of cost or expense in the operating of business enterprises overtake the increase in profits, the amount of profit is usually proportionally larger than the increases in wages.

(7) The effects of price changes on the value of investments. Price changes affect investors in bonds and stocks. As we recall, the income from bonds is fixed at a certain percent of face value. If bondholders feel reasonably sure of their interest and of the security of the principal, the prices of bonds do not decrease greatly when general prices fall. On the contrary, they are likely to increase. Bond prices are more stable than stock prices because bonds pay a stipulated amount of interest. The purchasing power of a given amount of bond interest increases, therefore, when prices fall; and the prices of bonds tend to increase. Of course, if there is uncertainty as to whether the interest will be paid as it becomes due, there may be a decline in the prices of the bonds.

The market prices of preferred stock tend to move in the same direction as those of bonds. The reason for this is that the income from preferred stock is more certain than that from common stock, although it is not as certain as is the income from bonds.

Common stocks, however, are very susceptible to changes in the prices of commodities in general. This is explained by the fact that the income from common stock, in the form of dividends, depends directly upon the profits earned by the corporation. Since rising prices tend to result in greater profits, the demand for common stocks is likely to increase when prices in general increase. But when commodity prices are declining, prospects for profits dwindle and market prices of common stocks fall.

WHAT CAUSES PRICES AND THE VALUE OF MONEY TO CHANGE?

There are several factors which may cause the general level of prices and the value of money to change. Moreover, the relative importance of each of these factors may be different at one time as compared with what it was at another time.

The factors that must be considered if we are to explain changes in the general level of prices are: (1) the amount of money and credit in circulation, (2) the velocity of money, and (3) the total volume of production and trade.

(1) The amount of money and credit in circulation. Since all goods are bought with either currency or credit, it is easy to see that the total quantity of purchasing power in use is a factor that is involved in both individual prices and prices in general or the general price level.

If the amount of money and credit in use doubles, while the amount of goods available for purchase remains the same, prices will tend to rise and the value of the dollar will tend to fall. On the other hand, under the same circumstances, a decrease in the amount of money and credit will tend to result in falling prices and a rise in the value of the dollar.

(2) The velocity of money. Mr. Ash receives his wages for the week, and he immediately pays his rent of $100. The property owner uses the $100 to pay a plumber who had installed a pump for him. The plumber uses the money to buy some supplies from a wholesaler — who uses the amount to pay one of his employees, who spends the money to buy a coat for his teen-age daughter. The $100 has changed hands six times, and it has been used to purchase several types of goods and services. The number of times that money changes hands is called the *velocity of money*. This is also a factor that is related to the demand for goods and, therefore, is related to the prices of goods.

(3) The total volume of production and trade. If the total number of units of goods and services to be purchased is small, the amount of money needed is not so great as it would be if the number of units were larger. As you can see, therefore, there is a relation between the quantity of goods and services to be exchanged and the amount of money needed.

DO CHANGES IN THE QUANTITY OF MONEY ACTUALLY AFFECT PRICES?

Without attempting to explore all the angles to the question, we may state the following conclusions, which are accepted by most people who have seriously studied the subject of the causes of changes in the price level: (1) Over a long period of time — a year or more — if other factors in the economy remain the same, a change in the amount of money in circulation will result in a change in prices, but the change in prices may not be in proportion to the change in money. (2) Over a short period of time, say, a period of several weeks or months, an increase or a decrease in money in circulation may have little effect on prices.

An attempt is sometimes made to sum up the discussion above as to the factors involved in changes in the level of prices by means of the *quantity theory of money*. Briefly stated, this theory holds that the average level of prices varies directly with the quantity of money and credit in circulation and the velocity of circulation, and inversely — in the opposite direction — with the volume of trade.

This explains why we should be concerned when government is spending a great deal more money than it is collecting from taxes. For, if too much money or credit is created by government borrowing and spending and the volume of goods produced does not increase proportionately, a rise in prices is bound to result. For instance, expenditures of billions of dollars for missiles result in an increase in personal incomes, but may not result in a corresponding increase in consumer goods.

CAN PRICES BE STABILIZED?

Under a system of free enterprise, prices of particular commodities are relied on to indicate the relative needs for certain kinds of goods. When supply is constant, an increase in the price of a commodity indicates a greater need and demand for that kind of good; a decrease in the price of a commodity indicates a decreasing demand for that type of good. But most people think that rapid fluctuations in the price level should be eliminated if possible. Accordingly, various proposals have been put forth to eliminate, or at least to minimize, changes in the price level.

Managed currency. One proposal that has been made calls for the abandonment of the gold standard. According to this proposal, the national government would be authorized to issue only paper money. As the price level tended to rise, the amount of money issued would be reduced; and, conversely, as the price level decreased, the amount of money issued would be increased. This proposal is known as *managed currency*. As the name implies, the plan would rely upon adjusting the supply of money so as to establish stable prices.

In order to give the government full control over the quantity of all money and credit, the federal reserve banks would be required to raise discount or interest rates when prices were rising, so as to discourage merchants and other businessmen from borrowing as much as they would if the discount rates were lower. The banks would likewise be required to decrease the rates when prices were falling. A decrease in the discount rates, it is said, would encourage the borrowing of funds for use in the purchase of goods and the operation of industries. Thus, it is claimed, prices would tend to rise.

The compensated dollar. Another suggestion for controlling changes in the general price level is that of the *compensated dollar*. In brief, the proposal is as follows:

1. At any time the dollar would consist of a certain amount of gold, but this amount would not be fixed.
2. Gold would not be coined. The United States Treasury would keep a supply of gold and would issue certificates that would be redeemable in gold. The metal could be used for commercial purposes.
3. If the price level rose, the amount of gold in the dollar would be increased by the same percentage. Likewise, a decrease in the price level would call for a proportionate decrease in the gold content of the dollar. By increasing the gold content of the dollar, fewer dollars in money could be put into circulation, and vice versa.

The idea of the compensated dollar might work. But most buying and selling is done by means of credit. Therefore, unless the amount of bank credit varied with the amount of money, controlling the number of gold dollars could hardly do much good. At present the government and the federal reserve banks can regulate the amount of bank credit, so it is questionable whether new controls of gold dollars would do much good.

WHAT IS INFLATION?

Inflation is the result of a more rapid increase in the amount of money and credit in circulation than in the supply of goods available for purchase. As has been said, inflation is the result of "too many dollars chasing too few goods." When inflation occurs, there is a rise in the price level. Sometimes such a rise may be rapid, as was the case in the United States from 1941 to 1948, from 1950 to 1951, and during the last half of the 1960's and early 1970's. It might be catastrophic, as it was in Germany in 1923, as we shall see in Chapter 19.

SOME GENERAL CAUSES OF INFLATION

The causes of inflation include the following: (1) increases in demand at a time when employment is very high, when industrial capacity is in full use, and when the supply of raw materials is low; (2) increases in the amount of money in circulation that exceed the increases in the production of goods and services; (3) increases in wages that surpass the increases in labor productivity. In general, whatever increases the amount of money in circulation as compared with the amount of goods and services to be purchased will eventually cause a rise in prices.

Borrowing and spending by government in excess of the amount of taxes collected or the rapid increase of bank credit and spending by business for capital goods will cause a rise in the general price level. Likewise, an increase in production costs that is greater than the increase in labor productivity will cause prices to rise, especially where prices are determined under conditions of monopoly or imperfect competition. It is claimed that raising wages in major industries more rapidly than labor productivity increases may compel employers to raise the prices of what they sell. A rise in prices resulting in this way has been referred to as *cost-push inflation*. On the other hand, it has been noted that whenever businesses can regulate the supply of their goods, they have some degree of control over the prices they can charge. Thus, it is claimed that the power to administer prices results in inflationary pressures when it is used to raise prices.

WHAT BANKS AND GOVERNMENT CAN DO TO CONTROL INFLATION

As we have seen, the amount of hand-to-hand money can increase or decrease in response to the needs of business. Also, the federal reserve banks can increase the amount of loans that can be made to business by lowering the interest rate and by buying government securities from banks; or they can discourage such loans by raising interest rates and by selling securities to banks. Moreover, the federal government and other levels of government can increase or decrease spending, and taxes can be raised or lowered.

All of these possibilities on the part of banks and the government may be utilized in an attempt to control the amount of money in circulation and thus to control prices in general. And it is the policy of the federal reserve banks and the government to attempt to exert an influence on prices by managing the amount of money and credit in circulation.

WHAT BUSINESS AND LABOR CAN DO TO HELP CONTROL INFLATION

During the late 1950's and early 1960's, economic policy makers in the federal government became increasingly concerned over the problems of maintaining growth in the nation's economy and of improving the competitive position of American industry in world markets. One requirement for achieving these goals was to prevent inflation.

To this end, in 1962, the President's Council of Economic Advisers first formally suggested certain standards or *guideposts* to help business and organized labor to make price and wage decisions that would not be inflationary. The guideposts, which were designed to relate price and wage changes to the average annual rate of increase in output per man-hour for the economy, were restated as follows in *The Annual Report of the Council of Economic Advisers* for 1966:

> 1. The general guidepost for wages is that the *annual rate of increase of total employee compensation* (*wages and fringe benefits*) *per man-hour worked should equal the national trend rate of increase in output per man-hour.*
>
> 2. The general guidepost for prices is that *prices should remain stable in those industries where the increase of productivity equals the national trend; that prices can appropriately rise in those industries where the increase of productivity is smaller than the national trend; and that prices should fall in those industries where the increase of productivity exceeds the national trend.*

The policy of publishing guideposts proved to be relatively ineffective and was abandoned after 1967. But the guidelines offered a challenge to private decision makers (management and labor leaders) to consider the interests of the general public in exercising whatever economic power they possess. It is only reasonable to expect business and labor to strive for more income in the form of profits and wages. The opportunity to do so is essential to the orderly functioning of the enterprise system. But both of these economic groups should exercise their powers over prices and wages in a responsible way. If they do so, one of the sources of inflation will be controlled. Presidential pleas that emphasize the responsibility of private decision makers are not adequate substitutes for the positive action that the control of inflation requires.

SUMMARY

The price level is the average of the prices of the more important types of goods for which people spend their money. A consumers' price index is the average price of the consumers' goods at a given time as compared with the average price at some previous time.

The price index can also be used to determine the value of a dollar at a given time as compared with that of a previous date or time. For example, a 100 percent increase in the price level indicates a 50 percent decrease in the value of the dollar.

An increase in prices hurts those whose incomes are fixed and those whose incomes do not increase as rapidly as prices rise. Conversely, those with fixed incomes benefit by a fall in prices. If government continues to provide the same amount of services, taxes may have to be increased when the price level rises — or the government must borrow money with which to meet its increased expenses.

At the present time we have a sort of managed money system, which is used to some extent in an attempt to prevent or to control wide fluctuations in the price level by controlling the amount of money in circulation.

By and large, the underlying cause of an increase in the price level is the fact that the quantity and velocity of money in circulation increase more rapidly than does the amount of goods and services that are available in the marketplace. When the reverse of this occurs, the price level tends to decline.

Unjustified wage increases and monopolistic price increases both tend to create inflationary pressures in the economy. The issuance of wage-price guideposts may serve to help business and labor evaluate their private economic decisions, but their effectiveness as a means of checking inflation has been subject to serious question.

NEW TERMS

base date
compensated dollar
Consumer Price Index
cost-push inflation
guideposts
inflation

managed currency
price index number
price level
quantity theory of money
velocity of money
weighted index number

QUESTIONS ON THE CHAPTER

1. How are changes in the price level measured?
2. How would you illustrate the construction of a simple arithmetical average price index number?
3. What is the significance of "weighting" expenditures?
4. What is the CPI?
5. What is meant by the expression "cost of living"?
6. Why do changes in the consumer price level affect different people in different ways?

7. How do changes in the consumer price level affect the following: (a) the value of debt payments; (b) the value of fixed incomes; (c) the amounts of investments; (d) governmental expenditures; (e) the value of wages; (f) profits; and (g) the value of investments?
8. What factors help to cause changes in the price level?
9. What is your understanding of the quantity theory of money?
10. Do we have a managed currency? Explain.
11. What is inflation, and what are its causes?
12. What is the significance of the price-wage guideposts?

APPLYING YOUR ECONOMIC UNDERSTANDING

1. The chart below lists certain economic goods with their prices in 1950 and in 1971. Using 1950 as the base year calculate the simple price index of each good for 1971.

Economic Good	1950 Price	1971 Price	1971 Price Index Number
(a) 1 bottle of coke	$ .05	$ .10	(a).......
(b) 1 pair of shoes	5.00	12.50	(b).......
(c) 1 movie admission	.50	1.25	(c).......
(d) 1 local telephone call	.10	.10	(d).......
(e) 1 local bus fare	.10	.30	(e).......

2. Refer to the application above and your calculated answers; then answer the following questions. (a) Did all prices rise between 1950 and 1971? (b) Which economic good showed the greatest percentage increase in price? (c) Which economic good showed the greatest dollar increase? (d) Which economic good showed no price change?
3. Interview several persons who are retired and are living on pensions or annuities, with specific reference to the effect of present prices on their level of living. Report your findings to the class.
4. Interview several wage earners who are union members to learn about the changes in their wage incomes for the past five years relative to their level of living. Report your findings to the class.

CHALLENGES TO ECONOMIC COMPETENCE

1. Prepare a display of articles that were advertised ten years ago with the same type of articles that are advertised today. Prepare an analysis to accompany the display. Should changes in quality be studied in relation to prices?
2. Have a representative of a local bank explain how a bank puts credit into circulation. Serve as a moderator for the class discussion which follows.
3. Organize a debate on the topic "Government Spending Maintains National Prosperity."

Unit 4

Distribution of National Income

Chapter 13 Sharing the National Income
Chapter 14 Wages for Labor
Chapter 15 Rent for Land
Chapter 16 Interest for Capital
Chapter 17 Profits for Enterprisers
Chapter 18 Labor Unions and Employers

Harold M. Lambert

Duke Power Co.

Inland Steel Company

Cominco Photo

You will recall that in our modern industrial economy there are resources that are called "factors of production" when they are used in the productive process. Those who provide land, the services of labor, capital, and the services of management for purposes of production share in the distribution of the national income.

Chapter 13

Sharing the National Income

What determines how much income shall go to the owners of each of the factors of production?
What determines how land, labor, and capital shall be used in the productive process?
How does the method of allocating productive resources under the free-enterprise system differ from that of communism?
How is the amount of rent, wages, interest, and profit paid to individuals determined?

You will recall from Chapter 4 that in our modern industrial economy there are resources that are called "factors of production" when they are used in the productive process. The owners of the resources of labor, land, and capital share in national income in payments that are known respectively as wages, rent, and interest. But these factors are worthless economically unless they are employed in production. In a capitalistic economy, an enterpriser or entrepreneur — a private individual or functional group — employs these factors to produce goods and services. The share of national income going to the entrepreneur is profit when circumstances are favorable, or loss when conditions are adverse.

Economists do not agree among themselves as to the number of factors of production. One group considers that there are four — labor, land, capital, and the entrepreneur. Another group classifies the first three as the primary factors and thinks of the entrepreneur as a special form of labor, albeit one of vital importance in his role as organizer, innovator, and risk taker in our economy.

As we said in Chapter 3, the production of the goods we need is a cooperative undertaking. That is, we cooperate by means of specialization and by pooling the types of resources that we may have. The amount of goods and services produced through our cooperative efforts constitutes the real income of the nation, and how well the people will live depends upon the nature and amount of production and how much income each person receives. The total net earnings received by those who supply labor, land, capital, and entrepreneurship for production is called the "national income." The value of each individual's contribution to production is also expressed in terms of dollars and becomes his *personal income*.

DISTRIBUTION OF INCOMES IN THE UNITED STATES

As we know, the money incomes of families in this country vary greatly. Of the 51.1 million families in this country in 1969 the Bureau of the Census estimated that the percentage distribution was that shown in the table below. (Median income is the amount of income above which there were as many recipients as there were families with incomes of less than that amount.) Why do incomes vary so markedly? Is it simply a matter of color as one might judge from the table? What are the factors that determine how much income an individual or a family may receive?

DISTRIBUTION OF FAMILY INCOME, 1969

Total Money Income	Total Families	White Families	Negro Families
Number........Thousands..	51,110	45,929	4,744
Percent..........	100.0	100.0	100.0
Under $1,000................	1.5	1.3	3.1
$1,000 to $1,499............	1.3	1.0	4.0
$1,500 to $1,999............	1.8	1.5	4.6
$2,000 to $2,499............	2.4	2.2	4.7
$2,500 to $2,999............	2.2	2.0	4.5
$3,000 to $3,499............	2.6	2.2	5.8
$3,500 to $3,999............	2.7	2.5	4.5
$4,000 to $4,999............	5.4	4.9	9.6
$5,000 to $5,999............	5.9	5.6	9.0
$6,000 to $6,999............	6.4	6.2	8.6
$7,000 to $7,999............	7.3	7.2	7.6
$8,000 to $8,999............	7.4	7.5	5.9
$9,000 to $9,999............	7.0	7.2	6.1
$10,000 to $11,999..........	13.0	13.6	7.9
$12,000 to $14,999..........	13.7	14.4	7.0
$15,000 to $24,999..........	15.7	16.6	6.5
$25,000 to $49,999..........	3.3	3.5	0.6
$50,000 and Over...........	0.4	0.5	0.1
Median Income....Dollars..	9,448	9,806	6,036
Mean Income......Dollars..	10,594	10,967	7,006

Source: U.S. Department of Commerce, Bureau of Census.

Ch. 13   SHARING THE NATIONAL INCOME

NUMBER OF FAMILIES BY FAMILY INCOME IN 1947 to 1969

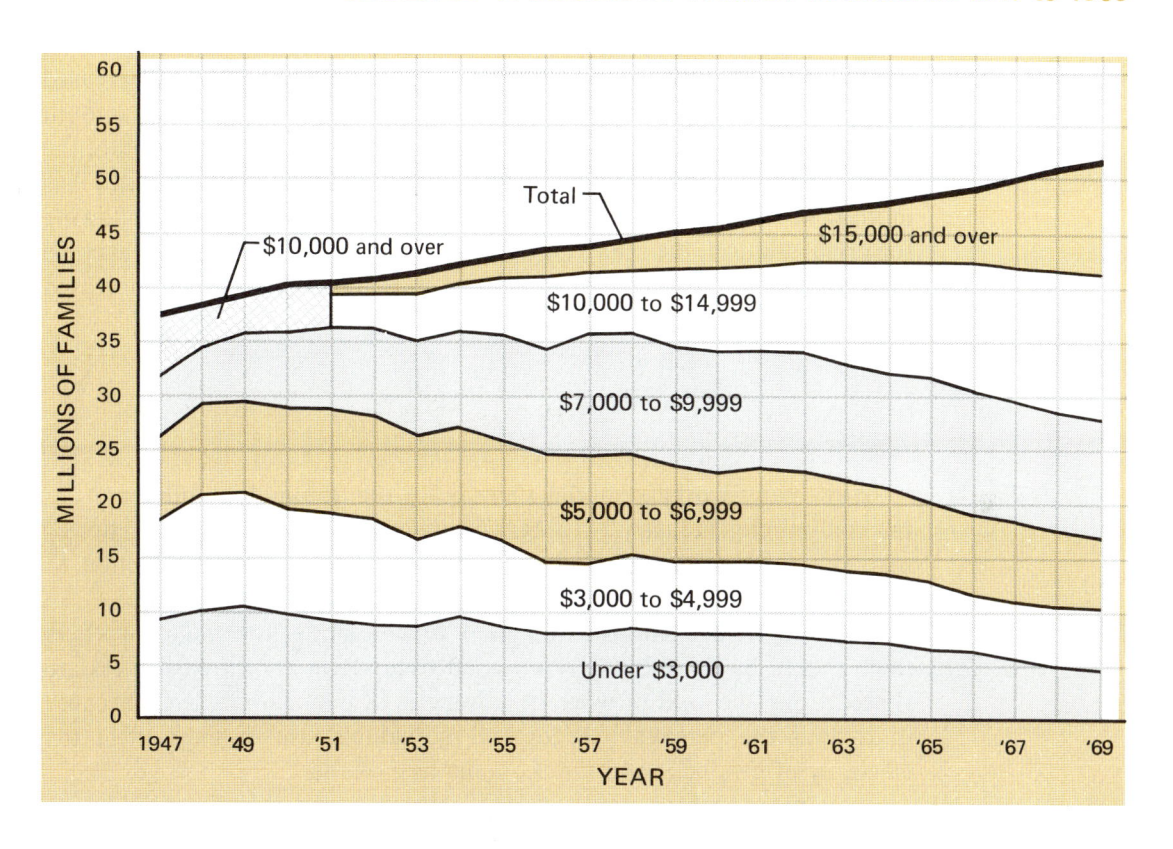

Figure 13-1.

SOURCE: U.S. Department of Commerce, Bureau of Census.

The methods used to distribute the national income are forms of pricing in the case of labor, land, and capital. It is assumed that the prices that are received by labor, land, and capital are determined by the forces of demand and supply. Therefore, an understanding of the problems relating to wages, rent, and interest involves a study of matters that pertain to the demand for and the supply of factors of production. Chapters 14, 15, and 16 deal individually with these distributive shares of national income. In the present chapter, reference to factors of production means labor, land, and capital unless the entrepreneur is specifically included. In a number of ways the latter productive function requires a different treatment and analysis, which will be explained in Chapter 17.

PER CAPITA DISPOSABLE PERSONAL INCOME

In the United States, annual disposable personal income per capita (average number of dollars available for expenditure per person) increased by more than 72 percent from 1960 to 1970. In current dollars, this amount was $3,344 in 1970 compared with $1,937 in 1960. But a large part of the increase was offset by higher prices since the Consumer Price Index was more than 30 percent higher in 1970 than it was in 1960. After allowing for price inflation, the real gain in purchasing power of disposable income per capita was about 37 percent for a population that had itself increased 13 percent.

THE IMPORTANCE OF PRODUCTIVE-RESOURCE PRICING IN OUR ECONOMY

How many workers should there be in the automobile industry? In the coal-mining industry? In agriculture? In the different branches of marketing? How are workers shifted from one kind of production to another? These are questions that must be answered in any kind of an economic system. The method used to determine how many workers there should be in an industry or in an occupation and how workers are shifted from one kind of work to another is of major importance because it involves the personal freedom of individuals, and it may affect the efficiency of production in the economy as a whole.

In a planned economy and one operating under a dictatorship, as in the Soviet Union, the problem of shifting factors of production from one use to another is a relatively simple matter. Production of practically all kinds in the economy is planned for a period of five or seven years. Then, by means of pressure of one kind or another exerted by the central government, labor, land, and capital are utilized in certain fields of production.

In the free-enterprise economy, market prices are relied upon primarily to allocate the several factors of production to particular fields of endeavor. For the most part, productive undertakings are the result of someone's desire for profit. In order to make a profit, both self-employed producers and employers seek to keep their total cost of production at the lowest level possible. Therefore, the demand for productive resources is related to the possibility of making a profit by each of the productive establishments. At the same time, owners of the factors of production are free to sell or not to sell the factors that they own. In our economy, then, productive enterprises compete for the use of the factors of production —

Ch. 13 SHARING THE NATIONAL INCOME 217

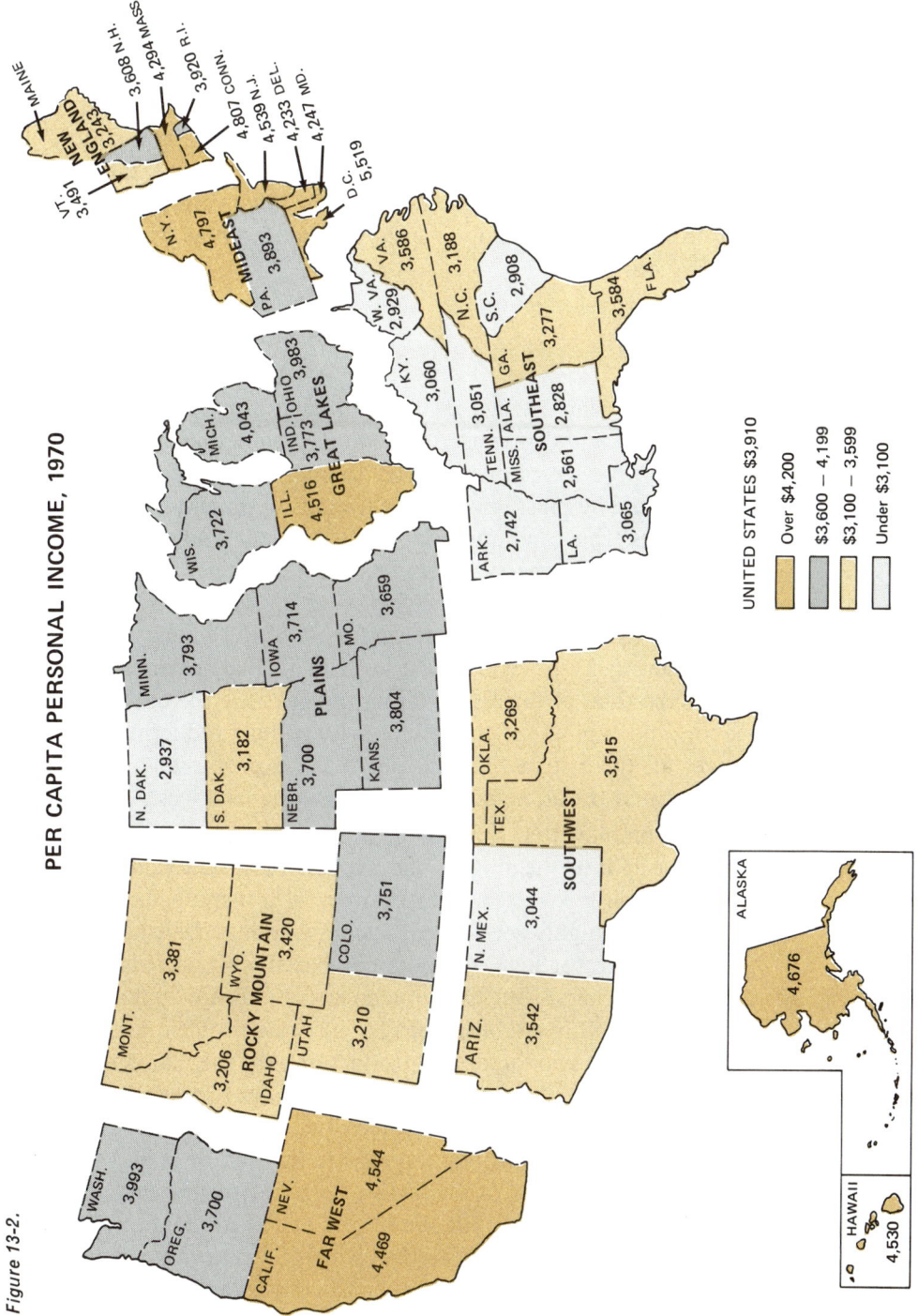

Figure 13-2.

PER CAPITA PERSONAL INCOME, 1970

New England
- MAINE 3,243
- VT. 3,491
- N.H. 3,608
- MASS. 4,294
- R.I. 3,920
- CONN. 4,807

Mideast
- N.J. 4,539
- DEL. 4,233
- MD. 4,247
- D.C. 5,519
- N.Y. 4,797
- PA. 3,893

Southeast
- W. VA. 2,929
- VA. 3,586
- N.C. 3,188
- S.C. 2,908
- GA. 3,277
- FLA. 3,584
- KY. 3,060
- TENN. 3,051
- ALA. 2,828
- MISS. 2,561
- ARK. 2,742
- LA. 3,065

Great Lakes
- MICH. 4,043
- OHIO 3,983
- IND. 3,773
- ILL. 4,516
- WIS. 3,722

Plains
- MINN. 3,793
- IOWA 3,714
- MO. 3,659
- N. DAK. 2,937
- S. DAK. 3,182
- NEBR. 3,700
- KANS. 3,804

Southwest
- OKLA. 3,269
- TEX. 3,515
- N. MEX. 3,044
- ARIZ. 3,542

Rocky Mountain
- MONT. 3,381
- WYO. 3,420
- IDAHO 3,206
- UTAH 3,210
- COLO. 3,751

Far West
- WASH. 3,993
- OREG. 3,700
- CALIF. 4,469
- NEV. 4,544

ALASKA 4,676
HAWAII 4,530

UNITED STATES $3,910
- Over $4,200
- $3,600 – 4,199
- $3,100 – 3,599
- Under $3,100

SOURCE: *Survey of Current Business*, April 1971.

and, in turn, the owners of such factors have the freedom to decide how, when, and where their contributions to production will be made.

Under conditions of competition the demand for and the supply of a factor of production determine the share of income that goes to the owner of the factor. But merely to say "demand and supply" does not give a very helpful explanation of how any one of the three kinds of income is determined. Although we know that prices tend to vary according to demand and supply, we should like to know why they tend to vary as they do.

INCOME IS LIMITED BY PRODUCTIVITY

Anyone who is engaged in producing a good needs land, materials, labor, and capital because these things enable him to make the good he wants to produce. For example, a manufacturer must have a site for his factory, and he must have the right kinds of materials. He must also have employees who can supply labor of different kinds. And he must have various kinds of machines, tools, and buildings. He expects to sell the goods that are produced in his factory at a price that will yield him a profit. Since he cannot have without cost most of the things needed to carry on his business, the price at which he sells his product must be one that will cover the total of the amounts that he pays for the use of land, materials, labor, and capital. If the selling price of his product does not more than cover all these items, he will not make a profit; and he may find that, instead of a profit, he actually suffers a financial loss.

The amount that a factor of production is worth depends upon how valuable it is in helping in the process of production. This fact is, in general, well recognized. For example, if a manufacturer needs a worker to operate a highly specialized machine, he may feel that he can afford to pay this operator high wages as compared with what he pays a majority of other workers. But how much can he afford to pay the various kinds of workers in his establishment? The same problem arises in connection with the other two factors of production that the manufacturer must buy.

The amount of money payment that goes to the owner of a factor of production — other than the enterpriser — as has been noted previously, is determined by a process of valuation; that is, someone must place a money value on units of the factor. In a free society this process of valuation is engaged in by both the buyers and the sellers of the factors. The amount or price to be paid to the owner of a factor of production is usually the result of an agreement between the buyers and the sellers of the factor.

HOW IMPORTANT IS MARGINAL PRODUCTIVITY?

The term *productivity* refers to the amount of output of goods that results from the use of a unit of a factor of production. For example, the productivity of one worker in a factory may be 100 articles a day, while that of another worker may be 150 articles. Or the productivity of one acre of land may be 30 bushels of wheat, and that of another acre, 20 bushels.

By *marginal productivity* we mean the amount or value added to the total product by the use of one more or an extra unit of a factor of production, while the number of the other factors remains as before. For example, suppose that a brick manufacturer has 100 employees. How much would his total production of bricks be increased if he hired one more worker? The answer to this question would indicate the marginal productivity of a worker of this kind when 100 workers are employed.

In thinking of marginal productivity we must keep in mind that we are thinking of units of factors and that all the units are assumed to be alike. Of course, we know that some land is more fertile than other land; that some workers are more efficient than others; and that a new machine in good condition is better than an old one. But to simplify our problem, imagine that we are dealing with a factor where the units are all alike.

The law of diminishing returns cannot be ignored. In all productive establishments — big and small — there is a point beyond which the utilization of a unit of a factor of production tends to result in less than a proportionate increase in output. This is the *law of diminishing returns*.

Every experienced farmer knows something about how the law of diminishing returns works. For example, a farmer may apply 100 pounds of fertilizer to a plot of land and get an increase in the yield of possibly 100 percent. And the application of a second 100 pounds might result in an increase in yield of, say, 25 percent. Still further applications would probably not produce any increase at all. Of course, if the second 100 pounds were applied to another plot, the yield might be as large as that for the first 100 pounds.

Likewise, a factory employer might find it desirable to employ 100 workers in his factory. But he knows that he cannot go on indefinitely employing additional workers because it would not be profitable to do so. A point would be reached where an additional worker in the plant could not add enough to the total production to justify the owner in hiring him, even at a very low wage.

In any productive establishment, total production is the result of all the units of production working together. The decrease in production that would result if one unit of a factor of production were eliminated is the marginal productivity of that factor in the establishment.

THE PROPORTIONS OF THE FACTORS OF PRODUCTION AFFECT MARGINAL PRODUCTIVITY

If a man who wishes to farm has a plow and a horse, he can utilize a certain number of acres of land to advantage. If he has more equipment, say two plows, two horses, and a hired man, he can make use of more land. If he did not have enough land of his own, he could afford to pay rent for additional land. Under the circumstances, an additional acre of land would have higher marginal productivity for him than it had before.

Likewise, a manufacturer may have space and a labor force sufficient to make use of another machine. He might conclude that another machine would add a great deal to his total output. Under these circumstances an additional unit of capital would have higher marginal productivity than would another unit of labor.

As you can see, the proportions of the factors of production in an establishment affect the marginal productivity of a unit of any one of the factors. If labor is being used generously and the other factors sparingly, the marginal productivity of labor is comparatively low. If capital is being used generously and the other factors sparingly, the marginal productivity of capital is low in comparison with that of the other factors. Finally, if land is being used generously and the other factors sparingly, the marginal productivity of land is comparatively small. In short, the smaller the number of units of a factor that are used, the greater will be the marginal importance of this factor.

DOES MARGINAL PRODUCTIVITY DETERMINE INCOMES?

Under conditions of pure competition in the markets for land, labor, and capital, marginal productivity would doubtless determine actual income for these factors. The marginal productivity of the workers on different levels would fix the total amount that could be paid in wages, and so with land and capital. And the competition between entrepreneurs would no doubt tend to cause rents, wages, and interest to approximate the marginal productivity of the land, labor, and capital used in these particular enterprises.

But competition in the demand for and the supply of the factors of production is not perfect. And to the extent that it is not pure or perfect, the amounts received in the way of rent, wages, and interest may not correspond to the marginal productivity of one or all the factors of production. On the other hand, there is usually at least some competition among those who desire to use land, labor, and capital and among those who supply these factors. Therefore, to the extent that competition exists, and bargaining positions permit it, marginal productivity tends to correspond to the share of income that goes to the owners of the factors of production.

SUMMARY

The production of goods and services results in the creation of income. The prosperity and well-being of the people of a nation depend upon the quantity and the variety of goods and services produced and the way incomes are distributed. The volume of production in the nation is measured in terms of money value. The national income is the amount of income apportioned to those who supply the factors of production needed. Personal income is the amount of income received by individuals and families.

Those who share in the distribution of the national income are the owners of the factors of production. The distribution of the national income involves the valuation of the amount of the factors of production that the owners of the factors contribute to productive processes. The amount of income that an individual receives is supposed to depend on the price and the quantity of the factor that he supplies.

In a free-enterprise society the prices of the factors of production, excluding the entrepreneur, are determined in the market by demand and supply. Therefore, impersonal market forces are depended upon to allocate the factors of production to particular uses. In a planned economy, like the Soviet Union, production is planned and resources are allocated accordingly.

In trying to understand how shares of the national income are determined, we must give attention to the following matters: the demand for and the supply of the factors of production; the productivity of the factors of production; marginal productivity; the law of diminishing returns; the proportions of the factors of production in given situations; and the fact that competition for the use of the factors of production is not perfect.

NEW TERMS

law of diminishing returns   personal income
marginal productivity   productivity

QUESTIONS ON THE CHAPTER

1. What are the factors of production, and what is their economic significance?
2. To what extent is there inequality in the distribution of income?

3. What is a median income?
4. How does the allocation of productive resources within the economy differ between the United States and the Soviet Union?
5. How does each of the following affect the amount of one's income as wages, rent, and interest: (a) demand and supply, (b) productivity?
6. Does marginal productivity refer to the productivity of any particular unit of a factor of production? Explain.
7. What is the difference between the law of diminishing returns and marginal productivity?
8. Does the law of diminishing returns have any effect on marginal productivity? Explain.
9. Should we conclude that marginal productivity always determines the amount of income that goes to labor, land, or capital?

APPLYING YOUR ECONOMIC UNDERSTANDING

1. What causes differences in the incomes of persons and families in your community?
2. Cite some specific social and economic problems in your community that result from the way incomes are distributed.
3. Check data on personal incomes in your state. How does per capita income in your state compare with that for the nation? How do you account for the difference?
4. The Roget Company uses a timed typing test in hiring new typists. Applicants must type a certain minimum number of words per minute as an employment requirement. How may this requirement relate to marginal productivity?
5. The Red Rover Trucking Company was a new small concern. Its owner made a decision to add another truck and driver to the company's fleet. Six months later it was discovered by an accountant that the revenues had increased by a lesser amount than the costs of the new truck and the driver's wages. How might a knowledge of the law of diminishing returns have helped this company?
6. Are increased output per man-hour and increased real income per capita both related to income distribution? Explain your answer.

CHALLENGES TO ECONOMIC COMPETENCE

1. Prepare a large display chart depicting the distribution of the national income for last year.
2. Arrange a panel discussion on "Predictions for Incomes in the Form of Wages, Rent, Interest, and Profits During the Next Decade."
3. Read the Foreign Policy Association's (Headline Series) pamphlet, *Technology and World Power*, by Victor Basiuk. Prepare an oral review of the pamphlet for presentation in class or in a local service organization.

Chapter 14

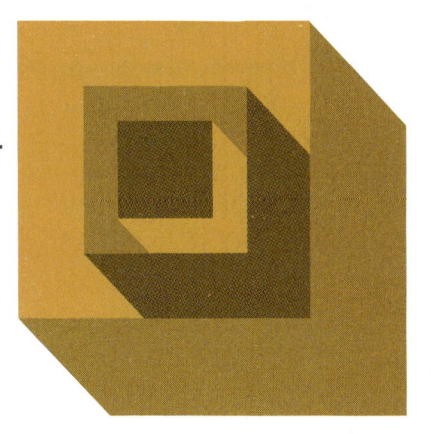

Wages for Labor

What is the essential nature of wages?
How is the price of labor determined?
How may one's standard of living affect his wages?
What laws relate to wages?

Employees get slightly more than three out of every four dollars of the total amount of all income paid to the owners of the factors of production. Included in the list of those who receive compensation for their services are not only employees in factories, stores, and elsewhere, but also the presidents of corporations and high government officials. Economists also sometimes talk about *imputed wages*, which denotes an estimated value placed upon the labor of self-employed persons when no cash payment for wages is made.

What — or who — decides how much of the national income is paid to those who supply labor? Why do incomes from labor differ so much? These are only two of the important questions that we might ask concerning how payments for labor are determined.

WHAT ARE WAGES?

Wages are prices that are paid for labor. Labor, as we recall, is human effort — physical or mental — that is expended in the production of material or nonmaterial economic goods. Thus, the term includes not only wages in the customary sense of the word, but also payments that are referred to as fees, commissions, and salaries.

Wage rates are prices for labor per hour, per week, per month, or for some other unit of time; or they may be prices for units of work. *Money wages*, or *nominal wages*, refers to the amount of money paid for given amounts of work. *Real wages* implies the amount of goods and services that money wages will purchase. *Wages of management* is a term that is sometimes used to indicate the value of the labor of a self-employed worker in performing managerial functions himself rather than hiring someone else to do this for him.

DOES MARGINAL PRODUCTIVITY FIX THE WAGES OF THE GROUP?

Under conditions of pure competition, employers tend to hire additional workers up to the point where the amount of wages becomes equal to the value of the product that would be lost by the employer if one less worker were employed. This idea is known as the *marginal productivity theory of wages*. Under pure competition, the wages of the last worker hired — which equals the marginal productivity of the workers — fixes the wages for the group when all the workers have approximately the same ability, for each worker will demand as much as the others are getting. Therefore, the employer pays the same amount of wages to all the workers of the same kind and of similar ability; and the amount paid is usually less when there are many employees of a given kind than when there are fewer. The amount paid is less because, after the law of diminishing productivity comes into operation, the productivity of a worker is smaller when there are many workers than when there are not so many. Since, as it is assumed, the other factors of production are fixed in quantity, the larger number of workers will have at their disposal a smaller quantity of these factors per worker. The output per worker, therefore, is smaller with the larger number of workers than with the smaller number.

MARGINAL PRODUCTIVITY LIMITS WAGES

The value of the productivity of a worker in any establishment limits the amount that the employer can pay in wages. But it is not always necessary for the employer to pay wages that are equal in value to what the services of a worker are worth to the employer. For example, suppose that there is only one employer and a great many persons are looking for work. Necessity may compel a worker to take a job at a wage rate that is very much less than the employer could afford to pay. Thus, marginal productivity sets the maximum wage, and the supply of labor helps determine the minimum the employer tends to pay.

HOW CAN WE EXPLAIN WAGES AND WAGE RATES?

As a general statement, we may say that under competitive conditions wages and wage rates are determined largely by demand and supply. But

CHANGES IN PRODUCTIVITY, 1850-1975

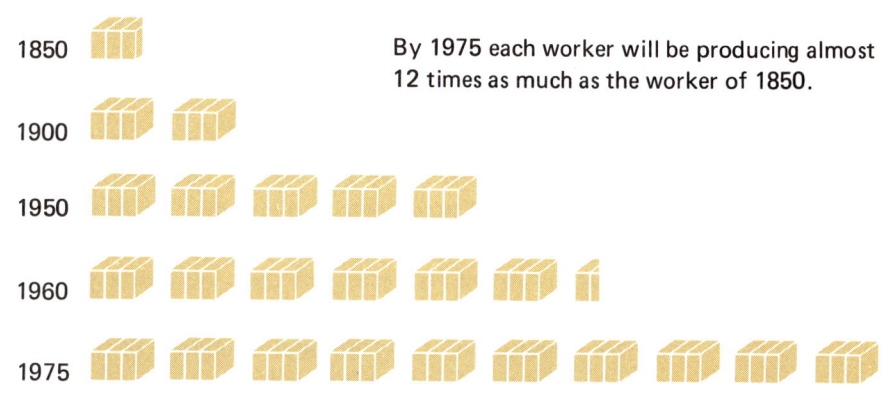

1850

1900   By 1975 each worker will be producing almost 12 times as much as the worker of 1850.

1950

1960

1975

Each symbol represents 50 cents, at 1960 prices, of national income per man-hour of private employment.

Figure 14-1.

The Twentieth Century Fund

this is an oversimplification. We can, however, get a good general idea about how wages are determined by understanding the factors that relate to the demand for and the supply of labor. Let us see what some of these factors are.

WHAT IS MEANT BY THE DEMAND FOR LABOR?

Employers in industry and business hire workers because they need certain kinds of human services. The textile manufacturer needs employees to tend spinning machines and weaving machines; the automobile manufacturer needs workers to use certain tools, run machines, or help assemble cars; and the manager of a store needs persons to sell goods.

Thus, the demand for labor is said to be a *derived demand;* that is, the demand for labor comes about because there is a demand for the things that labor can produce. It is true that in industry and business the demand for labor depends largely upon the demand for goods. When the demand for goods is great, employers tend to hire more workers; and when the demand for goods decreases, fewer workers are hired and frequently some that had been employed are laid off.

We should also note that the demand for labor is specific. Workers are employed to do certain kinds of work. A manufacturer does not just hire a worker; he hires a man to run a lathe, to keep the stock room, or to do some other particular kind of work. We also sometimes speak of the general demand for labor, as when someone says there is an increase in the general demand for labor. All this expression means, however, is that there has been an increase in the specific demands for a great many different kinds of workers.

THE EFFECT OF AUTOMATION ON THE DEMAND FOR LABOR

The word "automation" refers here to the automatic control of a productive process. It may refer to the integration of machines with each other, so that one machine completes an operation and passes the product along to another machine. Or it may refer to a system of self-correcting controls, as in oil refineries, so that the entire process of production is carried on continuously with little manual labor. In a sense, automation is a continuation of the technological change of the past but in a new form and at a greatly increased rate.

The effects of automation on the demand for labor are often hotly debated. Some say that automation will result in the creation of more

STATUS OF THE LABOR FORCE

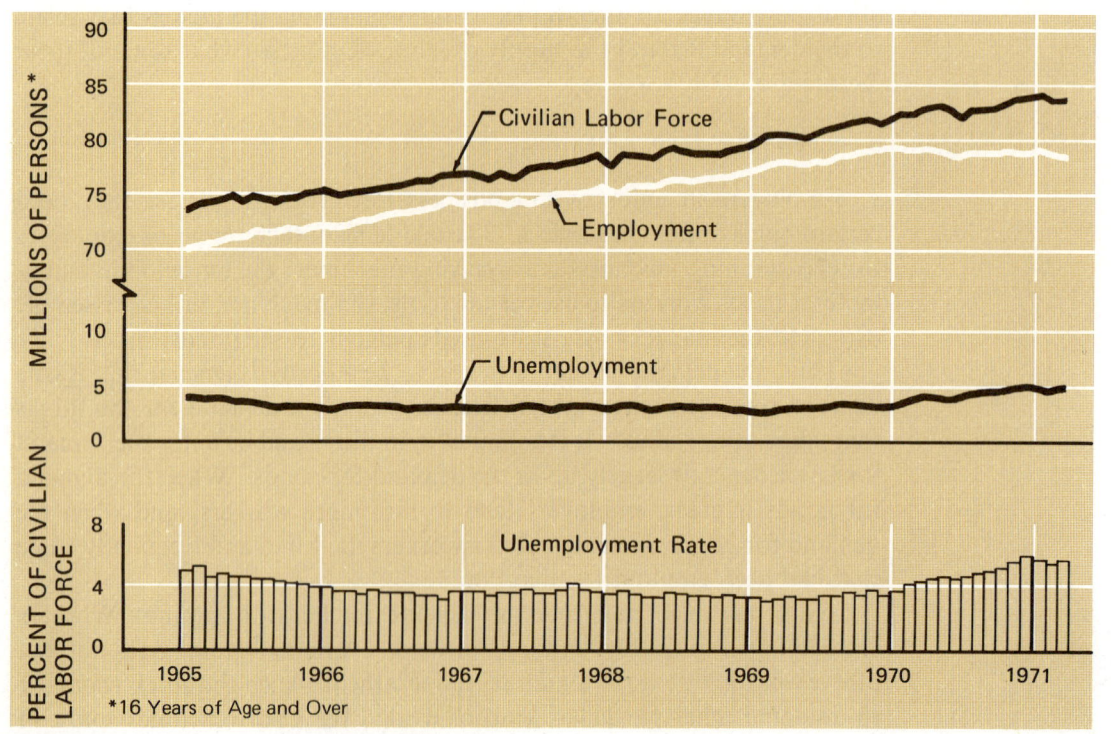

Figure 14-2.   SOURCE: Department of Labor.

LABOR FORCE

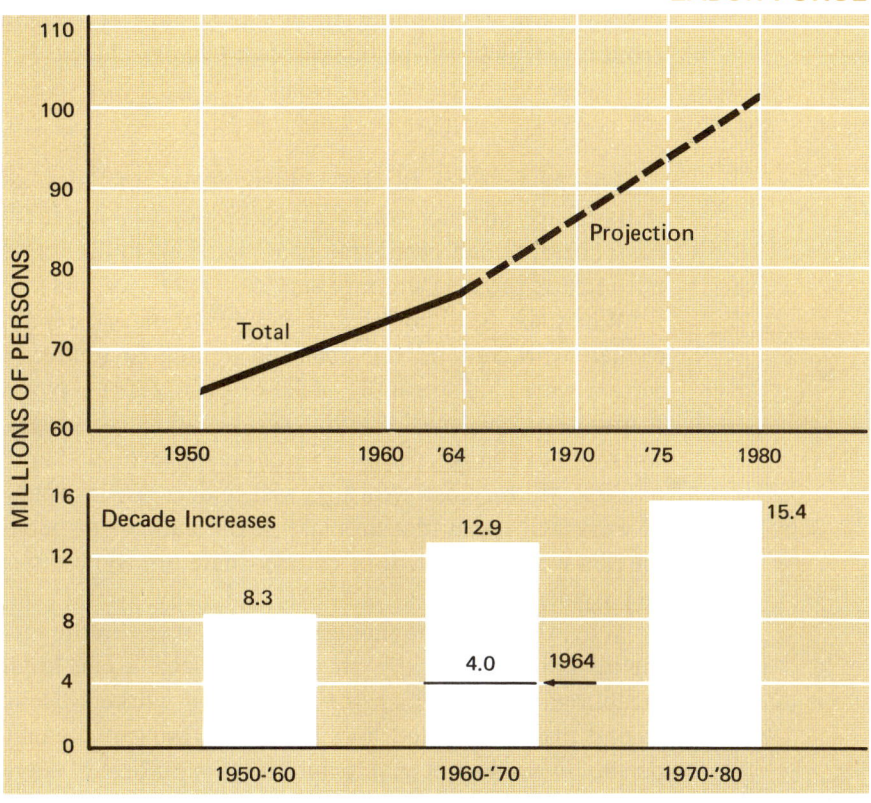

Figure 14-3.

National Industrial Conference Board, Inc.

An annual average addition of 1½ million to the labor force was expected between 1964 and 1970. (The civilian labor force consists of those persons 16 years and over who are employed or looking for work.) This increase represented a substantial change from our 1960–64 experience, when annual additions to the labor force averaged under 1 million. The 1964–70 rate of addition is expected to carry over into the 1970–80 decade.

A projection of labor force depends on two other projections: that of population and that of the labor force participation rate (percentage of the population in the labor force).... The labor force participation rates, in the aggregate, are expected to change only slightly from 56.5% in 1964 and 57.5% in 1970 to 58.3% in 1980.

jobs than are abolished. Others maintain that it decreases the need for workers and therefore reduces the demand for labor; and the reduction, according to many observers, will become much more pronounced in the future. One important viewpoint on this subject was expressed by the President's National Commission on Technology, Automation, and Economic Progress when it stated, "If unemployment does creep upward in the future, it will be the fault of public policy, not the fault of technological change."* Among other things, the commission emphasized the necessity for maintaining an adequate rate of economic growth in the economy, which will be discussed in Chapter 23.

WHAT IS MEANT BY THE SUPPLY OF LABOR?

The *labor force* in the United States includes all persons sixteen years of age or older who are working or looking for work. The *civilian labor force*, which numbered more than 84 million persons in 1971, does not include those in military service.

When we speak of the supply of labor, we refer to the number of civilian workers who are able and willing to render certain services for certain wages. The supply of labor of any given type varies with wages. If wages for one kind of work increase while the wages for other kinds of work do not change, the number of persons who will apply for the first kind of work will increase also. Likewise, a decrease in wages for a certain kind of work will result in a decrease in the number of persons who will apply for this work, provided, of course, there are some other opportunities for employment.

Why, then, do not changes in wages result in an equal supply of labor for all kinds of work? In the first place, some kinds of work require exceptional talent, which the majority of workers do not possess. In the second place, rules and laws frequently prevent the employment of those persons who do not give evidence of a sufficient degree of skill or who have not otherwise met the established requirements. In some of the professions, certain requirements under the law must be met before one may practice the profession.

As is shown in Figure 14-4, people as a rule have a longer work-life expectancy than they used to. This tends to increase the labor supply, although the percentage of teen-agers in the labor force is smaller than formerly, and more workers retire at an earlier age than was true before the passage of the Social Security Act in 1935.

What are the characteristics of labor? Labor possesses certain characteristics that we should understand when considering problems relating to the supply of labor.

(1) Labor is perishable. Although the employer must look upon the cost of labor much as he does upon the cost of raw materials, labor is

---

*Report of the National Commission on Technology, Automation, and Economic Progress — Technology and the American Economy, Vol. 1 (February 1966), p. 27.

INCREASE IN PRODUCTIVE YEARS

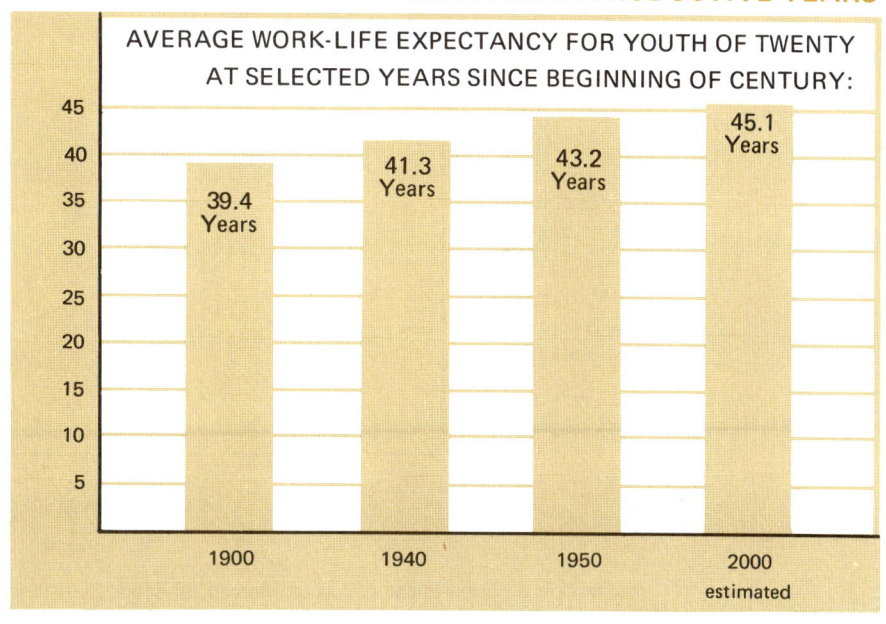

AVERAGE WORK-LIFE EXPECTANCY FOR YOUTH OF TWENTY AT SELECTED YEARS SINCE BEGINNING OF CENTURY:

1900	39.4 Years
1940	41.3 Years
1950	43.2 Years
2000 (estimated)	45.1 Years

Figure 14-4.

SOURCE: U.S. Bureau of Labor Statistics.

different from materials. It is absolutely perishable. It cannot be stored. A day lost by a worker can never be regained.

This characteristic of the labor supply is important for two reasons. In the first place, the worker is at a disadvantage in trying to bargain with an employer. He cannot hold out for higher wages without losing forever a part of the labor that he has to sell. In the second place, lost labor results in the production of a smaller amount of goods and services than might be produced if all labor were utilized. This fact is of importance to all consumers of goods and services.

(2) Labor cannot be separated from the person. Unlike goods, labor is always associated with a person. When an individual sells his labor, something more than the labor is involved. For example, the worker must consider working conditions when he offers to sell a day's services. To work a day for $20 in a poorly ventilated, evil-smelling factory is quite different from working for the same amount of money in a well-lighted and well-ventilated factory.

(3) The supply of labor does not change quickly. From 10 to 15 years of work experience are sometimes required for individuals to become sufficiently qualified to hold certain kinds of jobs. Of course, in time of war

PROJECTED PERCENT CHANGE IN EMPLOYMENT OF WORKERS IN MAJOR OCCUPATIONAL GROUPS, 1968 - 1980

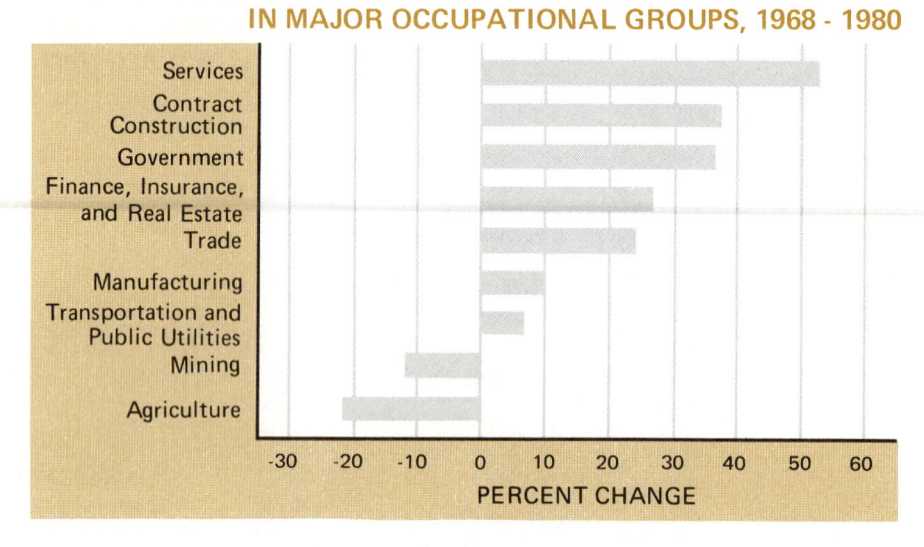

Figure 14-5.

SOURCE: U.S. Department of Labor, Bureau of Labor Statistics, *Occupational Outlook Handbook*.

women and retired workers not ordinarily employed in business and industry may go to work in factories and offices, and as a result the total supply of labor may quickly increase. But under normal conditions the supply of labor does not change greatly within a brief period of time.

(4) Most workers do not like to move from one community to another. Such goods as wheat, cotton, or articles of wearing apparel can be shipped easily from one place to another. But individuals as a rule do not like to move from one community to another, even when they can obtain higher wages by doing so. Family, friends, church affiliations, customs, and community ties tend to keep the worker where he has lived.

Standards of living and the labor supply. We shall avoid confusion and misunderstanding if we make clear what we mean by the expression "standard of living." Therefore, let us say that by *standard of living* we mean the way that one aims or expects to live, and by *scale of living*, the way he actually lives.

Those who have high standards of living seek to earn incomes that will enable them to bring their scales of living up to their standards of living. For example, they work hard, try to increase their skill and their

Illus. 14-1. Although the employer must look upon the cost of labor much as he does upon the cost of raw materials, labor is different from materials. It is absolutely perishable. It cannot be stored. A day lost by a worker can never be regained.

Thiokol Chemical Corporation

knowledge of their jobs, and may join a labor union. Or they may postpone marriage until they are in position to earn more income.

Although the rule has exceptions, it is noticeable that the lower the standard of living, the earlier people get married and the larger are their families. Consequently, as the standard of living increases, population tends to increase more slowly than it does when standards are lower. Meanwhile, the amount of capital and laborsaving machinery increases, which enables workers to produce more per worker. In other words, because of the increase in capital and because the number of workers becomes smaller in relation to the amount of capital available for productive purposes, the marginal productivity of workers rises, which makes higher wages possible.

LAWS AFFECT THE SUPPLY OF LABOR

One function of government is to "promote the general welfare." To do this, it is desirable to have certain laws that limit or prohibit the employment of children, and other laws that impose certain regulations over the employment of both men and women. Such laws affect the labor supply by limiting either the number of individuals who may work or the amount of work they may do under certain conditions.

Child labor. As a rule *child labor* has been defined as the gainful employment of persons between ten and fifteen years of age. Workers between fifteen and eighteen years of age are often referred to as young persons, rather than as children.

Even before the Industrial Revolution there were children who worked. But the coming of the factory system increased the number of kinds of work that children could perform. Operating many of the types of machines in factories requires comparatively little skill or training. As a rule, the wages necessary to induce children and young persons to work are less than those paid to older workers. In many cases the need to earn additional money with which to aid in supporting themselves and their families influences children and youths to seek work. And in some instances students lose interest in school activities. For these reasons there is a strong tendency for great numbers of children and young persons, who should be in school, to try to find work in industry unless there are laws that prohibit such employment. The situation of the school "dropout" is especially tragic in an era when the young person can most easily afford to remain in school and when society can least afford to lose the skills and knowledge that more years of schooling will provide him.

For a long time it was believed that the federal and the state constitutions did not permit the passage of laws that would prevent child labor. But during the last fifty to sixty years there has been a growing sentiment on the part of the public against the regular employment of children and young persons. As a result, federal and state laws have been enacted and upheld by the courts which discourage the practice of gainful employment by children.

Common features of the laws regulating child labor are: (1) a minimum-age limit, usually 14, under which employment for wages is prohibited; (2) the prohibition of work in dangerous occupations for persons under 18 years of age; (3) a maximum number of hours per day or week beyond which young persons may not work for wages; (4) the prohibition of night work; and (5) the necessity for attendance at school during a part of the year. In some of the states the standards are not so high as these. Most of such regulations do not apply to agriculture.

The federal Fair Labor Standards Act (1938) attempts to discourage the employment of young persons in interstate industries and commerce. The law prohibits the employment of persons under 16 years of age in industries and commercial businesses engaged in interstate commerce, except when the person is employed by his parents in an occupation other than manufacturing or mining. It also prohibits the employment of

Ch. 14 WAGES FOR LABOR

MORE JOBS WILL REQUIRE EXTENSIVE EDUCATION AND TRAINING

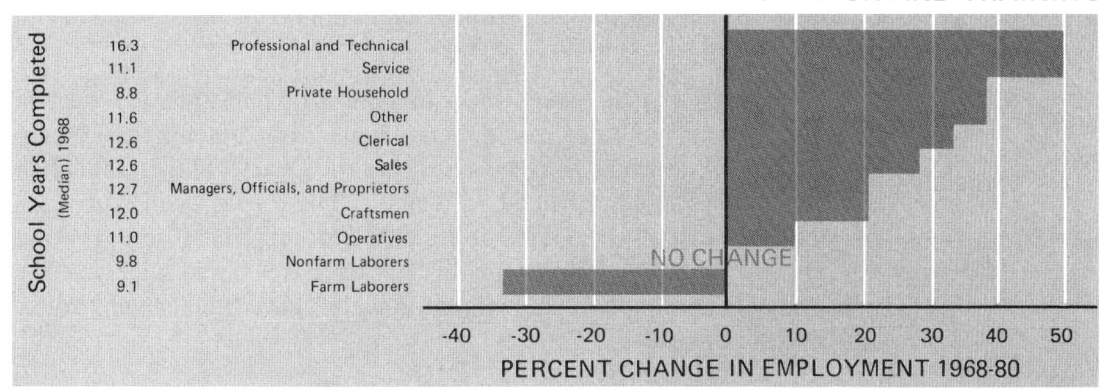

School Years Completed (Median) 1968

16.3	Professional and Technical
11.1	Service
8.8	Private Household
11.6	Other
12.6	Clerical
12.6	Sales
12.7	Managers, Officials, and Proprietors
12.0	Craftsmen
11.0	Operatives
9.8	Nonfarm Laborers
9.1	Farm Laborers

PERCENT CHANGE IN EMPLOYMENT 1968-80

UNEMPLOYMENT RATES ARE HIGHEST FOR YOUNG WORKERS

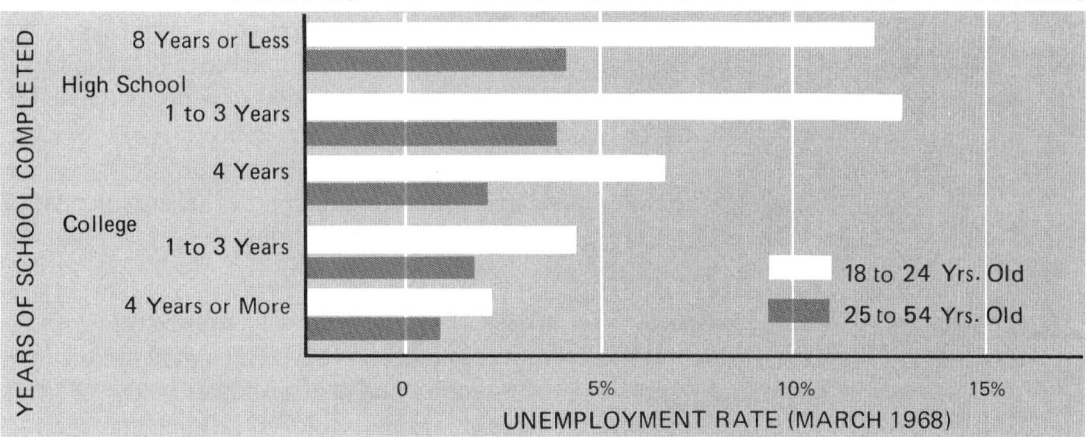

YEARS OF SCHOOL COMPLETED:
- 8 Years or Less
- High School: 1 to 3 Years
- 4 Years
- College: 1 to 3 Years
- 4 Years or More

□ 18 to 24 Yrs. Old
■ 25 to 54 Yrs. Old

UNEMPLOYMENT RATE (MARCH 1968)

ESTIMATED LIFETIME EARNINGS FOR MEN ARE HIGHER FOR THOSE WITH MORE EDUCATION

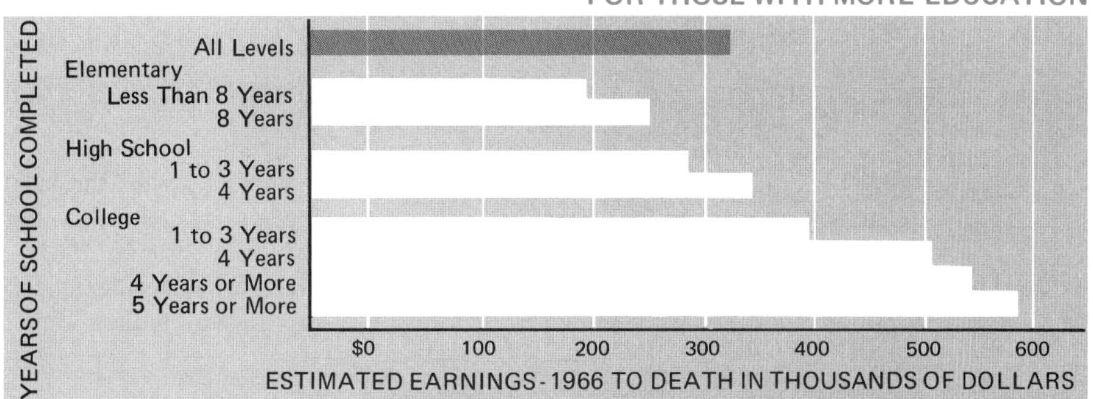

YEARS OF SCHOOL COMPLETED:
- All Levels
- Elementary: Less Than 8 Years
- 8 Years
- High School: 1 to 3 Years
- 4 Years
- College: 1 to 3 Years
- 4 Years
- 4 Years or More
- 5 Years or More

ESTIMATED EARNINGS - 1966 TO DEATH IN THOUSANDS OF DOLLARS

Figure 14-6.   SOURCE: U.S. Dept. of Labor, Bureau of Labor Statistics.

persons under 18 years of age in occupations that are considered by the Children's Bureau of the Department of Labor as being detrimental to health.

The regulation of the employment of women. The Supreme Court of the United States has ruled that the employment of women may be regulated by law. As early as 1935, 44 states and the District of Columbia had laws regulating the employment of women. These laws dealt with such matters as hours of employment, restricted occupations, and working conditions. State regulations on this matter have varied widely. The trend today is to eliminate these regulations that have been enacted solely on the basis of sex.

The regulation of the employment of men. For many years the right of government to regulate the hours and working conditions of men has been recognized. But the question of just how far government can go in the exercise of this power is not clear. Except to a limited extent, the federal government cannot regulate labor in a state if the labor is not employed in interstate industry or commerce. That right is reserved to the state legislatures.

Nearly all the states have laws for the regulation of the employment of men. There is, however, so much diversity among these laws that we cannot enter upon a discussion of their provisions.

The Walsh-Healey Act of 1936. This federal law requires that persons working on government contracts in excess of $10,000 be paid no less than the prevailing wages in the community and that no males below 16 years of age or females below 18 years of age be employed on such contracts.

The Fair Labor Standards Act of 1938. This law is popularly known as the federal Wage and Hour Law. In some respects it is the most important law dealing with labor and wages ever passed by Congress. The law applies to employees who are engaged in manufacturing, mining, transporting, handling, or in any way having anything to do with goods or services that move in interstate commerce.

The Act fixes the standard workweek at 40 hours. Under the 1966 amendment to the law, minimum wages for most of the covered employees are established according to the following schedule: February, 1967 — $1.40; February, 1968 — $1.60.* Coverage of the law has been extended to include not only industrial workers but also several million retail,

---

*Proposed amendments to the law would increase the minimum hourly wage to $2 or $2.50 and broaden the coverage by eliminating some of the minimum wage and overtime requirements.

service, and farm employees. Many states also have minimum wage laws covering persons who are not engaged in interstate commerce.

The federal law attempts to lessen the amount of employment of children. No distinction, however, is made between the employment of men and the employment of women.

The Civil Rights Act of 1964. This law includes a section on fair employment practices. It forbids discrimination in employment on the basis of race, religion, color, sex, or national origin.

HOW, THEN, DO DEMAND AND SUPPLY ACTUALLY AFFECT WAGES?

Let us see now what are the conclusions concerning the influence of the demand for and the supply of labor on the wages that individuals actually receive under conditions of free competition.

(1) The productivity of workers determines the maximum wages that employers can pay; but it does not always indicate the amount that they do actually pay.

(2) When the labor supply in a particular industry is small relative to demand, the marginal productivity will be high; conversely, an increase in the labor supply results in an increase in the number of workers that will be employed, which will cause a decrease in the marginal productivity of workers in that industry.

(3) Under conditions of pure competition, employers would be inclined to continue to employ workers up to the point where the marginal product — the value of the product of the last worker hired — would just equal the value of the wages necessary to induce the employee to work.

In a purely competitive labor market, wages would equal the value of the product of the last worker employed. But in order to have pure competition, there would have to be a great number of employers so that no one employer would have even a partial monopoly of jobs. Workers in each class or kind of work would be alike, so that it would not matter to an employer which one he hired. Workers would have to be willing to move freely from one place to another; and it would be necessary for them to have information as to where they could obtain the highest wages possible. There would have to be a large number of workers, so that no one worker could have even a partial monopoly of the supply of labor. And, finally, there could be no labor unions.

In actual practice, these conditions usually do not exist. For example, there may be only one or only a few employers in a community. Usually there are considerable differences in the quality of workers. Wage earners do not like to move from one locality to another, nor do they always know where they can obtain higher wages. In some cases the number of skilled workers is very small; and in some cases a labor union may be able to limit the number of workers who are available for particular jobs. For these reasons we can see that the price that is paid for most kinds of labor is not fixed by the same high degree of competition that determines some commodity prices. In most cases there is an element of competition, but there are other factors that help to determine just what contractual wages are paid.

OTHER FACTORS AFFECT WAGES

In most localities, custom has an important influence on wages. For example, there is likely to be a customary average for the wages paid domestic and farm helpers, teachers, physicians, and others, as well as many industrial and business workers. Even though custom has an influence on wages in many cases, a marked change in demand for or supply of labor can upset the customary wage. In the case of most employees, minimum wages are fixed by law or government agencies.

Bargaining power also affects wages. Where the number of employers is few and the number of workers many, the actual wage rate may be considerably below the actual productivity of the workers in a group. It is easy to see why this is true. Since there are many workers, an employer who has a large degree of monopoly in the labor market is not compelled to hire any particular worker. It makes little difference to him whether he hires Jones or Smith as long as they are of about the same ability. Therefore, if the wage rate is to be determined by bargaining, the employer will hire the worker who is willing to accept employment at the lowest wage. On the other hand, since there may be few or even no other opportunities for employment, it does make a great deal of difference to the individual worker whether he gets the job.

Those who believe that workers should organize say that only by belonging to a labor union can the individual become equal in bargaining power to the employer. It can be noted that union bargaining power sometimes exceeds that of employers. We shall discuss the aims and accomplishments of labor unions in Chapter 18.

WHAT DO WE MEAN BY GAW AND SUB?

Theoretically the two are distinctly different, but in practice they are closely related. A *guaranteed annual wage* (GAW) agreement means that the employer agrees to pay his employees a specified wage for a certain number of weeks even if the workers are laid off because of lack of work. The number of weeks is fixed by agreement between the employer and the employees. *Supplementary unemployment benefit* (SUB) plans provide for employer-financed funds out of which benefits received from state unemployment compensation are supplemented according to a negotiated formula. Several large companies have SUB contracts of one kind or another with their employees.

Those who advocate the guaranteed annual wage plan say that: (1) it will provide incomes for workers who are laid off, which will be good for business, since unemployed workers will still have money to spend; (2) it will cause management to regularize or stabilize employment by diversifying their production, that is, producing more than one kind of seasonable merchandise; and (3) it is only fair that employees have greater security of income.

Those who oppose the guaranteed annual wage plan argue that: (1) it is incorrect to think that all industries can operate the year round at a constant level of production and employment; (2) the annual wage plan will discourage employers from adding a larger number of workers to their labor force in times of prosperity, when they know that it will probably be necessary to lay off workers at some future time; and (3) it will result in inflation and higher prices, which will be unfortunate for persons not covered by an annual wage agreement. In fact, some critics of the plan have asserted that the adoption of the plan may inevitably lead to some form of a planned economy or socialism.

Cost-of-living wage agreements. Some collective-bargaining agreements between employers and unions contain *cost-of-living* or *escalator wage clauses*. Such clauses require that specified wage adjustments be made according to changes in the cost of living as indicated by the Consumer Price Index issued by the Bureau of Labor Statistics. Cost of living clauses may be an important part of the wage contract, especially in periods of inflation.

The annual improvement factor. Wage negotiations generally provide for a minimum increase for all workers covered by the agreement. The agreements between employers and unions sometimes provide for an additional annual percentage increase in wages. This latter provision for an annual increase is based on the assumption that the productivity of workers will constantly increase due to improved methods of production. It is referred to as the *annual improvement factor*.

SUMMARY

About three fourths of the national income goes to those who work for wages and salaries. Wages — including fees, commissions, and salaries — are prices that are paid for labor that is expended in the production of economic goods and services.

Real wages — the amount of goods and services that money wages will purchase — must be earned before they can be paid. Marginal productivity limits the amount that can be paid to workers, but it does not always determine the amount that employers actually pay.

One explanation that has been advanced to explain wages and wage rates is the demand-and-supply theory.

The demand for labor means the amount of labor of a certain kind that will be used in production at various wage rates. This includes the labor of both employees and self-employed workers. The demand for labor is derived from the demand for what labor produces.

The supply of labor means the amount of labor that will be offered for use in production at different wage rates. Like demand, the supply of labor is always specific. These characteristics affect the supply of labor: labor is perishable; labor cannot be separated from the person; the supply of labor does not change quickly; and labor is not highly mobile. Standards of living affect the supply of labor, and certain laws for the control of wages and the regulation of labor may also affect the supply of labor.

Several federal and a number of state laws affect the supply of some kinds of labor. Among these laws are those that pertain to child labor, the regulation of the labor of women and of men, the Walsh-Healey Act, and the Wage and Hour Law.

Keeping in mind what we have said, we may say that wages and wage rates depend upon the demand for and the supply of labor. At the same time, the following other factors usually affect wage rates: custom, public authority, monopoly, and bargaining by employers and employees.

The movement toward the adoption of guaranteed wage plans and supplementary unemployment benefits is gaining momentum in large segments of industry and business. We do not know now just how far the movement will go and what its effects on the different kinds of workers will be.

NEW TERMS

annual improvement factor
child labor
civilian labor force
Civil Rights Act of 1964
cost-of-living *or* escalator wage clauses
derived demand
Fair Labor Standards Act
guaranteed annual wage
imputed wages
labor force
marginal productivity theory of wages

money *or* nominal wages
real wages
scale of living
standard of living
supplementary unemployment benefits
Wage and Hour Law
wage rates
wages
wages of management
Walsh-Healey Act

QUESTIONS ON THE CHAPTER

1. What portion of the national income is usually distributed in the form of wages?
2. What is meant by "imputed wages"?
3. What are some of the types of income that may be included in "wages"?
4. What is "automation"? Why are its probable effects controversial?
5. What is the relation of marginal productivity to wages?
6. What effect do demand and supply have on wages?
7. What is meant by the expression "labor is perishable"?
8. What are the several characteristics of labor? Which do you consider the most important?
9. In what way do standards of living affect the supply of labor?
10. What factors other than demand and supply affect wages? Explain.
11. What is the nature of each of the two types of automatic wage changes that are provided in some bargaining agreements?

APPLYING YOUR ECONOMIC UNDERSTANDING

1. A student purchased a powered snowplow and contracted to clear driveways and walks at prices which varied with the size of the job. Is his net income after paying expenses a form of wage? Is it a wage of management? Why or why not?
2. A drive-in restaurant owner can increase his business by adding another worker. How can he determine whether he should hire the extra worker in order to increase his business income?
3. Although the total number of persons employed each year increases, the total number of unemployed persons may remain at a high level. Does this confirm the idea that the supply of labor does not change quickly? Explain your answer.
4. Do the Wage and Hour Act and its amendments affect workers in your community? Why or why not?
5. What is one of the lowest wages paid in your community? What is one of the highest wages paid in your community? Explain.
6. Is the labor in your area mobile or immobile? Defend your answer. How does the mobility or immobility affect the rates paid for local labor?
7. Would you personally prefer a job paying piece-rate wages or fixed wages? Give the reasons which support your answer.
8. Does the increase in the minimum wage rate set by Congress increase real income? Why or why not?

CHALLENGES TO ECONOMIC COMPETENCE

1. Present a mock Senate committee hearing on a proposed bill to increase the minimum wage rate.
2. Prepare a graph showing the major occupational groups in your community.
3. Select one of the major federal laws affecting labor and prepare both a synopsis of it as well as conclusions concerning its importance.
4. Write an article about the Guaranteed Annual Wage (GAW) or the Supplementary Unemployment Benefits (SUB).
5. Prepare an oral report on the topic "Is the Escalator Clause a Boon or a Burden?"

Chapter 15

Rent for Land

Exactly what do we mean by rent?
What relation exists between the price paid for land and the rent from the land?
What are the factors that affect the demand for and the supply of land?
Which of our social problems are related to the rent of land?

Manhattan Island is a part of New York City. It has an area of about 22 square miles. In 1626 when Peter Minuit, the Dutch colonizer, purchased the island from the Indians, he paid for it in merchandise — cloth and trinkets valued at 60 guilders. It has been estimated that at the time of the purchase, the price was $24!

Today on this island stand the Empire State Building, Lincoln Center, Rockefeller Center, the United Nations buildings, railroad terminals, and other well-known structures of which you have heard and which you have possibly seen. At the lower end of the island are Wall Street, the New York and the American stock exchanges, the offices of some of the world's largest banks, and many other kinds of business. Fifth Avenue is famous as a shopping center, and Broadway is the heart of the theatrical world.

What do you suppose Manhattan Island is worth today? No one knows. But a fair estimate of its value would run into many billions of dollars. In most places on the island, if you owned only a very small lot of land, you could sell it for a great deal of money. Or you could probably rent it to some business concern and receive a handsome income.

Why is the land so valuable now? The answer is that the rent of the land has increased. Moreover, it is the rent of land that determines the value of land in your city or community. Since this is true, you will agree that the subject of rent is important. If we could calculate accurately the amount of the rental value of all the urban and rural land in the United

242   DISTRIBUTION OF NATIONAL INCOME   Unit 4

Illus. 15-1. Manhattan Island is a part of New York City. In 1626 when Peter Minuit, the Dutch colonizer, purchased the island from the Indians, he paid for it in merchandise — cloth and trinkets valued at 60 guilders. It has been estimated that at the time of the purchase, the price was $24!

Culver Pictures

Illus. 15-2. What do you suppose Manhattan Island is worth today? No one knows. But a fair estimate of its value would run into many billions of dollars.

American Airlines

States for one year, we would find that the total would amount to many billions of dollars.

WHAT IS THE NATURE OF RENT?

The term *rent* is often used in various contexts. One may rent a house, an automobile, a city lot, a book, a tuxedo, a motorboat, or a farm. In each case, we note that the supply of what is rented is limited and that in most cases it is rather durable — it does not wear out quickly.

In Chapter 4 we saw that land consists of all natural resources that have been created without man's labor. Since land is durable and the arable supply remains about the same from year to year, the return from the use of land is often referred to as *economic rent*, or simply as *rent*. In this chapter let us restrict our study of the returns from the use of durable goods to that of land. For certain purposes of study it is convenient to define rent as income from land — natural resources — and interest as the return from the use of capital — man-made goods used to produce other goods and services.

Contract or commercial rent. If I rent a plot of farmland or a city lot from you, I pay an amount of money for the use of the land for a certain period of time, such as a year or longer. The amount is fixed by agreement and may be referred to as *contract* or *commercial rent*.

Economic rent. What determines the amount of contract or commercial rent that one is willing to pay for a piece of land? It depends upon one's estimate of the value of the economic rent of the land.

But what is economic rent? *Economic rent* is the annual value of the income or product from a plot of land in excess of the cost of producing that income. For example, if the income from a plot of land over a period of a year is $1,000 and if the cost of producing that income amounts to $900, the economic rent is $100, which is imputed to the land for its productive contribution.

MARGINAL, SUBMARGINAL, AND SUPRAMARGINAL LAND

Marginal land is land from which the product or income is just equal to the cost of producing that product or income. It is no-rent land. For example, if a farmer applies $100 worth of labor and capital to a plot of land and the yield is an amount of wheat that can be sold for $100, the land is said to be *marginal*. If the value of the wheat was only $90, the land would be *submarginal*. That is to say, submarginal land is land the product or income from which is less than the cost of producing the product or income.

If the value of the product or income was, say, $110, the land would be *supramarginal*, which means that the return from the land would be greater than the cost of production. What we have said can be illustrated by the use of the table at the top of the next page.

SUBMARGINAL, MARGINAL, AND SUPRAMARGINAL LAND

Land plot	Cost of utilizing land	Value of wheat produced	Amount of rent	Classification of the land
A	$100	$90	$–10	Submarginal
B	$100	$100	0	Marginal
C	$100	$110	$10	Supramarginal

THE LAW OF DIMINISHING RETURNS AFFECTS RENT

Now let us see how the law of diminishing returns would cause rent to arise even if all land were equally good but limited as to supply. Suppose that Mr. Ray has two units of labor and capital of $100 each, making a total of $200 of labor and capital, that he wishes to spend on the cultivation of land. Let us say that he owns a parcel of land and that Mr. Mason owns a similar parcel of equally productive land which he would allow Mr. Ray to use if Mr. Ray would pay him something for its use.

Now suppose that from past experience Mr. Ray knows that, if he spends $100 on his own land, his return will be about 200 bushels of wheat. If he spends $200 on his land, he will probably get 375 bushels. But, since Mason's land is equally productive, he would get a total of 400 bushels if he spent $100 on his own land and $100 on Mason's land, or 25 bushels more than if he spent the whole amount on his own land.

Now assume that the price of wheat is $2 a bushel. As you can see in the following table, the extra 25 bushels would be worth $50. Therefore, he could afford to pay Mason any amount up to $50 for the use of the latter's land and still be better off than if he had spent the $200 on his own land. In this example it is the operation of the law of diminishing returns that makes it worthwhile for Ray to pay Mason something for the use of the latter's land. It is not because of a difference in the fertility of the two parcels of land.

Ray's Expenditure Possibilities	Bushels of Output	Value of Output	Amount Available for Rent
On own land: $200	375	$750	
OR { On own land: $100 plus Mason's land: $100	200 200	$400 $400 } $800	$50

When people are free to engage in agriculture and other kinds of industry and business, some will continue to employ capital and labor in the utilization of land even after the law of diminishing returns sets in; that is, some will continue to add units of labor and capital until the value of the returns from the land is only equal to the cost of producing the product. In such cases the land is being used intensively.

It is the operation of the law of diminishing returns that limits the height of buildings in our cities. The rent received from the twentieth story may not justify the cost of adding that story to a building.

The preceding discussion explains how rent can arise from either or both of two causes: (1) differences in the fertility or productivity of land and (2) the working of the law of diminishing returns. In actual practice in the world of business and industry, both the differences in the productivity of land and the operation of the law of diminishing returns work together to produce rent.

WHAT IS MEANT BY THE DEMAND FOR LAND?

The most obvious function of land is that it provides "standing room." In spite of the fact that man has learned to fly — that he has gone to the moon, and that he is able to live under the surface of the water in submersible ships — we are still bound pretty closely to the earth's surface. Most of us stand on or move over the surface of the earth most of the time. In addition, our houses, factories, highways, railroads, playgrounds, schools, and other structures are on sites provided by the land.

As a factor in production, land contributes all the original material things that are used in the production of goods. Man creates greater utility in the materials supplied by nature when he changes the form of the materials into goods. But he is still dependent upon the storehouse of nature for the materials he uses.

Therefore, the demand for land arises from the fact that it furnishes standing room and that the resources of nature are capable of being used in various ways to satisfy our wants. In some cases land can be used directly to meet our needs, as in the case of playgrounds and natural parks. In other cases it can be used indirectly, as when we take ores and convert them into different kinds of goods.

Land in residential districts is not wanted for the production of goods. The demand for this land, particularly where separate residences are the rule, arises largely because of the utility of the land for consumer uses. The user, whether a tenant or an owner, wants the land because it possesses certain qualities that are desirable for residential purposes.

Land that is wanted for the growth of agricultural crops, the erection of factories, the cutting of lumber, or the erection of stores and other kinds of business structures is wanted for productive purposes.

THE SUPPLY OF LAND IS LIMITED

Land is always wanted for some particular purpose. For example, if one wants to grow oranges, he must go to Florida or California or some other place where the soil and the climate are suitable. But land in these regions is not unlimited. Or if he wants to open a store in the very best business district in a town or a city, he will find that the number of better sites is also limited.

Unlike the supplies of most goods, such as automobiles, shoes, lathes, and bread, we cannot readily increase the supply of arable land. In Holland some areas of land have been reclaimed from the ocean by building sea walls. Irrigation has made some additional land available for agricultural purposes. But instances such as these are exceptions to the rule. Moreover, they do not represent examples of creating land, but simply result in changing the form or the utility of existing land by making it available for man's use.

DEMAND AND SUPPLY DETERMINE COMMERCIAL RENT

Like the prices of commodities, the prices that owners of land receive for the use of their lands are fixed by the demand for and the available supply of land that may be used for particular purposes. As a rule, the amount of commercial rent that a tenant pays is fixed by agreement. Both the owner and the prospective tenant form their opinions as to the productivity of a given piece of land. The owner endeavors to obtain as high a rental price as he can; and the prospective tenant tries to obtain the use of the land for as low a price as possible.

SOME AGRICULTURAL PROBLEMS ARE CONNECTED WITH RENT

For many years the government has followed a policy of supporting the prices of farm products. In justification of this policy it was pointed out that the incomes of many farmers had declined as compared with other classes of incomes from industry and business. It was asserted that, because of the nature of the agricultural industry, the farmers were unable to help themselves.

Changes in prices cause changes in rent. In recent decades farms in the United States have become much more productive than formerly. Among the reasons for this increased productivity have been the rapid increase in the use of mechanical power and machinery, crop rotation, fertilizers, improved kinds of plants and livestock, better transportation facilities, and the increased utilization of irrigated lands in some parts of the country. All these things have increased the supplies of farm products, and often at a reduced cost.

As a result, farm prices, especially as compared with the prices of the things farmers had to buy, declined. As farm prices declined, the economic rent of farmland decreased, which reduced the farmer's net income. So, by guaranteeing minimum farm prices, the government, in effect, undertook to keep the economic rent of farmland high, or at least to keep it from falling too low.

This experience suggests a fact recognized by economists, namely, that high rents do not cause high prices. But high prices may result in high rents. In other words, the prices of the products or services of land determine the amount of land rent. A rise in the amount of income from land causes rent to rise; a decline in income results in a decrease in rent.

The use of irrigated lands creates a problem for the cotton states. Irrigation projects in the western states have opened up vast fertile areas suitable for growing cotton that are also well adapted to the use of tractor power and machinery. As a result, and partly because of the high price of cotton fostered by the government, much of the cotton produced in the United States is grown in the western states. About 50 percent of the cotton produced in this country is grown in Texas, New Mexico, Arizona, and California, much of it on irrigated farms. The states east of the Mississippi River, which long composed the most important cotton-growing region in the world, produce relatively less cotton than formerly.

As it becomes more and more profitable to employ the use of machinery in the larger and more fertile fields, other fields that are smaller and less fertile may sink to the marginal or submarginal level when used for cotton production. Consequently, more and more southern cotton farmers are faced with the necessity of deciding whether they will (1) continue to try to grow cotton and lower their scale of living, (2) find employment in some other industry, (3) adopt some other kind of agricultural crop, (4) turn to cattle raising, or (5) allow their land to grow pine trees for use as pulpwood or sawtimber. In any event difficult adjustments are involved.

Land erosion reduces the rent from agricultural land. From colonial days until comparatively recently few farmers attempted to do much about the washing or erosion of their land. In the early days of Virginia, Thomas Jefferson once wrote, "... we can buy an acre of new land cheaper than we manure an old acre. ..." But those days have long ago passed into history.

Much of our land is rapidly being damaged by erosion, which is a source of increasing social concern as population increases. Many farmers are making attempts to prevent their land from washing away and to restore its fertility. The Soil Conservation Service provides advice and seedlings to farmers willing to undertake a conservation program.

THE CITY SLUM PROBLEM IS CONNECTED WITH RENT

Among the problems which most cities have in common is that of poor-residential and slum, or ghetto, areas. Why do these areas exist?

The underlying reason for the existence of the poor-housing and slum areas in cities is that most of the people who live there cannot afford to pay enough rent to make it profitable for owners to construct and maintain better houses. That is to say, the income that can be obtained from improved or modern housing facilities would not be enough to cause the land to yield sufficient rent to justify the building of better housing facilities.

In recent years the government has undertaken to do something about the improvement of housing conditions in both cities and rural areas. The government has made long-term loans available to cities and to farmers for the construction of new and modern houses. City and state governments are carrying on programs for better housing for their people.

Illus. 15-3. Among the problems which most cities have in common is that of poor-residential and slum, or ghetto, areas.

AFL-CIO

DO LANDOWNERS EARN RENT?

As population increases, the amount of available land decreases in proportion to the number who need land. As population increases, the rent of land tends to rise. Because of these facts it has been claimed by some that the rent and increases in wealth due to increases in land values are forms of *unearned income;* that is, those who receive commercial rent as a form of private income do not earn it.

Those who take this position maintain that the owners did not create the land; that income in the form of rent that the owners receive is the result of population increase.

From earliest times there have been people who have argued that it is not right for private individuals to receive rent from land. But it was Henry George, in his book *Progress and Poverty* published in 1879, who at that time popularized the idea of taking away the rent of land by means of a single tax. He insisted that the private ownership of land is the underlying cause of poverty. He argued that those who own land can compel tenants to pay the owners incomes to which they are not entitled.

George contended that all income from land ownership should be taxed 100 percent. He maintained that, if this were done, the income to government would be sufficient to defray all the expenses of government, which would make it possible to do away with all other kinds of taxes. Hence, the proposal is often referred to as the *single-tax proposal*.

Before the arguments against the single tax are reviewed, it can be noted that the single-tax movement has had some important effects. For one thing, it called attention to the political and social power that ownership of land gives the owners of a great deal of valuable land. For another thing, discussions of the single-tax proposal have helped to cause students of taxation to study real estate taxes more carefully. However, there are those who feel that the tax on land that is not being used should be increased and that the tax on land that is being used for residential buildings should be decreased. This, it is contended, would help to eliminate slums.

But the single-tax argument carries little weight with most of the people today. Why? In the first place, it is argued that the single tax would violate our basic institution of private property. From the social standpoint, land is a gift of nature, but this is not the case for the person who has purchased land. Those persons who originally acquired ownership of free land died long ago, and in many cases, present owners have purchased land through savings just as one might purchase ownership of any other form of wealth.

Second, it is argued that if income from one form of natural creation is to be confiscated, in equity the principle must be extended to other forms of natural advantage. For example, the principle would justify confiscation of most of the earnings of the singer who is endowed by nature with unusual talents and of the actress whose beauty charms millions of theatergoers.

Third, it is argued that it would be impossible to determine accurately what amount of national income can be called land rent. And if this were possible, the amount would be wholly inadequate to meet the needs of all levels of modern government, which together spend approximately 40 percent of all income produced.

RENT ALLOCATES SCARCE RESOURCES ECONOMICALLY

Our discussion of rent offers an opportunity to review the function of factor prices in allocating scarce productive resources. But first, one might ask if rent can be abolished. This is comparable to asking if land can be used without its making a contribution to the productive process. As has been noted, due to the law of diminishing returns, rent would appear in a growing society even if all land were of equal fertility. But land is of different fertility, and, of course, no two plots of land occupy the same site. Therefore, the question is not that of the existence or the nonexistence of rent, but that of who is to receive it.

Since arable land is supplied in almost fixed quantity and its existence is, therefore, not dependent upon a payment of rent, we have seen that rent can be confiscated without destroying the land resource. This is true, but in our capitalistic, price-directed system this argument is beside the point. We have also seen that, like the prices of commodities, the prices that owners of land receive for the use of their lands are fixed by the demand for and the available supply of land that may be used for particular purposes. Prospective users of land will bid for its use on the basis of anticipated marginal productivity. Thus, land that is best suited for the growing of corn will be rented by the corn farmer rather than by the peanut farmer.

We see, therefore, that rent serves the purpose in a private-enterprise economy of allocating land to the most economically productive uses. Rent is the price paid for the use of land; and under competitive conditions, rent will be determined by the value that society places upon the goods or services flowing from the particular land use.

SUMMARY

Ordinarily, the term "rent" refers to the price paid for the use of a durable economic good of any kind. As used in this chapter, the term refers to the return from land. Economic rent is the value of the product of land that is in excess of the cost of utilizing the land. Marginal land is no-rent land. Submarginal land yields a return that is of less value than it costs to utilize the land. Supramarginal land yields rent.

The demand for land is derived from the demand for what land will produce. The demand for land is always specific — it is wanted for certain purposes.

The supply of land — land that can be used for specific purposes — is limited. Unlike man-made goods, the supply of arable land cannot ordinarily be readily increased. Of course, in some cases the supply of land that is available for use may be increased by means of irrigation.

Changes in the prices of goods or services resulting from the use of land cause changes in the amount of economic rent and contract rent.

Many of our social problems, such as the plight of many low-income farmers and those living in slum areas, arise partly from the facts that relate to the rent of land.

The rent of land and increases in the value of land, it has been said, are "unearned increments" of income and wealth, and such income and wealth should be taken by means of taxation and used by government. This is the idea of the "single tax." Arguments for the single tax once attracted considerable attention, but not much is said about it now except by those who would adopt drastic means to reform our economic order.

Rent arises in any economy where land is scarce relative to society's needs for it. In our economy rent accrues to the landowner and serves the social function of allocating scarce land to purposes for which it can be used most economically.

NEW TERMS

contract *or* commercial rent
economic rent
marginal land
rent

single-tax proposal
submarginal land
supramarginal land
unearned income

QUESTIONS ON THE CHAPTER

1. What is the difference between commercial rent and economic rent?
2. What is the difference between submarginal and supramarginal land? Which must pay rent?
3. How is the height of buildings related to the law of diminishing returns?
4. What gives rise to the demand for land?
5. Why is the supply of land fixed? Is this true of capital equipment?
6. What agricultural problems arise in connection with rent?
7. Which statement is more nearly correct: (a) High rents cause high prices; (b) High prices cause high rents? Explain.
8. How has the irrigation of land in the United States affected rent?
9. How may the erosion of land affect rent?
10. What is unearned income?
11. What urban problems arise in connection with rent?

APPLYING YOUR ECONOMIC UNDERSTANDING

1. Bernard rented a formal outfit to wear at his wedding. George rented a U-Haul to bring some things to his college dormitory room. Ethel rented an efficiency apartment. Frank rented 5 acres of land to use for producing melons. Does the word "rented" have the same economic meaning for each of the four situations stated above? Explain your answer.
2. Maburn rents a farm from Williams for $1,200 a year. The price of products grown on the farm increases 50 percent. Could Maburn afford to pay more rent when he renews his rental contract? Suppose Maburn was paying about all he could afford for the rent and prices of farm products had remained the same, but under pressure he agrees to pay $1,500 per year on a re-leasing of the land. Can he recover the increased rent by raising the prices of his products?
3. A suggested solution to the farm problem is to have the government buy up all of the marginal agricultural land. (a) If this proposal were carried out, and if agricultural prices were to fall, what would be the result? (b) If farm prices were to rise 25 percent and the government were not to buy the marginal land, what would result relative to the marginal land?
4. Martin Warner signed a one-year lease to use 320 acres of Herman Anstine's pasture land to graze cattle. Were both commercial and economic rent involved in this transaction? Why or why not?
5. Mr. Jenkins inherited the family home. It is a large 18 room urban dwelling. He does not wish to move into the house; consequently, he plans to rent out the property. For approximately the same remodeling costs, he can renovate it into two or more apartments. After the renovation he can expect annual contracts to bring in total rents of $3,000 for 2 apartments, $3,600 for 3 apartments, $4,000 for 4 apartments, or $3,750 for 5 apartments. Is the law of diminishing returns applicable in this situation? Explain.
6. A friend discusses with you his support of Henry George's proposal that government tax all economic rents up to 100 percent. What ideas could you present to him concerning the disadvantages of adopting the proposal?

CHALLENGES TO ECONOMIC COMPETENCE

1. Make a collection of the forms used in the rental and leasing of property, and arrange them for a bulletin board display.
2. Prepare a bar graph showing the changes in the average rental of different types of property in your community. (Consult a real estate firm.)
3. Prepare as an article suitable for your school newspaper a feature story on one of the following: (a) Land Shortage — The Coming Crisis, (b) How FHA Influences Land Rents, (c) Are the Causes for Slums Economic? (d) Forces That Change Land Values.

Chapter 16

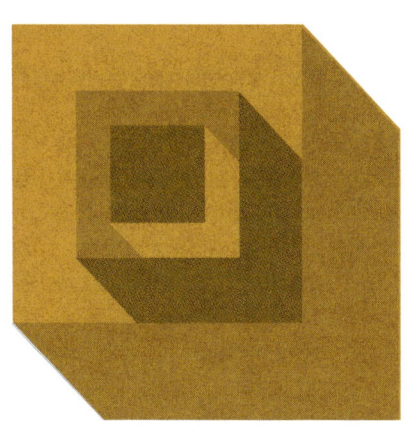

Interest for Capital

Why is interest considered one of the shares of the national income?
How has society's attitude toward the taking of interest changed?
What are the sources of loanable funds?
What determines interest rates?

In the distribution of the national income, a certain amount of the total payments goes to those who are the recipients of income in the form of interest. Interest is the compensation for the owners of capital or man-made goods that are used to produce other goods. It is also said that interest is the price which is paid for the use of a loan of money. Thus, there seem to be two different ideas of the meaning of interest.

This difference, however, is more apparent than real, for a little consideration of the matter will enable you to see the relation between loans of money and the creation of capital goods. In this connection it may be worthwhile to say a word about how interest on loans of money came to be regarded as a respectable way of earning an income.

SOCIETY HAS CHANGED ITS ATTITUDE TOWARD INTEREST

In ancient Greece the word *tokos* meant "offspring" or "increase." Since cattle and land are capable of producing offspring or an increase, it was considered moral for the owners of these types of wealth to accept payment for their use. But money, so it was thought, could not increase by use. According to Aristotle, "Money is intended to be used in exchange, but not to increase at interest." Hence, one who accepted interest was considered to be taking advantage of the need or destitution of the borrower. People did not understand how, by borrowing a sum of money, one might be able to earn enough money with which to repay the principal of the loan and also an extra amount with which to pay interest. This attitude continued in Europe through the Middle Ages.

The increasing use of capital goods gradually brought about a change in this traditional attitude. The possibilities for using a loan of money with which to create or to buy an improved tool or machine that would result in an increase in production came to be recognized. Take the case of the "flying shuttle," an invention by John Kay in 1733. By the use of such a shuttle a weaver could turn out many times as much cloth in a given time as he could before. Now if a weaver could borrow the money needed to buy the improved tool or machine, he might increase his production enough to pay for the machine plus an extra amount in the form of interest and still have something left.

As time went on, the increasing demand for capital goods resulted in greater emphasis on the importance of interest. There was a better understanding of the fact that an increase in the amount of capital goods results from the savings of labor and resources, and that the original source of loanable funds is this saving. Such saving is represented by the savings of money by individuals and business organizations. As an inducement to save money, the payment of interest on loans came to be a common practice and to be considered socially desirable — a contrast to the earlier years when interest earning was not allowed.

ARE THERE DIFFERENT KINDS OF INTEREST?

Interest is the compensation that belongs to the owner for the use of his capital or loans of money. If the interest is paid according to agreement, as when one borrows money at a bank, we may speak of it as *contractual interest*. If one uses his capital in his own business and receives income from its use, that part of his income may be considered as *imputed interest;* that is, a part of his income is really obtained from the use of his own capital.

Pure interest or *net interest* is the net return for the use of capital. It is the amount of one's income that results solely from the use of an amount of capital. *Gross interest* is the net interest on a loan plus any charge that may be added to compensate the lender for his risks and expenses incurred.

DEMAND AND SUPPLY DETERMINE INTEREST RATES

An *interest rate* is the price for the loan of funds. For example, if the amount of interest is $9 for the use of $100 for one year, the annual interest rate is 9 percent (9/100).

Unless controlled by law, interest rates are set by the demand for and the supply of loanable funds. Competition perhaps plays a more important part in the determination of prices in the money markets than in most other markets. Purchasing power in the form of money and credit tends to move to the place where people are willing to pay the highest price for its use. Therefore, as in the case of the prices for the use of labor and land, our problem in trying to understand interest largely relates to a study of the nature of demand and supply.

WHAT IS MEANT BY THE DEMAND FOR LOANABLE FUNDS?

The *demand for loanable funds* is the total number of dollars or the amount of money and credit that will be borrowed at specific prices (interest rates) at a given time. The total demand for loanable funds comes from three sources: (1) borrowing by consumers, (2) borrowing for productive purposes, (3) borrowing for speculation.

(1) Borrowing by consumers. There are various reasons why individuals borrow money with which to buy consumers' goods and services. These reasons include such things as illness in the family, inability to balance the individual or family budget, the purchase of durable consumers' goods, the desire to secure a college education, and the attempt "to keep up with the Joneses." Borrowing for the purchase of durable consumers' goods or for educational purposes is sometimes regarded as borrowing for investment purposes because such goods render services over long periods of time, and education increases the productivity of a person.

As we saw earlier in this study, commercial banks often make loans to consumers. The borrower may be asked to pledge some kind of *collateral* — such as stocks, bonds, or other personal property — to secure the loan. Or he may be able to have a friend whose credit is good at the bank sign his note as a *comaker* or *surety*, in which case the friend also becomes liable for the payment of the note. The rate of interest charged by commercial banks for consumers' loans is reasonable but sometimes higher than that charged for business loans.

Small-loan companies, including *industrial banks*, *consumer finance companies*, *credit unions*, and others make loans to consumers for periods up to 12 or more months. They accept notes that are signed by a comaker or surety, and usually require that a loan be repaid in monthly installments. Service and other charges made for loans by industrial banks are added to the interest on the loan.

Small-loan companies specialize in making loans of amounts up to $600 or even more to consumers. Such loans are often referred to as *consumers' loans*, *small loans*, or *remedial loans*. Maximum small-loan interest rates fixed by about three fourths of the states usually range from 1 to 3½ percent per month. For example, if you borrow $100 and repay

CAPITAL INVESTED PER EMPLOYEE IN MANUFACTURING

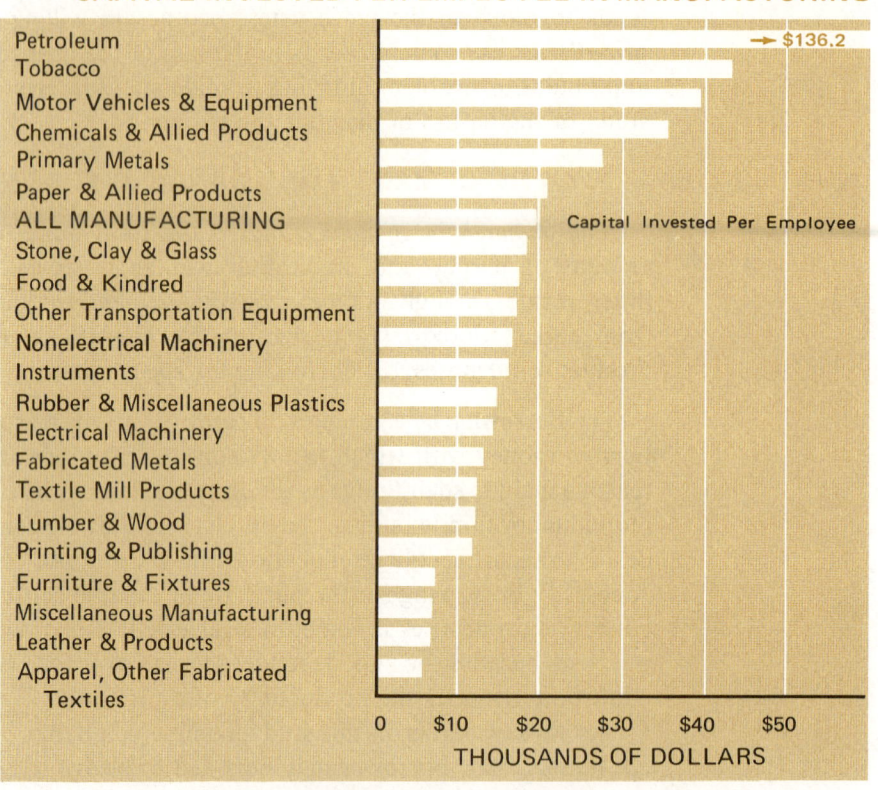

Industry	Capital Invested Per Employee (Thousands of Dollars)
Petroleum	→ $136.2
Tobacco	
Motor Vehicles & Equipment	
Chemicals & Allied Products	
Primary Metals	
Paper & Allied Products	
ALL MANUFACTURING	
Stone, Clay & Glass	
Food & Kindred	
Other Transportation Equipment	
Nonelectrical Machinery	
Instruments	
Rubber & Miscellaneous Plastics	
Electrical Machinery	
Fabricated Metals	
Textile Mill Products	
Lumber & Wood	
Printing & Publishing	
Furniture & Fixtures	
Miscellaneous Manufacturing	
Leather & Products	
Apparel, Other Fabricated Textiles	

Figure 16-1.

Adapted by permission from *Road Maps of Industry*, Conference Board, 1970.

the loan in 12 equal monthly installments of $8.33 plus interest at 3½ percent per month on the unpaid balance, the total amount of interest cost will be $22.75.

(2) Borrowing for productive purposes. Businessmen borrow for the purpose of increasing their profits. Therefore, unless they think they see an opportunity to make enough additional money with which to repay the loan, together with interest, they are not interested in borrowing money.

Here we have a clue to the question, "What is it that enables a borrower, as a result of a loan, to repay the loan?" It is the productiveness of the borrowed funds. Let us see what this means.

Suppose that a manufacturer has a supply of labor and factory space sufficient to enable him to use another machine that would cost $5,000, but which would not last more than one year. He estimates, however, that if he had the machine, he could probably increase the value of his production over and above all expenses, including the cost of the machine, by $500. He talks the matter over with a friend who has some money that he would lend and finds that he could borrow the amount by paying $250 in interest. If his estimate is correct, he could afford to pay $250 for the $5,000 he would have to borrow. Since he might increase his production by even more than he had estimated, he may decide to borrow the money and install the machine.

His friend then tells him that he will lend him another $5,000 for the purchase of another machine. But the manufacturer may be unwilling to borrow more because he thinks that the additional machine would not pay for itself and the interest on the loan.

Now if we consider that these amounts of $5,000 each represent units of capital, we can see that the law of diminishing productivity is in operation in the factory. Moreover, the unit of $5,000 that the owner borrowed indicated the last unit which could be used without a loss to the borrower because the estimated returns on an additional loan of $5,000 would not be enough to repay the loan together with interest.

As you can see, then, the marginal productivity of capital — the productivity of the last unit employed — determines the maximum amount that a borrower for productive purposes can afford to pay for funds. But it does not always fix the amount or the interest rate that he actually pays.

Borrowing by businessmen. Men in various types of business borrow money. The loans made to businessmen may be classed as (1) short-time loans and (2) long-time loans.

When a merchant does not have the money with which to pay for goods, he either buys the goods on account or borrows the amount needed from a commercial bank. Such loans usually extend from 15 to 60 days, although sometimes they are for a longer period of time.

Large companies, like manufacturing concerns and railroads, often find it desirable to borrow huge sums for the construction of plants and for the purchase of equipment. These funds are obtained for long periods of time, which may extend from several years to fifty years, or even more.

Borrowing by governments. Nearly all forms of government find it desirable to borrow funds for the purpose of erecting buildings and making permanent improvements of various kinds. Money spent for such purposes may be regarded as investments. These investments are undertaken for the sake of the educational and social advancement or the convenience of people in general. Examples of investments made by governments are

Illus. 16-1. Nearly all forms of government find it desirable to borrow funds for making permanent improvements of various kinds. An example of this is government-operated power dams.

Bureau of Reclamation, Department of the Interior

to be found in school buildings, parks and playgrounds, roads and streets, and many kinds of fixed equipment and buildings. Besides these we may add those examples of government industries, like government-operated power dams, the postal service, and facilities of the National Aeronautics and Space Administration.

(3) Borrowing for speculation. *Speculation* may be defined as buying goods or property with the expectation of selling at a profit as a result of a change in the market price. Speculation, strictly speaking, is not a form of production, although the purchase and the sale of stocks and bonds are often associated with the raising of money for productive purposes.

Many of the stocks and bonds bought on the New York Stock Exchange, as well as on other exchanges, are bought *on margin*. That is, the customer pays the stockbroker, who does the actual buying, only a part of the purchase price of the securities. The broker borrows from a bank the remainder needed to pay for the securities. In effect, he lends this amount to the person for whom he bought the securities. The broker holds the stock certificates or the bonds, whichever are bought, as security that the buyer will pay the remainder. At any time the buyer requests, the broker will sell the securities and deduct the amount of the loan.

Speculators often buy on margin, say 50 or 75 percent of the total cost of the securities purchased. (The Board of Governors of the Federal Reserve System fixes margin requirements.) Sometimes such purchases are profitable; on the other hand, they may result in financial loss. For example, suppose that Mr. Hopkins has $5,000 in cash with which he wishes to buy some shares of the stock of the East-West Corporation and that these shares are selling on the exchange at $10 a share. He feels that the price of the stock will go up shortly and that if he buys now, he will be able to sell at a profit. As you can see, he can buy 500 shares, not counting the commission that he would have to pay the broker. If the price of the stock should rise to $11, he would make $500 by selling it.

The broker, however, is willing to borrow $5,000 and lend Mr. Hopkins the additional amount needed to buy 1,000 shares. Then, if the price of the stock should rise to $11, Mr. Hopkins would make $1,000 by selling. On the other hand, if the price of the stock on the market should fall, Mr. Hopkins would have to increase his margin by depositing more money with the broker. If he did not do so, the broker would sell the stock, keep the amount of his loan, and return to Mr. Hopkins whatever was left.

WHAT IS MEANT BY THE SUPPLY OF LOANABLE FUNDS?

By the *supply of loanable funds* we mean the amount of dollars that individuals and business concerns will offer to lend at specific rates of interest at a certain time. The quantity of loanable funds supplied usually increases as the interest rate rises, and decreases as the interest rate falls.

WHAT ARE THE SOURCES OF THE SUPPLY OF LOANABLE FUNDS?

There are three general sources of loanable funds: (1) savings of individuals and families, (2) savings of business firms, and (3) extensions of bank credit.

(1) Savings of individuals and families. A majority of individuals and families find it impossible to save more than a very small part of their incomes each year, regardless of how high the interest rate may be. In fact, there are many who are unable to save anything. On the other hand, there are some who find it easier to save a great deal of their income than to spend it all; but there are relatively few such individuals and families. Most of the savings by individuals and families are made by those who belong to the middle and upper economic classes.

It has long been accepted that the higher the interest rate, the more people will save; and, vice versa, the lower the rate, the less they will save. Some economists, however, now hold that interest rates do not greatly affect the amount of savings. They say that equally important with interest rates is *liquidity preference*, which means the preference of people to keep savings in the form of cash for current purchases as a precaution against need and for possible investment or speculation in the future.

(2) Savings of business firms. A considerable part of the total savings in this country is in the form of the savings by business concerns, especially corporations. The decision as to what part of the profits of a corporation shall be retained by the business rests with the board of directors. As a rule, most of the savings are used for the purchase of new or additional equipment and for extensions of the business. Often, however, much of the amount not paid out to stockholders is invested in securities of other corporations and thus becomes available for use in the construction of capital goods. Some of the savings may also be deposited in banks.

(3) Extensions of bank credit. Most of the funds available for loans are provided by banks. These funds are created by extensions of credit to borrowers. For example, a merchant desires to borrow $1,000 for 60 days. He goes to his bank and gives acceptable evidence that he will be able and willing to repay the loan at the end of that time, and he gives the bank his promissory note. The bank then extends him credit for $1,000, less the amount of discount (interest collected in advance). Thus, the bank does not always have to save funds before it lends them.

GOVERNMENT POLICY AFFECTS THE SUPPLY OF LOANABLE FUNDS

The Federal Reserve System and the United States Treasury Department cooperate in carrying out the financial policies of the government. For many years one phase of the financial policy of the government has been to make it easy for businessmen to borrow funds for investment purposes. One of the methods for achieving this purpose has been to keep interest rates low.

To do this, as we shall learn in Chapter 21, federal reserve banks make use of three practices: (1) They lower the interest rate at which member banks can borrow from the federal reserve banks so that the member banks can make increased loans to their customers. (2) They bid up the price of government bonds held by the commercial banks and others; and when they buy bonds, the commercial banks and others who sell the bonds have more money to lend or to invest. (3) They lower reserve requirements.

If it appears that there is too much money and credit in circulation, the federal reserve banks adopt opposite measures.

Also, the federal government often encourages banks to lend to certain types of borrowers. For example, the Federal Housing Administration (FHA) guarantees bank loans made to families for the construction of homes. Billions of dollars of bank credit have been created in this way. Some loans for education are also guaranteed by the government.

The extent to which government, in cooperation with banks, should create and increase the supply of loanable funds is a major question. Some argue that it is the duty of government to help to increase the supply of money and loanable funds, and thus promote business prosperity and the general welfare. Others contend that such a practice is likely to lead to inflation, rising prices, and false prosperity.

HOW DO DEMAND AND SUPPLY AFFECT INTEREST RATES?

We are now prepared to summarize what has been said about the relation of the demand for and the supply of loanable funds. On the side of demand, we found that it is the marginal productivity of capital that determines how much a borrower of money for productive purposes can afford to pay for the use of a loan. On the supply side, we found that it is often necessary to pay some people and business concerns to save in order that the supply of funds may be sufficient to satisfy the demand for funds. Of course, there would be some saving even if there were no chance of getting interest on loans. Moreover, as we have seen, it is possible for the federal government in cooperation with banks to increase the amount of loanable funds.

Like the price of a commodity where competition exists, the price of funds — the interest rate — tends to be fixed at the point where demand and supply are equal, or in equilibrium. Anything that affects either the demand for or the supply of loanable funds will tend to result in a change in the interest rate.

As we have seen, the government sometimes helps to provide loanable funds, and the Federal Reserve System controls interest rates for borrowing by member banks. As a result, interest rates are affected by factors other than those we might call natural demand and supply.

HOW INTEREST ALLOCATES RESOURCES

We have seen that interest is a price, just as wages and rent are prices. The lender charges interest as a price for the use of funds, and the borrower must pay this price or be denied the loan. In the long run, businesses that are unable to repay loans and the required interest will be denied further use of borrowed capital funds. Banks must exercise judgment in determining which applicants for loans are most likely to be able to put the funds to work in sound enterprises. In so doing, an estimate must be made of the earning capacity of the business relative to the interest rate. Having secured his loan, the successful loan applicant then invests the funds in capital resources for the production of goods and services.

Thus, the rate of interest helps to determine how resources will be employed. Where the demand for a firm's goods is strong, productivity of capital tends to be high. This increases the ability of the borrower to pay the interest. Where demand is weak, the opposite is true. The interest rate, therefore, tends to channel loanable funds and capital resources into the production of goods that have the strongest consumer demand.

We should recognize, however, that the interest rate itself does not allocate loanable funds perfectly. Since the rate does not respond freely to every change in demand and supply, lenders must often decide who among numerous loan applicants are to receive a portion of the supply of scarce funds. Unless the banks can estimate potential productivity accurately, which is unlikely, some worthwhile but unproven enterprises may find it difficult to raise capital funds, while some less productive but older firms are supported adequately. In spite of this imperfection, however, the interest rate does help to allocate scarce funds to their economically most desirable uses.

THE VALUE OF INVESTMENTS IS DETERMINED BY CAPITALIZING INCOME AT A RATE OF INTEREST

By *capitalizing income* we mean finding the principal that will produce a certain amount of income at a certain percentage or interest rate. For example, suppose that a corporation bond with a face value of $1,000 pays 7.5 percent, or $75, interest annually. Suppose, further, that the corporation has the highest possible financial rating so that there is little question that it can pay the bond when it is due. Finally, suppose that such bonds are selling at a price that causes the yield to amount to only 6 percent on the investment. What is the market value of the bond? The answer is $1,250. ($75 divided by .06 equals $1,250.)

Of course, where the amount of risk is greater, the market price of the bond will be such that the yield on the investment will be larger. For example, suppose that investors thought the risk so great that they would buy the bond only at a price that would result in a yield of 9 percent on the price they would pay for it. The market value of the bond is $833.33, which is the amount of a principal that will yield $75 at 9 percent.

SUMMARY

At one time the taking of interest was considered to be unethical and immoral. Gradually, as the relation between saving and the accumulation of capital goods became apparent, the attitude toward the practice of lending money and the receipt of interest changed.

Ch. 16 INTEREST FOR CAPITAL

Interest is a price paid for the use of capital. If it is paid according to an agreement, as in the case of a loan of money, it is contractual interest. If the owner uses his capital himself and receives an income, that part of his income which is due to the use of his capital is imputed interest. Pure interest is the net return on capital; it does not include a reward for risk taking. Gross interest is pure or net interest plus an additional amount for costs in making the loan or for taking a risk that the loan will not be repaid when due.

The interest rates are determined by the demand for and the supply of loanable funds. The sources of demand for loanable funds are borrowing (1) by consumers, (2) for productive purposes, and (3) for speculation. The supply of loanable funds arises from (1) savings of individuals and families, (2) savings of business firms, and (3) extensions of bank credit. Government policy also affects the supply of loanable funds.

The value of investments is found by capitalizing the income from the property at a rate of interest.

NEW TERMS

capitalizing income
collateral
comaker *or* surety
consumer finance companies
consumers' loans
contractual interest
demand for loanable funds
gross interest
imputed interest
industrial banks

interest
interest rate
liquidity preference
margin (buying on)
pure *or* net interest
remedial loans
small loans
speculation
supply of loanable funds

QUESTIONS ON THE CHAPTER

1. Why is part of the national income distributed in the form of interest?
2. What is the meaning of interest?
3. Why was taking of interest formerly regarded as immoral or unethical?
4. Why did the attitude of the public toward interest change so that now interest income is regarded as being respectable and moral?
5. Does gross interest include net interest?
6. What is an interest rate?
7. What is meant by "the demand for loanable funds"?
8. What are some reasons why consumers borrow funds?
9. Have any of the states passed small-loan laws?
10. What are some examples to illustrate why businessmen borrow funds?
11. How does the productiveness of capital affect the interest rate? Explain.
12. What is meant by "buying on margin"?

13. What is meant by "the supply of loanable funds"?
14. What are the three general sources of loanable funds? Discuss each.
15. What is the relationship of interest rates and the supply of loanable funds?
16. How do interest rates affect the value of investments?

APPLYING YOUR ECONOMIC UNDERSTANDING

1. Does your state have a usury law? What are its main provisions? Is it based on the moral attitude toward the taking of interest that existed in the Middle Ages?
2. What are some examples in your community of capital which is earning imputed interest?
3. What are some of your local agencies that accept money as deposits and lend funds? (a) Do the depositors earn pure interest? (b) Do the borrowers pay contractual interest?
4. On June 8, 1968, the Board of Governors increased the margin requirement for purchasing stocks from 70 percent to 80 percent. On May 6, 1970, the Board reduced the margin requirement to 65 percent. Assume that Mr. Smith wished to purchase stocks with a market price of $40,000. (a) For a sale on June 7, 1968, what would be his minimum cash down payment? (b) For a sale on March 3, 1970, what would be his minimum cash down payment? (c) For a sale on May 7, 1970, what would be his minimum cash down payment?
5. Many prospective home buyers have very little cash for purchasing a home; they require mortgage loans. The debt on mortgages is long term and is paid off slowly. Before mortgage debt is paid off the incomes of home owners change. Consequently, unemployment or other conditions may result in nonpayment of mortgage debt. How might these statements be related to the establishment of FHA by the federal government?

CHALLENGES TO ECONOMIC COMPETENCE

1. Using the *Statistical Abstract*, prepare a graph comparing interest's share of the national income with total national income at five-year intervals from 1900 to the present.
2. Moderate a panel discussion on "Government Regulation of Interest Rates" and present a summarization of the main points of the discussion.
3. Prepare a written report on one of the following: (a) Are Government Bonds Profitable Investments? (b) The Socialist Viewpoint on Interest Payments, (c) What Government Debt Costs in Interest, (d) Are the Small-Loan Laws of Our State Adequate?

Chapter 17

Profits for Enterprisers

Of what importance are profits in our economy?
How do profits arise in our economy?
How can we calculate pure profit?
What might be the result of limiting profits by law?

There is nothing certain about the future except that it is uncertain. The truth of this applies particularly to most business enterprises.

Take the case of the typical independent grocer. He wanted to be his own boss, and he probably had the hope that he could make a success of his business. He knew that he might not succeed, but he was willing to take the chance. He invested most of his capital in the business. From time to time he borrows additional funds from the bank, which he must repay promptly according to his promise. He may rent the store building and the lot on which it is located. He must pay the salary of his clerk, and he has a number of other expenses. In addition, he is constantly carrying a number of risks, some of which he cannot avoid by means of insurance. He will realize his hope of making a profit only if he can keep his income greater than his actual outgo.

What is true of the corner grocer is likewise true of all who go into business for themselves, regardless of whether they set up in business as sole proprietors or organize great corporations.

PROFIT IS THE REWARD FOR INITIATIVE AND RISK BEARING

The enterpriser initiates the enterprise, assembles the factors of production, and carries the risk of financial loss. He may rent land, hire labor, and borrow the capital needed to run the business, or he may contribute all these factors himself.

Of course, if an enterpriser obtains land, labor, and capital from others, they, too, run some risk. It might be that he could not or would not pay them the agreed amount of rent, wages, or interest. But it is the *entrepreneurial risks* (risks assumed by an enterpriser) that justify profits. The enterpriser assumes the risk of paying the owners of land, labor, and capital and of being able to sell his product for more than he pays out in costs. Or if he furnishes part of these other resources himself, he will have to make an allowance for the value of the factors that he furnishes in calculating his profit.

THE TERM "PROFITS" HAS SEVERAL MEANINGS

In business the term "profits" has a number of meanings. For that reason it is necessary that we understand what is meant when the term is used.

Competitive profits are profits that are earned by a business or an industrial concern that competes with others in the sale of its products. *Monopoly profits* are those that are received by a concern that controls the supply or the prices of the goods or the services that it sells. *Speculative profits* are profits that are made as a result of a change in price after one has bought something — land, corporation stocks, or merchandise, for example. Speculators on organized markets sometimes sell "short" in the hope of making a profit. For example, one may sell — agree to deliver title to — 10,000 bushels of wheat two months hence at $1.60 a bushel, which he hopes to buy before the date of delivery at a price less than the price at which he sells it.

Gross profit is the difference between the amount that is paid for goods and the amount that is received when the goods are sold. *Net profit* is the amount remaining after the total amount of all expenses has been deducted from the gross profit. Such expenses include payment for the services, land, and capital belonging to others that may have been employed in the enterprise.

Pure profit, or *economic profit*, is the amount remaining to the owner after an allowance has been made for the use of the owner's own services, his land, and other capital.

WAGES OF MANAGEMENT ARE NOT PURE PROFITS

When one manages his own business enterprise, he is entitled to think that a part of his net profit, if any, above expenses should be considered as wages of management (See Chapter 14). When calculating the amount of pure profit, the owner should make allowances for the use of any or all of the factors of production that he furnishes. Therefore, pure or economic profit does not include wages of management. For this reason we say that the manager of a corporation, unless he gets part of his compensation from profits, is not an entrepreneur. His salary is considered to be only a form of wages.

HOW IS PURE PROFIT CALCULATED?

A simple example will illustrate how pure profit is calculated. Suppose that Fred Johnson engages in a grocery business. At the end of the year he determines (1) the sales, (2) the cost of goods sold, (3) the gross profit, (4) the expenses, and (5) the net profit. After the amount of net profit has been found, allowances are made for imputed interest on Johnson's capital (6) and for his own labor (7). The total amount of these allowances is deducted from the amount of net profit, and the remainder is considered pure profit (8).

(1) Sales..			$41,000
(2) Cost of goods sold...............................			30,100
(3) Gross profit..................................			10,900
(4) Expenses:			
Rent on lot and storehouse..........................		$2,000	
Wages of a part-time salesman.......................		2,400	
Interest on bank loans..............................		300	
Taxes and other expenses...........................		2,000	6,700
(5) Net profit.....................................			4,200
To calculate amount of pure profit, allow:			
(6) Interest at 5% on owner's capital of $10,000.............		$ 500	
(7) Value of owner's wages............................		3,600	4,100
(8) Pure profit....................................			$ 100

This example illustrates the residual nature of profits. It shows that net profit is the amount of income that remains after each of the owners of the other factors of production has been allowed his share of the income of the business. Pure profit is what remains after allowances have been made for the use of the owner's resources. But ask yourself if this $100 is all that Johnson can claim for himself out of the total receipts of $41,000.

WHAT ARE THE SOURCES OF PROFITS?

Ordinarily, there are four principal sources of profits, which are discussed in the following sections:

(1) Superior efficiency in management. Some men and women are better business managers than others. This is true whether they own their own businesses or whether they work as hired managers, as do those who run corporations. Those who possess exceptional managerial ability know how to keep down expenses so that the unit costs of production are kept at a minimum. They know where, when, and how to buy goods and materials at low prices; how to bargain successfully with workers; how to obtain the use of capital at low interest rates; and how to put new ideas into practice.

Those enterprises that are fortunate in having good management are more likely to make larger profits than are those whose management is inferior. For example, if the stockholders of a corporation elect a capable board of directors, who in turn employ efficient managers, the profits to the stockholders are likely to be larger than if less efficient managers were chosen.

(2) Imperfect competition. As we have said in several connections, pure competition seldom, if ever, exists. In order to have pure competition in the sale of a certain kind of a good, everyone would have to know exactly where he could buy at the lowest price or sell at the highest price, and there would need to be so many buyers and sellers that the amount anyone bought or sold would make no important difference in the market price. In no case is it likely that all of these conditions are met.

As you will recall from Chapter 10, nearly all manufactured products of any kind are different in some respect. Sometimes the only important distinguishable difference is in the brands. But some people learn to prefer one brand of flour, bread, or coffee to others. So, regardless of whether there is any real difference between two or more brands of a product, as long as people think there is, the maker has a better chance of selling the product if buyers prefer his brand. And the more people who prefer his product, the more nearly the maker comes to having a monopoly on the sales of his product.

(3) Pure monopoly. Of course, if the maker is the only one who can supply a particular product or service, the price he can charge for what he sells depends only upon how badly people want the product and their ability to pay for it; that is, the amount that he can sell depends upon the level of demand and its elasticity.

As we know, there are few cases of absolute monopoly. For the most part, business is neither purely competitive nor purely monopolistic; it is usually somewhere between these two extremes.

(4) Luck. For want of a better term to describe it, we may say that profits sometimes result from luck or chance. For example, a few farmers who owned poor farms and did not suspect that their land possessed valuable mineral resources have become rich because of the discovery of oil on their property. Some landowners have made large profits because of an unforeseen increase in population. Other unexpected developments have resulted in profits to individuals.

Of course, events that bring profits to individuals are always caused; they do not "just happen." But, because the person affected did not anticipate the event which brings him profit, he is said to be lucky and his profit is said to be a "chance gain." As we recognize, however, luck may bring losses as well as gains.

IN OUR SOCIETY PROFITS ARE NECESSARY

It is sometimes said that profits are necessary if goods are to be produced. This statement, however, is not exactly true in every particular case, for it is the hope of making a profit that causes enterprisers to undertake production. Some concerns have never made any profit, but they go on producing goods, at least for a while, hoping to do somewhat better in the future.

But if everyone were convinced that there was no reasonable hope for making any profit, there would be no incentive for anyone to organize the

VALUE OF THE PRODUCTIVE PLANT PER PERSON

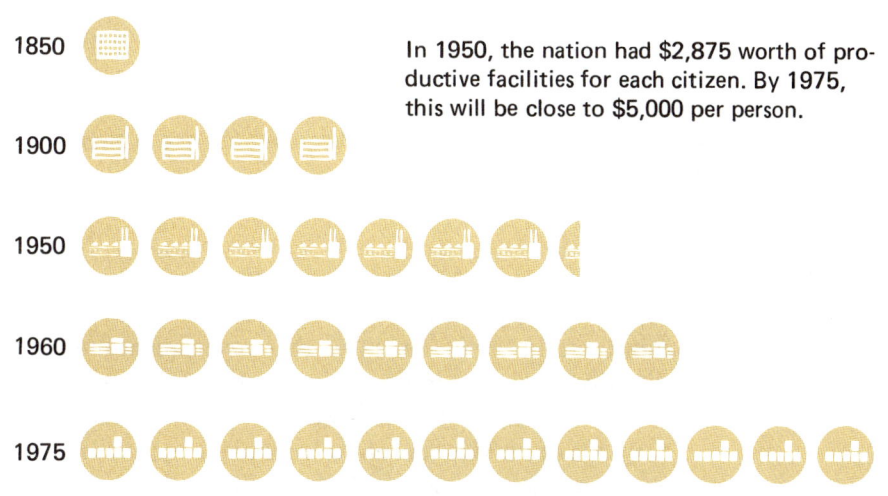

In 1950, the nation had $2,875 worth of productive facilities for each citizen. By 1975, this will be close to $5,000 per person.

Each symbol represents $400 per person, at 1960 prices.
Includes all civilian, productive, and commercial facilities except farms.

Figure 17-1.

Twentieth Century Fund

Without the opportunity to make a profit, people will not undertake the risks of production that are necessary in order to produce the goods that are wanted.

factors of production and to engage in business or industry except to a very limited extent. Therefore, there must be reasonable possibilities for enterprisers to make profits if production is to continue under the free-enterprise system, for under this system the hope of making a profit is the underlying motive for the organization and operation of business.

Just how much profit is necessary to cause enterprisers to assume the risks of production? Where risks are great, the amount of possible profits must be larger than when the risks are considered to be less. For example, private individuals and companies would seldom risk their capital in drilling for oil if the profits they could make were small. On the other hand, some public utilities whose profits are regulated by government have little trouble in obtaining the use of all the capital they need. The reason in this case, however, is that, since the business is a monopoly and is protected from competition, the risks are less and owners of capital are more willing to buy stocks and bonds in the enterprise.

SHOULD PROFITS BE LIMITED BY LAW?

From time to time, especially during a war, laws to limit profits have been enacted. Even in times of peace, there are those who would limit profits in one way or another. For example, it has been argued that, if a big company is making large profits, the company should raise wages without raising the prices of the goods it sells. Then there are those who maintain that in addition to the regular or normal tax on corporation profits, there should be an *excess-profits tax*, which is a heavy tax on profits above a certain percentage of the total assets of the business. Through the years a number of other methods of limiting profits have been proposed.

How should we regard proposals to limit profits? A detailed answer cannot be given here. But in considering the question, we should keep in mind certain things. It is true that government must sometimes control or fix prices and thus indirectly control profits to some extent. At the same time, we should not forget that in the free-enterprise system we depend on the hope of making a profit to encourage individuals and groups to initiate and carry on production. Without the opportunity to make a profit, people will not undertake the risks of production that are necessary in order to produce the goods that are wanted. And if too many restrictions are imposed on profit-making opportunities, the entrepreneurial services that are necessary will not be forthcoming. This is another example that illustrates the vital relations between economics and politics.

Finally, although our economy is often called a profit system, we should call it a profit and loss system. Fortunately, most enterprises are successful; but each year large numbers of businesses, both new and old, fail because they suffer losses instead of making profits. This is not only true of small businesses but it also occurs in some relatively large firms. If the possibility of receiving substantial profits were not present in our economy, the enterprising spirit of the capitalistic system would for the most part disappear.

SUMMARY

Profit is the possible reward to individuals who assume entrepreneurial risks. Pure profit does not include the wages of management. Competitive profits arise from conducting a business under a condition of competition. Monopoly profits are those profits that are received by a firm which has exclusive control of the supply or the price of a good. Speculative profits result from speculation. Gross profit is the difference between the cost and the selling price of a good, before operating expenses have been deducted. Net profit is the amount of gross profit less operating expenses. Pure profit is net profit less proper allowances for the use of the owner's land, capital, and services used in the business.

Ordinarily, there are four sources of business profits: (1) superior efficiency in management; (2) imperfect competition; (3) pure monopoly; and (4) luck.

The hope of making a profit is necessary to induce enterprisers to undertake the risks of business. In a free-enterprise economy such as ours, the hope of making a profit is relied on to induce individuals to undertake the production of most of the different kinds of goods and services that the people want. There have been instances where the desire to make profits resulted in unfortunate practices. On the other hand, it is commonly recognized that the free-enterprise system in Western nations, and especially in the United States, has led to unprecedented economic progress.

It is generally accepted that government controls over prices and certain practices of some types of business enterprise are at times necessary. But, as citizens, we should understand that too many restrictions of this kind would weaken or destroy the spirit of free enterprise. If this should happen, it would become necessary for government to take an increasingly important part in the initiation and conduct of production.

NEW TERMS

competitive profits
entrepreneurial risks
excess-profits tax
gross profit

monopoly profits
net profit
pure *or* economic profit
speculative profits

QUESTIONS ON THE CHAPTER

1. Why do men and women go into business for themselves?
2. What are some examples of business risks?
3. What part does risk play in relation to profit?
4. What is the difference between competitive profit and monopoly profit?
5. How can a speculator make a profit?
6. What is the difference between net profit and pure profit?
7. Why are wages of management not included in the amount that may be considered as pure profit?
8. Why is profit called a residual return?
9. How can each of the following be a source of profit: (a) superior managerial ability; (b) imperfect competition; (c) monopoly; and (d) luck?
10. Is the actual receipt of profits necessary if individuals are to undertake production? Explain.
11. Should profits be limited by law? Discuss.

APPLYING YOUR ECONOMIC UNDERSTANDING

1. The ABC corporation pays its president an annual salary of $50,000. The XYZ corporation pays its president an annual salary of $35,000 and a bonus in the form of shares of stock in the XYZ corporation. Do both presidents receive their income from profits? Why or why not?
2. Mr. Brooks owns $5,000 worth of XYZ company stock and $5,000 worth of XYZ company bonds. He receives $150 as dividends and $150 as interest. Are both payments to Mr. Brooks a form of profit? Discuss.
3. The chart below shows data for two different public utilities companies. (a) During 1970 which company's stockholders were furnishing the greater percentage of capital funds? (b) Between 1969–1970 what was the percentage increase in the capitalization of Company A? (c) Was the percentage increase in capitalization greater for Company A or Company B between 1969–1970? (d) Would profits from the increased capitalization be shared between the stockholders and the owners of the long-term debt?

A CAPITALIZATION COMPARISON
(millions of dollars)

	Company A		Company B	
	1970	1969	1970	1969
Total Stockholders' Equity	$ 700	$ 700	$25,000	$24,500
Total Long-Term Debt	950	850	20,500	16,000
Total Capitalization	$1,650	$1,550	$45,500	$40,500

4. The chart below reports data from the annual report of a banking corporation. (a) Does it indicate that profits vary from year to year? (b) In what year was a greater dollar amount of profit per share used for reinvestment? (c) What was the percentage increase in cash dividends between 1969–1970? (d) Was this percentage increase as great as the percentage increase in the cost of living in 1970?

A COMPARISON OF STOCK SHARES

	1970	1969	1968
Dividends declared per share	$ 2.84	$ 2.83	$ 2.62
Book value at end of year per share	44.64	42.53	42.17

5. Interview a person who has been successful and whose business has been expanding. Find out where the capital for his expansion came from. What part was derived from previous profit? Would the business have been expanded if there had not been previous profit? Give the reasons for your answer to the last question.
6. Look for either the book "Robber Barons" or a digest of it. According to the author, what were the results of uncontrolled profit seeking? Are similar possibilities present in the United States today? Why or why not?
7. Many people believe that the American scale of living is a result of our acceptance of the profit motive. What facts would support this belief?

CHALLENGES TO ECONOMIC COMPETENCE

1. Arrange for a bulletin board display centered around the theme "The Economic Role of Profit."
2. Select five key industries and prepare a graph showing the gross income, the cost of operation, the corporate income tax, and the net profit of the past year for each company you selected. (Use annual reports as source data.)
3. Prepare a large display poster which depicts how the national income for the past year was shared. (See issues of *Federal Reserve Bulletin* or *Survey of Current Business*.)
4. Prepare an outline suitable for an oral report on one of the following: (a) Are Profits Today's Scapegoat?, (b) When Profits Fell, These Businesses Failed, (c) The What and Why of Excess-Profits Taxes, (d) Guidelines for Success in Business, (e) My Own First Attempts as a Business Operator.

Chapter 18

Labor Unions and Employers

Why are labor unions organized?
What are the different kinds of unions?
What methods do unions and employers use in dealing with each other?
What laws are there that relate to labor unions?

There was a time when nearly everyone took it for granted that agreements as to wage rates and working conditions should be arrived at by individual bargaining between the employer and each employee. True, there were some exceptions to this general idea. Here and there a group of employees would organize and attempt to put pressure on their employer to raise wages and perhaps to make certain changes in their working conditions. One of the earliest of these cases in this country occurred in Philadelphia where a union of cordwainers tried to get an increase in wages for its members. But instead of getting what they wanted, some of the members were indicted and tried in court in 1806 for a violation of the common law. The name given to the trial was "The Trial of the Boot and Shoemakers of Philadelphia on an Indictment for a Combination and a Conspiracy to Raise Their Wages." The court decided that "A combination of workmen to raise their wages may be considered from a twofold point of view: one is to benefit themselves, the other to injure those who do not join their society. The rule (law) condemns both."

For a long time the enforcement of the law against the "combination" and "conspiracy" of workers who formed unions discouraged the growth of organized labor. But times have changed. Now laws specifically give workers in private industry and certain public employment the right to organize, and unions have the right to bargain with employers. In some industries, from 90 to 100 percent of the employees belong to unions. In nearly all other major industries — outside of agriculture, government, and some service industries — many, if not most, of the employees are organized.

WHAT ARE THE GENERAL AIMS OF LABOR UNIONS?

The general objective or aim of labor unions is the betterment of the economic lot of the members of the unions by means of collective bargaining with employers. *Collective bargaining* means the making of agreements between the employer and the union as to wage rates, hours, and other matters. In employees' relationships with employers, union leaders feel that only by means of collective bargaining can labor secure its rightful share of the national income.

In order to accomplish this major objective, unions maintain that four things are necessary:

(1) The union must be recognized by the employer. This means that the employer agrees to deal with the union as the agent of the employees.

(2) The union must have strength and security; that is, the union feels that it should represent the workers and that the employer should not do anything to weaken the union.

(3) The union must be able to get a satisfactory agreement with the employer as to wages, working conditions, pensions, and other things in which the members may be interested.

(4) Unions feel that they must be fully accepted by the employer. This means that they not only want to be recognized by the employer, but they want the employer to go further and show a real willingness to work with the union.

WHAT ARE THE MORE SPECIFIC AIMS OF UNIONS?

In pursuing these four general objectives, unions seek to achieve certain specific aims.

(1) Standard wage rates. One of the main objects of unions is to bring about *standard wage rates* for particular types of work. The union endeavors to fix the hourly rate or piece rate and the number of hours that may be worked without an increase in the wage rate. The aim of the union is to prevent too much competition among workers for jobs.

Standardized wages probably tend to stabilize labor costs in an industry. For example, if all employers in the automobile industry have to pay certain minimum wages for particular kinds of work, wage cost per worker for all employees in an industry will be about the same.

Some labor leaders are now proposing or demanding that employees be paid salaries instead of hourly, piecework, or daily wages. They contend that the rapidly growing use of automatically controlled processes in production justifies the use of salaries instead of the usual methods of calculating wage rates. A few, but not many, corporations and employees are in favor of sharing the profits of business with employees.

(2) Raising and maintaining wages. Has there ever been a strike in your community? If so, it is very possible that it was brought about by a demand by workers for higher pay or in an attempt to prevent a reduction in pay. Disputes over wages are the most frequent causes of strikes.

In periods of rising prices, labor unions insist on higher wages for their members if for no other reason than to maintain real wages. As the cost of living goes up, labor unions claim that the amount of money wages should increase at least in proportion. Otherwise, the workers suffer a loss in real wages. When this is the case, what the labor unions demand is the maintenance of the amount of real wages by means of an increase in the money wages. If the amount of money wages is increased only sufficiently to enable wage earners to buy the same amount of goods as they could before the rise in prices, there is no increase in real wages. Under such circumstances, the function of the union is to maintain wages.

When business depressions occur, employers may try to cut expenses by lowering wages. Workers naturally oppose the efforts to reduce their wages. The aim of labor unions in resisting the efforts of employers to reduce money wages is really to secure an increase in the real wages of members. For if the cost of living goes down while money wages remain the same as before, real wages increase. For example, if Patrick McGuire is receiving $20 a day and the cost of food and other things that he buys falls 20 percent, he could buy as much with a day's wages as he did before and have $4 left.

(3) Improvement of working conditions. Labor unions encourage employers to improve the surroundings in which employees work. Unless factories and offices are properly lighted, the eyes of workers may suffer. If unhealthful fumes and dust accumulate, the health of workers may be impaired. If washrooms are untidy and inconveniently located and if drinking-water facilities are unsanitary, the morale of the employees suffers. And unless adequate safety precautions exist, accidents may result in the injury or the death of workers.

Nearly all the states have laws that require employers to give attention to working conditions in their establishments, and labor unions have frequently been among the leaders in the drive to secure passage of this legislation. Visits are made by state inspectors to see that the minimum requirements set up by the law are being met. In some of the states the standards set by the state laws are much higher than are those in other states. But in some cases inspections are not carefully made.

(4) Increasing the security of jobs. Workers want jobs that will last. But workers are sometimes discharged without being given a satisfactory reason. Therefore, organized labor seeks general agreements with employers that require specific grounds for discharge.

Unions also try to establish rules for *seniority rating* of workers. Then if the working force is to be cut, those who have been employed longest are the last to be discharged. If workers are laid off temporarily, those with the highest seniority rating are rehired first. Likewise, those workers with the highest seniority rating are promoted first, provided they possess the minimum skill required for the job.

Unions often try to obtain greater security for workers by demanding that only union workers be employed in an establishment. If the employer is free to employ nonunion workers, union employees may be in constant danger of being replaced by other workers who are willing to accept jobs at wages lower than those set by the union.

(5) Industrial jurisprudence. This term refers to the methods of governing employee-employer relations in a plant. It is the objective of most unions to develop a system whereby the rights and duties of both the employee and management are determined under negotiated rules rather than by the decisions of management alone. To accomplish this goal a *grievance procedure* is established to handle day-to-day complaints that may be brought by individual employees, the union, or management. Collective bargaining thus becomes a continuing process under this procedure rather than a matter of only occasional negotiations.

(6) Fringe benefits. This term refers to compensation for employees other than the regular wages for time spent on the job, or for pieces of work done. For example, vacation pay, hospital or life insurance, and company pension plans are types of fringe benefits.

THERE ARE TWO TYPES OF UNIONS

Two types of labor unions have grown up in this country, the craft union and the industrial union.

The craft union. The craft union is the older type of labor organization. In some ways it resembles the guilds of the Middle Ages. A *craft union* is composed of those wage earners who are engaged in doing a particular kind or related kinds of work. Unions of carpenters, bricklayers, painters, tile setters, and cigar makers are examples of craft unions. The craft union tries to obtain for its members what is claimed to be a fair wage, to limit the length of the working day and week, to cause the employer to provide what are considered satisfactory working conditions, and, in some instances, to restrict work to those who have met apprenticeship requirements. Some craft unions undertake certain fraternal activities, such as providing aid for unfortunate members.

The industrial union. The other common form of labor union found in this country is the industrial union. The *industrial union* differs from the craft union in that it endeavors to include in its membership all the workers in a given industry, whereas the craft union aims to include in its membership those wage earners who are doing a particular kind or related kinds of work. For example, the United Mine Workers of America is intended to embrace all the workers in the mining industry, including teamsters, drillers, electricians, engineers, and other special types of workers. Other important industrial unions include the Amalgamated Clothing Workers of America, United Automobile Workers of America, United Steel Workers of America, International Union of Electrical, Radio, and Machine Workers of America, and the Textile Workers Union of America.

WHAT ARE THE REASONS FOR THE TWO TYPES OF UNIONS?

The general objectives of both types of unions are the same. The reason for the two types is a difference in belief as to which method will accomplish the best results. The idea of the craft union is that the organization and the methods of the union will be more effective if only those of a particular trade are included.

On the other hand, those who advocate the industrial union maintain that the united effort of all the workers in an industry toward a common purpose is necessary if the objectives of unionism are to be achieved. In the case of mine workers the isolation of the mines makes it desirable to include all the workers, for in some instances the number of workers engaged in a particular trade in the mine is small.

HOW ARE UNIONS ORGANIZED AND GOVERNED?

The organization and control of unions may be compared to that of our units of political government — those that make up our local, state, and national governments. On the lower level is the local union to which

Ch. 18 LABOR UNIONS AND EMPLOYERS

STRUCTURAL ORGANIZATION of the AMERICAN FEDERATION OF LABOR AND CONGRESS OF INDUSTRIAL ORGANIZATIONS

GENERAL BOARD
Executive Council and one principal officer of each international union and affiliated Department

STANDING COMMITTEES
Civil Rights
Community Services
Economic Policy
Education
Ethical Practices
Housing
International Affairs
Legislative
Organization
Political Education
Public Relations
Research
Safety and Occupational Health
Social Security
Veterans Affairs

STATE CENTRAL BODIES in 50 States and 1 Commonwealth

LOCAL CENTRAL BODIES in 764 Communities

NATIONAL CONVENTION (Every 2 Years)

EXECUTIVE COUNCIL
President, Secretary-Treasurer, 33 Vice Presidents

OFFICERS
President and Secretary-Treasurer
Headquarters, Washington, D. C.

120 NATIONAL AND INTERNATIONAL UNIONS

60,000 Local Unions of National and International Unions

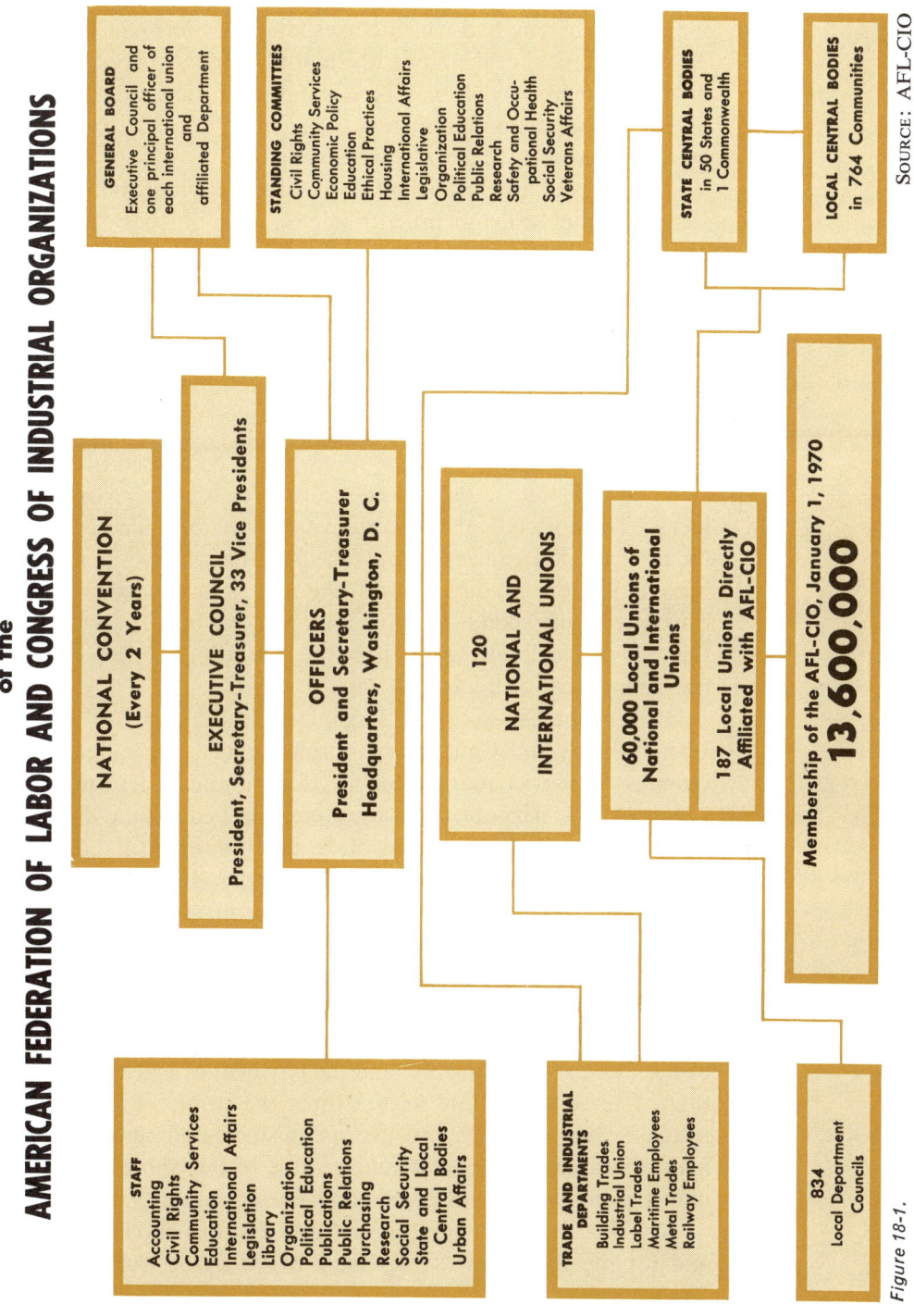

187 Local Unions Directly Affiliated with AFL-CIO

Membership of the AFL-CIO, January 1, 1970
13,600,000

STAFF
Accounting
Civil Rights
Community Services
Education
International Affairs
Legislation
Library
Organization
Political Education
Publications
Public Relations
Purchasing
Research
Social Security
State and Local Central Bodies
Urban Affairs

TRADE AND INDUSTRIAL DEPARTMENTS
Building Trades
Industrial Union
Label Trades
Maritime Employees
Metal Trades
Railway Employees

834 Local Department Councils

SOURCE: AFL-CIO

Figure 18-1.

individuals belong and which corresponds to our municipal governments. Next above the local unions are union regional offices, joint boards, or district councils, which may be compared to the states. On the top level are the national (and sometimes, the international) unions, which may be compared to the federal government.

Members of a union belong to the local organization, which is organized according to democratic principles. The officials of the local usually consist of a president, a secretary-treasurer, a shop steward, and possibly others. The function of the regional offices, district councils, or joint boards is to coordinate the activities of a number of locals. The national union is made up of representatives of local unions of a particular kind, as in the case of the United Automobile Workers, the International Typographical Union, and the United Mine Workers of America.

Union federations. A *union federation* is composed of national unions of different kinds. It also includes certain district union organizations and locals. The objects of the federation are to aid local unions and to promote the progress of organized labor. The governing body of a union federation is composed of representatives of the unions that make up the federation. This governing body functions at the biennial national convention. Between conventions the affairs of the federations are conducted by executive committees or boards.

In 1881 the Federation of Organized Trades and Labor Unions of the United States and Canada was formed under the leadership of Samuel Gompers. It was reorganized in 1886 as the American Federation of Labor (AFL). The objects of the American Federation of Labor included the confederation of national craft and industrial unions and of other unions not national in their scope. The Federation encouraged the organization of local unions and helped to form such unions; it promoted publicity favorable to the cause of labor; it attempted to settle disputes arising over the jurisdictions of craft unions; and it attempted to obtain in the courts what it considered justice for labor.

More specifically, it contended for a shorter working day, the adoption of the shorter working week, and the payment of higher wages. It claimed that, if there were more leisure time, the wants of the workers would increase. It argued that, because of their increased purchasing power from high wages, wage earners would be able to buy more of the products of industry and would thus promote business prosperity.

The Federation fought consistently for the abolition of child labor and for the limitation of the hours of labor for women. It supported factory legislation designed to provide for the protection of the workers

UNION MEMBERSHIP IN THE UNITED STATES BY STATE AND AS A PROPORTION OF TOTAL EMPLOYMENT IN NONAGRICULTURAL ESTABLISHMENTS, 1968[1]

State	Total membership (In thousands)	Ranking	Membership as a percent of employees in nonagricultural establishments	Ranking
All States	19,297	....	28.4	....
Alabama*	193	24	20.1	28
Alaska	27	48	34.0	10
Arizona*	89	32	18.9	33
Arkansas*	97	31	19.1	32
California	2,118	2	31.9	12
Colorado	149	27	21.8	24
Connecticut	275	17	23.7	23
Delaware	53	41	26.0	20
Florida*	279	16	14.4	44
Georgia*	239	19	16.6	43
Hawaii	70	36	27.5	19
Idaho	37	45	19.3	31
Illinois	1,538	4	36.0	8
Indiana	653	8	36.0	6
Iowa*	183	26	21.3	25
Kansas*	124	28	18.3	36
Kentucky	235	20	27.5	18
Louisiana	187	25	18.0	37
Maine	58	40	17.9	38
Maryland — District of Columbia	429	14	22.6	26
Massachusetts	562	10	25.5	21
Michigan	1,068	6	36.2	5
Minnesota	375	15	30.2	15
Mississippi*	76	35	13.8	47
Missouri	584	9	36.0	7
Montana	61	39	31.3	14
Nebraska*	79	34	17.2	40
Nevada*	52	42	29.4	17
New Hampshire	43	43	17.5	39
New Jersey	735	7	29.6	16
New Mexico	37	44	13.4	48
New York	2,539	1	36.2	4
North Carolina*	124	29	7.5	50
North Dakota*	29	47	18.8	34
Ohio	1,345	5	35.8	9
Oklahoma	121	30	16.7	41
Oregon	213	22	31.6	13
Pennsylvania	1,585	3	37.3	3
Rhode Island	83	33	24.1	22
South Carolina*	66	37	8.6	49
South Dakota*	24	49	14.4	45
Tennessee*	246	18	19.4	30
Texas*	474	11	13.9	46
Utah*	62	38	18.4	35
Vermont	29	46	20.7	27
Virginia*	230	21	16.6	42
Washington	454	13	41.4	2
West Virginia	213	23	41.9	1
Wisconsin	473	12	32.2	11
Wyoming*	20	50	19.5	29
Membership not classifiable	260	....	....	....

[1] Based on reports from 118 national and international unions and estimates for 71. Also included are local unions directly affiliated with the AFL-CIO, and members in single firms and local unaffiliated unions.

*Indicates a state with a right-to-work law.

Note: Because of rounding, sums of individual items may not equal totals.

SOURCE: U.S. Department of Labor, Bureau of Labor Statistics, *Directory of National and International Labor Unions in the United States*, 1969.

from machinery, for improved lighting and sanitation in factories, and for compensation to injured employees. It also advocated liberal support of public education, the creation of a department of education in the national government, free textbooks, and larger appropriations for public libraries. It advocated the use of a public works program by the government to provide employment in periods of business depression.

The Federation was not affiliated with any political party. Its policy was to advocate the election of public officials favorable to labor.

The AFL and the CIO. In 1935 some of the leaders in the AFL decided to organize a committee for the purpose of encouraging the formation of industrial unions. The committee took the name of Committee for Industrial Organization, which name was later changed to Congress of Industrial Organizations (CIO).

A bitter dispute developed among the leaders of the AFL. Some claimed that the proposal to organize industrial unions was an attempt to set up a rival organization to the AFL. Finally, several of the industrial unions were expelled from the AFL. As a result of the fight two big federations, the AFL and the CIO, developed; and each sought to increase its membership by organizing more unions and workers. Each organization undertook to establish new locals that would become affiliated with the national unions and federations.

AFL-CIO. In 1955 the two federations were merged under the title of the AFL-CIO. The ultimate consequences of this merger remain to be seen, but the former conflicts do not now appear to threaten the merger.

Independent unions. A union that is not affiliated with a federation is an *independent union*. Among the largest independent unions are the United Mine Workers of America, the United Electrical, Radio, and Machine Workers of America, and the International Brotherhood of Teamsters, Chauffeurs, Warehousemen, and Helpers of America.

ORGANIZED LABOR AND POLITICS

Organized labor in the United States has not always tried to achieve its objective by taking an active part in politics. In recent decades, however, the policy of remaining aloof from politics has been abandoned. The actions of the union leaders show a growing interest of organized labor in politics. In several national and state elections, the Political Action Committee (CIO) and the Labor's League for Political Education (AFL) were very active in raising funds for political purposes and in "getting out the vote" for candidates favorable to labor. The AFL-CIO has now established a Committee on Political Education (COPE).

HOW DO UNIONS TRY TO GET WHAT THEY WANT?

Labor unions use many methods. They attempt to enforce collective bargaining. They contend that the employee is at a disadvantage when bargaining over the wage contract and that for this reason a wage earner can get justice only by the collective action of groups of employees.

Union recognition and the trade agreement. After a labor union has been recognized as the bargaining agent for the employees, it asks for a *trade agreement* or labor contract. This agreement, which is usually written, sets forth the terms under which union workers are to be employed, including wages, hours, working conditions, and the order in which employees may be discharged (which refers to the seniority of employment). It usually contains provisions for "fringe benefits" — pensions, hospitalization payments, and perhaps other things.

Some trade agreements are between the union and only one employer. But other agreements outline the terms and the conditions of employment for a whole industry.

Union security arrangements. *Union security* is a term applied to any of several contractual devices used by a union to acquire a stronger position within a firm. A *closed shop* is one in which only union members are employed. Formerly it was more often the policy of unions to insist upon a closed-shop contract with employers. Frequently now, however, unions are content with a *union-shop agreement*, whereby the employer is free to hire anyone he chooses provided the employee agrees to become a union member within a specified time, say 30 days. Sometimes the union will accept a *preferential-shop arrangement*, whereby the employer agrees to give preference to workers who are members of the union. In some cases the union contract contains a *maintenance-of-membership clause*, which means that each employee who is a union member at the time the contract was adopted must keep up his membership or be discharged. The Taft-Hartley Act (1947) outlawed closed-shop contracts, and by subsequent legal interpretation, the preferential shop also.

Sometimes unions ask for a *checkoff* agreement with the employer, whereby the employer agrees to deduct union dues from the employees' pay and turn the money over to the union. The object is to prevent lapses in membership, and to provide a convenient means for collecting dues. At present the company cannot deduct such dues unless approved by individual union members.

After the enactment of the Taft-Hartley Act, unions sometimes entered into *agency-shop contracts* with employers. This type of union security contracts required all employees in the bargaining unit to pay regular dues and fees, but they were not required to join the union. The union thus became the "agent" for the employees, although not their "representative." The agency shop was intended to circumvent state *right-to-work laws* which are designed to make union and closed shops illegal. Many of the states have passed such laws.

The strike. The strike is a common means of trying to enforce the demands of organized labor. A *strike* occurs when a group of workers, through agreement, stop work as a means of enforcing their demands for increased wages, shorter working hours, better working conditions, or whatever they may desire. Sometimes a strike is called in order to help another group of workers, even though the strikers do not have any grievance of their own. In such a case the strike is a *sympathetic strike*, which is illegal under the Taft-Hartley Act.

Organized labor contends that a strike is often the only method by which it can control the supply of labor. On the other hand, the employer may feel that if the workers stop work, he has a right to employ others to take their places. If other employees are hired, the strikers naturally feel resentful because they are then not able to control the supply of labor as they had hoped to, and the success of the strike is thereby threatened. Usually, through the use of pickets (union employees) placed near the entrance to the factory, the construction job, or other place of work, the strikers attempt to dissuade others from taking their places. Strikers often refer to those who refuse to strike as *scabs;* and those who would take their places as *strikebreakers*.

The boycott. A *boycott* is a concerted agreement by a union group to have nothing to do with an individual or concern. A *secondary boycott* occurs when a labor union prohibits its members from entering the premises of or having any dealings with an employer against whom another union has struck. By the passage of the Taft-Hartley Act, secondary boycotts were made illegal.

Union labels. A *union label* is a tag or label stating that the article on which it appears was made in a union shop and according to union requirements.

Limitation of output. It has sometimes been said that it is to the worker's advantage to limit output. *Limiting output* means that the worker does not produce all that he is reasonably capable of producing. Those who advocate the deliberate restriction of output feel that there is

Ch. 18 LABOR UNIONS AND EMPLOYERS

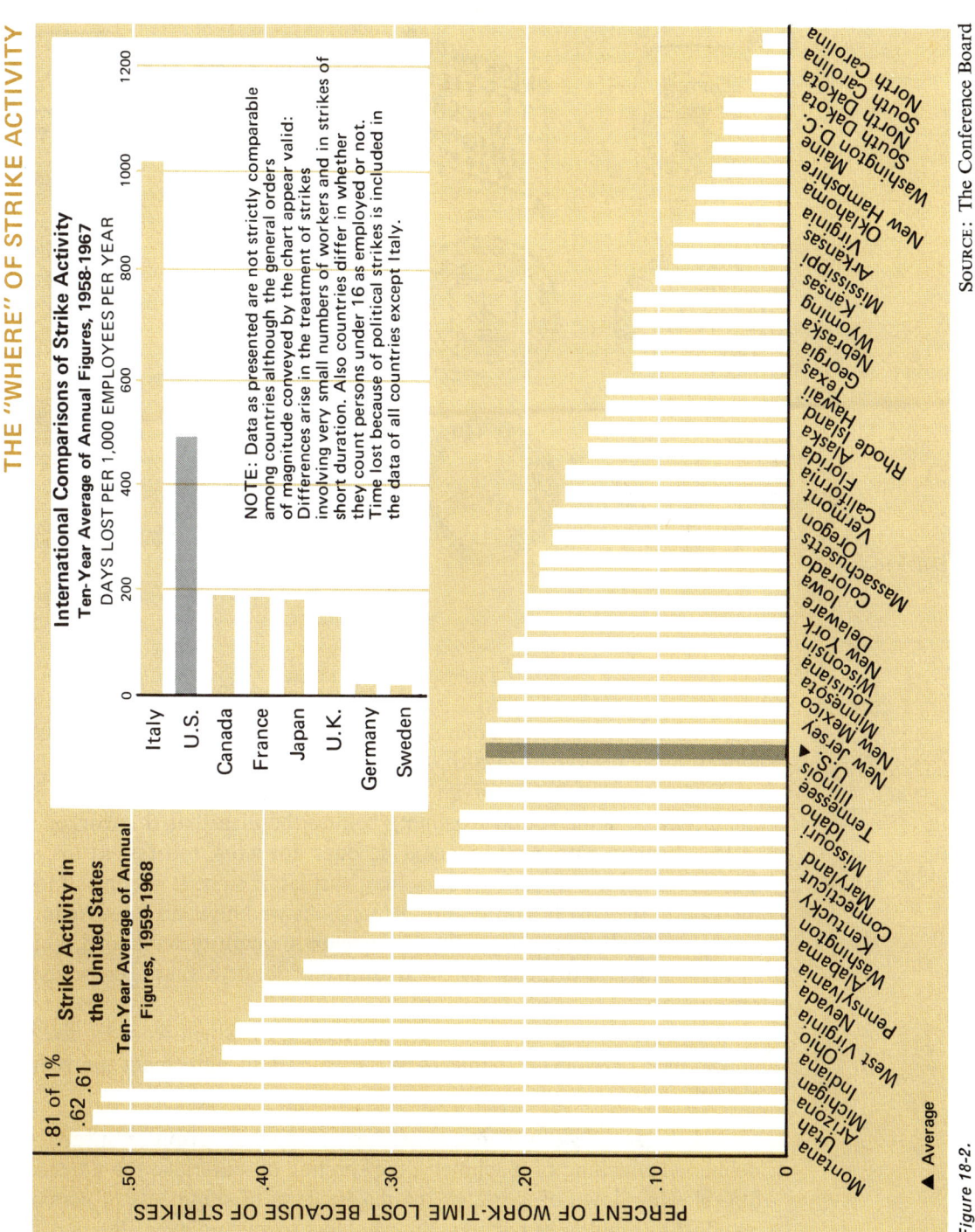

THE "WHERE" OF STRIKE ACTIVITY

International Comparisons of Strike Activity
Ten-Year Average of Annual Figures, 1958-1967
DAYS LOST PER 1,000 EMPLOYEES PER YEAR

NOTE: Data as presented are not strictly comparable among countries although the general orders of magnitude conveyed by the chart appear valid: Differences arise in the treatment of strikes involving very small numbers of workers and in strikes of short duration. Also countries differ in whether they count persons under 16 as employed or not. Time lost because of political strikes is included in the data of all countries except Italy.

Strike Activity in the United States
Ten-Year Average of Annual Figures, 1959-1968

PERCENT OF WORK-TIME LOST BECAUSE OF STRIKES

▲ Average

SOURCE: The Conference Board

Figure 18-2.

Figure 18-3.

Union Label and Service Trades Dept., AFL-CIO

Examples of Union Labels

just so much work to be done and that the worker can make his job last longer, and preserve his health, if he does not hurry.

From the standpoint of an individual worker and a particular job, there may be some sound reasoning behind the idea that the worker can at least remain employed longer if he does not work too fast at his job. But it is possible that such a policy may hurt labor since it may result in an increase in the cost of goods and services. As we know, an increase in the price of a good or a service causes a decrease in quantity demanded, which, in turn, causes a decrease in the quantity of labor demanded for use in production.

The Taft-Hartley Act prohibits *slowdowns*, by which workers give the appearance of working while they are in fact in agreement to reduce output.

Sabotage. *Sabotage* in connection with labor disputes means the deliberate wrecking of machinery, the spoiling of materials, the unreasonable slowing down of work, or the misdirecting of shipments of goods in an effort by employees to create financial loss to an employer. Responsible labor leaders do not advocate and do not condone the willful destruction of property.

SOME EMPLOYERS HAVE OPPOSED UNIONS IN MANY WAYS

In order to protect what they consider to be their rights with reference to wage contracts, employers make use of various devices.

Employers and business associations. Employers usually are organized into associations according to the nature of the product that they manufacture or sell. For example, automobile manufacturers, shoe manufacturers, iron and steel manufacturers, owners of drygoods stores and grocery stores, as well as other businessmen, have their own organizations. These organizations, in turn, are sometimes combined into a more or less loose federation or association. In this way employers are able to exchange information and to take collective action with regard to policies, and especially with reference to obtaining favorable publicity.

The object of these associations is not primarily to fight unions. But, at the same time, membership in an association does enable employers to establish more or less uniform policies for dealings with labor.

Blacklists. In the past some employers have made use of *blacklists*. These lists contained the names of employees who were, for one reason or another, unsatisfactory to the previous employer. Union activity was often a reason for blacklisting. The lists were sometimes exchanged among employers. Blacklisting is now illegal.

The lockout. Another method used by certain employers in their contest with labor is the lockout. By a *lockout* is meant the shutting down of the factory or other place of employment by the employer. Although lockouts have not been used frequently, the threat to close the factory has sometimes been used in the hope that employees would be influenced to meet the demands of the employer. A lockout in violation of an agreement with a union may be prohibited by a court.

Company unions. A *company union* is an organization of employees in a particular establishment that has no affiliation with any other organized group of workers. At one time some employers encouraged the formation of company unions. But under the National Labor Relations Act (1935) employers are not permitted to encourage by financial aid or to discourage the formation of a union in their plants.

Yellow-dog contract. Years ago it was not unusual for an employer to ask wage earners to sign a contract by which the latter agreed not to join a labor union. Or, if the wage earner was a member of a labor union, he agreed to sever his connection with the labor organization. Such contracts were popularly known in labor circles as *yellow-dog contracts*. They were declared unenforceable by the Norris-LaGuardia Act (1932) and outlawed by the National Labor Relations Act.

The injunction. Formerly one of the most effective means that the employer had in combating strikes was the injunction. An employer could ask a judge to issue an *injunction*, or order, enjoining strikers from doing certain acts or commanding them to refrain from certain acts.

The Norris-LaGuardia Act was designed in part to prevent federal judges from issuing injunctions against strikers when the employers claim that the strikers are conspiring to injure their property. Merely quitting work and urging others to refuse work is not to be considered as conspiracy. Several states also have laws limiting the use of injunctions in labor disputes.

WHAT ARE WAYS FOR SETTLING LABOR DISPUTES?

Most questions arising over wages and working conditions are settled by peaceful means.

Mediation and voluntary arbitration. With the help and encouragement of a third party the workers and the employers in a plant or an industry may come together, discuss their troubles, and arrive at a satisfactory solution. This method of settling disputes is called *mediation* or, sometimes, *conciliation*.

The federal government maintains the Federal Mediation and Conciliation Service, an organization that is designed to mediate all kinds of labor disputes except those in the railroad and airline industries. During recent years the Conciliation Service has handled hundreds of labor disputes each year. The National Mediation Board undertakes to settle disputes between railway employees and their employers. Some of the states have set up boards to attempt the solution of disputes between wage earners and employers.

When the two sides to a controversy are unable to settle the difficulties themselves, an outside individual or a group of individuals may be asked to consider the claims of both sides and to attempt to effect a peaceful solution. If both sides agree to submit their difficulties to an individual or a group and to abide by the decision, the method of settlement is known as *voluntary arbitration*.

Compulsory arbitration. Some persons and organizations have proposed compulsory arbitration as the best method of settling labor disputes. They contend that there should be a government board of arbitration that would have the right to enforce its decisions in labor disputes. This method would be *compulsory arbitration.* Most employers and unions are opposed to this method of settling labor disputes.

THE NATIONAL LABOR RELATIONS ACT OF 1935

This law is sometimes referred to as the Wagner Act because it was sponsored by Senator Robert F. Wagner, of New York. The Act was designed to insure to workers the right to organize and to bargain collectively with their employers. The law applies to all employers and employees in establishments whose activities affect interstate commerce, excluding those covered by the Railway Labor Act of 1926. The measure provides for the creation of the National Labor Relations Board, appointed by the President and confirmed by the Senate. Under the law employees may join labor organizations without interference from employers, and they may choose representatives for the purpose of collective bargaining. The Board may order an election by secret ballot to determine which union, if any, shall represent workers in a plant. The NLRB has been very successful in settling disputes brought before it.

The statute declares that it is "unfair" for employers to:

1. Interfere with, restrain, or coerce employees in connection with their desires to belong to labor organizations.
2. Discriminate against employees or prospective employees because of union affiliations, except that employers are not restrained from entering into closed- or open-shop agreements with unions.
3. Attempt to influence the formation of any labor organization or contribute to its support.
4. Refuse to bargain collectively with the duly elected representatives of his employees.
5. Discharge or discriminate in any way against an employee for testifying before the National Labor Relations Board.

THE LABOR-MANAGEMENT RELATIONS ACT REVISED THE NLRA

Continued opposition to the NLRA by many employers finally resulted in the enactment in 1947 of the Labor-Management Relations Act, popularly referred to as the Taft-Hartley Act. The general intent of the law is to limit some of the rights enjoyed by labor organizations under the Norris-LaGuardia Act and the National Labor Relations Act. The more important provisions of the Taft-Hartley Act are:

1. Unions may be sued for damages arising from jurisdictional disputes or for failure to live up to their contracts with employers.
2. Closed-shop agreements are forbidden, but union shops are permitted under certain conditions.
3. Strikes that might endanger national health and safety may be postponed for 80 days by court injunction.
4. Unions and corporations may not use their funds for political purposes.
5. Certain union practices are declared to be "unfair."
6. Jurisdictional strikes and secondary boycotts are prohibited.
7. Unions must give their members a complete statement of union income, expenditures, and assets.
8. States may enact laws specifying that no person shall be denied or excluded from employment because of failure to join a union. Such a law is often referred to as a "right-to-work law."

The National Labor Relations Board was increased from three members to five. The Board has the power to investigate unfair labor practices of all kinds, to supervise employees' elections of their representatives, and to ask the Circuit Court of Appeals to enforce its orders. On the whole, labor organizations are very much opposed to the Taft-Hartley Act.

THE LABOR-MANAGEMEMENT REPORTING AND DISCLOSURE ACT OF 1959 (THE LANDRUM-GRIFFIN LAW)

The Act comprises seven "Titles" each of which covers a different phase. Title I is actually a "Bill of Rights" providing free speech and assembly by rank and file union members; (II) requires detailed reports on union finances and requires employers to file reports concerning payments made to unions or union officials; (III) requires semiannual reporting on trusteeships over subordinate labor organizations; (IV) outlines provisions in regard to election procedures; (V) prohibits persons with records of crime or communist affiliation from holding union office; (VI) contains a number of miscellaneous provisions; and Title VII contains a number of amendments to the Taft-Hartley Act.

WHAT IS UNION-MANAGEMENT COOPERATION?

By *union-management cooperation* is meant a program by which a union agrees to cooperate with management in reducing costs, and union members and management work together in a spirit of cooperation, friendship, and trust toward each other. Under such a program each one endeavors to promote the interests of both the employer and the employees. The general idea is that, if the employer can reduce his costs of production, he can pay better wages and, at the same time, sell a greater quantity of his product and thereby make more profit.

There have been several successful attempts at union-management cooperation, and many thoughtful persons are convinced that the idea is growing.

COLLECTIVE BARGAINING IN GOVERNMENT EMPLOYMENT

Until fairly recently collective bargaining has generally been restricted to private business and industry. Now, however, the federal government and some states provide for unionization and collective bargaining for public employees. In 1962, through Executive Order 10988, President Kennedy opened the way for unionization and bargaining activities among employees in the Executive branch of government. President Nixon extended the privilege in 1969 through Executive Order 11491. In general these Executive Orders provided for many of the usual features of collective bargaining to apply to federal employment but with certain limitations such as no recognition of a right to strike. Some states also have opened the door to organization among their employees. Although these developments are in their infancy, their growth may be expected throughout the next few years.

SUMMARY

At one time labor unions were regarded as illegal combinations and "conspiracies." Now employees in private industry are given the right by statutory law to organize and bargain collectively with employers.

The major purpose of unions is the betterment of the economic condition of their members. In seeking this main objective, unions maintain that four things are necessary: (1) recognition of the union by the employer; (2) union strength and security; (3) satisfactory employment contracts for their members; and (4) acceptance of the union by the employer.

More specifically, unions aim to (1) standardize wage rates; (2) raise and maintain wages; (3) improve working conditions; (4) increase the security of jobs for members; (5) establish industrial jurisprudence; and (6) secure certain fringe benefits.

A craft union is composed of workers of a certain type. An industrial union is made up of all the workers in a plant or industry. Arguments can be advanced for each type of union.

The organization of unions includes local unions, district councils, state councils, national and international unions, and national federations.

An independent union is one that is not affiliated with a national federation. A company union is made up of the employees in a certain plant and has no connection with a national organization of workers.

Unions make or have made use of various devices, including trade agreements; restrictions on the right of the employer to hire workers, including closed-shop, union-shop, preferential-shop, maintenance-of-membership agreements, and the checkoff system; strikes; union labels; limitation of output; and sabotage.

Employers have opposed unions in different ways, including informal agreements as to policies in dealing with unions, blacklists, lockouts, company unions, yellow-dog contracts, and court injunctions.

Laws and devices for settling labor disputes and promoting peace between employers and employees include mediation, arbitration, the National Labor Relations Act, the Labor-Management Relations Act, and the Labor-Management Reporting and Disclosure Act. Union-management cooperation is an attitude and a formalized plan whereby employees and the employer work together for the mutual benefit of all concerned. Collective bargaining is relatively new for public employees, but it has gained official recognition at both the federal and state levels in recent years.

NEW TERMS

AFL-CIO
agency-shop contracts
blacklists
boycott
checkoff
closed shop
collective bargaining
Committee on Political Education
company union
compulsory arbitration
craft union
Federal Mediation and
   Conciliation Service
grievance procedure
independent union
industrial union
injunction
Labor-Management Relations Act
Labor-Management Reporting and
   Disclosure Act

Labor's League for
   Political Education
Landrum-Griffin Act
limiting output
lockout
maintenance-of-membership clause
mediation *or* conciliation
National Labor Relations Board
Norris-LaGuardia Act
Political Action Committee
preferential-shop arrangement
right-to-work laws
sabotage
scabs
secondary boycott
seniority rating
slowdowns
standard wage rates
strike
strikebreakers

sympathetic strike
Taft-Hartley Act
trade agreement
union federation
union label
union-management cooperation

union security
union-shop agreement
voluntary arbitration
Wagner Act
yellow-dog contracts

QUESTIONS ON THE CHAPTER

1. What are the objectives of labor unions?
2. What is meant by "standard wage rates"?
3. What proposal made by some unions could, if adopted, change pay systems drastically?
4. What efforts have been made by unions to raise and maintain wage rates?
5. How do seniority ratings enhance job security?
6. What is meant by a system of "industrial jurisprudence"?
7. What are some examples of "fringe benefits"?
8. Why was the Congress of Industrial Organizations formed?
9. What is the AFL-CIO?
10. What are some of the independent unions?
11. Does organized labor take any part in politics? Explain.
12. What is meant by union security?
13. How may labor disputes be settled by means of (a) mediation; (b) voluntary arbitration; (c) compulsory arbitration?
14. What are the main provisions of the National Labor Relations Act?
15. What are the relations of the Labor-Management Relations Act to the National Labor Relations Act and the Norris-LaGuardia Act?
16. What are some of the requirements of the Landrum-Griffin Act?
17. What does union-management cooperation mean? What does it require for success?
18. In what way has collective bargaining been recognized for public employees?

APPLYING YOUR ECONOMIC UNDERSTANDING

1. Certain labor-management contracts have escalator clauses with automatic increases when the Consumer Price Index rises. Is this related to both raising and maintaining wages? Why or why not?
2. Visit the personnel manager of a local plant and find out what state laws are in effect concerning working conditions in that plant. Report on your findings to the class.

3. Make a tabulation of the kinds of unions which are operative in your community. Classify them as to whether they are craft unions or industrial unions.
4. Organize a number of student committees to visit different labor organizations and collect information on (a) how each union is organized, (b) how each union is governed, and (c) its relationship to the state and national organization. Have each committee report its findings to the class. Have the class summarize the similarities in each union as based upon the committees' reports.
5. What are some examples of articles used in your community that carry union labels? What is the purpose of such labels?
6. Using newspaper or magazine references, select several recent or current labor-management disputes in your area. Which methods did labor use in the dispute? What devices did management use? What brought about, or is likely to bring about, a settlement?
7. Why does AFL-CIO oppose compulsory arbitration? Would management hold a similar view? Why or why not?
8. Using the *Reader's Guide to Periodical Literature* as a reference, locate some articles written by labor leaders at the time the Taft-Hartley Act was proposed and passed. What fears were expressed by some labor leaders? Has the operation of the law justified their fears?
9. Is it correct to say that the Landrum-Griffin Act is labor's "Bill of Rights"? Why or why not?
10. What is the role of government in the area of labor-management relations? Do you believe that this role should be expanded? Why or why not?

CHALLENGES TO ECONOMIC COMPETENCE

1. Arrange for a representative of the Labor Department of your state or the federal government to discuss in class the economic losses caused by strikes. Lead the summary discussion at the conclusion of the talk.
2. Prepare a biography on the life of a prominent leader from government, a national union, or management, who has made a significant contribution in labor-management relations.
3. Organize a bulletin board display centered upon "Labor-Management Relations."
4. Prepare a theme on one of the following: (a) The People vs. Labor Unions, (b) The History of the Labor Union Movement, (c) To Protect These Rights, (d) The New Look in AFL-CIO.

Unit 5

Money, Credit, and Banking

Chapter 19 Money and Its Use
Chapter 20 Credit and Its Use
Chapter 21 Money, Credit, and Banking

Long before coins and paper money came into existence, goods of several kinds were used for money. In olden times some good that was desired by nearly everyone came to be used as a medium of exchange.

At the left are stone discs from the island of Yap. What would be some of the reasons why this kind of money could not be used successfully in our present economic system?

Chase Manhattan Bank Money Museum

At the right is a double coil of feather money. It is 27 feet in length, and was made by natives on Santa Cruz Island from the red feathers of over 500 tiny honey birds. Until the early years of the 20th century such coils were used in the payment of special fines, the purchase of ocean-going canoes, and for paying for a wife.

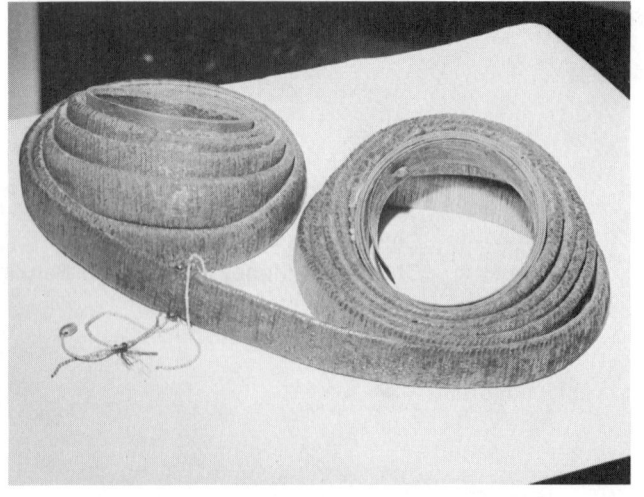

Chase Manhattan Bank Money Museum

Chapter 19

Money and Its Use

What is money?
What are the functions of money — how is it used?
What qualities must a satisfactory money possess?
How is government related to money?
What kinds of money are in use in the United States?

No one need tell you that money is important. You have learned that simple fact by experience. You, or your family, must have some money if you are to have the barest necessities of life. If you have enough money, you can enjoy the use of some luxuries. Some critics accuse Americans of being too much concerned with the getting of money. It is true that in our culture the possession of money sometimes affects an individual's status in his group. Yet this recognition of the power of money is not new. In Shakespeare's *Merry Wives of Windsor* one of the characters says, somewhat cynically, ". . . if money go before, all ways do lie open."

Since money is so important, we should want to know a great deal about it — what it is, how it originated, what gives it purchasing power, and how it may gain or lose value. How to get it is another problem!

WHAT IS MONEY?

On first thought it might seem easy to give a simple and correct answer to this question. For example, after thinking about it a little, we might say that *money* is anything that is generally used to pay for the purchase of goods and services and to discharge debts.

At the same time, it is estimated that about 90 percent of all goods and services that are sold are paid for by means of checks on bank deposits. Are these deposits money? According to our definition it would be reasonable to say that they are. Therefore, among economists, it is generally held that the term "money" includes not only coins and the paper money that is printed by the government, but also bank deposits that may be withdrawn by check at any time.

In this chapter, however, we shall be primarily concerned with the coins and paper money that are issued by the government and put into circulation by the banks. Money of this kind is usually referred to as *currency*. It includes pennies, nickels, dimes, quarters, half-dollars, silver dollars, and paper bills of various denominations.

VARIOUS THINGS HAVE BEEN USED FOR MONEY

Long before coins and paper money came into existence, goods of several kinds were used for money. In olden times some good that was desired by nearly everyone came to be used as a medium of exchange. Early writers tell us that the Latins often used cattle as money. In this connection it is interesting to know that our word "pecuniary," which pertains to money, is derived from the Latin word *pecus*, which means "cattle." Homer, a famous Greek writer, stated that the value of the armor of one of the ancient heroes was so many head of oxen.

Among the American Indians, wampum, or colored beads and shells, was used in trade. Eventually, wampum was often used as a medium of exchange by the American colonists. In 1619 the General Assembly at Jamestown, Virginia, passed a law that resulted in making it possible to use tobacco as money. A little later corn and musket balls were often used as money in Massachusetts. In 1719 the Assembly of South Carolina passed a law providing that rice should be receivable for taxes. Subsequently, rice came into general use as money in that colony. In Tennessee and Kentucky, as well as in other settlements, deer and raccoon skins circulated in the place of coins.

MONEY PERFORMS SEVERAL FUNCTIONS

The primary function or use of money is to serve as a medium or means of exchange. As we know, sellers ordinarily exchange their goods for money, and buyers usually exchange money for goods.

In order to be a satisfactory medium of exchange in the modern business world, anything that serves as money must perform several secondary or incidental functions, which are (1) a measure of value; (2) a store of value; (3) a basis for credit; and (4) a standard of deferred payment.

(1) Money as a measure of value. Individuals who wish to exchange goods must form estimates of the value of the respective utilities of the goods. For this reason, where most transactions involve the exchange of money for goods, a standard for stating values is needed. The usual standards for measuring volume, distance, or weight — such as a bushel, a foot, or a pound — would be of little use. These are not suitable as measures of value. We can, however, take some one good (gold, for example), divide it into units, and compare our desire for a unit of the good with our desire for units of other goods or services. In this way the unit becomes a "unit of value."

Essentially that is what occurred when we adopted the dollar as our unit of value. In 1792 Congress authorized the fixing of either 24.75 grains of pure gold or 371.25 grains of pure silver as our money unit, and it decreed that these quantities of gold or silver should be called a "dollar." As we shall see, the weight of the gold dollar was changed later. Other kinds of money were also authorized, but in each case the value of the money was based on the gold or silver dollar.

Since one may not want to pay as much as a whole dollar for some things, it is convenient to have the dollar broken down into fractional parts, just as the foot measure is divided into inches. In our monetary system, therefore, the dollar has been divided into a hundred parts; and coins ranging from 1 cent (one hundredth of a dollar) to $1 have been adopted. We are thus able to buy and sell conveniently things that are valued in fractions of a dollar.

(2) **Money as a store of value.** If you perform a day's work for another person, you expect to receive something in exchange for your labor. If you sell a bushel of wheat or a bale of cotton, you expect something of value in exchange for your commodity. In either case you will probably receive payment in the form of money. Since the money has purchasing

Chase Manhattan Bank Money Museum

Illus. 19-1. Since one may not want to pay as much as a whole dollar for some things, it is convenient to have the dollar broken down into fractional parts, just as the foot measure is divided into inches. Above is pictured the first coin issued by the United States, referred to as the Franklin Cent because of its inscription "Mind Your Business," a phrase attributed to Benjamin Franklin. The closed chain of thirteen links on the coin's reverse symbolizes the unity of the thirteen original colonies.

power, it might be said that, in effect, you converted the value of your labor or your wheat into money. You can put the money in your pocket, deposit it in a bank, or spend it. As long as you keep it and it retains its purchasing power, the value of what you sold will remain stored in it.

(3) **Money as a basis for credit.** In order for business concerns to meet their financial obligations when they fall due, they must build up a reserve of money. Likewise, banks must maintain a reserve of cash with which to pay depositors. If it were known that the bank on which a check was drawn had no cash on hand, no one would want the check. The reason why the check would not be acceptable would be that the credit of the bank had disappeared because it had no money.

(4) **Money as a standard of deferred payment.** If I wish to buy $1,000 worth of goods, the seller may be willing to sell them to me on account for sixty days. At the end of that time I shall have to make payment in money or something equally acceptable. Or I may be able to borrow the amount at a bank and pay cash for the goods. Of course, if I borrow the money at a bank, later I shall have to return the amount agreed upon. So in either case, payment is deferred until a later date, and money is used as the standard to indicate the amount to be repaid.

It may be that, when I return the $1,000, this amount of money will not buy as much as it would have bought when I borrowed it. On the other hand, it may buy more. But, because I repay the same number of dollars, a disagreement as to the amount of purchasing power to be repaid is avoided.

MONEY AS A MEDIUM OF EXCHANGE

Before a thing can become a medium of exchange, it must be capable of performing the four functions that we have just discussed on this and the two preceding pages. Anything that may be used satisfactorily as (a) a measure of value, (b) a store for value, (c) a reserve for credit, and (d) a standard for deferred payment can be used as a medium of exchange.

MONEY MUST POSSESS CERTAIN QUALITIES

Anything that is used successfully as money must possess the following qualities:

1. *Acceptability.* Individuals and business concerns must be willing to accept the object in exchange for what they wish to sell.
2. *Portability.* It must be possible to carry the object around without too much inconvenience.

3. *Durability*. It must not wear out too quickly. Or if it wears out rather quickly, it must be possible to replace it without great expense for another of equal value, as is the case with our paper money.
4. *Homogeneity*. All the units must be of equal value.
5. *Divisibility*. It must be possible to calculate values in terms of fractions of the unit and also in terms of multiples of the unit. In the case of our money, we have fractional coins, as 1-cent and 10-cent pieces, and multiple notes, as the $5 or the $10 federal reserve notes.
6. *Cognizability*. It must be possible to recognize the object easily. This is one reason why metal and paper intended for use as money are given standard designs by the government.
7. *Stability of Value*. To be used successfully as money, the value of the object must not fluctuate too much.

WHY ARE GOLD AND SILVER FAVORITE MONEY METALS?

By considering the qualities needed in money, we can see why gold and silver are widely used as money. Before paper money came into existence, gold was wanted by nearly everyone. It was not necessary to sustain life, but it could be worked into various kinds of ornaments. Its possession in any great quantity gave distinction to a person because with the gold he could obtain almost anything he wanted. The same thing was true of silver, only to a lesser degree.

Neither gold nor silver can be used as perfect money. But both metals possess the desired qualities in a higher degree than other metals.

ONLY THE GOVERNMENT COINS AND PRINTS MONEY

Only the federal government may coin or print money. It is easy to see why individuals, corporations, and state and local governments are not permitted to issue money. If they did so, the different kinds of money in use would vary as to value, and it would be difficult to buy and sell goods. Most money would not be readily acceptable.

The Constitution of the United States says, "No State shall . . . coin money . . . make anything but gold and silver coin a tender in payment of debts . . . ." And "The Congress shall have power . . . To coin money, regulate the value thereof . . . ." Thus, the coinage of money became a monopoly of the federal government.

When the national government was founded, there was a scarcity of gold in this country. For that reason it was decided to use both gold and silver for the coins of larger denominations and less valuable metals for those of smaller denominations. The dollar was established as the monetary unit. As we stated before, its weight was fixed at 24.75 grains of pure gold, and the weight of the silver dollar was fixed at 371.25 grains of silver.

Illus. 19-2. Only the federal government may coin or print money. The Bureau of Engraving and Printing designs, engraves, and prints all major items of a financial character issued by the United States Government.

In 1837, however, the content of the gold dollar was fixed at 23.22 grains. The weight content was reduced in 1934 to 13.71 grains and in 1972 to 12.63 grains, but gold was not to be coined. Since it was first coined, the silver dollar has contained 371.25 grains of pure silver.

WHAT IS FREE COINAGE?

Until we abandoned the gold standard, we had always had the "free coinage" of gold. Until 1873 we also had the free coinage of silver.

Free coinage does not mean that the money metal or metals will be coined gratis. A charge may be made when the owner of bullion takes his metal to the mint to be coined. *Free coinage* means that anyone is free to take his metal to the mint to have it coined into money. If the government charges just enough to pay for the work of coinage, the charge is called *brassage;* if an extra amount is charged, that is, anything in excess of brassage, this amount is called *seigniorage*.

WE FIRST ADOPTED THE BIMETALLIC STANDARD

When the Constitution of the United States went into effect (1789), we had no national coins. Foreign coins were in circulation, including many Spanish silver dollars. These dollars averaged about 371.25 grains of pure silver in weight. As a rule, they could be exchanged for 24.75 grains of gold. Upon the recommendation of Alexander Hamilton, the first Secretary of the Treasury, the United States adopted a bimetallic standard in 1792. *Bimetallism* is the use of two metals at a fixed ratio of value as a monetary standard. In the United States, gold and silver were the metals adopted.

Mint ratio and market ratio. The monetary standard was established as a gold dollar containing 24.75 grains of gold and a silver dollar weighing 371.25 grains of silver. The ratio between these two amounts was exactly 15 to 1. In other words, one ounce of gold was worth 15 ounces of silver. This ratio was established as the *mint ratio.*

But when people are free to trade gold and silver, as they were then, there is a *market ratio,* as well as a mint ratio, for the values of gold and silver; that is, since it is possible to use gold and silver for purposes other than money, there is a price for each metal in terms of the other that is fixed by demand and supply. The mint ratio may be fixed by the government, but the market ratio depends upon the demand for and the supply of each of the two metals.

Gresham's law. The chief difficulty in using a bimetallic standard arises from the operation of Gresham's law. The first definite statement of this principle is usually attributed to Sir Thomas Gresham, the financial adviser to Queen Elizabeth I. *Gresham's law* may be stated as follows: When two kinds of money having equal stated (or nominal) values — but not being in equal demand — are in circulation, the less desirable kind tends to drive the other out of circulation. If the market price, or ratio, does not agree with the government price, or mint ratio, one of the metals of a bimetallic standard will cease to be used as money.

Let us suppose that, when the bimetallic standard was adopted, a coat could be bought for $10. If the buyer had both kinds of money, he would as soon pay for it in gold as in silver because the two metals were equal in value both at the mint and in the market. Payment would require 247.5 (10×24.75) grains of gold or 3712.5 (10×371.25) grains of silver in coin.

Suppose, however, that the market price of silver in terms of gold rose and that in the market it would require $11 in gold (272.25 grains) to buy $10 worth of silver. The mint ratio would still remain at 15 to 1. But anyone owing a debt and having both gold and silver in his possession would pay the debt in gold because that metal would be worth less in the market than silver; that is, the gold in $10 worth of gold money would not buy 15 times as much silver in the market. The creditor could not compel payment in silver. Under these conditions gold would be used to pay debts because the debtor would have the choice of paying in either gold or silver. According to the mint ratio, gold would be overvalued, as compared with the ratio at which it could be exchanged for silver in the market. If gold thus remained overvalued for a considerable time, silver would cease to be used as money because people would use gold in paying their debts. Silver would eventually disappear from circulation.

HOW GRESHAM'S LAW OPERATES

Assume that the mint ratio is 15 to 1; that is, 1 ounce of gold buys 15 ounces of silver at the mint.

When the Market Ratio Is —	Gold Is —	Silver Is —	The Reason for These Effects Is —
15 to 1	Coined	Coined	The two metals have the same values on the market and at the mint.
16 to 1	Not coined — disappears from circulation	Coined	Gold buys more silver on the market than at the mint.
14 to 1	Coined	Not coined — disappears from circulation	Silver buys more gold on the market than at the mint.

On the other hand, if the mint ratio of silver to gold was 15 to 1 and the market ratio was 16 to 1, silver would be overvalued; and it would tend to be used in paying debts. This practice would have a tendency to drive the more valuable money, gold, out of use.

Although there were some persons who felt that bimetallism was desirable, our experience with it was not satisfactory. Therefore, in 1900, we adopted the gold monometallic or gold-coin standard.

WHAT IS MEANT BY THE GOLD-COIN STANDARD?

To explain exactly what is meant by this expression, we may say the *gold-coin standard* means that:

(1) A unit of gold is the measure of value for goods, services, and other money. Every country that adopts the gold standard designates the amount of gold that is to serve as the unit of value. The unit is given a name, as dollar, pound sterling, franc, or mark.

(2) The government will coin an unlimited amount of gold bullion. Gold bullion is gold in a nonmonetary form, usually bars. As long as the nation is on the gold-coin standard, anyone may have gold bullion coined into money by paying a charge for brassage or seigniorage. If silver is also used for money, the government buys only the amount that is needed.

(3) All other money can be exchanged for gold at its face value. As long as the nation is on the gold standard, anyone may take his other kinds of money to a bank and have them exchanged for gold.

(4) Gold is legal tender. This means that if you owe a debt, you may offer to make payment in gold. If the creditor refuses to take the gold, he cannot claim that you have not made an acceptable offer to pay the debt. If payment were offered in money that was not legal tender, he could claim that a satisfactory offer to pay the debt had not been made, and he could bring suit in court for collection of the debt. Other forms of money also may be legal tender.

(5) People are free to own and use gold as they do any other commodity. That is to say, they can buy or sell it, or use it to manufacture such things as rings and watch cases.

WHY WE ABANDONED THE GOLD-COIN STANDARD IN 1933

In 1929 business the world over suffered a severe decline. Conditions grew worse for several years. By 1932 fewer than one-half dozen important nations remained on the gold standard. During the early months of 1933 a general money panic seized the people, and they began to convert their money and bank deposits into gold. At the same time poor business conditions made it difficult for many banks to remain open.

Because of the large number of bank failures and the growing demand for gold for hoarding purposes, in 1933 the President of the United States declared a bank holiday, by which all national banks were closed in order to give people time to recover from their panic and to enable the federal government to try to do something to help the banks. All persons owning gold or gold certificates were ordered to turn them in to the Treasury of the United States and to receive in exchange other kinds of money. Although payment in gold may have been promised, the President declared that all public and private debts could be paid with other kinds of money. Thus, we "went off the gold standard."

THE DOLLAR DEVALUATION OF 1934

In 1934 the Gold Reserve Act was passed by Congress. This act provided that:

1. All gold held by federal reserve banks had to be transferred to the Treasury of the United States; in exchange the banks would receive gold certificates

which, however, could not be redeemed in gold. The certificates could be used only by the banks in dealing with the government or with other federal reserve banks.
2. Coinage of gold was forbidden. All gold coins owned by the government had to be melted into bars.
3. With the approval of the government, gold in limited quantities could be purchased by private individuals and concerns for manufacturing uses. Also under certain conditions gold could be bought by foreign countries and shipped abroad.
4. The President could reduce the weight of the dollar by not more than 50 percent of its former weight.

Immediately after the passage of the act, the President declared that the United States Treasury stood ready to buy gold at a price of $35 per ounce. This meant that the weight of the gold dollar was now 13.71 grains instead of 23.22 grains. (The weight of an ounce of gold, 480 grains, divided by 35 equals 13.71.) The gold in the new kind of dollar is only 59.06 percent as much as it was. This reduction is called *devaluation*.

This means that since the weight of the dollar was reduced, the number of dollars that could be made from the gold held by the government was greater, although the actual amount of the gold was the same as before. As a result of devaluation, the gold stock held by the Treasury increased in value by two billion dollars.

THE EFFECTS OF DEVALUATION

One of the objects in devaluing the dollar was to raise prices. The government believed that, if the value of money was reduced and prices were increased, people could sell goods at higher prices and thus pay their debts more easily; businessmen would be able to make more profits; production would be stimulated; and recovery from the depression would be hastened. After we left the gold standard and the dollar was reduced in value, prices began to rise. Production of consumer goods increased, and many corporations were able to show marked increases in profits. There was some increase in employment and in wages.

Government also was engaged at this time in a huge spending program. It is not known whether the increased spending or the devaluation of the dollar had the greater effect on prices.

For some time devaluation tended to increase the sale of goods and corporation securities to foreigners because a given amount of foreign money would now buy more dollars to pay for American goods. Chapter 27 will discuss how the dollar was again devalued in 1972 when gold was officially repriced at $38 per ounce.

WHAT IS FIAT MONEY?

Some persons question the necessity for using either gold or silver as standard money. They insist that the principal use of money is that of a medium of exchange. They say that paper money would, therefore, be just as good as any other kind. They argue that the government should print what money is needed and thus avoid the difficulties of a gold, or any other metallic, standard. Such money could not be converted into gold, for gold would not be standard. It would be *fiat money* because it would circulate by the decree, or fiat, of the government.

Fiat, or inconvertible paper, money would be satisfactory (1) if people would accept it in transactions, (2) if the quantity printed could be controlled, and (3) if all nations would adopt a uniform fiat money standard. But custom is strong; and, although they may never see the gold, people like to feel that, in some way or other, their paper money is backed up by gold. Moreover, the printing of money by a government without any relation to the amount of gold reserve has always proved disastrous to the nations that have tried the plan. As long as money is based on gold (even though the relation is indirect), governments are, as a rule, not likely to print so much money as they would if the paper money were not related to gold.

People do not like to pay taxes. Hence, rather than impose more taxes, a government that has the right to print irredeemable money may be tempted to print money with which to carry on its work.

Our experience with fiat money. In 1862 the United States government was authorized by Congress to print paper money with which to carry on the war. It was thought that it would be possible to print enough money to run the war without increasing taxes. So, within a short time, several hundred million dollars of United States notes, or "greenbacks," as they were called, had been printed. In 1864 there were $431 million of these notes in circulation.

As soon as the government began issuing the greenbacks, Gresham's law came into operation. The paper notes came into use, and gold and silver dollars disappeared. In business transactions the paper dollar was the actual standard of value. The value of the paper dollar fell to about 35 cents in terms of gold. In 1879 the government began to redeem the paper notes in gold. Naturally, when the redemption of these notes began, the value of the greenbacks rose until it was equal to that of gold. But from 1863 to 1879 the operation of Gresham's law placed this country on a paper standard, although legally the country was on a bimetallic standard.

Germany's experience with printing-press money. As a result of World War I Germany was heavily in debt, and business conditions were bad. It was decided to print the money needed by the government rather than to try to collect it by means of taxes. At the beginning of the war there were about 3 billion paper marks in circulation in the country. In 1923 the number had increased to more than 496,000,000,000 billion, and prices had risen to astronomical heights.

The situation became intolerable; something had to be done about it. The old money was withdrawn from circulation and replaced by a new kind. This was done by issuing new mark notes, and the old mark notes were "redeemed" in new notes at the rate of 1 trillion paper marks to 1. In this way many people and businesses lost all their savings.

WHAT KINDS OF MONEY DO WE HAVE?

We have many kinds of money in the United States, some of which are coins and the others paper money. Although all of these kinds are not in circulation for use by individuals, we cannot understand our complete monetary system unless we are familiar with each kind of money.

Gold bullion. After the government went off the gold standard in 1933, very few gold coins were left in circulation. People were required to exchange their gold coins and gold certificates for other kinds of money. Now all monetary gold is held by the government in the form of bullion.

Gold certificates. Between 1933 and 1964 only the Treasury and federal reserve banks were authorized to hold gold certificates. In 1964, however, the Secretary of the Treasury removed the restrictions on the general public's holding of gold certificates that were issued prior to January 30, 1934.

Silver bullion. Both silver bullion and silver dollars are held by the Treasury as security for silver certificates.

Silver certificates. In the past, silver held by the Treasury has served as security for silver certificates, which comprised an important portion of our paper money of small denominations. The printing of silver certificates was discontinued in 1963, and this kind of currency is being replaced gradually by federal reserve notes.

Silver and new nonsilver coins. The silver dollar weighs 412.5 grains, 41.25 grains being alloy. Most of the silver acquired by the government is held in the Treasury in the form of bullion, and comparatively few silver dollars are in circulation.

All half-dollars, quarters, and dimes were coined with a 90 percent silver content until 1965 when Congress authorized and the Treasury introduced a new system of coins to replace these old ones over a period of years. The new half-dollars look much like the old ones but are only 40 percent silver. The new nonsilver quarters and dimes are of a so-called "sandwich" construction in which a core of pure copper is centered between outer layers of a copper-nickel alloy as shown below.

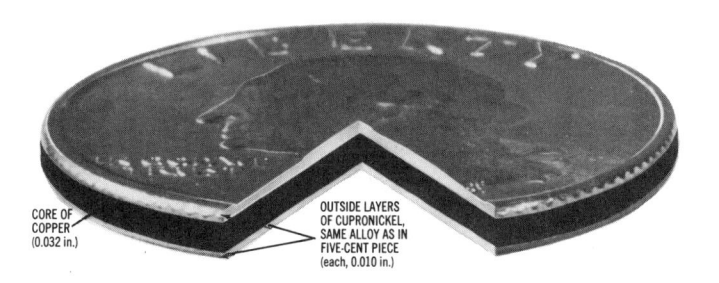

Illus. 19-3. SOURCE: Popular Science Monthly.

A world shortage of silver made the new coin system necessary as a conservation measure. Increasing business needs for coins and the growing demands for silver for industrial, defense, professional, and artistic uses had resulted in a critical drain on the national stock of silver.

Minor coins. The minor coins consist of the nickel and the one-cent piece. The nickel is composed of 25 percent nickel and 75 percent copper. The one-cent piece is composed of 95 percent copper and 5 percent tin and zinc. These coins are made by the government as business demands them.

United States notes, or greenbacks. Any kind of paper money is sometimes called a greenback because of its usual color. In reality the term *greenback* is applicable to only one kind of paper money — United States notes.

National bank notes. The National Bank Act was passed in 1863. This law provided for the organization of banks under a federal charter. Banks so organized were required to buy certain amounts of government bonds, the amount depending upon the size of the bank. Some much-needed money was obtained by the government in this way. The banks were given the right to issue national bank notes and were required to leave the government bonds on deposit with the Treasurer of the United States as security that the notes would be redeemed. National bank notes were acceptable anywhere in the country, and for a long time they served as an important part of our monetary system. In 1935 the government redeemed the bonds that the banks had on deposit with the United States Treasury, and the issuance of national bank notes was discontinued.

Treasury notes of 1890. By the provisions of the Sherman Act of 1890, the government was required to purchase certain quantities of silver. To pay for the silver, the government issued notes similar to greenbacks. They are the promissory notes of the government and are payable "in coin." Until 1933 they were, in practice, ordinarily redeemable in gold.

Federal reserve currency. In an attempt to improve the banking system, Congress passed the Federal Reserve Act in 1913. The purposes of the Federal Reserve System were several, but only one need be considered at this point.

Under the former banking system the amount of money had been limited to the kinds described in the preceding paragraphs. It was felt, however, that the amount of money should be elastic, that it should be possible for the amount to increase when business needs required more money and to decrease when the same amount of money was not needed. The Federal Reserve System therefore provides that a commercial bank belonging to the system may borrow from the federal reserve bank in its district by pledging government securities or commercial paper as surety for the loan. The commercial paper consists of promissory notes and other kinds of written promises and orders to pay that arise from business transactions and that have been received by the commercial bank from its customers. When this commercial paper is pledged as collateral, the transaction is known as a *discount*. For the most part, however, the borrowing takes the form of a loan that is secured by government obligations. In this case the transaction is known as an *advance*. In both cases the loan results either in an increase in the deposit of the commercial bank with the federal reserve bank or in the issuance of federal reserve notes to the borrowing institution.

By meeting certain conditions, each federal reserve bank may issue federal reserve notes, our main form of currency. Thus, the money issued by a federal reserve bank has behind it (1) the promises of those who signed the rediscounted commercial paper; (2) the promise of the local bank; (3) the credit of the United States because the federal reserve notes are obligations of the government. The previous 25 percent gold reserve

STATEMENT OF UNITED STATES CURRENCY AND COIN — APRIL 30, 1971
AMOUNTS OUTSTANDING AND IN CIRCULATION

	Amounts Outstanding	Amounts in Circulation
Total Currency and Coin	$60,781,635,817	$56,591,932,816
Currencies Presently Being Issued[a]		
Total	53,775,254,425	49,935,027,220
Federal Reserve Notes[b]	53,452,715,409	49,617,793,404
United States Notes	322,539,016	317,233,816
Coin		
Total	6,709,323,600	6,360,168,397
Standard Silver Dollars	484,719,600	481,675,128
Fractional Coin	6,224,604,000	5,878,493,269
Currencies No Longer Issued		
Total	297,057,792	296,737,199
Federal Reserve Notes[c]	847,480	835,060
Federal Reserve Bank Notes	54,232,466	54,162,935
National Bank Notes	20,151,935	20,145,318
Gold Certificates[d]	3,800,809	3,677,879
Silver Certificates	218,014,568	217,905,473
Treasury Notes of 1890	10,534	10,534

COMPARATIVE TOTALS OF MONEY IN CIRCULATION —
Selected Dates

Date	Amounts (in millions)	Per Capita[e]
April 30, 1971	$56,591.9	$273.80
June 30, 1970	54,351.0	264.62
June 30, 1965	39,719.8	204.14
June 30, 1960	32,064.6	177.47
June 30, 1955	30,229.3	182.90
June 30, 1950	27,156.3	179.03
June 30, 1945	26,746.4	191.14
June 30, 1940	7,847.5	59.40
June 30, 1930	4,522.0	36.74
June 30, 1920	5,467.6	51.36
June 30, 1915	3,319.6	33.01
Jan. 1, 1879	816.3	16.76

[a]Excludes gold certificates, Series of 1934, which are issued only to federal reserve banks and do not appear in circulation.

[b]Issued on and after July 1, 1929.

[c]Issued before July 1, 1929.

[d]Issued before Series of 1934.

[e]Based on Bureau of the Census estimates of population.

SOURCE: Adapted from a report of the Treasury Department.

requirement, which served to limit the amount of federal reserve notes that might be issued, was removed by Congress in March, 1968.

In addition to the federal reserve notes the federal reserve banks formerly issued a small amount of federal reserve bank notes. Few of these notes are now in circulation.

SUMMARY

Money may be defined as anything that is generally used to pay for the purchase of goods and services and to discharge debts. In this chapter the discussion is confined largely to money in the form of currency that is issued by the federal government and federal reserve banks.

Money serves as (1) a measure or standard of value, (2) a store of value, (3) a basis for credit, (4) a standard of deferred payments, and (5) a medium of exchange.

The qualities of good money are (1) acceptability, (2) portability, (3) durability, (4) homogeneity, (5) divisibility, (6) cognizability, and (7) stability of value.

Free coinage exists when one is free to take money metals to the government and have them made into money. Brassage is a charge for coinage that is just enough to pay for the work of coinage. Seigniorage is a charge for coinage that is more than sufficient to cover the cost of coinage.

We adopted a bimetallic standard of gold and silver in 1792, with a mint ratio of 15 parts of silver to 1 part of gold. The bimetallic standard was formally abandoned in 1900.

According to Gresham's law, an "inferior" (one that is in less demand) type of money will drive a better type out of circulation.

The gold-coin standard of money means: (1) a unit of gold is the measure of value; (2) government will coin unlimited amounts of gold bullion; (3) all other money in the system may be exchanged for gold at its face value; (4) gold is legal tender; and (5) people are free to own and use gold for both money and industrial purposes. At present we are on what might be called a limited gold-bullion standard.

In 1934, in an attempt to raise prices and to stimulate trade, the federal government devalued the dollar from 23.32 grains of fine gold to 13.71 grains. It is not possible to say exactly what all the effects of devaluation were.

Fiat money is money that has nothing except the decree or fiat of the government to back it. A type of fiat money was issued by the government during the 1860's. If too much fiat money is issued or too much spending of borrowed money by government takes place, prices may rise so high that money will become valueless.

Among the kinds of money presently in circulation in the United States, one kind of paper currency — federal reserve notes — is predominant, and silver is playing a decreased role in our coins.

At present nearly all the money in circulation in the United States consists of three kinds of paper money and a variety of coins.

Our currency system is related to gold, but none of our money is redeemable in gold. The amount of money in circulation has little relation to the amount of gold owned by the government. And for this reason our monetary system is a kind of managed-money system.

Ch. 19   MONEY AND ITS USE

NEW TERMS

acceptability
advance
bimetallism
brassage
cognizability
currency
devaluation
discount
divisibility
durability
fiat money

free coinage
gold-coin standard
greenback
Gresham's law
homogeneity
market ratio
mint ratio
money
portability
seigniorage
stability of value

QUESTIONS ON THE CHAPTER

1. What is money? Are bank check deposits money? Explain.
2. What are some of the things that have been used as money?
3. What qualities should money possess? Why?
4. Why are gold and silver so often used as money metals?
5. Why does the government have a monopoly on the coinage and printing of money?
6. How do you distinguish between *brassage* and *seigniorage*?
7. When a country is on a bimetallic standard, does the government fix the market ratio of value for the money metals? Discuss.
8. Why did we abandon the bimetallic standard?
9. Did Gresham's law have anything to do with our decision to abandon the bimetallic standard? Explain.
10. What is meant by the gold-coin standard? Explain in detail.
11. How would you summarize the major provisions of the Gold Reserve Act of 1934?
12. What is meant by devaluation of money?
13. What is fiat money?
14. Have the American people ever had any experience with fiat money? Explain.
15. What was Germany's experience with fiat money and inflation after World War I?
16. Could the dollar become as worthless as the old German mark?
17. How many kinds of money do we have? Discuss each kind.
18. What changes were made in our coins in the mid-60's? Why were these changes necessary?

APPLYING YOUR ECONOMIC UNDERSTANDING

1. Some unusual terms used with reference to money in literature are the following: (a) *two bits*; (b) *filthy lucre;* (c) *jack;* (d) *hard cash;* and (e) *ducat.* What is the meaning and the origin of each term?
2. Interview several people who were of adult age in 1933 concerning their experiences when the bank holiday was declared. Report your findings.
3. Do some research reading on life in Germany during its experience with printing-press money. How did this affect the life savings and insurance reserves of persons who had retired?
4. Prior to 1970 the Treasury Department ordered the withdrawal of all one-dollar silver certificates from circulation and their replacement with one-dollar federal reserve notes. When this was accomplished what effect did it have on the buying power of one-dollar bills?
5. From 1965–1966 the U.S. Treasury Department's potential seigniorage on coin and silver bullion shifted from $6.5 million to $950 million. In what way did the withdrawal of silver certificates and coins add to the federal government's income?
6. Review some articles on the importance of the use of gold as a basis for our money standard. Do you agree with the evidence presented?
7. In some communities it is difficult to find a two-dollar bill. Does this fact relate to Gresham's law?
8. The Netherland guilder has a value of 3.83 grains of gold. If the gold content was reduced to 1.915 grains of gold and the paper currency for circulation was doubled, what would be the effect on prices in the Netherlands? How would it affect the money saved in banks, in life insurance policies, or in bond holdings by Hollanders?

CHALLENGES TO ECONOMIC COMPETENCE

1. Prepare a bulletin board exhibit of magazine and other forms of illustrations showing the historical development of money in the United States.
2. Prepare an exhibit of coin savings banks for use as a display when parents visit your school during Education Week. Include, if possible, examples of cast-iron mechanical action banks of the past and others which might illustrate the evolution of coin savings banks. As part of the exhibit prepare a narrative account emphasizing the origin and importance of such banks.
3. Arrange to have a representative from a local bank meet with the class and discuss counterfeit money and how to detect it. Summarize the discussion.
4. Prepare a theme on one of the following topics: (a) Gold and the Public's Confidence, (b) An Unusual Form of Money, (c) The Art of Coin Collecting, (d) From Tree to Me — The Journey of a Dollar Bill.

Chapter 20

Credit and Its Use

What is credit?
Upon what is credit based?
What are the various ways in which credit is used?
What are the advantages and disadvantages of the use of credit?

"Charge it, please." It would be impossible to estimate with any degree of reliability how often that phrase is used in a day. For more than $7 billion worth of merchandise is sold through charge accounts in this country each year. It has been estimated that credit is used in from 80 to 90 percent of all purchases and sales of goods and services in the course of a year. In 1971 it was reported that the amount of consumer credit of all kinds totaled more than $123 billion, of which approximately 28 percent was the result of the installment buying of automobiles.

It might appear, therefore, that credit is more important than money. Sometimes, however, it is difficult to distinguish clearly between the terms "money" and "credit" as they are used in considering the nature and functions of our monetary system.

WHAT IS CREDIT?

Credit has been defined in many ways. It has been said that *credit* is "trust"; the "promise to pay for present goods in the future"; the "right to future payment"; the "act of obtaining goods in exchange for a promise"; the "power to borrow goods or money"; the "power to purchase goods"; and so on. At any rate, in a credit transaction there is a present exchange of something valuable — goods, services, or money — for a promise of a sum of money or some other return in the future.

When one buys groceries with the understanding that he will pay for them at the end of the month, he is using his credit. When a businessman borrows from a bank, he gives his written promise to pay the bank a certain number of dollars on or before a certain date. In exchange for this promise the bank either gives the borrower a sum of money or places the amount to the credit of his checking account. If the latter is done, the borrower can withdraw any part of the amount in money or transfer it to someone else. Hence, the borrower from a bank obtains purchasing power in the form of either currency or bank credit in exchange for his promise to pay the bank at a later date; in other words, the borrower's personal credit is exchanged for currency or bank credit.

CREDIT IS BASED ON CONFIDENCE

The extent of one's credit is limited by the confidence of sellers or lenders as to one's ability and willingness to pay his debts. Or, as is sometimes said, one's credit depends on his character, capacity, and capital.

In connection with the credit rating of an individual, *character* refers to an individual's willingness to pay. *Capacity* relates to his ability to pay his debts out of his current income. *Capital* refers to the amount of property, such as land, houses, or stocks and bonds, that he owns. All of these factors are important, but character is usually the first consideration.

There are various sources from which sellers and lenders may obtain information as to an individual's character and ability to pay his debts. For example, in cities retailers maintain a retail merchants' credit bureau. This bureau collects information that can be used in determining the rating of many, if not most, of the customers of the local stores. Simply by telephoning the bureau, a merchant can find out what a customer's credit rating is. It is obvious why a business firm or an individual should acquire and maintain a good credit rating.

Credit ratings for businessmen and firms — merchants and manufacturers, for example — are also established by private commercial credit concerns, the best known of which is Dun and Bradstreet, Incorporated. This agency carries on a continuous study of the credit standing of several million businesses located in more than 50,000 cities and towns in the United States. A book of ratings is published periodically, which is available to subscribers. Detailed individual reports may also be obtained for a fee.

THERE ARE DIFFERENT KINDS OF CREDIT

Credit is used by various people and concerns to obtain goods and funds for different purposes. For this reason we often hear references to different kinds of credit, such as personal or consumer credit, commercial or bank credit, investment credit, agricultural credit, and others.

Personal or *consumer credit* is credit that is used for the purpose of obtaining goods or funds for the satisfaction of personal wants. Charge purchases of groceries, clothing, or articles for the home, and borrowing from a bank in order to pay for such things are examples of the use of personal credit. *Installment credit*, which is used to obtain goods for personal consumption by making payments in installments, is a form of personal or consumer credit. *Commercial* or *bank credit* refers to loans made by banks to proprietors and business concerns for relatively short periods of time, say from thirty to ninety days. Such loans are used for the payment of wages, the purchase of merchandise, and other business expenses. *Investment credit* is used to obtain funds for long periods of time for the purchase of land and capital goods. *Agricultural credit* is used by farmers for such purposes as the purchase of agricultural land, the erection of farm buildings, the purchase of livestock, and the marketing of crops.

In this chapter we shall be concerned with only two types of consumer credit — charge accounts and installment buying — and credit instruments.

WHAT IS A CHARGE ACCOUNT?

A charge account is a common form of consumer credit. When one buys goods on a *charge account*, he obtains the goods at the time of the purchase but pays for them at a later date. With a thirty-day, or regular, charge account the entire balance comes due within a month. On a revolving charge account the customer establishes a maximum credit limit, and he is billed monthly for a fraction of the balance. The number of months allowed for paying off a given charge determines the fraction of the balance that comes due each month. The customer can add to his account at will so long as it does not exceed his established limit. For this convenience he pays a monthly service charge, commonly 1.5 percent of the unpaid balance, which amounts to an annual rate of 18 percent.

Advantages of charge accounts. The possible advantages of charge accounts include the following: (1) Charge accounts are convenient because the bother of paying for a small item at the time of purchase is avoided; (2) buyers are able to obtain and use the goods before they pay for them; (3) in some cases merchants give charge customers who pay their bills promptly more and better service; (4) charge customers frequently find it easier to return merchandise and to secure an adjustment

TOTAL CONSUMER CREDIT

(In millions of dollars)

End of period	Total	Installment					Noninstallment			
		Total	Auto-mobile paper	Other consumer goods paper	Repair and modernization loans[1]	Personal loans	Total	Single-payment loans	Charge accounts	Service credit
1939	7,222	4,503	1,497	1,620	298	1,088	2,719	787	1,414	518
1941	9,172	6,085	2,458	1,929	376	1,322	3,087	845	1,645	597
1945	5,665	2,462	455	816	182	1,009	3,203	746	1,612	845
1950	21,471	14,703	6,074	4,799	1,016	2,814	6,768	1,821	3,367	1,580
1960	56,141	42,968	17,658	11,545	3,148	10,617	13,173	4,507	5,329	3,337
1965	90,314	71,324	28,619	18,565	3,728	20,412	18,990	7,671	6,430	4,889
1966	97,543	77,539	30,556	20,978	3,818	22,187	20,004	7,972	6,686	5,346
1967	102,132	80,926	30,724	22,395	3,789	24,018	21,206	8,428	6,968	5,810
1968	113,191	89,890	34,130	24,899	3,925	26,936	23,301	9,138	7,755	6,408
1969	122,469	98,169	36,602	27,609	4,040	29,918	24,300	9,096	8,234	6,970
1970	126,802	101,161	35,490	29,949	4,110	31,612	25,641	9,484	8,850	7,307
1971—Mar.	123,604	99,168	35,028	28,591	4,045	31,504	24,436	9,557	7,207	7,672

[1] Holdings of financial institutions; holdings of retail outlets are included in "other consumer goods paper."

Note: Consumer credit estimates cover loans to individuals for household, family, and other personal expenditures, except real estate mortgage loans.

SOURCE: *Federal Reserve Bulletin*, May, 1971.

for an unsatisfactory purchase; and (5) it reduces the need for carrying as much money as would be necessary otherwise.

Disadvantages of a charge account. In criticism of buying on account, several disadvantages are sometimes pointed out.

(1) When some people buy on account, they are inclined to be careless in the selection of what they buy. The explanation for this carelessness is that merchants find it difficult to refuse to accept goods that are returned.

(2) Because they do not have to make payment at the time of purchase, many persons seem unable to resist the temptation to buy more goods than they would buy if they paid cash.

(3) Many people contend that because of charge accounts a merchant is compelled to sell his goods to all customers at a higher price than if he sold for cash only. Selling on account involves a great deal of bookkeeping, the mailing out of monthly statements, in some cases the carrying on of investigations of the credit standing of customers, and other clerical

expenses. In addition, the losses due to returned merchandise and uncollectible accounts constitute an expense. In order to make up for the total amount of all these expenses, the merchant must either add enough to the selling prices of some or all of his goods to cover these expenses during the year or recover these outlays through service charges.

MANY ARTICLES ARE BOUGHT ON THE INSTALLMENT PLAN

Consumers buy a great many goods on the installment plan. Installment credit is most widely used in the purchase of the more durable consumers' goods, including automobiles, household appliances, and furniture, although it is sometimes used in the purchase of nondurable consumers' goods. In a recent year purchases on the installment plan amounted to more than $100 billion.

Differences between account and installment purchases. An installment purchase differs from a purchase on a charge account in several ways. (1) As we have just said, installment buying is largely confined to durable consumers' goods, while both durable and nondurable consumers' goods are bought on account. (2) The title to goods sold on the installment plan usually does not pass to the buyer until final payment has been made; title passes immediately when goods are bought on account. If the customer fails to meet his payments on the installment plan, the seller usually may take possession of or "repossess" the goods, in which case the buyer loses the amount he has already paid. (3) Goods bought on the installment plan are paid for by means of a series of payments, whereas several purchases of goods bought on account may be paid for in one lump sum. (4) Customers who buy on the installment plan nearly always have to pay a *carrying charge*, which usually includes interest.

In many cases the cost of goods bought on the installment plan is much more than the cost of the same goods when bought for cash or on account. One reason for this is that the seller usually charges interest on the unpaid balance or on the total amount of the account. In addition, he adds enough to the price of the article to cover bookkeeping costs and other expenses, including the expense of investigating the credit standing of the customer, the increased expense of collecting from "slow-pay" customers, the cost of repossessing and reconditioning goods that are not paid for by some buyers, losses in resale prices of repossessed goods, and insurance on goods in the hands of customers who have not made final payments.

How costly are carrying charges? Sometimes the carrying charge is stated as "only" 6 percent, or some other percent. The actual rate is usually much higher. Suppose, for example, that the price of an article is $120 plus 6 percent ($7.20) for carrying charges, which are paid at the time of the purchase, and that the buyer is to pay the $120 in equal installments of $10 at the end of each month. The average monthly amount he owes is $65. (Add the amounts owed at the end of each month and divide by 12.) Then $7.20 divided by $65 gives 11.08 percent, the rate of carrying charge, which is almost double 6 percent. Of course, terms of installment sales vary, but this example shows the method of calculating the true rate of carrying charges on all kinds of installment sales and purchases.

Advantages of installment buying. Installment buying may have one or more of the following advantages: (1) The buyer is able to obtain the possession and the use of an article before he has accumulated the amount of the full purchase price; (2) installment buying is a form of saving; (3) it is a convenient method for the customer; (4) many goods bought on the installment plan "pay for themselves" because they save expenses; (5) installment buying makes it possible for families to "spread out" expenditures and thus budget expenses more satisfactorily.

Disadvantages of installment buying. Installment buying may have several serious disadvantages: (1) Installment purchases often cost more than articles purchased for cash or on account; and (2) people frequently overbuy and become too heavily burdened with debt.

THERE ARE VARIOUS KINDS OF CREDIT INSTRUMENTS

A *credit instrument* is a written or printed form that is used in creating or in transferring credit. Among the more commonly used credit instruments are: (1) credit instruments drawn on banks; (2) promissory notes; (3) commercial drafts; and (4) credit cards.

(1) Credit instruments drawn on banks. Several kinds of credit instruments are drawn on banks by individuals, business concerns, or other banks for use as a substitute for cash in settlement of business transactions. Those commonly used are checks, bank drafts, cashier's checks, and certified checks.

A *check* is an order written by a *depositor* (one who has funds in a bank), directing the bank to pay a certain amount of his funds to the person named in the check or to the order of that person.

A *bank draft* is an order written by one bank, directing a second bank to pay a certain sum of money to the order of the person named in the draft. All banks keep deposits in some other banks against which they can

A Check

A check is an order written by a depositor directing the bank to pay a certain amount of his funds to the person named in the check or to the order of that person.

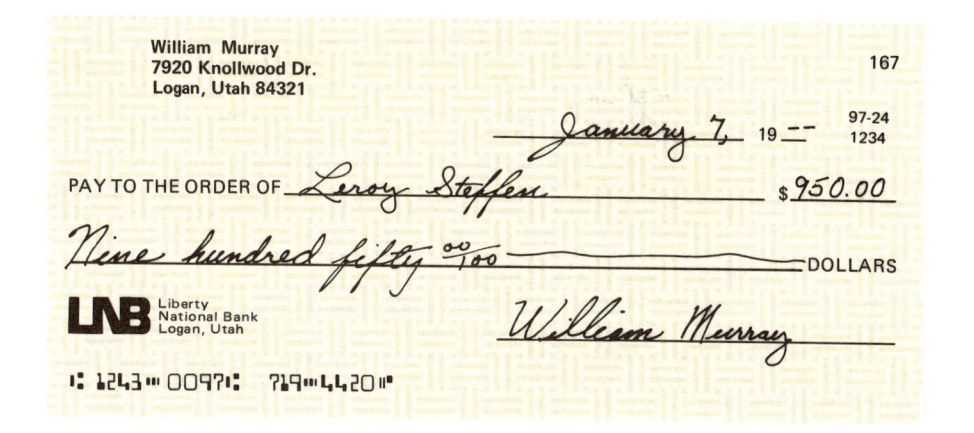

Figure 20-1.

draw drafts. Since banks are better known to the public than are most individuals, bank drafts are more readily acceptable than personal checks. By the payment of a small fee, bank drafts may be purchased from any commercial bank.

A *cashier's check* is one drawn by a bank on its own funds in the bank. Cashier's checks are, as a general rule, used by banks in paying their own debts.

A *certified check* is a depositor's check on which the cashier of the bank writes or stamps the word "certified" and signs his name. The amount of the check is deducted immediately from the depositor's account, and the bank assumes the obligation of paying the check.

(2) Promissory notes. A *promissory note* is a written promise to pay a certain sum of money on or by a definite date. In many cases where the buyer does not pay for goods at the time of purchase, he is required to give the seller a promissory note. Then there is less likelihood that a dispute will arise as to the amount of the debt. Also, when one borrows funds from a bank, he gives a written promise that the amount will be paid.

Sometimes promissory notes are supported by a *mortgage* of certain property of the maker of the note. The usual type of mortgage is a formal conditional transfer of rights — but not necessarily possession — of the property. The mortgage terminates upon the payment of the note.

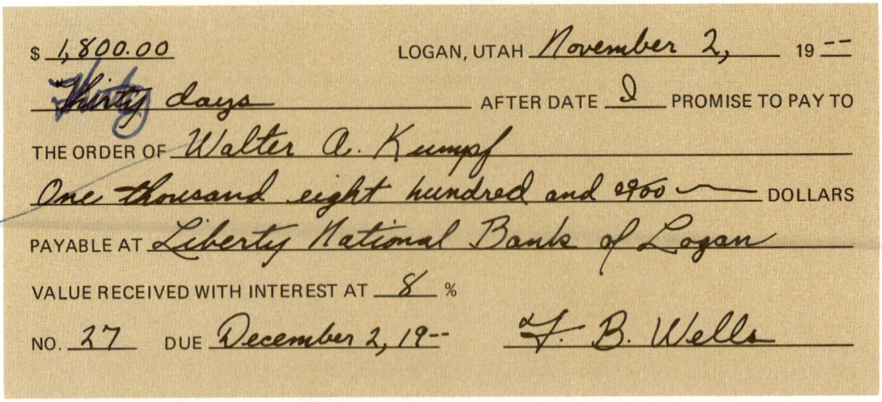

Figure 20-2.

A Promissory Note

A promissory note is a written promise to pay a certain sum of money on or by a definite date.

(3) **Commercial drafts.** A *commercial draft* is an order written by one person or business concern directing another to pay a certain sum of money to the person or concern named in the draft, or to his "order." If the draft is payable to the order of the person named, it is easy to transfer the draft to another by means of an *indorsement;* that is, by writing one's name on the back of the draft. Promissory notes and checks also may be transferred in this way.

A commercial draft drawn by a person or a business concern in one state or country on another person or concern in another state or country is sometimes referred to as a *foreign bill.* One drawn on another person or business concern in the same state may be referred to as a *domestic* or *inland bill.*

The person on whom a commercial draft is drawn does not have to pay it until he accepts it. If he is willing to pay the draft, he writes the word "Accepted," together with his name and the date, on the face of the instrument.

A time draft drawn by the seller of goods and accepted by the purchaser is termed a *trade acceptance.* Trade acceptances contain the following statement or its equivalent: "The transaction that gives rise to this instrument is the purchase of goods by the *acceptor* (the person on whom the draft is drawn) from the *drawer* (the person who draws the draft)."

(4) **Credit cards.** A *credit card* authorizes hotels, airlines, filling stations, or stores to sell goods or services to the holder who agrees to pay later, usually within a month. These cards are issued to persons and business

concerns whose credit ratings are good. Depending on the type of card and the company issuing it, the holder may charge his hotel room rent, meals, car rental, gasoline, airplane fare, and other expenses and even get his checks cashed when away from home. Several credit card companies now issue cards that can be used by travelers in many foreign countries. With such a card the traveler is able to obtain hotel and other services and pay later.

WHAT ARE THE ADVANTAGES AND THE DISADVANTAGES OF CREDIT?

Whether advantages or disadvantages result from the use of credit depends on the way it is used. Among the advantages to be derived from the proper use of credit are the following:

(1) Credit enables business firms and consumers to obtain goods at the present time in exchange for a promise to pay for them sometime in the future.

(2) It may be more convenient to have a charge account and to pay for goods monthly rather than at the time of purchase, as often happens in the case of some kinds of consumers' goods.

(3) It is often possible to buy goods from distant sellers and to make payment by check rather than by sending money. It is comparatively easy to send almost any amount of money to distant parts of the world by telegraph.

(4) Most merchants feel that credit is good for business because its use induces many persons to buy more than they otherwise would.

(5) The use of credit makes it possible for banks to transfer purchasing power from one person to another by the use of bookkeeping entries rather than by handling cash.

The disadvantage of credit arises from its misuse. For example, consumers may overbuy and thus become so involved in debt that they cannot meet their obligations. If consumer credit becomes overextended, there may be a marked decrease in consumer purchases, which may produce a decline in business prosperity. If a business firm overextends credit, it may go bankrupt. And if government borrows too heavily — especially when there is a high level of employment — there will be a rise in prices. This means a decrease in the value of money, which results in hardship for those whose incomes do not keep pace with the general rise in prices.

SUMMARY

Credit is used in 80 to 90 percent of total purchases and sales in the United States.

Credit may be defined as the ability to borrow money or to buy goods or services in exchange for a promise to pay money or its equivalent at some time in the future.

Credit is based on confidence. The elements of one's credit are character, capacity, and capital. Credit agencies provide credit ratings of individuals and business firms.

Advantages result from the proper use of credit. But when credit is misused, difficulty results. Credit enables buyers — consumers and businessmen — to obtain goods before they are able to pay cash, which may be beneficial. Credit also makes it possible to make payment for a number of purchases at one time. The use of credit and credit instruments makes possible payment to distant sellers easily and quickly. Charge accounts enable merchants to sell more goods, and it is easy to create purchasing power merely by making bookkeeping entries.

There are several types of credit, including personal, installment, commercial, investment, and agricultural credit. A charge account is evidence of consumer credit or personal credit. Goods bought on an installment plan usually cost more than if purchased for cash.

A bank check is an order by a depositor on his bank to pay a certain amount of money to the holder of the check. A bank draft is an order by one bank on another bank to pay the holder a certain amount of money. A cashier's check is a check drawn by the cashier of the bank on the funds of the bank. A certified check is a depositor's check that has been certified for payment by the bank in which he has a deposit. A promissory note is a written promise signed by the maker to pay a certain amount of money at some future date. An indorsement is the signature of the holder of a credit instrument. A commercial draft is an order to pay money drawn by a person or a firm on another person or firm. A trade acceptance is a form of draft.

An overextension of credit by banks or government may lead to inflation and a rise in prices in general.

NEW TERMS

acceptor
agricultural credit
bank draft
capacity
capital
carrying charge
cashier's check
certified check
character
charge account
check
commercial *or* bank credit
commercial draft
credit
credit card
credit instrument
depositor
domestic *or* inland bill
drawer
foreign bill
indorsement
installment credit
investment credit
mortgage
personal *or* consumer credit
promissory note
trade acceptance

QUESTIONS ON THE CHAPTER

1. What is credit?
2. On what is credit based?
3. What are the classes or kinds of credit that are referred to in the chapter? Define each.
4. How does a thirty-day charge account operate? A revolving charge account?
5. What are (a) the advantages and (b) the disadvantages of buying on account?
6. What is installment credit?
7. How are carrying charges often understated in terms of actual cost to the customer?
8. Is it wise to buy goods on installment terms? Why or why not?
9. What is a credit instrument? Give examples.
10. What type of security is sometimes used to back a promissory note?
11. How does a promissory note differ from a commercial draft?
12. What relationship is there between prices and the use of credit by consumers and business?

APPLYING YOUR ECONOMIC UNDERSTANDING

1. Three important factors in a credit rating are character, capacity, and capital. For each of the following situations which factor is predominant? (a) Mr. A plans to make a credit purchase; he has no current debts. He owns his own home, an automobile, and has some savings. (b) Mr. B is slow in paying his debts and has a number of unpaid bills. (c) Mr. C has consistently paid his bills in the past and has never been behind in any previous time payments. (d) Mr. D has a take-home income of $900 monthly. His present debts and current payments use up $800 of his monthly income. He plans to make some additional credit purchases. (e) Mr. E is unmarried and just graduated from college. He intends credit purchases of a car and furniture for his new apartment. He presently owns only his clothing and some books valued about $400. (f) Mr. E, above, will have a monthly net income of $600 and his credit purchases would require total payments of $150 monthly.
2. Types of credit differ. How might each of the following be classified? (a) The Novelty Shop arranges a short-term business loan to buy a stock of Easter novelties. (b) Mr. Rolf makes a loan from his credit production association to buy a herd of feeder cattle. (c) Jim buys a new suit and charges it on the family's charge account. (d) The Airflot Corporation sells some 10-year term bonds to purchase some B747 jets. (e) Bob buys a Mercury Montego automobile and agrees to pay for it with monthly payments to the dealer.
3. In a college community local merchants extend credit to new faculty members who merely state that they are employed by the college. Merchants are also liberal in extending credit to college students. Why?

4. What are some of the major areas of consumer credit used by families in your community? How do the dollar amounts of credit for durable goods and for nondurable goods compare?
5. An automobile dealer sells the same model car at the same price to two customers who trade in cars with the same trade-in values. One customer pays cash for the balance, the other pays in installments. How does the real cost differ for each owner?
6. A mail-order house follows the practice of immediate shipment for goods ordered with an accompanying bank draft. It delays shipment for 5–7 days on orders accompanied by a check. Why?
7. A seller of real estate will accept cash or a certified check before transferring title. He will often delay or refuse to transfer title when paid with a personal check. Is this a sound business practice? Why or why not?
8. Many business firms prefer that their employees use credit cards when they travel. Why?
9. What are some of the ways in which the government can influence or control installment credit?
10. A speaker at a conference stated that installment buying has been the basis for the success of the American economy. Do you agree? Why or why not?

CHALLENGES TO ECONOMIC COMPETENCE

1. Arrange for a bulletin board display of the uses of credit in your community. Include the various contract applications and forms which are most commonly used by borrowers in your community.
2. Many banks require a minimum deposit or they charge the customer on the basis of the number of checks written. From a money cost standpoint, is it always advisable to use checking accounts? Why or why not?
3. Consult the *Survey of Current Business* or the *Federal Reserve Bulletin* and make a current tabulation of the major forms and amounts of credit used in the United States.
4. Prepare a panel discussion on: Consumer Credit — Friend or Foe?
5. Develop a written report on one of the following: (a) Credit Growth in America, 1910 to the Present; (b) Credit Agencies for Farm Families; (c) Why I Use Credit; (d) Credit Cards and Social Prestige; (e) Are American Families in the Quicksand of Debt?

Chapter 21

Money, Credit, and Banking

What is the role of the commercial bank in our economy?
Where do banks get money or credit to lend?
What is the significance of multiple bank credit expansion?
Why are cash and legal bank reserves important?
What is the Federal Reserve System and what are its functions?

Business firms that specialize in the transfer of money and credit are known as banks. The modern term "bank," when used in this sense, comes from the Italian *banca*, which meant a bench or table used by money changers. In Italy during the Middle Ages, as in other European countries, there were market centers in the larger cities where people came to buy merchandise. Because both domestic and foreign coins were used, there was a need for some agency that could exchange one kind of money for another. Also, it was often necessary to exchange coins of one denomination for those of another denomination. The money changers provided these services, and across their benches or tables they received and gave out money.

Our modern commercial banks deal in both coined and printed money and credit, but most of their activities have to do with credit. In fact, in comparison with the total volume of the business they do, little money is used.

THERE ARE DIFFERENT KINDS OF BANKS

There are many kinds of financial institutions that deal in money and credit. For example, *investment banks* arrange for an extension of credit to large borrowers, such as governments and big corporations. *Savings banks* accept the small deposits of persons who want a safe place in which

Illus. 21-1. The modern term "bank" comes from the Italian *banca*, which meant a bench or table used by money changers. Contrast the scene, which is a medieval Italian banking house (from a Florentine woodcut, 15th century) with a modern commercial bank shown on the opposite page.

Bettmann Archive

to keep their money and at the same time to receive some interest on their savings. *Savings and loan associations* conduct a limited savings-bank business and make loans to members for the purchase, construction, or modernization of residences.

In this chapter, however, we are concerned primarily with commercial banks. Perhaps most people are more familiar with this kind of financial institution than with the other businesses that deal in money and credit.

WHAT IS A COMMERCIAL BANK?

A *commercial bank* is a financial institution the main functions of which are: (1) to receive deposits of money and credit and (2) to lend money or credit to individuals and business firms.

If one deposits money or checks in a bank, the deposit is a *primary deposit*. If he borrows an amount from the bank and leaves it on deposit until he checks it out, the deposit is a *derivative deposit* because it was derived from money held by the bank in the form of primary deposits.

In addition to receiving deposits and making loans, however, commercial banks engage in other activities. For example, banks provide safety-deposit boxes in which individuals and business concerns may keep valuable documents, jewelry, and coin collections; they provide for

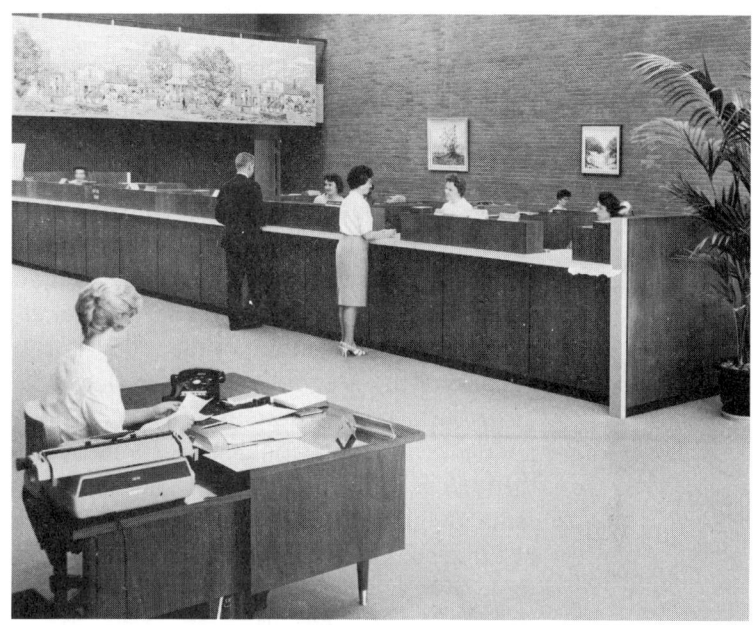

Illus. 21-2. A commercial bank is a financial institution the main functions of which are: (1) to receive deposits of money and credit and (2) to lend money or credit to individuals and business firms.

Sterling Savings

the purchase and sale of foreign exchange (money); they buy and sell government and corporate securities; they collect checks drawn on other banks; they give advice on financial matters; and other services.

Bank loans are extensions of credit. We have seen how credit may be a convenient method of obtaining goods for personal use. If, however, a retailer allows you to buy goods on account and if he sells a great deal of goods in this way, he will probably have to borrow money with which to pay for the goods that he buys from wholesalers. If he does not have the money and does not borrow it, he will have to ask for credit from the wholesalers. If the wholesalers sell on account, they will have to borrow from their banks or ask for credit from manufacturers. As a matter of fact, retailers, wholesalers, and manufacturers all borrow large amounts from banks.

A bank ordinarily lends purchasing power in the form of credit. For example, if a merchant wants to borrow approximately $1,000, he signs a note for that amount payable to the bank. The bank deducts in advance the interest, which it calls "discount," and credits the merchant's account for the balance. Thus, if the loan is for 60 days and the interest rate is 9 percent, the amount of the interest is $15. The bank therefore credits the merchant's checking account for the balance, or $985.

The merchant will then be able to write checks to the amount of $985. These checks can be used to pay for goods purchased from wholesalers and to pay other accounts. Thus, credit serves the purpose of a medium of exchange quite as well as, or even better than, coins and printed money.

Banks clear and collect checks. Suppose that you and I have accounts in the same bank, that your bank balance amounts to $200, and that mine amounts to $176.50. Assume that you give me a check for $20. If I deposit your check, the bank will subtract $20 from your bank balance and add the same amount to mine. If I cash your check, the bank will give me the money and subtract the amount from your bank balance; and the balance of my account will not be changed.

If our accounts were in different banks and I deposited your check in my bank, my bank would send the check to your bank. Your bank would then deduct the amount from your account, and my bank would add the same amount to my account. In smaller towns where there are only two or three banks, an employee of one of the banks each day gathers together the checks which were presented to his bank for deposit but which were drawn on the other bank or banks and delivers them to those banks. In turn he collects from those banks the checks drawn on his bank. The debtor bank, as a result of the difference between the totals of incoming and outgoing checks, pays the creditor bank the amount due it.

In larger cities where there are many banks, checks are collected and cleared in a *clearinghouse*, which is a room or a building set aside for this purpose. One of the functions of the federal reserve banks is that of clearing and collecting checks deposited in banks in different parts of the country.

WHERE DO BANKS GET THE MONEY OR CREDIT THEY LEND?

We can best answer this question by describing briefly the organization and operation of a bank. A commercial bank is usually a corporation. It receives its charter either from the state in which it is located or from the national government.

Organization and operation. Let us say that a bank has received its charter and that it has a capital stock of $100,000, all of which has been sold and paid for in cash. The condition of the bank is then:

Assets	Capital Account
Cash (Paid in by stockholders). $100,000	Capital Stock (Owned by the Stockholders) $100,000

The bank must have a place of business and equipment with which to carry on its operations. Let us say, therefore, that it rents a building and buys a vault, desks, and other equipment for $25,000. The condition of the bank is then:

Assets		Capital Account	
Cash ($100,000 minus $25,000)	$ 75,000	Capital Stock	$100,000
Equipment (Vault, etc.)	25,000		
	$100,000		$100,000

Since the bank is owned by responsible men who are well known in the community, many persons will probably desire to deposit money. Some of the depositors will want the privilege of withdrawing the money by check. Suppose, therefore, that during the first week the deposits are all in cash and amount to $15,000. The condition of the bank is then:

Assets		Liabilities	
Cash ($75,000 plus $15,000)	$ 90,000	Deposits (Owed to Depositors)	$ 15,000
		(a) Demand $10,000	
Equipment	25,000	(b) Time 5,000	
		Capital Account	
	$115,000	Capital Stock	100,000
			$115,000

The bank now has $15,000 more than was supplied by the owners, and it owes the depositors that amount.

Demand and time deposits. When people deposit money in a bank, they often do so with the idea of allowing at least part of it to remain for several days or possibly for months. The bank becomes indebted to the depositors for the amount of the deposits and the term *deposits* represents the amount that the bank owes the depositors which may be withdrawn in cash or transferred by check.

If money is deposited with the understanding that it may be withdrawn at any time without previous notice and that it will not earn interest, the deposit is called a *demand deposit*. But if the depositor wishes to leave his money with the bank in a savings account, the bank will pay a small rate of interest — from 4½ to 5½ percent — for the use of the money. In case the depositor desires to withdraw his savings deposit, the bank reserves the right to receive several days' notice. Deposits made under these conditions are called *time deposits*. Most of the savings deposits are invested by the bank in some kind of interest-bearing notes or other commercial paper or securities. Therefore, if several depositors wanted to withdraw large amounts from their savings accounts, the bank might need several days in which to sell some of its investments. Usually, however, savings deposits may be withdrawn at any time.

Many commercial banks also encourage their depositors to purchase *savings certificates of deposit*. Often these certificates are available only in minimum denominations, such as $1,000, and in multiples of $100 above the minimum. To induce the purchaser to leave his funds with the bank for an extended period of time, the bank pays a rate of interest on the certificates that is higher than the rate that it pays on regular time deposits.

BANKS MUST KEEP RESERVES

A bank must keep available a sufficient amount of money with which to meet cash withdrawals and to pay checks that will likely be drawn on it. This amount of money usually consists of (1) cash in vault, (2) reserve with the federal reserve bank, and (3) balances with other banks. This amount of money is known as its *working reserve*. How much this reserve should be depends upon the experience of the bank. For example, if the bank finds that it can meet ordinary demands by keeping on hand cash amounting to 10 percent of its deposits, it will see that the cash on hand does not fall below that amount. On the other hand, it will not want to keep on hand much more than that amount because cash in the vault does not earn an income. Many banks find that cash to the amount of 1½ percent of the total time and demand deposits is sufficient. In addition, banks keep deposits in certain other banks, called *correspondent banks*. If needed, these deposits may be called for and used to pay depositors' checks.

National banks and state banks that are members of the Federal Reserve System are required to keep on deposit with the federal reserve banks of which they are members a *legal reserve* equal to a certain percentage of their deposits. The amount that is set aside as a legal reserve reduces the amount of deposits of cash that a bank can lend and pay out to its customers who borrow from the bank. The amount of legal reserves required for banks located in the larger cities constitutes a greater percentage of deposits than is required for banks in other cities or communities.

As we have indicated, the purpose of legal reserves is to prevent banks from overextending loans to their customers. If a bank should lend too much, it would not have enough money to cash the checks of its customers. The function of legal reserve requirements may be illustrated as follows: Suppose the legal reserve required is 20 percent of the total of the deposits. These total deposits include not only money left in the bank when deposits

Ch. 21 MONEY, CREDIT, AND BANKING

of money and checks are made but also deposits arising from funds borrowed from the bank and left with the bank to be checked out later.

Now assume that the member bank has total deposits of $100,000 and has a legal reserve of $20,000 on deposit in the federal reserve bank. If it makes any further loans or receives any other deposits, it must increase its legal reserve so that it will not be less than 20 percent of the new total of deposits.

BANKS CAN CREATE DEPOSIT CURRENCY

The owners of a bank put some money in the bank when they pay for their shares of capital stock. Individuals and business firms also make deposits in the bank. These two factors together enable the bank to extend loans to individuals and firms which can be withdrawn by checks. In this way banks create deposit currency.

Illustration of the creation of deposit currency. By *deposit currency* we mean bank credit that circulates in the form of bank checks, which are payable on demand by the banks on which the checks are drawn. Suppose that on June 1, William Jones, a merchant, wishes to borrow $500 for 30 days from the bank used as an illustration on page 331. If his character is good and his business promising, the bank will let him have either money or credit and will charge interest for the time of the loan. Ordinarily, under these conditions the merchant will not take the money but will be content to have the amount of the loan credited to his checking account in the bank. In this example we shall ignore the discount, or interest. Immediately after the loan is made, the condition of the bank may be illustrated by the following statement:

ASSETS		LIABILITIES	
Cash	$ 90,000	Deposits ($15,000 plus Jones's Deposit)	$ 15,500
Equipment	25,000	(a) Demand $10,500	
Loans and Discounts (William Jones's note)	500	(b) Time 5,000	
		CAPITAL ACCOUNT	
		Capital Stock	100,000
	$115,500		$115,500

We can see that the "Cash" item remains unchanged as a result of the loan; however, an additional $500 demand deposit, not previously in existence, has been created. Thus, the bank has created money in the form of bank credit, and Jones can now write checks which transfer to others ownership of the demand deposit that was credited to his account.

How much can banks lend to their customers? At any time, if all those who have a right to draw checks on the bank were to demand payment, the bank would have insufficient cash to meet the demands of the depositors. But the individual depositors usually withdraw their deposits by checks only as funds are needed, and not all at once. As borrowers' notes fall due and are paid, about as much money is coming into the bank as is going out. Depositors usually leave their funds in their accounts for a more or less extended period of time, and borrowers are constantly repaying loans. The single bank finds, therefore, that it needs to keep only a fraction of the amount of deposits on hand. All other commercial banks have similar experiences, and this results in the possibility of multiple bank credit expansion.

Multiple bank credit expansion. We have seen that a single bank must keep a fraction of its deposits as required reserves, but it can lend the remainder, known as *excess reserves*. Since the bank's earnings come primarily from the lending of these excess reserves, it will welcome opportunities to make sound loans.

You have already learned that in most cases the individual bank creates derivative deposit money when it makes a loan. In doing so the bank lends only what it has on hand, a portion of its excess or loanable reserves. If the reserve requirement is 20 percent, this means that the bank can lend the remaining 80 percent of its deposits, or four times the amount it holds in reserve. Thus, the single bank can lend only part of what it has on hand.

However, the commercial banking system as a whole can lend several times the amount of any new deposits it acquires. This process is known as *multiple bank credit expansion* and can be best understood from a simple illustration. Suppose that a new deposit of $1,000 is made in Bank A, which holds $200 of it in reserve (20 percent) and lends $800 to Brown. Suppose further that Brown buys a console stereo and that the dealer deposits Brown's $800 check in Bank B. Now Bank B, also interested in making sound loans, holds $160 of the deposit in reserve and lends Smith the remaining $640 (80 percent) of excess reserves. As a result of Smith's spending of the $640 and the subsequent depositing of the check in the seller's bank, say Bank C, this bank is now in a position to lend $512, retaining $128 as reserves. If this process should be carried to the limit of its possibilities, the entire original $1,000 deposit would be spread throughout the banking system as reserves. In the process, however, it would serve as the basis for creating $4,000 of additional new demand deposits that did not previously exist.

The multiple bank credit expansion process can be summarized as follows:

Bank	New deposits received	Required reserves on new deposits	Available for loans in the form of demand deposits
A	$1,000	$ 200	$ 800
B	800	160	640
C	640	128	512
All other banks	2,560	512	2,048
Total for system	$5,000	$1,000	$4,000

Note that the $4,000 of loans result in $4,000 of deposits which, with the original $1,000 deposit, add up to $5,000 of new deposits. Thus, the banking system is a powerful instrument through which new bank money is created. In fact, this process of multiple bank credit expansion is the mechanism through which most of our money supply has been generated in recent decades. For example, our coins and paper money increased from $26.4 billion in 1947 to only $48.9 billion in 1970. During the same period, however, demand deposits increased from $86.7 billion to $165.6 billion.

Unfortunately, banks sometimes extend too much credit during periods of business prosperity. When a great many banks do this, the creation of so much credit helps to produce an unhealthy business boom. As a result many people become so deeply involved in debt that they cannot meet their financial obligations when they fall due. If banks begin to require repayment of more loans than they are currently making, the credit expansion process will then work in reverse, which results in *multiple bank credit contraction*. In the example above, this process could end in the canceling of $4,000 of loans and $5,000 of deposits.

THE BANK'S STATEMENT OF CONDITION

By reading the bank statement on page 336, we can see that the total amount of deposits is much greater than the cash assets of the bank. However, the depositors are protected because the assets in the form of government obligations and securities can be sold for cash. The loans and discounts can also be sold for cash, or the bank can wait until due dates when the loans will be repaid in cash. In the meantime, the bank's loans to governments, businesses, and others made more production and consumption possible than if the bank had not purchased the obligations and loaned credit based upon the security of the notes.

THE FIRST NATIONAL BANK
Statement of Condition June 30, 19--

Assets		Liabilities	
Cash and Due from Banks	$1,152,999.72	Deposits	$3,838,609.28
U. S. Government Obligations	1,979,800.00	Demand 3,220,304.15	
Municipal Securities	35,200.00	Time 618,305.13	
Corporate Securities	191,744.22	Reserve for Taxes	7,000.00
Federal Reserve Bank Stock	6,000.00	Bank Checks Outstanding	16,468.96
Loans and Discounts	772,763.87	Other Liabilities	6,948.53
Banking House	31,500.00	Total Liabilities	$3,869,026.77
Furniture and Fixtures	4,500.00	**Capital Accounts**	
		Capital Stock	50,000.00
		Surplus	150,000.00
		Undivided Profits	105,481.04
	$4,174,507.81	Total Capital Accounts	$305,481.04
		Total Liabilities and Capital Accounts	$4,174,507.81

A Bank Statement of Condition

Explanation of terms used in this statement —

Cash and Due from Banks: Money in the bank's vaults and money owed to it by other banks.
U. S. Government Obligations: U. S. bonds and notes owned by the bank.
Municipal Securities: City bonds owned by the bank.
Corporate Securities: Corporation bonds owned by the bank.
Federal Reserve Bank Stock: Stock of the Federal Reserve Bank that the bank owns.
Loans and Discounts: Total amount of notes owed to the bank, mostly by local businessmen.
Banking House: The estimated value of the bank building, which is owned by the bank.
Furniture and Fixtures: Estimated value of the vault and other equipment.
Deposits: Total of the time and demand deposits.
Reserve for Taxes: Funds retained for the purpose of paying taxes.
Bank Checks Outstanding: Checks issued by the bank or certified checks which have not been presented for payment.
Other Liabilities: Various kinds of small debts that have not been paid.
Capital Stock: Par value of the issued capital stock of the bank.
Surplus: Part of the bank's permanent capital.
Undivided Profits: Profits not paid out to stockholders.

WHAT IS THE FEDERAL RESERVE SYSTEM?

The Federal Reserve System includes the Board of Governors, the Federal Advisory Council, the Federal Open Market Committee, the 12 federal reserve banks and their 24 branches, and the member banks. These *member banks* consist of all national banks and such state banks and trust companies as desire to become members and can meet the requirements for membership.

Organization. Under the Federal Reserve Act of December 23, 1913, the United States was divided into 12 districts. A federal reserve bank is located in each district. The numbers of the federal reserve districts and the cities in which federal reserve banks are located are as follows: 1, Boston; 2, New York; 3, Philadelphia; 4, Cleveland; 5, Richmond; 6, Atlanta; 7, Chicago; 8, St. Louis; 9, Minneapolis; 10, Kansas City; 11, Dallas; and 12, San Francisco.

It was believed that each region that makes up a federal reserve district has special banking needs because of its particular kinds of economic activities. Thus, the general banking needs of an agricultural region, like that surrounding St. Louis, for instance, are different in some respects from those of a business community like that of New York.

All the national banks in each district are required by law to become members of the federal reserve bank in the district. State banks may also become members by meeting the requirements imposed on the national banks with respect to such matters as (1) inspection by federal bank examiners, (2) reserve requirements, and (3) subscriptions to the capital stock of the federal reserve bank of the district.

Each member bank must subscribe for stock in the federal reserve bank to the extent of 6 percent of its own capital stock, although so far it has been required to buy an amount equal to only 3 percent. The stock of each federal reserve bank is therefore owned by the member banks in the district.

Management. The Federal Reserve System is under the management of the Board of Governors, consisting of seven members appointed by the President and confirmed by the Senate. The Board is kept informed of the financial conditions in the various banking districts by the Federal Advisory Council, composed of one member from each district.

Each federal reserve bank is under the direction of a board of directors made up of nine members, three of whom are appointed by the Board of Governors and six of whom are elected by the member banks of that district.

Functions. There are five main functions of the Federal Reserve System.

(1) Holding of reserves for member banks. The Federal Reserve System was created partly for the purpose of providing a safe means of keeping the reserves prescribed by the Board of Governors for member

Figure 21-1.

THE FEDERAL RESERVE SYSTEM

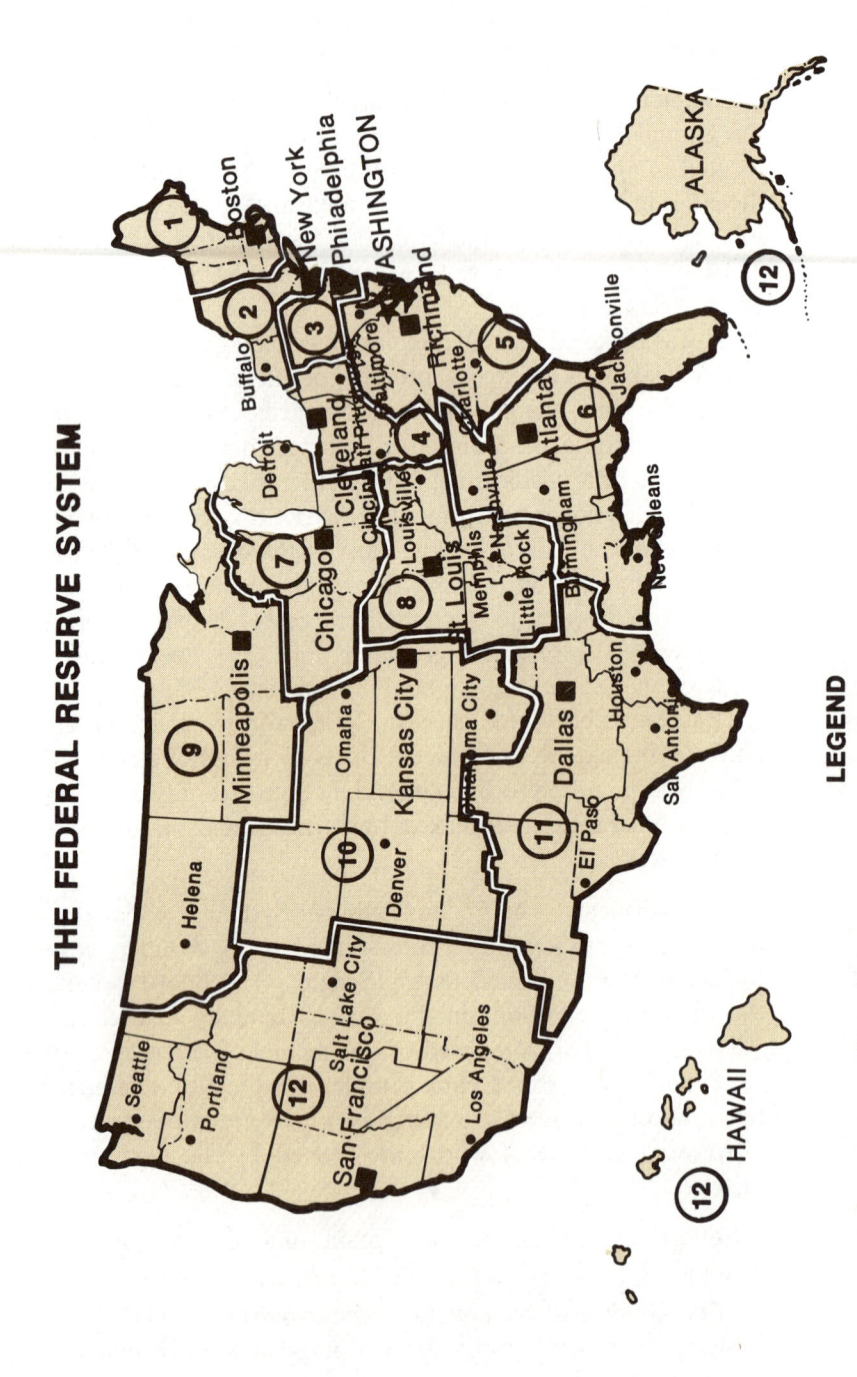

LEGEND

— Boundaries of Federal Reserve Districts   — Boundaries of Federal Reserve Branch Territories
★ Board of Governors of the Federal Reserve System   ■ Federal Reserve Bank Cities   • Federal Reserve Branch Cities

SOURCE: *Federal Reserve Bulletin*, Board of Governors of the Federal Reserve System, Washington, D.C.

banks. Each member bank must keep a specified amount on deposit with the federal reserve bank to which it belongs. In addition to these reserve deposits specified by law, banks usually keep other kinds of deposits in the federal reserve banks. Then, if the need arises, the bank can call upon the federal reserve bank for the amount of the money required to meet the demands of its depositors.

(2) Supplying public needs for cash. The need for hand-to-hand money in the form of coins and paper money varies. For example, just before and during the Christmas season many people make more cash purchases, and merchants have to keep more cash on hand with which to "make change" for their customers. As a result, the amount of cash withdrawn from banks increases, which makes it necessary for banks to acquire additional supplies of money.

In order to replenish its cash reserves, a bank that is a member of a federal reserve bank asks the latter for a shipment of cash in the form of coins, federal reserve notes, or other kinds of paper money. The federal reserve bank immediately makes the shipment, and the amount is deducted from the member bank's account. Later, when less cash is needed, the bank will return part of its cash to the federal reserve bank.

Merchants and other businessmen who hold notes and trade acceptances that they have received from the sale of goods can take these credit instruments to the bank and borrow on them, that is, sell them to the bank. If the bank then needs additional funds, it can send these notes and trade acceptances to the federal reserve bank in the district and can rediscount (or sell) them. Or it may give its own promissory note to the federal reserve bank and pledge its customers' notes and other commercial paper that the note will be paid.

In either case, the federal reserve bank will give the bank federal reserve notes and other kinds of money or credit the bank's account. If the bank takes cash, it in turn pays it out to its customers.

When the notes and trade acceptances are paid by those who signed or accepted them, there is a decrease in the amount of money in the hands of individuals. Thus, the Federal Reserve System makes an elastic currency system possible, which tends to prevent the extreme fluctuations in prices that would take place without such elasticity. The amount of money and credit tends to correspond to the needs of business.

(3) Control of the amount of bank credit. There are several ways by which federal reserve banks may attempt to control the volume of bank credit in the United States. One of these methods is by changing the discount or interest rate that the federal reserve banks charge member banks

MONEY SUPPLY CREATED BY BANK LOANS

BRAKE
1. Raise in reserve requirements by Board of Governors.
2. Raise in rediscount rate by federal reserve banks.
3. Sale of securities in the open market by the Federal Reserve System.

ACCELERATOR
1. Lowering of reserve requirements.
2. Borrowing by member banks from Federal Reserve.
3. Purchase of securities in the open market by Federal Reserve System.

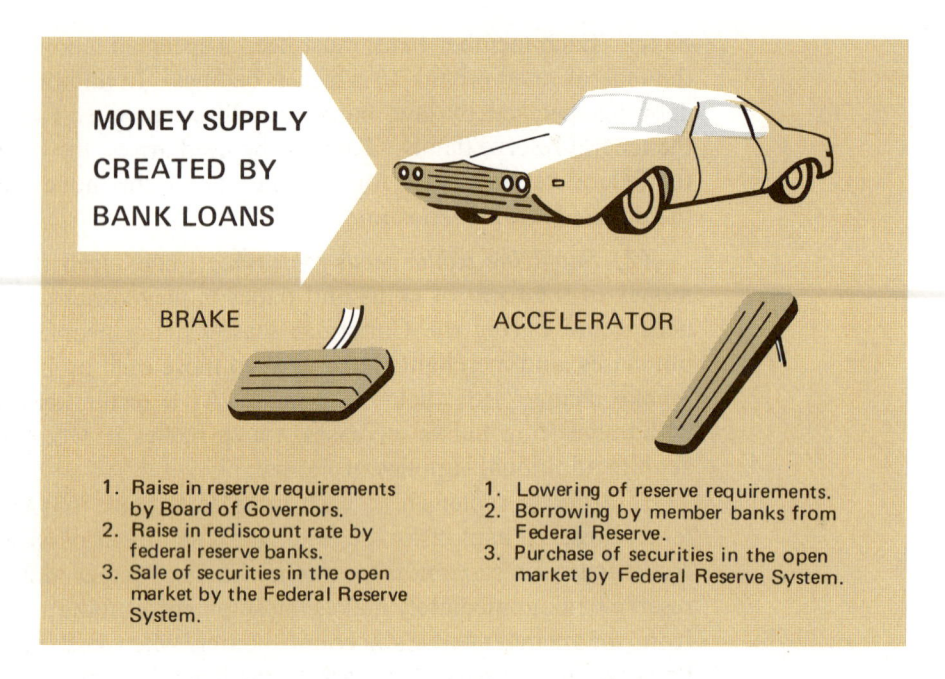

Figure 21-2.

There are several ways by which federal reserve banks may attempt to control the volume of bank credit in the United States.

for loans. By raising the discount rate, member banks may be discouraged from borrowing at the federal reserve banks. When this happens, the amount of member bank loans becomes more limited.

On the other hand, by lowering the discount rate, the federal reserve banks may encourage member banks to borrow. As borrowing by member banks becomes easier, the amount of the loans that may be made to business concerns by member banks increases.

Open-market operations offer the Federal Reserve System another means of controlling the volume of credit. *Open-market operations* refer to the buying and selling of bonds and certain kinds of commercial credit instruments. When the federal reserve banks buy bonds and commercial paper, more money and credit are put into circulation.

Commercial banks keep part of their funds invested in bonds and other kinds of credit instruments. If the federal reserve bank in your district should buy $100,000 worth of bonds from the First National Bank, that would give the commercial bank an additional amount of money that could be used as a reserve for loans to businessmen in the community. Thus, the amount of bank credit would be expanded.

But when the federal reserve banks sell bonds and commercial paper, less money and credit are available for use by businessmen. For example, if the federal reserve bank sells $100,000 worth of bonds to the First National Bank, the commercial bank will have to use its money or credit to buy the bonds. It will, therefore, have a smaller reserve from which loans can be made to local business concerns.

Finally, federal reserve banks can discourage member banks from extending loans (which become deposits) to their customers in another way — by increasing reserve requirements. For example, an increase of say from 12 to 13 percent might make it difficult for member banks to supply the increased reserve, which would discourage banks from making loans (which increase deposits). By reducing reserve requirements, federal reserve banks can encourage banks to increase loans.

Thus, by changing reserve requirements or the discount rate or by buying or selling government securities in the open market, the Federal Reserve System can increase or decrease the amount of money in circulation. In this way the System encourages or discourages economic activities in the nation, especially since the changes in money supply have the multiplying effect on credit expansion or contraction as has been previously discussed.

(4) Clearinghouse for member banks. The Federal Reserve System greatly simplifies the clearing of checks or the method by which checks that have been deposited in banks or paid by banks are transferred to the banks on which they are drawn. For example, Jones, who lives in the city of Fredericksburg, Virginia, 50 miles north of Richmond, and in the fifth reserve district, sends his check to Smith, who lives in Chicago. Smith deposits the check in his Chicago bank, the First National Bank. The First National Bank sends the check to the Federal Reserve Bank of Chicago, which in turn sends it to the Federal Reserve Bank of Richmond. The latter bank then sends the check to Jones's bank in Fredericksburg, where the amount of the check is deducted from Jones's account. Thus, the collection and clearing of checks deposited in thousands of banks all over the country is facilitated.

(5) Fiscal agent for the United States government. Every year the federal government collects billions of dollars in taxes and from loans. All this money is paid out for the maintenance of the armed services, for the improvement of harbors and navigable streams, for pensions, for the aid of industry, and for other activities that are considered to be of benefit to the general public. So great, therefore, are its financial activities that the government must have some *fiscal*, or financial, *agent* to hold and

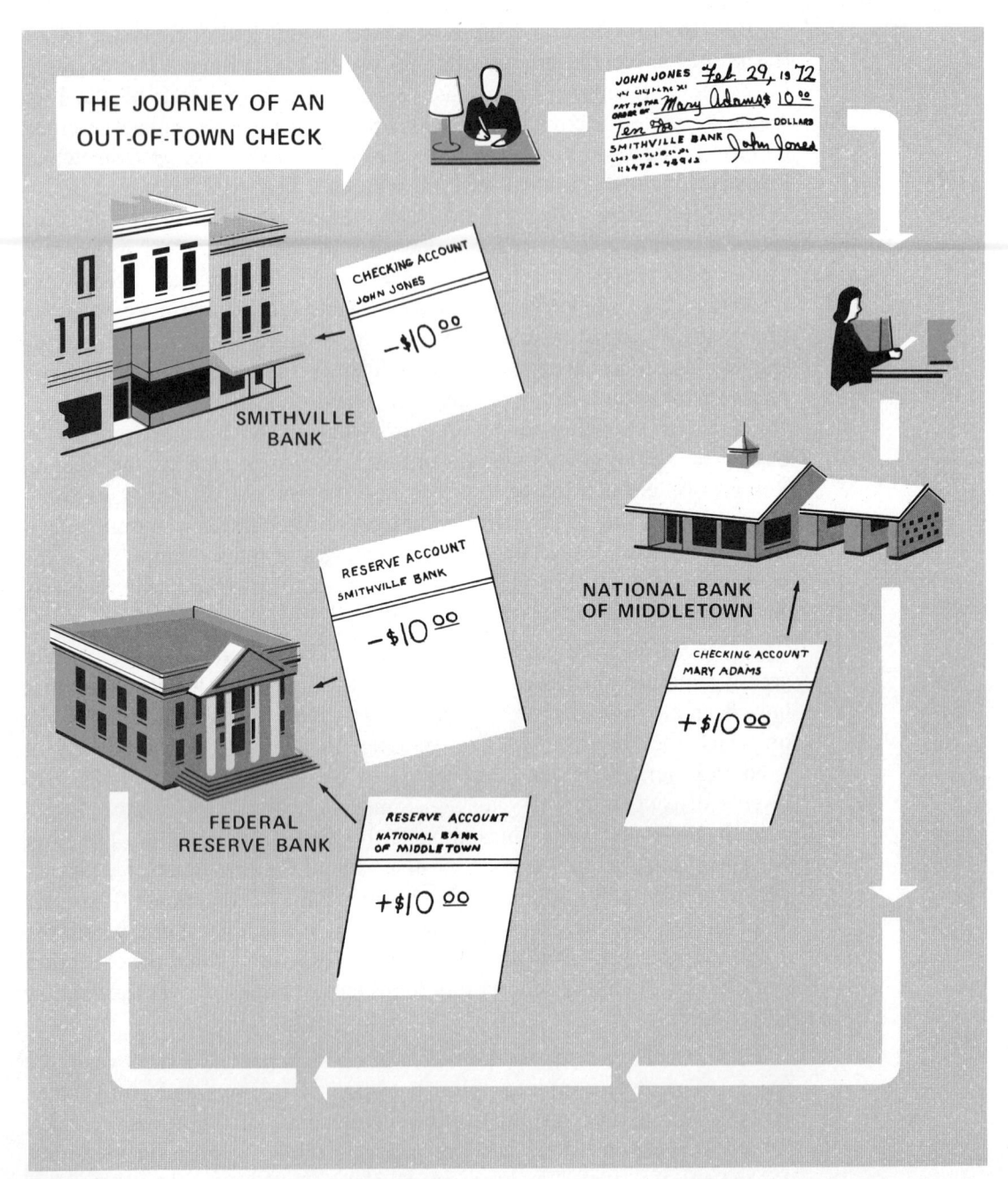

Figure 21-3.

The Federal Reserve System greatly simplifies the clearing of checks.

pay out its money. These services are performed by the Federal Reserve System.

Federal reserve banks handle the billions of dollars worth of United States bonds and notes that have been sold since those banks were organized. The bonds and the notes are sold through the reserve banks, which also reimburse commercial banks for bonds paid off or cashed by the holders.

THE F.D.I.C. INSURES DEPOSITS

Laws passed by Congress beginning in 1933 provided a plan for the insurance of bank deposits. Deposits are now insured to a maximum of $20,000. Under the plan, all national banks and state banks that are members of the Federal Reserve System are required to insure their deposits with the Federal Deposit Insurance Corporation. The insured banks pay premiums or assessments that provide an insurance reserve. The capital stock of the F.D.I.C. is owned by the federal reserve banks, but it pays no dividends.

BANKS ARE VITALLY IMPORTANT

The services that banks perform are so essential in their nature and so far-reaching in their effects that it is difficult to overemphasize the importance of good banking practices. By granting loans to certain concerns and individuals, banks may encourage particular kinds of businesses; or, by denying loans, they may discourage other business undertakings.

Banks also tend to stimulate saving by providing a comparatively safe place for deposits. And, as we have seen, they manufacture credit, which is used as a medium of exchange in carrying on business transactions. The credit thus created is far greater in amount than the value of all the gold and silver owned by the government.

SUMMARY

A number of different kinds of financial firms specialize in dealing in money and credit. These include investment banks, savings banks, savings and loan associations, and commercial banks. The main functions of commercial banks are to accept deposits and to make loans.

A bank deposit is an amount of money (or credit) that a bank is obligated to pay to the depositor. A demand deposit may be withdrawn by check at any time without advance notice by the depositor to the bank. It does not draw interest. In the case of a time deposit, the bank may require advance notice before the amount is withdrawn. A low rate of interest is usually paid on time deposits.

A bank may lend several times as much credit as it has money on reserve in its vault or in a federal reserve bank. In doing so, a minimum ratio between loans and reserves must be maintained. The banking system as a whole can create deposit currency several times as great as the amount of new reserves it receives. The process also works in reverse.

The Federal Reserve System is composed of the Board of Governors, the Federal Advisory Council, the Federal Open Market Committee, the 12 federal reserve banks and their 24 branches, and the member banks. The main functions of the Federal Reserve System and its central banks are to hold reserves of member banks, to issue federal reserve currency, to control the amount of bank credit in the country, to clear checks, and to act as fiscal agent for the federal government. The federal reserve banks are owned by the member banks. All national banks must belong to the Federal Reserve System, and state banks may belong.

The F.D.I.C. insures deposit accounts up to a maximum of $20,000.

NEW TERMS

clearinghouse
commercial bank
correspondent banks
demand deposit
deposit currency
deposits
derivative deposit
excess reserves
fiscal agent
investment banks
legal reserve
member banks

multiple bank credit contraction
multiple bank credit expansion
open-market operations
primary deposit
savings and loan associations
savings banks
savings certificates of deposit
time deposits
working reserve

QUESTIONS ON THE CHAPTER

1. What are the two main functions of commercial banks?
2. What does one get when he borrows from a bank?
3. Is discount a form of interest? Explain.
4. What is meant by "clearing and collecting checks"?
5. What is a bank deposit? a demand deposit? a time deposit?
6. What is the distinction between a bank's working reserve and its legal reserve?
7. What is the purpose of legal reserves?
8. What do you understand by the term "deposit currency"?
9. What are a bank's assets and liabilities?
10. How much can a bank lend to its customers?

Ch. 21 MONEY, CREDIT, AND BANKING

11. How are individual banks able to lend safely more purchasing power, or money, than they keep on hand as reserves?
12. How do banks create, or manufacture, deposit currency?
13. What is the significance of multiple bank credit expansion and contraction?
14. What is a federal reserve bank?
15. What is the Federal Reserve System?
16. By whom and in what manner are the 12 federal reserve banks owned?
17. What are the functions of the Federal Reserve System?
18. Can federal reserve banks control the total amount of commercial bank credit? Explain.
19. What is the F.D.I.C. and how does it operate? Why is it important?
20. Why are commercial banks so important?

APPLYING YOUR ECONOMIC UNDERSTANDING

1. How many and what types of financial functions does your local commercial bank perform? Explain each function.
2. Secure permission to visit a bank clearing or a clearinghouse in a city. Explain the procedure of clearing that you observed.
3. Examine the latest annual report of your local commercial bank. What percentage of its total funds belongs to (a) the owners of the bank, and (b) the depositors?
4. According to the latest annual report of your local bank, how do the demand deposits compare with time or savings deposits? What might account for the relationship which you discovered?
5. A recent trend has been the issuance of certificates of deposit by banks and savings institutions. The depositor agrees to nonwithdrawal of his deposit for 6 months, a year, or a longer time period. The depositor also receives a higher rate of interest than he would receive on a regular savings account deposit. Why would your local bank adopt this trend?
6. Compare the rediscount rate of the federal reserve bank in your district with the interest rate your nearest member bank charges its borrowers. Does the difference have anything to do with determining whether the member bank will borrow reserves so that it can lend money to its customers? Explain.
7. Under what circumstances could a husband, a wife, and a teen-age son have more than $20,000 on deposit in an F.D.I.C. insured bank and still be covered for their total savings exceeding $20,000?
8. Discuss with your local banker the various ways in which a bank can invest its funds. Compare what are considered safe percentages for each type of bank investment based on total bank investments. Report your findings to the class.

9. Assume that you are a member of a board of directors of a bank with a responsibility for selecting a new president for the bank. What qualifications would you establish as being most important?
10. Does your local bank participate in multiple bank credit expansion? Why or why not?

CHALLENGES TO ECONOMIC COMPETENCE

1. Prepare a display showing the various roles your bank plays in aiding the economic life of your community.
2. Make a book of clippings and forms related to your local bank's operations and include a written article to explain the operations.
3. Prepare and present a debate on the issue: Federal Reserve Banks Should Be Owned by the Government.
4. Write a report on one of the following: (a) The History of Our Local Bank, (b) How the Federal Reserve System Operates, (c) Credit Control: How and by Whom? (d) Banking Has a New Look.

Unit 6

National Income — Growth and Stability

Chapter 22 Measures of Our National Income and Production
Chapter 23 Business Cycles and Economic Growth

Humble Oil & Refining Co.

Whether a nation — and not merely some group of individuals — is rich or poor depends upon the value of total production relative to the number of people in the nation. The question as to whether a nation is making economic progress also depends upon the increase in the amount of production that is taking place relative to the size of the population. The stability of the economy depends upon the extent to which a sound level of production is maintained.

U.S. Department of Agriculture

Bethlehem Steel Co.

Chapter 22

Measures of Our National Production and Income

How can we measure the volume of production and income in the economy?
What do GNP, NI, PI, and DPI stand for?
How do changes in prices affect the size of the national production?

By this time we understand that real economic income consists of goods and services that are produced by the employment of economic resources. We measure the value of goods and services in terms of money. If we have enough money and if the goods and services are available, we can buy the things we need to satisfy our wants. It is important, however, to keep in mind the fact that production gives rise to money income and that money is valuable only to the extent that it can be used to buy goods and services now or in the future.

Whether a nation — and not merely some group of individuals — is rich or poor depends upon the value of total production relative to the number of people in the nation. The question as to whether a nation is making economic progress also depends upon the increase in the amount of production that is taking place relative to the size of the population. Finally, the stability of the economy depends upon the extent to which a certain level of production is maintained.

Probably most of us are more interested in matters that relate to our own personal income than we are in those that relate to the income of the nation as a whole. But it does not take an expert economist to recognize some of the relations between total production and income in the nation, and the amount and value of the income that each one of us receives. No matter whether we contribute land, labor, capital, or entrepreneurship to production, in our free society the larger the total amount of goods and services produced, the larger our individual incomes are likely to be.

It is obvious, therefore, that if we are to get an overall idea as to how well the economy is performing, we must be able to understand how we can measure the amount of total production that is taking place or has taken place. How can total production in a nation for a period of time, such as a year, be calculated? What is the relation between total production and the total amount of personal income? Of the total income that the people receive, how much can they spend? Or save? What, if anything, can be done to increase the amount of total income of a people? Such questions are certainly worthy of our consideration, for they are directly related to the well-being of the people in the nation.

THE GROSS NATIONAL PRODUCT AND INCOME

The *gross national product* (GNP)[1] is the term used to refer to the total market value of the amount of goods and services produced in the nation during a given period of time, say a year. The gross national product is also the measure of the gross national income. The information that is needed to determine these measures must be gathered from many sources. This work is therefore undertaken by several federal government agencies, but most extensively by the Department of Commerce.

Illus. 22-1. The gross national product (GNP) is the term used to refer to the total market value of the amount of goods and services produced in the nation during a given period of time. New construction constitutes a part of the GNP.

Housing and Home Finance Agency

---

[1] In studying the GNP and its component parts you should make use of the current monthly editions of the following publications: *Survey of Current Business,* U.S. Department of Commerce, and the *Federal Reserve Bulletin,* Board of Governors of the Federal Reserve System, both of Washington, D.C. These publications should be in your school library.

HOW GNP IS MEASURED

In order to be able to calculate what the total production or income amounts to, a common denominator of value must be utilized. Obviously, if the gross national product consists of goods and services, we cannot add together numbers of space vehicles, bales of cotton, dozens of shirts, numbers of teeth filled, and days of clerical service. Therefore, in trying to get an idea of the volume of the GNP, we think in terms of the money value of total production.

We can measure GNP in either of two ways: (1) we can measure the value of the goods and services produced by adding together the total expenditures made in producing them; or (2) we can add the total incomes resulting from the expenditures for total production in the economy.

In calculating the gross national product by adding total expenditures, only expenditures on *final products* are included. For example, in calculating the cost of a loaf of bread — which is the final product when purchased by a consumer (and not for resale) — care must be taken to avoid "double counting." One can imagine all the costs involved if the value of each of the steps in the production were considered. The wheat grower pays the costs which arise in preparing the land. Planting, cultivating, and reaping call for the use of capital goods in the way of equipment; services too, in the form of labor, are purchased. The wheat is sold and transported. The milling company adds its cost as wheat is turned into flour. As the product continues to move from mill to bakeries, other costs must be met. And so the bread as a final product in the housewife's marketing basket involves other products — milk, shortening, eggs, yeast, salt, sugar, and, if enriched, vitamins thiamin, riboflavin, and niacin — all of which have been subjected to intermediate stages of production. Thus, the value of the final product is the value of the raw material plus the value added by expenditures at each stage of production.

COMPONENTS OF THE GNP

In calculating GNP for a given period of time the United States Department of Commerce classifies all expenditures in the economy into four categories: (1) personal consumption expenditures, (2) gross private domestic investment, (3) net exports of goods and services, and (4) government purchases of goods and services.

Personal consumption expenditures. The total amount of these expenditures includes all expenditures at market value for goods and services purchased. This classification includes expenditures for both durable and

GROWTH IN REAL GNP, TOTAL AND PER CAPITA 1910 - 1970

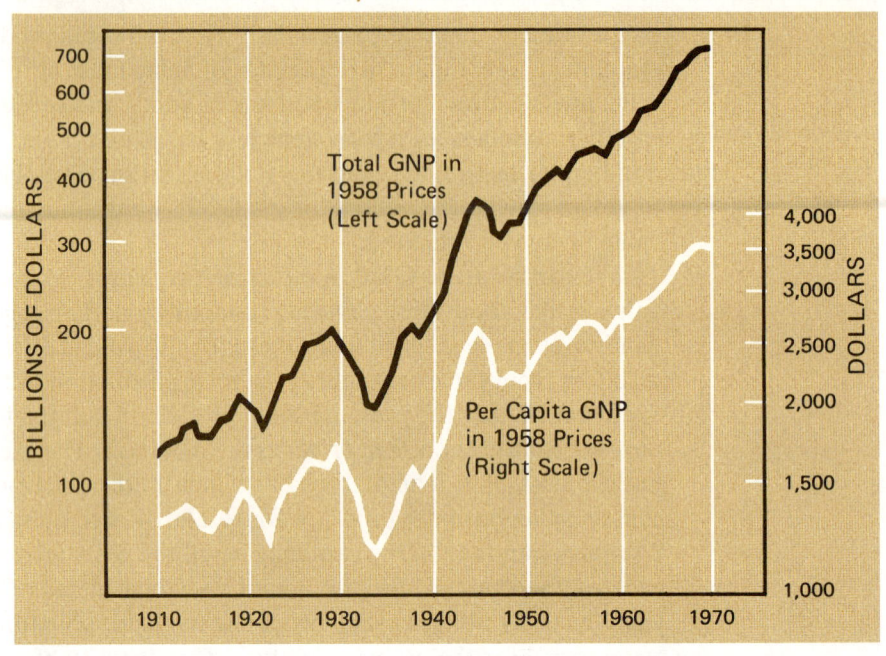

Figure 22-1.

SOURCE: U.S. Department of Commerce. Reprinted in *Economic Report of the President*, February, 1971.

nondurable goods — refrigerators and food, automobiles and gasoline— purchased by individuals, families, and by nonprofit institutions, such as schools and hospitals. Roughly speaking, about two thirds of the gross national product is made up of personal consumption expenditures.

Gross private domestic investment. This classification includes expenditures for new capital equipment bought to replace worn-out machines, tools, and buildings, or to increase production. It includes new houses built for individuals and families since such expenditures are considered investments rather than consumption expenditures. Houses are planned to last several lifetimes. Business and industrial structures, such as new office buildings or factories, which are designed to increase production, are placed in this category. It also includes goods that have been purchased by merchants but not sold to final users, provided they were produced during the period studied. The measure of the expenditures for such goods is indicated by the total amount of the increase in the value of inventories — goods on hand — at the end of the period. In case the

Illus. 22-2. The total amount of personal consumption expenditures includes all expenditures at market value for goods and services purchased. Roughly speaking, about two thirds of the gross national product is made up of personal consumption expenditures.

amount of inventories is less than at the beginning of the period, a deduction from the total amount of gross private investment is indicated.

Net exports of goods and services. Goods and services produced in this country but sold abroad constitute a part of the gross national product. On the other hand, goods purchased by the people of the United States from abroad are not part of our GNP. Therefore, we deduct the value of our purchases of foreign-made goods — German cars, Japanese transistor radios, British wools, or services such as rail transportation in Austria, hotel accommodations in Switzerland, or voice lessons in Italy — from that of our exports or sales abroad. This gives us the amount of our *net exports*.

Government purchases of goods and services. These purchases include those made by the federal, state, and local governments. Examples of such purchases are those for state-owned cars, public library buildings, desks, typewriters, and other office equipment; military and police services; and the services of millions of employees, from unskilled laborers working on the roads to highly trained experts in research laboratories. It includes the salary of the President of the United States. It does not, however, include all of the expenditures for government-produced services, such as those provided by the postal service and certain other government-owned and operated businesses, as power companies and waterworks. These are considered as consumer expenditures.

We can summarize what we have just said as to the expenditures that make up the gross national product by using the figures for the year 1971.

THE GROSS NATIONAL PRODUCT

Year 1971

(First Quarter Annual Rate)

(Billions of dollars)

Personal consumption expenditures..............	$ 646.4
Gross private domestic investment...............	142.4
Net exports of goods and services................	3.3
Government purchases of goods and services......	228.7
Gross national product (in current dollars)....	$1,020.7*

*Slight discrepancy due to rounding of figures.

SOURCE: *Federal Reserve Bulletin*, June, 1971.

DISTRIBUTION OF THE GROSS NATIONAL PRODUCT AND INCOME

Most of the income resulting from the expenditures in creating the gross national product goes to the owners of the factors used in producing the product. The total amount of income going to the owners of these factors is the national income (NI).

National income. The national income and the GNP are not equal because certain deductions from GNP must be made before it can be distributed. In the producing of the goods and services which constitute the gross national product during the year, part of the capital equipment used is consumed and therefore depreciates in value. Some of it is worn out entirely; some of it becomes obsolete, or out of date. A newspaper printing press depreciates (although not noticeably) with each edition issued. A truck depreciates with each day's use. So a part of the goods produced during the period is used to replace depreciated capital. Even though the capital goods are not actually replaced with new equipment, funds are set aside for this purpose and not paid to the owners of the factors of production. This does not mean that the depreciation allowance is placed in an idle account; on the contrary, the funds are kept at work through reinvestment in many forms. After deducting the amount of depreciation from GNP, the amount remaining is called *net national product* (NNP).

The cost of the items that make up the net national product includes certain indirect or business taxes, which do not add to the national income but which may enable the government to provide certain services. Therefore, these indirect taxes and certain other minor items are deducted from NNP. What remains is national income, which, as we said before, goes to the owners of the factors of production.

The national income is distributed as follows: (1) compensation for employees, (2) proprietors' incomes, (3) rental income of persons, (4) corporate profits, and (5) net interest.

The total amount of wages and salaries paid to employees, including contributions by employers to the social security program, is classified as the *compensation of employees.* It is by far the largest portion of the national income. *Proprietors' income* is the amount earned by sole proprietorships, partnerships, and self-employed persons. Sometimes this amount is referred to as the "income of unincorporated enterprises." *Rental income of persons* is the measure of the rental income received by property owners, including the estimated rental value of nonfarm residential and business property. The estimated rental value of owner-occupied farm property is included in the income of unincorporated enterprises.

Corporate profits is the net amount of income earned by corporations before the payments of corporate taxes or the payment of dividends to stockholders. Net interest is the amount of interest received by persons from sources other than units of government. Interest paid by units of government is not considered as payment for productive contributions by those who lend money to government.

The table at the top of page 356 illustrates how the net national product and the national income are related to the gross national product.

PERSONAL INCOME AND DISPOSABLE INCOME

The amount of the national income shows how much of the gross national product is distributed among the owners of the factors of production. But it does not show how much is distributed to persons. For example, some of the national income is in the form of profits retained by corporations and not distributed to the stockholders, and some of the national income is in the form of contributions by employers for the social insurance of their employees.

Personal income (PI). As we are using the term here, personal income is the aggregate income of all persons in the country from all sources. Except for a few minor items, it is the amount of the national income, *minus*

GROSS NATIONAL PRODUCT, NET NATIONAL PRODUCT,
NATIONAL INCOME — 1971 (First Quarter Annual Rate)

(Billions of dollars)

GROSS NATIONAL PRODUCT....................		$1,020.7
Deduct: Capital consumption allowances (depreciation, etc.)..................		88.4
NET NATIONAL PRODUCT.....................		932.3
Deduct: Indirect business taxes and make other minor adjustments........		99.1
NATIONAL INCOME...........................		833.2
Compensation of employees..................	625.2	
Proprietors' income.........................	67.0	
Rental income of persons....................	23.1	
Corporate profits...........................	82.7	
Net interest................................	35.2	
		$833.2

SOURCE: *Federal Reserve Bulletin*, June, 1971.

the amount of corporation profits not paid to stockholders, corporation taxes, and social insurance contributions; *plus* government interest and social security payments, pensions, and corporation dividends. If a person owns government bonds, he receives an amount of interest each year, or he may be receiving a government pension or social security benefits, which adds to whatever income he may have from other sources. Personal income, however, is not the total amount that individuals are free to use as they please.

Disposable personal income (DPI). By total *disposable personal income* we mean the total amount of personal income remaining after individuals have paid their federal, state, and local government taxes on property and income, and after compulsory payroll deductions for retirement and unemployment compensation have been made. What remains after these payments have been made is the amount that may be spent or saved. The amount of disposable income *minus* what is saved equals the amount that is spent for consumption goods and services. Or, conversely, the amount of disposable income *minus* what is spent for consumer goods and services equals the amount that is saved. Most of what is saved is spent for capital goods, either by the owner himself who makes his own investments or by some company, bank, or government agency to which the owner lends the money.

The chart on the following page represents the flow of income and expenditures in the national economy. As you can see, the flow goes around and around. Let us trace the relations of the components that are involved in the flow of income and expenditures. Each factor is explained in the following sections.

1. Gross national product (GNP) is the market value of all the goods and services produced in the nation's economy for a given period of time, say, a year. It is equal to the total expenditures made for those goods and services by (1) consumers, (2) business, and (3) government, which are indicated on the chart as "personal consumption expenditures," "gross investment," and "government purchases of goods and services."

2. Net national product (NNP) is the amount of GNP remaining after deducting the amount of depreciation or the value of the products used up (capital consumption) in producing GNP.

3. National income (NI) is the amount of NNP remaining after we deduct the total amount of indirect business taxes, which do not increase the market value of goods and services and which are not necessary to production. National income is equal to the total amount of (1) compensation paid to employees, (2) proprietors' incomes, (3) profits of corporate and noncorporate enterprises, (4) net interest, and (5) rental income paid to persons.

4. Personal income (PI) is the amount of NI *less* the total amount of corporate taxes and savings, and social security contributions (or taxes), *plus* the amount of interest payments by government and the amount of transfer payments. *Transfer payments* refer to income received by individuals from government and business for which no productive services are currently rendered — as, for example, old-age and survivors' and veterans' pensions, as well as private pensions.

5. Disposable personal income (DPI) is the amount of PI remaining after we deduct the total amount of personal taxes.

Personal consumption expenditures is the amount of DPI less the amount of personal savings.

Now note that (1) personal consumption expenditures, (2) investment of gross savings by persons and business, and (3) expenditures by government result in the creation of the gross national product (GNP). Thus, we are back at the point from which we started, and we see that the flow of income and expenditures goes on.

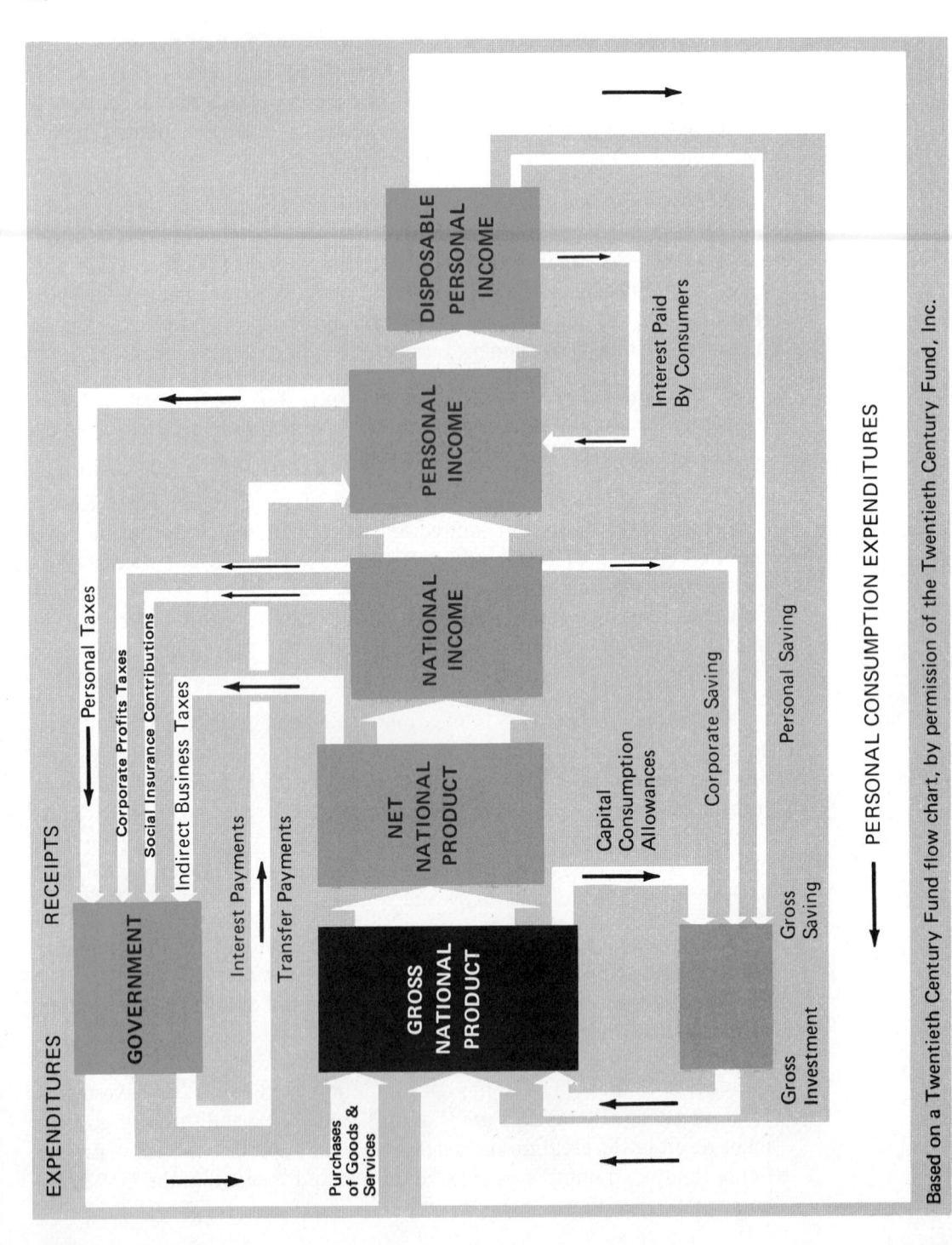

Figure 22-2. Based on a Twentieth Century Fund flow chart, by permission of the Twentieth Century Fund, Inc.

Ch. 22 MEASURES OF OUR NATIONAL PRODUCTION AND INCOME 359

To continue our illustrations with figures for 1971 we have the following items (in billions):

NATIONAL INCOME..............................		$833.2
Deduct: Corporate profits and increases or decreases in inventory...............	82.7	
Contributions for social security........	63.2	145.9
		687.3
Add: Government transfer payments............	82.3	
Net interest paid by government and consumers.......................	32.5	
Corporate dividends.....................	25.8	
Business transfer payments................	3.7	144.3
PERSONAL INCOME.............................		831.5*
Deduct: Personal tax and nontax payments......		116.4
DISPOSABLE PERSONAL INCOME....................		$715.1
Deduct: Personal savings......................	49.8	
Equals: Personal outlays......................	665.3	
Consumer interest payments..	17.9	
Personal transfer payments to foreigners.............	1.0	
Personal consumption.......	646.4	

*Slight discrepancy due to rounding of figures.

SOURCE: *Federal Reserve Bulletin*, June, 1971.

The diagram on page 358 illustrates each of the steps discussed. Thus, we see that the amount of personal consumption for durable and nondurable goods and services takes us back to our starting point — expenditures for personal consumption as the largest portion of the GNP.

In studying the structure of GNP and NI, we might draw an analogy between the individual and the economy. The health of the individual depends in large part on the adequate functioning of the circulatory system which furnishes all parts of the body with necessary nourishment. Some of the blood vessels carry blood from the heart; others carry blood to the heart. Since the circulatory system is an integrating system, it is important that every part be in good working order. If any organ of the body does not receive the proper blood supply, it cannot function; illness or death results.

So, too, the health of the economy depends upon the adequate functioning of the flow of income. If the government were not to receive certain funds, then its functions would have to be curtailed. If the protective functions were curtailed, the result could be disastrous. If, on the other hand, insufficient funds are available for investment by private business, economic growth is impossible.

To carry our analogy a bit further, a young person — such as you — who is experiencing a period of rapid growth needs a greater intake of food to make that growth possible. So too, in the economy, growth requires the production and utilization of more goods and services.

The increase in population naturally demands a greater number of goods — starting with more cans of baby food, more gallons of milk, more cotton materials, more toys, and the services of a greater number of pediatricians and baby-sitters. But as a people begin to demand more of the good things of life, as their scales of living begin to approximate their standards of living — more goods and services must be provided. In the decade of the fifties many families became two-car families. Now we are being encouraged to become a nation of new-home owners, with elaborate kitchen equipment and perhaps a swimming pool in the backyard. As our demands for consumer goods increase, the GNP can also increase.

GNP IN CURRENT DOLLARS AND CONSTANT DOLLARS

Changes in the value of money and prices affect the size of GNP for a given year compared with that for a previous year. This is also true of the income of any individual or firm in business or industry. For example, suppose that the price of corn in 1960 was $1 a bushel and that farmer Jones grew 100 bushels of the grain. The value of his corn would be $100. Then suppose that at the present time the price of corn is $2 a bushel and that he grows 100 bushels. The value of his corn this year would be $200, although the quantity produced is the same as it was in 1960. In this case, his corn crop is being valued in terms of *current dollars* — the value of the dollar at present. In terms of current dollars, then, it would appear that his corn crop is worth twice as much as it was in 1960, although in terms of physical quantities (bushels) the size remains the same.

In order to compare farmer Jones' real contribution of corn to the gross national product for any series of years, it is necessary to compare the money value of the corn in terms of *constant dollars*. By this we mean that we select the price of corn in a given year and use this price as the base. The price for any other year is then compared with the base year in terms of constant purchasing power. Crop size remains the same.

Usually the size of the GNP is stated in terms of current dollars. But in order to get a correct idea as to changes in the size of the real GNP for a year as compared with that of a preceding year, it is necessary to calculate the quantities of goods and services produced for each year in terms of constant dollars. The following table illustrates how the use of current dollars and constant dollars makes a difference in stating the size of the real GNP.

GROSS NATIONAL PRODUCT IN CURRENT AND CONSTANT DOLLARS
(billions of dollars)

YEAR	GNP IN CURRENT DOLLARS	GNP IN 1958 DOLLARS (CONSTANT DOLLARS)
1929	103.1	203.6
1933	55.6	141.5
1941	124.5	263.7
1950	284.8	355.3
1955	398.0	438.0
1960	503.7	487.7
1965	684.9	617.8
1970	976.5	724.1
1971*	1,020.7	732.7

*First quarter estimates

SOURCE: *Federal Reserve Bulletin*, June, 1971; *Economic Indicators*, June, 1971.

As you can see, if you compare the GNP of 1965 with that of 1971 in terms of current dollars for each year, it would appear to have increased greatly — by close to 49 percent in a six-year interval. If, however, your comparison is made in terms of constant dollars, the increase is much smaller — just about 19 percent. Does this mean that the people in the United States had per capita a greater amount of goods and services available in 1971 than in 1965? Our problem is complicated, for we cannot answer this question until we consider the increase in population. But taking changes in population into consideration, we find that real disposable personal income per capita increased approximately 16.5 percent during the six years in question (from $2,240 to $2,610 in constant dollars).

The real GNP does not remain the same from one year to another. Over the period of American history the total amount of production has risen many times. For years the economists held a GNP of $500 billion as a goal worthy of our best efforts. Now, having attained it, the goal is considered by many of these economists to be an ever-rising objective.

The level of prosperity and the rate of growth of GNP are not fixed. From time to time there have been recessions and depressions in business and industry, as illustrated by the GNP data for 1929 and 1933. That is to say, there have been times when production and employment have greatly decreased. Eventually, however, each period of recession and depression has been followed by a period of increasing production and employment.

SUMMARY

The real income in the nation for any given period, such as a year, consists of all the goods and services produced during that time. The value of the total quantities of all the goods and the services produced is measured in terms of dollars.

Total production can then be measured by adding together all the expenditures made for the final products. The four components are (1) total personal consumption expenditures; (2) total investment expenditures by business firms; (3) net amount of goods and services sold abroad; and (4) total amount of goods and services purchased by government. The total is known as the gross national product (GNP).

Since the depreciation of capital goods resulting from use in production or from obsolescence is not actually a part of the national income, this sum is deducted from GNP; and the sum remaining is known as the net national product (NNP).

By deducting indirect business taxes from the NNP we have the amount of income that is received by the owners of the factors of production. This amount constitutes the national income (NI). The national income is distributed in several forms, as (1) compensation for employees, (2) proprietors' incomes, (3) rental income of persons, (4) corporate profits, and (5) net interest. Of these groups, by far the largest portion is received by employees as compensation.

Personal income (PI) is found by subtracting from the national income the (1) amount of corporate profits not paid to stockholders, (2) amount of corporate taxes, (3) change (increase or decrease) in the value of all inventories, and (4) social security taxes paid by employers. Since some persons are the recipients of interest payments, dividends, pensions, or social security benefits from government, these amounts of payments are added to the amount of personal income.

Before an individual can plan the amounts he may spend or save from his income, he must make provision for the payment of his taxes to the government. Therefore, by deducting the total amount of personal taxes from total personal income, the total disposable personal income is found. This is the amount of income that persons are free to spend or to save.

The amount of the GNP is expressed in terms of current dollars. It is usually considered an indication of the prosperity of the people of a nation. It is also an indication of national economic progress. In order to determine whether economic progress is being made, total production must be considered in relation to total population. It is also necessary to consider changes in the value of the dollar. For this reason, when the GNP for one year is being compared with the GNP for another year, both amounts are expressed in terms of constant dollars — which means in terms of dollars of constant purchasing power.

NEW TERMS

compensation of employees
constant dollars
corporate profits
current dollars
disposable personal income
final products
gross national product
net exports

net national product
personal consumption expenditures
proprietors' income

rental income of persons
transfer payments

QUESTIONS ON THE CHAPTER

1. In what three ways is the level of production important to individuals and to the nation as a whole?
2. Why is it desirable to understand how we measure total production in the economy?
3. What is gross national product (GNP)?
4. How can we measure GNP?
5. In using the total expenditure method of calculating GNP, how is "double counting" avoided? Explain.
6. What are the components of GNP?
7. How do we calculate net exports of goods and services?
8. Who receives most of the income resulting from expenditures on GNP?
9. How is national income (NI) derived?
10. In what forms is "rental income" included in NI?
11. What are the components of NI?
12. How should you define personal income?
13. Why is it often desirable to calculate GNP in constant dollars?

APPLYING YOUR ECONOMIC UNDERSTANDING

1. Between 1968–1969 the number of bushels of food grains produced in the United States increased. Would this indicate that food grains maintained their same percentage of importance in GNP? Why or why not?
2. A corporation had a year-end profit of $100,000. It paid $46,500 as federal corporate taxes and declared a cash dividend of $26,000 for stockholder distribution. (a) What percentage was left for corporate saving and investment? (b) How will this investment affect future GNP?
3. A parent has $100 of excess disposable personal income. (a) Would his purchase of a part of a company's bond issue have the same effect it might have if the parent were to purchase a United States government bond? (b) Why or why not?
4. Cite some illustrations of governmental transfer payments made in your community that make up part of the total transfer which adds to the nation's personal income.
5. In the 1960's individuals were allowed a $600 personal exemption in calculating their federal income tax return. In the 1970's this was increased to a personal exemption of $625. How does a change of this type affect the nation's disposable personal income (DPI)?

6. A company in which you are a stockholder retained part of its profit and will use it to complete a renovation of its plant. (a) Will this affect gross national product? (b) What economic reasoning supports your answer?
7. (a) What are some items which you recently used that will become a part of this year's national personal consumption of nondurable goods? (b) Why is personal consumption of nondurable goods in excess of the personal consumption of durable goods?

CHALLENGES TO ECONOMIC COMPETENCE

1. Read a current magazine article forecasting the GNP for this year. Summarize the article in a single paragraph for a school newspaper item.
2. Check the index of rental films in a motion-picture film catalog for a film which illustrates the national income accounts. Request permission to have it rented. Preview the film and arrange to show it to the class. After the class has viewed the film, lead a class discussion and a summary discussion about the film.
3. Prepare a folder and make a collection of news items that discuss the national income accounts.
4. Write a report on one of the following: (a) Trends in GNP Since 1930, (b) How GNP Affects My Family, (c) How Consumers Spend Their Disposable Personal Income, (d) What Causes GNP to Grow?

Chapter 23

Business Cycles and Economic Growth

What are business cycles?
What causes alternating periods of expansion and contraction in business?
What can be done to control the ups and downs in business activity?
Have our monetary and fiscal policies been successful?

The national economy of the United States has been in existence for about 200 years. During this time both total and per-capita production and income have increased many times over. The economy, as measured in terms of production and income, is still growing at an average rate of from about 3 to 3½ percent a year. As a result, from the standpoint of economic wealth and income, the United States is the richest nation on earth.

But the growth of the economy has not been continuous. There have been periods of great prosperity, at least for most of the people. During such periods, production has grown, employment has increased, and wages and profits have risen. Eventually, however, each period of prosperity has been followed by a period of recession in production and income. As a result of these alternating periods of prosperity and recession, the condition of the economy throughout its history has been described as "half boom and half bust."

Obviously, if the periods of business contraction could have been avoided or lessened, people would have fared better, and it would appear that our present level of wealth and economic leadership would be even higher than it is. For a long time, however, economists and people in general accepted the ups and downs in business activity as a matter of course. Many, if not most, persons seemed to feel that under a system of free enterprise, recurring periods of business prosperity and recession or depression were inevitable and that not much, if anything, could be done about it. During the last thirty years or so, however, the attitude of most economists and political leaders on this matter has changed greatly.[1] They no longer accept the idea that nothing can be done to prevent business recessions. At least they feel that certain policies can be adopted which will minimize recessions and possibly achieve the goal of a constantly growing and expanding economy. On the other hand, there are some who are convinced that the employment of such policies is fraught with grave danger to the continuation of the free-enterprise system. These differences in opinion frequently give rise to political issues that are debated vigorously in the press, on radio and television, and on the floor of Congress.

BUSINESS CYCLES

In economic terminology, the major fluctuations in business activity in the economy are referred to as *business cycles*. The term "cycle" suggests a characteristic and recurring sequence of changes in the condition of business from that of expansion to contraction to expansion and so on. Each period of expansion or prosperity and each period of contraction or recession is not necessarily the same as the preceding one. But what is implied is that certain conditions of business follow each other in sequence. The four phases of the business cycle are (1) *expansion* — optimism prevails and business is "picking up." The movement gains momentum and *prosperity* reigns. (2) A *peak* is attained after which expansion ends and contraction begins. (3) During the period of *contraction*, businessmen are

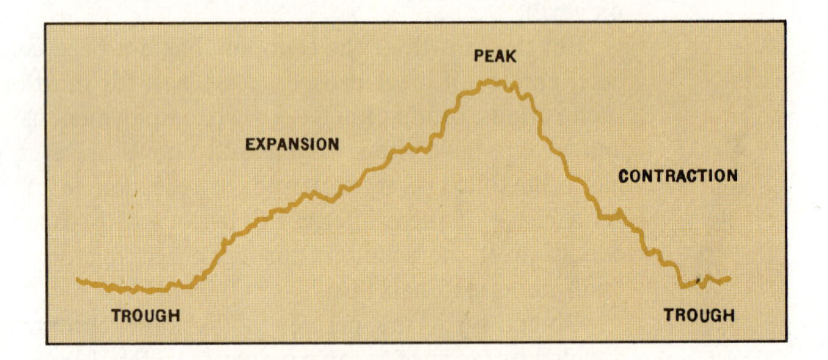

Figure 23-1.

The Phases of a Typical Business Cycle

The irregularities in the general trend of the cycle indicate monthly and seasonal changes in business activity.

---

[1] An English economist, John Maynard Keynes, is generally given credit for much of the change in the attitude and thinking of most present-day economists with regard to the causes and possible controls over business cycles. He set forth his ideas in his book *General Theory of Employment, Interest and Money*, which was published in 1936.

pessimistic and times are described as "bad." (4) Finally, a *trough* is reached — the lowest point of the *depression*. Having reached bottom, revival or expansion begins again. In most cases these cycles covered a period of three or four years, but economists have discovered that there have been general long-term upward and downward swings extending over periods of fifty or more years.

THEORIES AS TO THE CAUSES OF BUSINESS CYCLES

Many theories have been advanced to explain business cycles. Briefly stated these theories include the following: (1) overproduction — more goods have been produced than can be sold; (2) sunspots and weather — the appearance of dark spots that occur on the sun seem to be accompanied by magnetic storms on earth. The weather conditions definitely affect agricultural production and hence total income; (3) monetary — the amount of money in circulation varies and thus affects the demand for goods and services; (4) overinvestment — too much money has been spent for capital equipment and not enough for consumer goods; (5) psychological — the degree of optimism or pessimism on the part of entrepreneurs and consumers results in variations in investments and consumer purchases, which cause changes in the flow of income. If people feel that business is entering a period of "good times," they buy more freely, which sends sales up and in turn increases the demand for capital goods; (6) underinvestment — the amount of money spent for capital goods is less than the amount of savings of businesses and individuals, which means that part of the amount saved becomes idle and is not passed on as income to others.

Economists generally agree that no particular one of these theories is a complete explanation as to the causes of the business cycle. But many of them agree that there is some truth in most of the theories.

Most economists attach the greatest significance to the underinvestment theory, which can be used to explain changes in the total or aggregate demand for goods and services. This theory might also be called the aggregate demand theory because investment in capital goods plays such an important part in determining the amount of income in the nation.

AGGREGATE DEMAND, PRODUCTION, EMPLOYMENT, AND PRICES

As we saw in the preceding chapter, the amount of the gross national product is measured by the expenditures of four classes of purchasers of the goods and services produced in the economy: (1) consumers (personal

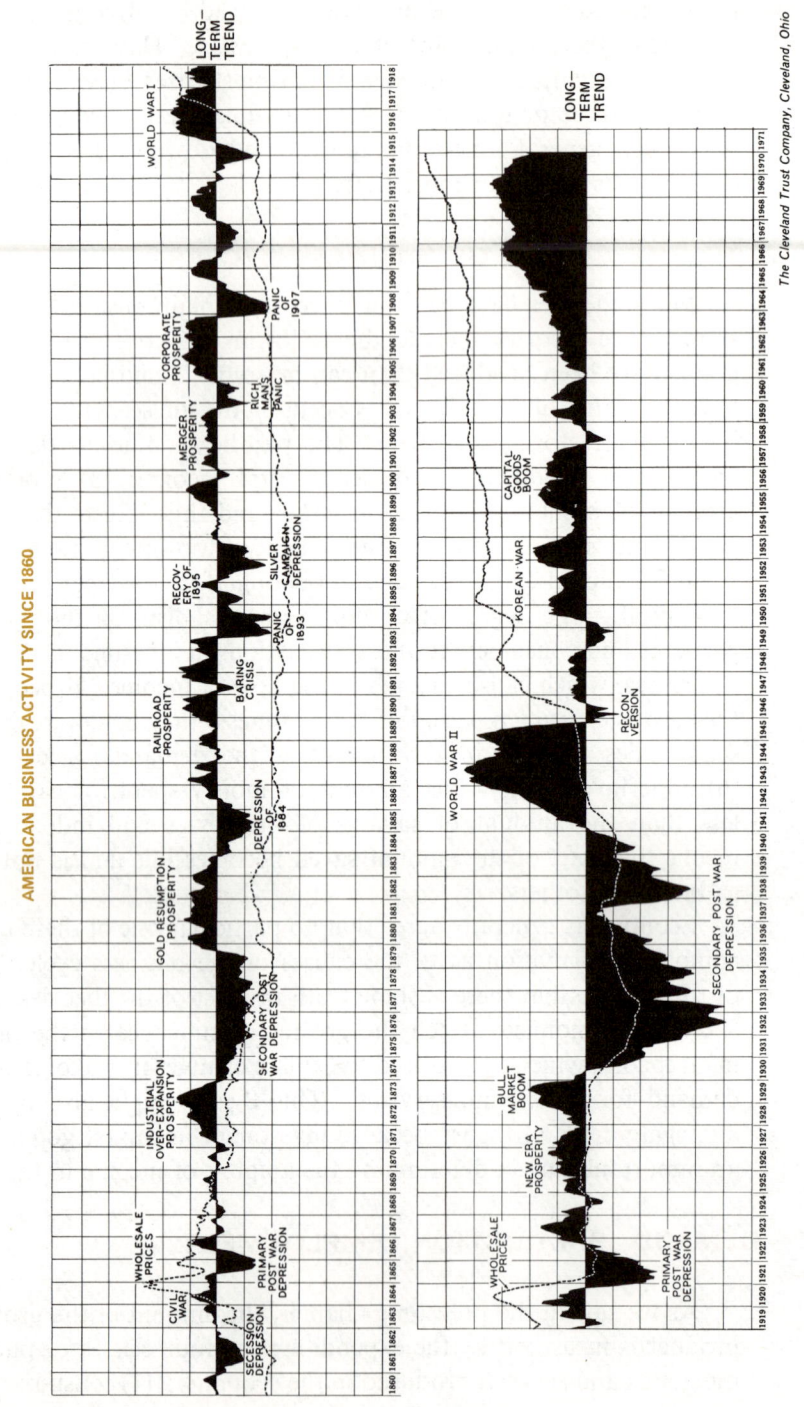

368 NATIONAL INCOME — GROWTH AND STABILITY   Unit 6

The dark parts of the chart above the line "Long-Term Trend" indicate periods when business prosperity was high or above average. Those below the line indicate periods of business depression or low prosperity. Note, too, the change in wholesale prices. Events and conditions recorded in American history help to add interest and meaning to the chart.

Figure 23-2.

consumption expenditures); (2) producers (gross private domestic investment); (3) foreign purchasers (net exports of goods and services); and (4) government (government purchases of goods and services). The total demand of these buyers for goods and services — all of the food and furniture bought by consumers; all of the machinery purchased by automobile manufacturers; all of the cotton purchased from the United States; and all the roads built by government — is *aggregate demand.*

Perhaps it is well to recall that market demand implies a want that is backed up with money or purchasing power. It is more than the mere need or desire for a good. As aggregate demand increases, total production tends to increase also. If aggregate demand increases faster than production, prices rise and inflation results because the amount of money in circulation has increased faster than the total supply of goods and services. If aggregate demand decreases — if consumers buy fewer goods, if families decide to continue to use the old car — manufacturers of cars need less steel, fewer workmen, and fewer salesmen; and, as production declines, unemployment increases. Even if prices of automobiles decline, they still may not be purchased. If this situation continues, a period of marked business contraction may develop.

What can be done to control aggregate demand? As we have learned, the national income is generated by expenditures for production. The owners of the factors of production used in producing GNP receive incomes in the form of wages and salaries, profits, rent, farm income, corporate profits, and net interest, as enumerated by the U. S. Department of Commerce.

As long as total spending of income in the nation equals the amount of income received, production will continue at a stable level. But if investment spending for capital goods by business is less than the amount of total savings in the economy, then the income stream becomes less than it was. For example, if consumers save 20 billion dollars in a year and only 15 billion dollars is invested in capital goods, the income stream is reduced by at least 5 billion dollars, which will result in a decrease in the demand for goods and services. For if plants are not working at capacity level, fewer workers are employed, and fewer goods are turned out. The increase in unemployment means more persons without paychecks, which means fewer expenditures for consumer goods and services. Conversely, if business firms borrow from banks or use funds that were hoarded from a previous year so that total spending is greater than total income for the current year, aggregate demand will increase. This demand will exert an upward pressure on production, prices, and employment.

Increases and decreases in aggregate demand. Why does aggregate demand fluctuate? That is to say, why do consumers, government, business, and foreigners increase or decrease their spending?

As a rule, the amount of spending by consumers does not fluctuate as much as does the spending by business firms for capital goods and for the production of goods and services. But there are times when such consumer spending changes quickly. During World War II when so much of the productivity of workers in this country was directed toward the production of war materials, consumer goods were definitely limited. When the shoe manufacturers were busy turning out shoes for millions of soldiers, the limited supply of shoes for civilians had to be rationed. The same thing was true also of meat supplies, sugar, nylon fabric, and gasoline and fuel oil. Steel had to be directed to uses other than automobiles and refrigerators, and so it was impossible to buy as many articles of this type as before. Even tin, paper, and soap were listed among scarce materials. To add to the problem, workers in war plants were making unusually high wages and were eager to make purchases. After the war, when restrictions were removed on purchases, there was a marked increase in prices as a result of the increase in buying.

Then in 1950 the Korean conflict was developing. Talk of war caused consumers to rush to the market and to stock up on goods because they remembered the restrictions on purchases during World War II.

At other times marked changes in consumer demand occur which are not so easily explained. The Board of Governors of the Federal Reserve System and a group at the University of Michigan have been engaged in a study of this question for some time. Perhaps before long we shall know much more about this matter.

From 1950 to 1970 consumer expenditures grew from about $191 billion to about $646 billion. During the great business depression after 1929, that is, in the thirties, consumers spent much more than they received in disposable income because they had to use much of their savings. Since World War II, consumer spending has been about 92 to 95 percent of disposable personal income.

The amount of our exports does not constitute a large part of the aggregate demand for our goods and services. Therefore, changes in the net exports of goods and services do not greatly affect aggregate demand.

Investment spending — spending by business firms — depends largely upon the businessman's expectations of profits. The factors that affect his expectations in this respect are many and complex. Among these factors, however, we may mention the following: *innovations* including new products, new types of industry, and new methods of marketing. Such innovations as television and such types of industry as plastics, electronics, and new methods of production and of marketing as automation and supermarkets have greatly influenced investments in the economy.

Several innovations may occur in rapid succession. But, as a rule, they do not. Usually after an innovation has been accepted and established, investment spending that resulted from the advent of the new product or method of production slows down.

The amount of spending by government sometimes depends upon what people think government should do. If the voters feel that government should undertake to perform only routine or traditional functions, then the level of government spending will remain relatively stable except in the advent of war. For some years national defense — veterans' payments, interest on the national debt, and other matters related to past or possible future wars — has claimed more than 50 percent of the federal budget expenditures.

Government spending has special significance because it is large and it can be controlled, while private spending is changeable and is not directed by any external authority. If more highways or school buildings are desired by the people, their construction can be authorized and undertaken. The money needed can easily be borrowed. Likewise, if the federal government administration and Congress feel that an increase or a decrease in spending by the government is needed in order to stimulate business or to reduce the danger of inflation, appropriate action may be taken. Whether the results desired will be achieved will depend upon whether such action is properly timed and whether it is properly integrated with other forces that affect production, income, and employment.

FLUCTUATIONS IN PRODUCTION AND INCOME MAY BE CUMULATIVE

In trying to account for changes in demand for goods and services, it is very important for us to know that changes in production and income are often the result of cumulative processes. That is to say, a given increase or decrease in investment or in the demand for goods may result in a total increase in production in the economy that is several times as great as was the increase or decrease in investment or demand. An understanding of (1) the multiplier principle and (2) the acceleration principle will enable us to understand how this occurs.

The cumulative effect of the multiplier principle on consumer spending. Suppose that $6 million of savings from last year — or from a loan from investment bankers of that amount — is invested by a business firm. How much would the investment add to the GNP? That would depend largely upon how much of the incomes received by wage earners and others is spent and how much is saved.

Let us assume that the $6 million is spent in the erection of a new plant. Building materials must be provided, and hundreds of workers employed. As the building nears completion, new machines are installed. They may have been ordered from plants hundreds of miles away — so transportation workers as well as manufacturing workers have added work. The workers — the carpenters, bricklayers, workers in cement mills, workers in tile, workers in steel, unskilled laborers, plumbers, plasterers, workers who produce panes of glass, as well as glaziers, electricians — all of these have increased incomes as a result of the construction of the plant. Let us assume further that these workers save about one fourth of their income and spend the rest for consumption goods — clothing for the family, a new car, perhaps new furniture or a vacation trip. You can easily see that those who work in textile mills, in department stores, in automobile plants, lumber mills, or who render services on trains, in motels, restaurants, or national parks are going to benefit. These workers in turn spend some of their added income and save some. If each person involved spent three fourths of the income he received and saved the rest, the effect on incomes and savings in terms of millions of dollars would be as follows:

	Increase in income	Increase in consumption	Increase in savings
Original Investment	$ 6. million	$ 4.5 million	$ 1.5 million
Second Group	4.5	3.375	1.125
Third Group	3.375	2.531	.844
Fourth Group	2.531	1.898	.633
Fifth Group	1.898	1.4235	.4745
Sixth Group	1.4235	1.217	.206
Seventh Group	1.217	.91275	.30425
Eighth Group	.91275	.68456	.12819
Ninth Group	.68456	.51422	.17014
Tenth Group	.51422	.38581	.12861
TOTALS	$23.05603	$17.44184	$ 5.51369

The table could be continued, but we have gone far enough to show that the increase in savings was fast approaching the initial investment of $6 million. When this point is reached, the total effect on the national income has run its course. But, as the figures indicate, the increase in the GNP would approach $24 million — four times the original amount invested. In such a case, the cumulative effect of investment on income would definitely be determined by the propensity or inclination to save, which in this case is ¼, and the multiplier becomes the reciprocal of the marginal propensity to save or $\frac{1}{\frac{1}{4}}$ equals 4 (the multiplier). We see, then, that under the *multiplier principle* the greater the propensity to save, the smaller the total effect of any given investment on the income.

On the other hand, the multiplier can work in reverse. Suppose, for example, this year people save $20 billion of their income and that $6 billion is not spent for the creation of new capital goods. This will result in a cumulative reduction in spending by a group of consumers, which will reduce the demand for goods and thereby affect production and employment.

Cumulative effects of the acceleration principle on the production of capital goods. What this "accelerator" means is that an increase in the demand for consumer goods may result in a greater percentage increase in the production of capital goods. Suppose, for example, that a taxi firm is operating at full capacity and that it has 10 cars. Assume further that each year one car wears out and has to be replaced by the purchase of a new car. Even a slight increase in the demand for taxi service — say 10 percent — will require that the taxi company buy two new cars that year. This would mean that for this firm a 10 percent increase in the demand for taxi service would result in a 100 percent increase in the demand for new cars, which are classified as capital goods. You can well imagine the acceleration in spending that would result if the automobile industry has an increased demand for cars which in turn calls for an increased demand for steel and chromium and radios and fans and nylon for seat covers — to mention just a few items utilized.

On the other hand, a 10 percent decrease in the demand for taxi service might mean that the firm would not have to buy even one new car this year. This would mean that a 10 percent decrease in the demand for consumer services would result in 100 percent decrease in the taxi company's demand for cars. This would result in a deceleration in spending.

We conclude, therefore, that it is possible that a given change in the demand for consumer goods or services may result in a much larger or a much smaller change in the demand for capital goods, depending upon whether demand for consumer goods increases or decreases. The cause for these facts is the operation of the *acceleration principle*.

It is easy to see how the operation of the acceleration principle can affect total production and employment in the economy. And in this case we have scarcely mentioned the resulting psychological effect. To refer once again to the taxi company: With the increase in business, the wages of a driver might increase, and with such an increase his family buys more than it previously could afford; merchants buy more goods, which causes factories to produce more, and so on. Since business "is good," the owner of the company may decide upon a real vacation trip — across the country. And if he drives, people in all parts of the country are likely to profit — those who own hotels, motels, restaurants, or gas stations; people who have entertainment to offer, or clothes, souvenirs, and postcards to sell. Even insurance companies may have added income!

CAN WE CONTROL THE UPS AND DOWNS IN PRODUCTION, EMPLOYMENT, AND INCOME?

As was mentioned earlier, before 1929 few economists or people in government felt that there was much that could be done to offset these ups and downs in business activity. But the Great Depression of the thirties demanded that some drastic action be taken, and the federal government did step in. Although there is much difference of opinion as to how effective the government's actions were in raising prices and in creating employment, government action tended to establish some precedent. This was evidenced a decade later in the passage by Congress of the Employment Act of 1946 which states:

> The Congress declares that it is the continuing policy and responsibility of the Federal Government to use all practicable means consistent with its needs and obligations and other essential considerations of national policy, with the assistance and cooperation of industry, agriculture, labor, and state and local governments, to coordinate and utilize all its plans, functions, and resources for the purpose of creating and maintaining, in a manner calculated to foster and promote free competitive enterprise and the general welfare, conditions under which there will be afforded useful employment opportunities, including self-employment, for those able, willing, and seeking to work, and to promote maximum employment, production, and purchasing power.

More briefly stated, the Act says that it is now the policy of the United States government to cooperate with private business and industry in an effort to promote a continuing high level of employment, production, and income. As you will notice, the Act declares that it is the policy of the federal government "to foster and promote free competitive enterprise...."

What can the federal government do to "promote maximum employment, production, and purchasing power"? For more than 25 years two types of policies or actions have been discussed at length as to what and how much these policies can do to promote the general economic welfare. These are (1) monetary policy and (2) fiscal policy. In addition, considerable discussion has been devoted to the relative merits of "automatic stabilizers."

Monetary policy. The amount of money and credit available to business firms affects the amount of goods and services produced and the plans of business and industry for production in the future. The supply of money and credit in circulation also affects consumer spending. Other things being equal, the less expensive it is to borrow from banks, the more business firms will borrow in order to increase production, and vice versa.

Monetary policy means the use of devices to control the supply of money and credit in the economy. It has to do with controls that are used by the banking system.

As you recall from Chapter 21, our banking system is made up of the Federal Reserve System, the member banks, and nonmember banks. The member banks hold about 80 percent of the total amount of business and personal checking accounts. The Federal Reserve System has the primary responsibility for conducting the monetary policy in this country.

Bank reserves and monetary policy. As you know, each member bank is required to maintain reserves in the federal reserve bank to which it belongs. These reserves are of two kinds: legal reserves, the amount of which is a certain percentage of the deposits of customers in the member banks; and "excess reserves," which are deposits of member banks in federal reserve banks in excess of the required amount of legal reserves. If a bank has an amount of excess reserves, it can make additional loans to its customers without sending in more deposits to increase its legal reserves. Member banks can also increase the amount of their excess reserves by borrowing from the federal reserve bank.

By controlling the amount of reserves of member banks, the federal reserve banks can exert control over the amount of loans made by the member banks. If the management of the Federal Reserve System thinks that banks are extending too much credit to business and that an unhealthy boom is developing, it may increase the amount of legal reserves. And it can raise the interest rate that is charged on loans to member banks.

This will tend to cause the member banks to raise the interest rate that they charge for loans to their customers, thus reducing borrowing. Lowering the interest rate will tend to have the opposite effect.

How much the interest rate will have to be changed in order to encourage or discourage loans to business firms will depend upon how optimistic businessmen are as to the future. For example, if a businessman feels that he could pay 9.5 percent on a bank loan and still make a profit from the use of the money, raising the rate from 7 to 8 percent would not discourage him from borrowing. Or, if he felt that he could make only about 5 percent on money he might borrow, lowering the rate from 8 to 6 percent would not induce him to seek a loan.

Federal reserve banks can increase the amount of money and credit in circulation by buying government securities in the open market (see Chapter 21). Such an increase in money and credit may help to stimulate business. Or these banks can reduce the amount of money and credit in circulation by selling securities in the open market. Buyers reduce their bank accounts when they make payment to the federal reserve bank for the securities. Selling securities in the open market takes place when the managers of the Federal Reserve System feel that the amount of bank credit is becoming too large and is tending to result in inflation.

Selective controls and "moral suasion." Selective controls are measures that are used during periods of national emergency by federal reserve banks to influence the demand for loans for the purpose of buying goods. Such controls affect indirectly the amount that individuals can borrow from banks to make down payments on purchases of durable consumer goods. Increasing the amount that banks can lend encourages consumers to buy more; decreasing the amount has the opposite effect. In either case, the demand for certain goods is affected, which has an effect on the amount of production as was discussed earlier in this chapter. Ordinarily, the Federal Reserve System does not control installment sales. *Moral suasion* means the making of suggestions by federal reserve banks to member banks to encourage or discourage loans to customers.

Fiscal policy. *Fiscal policy* refers to the use of the powers of taxation and spending by the federal government for the purpose of increasing or decreasing production, income, and employment in the economy. If the amount of taxes collected is more than that spent by the government, aggregate demand is reduced. If the amount of taxes collected is less than the amount spent, aggregate demand is increased.

Discretionary fiscal action. By *discretionary fiscal action* we mean the changes in taxing, borrowing, or spending by government programs that are designed to have an effect on production and employment. For example, personal income taxes may be increased, decreased, or allowed to remain at the same rate. If they are increased, consumer spending is likely to decrease; if they are decreased, spending is apt to rise. If they remain unchanged, the payment will affect spending, but the effect is unplanned.

In case of a contraction in business and employment, the government may outline a program of increased spending for public highways, hospitals, schools, dams, and other projects without increasing taxes. The money needed for such purposes would be obtained by borrowing from individuals, business concerns, and banks. Such borrowing and spending would increase incomes of certain business firms and individuals, but it would also increase the amount of interest that must be paid on the public debt. The increase in spending and income would be greater if the loans were obtained from banks rather than from individuals and business firms. This is because banks can "create money" (credit) by extending loans (see Chapter 21), while loans from firms and persons reduce the amount of money they have available for spending.

In order to stimulate business, the government may engage in "deficit financing" — borrowing — and reduce income taxes at the same time. This might increase consumer and business spending even more than by merely reducing taxes or increasing the national debt by borrowing.

Automatic stabilizers. These are devices that tend to operate automatically as stabilizing influences on production and income. Federal income taxes — individual and corporate — and social security taxes claim more revenue as GNP and NI increase. If these taxes thus collected are not spent immediately by the government, the size of the income stream in the economy is reduced. On the other hand, social security payments, subsidies to farmers, and unemployment compensation payments tend to prevent personal incomes from decreasing as much as they would without such payments. Therefore, they have a stabilizing effect on the economy without any special action by the government. They are often called *automatic stabilizers*.

WILL MONETARY AND FISCAL POLICIES ACTUALLY WORK?

To establish monetary and fiscal policy certain kinds of economic data must be available, some of which are known as *economic indicators*.

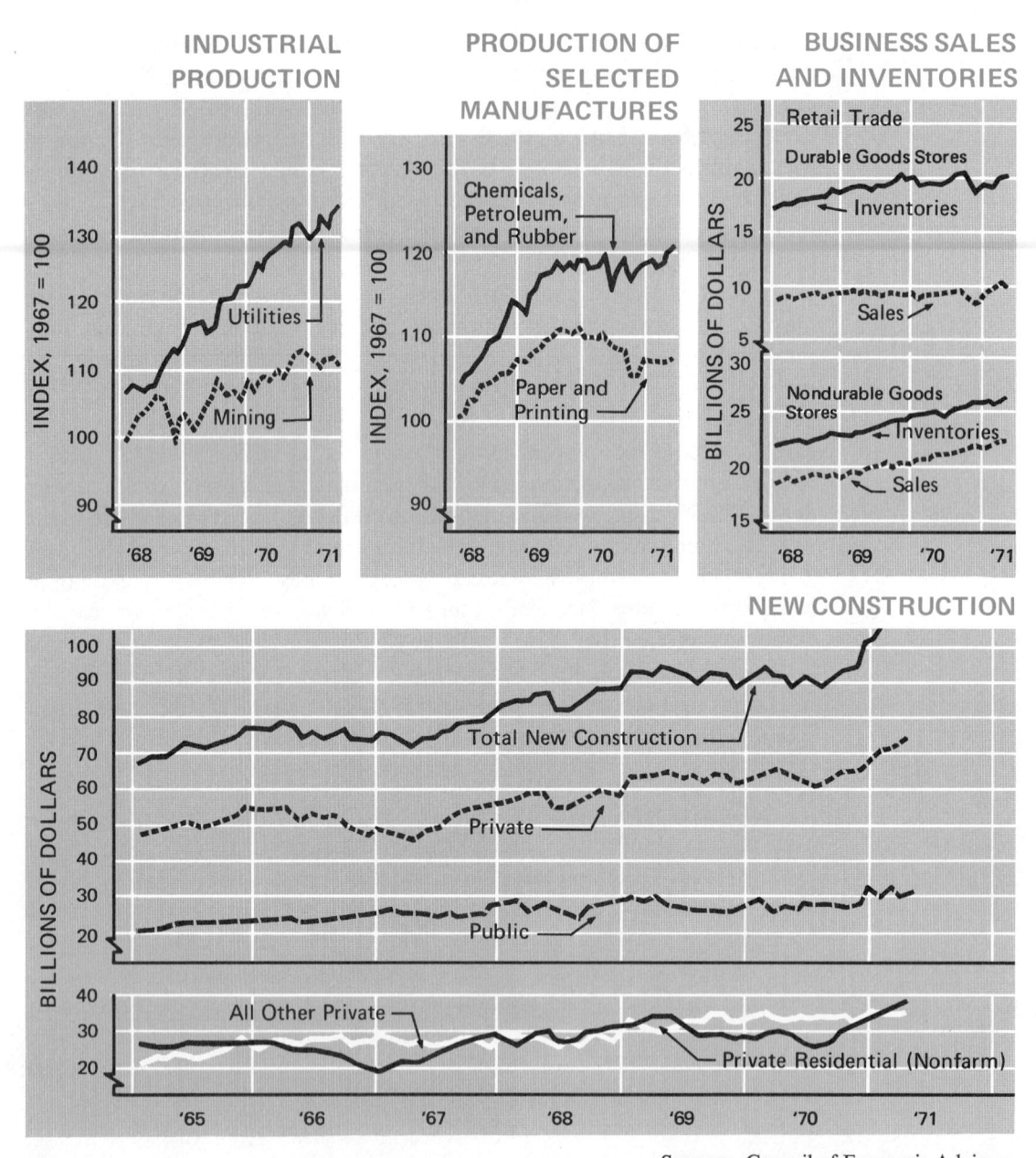

378   NATIONAL INCOME — GROWTH AND STABILITY   Unit 6

Figure 23-3.   SOURCE: Council of Economic Advisors.

SOME ECONOMIC INDICATORS

The position of the economy and direction in which it is moving — whether up, down, or sidewise — is suggested by data and charts having to do with expenditures and income in certain business areas and for the economy as a whole. These data and the charts that can be constructed from the data are indicators of what is taking place in the economy.

Economic indicators. In order to ascertain the direction of business activity, certain phases of economic life are studied. New orders for durable goods, for example, might indicate an optimistic outlook in this field. If this optimism is supported by other facts, such as a growing personal income or an increase in retail stores sales, the businessman, or the economist, or the government official might conclude that "expansion" is occurring. Such business activities are recognized as economic indicators.

Monetary and fiscal policy in practice. During and since the Great Depression of the 1930's, we have made use of several types of monetary and fiscal policies for the purpose of stimulating or restricting production, income, and employment in the economy. There are some who assert that these efforts have been highly successful. Others are equally convinced that there has been too much interference in private enterprise by government and that government has spent too much money, which, they say, has resulted in unnecessarily high taxes. They feel that as a result of deficit financing the national debt is larger than it should be.

How successful have we been in promoting and stabilizing economic prosperity and growth? That is impossible to say. Some argue that we have moved too far toward an economy that is controlled largely by government. Furthermore, it is sometimes said that the basis of the economy will remain strong if the forces that affect production, income, and employment are allowed to work themselves out without the use of monetary and fiscal policies.

Unfortunately, we do not have definite and unquestionable statistical proof as to just how successful we have been in the use of monetary and fiscal measures. This is true because there are so many interrelations between the factors and forces that operate in the functioning of the economy. For example, if government borrows and spends $1 million and ten months later GNP has increased by $4 million, it is difficult to prove the increase was due solely to the spending of borrowed money.

Most economists, however, believe that there is merit in the theories behind monetary and fiscal policies. It is probably safe to say that no economist subscribes to the idea of pure *laissez faire*. As to the nature and extent of the differences in opinion between the leaders of the two great political parties, the distinction is largely one of degree. That is to say, political leaders, as a rule, differ for the most part only as to the extent they think we should rely on money and credit management and government taxing and spending to stabilize and promote the growth of the economy.

It can be said with assurance, however, that the success of monetary and fiscal policies depends on: (1) the ability of the monetary experts and political leaders to recognize promptly the need for appropriate action, and (2) the ability of these experts and leaders to devise programs of action that will be effective.

SUMMARY

Throughout the existence of our economy there have been recurring periods of business prosperity and contraction. These fluctuations in the level of production, incomes, and employment are referred to as phases of "business cycles." It is apparent that these changes are due to changes in the aggregate or total demand for goods and services of all kinds.

The essential elements of demand are willingness to buy plus the ability to buy, which is made possible by the receipt of income. Income is derived from expenditures for production. Therefore, as long as aggregate demand is equal to production, total production, income, and employment will not decline.

Spending of savings or money borrowed from banks for new capital goods has a multiplying effect on consumer income, which, in turn, accelerates the demand for capital goods.

In a free economy such as ours the desire for profit is relied upon to encourage spending for production of goods and services. Such spending creates income for the owners of the factors of production. Economists believe, however, that the banking system and government can make use of certain policies that will stabilize and promote production and income. Such a policy on the part of the banking system is referred to as "monetary policy." It involves the changing of interest rates charged by banks, changing reserve requirements, and buying and selling government securities. Action by government to stabilize business conditions is called "fiscal policy." It has to do with government borrowing and spending, taxation, and the handling of the public debt.

To be effective, monetary and fiscal policies must be of the right type, they must be coordinated, and they must be used at the proper time.

NEW TERMS

acceleration principle
aggregate demand
automatic stabilizers
business cycles
contraction
depression
discretionary fiscal action
economic indicators
Employment Act of 1946
expansion

fiscal policy
innovations
monetary policy
moral suasion
multiplier principle
peak
prosperity
selective controls
trough

QUESTIONS ON THE CHAPTER

1. What is the average rate of growth of our economy? Is the process continuous?
2. During recent decades, what has been the attitude toward regulating business fluctuations?
3. What is implied by "cycle" in the term "business cycle"?
4. What are the theories of the business cycle?
5. What general evaluation do economists make of the business cycle theories?
6. What is the composition of "aggregate demand"?
7. What is the relation between aggregate demand and the level of economic activity?
8. How stable in amount are the component expenditures in aggregate demand?
9. What determines whether changes in government spending will contribute to economic stability and growth?
10. What is meant by the "multiplier effect"?
11. What is meant by the "acceleration principle"?
12. What is the objective of the Employment Act of 1946?
13. What is monetary policy, and of what importance is it?
14. What is the significance of "excess reserves"?
15. What devices are or have been used by the Federal Reserve System to regulate the supply of bank credit?
16. What is the purpose of fiscal policy?
17. How do automatic stabilizers operate? Cite examples.
18. How does discretionary fiscal policy differ from automatic stabilizers?
19. Why should government borrow from banks rather than from individuals and business firms if it wants to stimulate economic activity?
20. What are some examples of economic indicators?
21. What is "deficit financing"?
22. Will monetary and fiscal policies actually work?

APPLYING YOUR ECONOMIC UNDERSTANDING

1. How does the written history of the United States prove the economic growth of the United States? Cite some specific examples.
2. Some economic writers praise the Employment Act of 1946 as our "economic constitution"; some feel that it is an "economic Bill of Rights"; and others believe that it is as significant as the Declaration of Independence. Discuss the reasons for these viewpoints.

3. What types of evidence would tend to show that incomes of persons are being more evenly distributed today than formerly?
4. (a) What are some of the forms of technology which have influenced the nation's economic growth? (b) Cite some current illustrations of each form you named.
5. Using the annual reports of several corporations, cite examples of their proposed expansion programs. (a) What sources will be tapped for this expansion? (b) How will the proposed expansion affect employment? (c) How will the proposed expansion affect production and economic growth?
6. (a) Does the "psychology of fear" affect the economic decisions of people? Defend your answer. (b) How is fear or the feeling of insecurity related to changes in national prosperity?
7. During periods of economic slowdown, both businessmen and government officials are concerned. (a) What types of suggestions might businessmen advocate to restore prosperity? (b) What types of suggestions might legislators propose to restore prosperity? (c) Why would such suggestions probably become political issues?
8. What are some recent examples of governmental programs which were instituted to offset inflationary pressures?

CHALLENGES TO ECONOMIC COMPETENCE

1. Read the CED report of 1961, *Growth and Taxes*, and summarize its main points for an oral presentation to the class.
2. Prepare a bulletin board display centered on the theme "America's Economic Growth."
3. Beginning with 1909, prepare a chart for each decade which shows changes in (a) per capita annual income, (b) per capita annual output, (c) per capita annual taxes, (d) per capita annual savings.
4. Prepare a four-member panel discussion on Economic Growth, with one member representing each of the following areas: (a) industry-business, (b) labor, (c) government, (d) consumers.
5. Write a three-paragraph article suitable for a feature spot in a newspaper on one of the following topics: (a) Has the American Economy Matured? (b) Labor-Automation and Prosperity, (c) Roads to Economic Progress, (d) Is Security Curbing Our Economic Growth?

Unit 7

Government Finance and Taxation

Chapter 24 Government, Taxes, and the Public Debt
Chapter 25 Our Tax System

North Carolina Highway Commission

The Library of Congress

Tennessee Valley Authority

What government does affects us in some way, whether we know it or not. In addition, we have to pay for all the services the government performs. But many of the governmental services we enjoy are taken for granted. The building and maintenance of highways, the operation of libraries, and the construction and operation of dams for power production and flood control — these are examples of governmental services.

Chapter 24

Government, Taxes, and the Public Debt

Why is the cost of government mounting in this country?
What goods and services does government provide?
How does government get the money it spends?
How does government debt affect you?

Over the period of our national existence the trend of governmental spending has been upward. By 1970 the total annual expenditures by all levels of government — federal, state, and local — reached about $313 billion, or approximately $1,527 per capita. In the same year the total amount of revenue collected was approximately $303 billion, or about $1,478 per person. The difference meant an increase in governmental debt which continues to rise so that the total amount was more than $442 billion, or approximately $2,156 per capita.

Where does government get the money it spends? Who pays? What services do you receive from government? How much does your family pay for these services? Does everyone pay the amount he should? These and other questions concerning government income and expenditures are of importance to each of us.

WHAT ARE THE PROPER FUNCTIONS OF GOVERNMENT?

It is difficult to answer this question to the satisfaction of everyone. Years ago it was usually thought that there were only three things that government should do. It should (1) protect the people against violence and crime and from invasion by the armed forces of other nations; (2) protect individuals from injustice and oppression by others; and (3) build and maintain certain public works that would be of great service to all the people and which it would not be profitable for private business concerns to undertake. This was the view expressed by Adam Smith (1723–1790), the British economist, in his *Wealth of Nations* about 200 years ago. And it is the view that is held by some people today.

On the other hand, there are some persons who hold that government should undertake to supply any and all services that will promote to the greatest degree the general welfare of the people. How far government should go in providing services for the people is a difficult question to answer. At any rate, we do know that the functions of government have expanded greatly since the days of Adam Smith.

In recent years over 50 percent of federal government expenditures have been for national defense and international affairs. For the fiscal year of 1972, the war in Vietnam remained a factor in the $82 billion of defense and international affairs expenditures. At the state and local level about 40 percent of governmental expenditures is for education.

MODERN GOVERNMENT PROVIDES MANY SERVICES

We need protection against those who would intentionally or unintentionally do us harm. But we do not hire armed guards to protect us and our property. We depend upon officers of the law to do that. We need protection against unscrupulous persons who would sell us food or medicine that would injure our health. But we do not employ a private chemist to analyze the groceries and the medicines we buy. Instead we expect government inspectors and other law-enforcement officers to discover and punish those who try to sell us those things the use of which would prove harmful. We could not get along very well without roads and streets. But, of course, we do not build them ourselves. We look to the city, the county, the state, or the federal government to provide them. Parents want their children to have an education. But very few of them hire private teachers. Most of them send their children to public schools that are built and kept up by government. And if a foreign military force tries to invade the country, our shores are protected by the soldiers, the sailors, the marines, and the airmen of the United States Government.

We do not have the space here to list all of the things that government today is called upon to do. The following, however, are some of the services provided by government — local, county, state, and federal — in this country:

Protects property
Protects individuals from violence by others
Protects the country from invasion by other nations
Engages in space research and exploration

Enforces business agreements
Prohibits unfair competition between business concerns

> Protects consumers against the sale of adulterated and misbranded goods
> Prohibits some kinds of false advertising
> Regulates the services and the rates of public utilities
> Prohibits business combinations that are intended to monopolize production and trade
> Regulates communication industries
> Maintains postal facilities
> Builds and maintains highways and streets
> Provides public sanitary facilities
> Licenses the use of automobiles
> Improves waterways

Conserves forests and other natural resources
Provides the governmental machinery for a system of social security
Gathers information at home and abroad that will aid business
Gathers and publishes information pertaining to labor and working conditions
Provides agencies for settling labor disputes

> Inspects banks and regulates credit supplied by banks
> Protects individuals from undue annoyance by others
> Provides schools and institutions of higher learning
> Aids individuals and groups who suffer disaster from floods and storms
> Regulates certain prices

Establishes qualification standards for certain occupations
Builds and maintains electric-power facilities
Provides certain kinds of banks
Provides hospitals and medical aid to individuals in certain situations
Extends financial aid to other governmental units

> Provides recreational facilities
> Maintains facilities for protection against fire
> Builds and maintains public waterworks and gas systems
> Attempts to control fluctuations in business prosperity
> Provides and regulates money and currency

Establishes pensions for war veterans
Carries on scientific experiments and research that is intended to aid agriculture and other industries
Conducts research designed to protect and to improve health
Maintains prisons for the segregation of lawbreakers
Provides street lighting

> Operates public libraries
> Requires employers to observe certain minimum standards as to safe and healthful working conditions for their employees
> Protects certain industries from competition from foreign producers

Some of the services that government renders are familiar to you, and you probably take them for granted. Some of the activities that are carried on by government, however, are matters of which you are probably not aware. But they should be of concern to you and to every citizen because what government does affects us in some way, whether we know it or not. And we have to pay for all the services the government performs.

OURS IS A THREE-LEVEL FORM OF GOVERNMENT

You recall that the Constitution was adopted in 1789. Before this time, each of the states was sovereign and independent. Many of the states were fearful of joining a union of the states because they wished to retain their freedom to act as they pleased. Even after the Constitution was adopted and the national government was established, the union was regarded by many as merely a sort of a confederation.

Among the most important reasons for forming the union was the need for regulating trade between the states and the desire for protection against designs any European nations might have on the territory claimed by the states. Therefore, when the Constitution was adopted, the states reserved the right to carry on certain activities within their own borders. They also retained the right to delegate to local governmental units the power to perform certain functions.

As a result, some services are supplied mostly by local government, such as a school district, a county, a township, a village, or a city; other kinds of services are furnished by the state; and still others, by the federal government. In some cases, there is an overlapping of the services supplied by different government units. For example, the federal government appropriates money for vocational education, health services, old-age assistance, and road building; and the state governments — and sometimes local governments also — appropriate funds for the same purposes. Other examples can be found to show how the responsibilities of different levels of government overlap.

(1) The services and expenditures of local governments. Most of the local governmental expenditures are made for schools, streets, and social welfare. Formerly more than half of all the money spent by the three divisions of government was expended by local governments.

As a rule the people wish to provide by local taxation for those things that seem to them to be of most direct and personal concern. For this reason local governments ordinarily spend more for education and streets than for most other things. Protection against most kinds of lawbreakers is considered a local matter, and the community taxes itself to maintain a police force. Of course, state police are constantly patrolling the highways,

TRENDS IN STATE GENERAL REVENUE FROM SELECTED MAJOR SOURCES: 1960 - 1969

TRENDS IN STATE GENERAL EXPENDITURE FOR SELECTED FUNCTIONS: 1960 - 1969

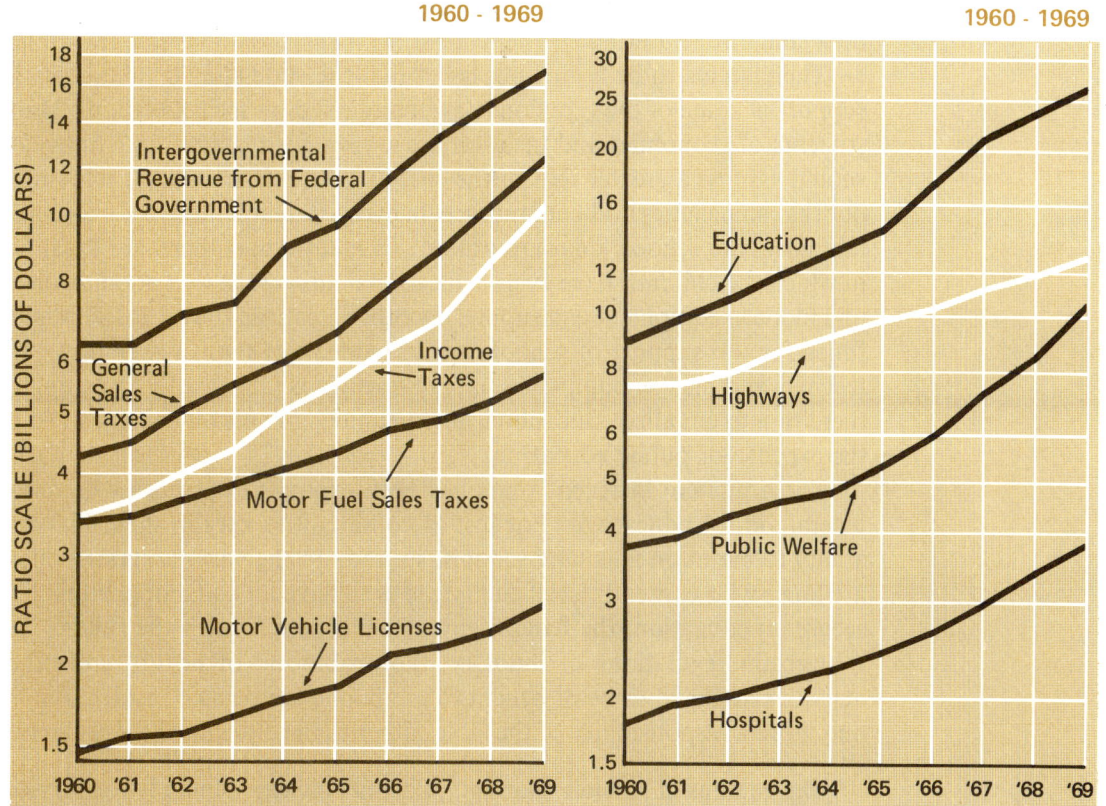

Figure 24-1.

SOURCE: U.S. Department of Commerce, Bureau of the Census, *State Government Finances in 1969*, June, 1970.

and the federal government maintains agencies, such as the Federal Bureau of Investigation (FBI), to protect the public against crimes that may extend across state boundaries.

Most of the benefits derived from streets, waterworks, and fire departments are received largely by the citizens in the community. For that reason such facilities are maintained by taxes derived from local sources.

(2) The services and expenditures of state governments. Since World War I total annual expenditures by the state governments have been less than those of the federal government. The greater part of the state governmental expenditures goes for education, highways, and social welfare, the importance of the expenditures being indicated by the order of naming. Other expenditures include those made for health, general government, protection, economic development, debt redemption, interest on the public debt, and public utilities.

There seems to be a growing belief that the state should take over the support of some of the functions now maintained by local taxation. Many students of economics and taxation are saying, for instance, that the state should assume a greater part of the cost of public education. It is pointed out that some cities and communities in every state are more able to maintain adequate schools than are others. In many states there are localities in which the children have every educational advantage that good teachers and modern equipment can supply. In other localities the means of raising funds for the support of schools are so inadequate that only poorly paid teachers and meager equipment are provided. It is said that the state ought, therefore, to equalize educational opportunities for all by bearing most of the expense of public education.

The argument in recent years has been expanded by those who favor federal aid for education. For just as communities vary in their financial ability to maintain adequate schools, so, too, do the various states. There are those who contend that if each child is to have an equal opportunity to secure an education, the federal government must furnish the funds.

Certain regulations of industry, the promotion of health, and other activities designed to be of benefit to the public are being considered more and more a responsibility of the state rather than of the local governments.

The concept of revenue sharing. Whereas greater demands for services are constantly being placed on local and state governments, their main sources of revenue are consumption and property taxes which do not grow as rapidly as the demands. Most students are familiar with the discussion of these growing needs, many of which are related to the urbanization of our society. The financial squeeze on many state and local governments has reached the critical stage, and leaders at all levels of government are searching for the best means of dealing with those needs that are faced mostly at the state and local levels.

The dimensions of the problem are illustrated by the record of growth in recent decades of state and local revenues, expenditures, and debt. From 1948 to 1969, annual tax revenues increased from approximately $20 billion to $98 billion; but expenditures grew from $21 billion to $119 billion. Thus, despite hundreds of tax increases that have been enacted during these years, state and local government debt grew from $19 billion to $135 billion, an increase of more than 600 percent.

Fiscal authorities have often discussed the merits of federal *revenue sharing* as one means of giving relief to the hard-pressed state and local budgets. Unlike the main sources of state and local revenue, the federal personal income tax has much elasticity. In our expanding economy, it automatically provides a source of increasing revenue to the federal government. Under revenue sharing, a portion of federal revenue would be turned over to the states and through them to local governments, possibly distributed to the states primarily on the basis of population. If adopted as national policy, revenue sharing would provide a large measure of support for state and local functions that suffer now from insufficient financing.

The President urged Congress to enact one form of revenue sharing to begin in fiscal 1972, but the future of this proposed legislation is uncertain. Alternate means of coping with the problems of state and local governments are thought by some authorities to be more desirable. Whatever the final outcome, however, the needs will undoubtedly become more acute until some satisfactory source of funds is provided.

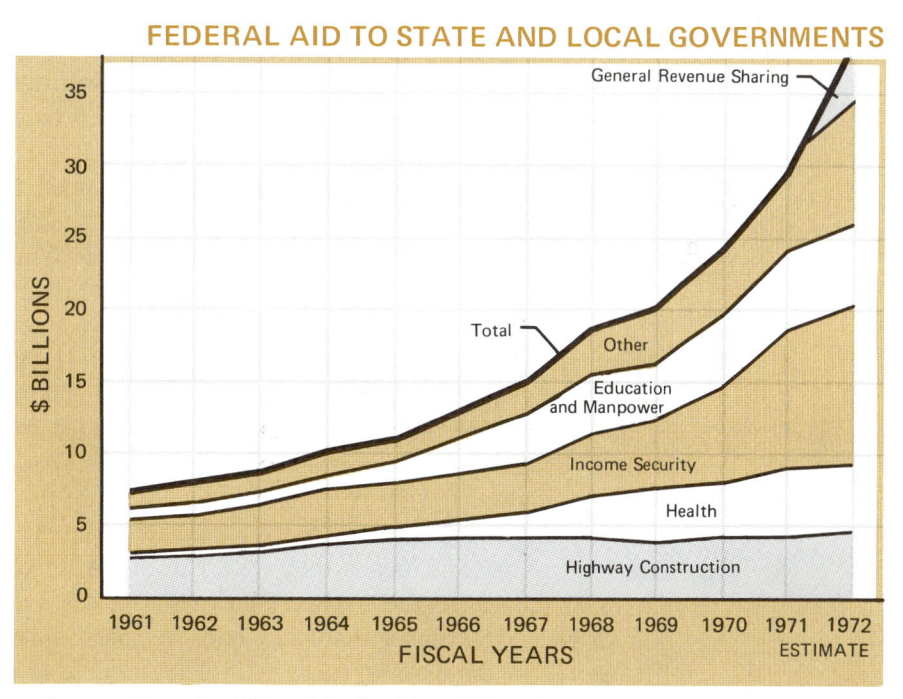

Figure 24-2.

SOURCE: Executive Office of the President, Office of Management and Budget, *The U.S. Budget in Brief, Fiscal Year 1972*.

(3) The services and expenditures of the federal government. Just what the federal government should or should not do is a question that is often debated. For example, does the government have the right and the power to say how a business shall be run? Should the government attempt to regulate child labor? Should it attempt to fix minimum wages of workers? These are some of the many questions over which there have been spirited disputes.

Article I of the Constitution gives the government, through Congress, power to provide for the national defense, to conduct diplomatic relations with other nations, to control immigration and naturalization, to regulate foreign and domestic trade, and to control the monetary system. The Constitution does not specifically give Congress power to pass laws for the construction of internal improvements, to aid agriculture or business, to appropriate funds for the relief of privation caused by unemployment, or to do most of the things that the government today undertakes to do.

But the same Article does state that Congress shall have the power "To lay and collect taxes, duties, imposts, and excises, to pay the debts and provide for the common defense and general welfare of the United States." This quotation is often referred to as the *general welfare clause* of the Constitution. Those who oppose an extension of the activities of the government are likely to contend that the proposal is unconstitutional because it is not specifically provided for in the Constitution. On the other hand, those who favor the measure will say that it is constitutional because of the "welfare clause."

Except for a short time during the War Between the States, the per capita expenditures of the federal government for the first 127 years of our national history never rose above $10. Then came World War I, when in 1919 annual per capita expenditures rose to more than $178 and then fell to a low of $24 in 1927. But by 1941, the year we entered World War II, the amount had risen to slightly above $102. By 1971, the per capita cost of the federal government was about $1,050, or $4,200 for a family of four.

In time of war the government naturally spends more money than it does in times of peace. But even before we entered World War II, the long-run tendency was for the per capita expenditures of the government to increase. The expenditures of the government after the War Between the States were never as low as they were before. After our war with Spain (in 1898) they increased. After World War I, the average expenditures were a great deal higher than they had ever been during times of peace. Therefore, on the basis of history, it is reasonable to think that the per capita expenditures of the federal government will never again be as low as they were in 1941.

Ch. 24　GOVERNMENT, TAXES, AND THE PUBLIC DEBT

THE BUDGET DOLLAR
Fiscal Year 1972 Estimate

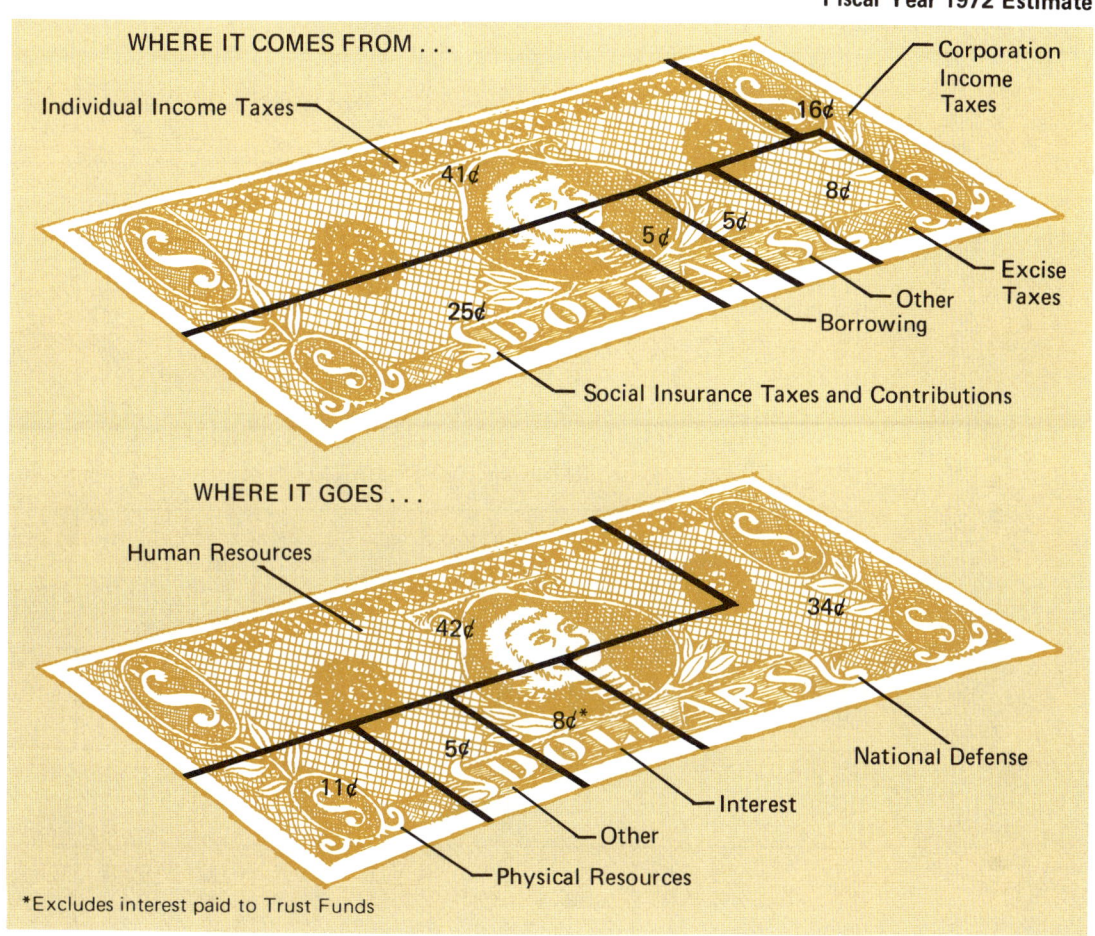

WHERE IT COMES FROM...
- Individual Income Taxes — 41¢
- Corporation Income Taxes — 16¢
- Excise Taxes — 8¢
- Other — 5¢
- Borrowing — 5¢
- Social Insurance Taxes and Contributions — 25¢

WHERE IT GOES...
- Human Resources — 42¢
- National Defense — 34¢
- Physical Resources — 11¢
- Interest — 8¢*
- Other — 5¢

*Excludes interest paid to Trust Funds

Figure 24-3.

SOURCE: Executive Office of the President, Office of Management and Budget, *The U.S. Budget in Brief. Fiscal Year 1972.*

HOW DOES GOVERNMENT GET THE MONEY IT SPENDS?

The funds that the government collects but does not have to repay (such as those received in the form of taxes) are called *revenues*. Money borrowed on bonds, however, is not revenue. The term *receipts* includes money and credit received from both taxes and loans from the people.

The sources of funds for governmental expenditures are: (1) taxes; (2) fees and licenses; (3) rates; (4) special assessments; (5) public domain; (6) gifts; and (7) borrowing.

FEDERAL GOVERNMENT

BUDGET RECEIPTS AND OUTLAYS, 1789–1972 (in millions of dollars)

Fiscal year	Receipts	Outlays	Surplus or deficit (−)	Fiscal year	Receipts	Outlays	Surplus or deficit (−)
ADMINISTRATIVE BUDGET							
1789–1849	1,160	1,090	+70	1920	6,649	6,358	+291
1850–1900	14,462	15,453	−991	1925	3,641	2,924	+717
1905	544	567	−23	1930	4,058	3,320	+738
1910	676	694	−18	1935	3,706	6,497	−2,791
1915	683	746	−63				
CONSOLIDATED CASH STATEMENT							
1940	6,879	9,589	−2,710	1948	45,357	36,493	+8,864
1941	9,202	13,980	−4,778	1949	41,576	40,570	+1,006
1942	15,104	34,500	−19,396	1950	40,940	43,147	−2,207
1943	25,097	78,909	−53,812				
1944	47,818	93,956	−46,138	1951	53,390	45,797	+7,593
1945	50,162	95,184	−45,022	1952	68,011	67,962	+49
				1953	71,495	76,769	−5,274
1946	43,537	61,738	−18,201				
1947	43,531	36,931	+6,600				
UNIFIED BUDGET							
1954	69,719	70,890	−1,170	1964	112,662	118,584	−5,922
1955	65,469	68,509	−3,041	1965	116,833	118,430	−1,596
1956	74,547	70,460	+4,087	1966	130,856	134,652	−3,796
1957	79,990	76,741	+3,249	1967	149,552	158,254	−8,702
1958	79,636	82,575	−2,939	1968	153,671	178,833	−25,161
1959	79,249	92,104	−12,855	1969	187,784	184,548	+3,236
1960	92,492	92,223	+269	1970	193,743	196,588	−2,845
1961	94,389	97,795	−3,406	1971 estimate	194,193	212,755	−18,562
1962	99,676	106,813	−7,137	1972 estimate	217,593	229,232	−11,639
1963	106,560	111,311	−4,751				

Notes.— Certain interfund transactions are excluded from receipts and outlays starting in 1932. For years prior to 1932 the amounts of such transactions are not significant.

Refunds of receipts are excluded from receipts and outlays starting in 1913; comparable data are not available for prior years.

SOURCE: Executive Office of the President, Office of Management and Budget, *The U.S. Budget in Brief, Fiscal Year 1972.*

(1) Taxes. A *tax* is a compulsory contribution from private wealth to be used in carrying on the functions of government. The principle underlying the right of the government to levy contributions from wealth is that the functions of government promote the welfare of all the people and that the existence of government is essential to the existence of wealth. Taxes constitute the main source of revenue for all sorts of government, whether local, state, or federal. The following are the most important kinds of taxes that are utilized by the local, state, and federal governments.

(a) The general property tax. The general property tax is based on the idea that the ownership of property carries with it the responsibility of supporting the government because the government renders services in the way of protection. Furthermore, the ownership of property is supposed to indicate the ability to pay taxes. The basis for the tax is the assessed value of property, the amount of the individual's tax being a percentage of the declared value of his property.

The tax is levied without any reference to the net income of the owner. From time to time tax assessors prepare lists of taxable property. In most states the personal property in a given district is reported annually by the owners to a tax official, while real estate is listed at intervals of two or three years. Many state governments derive revenue from taxes on property. The federal government does not make use of the general property tax.

This tax is the source of more than three fourths of all local revenues. Although it remains an important tax, its use as the means of raising most of the state revenue has been rather widely criticized and almost abandoned.

(b) Consumption taxes. A *consumption tax* is a tax that is levied upon a commodity or a service. Taxes on gasoline, tobacco, and imported goods are examples.

The arguments advanced in support of consumption taxes are that no one can escape payment because all are consumers and that such taxes are easy to collect.

Consumption taxes are divided into two classes: (1) excises and (2) customs duties, or import tariffs.

In general it may be said that *excises* are taxes imposed at the time of the sale of goods. They may be levied upon goods produced in this country or upon those of foreign origin. In any case, although an excise tax may be paid to the government by the seller, as in the case of the tobacco tax, the expense of the tax is usually passed on to the final consumer.

Within recent years many proposals for the adoption of a *general sales tax* have been made. These proposals have always been met by spirited opposition. But, in spite of the objections raised, most states and many local governments have adopted some form of sales tax.

The general sales tax is the outgrowth of excises or stamp taxes. It is frequently called a sales tax, a merchants' tax, a gross-sales tax, a turnover tax, a gross-receipts tax, a manufacturers' tax, a producers' tax, or by some other name. Whatever the name of the sales tax, the object is to collect taxes at the time of the sale of goods.

Customs duties, or tariffs (as the term is used here), are taxes imposed upon goods brought in from foreign countries. Such taxes are used for the purpose of raising revenue or of discouraging the importation of goods.

(c) Income taxes. As the term is usually understood, *income taxes* refer to taxes levied upon the net incomes of individuals or corporations.

Net income means the amount of income after certain deductions have been allowed. For example, both single persons and heads of families are allowed a certain amount of income upon which they do not have to pay taxes. Most gifts to charity and to educational institutions may be deducted from income before the tax is calculated.

Income taxes are of comparatively recent origin. Not until the adoption of an amendment to the Constitution in 1913 did the federal government have the power to levy taxes on incomes. Before that time an income tax law passed by Congress had been held unconstitutional by the United States Supreme Court. At present, taxes are levied on personal incomes as well as on the incomes of corporations. Income taxes constitute the main source of revenue for the federal government. Most of the states and many cities also derive a great deal of revenue from income taxes.

(d) Estate and inheritance taxes. The federal government and all the states, except Nevada, have laws imposing taxes upon property acquired through inheritance. The Federal Estate Tax Law provides a flat exemption of $60,000 on the net estate. The rate begins at 3 percent of taxable value of the first $5,000 and increases up to a maximum of 77 percent on $10 million or more. Considerable variation is found in the laws of the different states, but in general the rates are much lower than those imposed by the federal government.

The federal government imposes a *gift tax* with rates that are three fourths of those of the estate tax. The object of this tax is to make it impossible for an estate to escape taxation because it is given to his heirs by the owner before his death.

(e) Capitation taxes. A capitation tax is levied on the individual without reference to benefits received by him or according to his ability to pay.

It is sometimes called a *poll*, or *head*, tax. Formerly, the payment of a poll tax was frequently a requirement for voting. Capitation taxes are of ancient origin and were once an important source of governmental revenue.

(2) Fees and licenses. *Fees* are amounts collected from individuals in return for services performed by the government. By paying a fee, the individual receives a special benefit from the government. The charge for recording a deed for transfer of the title to real estate is an example of a fee.

A *license* is a form of fee. By the payment of the amount required, the individual is given the right to engage in a particular kind of business or to do a certain other thing. Licenses are issued for such purposes as the operation of stores, automobiles, taxicab companies, barbershops, and restaurants. Professional people, such as physicians and public accountants, also must take out licenses.

(3) Rates. The term *rates* may be applied to revenues that are derived from businesses operated by the government, such as waterworks. Frequently the income received from government-operated industries does not cover the costs of supplying the services. Whatever amounts are received, however, are classifiable as revenues.

In some cases the federal government engages in businesses that produce income. The outstanding revenue-producing enterprise operated by the federal government of the United States is the postal service. The postal service has generally operated at a loss. When a loss occurs, it is generally considered justifiable because the postal service is conducted in the interest of the public welfare.

The relatively small amount of revenue derived from public industry in this country does not justify our further consideration of the subject in this connection. But the question of the future extension of government into industry is likely to become an increasingly interesting topic.

(4) Special assessments. *Special assessments* are payments made by the owners of land to the government for improvements that are made by the government and that usually result in an increase in the value of the land. The building and the improving of streets are the most common occasions for the levying of special assessments.

(5) The public domain. The term *public domain* refers to all the land owned by the government. When the term is used, we usually think of agricultural, forest, and mineral lands that are owned by local, state, or federal government.

Although most of the area of the United States at one time belonged to the federal government, the public domain has never yielded any important amount of net revenue. Most of the land was sold to settlers for nominal amounts of money, the usual price being from $1 to $2 an acre. This liberal policy on the part of the federal government was considered wise because it encouraged the rapid settlement of the land.

Most of the public domain suitable for agricultural purposes has passed into the hands of private owners. The federal government and many of the states, however, still own valuable timber and mineral lands, the disposition of which constitutes a public problem. As long as these lands are undeveloped, they cannot produce an income. Some of the questions involved in the disposition of these lands are: Shall the lands be held for the use of future generations or until the exhaustion of our present privately owned resources demand their use? Shall they be disposed of to private individuals without restrictions as to development, or shall the government supervise their use? Shall the natural resources now owned by the state governments and the federal government be developed by the governments themselves?

(6) Gifts. It would probably be a surprise to many people to realize that our several types of government receive millions of dollars' worth of gifts every year. This is a fact, however, especially in the case of local governments. In nearly every town there are buildings, parks, art collections, or sums of money held in trust for specific purposes, that came into the possession of the government as the result of gifts from individuals. The total of all such donations amounts to many millions of dollars.

(7) Borrowing. Governments, like individuals, sometimes find it necessary or convenient to borrow funds.

Reasons for borrowing by government. Government units borrow for the following reasons: (1) in case of emergencies, like war or some other catastrophe, which make it necessary to obtain a large amount of funds quickly; (2) when it may be desirable to make a large outlay for a permanent improvement, such as school buildings, roads, streets, hospitals, or the development of power resources; and (3) when the people demand more services than they are willing to pay for currently by means of taxation.

Dangers of government borrowing. Governments, like individuals, can go bankrupt; that is, they can become so deeply in debt that they cannot pay what they owe from their usual sources of income. But unlike individuals, national governments can borrow unlimited amounts with which to pay their debts. In addition, if they choose to do so, they can print money. But if too much money is obtained by either or both of these ways, inflation of the currency will result and prices will rise so high that money will lose some or all of its purchasing power. Our experience since 1940 has demonstrated how government borrowing can affect prices. During that time the federal government borrowed and spent billions of dollars more than it collected from taxes. As a result prices more than doubled — money lost more than half of its purchasing power.

WHAT IS THE SIZE OF THE FEDERAL DEBT?

It is interesting to compare the size of the federal debt with what it was in certain years in the past. In May, 1971, it was about $397 billion. In 1940, it was about $48 billion; in 1930, a little over $16 billion; and in 1900, about $1.2 billion. The per capita amount of the federal debt in 1971 was approximately $1,936.

SHOULD WE TRY TO PAY OFF AND RETIRE THE NATIONAL DEBT?

The annual interest on the federal debt alone in 1971 was more than $20 billion, or about $90 for each man, woman, and child in the United States. Of course, some persons and families pay very little of these amounts, while others pay a great deal.

Why not pay off the debt and stop the expense of interest payments? If we should decide to pay off the national debt, it would be necessary to raise taxes to obtain sufficient money to retire a portion of the debt each year — unless we give up certain government services. Would we be willing to do that? What would be the effect on business and jobs?

If we decide not to redeem or pay off the government debt, those who hold government bonds will continue to receive interest. When a series of bonds falls due, the government can simply borrow the money and pay the bondholder, without increasing the total of the national debt. (This is called *refunding* the debt.) There will also be a regular market where the bonds can be bought and sold, provided people do not lose faith in the government. Then, if a bondholder needs the money he has invested in a bond, he can sell his bond in the market to anyone who wishes to buy it. Meanwhile we shall go on paying the interest on the debt.

Whether the national debt should be paid is a question about which you will hear more. The final solution to the question is important, for it will affect everyone.

SHOULD THE GOVERNMENT SPEND LESS?

Before we say that government spends too much and that taxes are too high, we must consider that many conditions in our national life have changed greatly during the past few decades. In 1900, for example, there were about 700,000 pupils in high school; now there are more than 18,000,000. Then the automobile was just coming into use, and little was spent for roads. Unemployment was not considered a national problem. Now the government has adopted a continuing policy of attempting to provide work or income for those who cannot find employment. In addition, poverty is no longer regarded as being purely a personal or individual problem; it is now generally considered the duty of the national government to aid — directly or indirectly — in trying to relieve want and insecurity when they are not due to laziness. Government is active in many other matters in which formerly it showed little or no interest.

At present military security and aid to other nations imposes a tremendous financial burden on the federal government, and hence, on the people. It seems that these expenditures are unavoidable. At the same time, they pose a danger to our national financial stability.

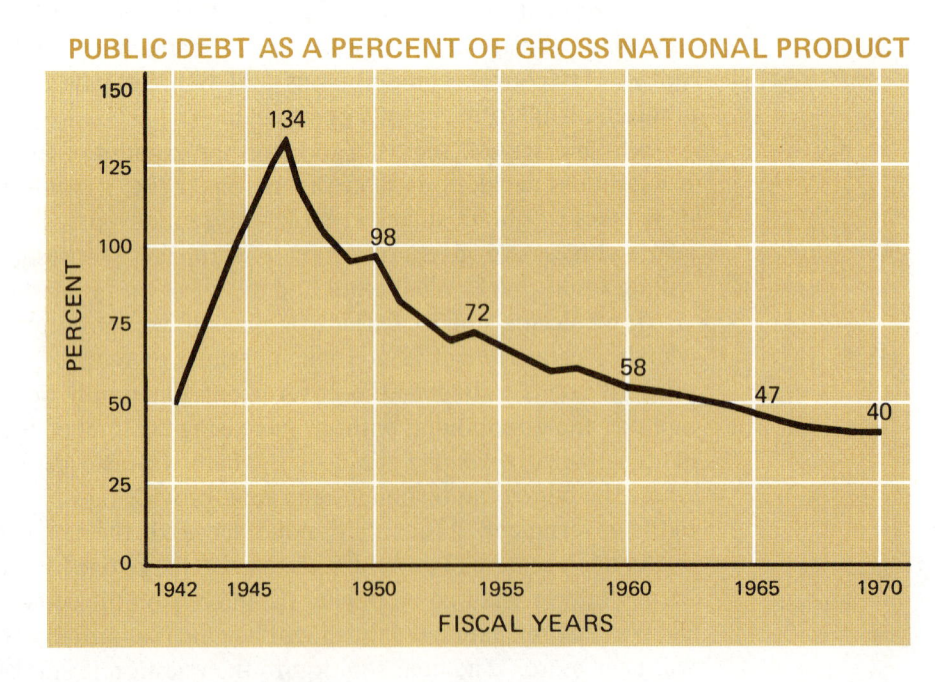

PUBLIC DEBT AS A PERCENT OF GROSS NATIONAL PRODUCT

Figure 24-4.

SOURCE: Adopted and updated from *The Budget in Brief*.

Government spending and public policy. It has become the policy of the federal government to use taxation and public spending as methods to control business fluctuations and to promote ever-increasing prosperity. The implication, of course, is that such a policy has the approval of the voters. Therefore, it is evident that government is becoming increasingly important in the lives of the people, which should arouse more intelligent interest in government on the part of the citizens.

The threat of war. Of great importance is the fact that military conflict, such as that in Vietnam, and the threat of expanded warfare make it necessary for us to spend billions of dollars annually for armed protection. The space race which is directly related to military supremacy demands annual expenditures of more billions.

Thus, we conclude that if we demand more services from government and if the threat of war continues, it is probable that both taxation and government debt will increase. And the increase will take place regardless of which political party is in power.

SUMMARY

Government is our biggest business. It spends at least one fourth of our total national income, and one out of eight employed persons is in government service.

Government is the supreme form of social organization that has the power to compel people to cooperate in providing certain services. There are three levels of government in the United States — local, state, and federal.

Government is engaged in many activities. Just what the proper functions of each level of government are is often a matter of dispute. Perhaps we might say that, in general, the more personal the service and the more the people feel that they should control the service directly, the more likely it is that it will be provided by local government. But this is not an infallible rule.

Government obtains the funds it needs from revenues, including: (1) taxes — general property, consumption, income, estate and inheritance, capitation, and other taxes; (2) fees and licenses; (3) rates; (4) special assessments; (5) income from public domain; and (6) gifts. It may also obtain funds by borrowing, which most governmental units frequently do.

The federal debt has become so large that it will be impossible to pay it off in the foreseeable future. It will probably be our policy to refund it — issue new bonds for the old ones as they come due.

The two reasons why the cost of government has increased so much in recent decades are (1) the people are demanding more services by means of government, and (2) war. Whether it will eventually be possible to reduce taxes in the future depends on the extent to which we decide to provide ourselves with various services by means of government and on whether war or the threat of war continues.

NEW TERMS

consumption tax
customs duties
excises
fees
general sales tax
general welfare clause
gift tax
income taxes
license
net income

poll (head) tax
public domain
rates
receipts
refunding (debt)
revenues
revenue sharing
special assessments
tax

QUESTIONS ON THE CHAPTER

1. What functions did Adam Smith think proper for government?
2. What are some of the services that are supplied by government?
3. What services do local governments render to citizens?
4. What services do state governments render to citizens?
5. What is meant by revenue sharing? What problem is it supposed to help solve?
6. What services does the federal government render to citizens?
7. Relatively, do the larger governmental units render more services than formerly?
8. Have expenditures by the federal government tended to increase over the years? Discuss.
9. What is the difference between governmental receipts and revenues?
10. Are income taxes usually levied on net or gross income? Explain.
11. What is the object of the federal gift tax?
12. Why do governments borrow funds?
13. What are some of the dangers that may arise from borrowing by government?
14. Should the national debt be paid off? What are the arguments for and against paying the debt?
15. Should government in this country spend less? Discuss.
16. Are there reasons to expect continued increases in governmental expenditures? Discuss.

APPLYING YOUR ECONOMIC UNDERSTANDING

1. Bring to class a copy of the latest tax budget of your own community. (a) Which of the services provide benefits to you directly? (b) Which of the

services provide benefits to you indirectly? (c) Are both types of benefits equally important?
2. Analyze a copy of the latest tax budget of your state. (a) How does the cost of the direct services you receive compare with the cost of the indirect services you receive? (b) Are all of the services equally important? Give the reasons for your answer.
3. The federal budget provides for various services for the public. What types of services use the major portions of federal income?
4. Secure a copy of the school budget for your community. (a) What unit of government is responsible for raising the major portion of school funds which are required? (b) What unit of government raises the smallest part of the required school funds?
5. What are some changes in our way of living during the past century that have required government to take on added duties? How do the added duties of government affect the amount of tax income which must be secured?
6. When taxes are not collected, or the amounts collected are insufficient, where does the governmental unit secure funds to pay its obligations? Does this affect the tax income needed in the future?
7. Many families save money for a "rainy day." Does the government do the same thing? Explain why it does or does not tend to build up surpluses.
8. Name some of the groups that are supporting federal aid for local schools. (a) Why do they favor federal support? (b) Why do other groups oppose federal support for local schools? (c) Which of the arguments use economic factors as a basis for consideration?
9. Governments secure revenue from various sources. What specific source is used in each of the following situations? (a) Many western settlers acquired federal land by paying the government one dollar an acre for it. (b) The county treasurer sent out statements to real estate owners which indicated a levy of 3 percent on the assessed valuations. (c) Mr. X gave his home and art collection to the state for perpetual use as an art museum. (d) John paid the city clerk $5 for a document which would permit an official to perform his forthcoming marriage ceremony. (e) Mr. Y received a bill from the county waterworks for water he used the previous month.

CHALLENGES TO ECONOMIC COMPETENCE

1. Prepare a series of pie charts which show the sources of income and the sources of expenditures for your local, your state, and the federal governments.
2. Arrange a bulletin board display centered on the theme "Tax Dollars Come, and Tax Dollars Go."
3. Prepare a scrapbook to include all the different types of tax forms which you can locate. Write an explanation to accompany each tax form.

Chapter 25

Our Tax System

What is equity or justice in taxation?
What are the basic principles of taxation?
On what basis should taxes be levied?
What are the merits of the various types of taxes?

Did you ever have a free lunch? Well, you probably have had a lunch for which you did not pay. But someone paid for it because lunches are not free goods. Neither are the services provided by government free services.

We may be free to use certain goods and services supplied by government — roads, street lighting, police protection, schools, parks, libraries, and the like. But we should not feel that no one had to pay for them.

Now, since all the costs of government services must be paid for by the public, how much should each one of us pay? Should each pay the same amount? If some should pay more than others, how much more? Are there any rules that we can follow in levying taxes? Should we be concerned with justice in taxation? Or should we simply adopt the rule of "plucking the goose" in such a way that we will have the least amount of "squawking," being guided only by the need of government to collect a certain amount of revenue?

WHAT IS EQUITY OR JUSTICE IN TAXATION?

Few people, if any, enjoy paying taxes. But they are less likely to resent having to pay if they feel that each one pays the amount he should. One may believe, of course, that government is spending too much, but that is another matter.

What is an equitable or a just tax? A number of theories have been proposed for the levying of taxes that are equitable. Of these theories the two best known are the benefit theory and the ability-to-pay theory.

(1) The benefit theory. According to the *benefit theory* of taxation, one should pay taxes in proportion to the benefits he receives from government. If Jones's farm is worth $5,000 and Smith's $100,000, then Smith should pay 20 times as much tax because he enjoys 20 times as much protective service from government.

But suppose Smith has no family, while Jones has a family of six children who are attending public schools. Then how much more benefit does Smith receive from government than does Jones?

It is hardly defensible, therefore, to base all taxes solely on the benefit principle.

(2) The ability-to-pay theory. According to the *ability-to-pay theory*, the amount of taxes that individuals should pay depends on their ability to pay the taxes. The theory assumes that one's ability to pay a tax is determined by the amount of wealth he owns or the income he receives.

But it is one thing to say that each of us should pay taxes according to his ability, and it is quite another thing to say how much ability to pay taxes each of us has. Consider, for example, the cases of Young and Heflin. Young has an income of $1,000, and Heflin, $100,000. If a tax of 1 percent is levied on the incomes of each, Young would pay $10, while Heflin would pay $1,000. Would each pay in accordance with ability to pay?

In order to answer this question intelligently, we would have to consider other factors in each case. For the purpose of illustration, suppose that Young has a wife and two children, while Heflin is a single man with no dependents. Obviously, these factors would have to be considered.

Assume, however, that neither of the men has the responsibility of dependents. Would the amount paid by each be in accordance with his ability? It evidently would not. In other words, Heflin could pay 1 percent of his income with less sacrifice than could Young. We conclude that the ability to pay taxes increases faster than the increase in income.

For this reason income tax rates usually, but not always, are progressive to a certain point. That is to say, the greater the amount of income received, the greater is the percentage of the tax, up to a certain point, demanded by the government. For a true *progressive tax*, the rate must increase at least as rapidly as does the amount of income. If the tax rate remains the same regardless of the amount of income or value of the property taxed, we have a *proportional tax*. For example, if the tax rate on real estate is $2 per $100, the tax is proportional because one who owns property assessed at $1,000 pays $20 in taxes, while another whose property is assessed at $2,000 pays $40.

A *regressive tax* is one for which the rate decreases as the tax base (income or assessed property value) increases. Such a rate is not used in modern tax systems. Sometimes, however, a tax that places a heavier burden on persons with low incomes than on those with higher incomes is said to be regressive. For this reason a sales tax is often said to be regressive in effect because its payment entails a relatively greater sacrifice on the poor than on the rich.

In the case of a *degressive tax*, the tax rate increases but at a slower rate than the increase in the amount of income or the value of the property to be taxed. For example, if the rate is 10 percent on $1,000 of income and 11 percent on $2,000, the tax is degressive.

Assume that the first $1,000 of property owned or income received is taxed at the rate of 4 percent. Then the burden of a tax on successive amounts of property or income would be as shown below.

Amount of taxable property or income	Tax rate — percentage			
	Proportional	True Progressive	Degressive	Regressive
$1,000	4	4	4	4
2,000	4	8	4.8	3.2
3,000	4	12	5.4	2.6
4,000	4	16	5.8	2.2
5,000	4	20	6	2

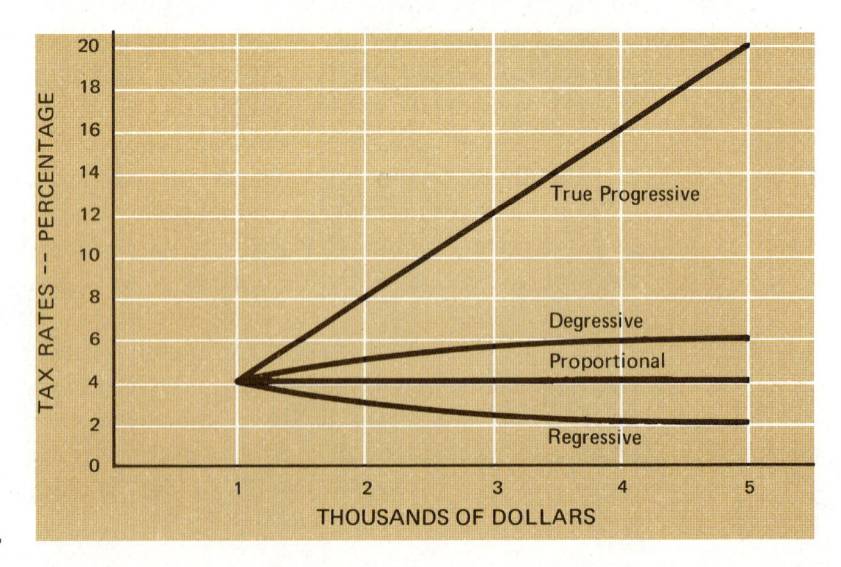

Figure 25-1.

ADAM SMITH PROPOSED FOUR CANONS OF TAXATION

In his *Wealth of Nations*, Smith laid down four *principles* or *canons of taxation* that he contended should be followed in levying taxes. These principles may be indicated by the words (1) justice, (2) certainty, (3) convenience, and (4) economy, although Smith did not use these exact terms.

(1) Justice or equity. Like most people, Smith thought that everyone should contribute to the support of government according to his ability to do so. He believed that people should pay taxes "in proportion to the revenue which they respectively enjoy" as citizens.

(2) Certainty. This term means that the amount, manner of payment, and the time of payment should be definite.

(3) Convenience. Taxes should be payable at a time that is most convenient to the taxpayer. A tax on gasoline which is payable by the consumer at the time of purchase is considered to be one that conforms to this principle.

(4) Economy. Everyone would probably agree with Smith that no more should be collected in taxes than is needed for the purpose or purposes for which the taxes are levied, plus a reasonable amount to cover the expense of collecting the taxes. In deciding what taxes shall be used, those that are expensive to collect should be avoided as long as possible.

These principles of taxation have been criticized as being inadequate. But each one of them is still recognized by most — but not all — people as being sound. Most students of taxation would add that a tax should produce enough revenue to make it worthwhile to collect, and it should be simple and easily understood.

FOR WHAT PURPOSES ARE TAXES LEVIED?

In the United States taxation has been used for two major purposes: (1) paying expenses of government, and (2) controlling the business cycle.

(1) Paying the necessary operating expenses of government. Traditionally, the general idea underlying taxation in this country has been that of obtaining funds with which to defray the necessary expenses of government. As a rule, the local lawmaking bodies, state legislatures, and Congress have professed that this idea should be followed in levying taxes. And the principle has usually been accepted that taxes should be levied according to the principles of ability to pay and of the benefits received from the government.

As the expenditures of government increase, it may be necessary to tax large incomes more heavily than small ones in order to get enough money to finance government activities. Progressive income tax rates accomplish such a purpose. One result of progressive taxation is the redistribution of national income to some extent. The proceeds from the higher taxes paid by those with larger incomes may be used to provide public service for all the people. However, most of the taxes collected by the federal government are used to provide military defenses or national security and to pay for past wars. The federal budget for fiscal 1972 called for an estimated expenditure of approximately $78 billion for defense, not counting about $4 billion for financial aid to other nations and more than $10 billion for veterans' benefits.

(2) Controlling the business cycle. As we have said in other connections, to some extent the federal government undertakes to use taxation as a means of controlling the ups and downs of business. For example, in a time of business recession or depression, a decrease in taxes leaves consumers with more money to spend, which may create more demand for goods, which, in turn, may stimulate production and business prosperity.

The Revenue Act of 1964, which substantially reduced income tax rates, was the first tax legislation adopted by Congress for the specific purpose of stimulating general economic activity. It is very possible that in the future increasing use will be made of taxation and governmental spending in an attempt to stabilize business and to promote economic growth. This topic was discussed more fully in Chapter 23.

TAXES ARE DIRECT OR INDIRECT

Sometimes the person from whom a tax is collected is not the real taxbearer. For example, in the case of the tax on tobacco products, the manufacturer pays the tax to the government, but he then adds the amount of the tax to the selling price of the cigars, cigarettes, or other forms of tobacco product. The final consumer bears the tax burden in the form of the increased price he pays for the tobacco. Apparently, the manufacturer pays the tax; in reality he merely acts as a tax collector. Taxes on commodities are added to the selling prices and in this way tend to become *hidden taxes*.

Shifting a tax means transferring the burden of the tax from one person to another. A tax is *indirect* when it can be shifted. It is *direct* if it cannot be shifted, as in the case of a personal income tax.

Should government get its money by direct or by indirect taxes? It is generally agreed that everyone should support the government in proportion to his ability to do so. Too, he should realize that he is helping to pay the cost of government because, so it is argued, he will then be more likely to take an interest in how public funds are spent. Therefore, it is said, direct taxes are desirable. Those who favor indirect taxes say that they are easy to collect, that people pay the taxes in small amounts, and that they do not feel the burden as much as if the taxes were direct.

WHAT ARE THE MERITS OF THE DIFFERENT MEANS OF OBTAINING REVENUE?

Let us examine briefly the merits and the demerits of each of the means or methods of obtaining governmental revenue.

(1) Fees, licenses, and special assessments. Each of these types of revenue is justified largely on the theory of special benefits conferred upon individuals. Little or no attempt is made to adapt the amount required to the ability of the individual to pay. Many local and state governments rely upon these sources for a great deal of revenue.

The use of fees as a means of compensating public officials is sometimes justifiable, but the fee system sometimes results in graft. Therefore, the payment of governmental officials by means of fees is not to be commended as a general policy.

(2) The general property tax. The general property tax has so many shortcomings, and the tax results in so much injustice, that, as a major source of revenue, it is generally condemned except for local purposes.

In the first place, the theory of the general property tax rests upon a false assumption. It assumes that the ownership of assessed property is an indication of the ability to pay taxes. If most of the wealth of the country existed in only a few forms, the ownership of property would be a fairly reliable indication of an individual's ability to pay taxes.

But when some people receive huge salaries, the ownership of property is only one evidence of taxpaying ability. For example, a farmer may own a great number of acres of land that yield him little or no profit. A professional person or businessman may have little property income but a large income because of his talent or ability. In these two cases property ownership does not indicate the relative abilities of the two men to pay taxes.

An evil that may arise from the general property tax is *tax evasion*. The idea behind the general property tax is the taxation of all personal property as well as real estate. An attempt is therefore made to discover and tax all land, houses, household furniture, jewelry, stocks, bonds, mortgages, and other forms or evidences of wealth not exempt from taxation. Some forms of wealth cannot be concealed, while others can be concealed easily. Naturally, in listing their property with the government, unscrupulous persons — perhaps most people are not overly conscientious in this connection — will fail to include all their property. The personal property tax may thus have the effect of a tax on honesty.

Moreover, if all property is reported, the tendency is to undervalue it. To report property at its full value means the payment of a larger amount of tax than if the property is undervalued. If the assessor tried to determine the fair valuation of all property reported, he would be confronted with an almost impossible task. The average assessor would find it very difficult to determine the value of a diamond or a stock of goods in a store.

Again, as an attempt is made to tax all property, double taxation frequently results. For example, if a tax is levied upon a factory building and also upon the capital stock or the bonds of the factory, double taxation is the result. Taxes are paid on the physical property and also upon the shares of stock or upon the bonds.

Finally, taxes on houses and factories can be shifted to tenants and to those who buy the products of factories. There is a tendency for owners of apartment houses to add the amount of the taxes they have to pay on the property to the rent they charge their tenants. And whenever he can, the factory owner naturally tries to collect the amount of taxes he pays by increasing the price he charges for his product.

These criticisms are made against the recognized defects of the general property tax as a means of obtaining any important portion of state or federal governmental revenue. They do not imply that for local taxation purposes the general property tax should be abandoned. The tax yields a comparatively certain amount of revenue, which recommends it for consideration. But students of taxation contend that it should not be made the chief source of state revenue.

(3) Consumption taxes. These taxes usually result in increasing the cost of commodities. They are used primarily for raising revenue and, except in a very general way, do not conform to the principle of ability to pay.

It may be argued that those who purchase the greatest quantity of gasoline, for example, are better able to pay the tax than are those who buy in smaller quantities. Even so, the tax rate is proportional and not progressive, that is, it does not increase in proportion to the ability to pay. And, in fact, the burden of the tax may be regressive if it takes a greater percentage of the total income of the poor than of the wealthy consumer.

Moreover, consumption taxes are nearly always indirect. They are shifted to the consumer. Again, such taxes are levied upon that part of the income that is spent, and not upon what is saved. Consequently, the more a person saves, the smaller is the amount of consumption taxes he pays. But the more he saves, the more able he is to pay taxes.

The justifications given for consumption taxes are that: (1) such taxes are convenient to collect; (2) they may be used as a means of discouraging the use of certain kinds of goods, such as tobacco and liquor; and (3) they yield large revenues.

(4) Business taxes. Business taxes are a favorite means of raising government revenue. There are several reasons why such taxes are frequently employed. They are comparatively easy to collect. They produce a relatively steady income to the unit of government that levies the tax. In many cases, because of the nature of the tax, businessmen feel that most or all of the tax can be shifted to someone else. And, finally, it is claimed that business enterprises enjoy many benefits from the existence of government, and for that reason they should be willing to pay for such benefits by means of special taxes.

The federal government levies a tax of 22 percent on the net corporate incomes of $25,000 or less; and 48 percent on additional income above that amount. Certain corporations with no more than ten stockholders may be taxed as sole proprietorships or partnerships. During World War II corporations paid excess-profits taxes on net incomes above specified amounts. There are three kinds of payroll taxes that are levied upon certain employers. The purpose of one of these taxes is to provide funds for general old-age security benefits as required by the Social Security Act; one is levied upon public carriers, such as the railroads, to provide a special kind of social security for their employees; and a third is imposed upon certain classes of employers to provide funds for unemployment insurance.

Most of the state governments have laws taxing corporations. Several states tax railroads and public-service corporations. Most of the states levy taxes on banks. All the states have taxes of one kind or another on insurance companies. Several of the states have *severance taxes*, which are taxes on natural resources that are removed and sold — such as coal, ores, oil, and timber. A few states impose special taxes on chain stores.

(5) Personal income taxes. As was stated previously, most of the revenue received by the federal government comes from personal income taxes. More than half of the state governments obtain some of their revenues from such taxes.

An income tax is one that is levied on the basis of income received. The amount of the tax is indicated as a percentage of the income.

The tax is levied only on taxable income, and not on gross income. *Taxable income* is calculated by subtracting certain allowable deductions and exemptions from the gross income. Among allowable *deductions* in calculating federal taxes are: contributions to charitable institutions; certain kinds of trade losses and expenses; business losses from theft, casualty, and bad debts; and depreciation of business property.

An *exemption* for tax purposes is a specific amount of one's income on which one does not have to pay any tax. It may be $600, $1,000, or some other amount. In addition to his own exemption, the taxpayer is allowed to claim exemptions for dependents, which may include a wife or husband, children, brothers and sisters, parents, grandparents, nephews, and nieces, if they are dependent on the taxpayer for at least half of their support. Special exemptions are also allowed for blind persons and for those who have reached the age of sixty-five.

Arguments for and against the income tax. There are several strong arguments in favor of income taxes as a means of obtaining governmental revenue. A tax on income may be graduated and the rate made progressive so as to levy the tax somewhat in accordance with the individual's ability to pay. The tax tends to "stay put," and is not easy to shift.

On the other hand, the amount of the yield of income taxes is uncertain because the total collected depends upon the incomes of the taxpayers. In periods of business depression the yield falls off; and it rises in periods of prosperity. The tax requires high-grade administration and supervision on the part of tax officials. If the rate that is set proves to be too high and too progressive, initiative and industry will, as a result, be discouraged.

Methods of collecting personal income taxes. There are two ways by which personal income taxes may be collected. First, they may be paid by the taxpayer sometime during the year following that in which the income was earned. In such a case the taxpayer files a report, or tax return, which shows the amount of his total taxable income and the amounts of his allowable deductions and credits. In these cases he pays the income tax at the time he files his tax return, although he may be permitted to defer part of the total payment until some time later.

Second, the income tax may be collected on the pay-as-you-go plan. Under this plan the amount of the tax is withheld at the time income is received. Under the federal law most wage earners have the amount of their income taxes deducted by the employer, who sends it to the Treasurer of the United States. If for any reason the amount withheld by the employer does not equal the tax that is due, an adjustment is made at the end of the year.

Self-employed individuals, who do not work for wages or salaries, estimate their incomes for the year and pay the tax in installments, usually four.

(6) Estate and inheritance taxes. An *estate tax* is a "death tax" that is levied on an estate before the property passes to the heirs. An *inheritance tax* is one that is levied on the share of an estate received by an heir. There is a federal estate tax. Most of the states also levy an estate or an inheritance tax.

(7) Capitation taxes. These taxes are a vestige of an ancient practice of granting immunity to persons from serving in the army by the payment of a "head" tax. In the early history of this country a "head" or capitation tax was imposed on all adult males old enough to vote, and thus became known as a "poll" tax. Since the receipts were used to build or maintain roads, persons who were short of money could "work out" their taxes by physical labor on the road.

Two weighty arguments may be advanced against capitation taxes: (1) These taxes bear no relation to the ability of the taxpayer to support the government, and (2) they are often difficult to collect.

CAN WE IMPROVE OUR TAX STRUCTURE?

Changes in the personal income tax that are advocated by some persons include revisions in the allowable deductions, changes in the rate structure, and modification of the per capita exemption. Some critics even suggest the adoption of a negative income tax under which a person would receive a check from the government if his exemptions and deductions exceed his income. Further reductions in corporation and other business taxes are proposed by some economists as means for encouraging economic growth. And at the local level, revision of the property tax has long been advocated by many tax experts, some of whom urge that the tax on personal property be abolished.

Anyone who has studied the various types of taxes imposed by the federal, state, and local governments is likely to conclude that the tax structure can be greatly improved. And in the interests of justice and the public welfare, each of us should be familiar with the principles of taxation. Such familiarity would prevent us from endorsing a plan of taxation simply because it is popular or seems expedient. Those who respond to slogans such as "soak the rich" or "tax the corporations" frequently do not understand who bears the real burden of any given tax, or to what degree these groups are already taxed.

SUMMARY

Government exists for the good of all the people. To carry on its activities, government needs money, which, for the most part, must be collected from the people by means of taxes.

Tax rates may be (1) proportional, (2) progressive, (3) regressive, or (4) degressive.

It is highly important that taxes should be levied in accordance with principles that are fair and sound. Four such principles that are widely recognized in democracies are those which relate to (1) justice, (2) certainty as to payment, (3) convenience as to time and manner of payment, and (4) economy in collection.

Taxation is necessary to obtain funds needed for the essential operating expenses of government, including the national defense. Taxation is also advocated by some as a device for helping to stabilize business conditions.

Taxes may be direct or indirect. Other things being equal, taxes should be direct so that each taxpayer will more fully appreciate the cost of government. But it may be expedient and practical at times to make use of indirect taxes.

The federal government gets most of its revenue from personal and corporate income taxes. By and large, most of the revenue to the states comes from sales, gasoline, and corporation taxes. Taxes on property are the main source of revenue to local government.

The usual sources of government revenue are fees, licenses, special assessments, general property taxes, consumption taxes, business taxes, personal income taxes, and estate and inheritance taxes.

Our tax structure probably can be improved. But such improvement is likely to come only as the result of serious thought by fair-minded and well-informed citizens.

NEW TERMS

ability-to-pay theory
benefit theory
deductions (tax)
degressive tax
direct (tax)
estate tax
exemption (tax)
hidden taxes
indirect (tax)

inheritance tax
principles *or* canons of taxation
progressive tax
proportional tax
regressive tax
severance taxes
shifting a tax
taxable income
tax evasion

QUESTIONS ON THE CHAPTER

1. How free is our "free school system"?
2. What is the benefit theory of taxation?

3. What is meant by "ability to pay taxes"?
4. If the tax rate increases at the same rate as income or the value of property on which the amount of tax payment is figured, is the rate progressive, regressive, or proportional?
5. Why should a tax be certain? convenient? economical?
6. For what major purposes have taxes been used in the United States?
7. What are some examples of (a) an indirect tax and (b) a direct tax? Which can be shifted?
8. Can you give an illustration of (a) a fee, (b) a license, (c) a special assessment?
9. What are the arguments for and against the use of the general property tax?
10. Who bears the burden of a consumption tax?
11. Why are consumption taxes used?
12. What are business taxes?
13. What are the arguments for and against the use of income taxes?
14. Is there a difference between an estate tax and an inheritance tax?
15. What arguments can be made against the capitation tax?

APPLYING YOUR ECONOMIC UNDERSTANDING

1. List some examples of revenue collected by your local government which are based on the benefit theory.
2. Name five sources of your state government's income and classify each as to whether it involves the benefit or the ability-to-pay theory.
3. Is the major source of federal government income in the form of a progressive, a proportional, a regressive, or a degressive tax? Defend your answer.
4. Data which showed national unemployment at high levels induced several prominent congressmen to advocate reductions in personal income taxes. What was the probable reasoning behind their proposal?
5. For many widows, inheritance of the family home is a major part of the wealth which they may receive following the death of a husband. Does the merit of the general property tax have any relationship to this type of situation? Why or why not?
6. A state has a 3 percent tax on sales to consumers. Mr. Apt makes six separate purchases costing 15 cents each. Mr. Smart makes a single purchase for a dollar. Will the same amount of taxes be collected from both customers? Is Mr. Apt paying a 3 percent tax? Explain your answer.
7. A current complaint of some businesses is that the federal government's tax policies are not so liberal as those of the governments of their foreign competitors. (a) How would lower tax rates on corporations and greater depreciation allowances affect the ability of American corporations to keep capital equipment modernized? (b) Would a liberalization of our government's tax policy toward corporations put them in a better competitive position?
8. The Constitution of the United States made a per capita tax legal and possible. Why doesn't the Congress of the United States use this tax power as a major or sole tax source?

9. Secure a copy of *Your Federal Income Tax*, published by the Internal Revenue Service. (a) What are some of the exemptions which are permitted to taxpayers? (b) Which exemptions apply to some forms of income but not to others? (c) To what extent may exemptions create inequity?

CHALLENGES TO ECONOMIC COMPETENCE

1. Arrange to have the class visit the office of the local tax collector to learn how property is assessed and taxed. After the visit summarize the information obtained.
2. Serve as chairman of a small discussion group which will report to the class on the topic "A Sound Tax Program."
3. Prepare a graph showing the average per capita income and the average per capita taxes for five-year intervals beginning with the year 1930.
4. Write a synopsis of an article which discusses one of the following: (a) Agriculture and Our Tax Program, (b) Taxes and Our Foreign Aid Program, (c) Are Estate and Inheritance Taxes Necessary? (d) How Federal Government is Financed.

Unit 8

International Economic Problems

Chapter 26 Buying and Selling Between Nations
Chapter 27 Making Payments Between Nations
Chapter 28 Nations With Other Economic Systems
Chapter 29 Our Interest in the Underdeveloped Nations

CrownZellerbach

It is frequently stated that a protective tariff is desirable in the United States to protect American labor against low wages prevailing in other countries. Yet those who oppose tariffs to protect labor say that the American worker, by using more efficient laborsaving machinery, is able to produce much more than the average foreign worker.

CrownZellerbach

Chapter 26

Buying and Selling Between Nations

How can we gain by trading with people in other nations?
How does the law of comparative advantage influence international trade?
How do a nation's imports limit the amount of its exports?
Is the European Common Market a threat to American industry?

Americans are confirmed tourists. By car, bus, train, ship, and plane they travel: to the mountains, to the ocean, to the lake regions, to resort spots, to the city, and to the country. Our national parks are visited by tens of millions annually. Other millions cross the borders into Canada and Mexico. And hundreds of thousands travel overseas.

All of these tourists have something in common. They seek a change of scene and experience. Most of them make some purchases which they bring home as mementos of that new experience. When an American tourist buys an article in any part of this country, with few exceptions, he may transfer it wherever he so desires without having to report the purchase.

The situation is different, however, when one visits Canada or Mexico, or some other foreign country. Upon returning to the United States, you are required to "declare" the kind and value of the purchases you have made abroad. If the total value of all of your purchases is more than a certain amount, you may have to pay a *duty* or tax on the amount of the excess value.

Likewise, trade that is carried on by merchants in different countries must observe a number of regulations and restrictions that do not apply to trade in the nation in which a merchant lives.

Why are there differences in the regulation of trade at home and abroad? If it is desirable that people be free to trade with each other in the home market, why should they not be equally free to trade with persons living in another nation?

WHY DO WE TRADE WITH OTHER PEOPLE?

The reason for trade between individuals, whether at home or abroad, is the same: Each one gains — or he thinks he will gain — from such trade. You secure some article you want, and the seller gains something he wants — which is usually your money.

In simple situations the reason for trade is so apparent that we seldom think about it. In the more complex situations of international trade, however, people often lose sight of the reason for trade. Furthermore, they are likely to feel that the justification for trade between people in different nations is not the same as it is for trade within a nation. Therefore, they are frequently willing — even eager — to impose restrictions on foreign trade that they would not tolerate if such restrictions were imposed on domestic trade.

WHAT IS THE LAW OF COMPARATIVE COST?

Each region within the United States tends to produce those goods which it can produce at less cost than the other regions can produce them. The goods thus produced are sold in the market, and much or most of the money received is used by the sellers to buy goods produced in other regions. For example, tropical fruits can be grown at lower cost in Florida and California than in Iowa or Nebraska. Iowa is better suited to the growing of corn or Nebraska to the growing of wheat. Therefore, a given amount of labor and capital expended for production produces larger returns if it is devoted to the type of good a given area is best fitted to produce. The advantage that one region or nation has over another may arise because of its supply of natural resources, skilled labor, capital, or efficient managerial ability.

Even when one state or nation enjoys an absolute advantage as to costs as compared with another, in the production of all commodities, it is to the mutual advantage of each for them to devote their labor and resources to the production of those commodities in which they have the least disadvantage. In this way, production costs in each state or nation will be minimized, and by exchanging commodities each will have more goods to use at lower costs than if each produced all it used. This fact or principle is called the *law of comparative advantage* or *comparative cost*.

NATIONS OF THE WORLD HAVE DIFFERENT RESOURCES

When we consider the whole world, we find that nations differ as to climate, soil, natural resources, and industrial development. In other words, the differences that account for specialization in production in the United States exist also among the nations.

Illus. 26-1. When we consider the whole world, we find that nations differ as to climate, soil, natural resources, and industrial development.

U.S. Department of Agriculture

Some nations have rich natural resources. As in the case of our states, some nations have a greater variety of natural resources and a more favorable climate than others. The United States and the Soviet Union possess vast territories that are rich in many kinds of ores and other resources needed for manufacturing. Considerable portions of the areas of both nations are still covered with forests. Because of the presence of much fertile land and a variety of climatic conditions, both nations are able to produce many kinds of agricultural products.

The British Commonwealth of Nations, composed of the United Kingdom and its dominions, embraces territory that supplies many materials for manufacturing. The agricultural lands in Canada, Ireland, Australia, New Zealand, South Africa, and elsewhere produce most of the farm products used by the people living within the Commonwealth, as well as much that is exported to other countries.

Some nations have limited natural resources. Most countries are very dependent upon others for some kinds of essential goods. Although they may possess rich resources of one kind or another, they are poor in other resources. For example, France is poor in nearly all kinds of metals other than iron, aluminum, and antimony; it has practically no copper, zinc, silver, lead, nickel, or tin. Germany must import a great many raw materials. Sweden is rich in iron ore, but only the southern third of the country is suitable for agriculture. Italy has to import the great majority of the materials used in her factories.

The desire to get unlimited control of all the natural resources they could was one of the main reasons why Germany, Japan, and Italy resorted to aggressive actions which led to World War II.

A study of the distribution of the natural resources of the earth enables us to see why foreign trade is desirable.

WHAT GOODS DO WE EXPORT AND IMPORT?

The most important kinds of goods that we *export*, or sell, to other countries consist of automobiles and parts, grains, raw cotton, aircraft and parts, machinery, iron and steel products, coal, coke, petroleum and its products, unprocessed tobacco, chemicals, manufactured rubber, paper and paper products. Our most important *imports* include coffee, petroleum, newsprint, copper, crude rubber, iron ore, wood pulp, cane sugar, wines and spirituous liquors, unmanufactured wool and woolen cloths, vegetable oils, precious stones, meats, and works of art.

The goods we import are important. All our coffee comes from foreign countries, most of it being imported from Brazil. Central America supplies us with large quantities of bananas. Much of our cacao comes from equatorial South America. Most of our natural rubber comes from the Far East. Much of the manganese, nickel, zinc, chromite, tungsten, lead, and other less commonly known metals and minerals, many of which are essential in the production of the new kinds of steel and of other manufactured products, is imported. Our own supplies of these materials are very limited.

What is the value of our exports and imports? Approaching the 1970's our sales to other countries accounted for only about 3.6 percent of the total of our gross national product. The people in the United States were buying about the same percentage of their goods and services from abroad.

But the size of exports and imports does not give a true idea of the importance of our foreign trade. Of some commodities, such as cotton and tobacco, we export a large percentage of the total amount produced.

U.S. MERCHANDISE IMPORTS AND EXPORTS WITH POPULATION FOR SELECTED YEARS

(Imports and Exports valued in millions of dollars)

Year	Imports	Exports	U.S. Population	Year	Imports	Exports	U.S. Population
1775	1	9	2,476,000	1875	533	513	45,073,000
1790	23	20	3,929,000	1900	850	1,394	76,094,000
1800	91	71	5,297,000	1925	4,227	4,910	115,832,000
1825	90	91	11,252,000	1950	8,852	10,275	151,234,000
1850	174	144	23,261,000	1969	32,964	33,588	202,711,000*

*(April, 1969)

SOURCE: Dept. of Commerce and Bureau of the Census.

MUST A NATION IMPORT IF IT WISHES TO EXPORT GOODS?

The money that is received for goods that are exported is used to pay for the goods that are imported from other nations. In the long run, therefore, the value of the total exports from a country tends to equal the total value of imports.

For many years most nations have wanted to buy goods of greater value from us than we have wanted to buy from them. As a result the value of our exports each year has generally exceeded the value of our imports. But this has been possible only because the government has loaned or given these nations money equal to the value of the excess of our exports over our imports, as will be noted in Chapter 27.

WHY ARE IMPORTS OFTEN DISCOURAGED?

We have seen that where the law of comparative cost is allowed to operate, a territorial division of labor results, and trade between regions follows as a matter of course. Some people hold that the law of comparative cost should be allowed to operate unhindered. Those who believe in *free trade* contend that goods should be permitted to enter this country without the imposition of any tax whatever. They assert that, if goods are thus allowed to move freely from one country to another, each country will reap the same benefits as those that come to a nation from free domestic trade. They claim each country would have more goods at lower cost.

On the other hand, those who oppose free trade admit that the theory of free trade sounds plausible, but they contend that it would not work out to the best interest of a nation. Accordingly, by imposing taxes or *tariffs* on imports, they would discourage the importation of nearly all kinds of goods that can be produced in this country. In other words, by taxing imports, they would "protect" home industry.

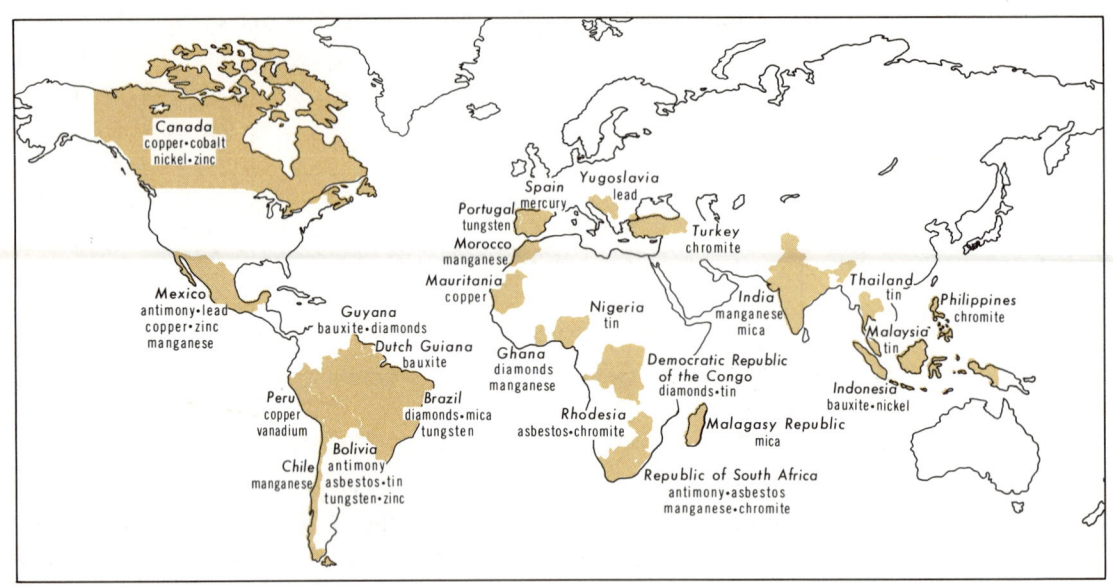

Figure 26-1. *Highway Highlights*

The goods we import are important. Much of the manganese, nickel, zinc, chromite, tungsten, lead, and other less commonly known metals and minerals, many of which are essential in the production of the new kinds of steel and of other manufactured products, is imported.

The preceding opinions represent the two extreme points of view with respect to imports. Between the two extremes are all shades of opinions. Some favor a tariff for revenue only; that is, they hold that taxes should not be imposed for the purpose of discouraging imports, but only for the purpose of raising money for the government. Others would levy taxes high enough to afford some protection to home production. On some items, they would support a tax high enough to prohibit imports of those items.

THERE ARE ARGUMENTS FOR AND AGAINST PROTECTION

There have always been restrictions on the trade between nations. In the case of the United States, the history of the tariff has been an interesting story. The debates over our foreign-trade policies have been long and sometimes bitter, and most of the arguments for and against a "protective tariff" have been repeated many times. Those who favor a protective tariff are frequently referred to as *protectionists*, while those who oppose such a tariff policy are known as *antiprotectionists*, or "free-traders." The arguments pro and con involve a number of points.

(1) Nationalism. One of the arguments advanced for protection is that this policy promotes *nationalism*. This argument assumes that an intensive spirit of nationalism is a good thing and that it should be encouraged. The nation that subscribes to nationalism exalts its own people and institutions and attempts to build up a spirit of national unity and independence. Emphasis is placed upon the desirability of making the nation self-sustaining and of encouraging the patronage of domestic industries. In order to appeal to the nationalism of the consumer, people are urged to buy home products.

The opponents of protection, on the other hand, insist that trade restrictions for the purpose of stimulating nationalism are undesirable for two important reasons. First, they assert that intense nationalism leads to a narrow outlook, to selfishness that breeds hatred, and eventually to the danger of war. Second, they state that no nation can restrict commercial intercourse between nations and at the same time promote to the highest degree the economic welfare of its people.

Moreover, it is pointed out that, unless we buy goods or services from other nations, the amounts of our exports will decrease. Many persons claim that high tariffs are especially harmful to the farmers because, as they maintain, the less we buy from abroad, the less wheat, cotton, and tobacco can be sold to other countries.

(2) The home market. Related to the argument for protection is the contention that protection builds up a *home market* for the sale of commodities. The home market constitutes a more reliable and constant demand for products than does a foreign market. The former cannot be interrupted easily by wars, by the trade restrictions of other countries, or by foreign economic upheavals.

There are several arguments against the "home-market" justification for protection. One argument is that tariffs lower levels of living because they cause goods to cost more. And it is pointed out that to the extent that tariffs protect the home market by keeping foreign-made goods out of the country, the ability of the country to export goods is reduced, for, in the long run, the value of exports and imports must balance.

(3) Military necessity. Protectionists argue that protection is justified upon the grounds of war and military necessity. They point out that in case of war a nation may be shut off from foreign supplies of raw materials and finished goods. Consequently, the people may suffer, and the lack of certain materials needed to carry on the war may result in defeat. Hence, a nation should be as self-sustaining as possible.

On the other hand, there are those who hold that protection is one of the principal causes of international hatred and war. They contend that the efforts of nations to become self-sustaining in anticipation of war only make war that much more probable. They claim this argument is based on a recognition of facts, for, they say, no nation can become independent of other nations unless it is able to get control of the resources that many other nations possess.

(4) Infant industries. Protectionists say that, because of resources and markets, certain industries would thrive in this country if those industries were given a start under favorable conditions. They contend further that once these infant industries have acquired strength and momentum, they could produce commodities as cheaply as similar industries in other countries. It is maintained that, during the early years of the life of these industries, protection from the competition of foreign industries which have been established longer is needed. Moreover, it is said that in this way the industries in the country can be diversified.

In answer to this argument, those who oppose protection contend that if *infant industries* have been given protection, they never seem to grow up. They are unwilling to give up the profits that a protective tariff enables them to make. It is said further that if protection encourages diversification in industry, there never would have been any great spread in the location of industries in the United States. As an example, it is pointed out that comparatively recently the cotton textile industry has tended to migrate from New England, where it was first established, to the southern states. It is claimed that if the infant-industry argument were sound, the textile industry could not have grown up in the South without protection from the competition of New England factories. However, in recent years some Southern congressmen have become strong protectionists, since the South has become increasingly industrialized.

(5) Dumping. *Dumping* refers to the sale of products in another country at a price lower than the cost of production at home. It is said that surpluses of goods are sometimes dumped on the foreign market at whatever prices can be obtained for them. It is charged that frequently a government, by offering a bonus or a subsidy, will encourage an industry to strangle or demoralize foreign competition by dumping its products on the foreign market.

In general, those who oppose protection agree with the protectionists in their attitude toward dumping. They point out, however, that the term "dumping" should not refer to the mere sale of goods at a price lower than that which can be obtained in the domestic market. Extreme free traders contend that only when goods are sold below the actual cost of production in a foreign country and in an attempt to demoralize our industries should protection be sought.

(6) The protection of labor. It is frequently stated that a protective tariff is desirable in the United States to protect American labor against low wages prevailing in other countries. This argument is widely held, even by workers themselves. It is maintained that in certain cases the highly paid labor in this country cannot compete with the poorly paid labor in other countries.

Those who oppose tariffs to protect labor say that the American worker, by using more laborsaving machinery, is able to produce much more than the average foreign worker who is engaged in the production of the same kind of commodity. Because he produces more units of goods of a given kind than does a similar worker in another country, the American employer can pay him higher wages than the foreign employer can pay his employees. Except in the production of certain handmade articles, such as artworks and laces, the American worker usually produces much more efficiently than does the foreign worker.

It has been pointed out that much improved machinery used in foreign countries was made in the United States. Many factories of different kinds have been established by Americans in other countries, partly for the purpose of using cheap labor. The result is that the goods thus produced abroad by American-owned factories compete in the markets of the world with the goods made in this country. Among the American corporations that have factories in other countries are the Ford Motor Company, General Motors, International Harvester, and some of the meat-packing concerns. In many cases foreign chambers of commerce and governments have encouraged Americans to build factories within their countries.

(7) Equalization of the cost of production. Another argument advanced by protectionists is that protection should be utilized for the purpose of equalizing the difference between the cost of production in the United States and that of production in the principal competing countries. It is said that protection thus prevents underselling in our markets by those foreign producers who are able to sell goods here more cheaply than our domestic producers can produce them.

Critics point out that, while this policy has attractive features, it cannot be carried out with any degree of justice. The cost of production varies greatly among domestic producers. For example, Gould may be

Illus. 26-2. The cost of production varies greatly among domestic producers.

able to produce a commodity for one dollar, while Johnson may not be able to produce it for less than one dollar and a half. Which of these costs shall be taken as the basis for the calculation of a tariff rate? In other words, in the establishment of a tariff rate, whose cost of production shall be used in comparison with foreign costs? Besides, it is contended that the cost of production for the many individual establishments in the foreign countries could not be ascertained.

(8) **Governmental revenue.** Some who favor protection argue that the revenue from a protective tariff helps to defray government costs. To this argument antiprotectionists reply that the policy of levying a tariff for revenue defeats its own purpose. If the protective tariff on any commodity is high enough to afford protection, then that commodity will not be imported, and hence no tax will be collected. It is conceded that a tariff for revenue only may be desirable. At the same time, a tariff for revenue is unsatisfactory as a source of income to the government because governmental costs usually are fairly constant, while revenues derived from foreign trade, which fluctuates a great deal, are uncertain.

In addition to these arguments against protection, it is contended that protection fosters monopoly by making it possible for some producers to build up large businesses that are able to crush the competition from smaller producers.

Politics and the tariff. Possibly it is desirable to have an import tariff on certain commodities, but just how much the tariff should be is difficult to say. Tariff making has long been a political issue. All too often tariff rates have been fixed by the lobbying of manufacturers and others who desire protection. The charge has often been made that tariff laws result from "log-rolling" or "back-scratching" by senators and representatives in Congress. That is, one will vote for the protection of an industry in another's state if the latter will vote to protect a certain industry in his state.

Individual and social viewpoints. The main root of the controversy over protection is the conflict between individual and social interests. To a New England manufacturer or to a Louisiana sugar grower a protective tariff may be beneficial. But protection will cause the prices of the protected articles to be higher for the consumer.

Moreover, a manufacturing establishment or an industry that has grown up under cover of a protective tariff may suffer if the tariff is removed or even lowered enough to permit foreign goods to enter this country and to compete with domestic goods. Stockholders and bondholders in the companies affected will suffer a loss in the value of their investments; wages in the protected establishments will have to be reduced; and workers in the industries that are affected may even be thrown out of employment.

Some have argued that it would be socially desirable for the government to subsidize or to buy and discontinue those industries that are unable to survive foreign competition. Others have suggested that the government should adopt the policy of gradually lowering all tariffs. This would give those in protected industries time in which to increase their efficiency or to go out of business.

CAN MORE SATISFACTORY TARIFF RESTRICTIONS BE MADE?

Complaints against tariff laws have led to two notable efforts by Congress to make our tariff laws more acceptable to the people. Those efforts resulted in the creation of the *Tariff Commission* in 1916 and the passage of the *Reciprocal Trade Agreements Act* of 1934.

(1) The Tariff Commission. This federal agency was created in 1916 to provide for "scientific" tariffs that among other things would "equalize the cost of production at home and abroad." But the cost of production of different producers varies, so that it is impossible to say just what is meant by the "cost of production" of shoes or wheat or some other commodity made in this or some other country. The efforts of the Commission to devise a "scientific" tariff have not accomplished a great deal.

(2) The Reciprocal Trade Agreements Act of 1934. This law gives the President, without the approval of Congress, the right to raise or to lower any tariff by as much as 50 percent. The general object of the Act is to increase our sales of various products in foreign markets. Where a reciprocal tariff agreement is reached with another country, we agree to lower our tariffs on certain goods imported from that country in return for the agreement of that country to lower its tariffs on certain goods imported from the United States. By 1970 we had entered into reciprocal trade agreements with most of the commercially important nations of the world. Many of these agreements are of considerable importance. But they do not mean that we have abandoned our traditional policy of protection of domestic interests.

As a result of the *Reciprocal Trade Agreements Act*, the nation's tariffs have been reduced from 18½ percent of the total value of imports to about 6 percent. It has been the practice of Congress to review and renew the Act every few years. In recent years, the Presidency has become more powerful through its exercise of the authority to negotiate tariffs. This presidential authority not only refers to economic matters, but it may also be used as a weapon or bargaining tool to strengthen the American position on international political affairs.

INTERNATIONAL CARTELS FIX PRICES AND LIMIT SUPPLY

An *international cartel* is a combination or arrangement between two or more business concerns located in different countries for the purpose of conducting their affairs in such a way as to make more profit. In other words, the cartel is a monopolistic device for eliminating competition between the members of the organization.

For example, a cartel of an American and an English firm provides that the English firm will not attempt to sell patented chemical products in the United States, and the American concern will not sell its products in any part of the British Empire. Since the big English firm controls most of the chemical industries in the British Empire, the cartel serves to keep out of the United States practically all the chemical products made in Great Britain. Likewise, the cartel prevents the American concern from selling its products in any part of the British Empire. As you can see, a cartel is a form of monopoly; and cartels often have the same effects as a protective tariff.

International cartels, tariffs, and other trade restrictions have long hampered trade between European nations.

THE ITO AND THE GATT

Following World War II, under the sponsorship of the United Nations, a number of nations undertook to form an International Trade Organization (*ITO*), which was intended to stabilize international trade. The main purpose of the ITO was to eliminate international cartels, trade quotas, protective tariffs, and other trade restrictions. This organization never came into existence since the proposal failed to be ratified by a sufficient number of countries.

The General Agreement on Tariffs and Trade (*GATT*) was signed at Geneva, Switzerland, in 1947 by the representatives of 23 countries. By 1964 a total of 62 nations had become members. The United States has participated in some of the agreements proposed by GATT. The Agreement provides for regular discussions of ways and means for the reduction of restrictions on international trade.

In 1968 the United Nations Conference on Trade and Development adopted procedures to encourage the export trade of developing countries and to alleviate trade problems that hinder the economic growth of the less-developed nations.

WILL THERE BE A UNITED STATES OF EUROPE?

For a long time the European nations have had protective tariffs and other trade restrictions against their neighbors. But until recently they were able to get along pretty well because (1) they had overseas possessions, which provided them with certain raw materials and a market for some of their goods, and (2) many of their citizens had large and profitable investments in other countries. These investments supplied funds with which goods could be bought from other nations.

Now most of the overseas possessions have become independent dominions, and the two world wars destroyed nearly all of the foreign investments of the nations. As a result, two regional trade associations were formed in Western Europe to promote its economic growth and development.

(1) The European Economic Community (EEC). The *EEC* was established in March of 1957 by a treaty signed by six nations — Belgium, The Netherlands, Luxembourg, France, West Germany, and Italy. It is often referred to as "the Sixes." The purpose of EEC is to form a "common market" in Europe by removing restrictions on trade between the nations and to promote the economic development of Western Europe as a unit. Restrictions on the movement of trade and labor were removed gradually within the community. The EEC also applies a unified tariff on developed countries outside of the community.

(2) The European Free Trade Association (EFTA). Since EEC planned eventually on a common tariff wall around the six countries, Great Britain recognized that to join that organization might weaken her political and economic ties with the Dominions. Later, however, she became one of the members — with Austria, Denmark, Norway, Sweden, Switzerland, and Portugal — of the European Free Trade Association (*EFTA*). "The Sevens" were interested in the abolition of tariffs within the organization but made no provision for a unified tariff wall against the rest of the world. Finland became an associate member in 1961. The general purposes of both EEC and EFTA are much the same, and efforts are being made by each organization to work with the other.

Twice in the 1960's, the British government desired to shift from EFTA to EEC and made application for membership in EEC. However, Britain

EFTA TRADE IN 1968
(in million U.S. dollars and percentage change 1967–1968)

Reporting country	Total EFTA $ mill.	%	Total EEC $ mill.	%	USA $ mill.	%
Imports (c.i.f.) —						
Austria	459.1	+8.9	1,433.1	+6.0	83.5	+3.6
Denmark	1,287.4	+3.5	1,051.4	+2.4	273.6	+1.5
Finland	594.2	−2.3	420.8	−8.7	72.3	−12.5
Norway	1,165.5	+3.9	667.5	−3.3	206.2	+17.1
Portugal	239.6	+1.4	355.8	+4.6	66.6	−6.5
Sweden	1,781.2	+7.6	1,756.0	+6.1	473.7	+8.5
Switzerland	741.6	+9.4	2,674.8	+9.5	402.0	+16.8
United Kingdom	2,784.5	+7.4	3,761.3	+8.2	2,551.2	+15.0
Exports (f.o.b.) —						
Austria	471.0	+15.9	801.5	+8.9	92.0	+18.6
Denmark	1,290.5	+3.3	602.0	+6.3	210.3	+16.4
Finland	641.9	+13.2	402.7	+11.6	96.3	+8.7
Norway	879.8	+7.8	453.1	+12.0	159.6	+13.6
Portugal	245.8	+9.1	123.0	+6.5	78.8	+12.6
Sweden	2,145.1	+8.3	1,338.5	+10.4	381.4	+14.7
Switzerland	842.1	+11.2	1,466.7	+14.6	412.0	+12.9
United Kingdom	2,121.3	−1.5	3,099.2	+7.9	2,182.8	+24.4

SOURCE: *Ninth Annual Report, EFTA;* 1969.

The general purposes of both the **EEC** and **EFTA** are much the same, and efforts are being made by each organization to work with the other.

requested a conditional admission to meet its Commonwealth obligations. France objected and blocked Britain's entry. Thus, any rapid political and economic integration of Western Europe in the near future has been delayed. If EEC and EFTA should merge — as some think they eventually will — there would be an economic "United States of Europe."

In the early 1960's, the economic and military needs of the United States seemed to indicate possibilities for a future unification of United States, Canada, and the western European countries into an expanded common market. Later events, such as the Cuban crisis, the Vietnamese war, and French political and English economic trade policies, have created many new conflicting economic interests. This would indicate that unification within a common market of this type is presently improbable.

OTHER REGIONAL TRADE ASSOCIATIONS

In Africa a twelve-nation conference took a stand in favor of a preferential system of tariffs, and in Southeast Asia similar action has been taken. Kenya, Uganda, and Tanzania renamed their common market the East African Community in 1967. It uses a common agricultural policy, coordinated economic planning, and a unified operation of postal and transport services.

In 1960 a treaty was signed in Montevideo, Uruguay, by representatives of seven Latin American countries, thus forming a type of Latin American Common Market. The participating countries include Argentina, Brazil, Chile, Mexico, Paraguay, Peru, and Uruguay. In this Latin American Free Trade Association, members retain their own external tariffs. The program provides for the gradual elimination of trade restrictions on at least three fourths of the trade within the area. Any Latin American country may join.

The Organization of American States (*OAS*) was formed in 1948 to provide security for the North and South American nations. In 1961 the program of the "Alliance for Progress" between the United States and Latin America was initiated by President Kennedy. The purpose of the Alliance was to encourage the economic development of the Latin American nations by means of financial aid by our government, other nations, and private business to the amount of $20 billion over a period of 10 years. Since then, Alliance representatives have been assured that the continuance and extension of aid to Latin America by the American people would not terminate at the end of the original period.

SUMMARY

A division of labor in production comes about as a result of the comparative advantage or least disadvantage that individuals, regions, and nations have with respect to the production of certain kinds of goods and services. The law of comparative costs is simply the fact that individuals, regions, and nations tend to devote their resources and efforts to the production of those goods which they can produce at a cost that is less than others can produce them.

Trade results as a matter of course because of the practice of a division of labor. As a rule, trade is beneficial to both buyers and sellers.

In international trade one thing which creates problems is that there are legal and economic restrictions on the movement of goods from one country to another. These restrictions take the form of tariffs, quotas, price fixing by cartels, and other interferences with free trade.

The United States can benefit by foreign trade because we do not have all the kinds of natural resources and certain other kinds of goods that we need. Furthermore, in order to export part of what we produce, we must buy from other nations as much as we sell abroad. If we do not, either our business firms or the federal government must lend foreign buyers the difference between what we sell and what we buy. Often in past years, our government has given other nations funds with which to buy our goods, which means, in effect, that the American people have given away the goods because they, as taxpayers, supplied the money with which to pay for them.

Arguments for and against a protective tariff relate to: (1) nationalism, (2) home markets, (3) military necessity, (4) young or infant industries, (5) dumping of goods from other nations, (6) protection of domestic wages, (7) equalization of the cost of production, and (8) governmental revenue.

The tariff is frequently a sectional political issue, and tariff laws have been passed by means of "log-rolling" methods.

The Tariff Commission studies international trade and makes recommendations for the passage or changing of tariff laws. The Reciprocal Trade Agreements Act of 1934 makes it possible for the United States to agree with another nation to lower certain of our tariffs on its goods if it will lower its tariff on our goods.

The International Trade Organization (ITO) was an effort to bring about a lessening of international trade restrictions, but the proposal was not ratified and hence failed to come into existence. The General Agreement on Tariffs and Trade (GATT), in some ways similar to ITO, has survived for more than a decade and has shown an increase in participating members.

Several efforts to create an economic "United States of Europe" by removing trade restrictions have been made. Considerable progress has been achieved within the framework of EEC and EFTA as regional groups.

NEW TERMS

antiprotectionists
dumping
duty
EEC
EFTA
export

free trade
GATT
home market
imports
infant industries
international cartel

ITO
law of comparative advantage *or* cost
nationalism
OAS

protectionists
Reciprocal Trade Agreements Act
Tariff Commission
tariffs

QUESTIONS ON THE CHAPTER

1. What is the principle of the law of comparative cost?
2. Is free trade within our fifty states desirable? Explain.
3. What is the basic reason for engaging in international trade?
4. Do differing resources of nations constitute a significant economic fact? Discuss.
5. How has the search for resources influenced military history of recent decades?
6. How basic for us is our foreign trade? Discuss.
7. How are ability to export and ability to import interdependent?
8. For what reasons do nations often discourage the importation of goods?
9. Do social and individual viewpoints on international trade sometimes conflict? Explain.
10. What is (a) the Tariff Commission? (b) the Reciprocal Trade Agreements Act of 1934?
11. What is an international cartel? What are its objectives?
12. What are the arguments for the formation of a United States of Europe? Explain.
13. What is (a) ITO? (b) GATT? (c) EEC? (d) EFTA? (e) OAS? What is the purpose of each?
14. What evidence is there, other than in Europe, of increasing interest in trade cooperation among nations?

APPLYING YOUR ECONOMIC UNDERSTANDING

1. In recent years the small types of foreign cars have been popular with the American consumer. How may the law of comparative cost be applicable to this situation?
2. The American steel industry has had severe competition from Japan in the sale of certain steel products. Explain what specific advantages the foreign producers may have which makes possible this inroad on our market.
3. Cite examples of food items that you use which come entirely, or in part, from other nations. Which of these cannot be produced economically in the United States?
4. Certain nations in southeastern Asia desire goods from the United States which they cannot produce themselves. To make these purchases possible the United States government has loaned or given money to these nations.

What direct effect do the loans have on our economy? What indirect economic effects does this policy have?

5. In a recent year, the value of United States merchandise exports was approximately $34 billion. (a) Use reference sources to find out which segments of the economy benefited by this trade. (b) What would some of the economic effects be if this trade had not taken place?
6. Although the sewing machine was invented in the United States, foreign housewives were using models in their own countries, which reversed and which made automatic fancy stitching possible, before such machines were available to the American housewife. What economic factors might have created this situation?
7. Since both technology and world population are expanding, what are some of the implications for world trade in the coming years?
8. In a Senate hearing on tariffs, representatives of two companies producing the same kind of product presented opposite viewpoints regarding a tariff on imports of the product they were producing. Discuss the possible reasons for their opposite stands.
9. Review some of the previous tariff laws adopted in the United States and indicate the support they received in Congress. How does this show that tariffs are sectional political issues?

CHALLENGES TO ECONOMIC COMPETENCE

1. Prepare a bulletin board display which shows products exchanged between your state and nations of the world.
2. Read about consular services and report your findings to the class.
3. Review a motion picture film on world trade. Show it to the class and then lead a discussion about its important points.
4. Prepare a booklet with collected clippings on world trade.
5. Write a report on one of the following: (a) The Purposes of ITO, (b) How GATT Aids Foreign Trade, (c) United States Tariff Policy, (d) Competition for World Markets.
6. Read *International Trade: Gateway to Growth*, a booklet published by the United States Department of Commerce. Prepare a written review which compares its main ideas with those presented in this chapter of the textbook.
7. Organize two teams to prepare and present a class debate on the topic: Resolved: *that the noncommunist nations of the world should work toward establishing an economic community.*

Chapter 27

Making Payments Between Nations

How can money payments between persons in different nations be made?
Why do nations use exchange controls?
Why was the International Monetary Fund established?
What is the purpose of the World Bank?

Each nation has its own monetary system. If an American merchant or manufacturer sells goods, he will ordinarily accept only dollars in payment. Likewise, an Englishman will expect to be paid in pounds sterling; a Frenchman, in francs; an Italian, in lire; and so on with sellers in each of the nations.

Here, then, in international trade is encountered a problem that does not arise in domestic trade. How can a seller in one nation, say, the United States, be paid in the money of his own country when the nation where the buyer lives has a different system of money? For example, how can Mr. Smith, in New York, be paid in dollars for a sale of typewriters to Mr. Jones, in London, if Jones has only pounds with which to pay? The answer requires an understanding of the processes for payment of exports and imports.

EXPORT AND IMPORT PAYMENT PROCESSES

Purchasing foreign exchange. Some banks in the United States keep deposits in banks in other countries, such as England, France, Italy, or Japan. Certain foreign banks, likewise, keep deposits in some American banks. These American banks are ready to sell pounds, francs, lire, or yen to anyone who wants to buy them, and the banks overseas are willing to sell dollars. One who buys pounds from the American bank pays for them with dollars, and one who buys dollars from the banks in other countries pays for them with the currency of the country. The amount paid in each case depends on the rate of exchange prevailing at the time.

FOREIGN EXCHANGE RATES

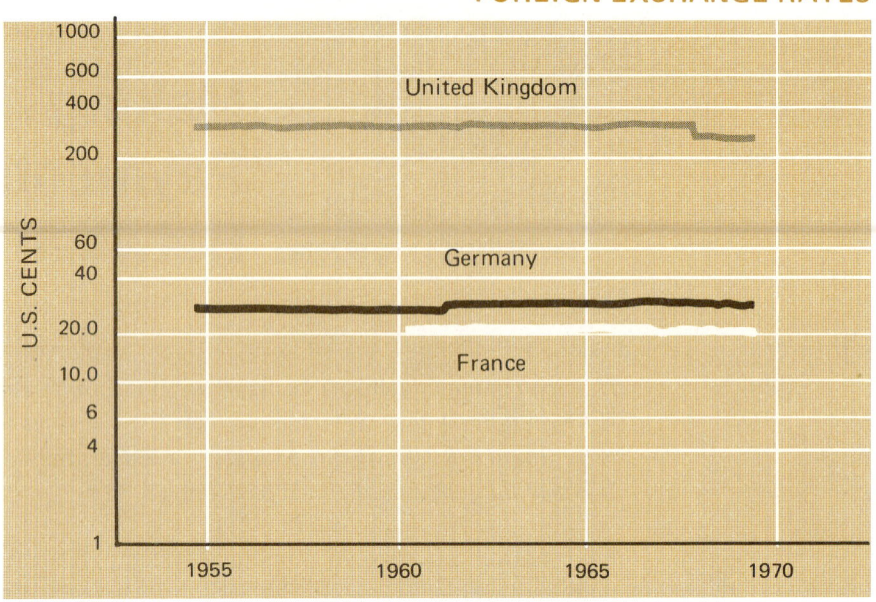

Figure 27-1.

SOURCE: *Historical Chart Book* (*1969*); Board of Governors of the Federal Reserve System.

In New York the value of the pound or the franc or the mark would be listed in terms of the dollar, although the rate of exchange may vary.

The *rate of exchange* between the currencies of two countries is the price paid in the domestic currency of one country for a unit of foreign currency. In New York the value of the pound or the franc or the mark would be listed in terms of the dollar, although the rate of exchange may vary from month to month, or day to day, by fractions of a cent. On a given day the pound of the United Kingdom might be listed at $2.404, the French franc at $.18005, and the German Deutsche mark at $.27126.

Payment for an export of merchandise. There are two simple ways by which Mr. Smith might be paid in dollars for his shipment of typewriters, which, let us say, are valued at $2,400.

Method 1. Suppose that the Midland Bank, in London, has dollars on deposit in the National City Bank in New York. When Mr. Jones orders the typewriters, he buys a draft from the Midland Bank on the National City Bank and has it made payable to Mr. Smith. Assume that £1 is worth $2.40. Then Mr. Jones pays his bank £1,000, and the draft is made out for $2,400.

When Mr. Smith receives the draft, he ships the typewriters and presents the draft to the National City Bank, which pays him in dollars. The bank deducts the dollars from the account of the Midland Bank.

Method 2. Mr. Smith might be paid in dollars by another method, somewhat as follows:

When Mr. Jones orders the typewriters, he directs Mr. Smith to ship the merchandise and to draw a *draft* on him for the amount of the cost.

> New York (Date)
>
> Pay at sight to the order of the *National City Bank of New York*
>
> One thousand pounds sterling — — — — — — — — — — — — — —
>
> To *R. P. Jones*   *A. R. Smith*
>   *London*

Then when Mr. Smith ships the typewriters, he obtains a *negotiable bill of lading* (a receipt that can be transferred only by indorsement) from the steamship company. Mr. Jones must have this receipt before he can get the typewriters when they arrive in England.

Mr. Smith draws the draft and presents it, together with the bill of lading, to the New York bank. The bank pays him $2,400. The bank then sends the draft and the bill of lading to the Midland Bank. Mr. Jones accepts and pays the draft and receives the bill of lading, which will enable him to get the typewriters from the steamship company.

The Midland Bank then adds the amount of £1,000 to the account of the National City Bank. Thus, the New York bank now has more pounds in the English bank, which it can sell to anyone who wants to make payment for goods or services purchased in England or elsewhere.

These simplified examples illustrate how exporters from any nation are paid in the money of their own country. The second example shows how exports result in an increase in the amount of foreign currency (often called *foreign exchange*) in a foreign bank that belongs to banks in the exporting country, and this currency is available for the payments of imports.

Payment for an import of merchandise. Let us say that Mr. Williams in New York wants to buy $2,400 worth of woolen goods from a London exporter. By reversing the procedures outlined with reference to the payment for the export of typewriters, you can see how the Englishman can be paid in pounds.

WHAT IS THE BALANCE OF INTERNATIONAL PAYMENTS?

In few cases does the total amount of sales by one nation equal the total purchases from another nation. But the amount of foreign exchange (bank balances in foreign banks) that any nation has which can be used to pay for the goods or services that it imports usually arises from payments for its exports. Therefore, if a nation buys more than it sells, it must obtain a gift or a loan of money from some other nation. Thus, a nation that sells more than it buys from other nations becomes a *creditor nation*.

Any transaction that calls for a payment by a foreigner to an American individual or business firm is an export. Any transaction that calls for a payment by an American to a foreign individual or firm is an import. The transactions that result in money payments between nations relate to visible and invisible items, exports and imports. A *visible item* is one that is tangible, such as typewriters or wheat. An *invisible item* is one that is intangible, such as tourists' services, earnings from investments, loans of money, and investments, including stocks and bonds.

The balance in the annual account (receipts and payments of money) of business transactions between the United States and all other nations is called our *balance of international payments* for the year. The following list of receipts and payments includes most of the items that enter into our balance of international payments.

THE BALANCE OF INTERNATIONAL PAYMENTS (UNITED STATES)

Receipts (Receipts from foreigners. Foreign currency is used to buy dollars with which to make payment.)	Payments (Payments to foreigners. Dollars are used to buy foreign currency with which to make payment.)
1. Exports of merchandise	1. Imports of merchandise
2. Services rendered to foreigners (shipping services, etc.)	2. Services rendered by foreigners (shipping services, etc.)
3. Travel by foreigners in the United States	3. Travel by Americans in other countries
4. Income from foreign investments	4. Income to foreigners on their investments in the United States
5. Capital movements (loans, etc.)	5. Capital movements (loans, etc.)
6. Gold exports	6. Gold imports

The totals of the receipts and payments are always equal because the amount that a country buys or imports is equal to the amount it sells or exports plus or minus the change in its foreign debits (capital movements), that is, the amount it borrows or lends.

It is often said that, if the value of a nation's exports of merchandise is greater than the value of its imports of merchandise, it has a *favorable balance of trade*. If the value of such imports exceeds that of its exports, it has an *unfavorable balance of trade*. But the amount of a nation's total international receipts and payments is always equal, for if it buys more merchandise and services than it sells, it borrows the difference. If a nation sells more than it buys, it must extend credit or gifts. Thus, the receipts and payments balance.

In 1971 nations were selling us more goods and services than we were selling to them. They acquired claims in the form of bank deposits which could be converted into gold. We were also making unilateral transfers — gifts of money — in addition to what we imported. So claims for our money exceeded our total claims for payments for our exports. The situation became dangerous since it increased the drain on our low gold reserves and posed an alternative undesired action, the devaluation of the dollar. By August 15, 1971, President Nixon was forced to announce the suspension of the convertibility of the dollar into gold. In May, 1972, Congress endorsed the devaluation of the dollar by raising the official price of gold to $38 per ounce.

THE NATURE OF EXCHANGE CONTROLS

At one time the rate of exchange between Great Britain and the United States was £1 for $4.87 ($4.8665). For some time prior to 1949 it was £1 for $4.03. Then in 1968, the pound was devalued and the rate was fixed at £1 for $2.40. What basic factors caused the change?

The gold-par rate of exchange. There was a time when most of the important commercial nations were on the gold standard; that is, each nation defined its monetary unit as a certain weight of gold. For example, the weight of the American dollar was 23.22 grains of fine gold, and the weight of the English pound was 113.0016 grains. As you can see, by means of a little arithmetic, the pound weighed slightly less than 4.87 times as much as the dollar. Therefore, £1 was worth about $4.87. This was the rate of exchange between the two countries (£1 for $4.87).

As long as both nations were on the gold standard, the rate of exchange did not fluctuate very much. The following example shows why the rate remained stable. Suppose you owed a debt of £100 to an Englishman, and that your bank asked you to pay as much as $4.95 a pound, or $495 for a draft which, at the *gold-par rate*, would cost only $487. And suppose that it would cost you only $5 to ship £100 worth of gold (11300.16 grains) to England. You could buy and ship the gold and thus save $3. The bank, therefore, could not compel you to pay much more than the gold-par rate, plus the cost of shipping gold, for a draft.

When nations were on the gold exchange standard, the point or price at which it would be more economical to ship gold than to buy exchange was called the *gold export point*.

Forms of exchange controls. The factors that determine exchange rates are many and interrelated. In the absence of use of a gold standard, maintaining stable exchange rates creates problems. Abandonment of a gold standard requires the adoption of direct and indirect agreements to establish the exchange value and use of each nation's currency relative to that of other nations. The adoption and application of such agreements is termed *exchange control*. Four commonly used forms of exchange control are:

1. Licensing or setting quotas.
2. Establishing official rates of exchange.
3. Using purchasing-power parity exchange rates.
4. Devaluating one's own currency.

(1) Licensing or setting quotas. A country has a recognized authority to determine how its own currency or gold reserve will be used. Therefore, it may refuse to grant an import license for jewelry, yachts, or other luxuries so that its currency or gold may be conserved for other more urgent uses than payments for luxury imports. A nation can also refuse to issue an export license for domestically produced capital goods, which would force the domestic manufacturer to sell them at home for internal capital use. A nation can encourage the use of its currency by certain countries and discourage its use by others through a quota system. Using a sugar purchase quota system as an illustration, the nation can allocate various percentages to favored nations and refuse to permit purchases from nonfavored nations. Some nations will also limit the amount of currency that their citizens may take out of the country when they travel abroad.

(2) Establishing official rates of exchange. Basically, exchange rates throughout the world are determined by the demand for and the supply of money of each country that may be bought and sold for use in paying for imports of goods and services. Most nations fix an official rate of exchange for their currencies, and then in one way or another make an effort to keep the market price of its money at or near the official or announced price.

Illus. 27-1. Basically, exchange rates throughout the world are determined by the demand for and the supply of money of each country.

For example, if the market price falls, the government may enter the exchange market and buy its own money with the purpose of reducing the supply held by banks, thus raising the price. Or, if the price is above the official rate, the government may sell exchange at a lower price.

Some nations establish different rates of exchange for various kinds of imports. An importer of luxuries might have to buy foreign currency from the government bank at a high rate of exchange. An importer of necessities might purchase it at a much lower rate. A number of nations permit tourists traveling in their country to exchange their currency at more favorable rates of exchange than is permitted at the official rate of exchange. A nation holding currency of Country A might refuse its sale to importers, while it offers its holdings of the currency of Country B at attractive rates to importers. Thus, importers are barred from purchasing from Country A and are encouraged to buy from Country B.

(3) Using purchasing-power parity exchange rates. It is obvious that the relative purchasing power of any kind of money (dollars, pounds, and francs, for example) determines its value in terms of other money. For example, if £1 will buy as much as $2.40, then £1 is worth $2.40. This is true regardless of what the government says either the dollar or the pound is worth.

It has been said that, where nations are not on the gold standard, the exchange rate of the moneys of two countries should be fixed by a comparison of the amounts of goods that units of each kind of money will buy in their respective countries. For example, if $2.40 will buy approximately as much in the United States as £1 will buy in England, then the exchange rate should be $2.40 for £1. This idea is known as the *purchasing-power parity theory*. As yet, however, there seems to be no generally acceptable and exact way of comparing the purchasing power of different kinds of money.

At the same time, the value of money depends on what it will buy. The relative value of two kinds of money depends upon how much each will buy. So we see that exchange rates, in the long run, do tend to be fixed according to the theory of purchasing-power parity.

(4) Devaluating one's own currency. If the price of a pound of English money is $2, it is easier for an American to buy and pay for English goods than it would be if the price of the pound were $3. Therefore, in order to induce people in other nations to buy more goods from it, a nation may reduce the price of its money in terms of gold or of the value of the money of some other nation. This is known as devaluation.

In order to understand how devaluation is supposed to bring about an increase in the exports of a nation, let us suppose that the price of a yard of English woolen goods is £2 and that the exchange rate is $4.03 for £1. The cost in dollars would, of course, be $8.06. Now suppose that the official rate is fixed at $2.40 for £1. The cost of the same material would then be $4.80 (2 × $2.40). Such a reduction in cost would probably result in greater sales of English woolen goods to the United States. But the increase in English woolen exports would be temporary because relative costs and prices would eventually be reestablished.

Whether devaluation will enable a nation to increase its exports so that their value will be equal to the value of its imports depends (1) on whether the devaluation is great enough so that it is cheaper for other nations to buy what the nation has to sell than it is to buy the goods elsewhere or to make them at home and (2) on whether exporters raise the price of their goods. After the devaluation in 1968, the prices of many goods intended for export by the devaluating nations were immediately raised. From this it is evident that devaluation of its money does not enable a nation to solve its international exchange problems.

INTERNATIONAL TRADE IS BESET BY MANY PROBLEMS

After World War II there was a great deal of talk of *dollar shortages* in other countries. This expression meant that other nations wanted to buy a great many goods from us but that they did not have enough dollars with which to pay for the goods. The real reason that they lacked dollars

U. S. RESERVE ASSETS

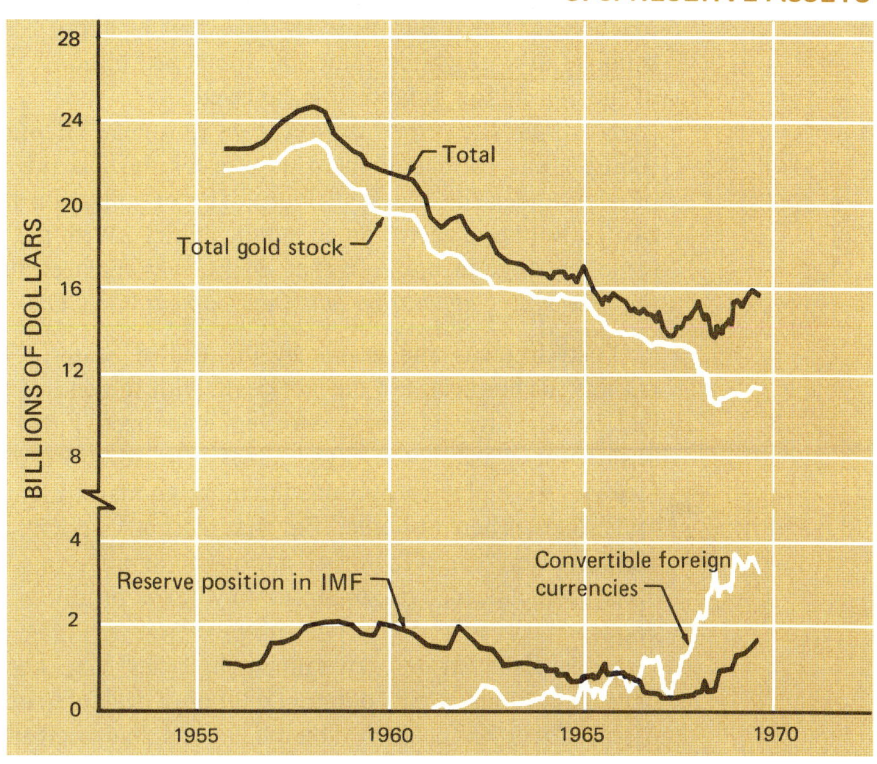

Figure 27-2.

SOURCE: *Historical Chart Book* (*1969*): Board of Governors of the Federal Reserve System.

In the late 1960's the excess or glut created a drain of our gold reserves as foreigners exchanged the excess of dollars for gold.

was that we were not buying from them as many goods as they wanted to buy from us. In the late 1960's, the process was reversed. Foreign nations had an excess of dollars which was termed a *dollar glut*. The excess or glut created a drain of our gold reserves as foreigners exchanged the excess dollars for gold.

The lend-lease program. In 1941 Great Britain and her allies were at war with Germany and were in great need of supplies that they could obtain only in the United States. Under the circumstances the nations at war with Germany could not pay us for the goods. So we set up a *lend-lease program* by which we undertook to advance supplies to Great Britain and other nations. The question of how they were to pay for the goods was deferred until the end of the war.

After we entered the war, lend-lease shipments were increased. Altogether we aided our allies to the extent of about $50 billion, and they supplied us with goods valued at about $10 billion. After the war, most of the $40 billion balance was canceled.

In 1948 the Organization for European Economic Cooperation (OEEC) was formed to help administer the aid the United States was offering under the Marshall Plan. The organization has been continued as a consultative agency in economic affairs. With the change in function came a change in name so that OEEC was replaced by the *Organization for Economic Cooperation and Development* (OECD).

Postwar loans and grants by the United States. The need of other nations for financial aid did not cease with the end of the war. Factories had been destroyed, many workers had been killed or wounded, and business in general was demoralized. In addition, our own farms and factories were able to produce far more goods of many kinds than could find a market here at home. For that reason American farmers and manufacturers were eager for other nations to arrange in some way to get the dollars they needed in order to buy farm products and manufactured goods.

Since 1940 various government agencies have been established that have made loans or gifts of many billions of dollars to other nations. Much of this money has been used by the nations that received it for the purchase of our goods and goods from other nations, including military equipment. Some of it has been used for rearmament by nations that are friendly to us. The money for the loans and gifts thus made has been obtained by the federal government from loans from banks, business firms, and individuals, and by taxation. Such loans and gifts that are not repaid become a burden on the American taxpayer.

As we recall from Chapter 26, the "Alliance for Progress" — a program of aid for Latin America — was proposed at a meeting of the economic ministers of 21 nations. The program proposed the most liberal help the United States has offered — $20 billion in low-interest loans over a period of ten years. Its purpose was to raise the living standards in the Latin American countries, and it called for land and tax reforms in those countries to which loans were to be extended.

THE E-IB, IMF, AND IBRD ARE INTENDED TO AID INTERNATIONAL TRADE

The *Export-Import Bank* was set up in 1934 to assist in financing exports and imports. The E-IB borrows funds from the Federal Treasury

EXPORT-IMPORT BANK (E-IB) LONG-TERM LOANS AND REPAYMENTS, FISCAL YEARS, 1962-1969

(Millions of dollars)

	Total	Near East and South Asia	Latin America	Vietnam	East Asia	Africa	Europe	Other and non-regional
Export-Import Bank long-term loans:								
Loan authorizations:								
1962-68 average	404	93	196	....	27	30	58	....
1969	537	68	289	....	40	58	81	....
Repayments and interest:								
1962-68 average	383	74	245	....	25	10	29	....
1969	546	113	317	....	28	24	64	....

SOURCE: *Economic Report of the President* (February, 1970).

The E-IB borrows funds from the Federal Treasury with which to make loans needed to finance trade between the United States and other countries.

with which to make loans needed to finance trade between the United States and other countries. Sometimes it guarantees private loans by business concerns for this purpose. Its work is complementary to that of the *International Bank for Reconstruction and Development* (IBRD), and the amount of its loans has been larger than that of the other institution.

In July, 1944, at Bretton Woods, New Hampshire, representatives of 44 nations signed the "Articles of Agreement" for the *International Monetary Fund* (IMF) and the International Bank for Reconstruction and Development. By 1971, 116 countries were members.

The International Monetary Fund. The main purposes of the Fund are: (1) to promote international monetary cooperation; (2) to assist in the growth of international trade; (3) to help stabilize exchange rates; and (4) to provide a place where the central banks of the nations may borrow funds with which to pay for imports, or may obtain special drawing rights.

Each of the member countries contributes capital to the Fund. The aggregate of members' quotas in 1971 exceeded $22.3 billion. The capital is in the form of gold, national currencies of the member nations, and SDR certificates. The Fund is managed by a board of governors, each member nation being entitled to at least one governor. The Board of Governors elect 18 executive directors, who elect the managing director.

The central bank in a member nation (in the U. S., the Federal Reserve Bank in New York) may borrow an amount of the foreign exchange needed to pay for imports. This exchange may then be sold to importers in the nation who want it to pay for their imports.

Each member nation agrees to allow importers and exporters in the nation to use foreign exchange without interference by the government. They further agree not to change the value of their currency more than 10 percent without first consulting the managers of the Fund.

The International Bank for Reconstruction and Development. This financial institution, usually referred to as the *World Bank*, is designed to encourage international lending by private individuals and concerns. It was expected that such loans would be made for long periods of time and would be used (1) to help restore the war-torn countries and (2) to help develop backward countries. More recently, by facilitating the investment of capital for productive purposes, it tends to promote the long-range growth of international trade.

The subscribed capital of the bank is more than $23 billion. The Bank does not receive deposits. It may (1) lend or (2) guarantee loans made to member nations, cities, or to "any business, industrial, or agricultural enterprise in the territories of a member."

For example, the Bank approved a loan to pay part of the cost of a $2 billion complex in Pakistan which includes the Mangla Dam and a project to irrigate 3 million acres of desert land.

WHAT IS THE FUTURE OF OUR INTERNATIONAL TRADE AND FINANCE?

Nearly all nations want more dollars with which to buy American products or goods produced in other nations. But the only way by which they can get more dollars is by exporting more goods and receiving payment in dollars, or by loans or gifts of dollars from other nations — especially from the United States.

Should we abolish our tariffs on certain kinds of imports, and allow foreign-made goods to enter the country in greater quantities? If we did this, other countries could sell us more goods, and in this way get more dollars with which to buy our goods or goods from other nations. But what would happen to American industries that now enjoy the benefit of a protective tariff? In some cases protected industries might not be able to meet the competition of foreign-made goods. If not, profits in such industries would decrease or disappear and many workers would have to seek other jobs. It has been suggested that, if an industry could not meet foreign competition after the removal of a protective tariff, the government might reimburse the owners for the loss of their business.

Ch. 27   MAKING PAYMENTS BETWEEN NATIONS

Illus. 27-2. The great majority of the people of the world live in the less-developed nations — those that are not advanced industrially.

Social Science Curriculum Resources

Then, too, the great majority of the people of the world live in the less-developed nations — those that are not advanced industrially. Most of these peoples are becoming restless and eager for more goods. Their leaders are seeking ways by which methods of production can be modernized. Nearly everywhere there are signs that an industrial revolution in the less-developed nations is beginning.

American capital by the billions is being invested in many parts of the world. Businessmen recognize that Africa and Asia may develop into enormous markets for the American manufacturer.

There is some possibility that, with the growth of the regional markets, American trade may suffer for a time. However, as the standards of living in many areas of the world increase, combined with the natural increase in population, world trade should become increasingly more important.

Most of the nations of the world, of course, have a long way to go before they overtake the highly developed economy of the United States. But as their production and trade increase and as we continue to turn out an increasing amount of goods, the problem of international trade may well become more acute. How will these problems be solved? This question is a challenge to the statesmen of all the nations and to the citizens of the free countries who have the opportunity to think and to express their opinions on public issues.

SUMMARY

If one exports goods or services, the buyer (importer) must make payment with money used in the exporter's country. Therefore, the importer exchanges his money for the other currency; that is, he buys money used in the exporter's country. The rate at which his money exchanges for the money of another country is the rate of exchange.

Exports of goods and services create supplies of foreign exchange, which can be used to pay for imports. There are two classes of exports and imports: visible and invisible items. The balance in the annual account of business transactions between a nation and all other nations is the balance of international payments of that nation for the year. When the total value of visible exports is greater than that of visible imports, it is sometimes said that a nation has a favorable balance of trade. But we should understand that imports pay for exports. That is to say, the money that is received by exporters for their exports is purchased (indirectly and through banks) by importers to pay for their imports.

At one time commercial nations were on the gold standard, which meant that the international rate of exchange was the ratio of the weight of the monetary unit of one nation to that of another nation. Now in most cases various forms of exchange control are used. These controls include: (1) licensing or setting quotas, (2) establishing official rates of exchange, (3) using purchasing-power parity exchange, and (4) devaluating one's own currency.

Since World War II we have loaned or given other nations many billions of dollars in an effort to help them to raise the level of living of their people. At the same time, such loans and gifts have been used largely to buy American goods.

NEW TERMS

balance of international payments
creditor nation
dollar glut
dollar shortages
draft
exchange control
Export-Import Bank
favorable balance of trade
foreign exchange
gold export point
gold-par rate of exchange
International Bank for Reconstruction and Development
International Monetary Fund
invisible (export and import) items
lend-lease program
negotiable bill of lading
Organization for Economic Cooperation and Development
purchasing-power parity theory
rate of exchange
unfavorable balance of trade
visible (export and import) items
World Bank

QUESTIONS ON THE CHAPTER

1. What is meant by "rate of exchange"?
2. How do exports increase the amount of our foreign exchange?
3. How do imports increase the amount of dollar exchange belonging to banks in other nations?
4. What is the meaning of the expression "exports pay for imports, and vice versa"?
5. What does it mean to be a "creditor nation"? Is the United States a creditor or a debtor nation? Explain.
6. Are invisible imports and exports ordinarily considered in the idea of a favorable balance of trade? Explain.
7. What may happen if, over a period of time, foreign claims for our money exceed our claims against foreign nations?
8. When the United States and Great Britain were on the gold standard, what was the rate of exchange between the two nations?
9. What is meant by the four forms of exchange control?
10. Basically, how are exchange rates determined at present?
11. According to the theory of purchasing-power parity, how do exchange rates tend to be fixed in the long run?
12. In 1968, what were many nations trying to accomplish by devaluating their currencies? How effective was devaluation?
13. What was the lend-lease program?
14. What is the OECD?
15. Why were postwar loans and gifts of money made to foreign nations?
16. What is the "Alliance for Progress"?
17. What is the Export-Import Bank? What is its purpose?
18. What is the International Monetary Fund? What are its objectives?
19. What is the International Bank for Reconstruction and Development (World Bank)? How does it work?

APPLYING YOUR ECONOMIC UNDERSTANDING

1. In 1965, Rhodesia declared its independence from Great Britain over the latter's objection. The UN Security Council placed an embargo in 1968 on trade and travel with Rhodesia. Oil shipments to Rhodesia and chrome shipments to the United States are now affected. In what ways were payments between nations involved in this situation?
2. An American automobile exporter shipped 100 automobiles (valued at $271,260, including shipping costs and insurance) to a German importer at Bremerhaven. How many marks must the importer deposit to cover a draft drawn by the exporter?
3. In a recent year, United States merchandise exports to South America amounted to $4,063 million. South American merchandise and other

imports into the United States amounted to $3,669 million. (a) To balance the trade, how many dollars of additional payment to United States would be necessary? (b) What are some methods by which this payment could be made?

4. At present the Treasury values gold at $38 an ounce or 480 grains. The Norwegian kroner is valued as equivalent to 1.92 grains of gold. The cost of shipping gold to Oslo is 36 cents an ounce. (a) If the bank charge for a draft of 250 kroner to Oslo was quoted at the price of $39, what method of payment would be cheaper? (b) By how much?

5. The American dollar is equivalent to 50 Belgian francs. (a) If the Belgian government devaluated the franc so that the rate of exchange was 55 Belgian francs to the dollar, what probable effect would it presently have on American imports of Belgian goods? (b) What effect, if any, would it have on Belgians who were importing American products?

6. A nation that borrowed money from the United States now wishes to repay the loan. State two methods that a nation can use to secure funds to repay the debt.

7. An organization proposes a campaign of "Buy American Goods." (a) Would this campaign affect a nation which sells us tin ore in the same way as a nation that sells us cotton clothing? (b) What effect would it have on debt repayments to the United States by the country which exported cotton clothing to us?

8. Certain administration leaders are advocating that we stimulate tourist travel and that we encourage tourists from other nations to visit the United States. (a) In what way would this affect invisible imports? (b) How would it affect the balance of payments?

CHALLENGES TO ECONOMIC COMPETENCE

1. Prepare and present a debate on the topic "Resolved That Foreign Trade Stimulates the World Economy."
2. Prepare a sociodrama showing a tourist faced with the problem of buying and spending a foreign type of currency.
3. Invite a representative from a local bank to discuss the uses of traveler's checks. Lead the summary discussion.
4. Prepare an oral report on one of the following topics: (a) American Trade or American Aid, (b) How the International Bank for Reconstruction and Development Operates, (c) The Economic Role of the Export-Import Bank, (d) Our Dwindling Gold Supply.
5. Make a collection of illustrations and other printed material concerning payments between nations. Prepare a bulletin board display using items from the collection.
6. Make arrangements to preview the Carousel film: *Exports, Imports, Dollars, and Gold.* Show the film in class and lead a discussion on how it illustrates easing the net outflow of gold.

Chapter 28

Nations With Other Economic Systems

How can we distinguish socialism, communism, and fascism?
What criticisms of our economic system are made by the socialists?
How do we reply to criticisms of our economic order?
How can we describe the political and economic order in the Union of Soviet Socialist Republics?

The volume of goods and services produced in the United States annually is valued at hundreds of billions of dollars. Occasionally there are stories about possibilities of Russian production surpassing ours in the near future. Both Russia and China are said to be plotting revolutions in noncommunist nations by promising economic miracles as rewards. It is constantly repeated that socialism has been a failure in Great Britain. We hear it said that some of the South American countries are under fascistic rule. Every now and then someone says that the United States is becoming socialistic — or maybe fascistic. Some say that capitalism will soon be a thing of the past. Comments such as these indicate a concern — or even a fear — related to the changing nature of economic systems.

THE CHANGING NATURE OF ECONOMIC SYSTEMS

In Chapter 2, you discovered that capitalism in some nations was evolutionary because it developed slowly over a long period of time. After World War I, a number of nations shifted rapidly from one form of economic system to another. This type of rapid change is revolutionary change. Such a change may be accomplished through peaceful democratic processes, as was evident in Great Britain's partial adoption of a democratic type of socialism. It may be instituted by radical and violent struggles, such as those which occurred during Russia's and China's change to communism. It may also be encouraged through an appeal to national pride, a method which gave birth to Nazism in Germany, seemingly peaceful at first but then brutal and immoral.

What does each of these "isms" mean — capitalism, socialism, communism, fascism, and Nazism? Capitalism has been discussed in several connections. Now our attention shall be given to other systems.

WHAT IS SOCIALISM?

Briefly stated, the doctrine of *socialism* advocates collective ownership, usually by government, of most of the land, capital, and other material means of production, and the abandonment of the private profit motive as an incentive for the production of goods. Socialists contend that under a system of socialism, individuals will contribute to the production of the national income in proportion to their ability and will receive incomes proportionate to their contribution to production.

There are many variations of socialism, including the Russian or Marxian brands. Each of these varieties differs in some way from the others. Even though socialists differ among themselves as to the details of carrying out their ideas, they all contend that:

1. Productive wealth — factories, stores, mines, telephone and telegraph lines and equipment, transportation facilities, electric power, banks, most of the land, and other forms of productive property — should be owned by the state, that is, by the government or by cooperative groups; production for profit, by employing wage earners, should be abolished and the state (government) should be the only employer in the major types of business and industry.

2. Production for use should be substituted for production for profit.

THE CHARGES OF SOCIALISTS AGAINST FREE ENTERPRISE

Socialism maintains that the private ownership of capital and the operation of business for profit results in many evils. The various charges of socialism against capitalism can be made in a series of brief statements. Socialists claim that:

(1) The private ownership of capital results in great differences in wealth and income. Because of this fact, some persons are able to obtain more than their fair share of the national income, while others receive too little.

INDIVIDUAL INCOME TAX RETURNS*

Income Classes (grouped according to adjusted gross income)	Number of Returns	Adjusted Gross Income	Taxable Income
Under $600	4,075,332	1,361,445,000	....
$600 under $1,000	3,320,487	2,642,120,000	35,153,000
$1,000 under $2,000	7,557,305	11,216,961,000	2,618,167,000
$2,000 under $3,000	5,902,715	14,725,779,000	5,373,562,000
$3,000 under $4,000	5,692,292	19,900,937,000	9,001,015,000
$4,000 under $5,000	5,453,958	24,534,106,000	12,148,963,000
$5,000 under $6,000	5'198,958	28,604,730,000	15,202,642,000
$6,000 under $7,000	5,222,780	33,949,381,000	18,893,089,000
$7,000 under $8,000	5,114,151	38,292,349,000	21,726,000,000
$8,000 under $9,000	4,489,519	38,126,584,000	22,624,470,000
$9,000 under $10,000	3,851,257	36,526,002,000	22,386,911,000
$10,000 under $15,000	10,406,370	124,684,024,000	82,860,313,000
$15,000 under $20,000	2,759,089	46,814,825,000	33,891,589,000
$20,000 under $50,000	1,947,384	54,781,117,000	42,669,635,000
$50,000 under $100,000	259,285	17,111,735,000	14,077,176,000
$100,000 under $200,000	51,122	6,735,449,000	5,504,930,000
$200,000 under $500,000	12,576	3,603,045,000	2,867,476,000
$500,000 under $1,000,000	2,038	1,370,240,000	1,089,313,000
$1,000,000 or more	813	1,624,600,000	1,269,156,000

*For a recent year

SOURCE: *Internal Revenue Service, Treasury Department.*

The private ownership of capital results in great differences in wealth and income.

(2) The wrong goods and services are produced. Under capitalism, production for profit is the motive. It is often more profitable for manufacturers to use capital and labor for the production of luxuries that can be bought only by the rich than it is to produce goods that are needed by the poorer classes.

(3) Competition in the manufacture and sale of goods and services is wasteful. There are more service stations, grocery stores, and other kinds of business establishments than are needed. Advertising, the cost of which must be added to the selling price, also is wasteful.

(4) Competition wastes and destroys natural resources. In order to "get rich quick," wasteful methods of production have been used in developing our oil, gas, coal, and timberlands. Under capitalism much of our agricultural land has been worn out or has washed away.

(5) The desire of employers to make profits results in overworking and underpaying labor. Cooperation instead of competition should be the rule. There would be less waste and strife among the people if competition were abolished.

(6) Competition in production results in periods of general prosperity followed by periods of business depression. Business cycles could be eliminated and regular employment provided if production were planned and directed by a central authority.

(7) The system of free enterprise does not allow all classes to enjoy equal liberty. Those who own the wealth determine the kinds of laws that are made. Often these laws are made to favor the rich and to discriminate against the poor. Socialism asserts that under capitalism the state is an agency for protecting property owners and for oppressing those who do not own property.

(8) Free enterprise tends to bring about war. The desire for raw materials and markets causes nations to try to gain advantages over other nations.

THE DEFENSE FOR FREE ENTERPRISE

The American people, on the whole, do not claim that our form of capitalism is a perfect system. But they do maintain that its advantages far outweigh its disadvantages and that the American way of life offers

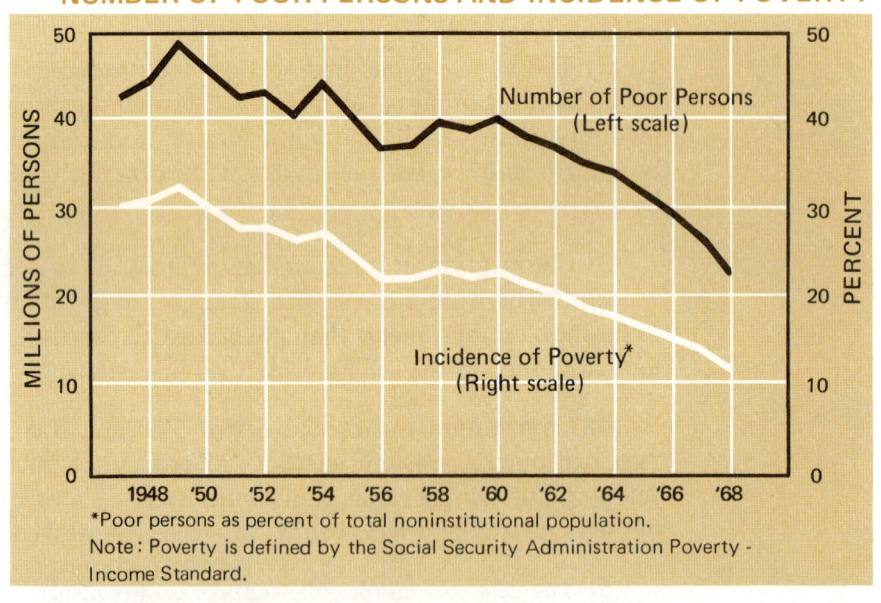

Figure 28-1.

NUMBER OF POOR PERSONS AND INCIDENCE OF POVERTY

*Poor persons as percent of total noninstitutional population.
Note: Poverty is defined by the Social Security Administration Poverty - Income Standard.

SOURCE: *Economic Report of the President, 1969.*

The American people, on the whole, do not claim that our form of capitalism is a perfect system. The American way of life offers opportunities for welfare and happiness.

opportunities for welfare and happiness that cannot be found in any country that has a different kind of economic system.

In reply to the charges of socialism, those who prefer American capitalism advance the following arguments:

(1) Private ownership of wealth is a positive good. The hope of accumulating wealth is a worthy incentive for effort; it stimulates initiative and causes individuals to work and save. Private savings accumulate and are invested in factories and other forms of productive equipment. As a result, the capital of the nation increases, which makes possible the production of more and more goods and services at lower costs.

It is a worthy desire for one to wish to accumulate wealth, some of which at least may be left to one's relatives or others. It is claimed that people will work harder to produce and save if their children or other relatives are permitted to inherit wealth.

(2) It is true that part of the nation's capital is used in the production of luxuries that only the rich can afford. On the other hand, what is a luxury today may become a necessity tomorrow. At one time bathtubs were regarded as luxuries and were taxed as such. Now they are considered essential to health. In many cases the well-to-do class has served to introduce and to popularize many kinds of goods that have aided in raising the average standard of living.

It is not true that most of the nation's wealth is used to produce luxuries. The greatest opportunity for making a profit lies in producing things that a majority of the people need and buy. For example, the automobile companies that have specialized in making low-priced cars have made the most profits. Therefore, most of the capital in the nation is used to produce goods and services for which there is the greatest need.

(3) On the whole, competition is the life of trade. While competition may sometimes result in the building of too many service stations or other kinds of business establishments, in the long run competition results in the production of goods at a lower cost than would be likely if competition were abolished. The desire to sell more goods causes producers to seek new and better methods of production in order that prices may be reduced and sales increased. Competition results in the production of a greater variety of goods and services. If competition were abolished, there would not be the same incentive to reduce the costs of production or to turn out a variety of goods.

Advertising may stimulate the production and use of more goods. As demand increases, production on a large scale becomes possible, which results in lowering the unit cost of production.

American Airlines   *Burlington Northern*

Illus. 28-1. On the whole, competition is the life of trade.

(4) Wastes of natural resources have occurred in the past. But government can and does take measures to conserve our natural resources of oil, coal, timber, and soils without abolishing private property. American capitalism has learned that the long-run benefits gained from the conservation of resources are greater than the short-run profits derived from wasteful use of resources. Timber companies now replant or farm their forest areas; mining companies rehabilitate strip mine areas to new uses; and the petroleum industry through science and technology has eliminated many of the noneconomic practices of the past. The urgencies of conservation involve problems not only for capitalism but also for other economic systems.

(5) Under our system the division of labor results in the organization of society on a cooperative basis. In the first place, different individuals and groups specialize in producing certain kinds of goods and services that are exchanged for money that, in turn, is exchanged for goods and services produced by other individuals and groups. Thus, indirectly, shoes may be exchanged for oranges or wheat or cotton. The general welfare of the country depends upon the total amount of all production.

In the second place, the owners of land, labor, capital, and the enterprisers are engaged in a form of cooperation, although the immediate aim of each is to get rent, wages, interest, or profits. There must be a

Illus. 28-2. Timber companies now replant or farm their forest areas.

Crown Zellerbach

combination of labor and capital before production can take place. On the whole, employers are willing to pay fair wages, and employees are willing that employers should make a fair amount of profit. Therefore, it is to the interest of both that as much should be produced as is reasonably possible. In spite of the fact that individuals and groups compete with each other, we are engaged in cooperation on a vast scale. Under competition the motive for work is largely self-interest. Under socialism the incentive would have to be, to a great extent, compulsion by government.

(6) It is true that business has always had its ups and downs. Periods of prosperity have been followed by periods of recession or depression. But business has always recovered and gone on to greater prosperity.

Many persons, however, now believe that out of our experience we are discovering how to prevent or control the business cycle and to maintain a high level of employment and production. To do this requires that we adopt and follow the correct public policy with respect to the relations of government to private enterprise. How to formulate and carry out such a policy is, of course, a great challenge to our intelligence and willingness to undertake the responsibilities of citizens in a modern democracy.

(7) Under our system an individual enjoys the greatest amount of freedom possible, where people live together. No one is absolutely free to do as he pleases. It is also true that great wealth gives the owner power over others. The owner of a factory, for example, has something to say about what will be produced and the amount of wages he pays his employees, and strong financial interests have sometimes influenced the making of laws.

On the other hand, under socialism there would be many individuals who would not be able to do as they pleased. Socialists claim that under socialism all rules for the control of business and for the payment of wages would be fixed by democratic means; that is, the people would say what should be done. But what would happen to those who disagreed with the majority? They would be compelled to do as the majority decided. Since the mass of the people would not understand how things should be run, it would be necessary to leave the decisions as to business matters to a small group. Even then, disagreements would likely arise, and the final decision would have to be left to a still smaller group or to an individual whose decision would become law. Therefore, while socialists advocate democracy, under socialism it would be impossible to satisfy everyone.

(8) The system of free enterprise is no more likely to result in war than is socialism. It is not so active in stirring up discontent and trouble in other countries as is radical socialism. Unless the whole world were under socialism, there would still be as much cause for war as there now is. Even if all nations adopted socialism, that would not mean the end of international friction and rivalry.

THE PROGRAM OF SOCIALISM

Socialism would place ownership and control in the hands of the government. The central government would own and control the big industries, like the railroads, the telegraph companies, and the automobile industry. Small local concerns, such as small factories or stores, might be owned and controlled by the state governments. Some industries, including farming, could be run by cooperatives.

Under complete socialism the government would be the only enterpriser, the only producer and seller of goods, the only fixer of prices. All who were able to work would have to work or go without income. Those who were unable to work would be provided for by the state. There would be differences in the amount of wages that would be paid to different kinds of workers.

The purpose of state ownership and control is to increase production and to give each deserving person a larger amount of goods and services. In order to do this, planning boards in communities and regions would be organized to decide what should be produced in the various parts of the country. The local board would report to the state board, which, in turn, would report to the national planning board. Thus, a plan for the whole nation would be mapped out. And when the plan was once established, everyone would be compelled to work in accordance with it. It is not likely that unrestricted criticism would be permitted, for if everyone were allowed the right of free criticism, the plan might be upset and confusion result.

THE POLICY OF SOCIALISM

The Socialist Party of the United States, which in recent years has had only nominal existence, usually represents the majority of the socialists in this country. It advocates the establishment of socialism by peaceful, lawful means. The leaders do not favor violent revolution as the desirable way to overthrow capitalism. They urge a gradual change to socialism. According to them, the people should be educated to desire a change in the economic order and to bring about the change by voting to give the federal, the state, and the local governments more and more power.

THE NATURE OF SOCIALISM IN GREAT BRITAIN

There is a strong socialist element in Great Britain. But the type of socialism is different from that which exists in Russia and Red China. British socialism is of the democratic type.

Almost immediately after the end of World War II, the Labor Party took control of the government in Great Britain. The nationalization (socialization) programs of the Labor Party developed rapidly. The major nationalized economic areas and the changes that were adopted included:

(1) Finance. The nationalization of the Bank of England and the governmental control of investment were completed.

(2) Fuel and Power. The nationalization of the coal industry, electric power, and the gas industry was put into effect.

(3) Transportation and Communication. The nationalization of all inland transportation facilities, such as railways, canals, dockyards, the London Passenger Transport Board, highway freight and civil aviation, as well as of cable, radio, and television was accomplished.

(4) Steel. The nationalization of the steel industry was carried out.

(5) Social Welfare. The National Insurance Act provided for sickness and disability pay, widow allowances, and old-age retirement benefits. The Industrial Injuries Act provided disability and death benefits as compensation for industrial accidents. The National Assistance Act provided financial aid to the aged, the disabled, and the infirm who were not otherwise covered. The Family Allowance Act gave a subsidy to each family for each child after the first-born.

(6) National Health Service. In effect, this is a socialization of the health facilities of the nation. It gives comprehensive health service to every resident for the prevention, diagnosis, and treatment of physical and mental health in professional offices, at clinics, or in hospitals. Less than 5 percent of the cost is paid by the individual directly; the remainder is paid through insurance plans or is paid through government subsidies or through payments derived from public taxation.

(7) Land-Use and Planning. Various acts provide for the efficient use of land, including farmland, with the imposition of penalties for noncompliance. The ultimate control over the utilization of all kinds of land is placed in the hands of the national government.

In 1951 the Conservatives returned to power. The government then took steps to denationalize (return to private ownership) the steel industry and highway freight transportation. With the Labor Party's return to power in 1964, the renationalization of steel became a crucial issue. The Labor Party's experiment with socialism was not effective in holding down wage rates when private workers became state employees. Nor did the adoption of socialism hold down the prices of products which Britain needed to sell competitively in world trade. Under the Labor Party's policies of socialism a devaluation of the pound was forced in 1949 and again in 1968. Great Britain has changed and is still undergoing economic change which creates conflicts between the goals of maintaining basic individual freedom and extending the program of socialism.

WHAT IS COMMUNISM?

It is not always easy to distinguish between socialism and *communism*. Karl Marx (1818—1883), a German, was the founder of modern communism. Marx insisted that only by revolution could definite social change be accomplished. In the *Communist Manifesto* he states that the "history of all hitherto existing society is the history of class struggles." Since history offered Marx no notable example where a major economic system freely gave way to another system, he felt that communism could be attained only through revolutionary measures.

Marx, however, saw in socialism merely the one step between capitalism and communism. He argued that the inherent weaknesses of capitalism would become apparent in the course of time and then chaos and anarchy would follow. At this point, Marx argued, the masses of the people would rise up, seize economic property and power, and set up a *dictatorship of the proletariat* (working people). The resulting order would be a form of dictatorial socialism. In theory those in charge of government would represent the working people, not the propertied classes as is the case, according to Marx, under capitalism.

After dictatorship of the proletariat has been established and the government has assumed control of all economic, social, and political activities, the people will be educated to understand and to believe in communism. The communists hold that eventually everyone will come to accept communism and to love it to such an extent that political government will not be necessary and will "wither away."

Communism makes no pretense of advocating freedom in the sense that we understand the term. It holds that, when socialism of the type Marx had in mind is established, freedom to oppose the policies established by the leaders in power could not be permitted. Religion is opposed, particularly the Christian religion, because it tends to prevent people from using violent means in resisting injustice. Religion is called an "opiate" of the working class because it teaches meekness and kindness rather than resentment when injustice occurs.

THE NATURE OF SOCIALISM IN THE UNION OF THE SOVIET SOCIALIST REPUBLICS (USSR)

After the revolution in Russia in 1917, the communists tried to set up a communistic state. There were fewer than 100,000 communists out of a population of 150 million, but they were well organized. By various methods they gained control of the army and government.

Under the new order all the features of communism that we have listed above were to be put into practice. The undertaking, however, was too great, although untold numbers were killed in an attempt to compel everyone to accept the new system. Lenin and Trotsky, who headed the Russian Revolution, advocated worldwide revolution and dictatorship by the proletariat. Eventually the leaders had to compromise by adopting a system of dictatorial socialism.

Government of the USSR. In Russia there is only one political party, the All-Union Communist Party. Positions in government are limited to those who are known to be "good" communists. Those who have not shown the right degree of enthusiasm for the government and its leaders are expelled from the party and in many cases punished with a loss of position, imprisonment, or even death. Organizations of the party are found in each community, and in every case they are under the leadership of a zealous communist. Theoretically, anyone may be nominated for public office, but in practically all cases the candidate favored by the Communist Party receives from 98 to 100 percent of all votes cast!

The USSR is made up of fifteen autonomous (self-governing) Union republics and a number of national areas or territories. The highest legislative body is the *Supreme Soviet* (Council), which is made up of the Soviet of the Union and the Soviet of the Nationalities.

The constitution of the USSR. The constitution of the USSR, adopted in 1936, states that the nation is "a socialist state of workers and peasants." It declares that "He does not work, neither shall he eat," and "From each according to his ability, to each according to his work." (Marxian socialism adopted the slogan "From each according to his ability, to each according to his need.") Under the constitution, freedom and religion are "guaranteed" — but, of course, the exercise of these rights must not interfere with the plans of the government. (No member of the Communist Party is a member of a church because communism has no place for religion.) Every citizen 18 years of age may vote.

The economy of the USSR. Although the Soviet economy is very complex, some indications of its nature can be found in statements from *Social Science: A Textbook for Soviet Secondary Schools.**

> In the Soviet Union the means of production belong to the Soviet society.
> State property is managed not by all of the people but by state establishments and enterprises which are part of the overall entity which is the state.
> Under socialism all production is subordinated to the task of boosting the economy.
> Hence the absolute necessity of a *preferential development of the production of the means of production over the production of consumer goods.*
> Socialist production, its scale and rhythm, demands an absolute and very strict *labor discipline.*
> To Each According to His Labor.
> The national economic plans express the policy of our Party and are an important means for the implementation of that policy.
> The production of commodities, their distribution and exchange takes place in the Soviet Union not without controls, but on the basis of unified national economic plans.

---

*G. Kh. Shakhnazrov, et al. Moscow: State Publishing House, 1963.

As indicated by these statements, all production is carried on according to plans which are set up under the direction of the national planning body, the *Gosplan*. These plans run from five to seven years.

Private property, such as tools or equipment used by an individual, is permitted; but any articles produced for sale by the individual with its use are heavily taxed. The hiring of labor to use private property for production purposes is illegal and heavily penalized. Thus, most of the economy functions through state industries, state factories, state farms, collective farms, state wholesale establishments, state retail stores, and state health, welfare, and other service agencies.

In the USSR the square miles of land resources are more than double, and the population is about 18 percent greater than that of the United States. However, Soviet gross national product is estimated to be one-half to two-thirds as large as that of the United States. Soviet emphasis is on capital goods production. Much of this must be used to provide military materials and other assistance to areas that are Soviet satellites or security buffer zones. Consequently, the consumption of personal products per capita tends to be less than consumer consumption in the United States.

COMMUNISM HAS GROWN RAPIDLY

The czarist regime in Russia was overthrown by the Communists in 1917. After several years of confusion and uncertainty, the New Economic

SOME ECONOMIC COMPARISONS — USA vs. USSR

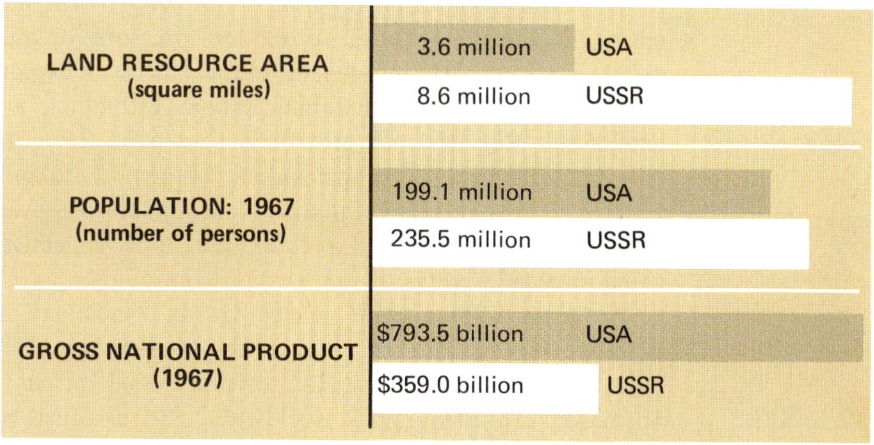

LAND RESOURCE AREA (square miles)	3.6 million	USA
	8.6 million	USSR
POPULATION: 1967 (number of persons)	199.1 million	USA
	235.5 million	USSR
GROSS NATIONAL PRODUCT (1967)	$793.5 billion	USA
	$359.0 billion	USSR

Figure 28-2.

SOURCES: *Statistical Abstract of the United States, 1969*, and *The Institute for Strategic Studies* (London).

In the USSR the square miles of land resources are more than double, and the population is about 18 percent greater than that of the United States.

ECONOMIC GROWTH RATES: USA vs. USSR (1940-1967)
Capital Investment, Personal Consumption, and Agricultural Production (1940 = 100)

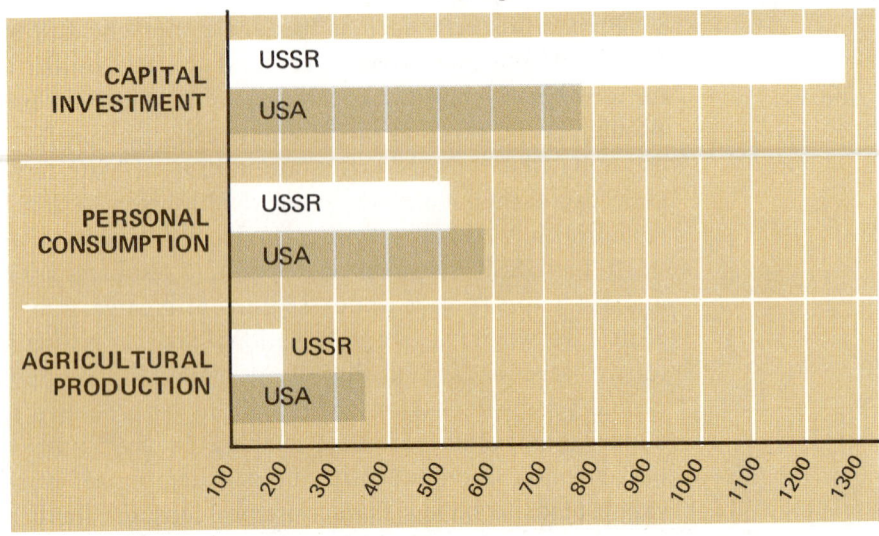

Figure 28-3.

SOURCES: *Statistical Abstract of the United States, 1969*, and official Soviet data.

Soviet emphasis is on capital goods production. Personal products per capita tends to be less than consumer consumption in the United States.

Policy (NEP) was established in 1921, partially restoring private enterprise. But by 1933 the government had practically established complete and ruthless control of all production. Following World War II, a number of nations in Europe, through subversion, pressure, or military action, were allied with Russian communism. In the process of expansion some nations were annexed, such as Estonia, Latvia, Lithuania, and parts of other countries. But the real growth is shown in the number of satellites, Albania, Bulgaria, Czechoslovakia, Hungary, Poland, Rumania, and Eastern Germany. The Cuban revolution in 1959 was followed by the establishment in 1962 of a communist-type collective leadership; and Cuba joined the ranks of the Russian communists.

Moscow holds to the belief that its "socialist" ideology must be dominant in the world. Consequently, the Brezhnev Doctrine of applying force in Czechoslovakia was to preserve "socialism" in the Marxian sense. Since socialist ideology is worldwide, Russia must back revolutionary socialist groups within all countries. The Soviets do not tend to supply military manpower. Support is given through foreign aid material programs in which the major Russian sacrifice is limited to lowered personal consumption at home.

Meanwhile, by 1950, practically all of China had been overrun by the communist forces of Mao Tse-Tung, the communist leader. Thus, more than half a billion Chinese willingly or otherwise accepted international revolutionary communism — along with China's satellites, North Korea, North Vietnam, and Tibet.

The communists also claim to have several million followers in non-communist countries. This number may be exaggerated, but in other European, African, and Asiatic countries, and also in some Latin American countries, there are enough communists and socialists to create constant concern and problems for the nations of the free world.

WHAT IS TOTALITARIANISM?

Under a system of *totalitarianism* the state takes possession of the rights of all, and no one has a right unless it is given to him by the state. In its glorification of the state, there is no respect for a democratic form of government; and there is a complete dictatorship of the economy under a leader. Germany, Italy, and Japan can be cited as three examples of the rise of totalitarian economies following World War I.

(1) Germany's Nazism. The term *Nazism* was used to refer to the teaching of the National Socialist German Worker's Party, which was founded in 1919. Its leader, the "Führer," was Adolph Hitler.

(2) Italy's fascism. The term *fascism* is derived from the Latin *fascis* meaning "bundle," which denoted the power of authority. It was a system originally designed to combat communism and disorder. Benito Mussolini, who was called *Il Duce* — the leader — exercised the control of the movement.

(3) Japan's co-prosperity. The term *co-prosperity* was used to designate the economic benefits for a united Asia under Japanese or Oriental control. The Japanese Samurai (militarists) supported the movement through their code of "bushido" or feudal loyalty to the Emperor. The Emperor, acting as the divine ruler, was a figurehead; actual power was exercised by Tojo, who represented the Samurai and upper classes.

The economy under totalitarianism. The common elements of these nations' economies included: (1) The right of private property and production for profit — as simulated capitalism — was under strict governmental control; (2) the organization of industries and businesses was under a leadership responsible to the government; (3) workers were organized and subjected to wage and other controls; (4) workers were forbidden to strike and were required to cooperate with management; and (5) all activities of production, exchange, and distribution were dedicated to the purposes of the state.

Totalitarianism is opposed to democracy. A reverence for militarism, a fervor for colonial expansion, and a belief in national or racial superiority are intended to provide its emotional appeal.

World War II was fought to abolish the dictatorships that had been established in Germany, Italy, and Japan. As we know, the war was won by the Allies, and the three dictatorships were destroyed. It would be a mistake, however, to assume that the ideas and philosophies of fascism and Nazism have disappeared from the world.

IS OUR ECONOMIC AND SOCIAL SYSTEM IN DANGER?

Communism holds that all nations should adopt dictatorial socialism as the next step toward communism. From Karl Marx to the present-day communists, communism has taught that practically any means are justified to hasten the downfall of capitalism — sabotage, the creation of class and group hatreds, measures that will increase government debt and produce inflation, the fomentation of strikes and industrial discontent, propaganda favorable to communism, and revolution by armed might.

After the end of World War II, communists redoubled their efforts to gain power in the world. In some cases they managed to gain control of government. In other cases they sought to win converts and to create conditions that would hasten the coming of communism, which they regard as inevitable. By 1950 our people had become alarmed by the threat of armed aggression by Russia and Red China and hurriedly began to rebuild our military strength.

Today many nations — the United States and the Soviet Union especially — are spending much of their labor and material resources in building up their military strengths on a scale that is almost beyond our imagination. One prominent Russian is reported to have said, "A communist has no right to be a mere onlooker." If this philosophy prevails in a country where the individual has little freedom of decision, how much more important it becomes in America that we be a nation of "doers" — active supporters of democratic principles.

The diversion of America's various resources to armaments has prevented the use of those same resources for other pressing domestic needs. Thus, strains that resulted from unmet needs in housing, urban development, mass transportation, environmental improvement, and other areas have contributed to social and economic domestic unrest and frictions. A similar situation prevailed in the USSR. For both nations

Ch. 28 NATIONS WITH OTHER ECONOMIC SYSTEMS

STRATEGIC MILITARY BALANCE — USSR vs. USA
September 1970

DELIVERY SYSTEM	USSR DELIVERY VEHICLES	USSR MEGATONNAGE (APPROXIMATE)	USA DELIVERY VEHICLES	USA MEGATONNAGE (APPROXIMATE)
Early Model ICBMs	220 SS-6s, SS-7s, SS-8s	1,100	54 Titans	270
Small ICBMs	800 SS-11s, SS-13s	800	1,000 Minutemen	1,000
Large ICBMs	300 SS-9s	7,500	0	0
Orbital Bombardment System and Fractional OBS	Developed, probably operational, number unknown	30-100 each	0	0
Sub Launched Ballistic Missiles	280 SSN-6s, Serbs and Sarks	200	656 Polaris	460
Sub Launched Cruise Missiles	300 Shaddocks	30	0	0
Intermediate and Medium Range Ballistic Missiles	700 SS-4s, SS-5s and SS-14s	700	0	0
Heavy Bombers	200 Bisons and Bears	Variable	550 B-52s	Variable
Medium Bombers	700 Badgers and Blinders	Variable	0	0
Totals*	3,500	10,330	2,260	1,730

*(Megatonnage totals do not include Heavy or Medium Bomber payloads or Orbital Bombardment System Warheads.)

Figure 28-4.

SOURCE: American Security Council.

Today many nations — the United States and the Soviet Union especially — are spending much of their labor and material resources in building up their military strength.

the production possibility theory indicates that a limitation of demand for armaments would make possible the shifting of armament resources to other possible economic uses.

Consequently, in 1970 the U.S. and the Soviet Union began a series of Strategic Arms Limitation Treaty (SALT) talks in Vienna. Should these talks result in a mutual treaty, a reallocation of resources could be made by both nations. This reallocation would relieve many of the tensions caused by domestic shortages. It would also enable the American economy to expand its role in lessening the external tensions which have been increasing in the underdeveloped nations.

SUMMARY

The economic system of any nation is subject to change. Change can be evolutionary or revolutionary. In recent years, certain nations have undertaken revolutionary changes in their economic systems which were accomplished in ways varying from peaceful and democratic to violent and dictatorial.

Socialism advocates collective ownership of land, capital, and other material means of production. Production for use of society is substituted for production for profit. Britain's socialism, which was democratically adopted, resulted in the nationalization of some or all of the areas of: (1) finance, (2) fuel and power, (3) transportation and communication, (4) steel, (5) social welfare, (6) national health, and (7) land-use and planning.

Communism was explained and advocated by Karl Marx. It is similar to socialism since it advocates the social and collective ownership of all instruments of production, the elimination of the profit motive, and the adoption of a program of cooperation through comprehensive planning. Unlike democratic socialism, it maintains a dictatorship over the people under the control of a minority power group. This system has spread rapidly since World War I. Some nations follow Russian communism which is presently less militant and violent than that of Chinese communism; all forms of communism use continuous efforts to bring about the common goal of total worldwide communism.

Totalitarianism, as expressed by fascism and Nazism, permits private ownership of production resources, but the state directs what will be produced and to whom production will go. The individual is subordinate to the state and owes all of his allegiance to the state and its dictator. The major forms have included Nazism in Germany, fascism in Italy, and co-prosperity in Japan. Dictators were eliminated by their defeat in World War II, but the totalitarian system still exists in certain nations.

Our society and economic system is not that of pure capitalism, as that term once implied. We do not practice a system of pure individualism in which everyone is free to do as he pleases. We use democratic government to restrain those who would disregard the rights of others; to provide certain services that can be best provided by government, and without unduly encroaching on the rights of individuals; and we adopt certain general public policies that are designed to encourage business. We emphasize the essential importance of individual freedom and private enterprise.

In this way we believe we can meet successfully the threat of totalitarianism and dictatorship. Whether we will be successful depends on our intelligence, our capacity for self-discipline, and our determination to live as a free people.

NEW TERMS

communism
Communist Manifesto
co-prosperity
dictatorship of the proletariat
fascism

Gosplan
Nazism
socialism
Supreme Soviet
totalitarianism

QUESTIONS ON THE CHAPTER

1. What differences are there between socialism and free enterprise or capitalism?

2. What are the socialist criticisms of, or charges against, capitalism?
3. How do those who believe in our economic system reply to the criticisms of the socialists?
4. What is "the program of socialism"?
5. What is meant by "the policy of socialism"?
6. What is the form of economic and political order in Great Britain?
7. How does British socialism differ from Soviet and Chinese socialism?
8. How did the Conservatives change the British economy following 1951?
9. Do "Marxian socialism" and "communism" mean the same thing? Explain.
10. What is meant by "the dictatorship of the proletariat"?
11. What did Karl Marx mean by a "withering away of the state" or government?
12. What differences are there between communism and free enterprise or capitalism?
13. How does communism differ from socialism?
14. Does Russia have a form of socialism? Explain.
15. To what extent does the constitution of the USSR profess to guarantee freedom to the individual? How meaningful is this guarantee?
16. What are the main features of the economy of the USSR?
17. What were the common elements in the economies of fascistic totalitarian states?
18. What were the common elements in the political systems of fascistic totalitarianism?
19. To what extent did fascistic totalitarianism resemble communism and socialism?
20. What, if anything, did fascism and Nazism have in common with capitalism?
21. What is the significance of the SALT negotiations?

APPLYING YOUR ECONOMIC UNDERSTANDING

1. Explain the connection between a cold war and the changing nature of economic systems. Cite some specific examples of involved nations.
2. Cite some specific examples of the ownership of productive wealth by governmental units in the United States. Are they forms of socialism? Defend your answer.
3. Socialism attempts to reduce the inequality of wealth and incomes of persons in society. To what extent has this been achieved in the Russian society?
4. Imperialism is a national policy in which one nation for its own interests seeks to control other nations. This can be accomplished by the exercise of military or physical force. Can it also be done by means of giving or lending money or the withholding of funds as a means of control? Cite some nations which are termed "imperialistic."
5. Name some nations which practice socialism in part in their economic system but have retained political democracy. In what ways do they differ from socialist countries which are undemocratic?

6. Judging from our practice in foreign economic policy, what does our nation believe is the surest safeguard against the adoption or continuance of socialism in the countries which we are aiding?
7. Some writers believe that "creeping" socialism is spreading in the United States. Do you agree with this viewpoint? What facts support your answer?
8. How does the charge that capitalism through competition wastes and destroys natural resources relate to present-day problems of ecology?
9. In 1956, Hungary attempted a revolution to break away from the Soviet Union. Discuss this in terms of the Moscow belief that its "socialist" ideology must be dominant in the world.

CHALLENGES TO ECONOMIC COMPETENCE

1. Prepare a bulletin board display showing a comparison between the United States and a nation with a different type of economy. Compare elements such as economic growth, national production, personal income, prices, cost of living, level of living, agriculture, labor, and personal freedom.
2. Arrange a panel discussion on the topic "Economic Growth With Freedom."
3. Prepare a five-minute oral report on one of the following topics: (a) The Conflicting Economic Interests of Russia and the United States, (b) The Rise and Fall of Nazism, (c) Italy under Fascism, (d) Life in Communist China, (e) A Review of the Fabian Society, (f) Karl Marx, A Prophet of Doom, (g) East Berlin — West Berlin: A Contrast of Economies.
4. Prepare a vertical file folder for each type of economic system. Collect appropriate materials and assemble them in each folder. Donate the completed projects to your school library for use as resource references.

Chapter 29

Our Interest in the Underdeveloped Nations

What is an "underdeveloped nation"?
What is necessary for the economic development of a nation?
Why do we have an interest in the developing nations?
What can or should we do to help other nations?

In practically every community in this country there are some unfortunate families whose impoverishment forces them to live in inadequate houses and to wear shabby clothing. Public and private welfare organizations, however, usually provide these poor people with at least a subsistence, if not an adequate, living. Thus, even in a country as affluent as ours, poverty is not unknown. Fortunately, however, the problem is recognized; and our resources permit us to take continuous action toward its solution.

It is hard for Americans to realize that hundreds of millions of people in some parts of the world today are always hungry; that such people are destined to a short life span because of malnourishment and disease; and that infants are born to die because adequate food is not available. Where are these people? Some are close enough to be regarded as our immediate neighbors; and in the jet age, even people on the other side of the globe are very close in terms of time.

With increased emphasis the world has been hearing and reading about the less-developed, developing, or underdeveloped nations. Their problems have, in a measure, become our problems, and their future may greatly affect the future of the United States.

WHAT IS AN UNDERDEVELOPED NATION?

It is rather difficult to draw a definite line of demarcation between a "developed" and an "underdeveloped" nation. Perhaps the best way to compare the degree of national economic development is by comparing the amount of per capita income in those nations that have achieved a high degree of economic development with the per capita incomes in those nations regarded as less developed. For example — using United States State Department 1970 data as the source of the latest comparative statistics — in 1969 the per capita income in the United States was over $3,750, whereas in India, Pakistan, and Haiti it was less than $200.

Of course, there are other nations — Guatemala in Central America; Brazil in South America; Indonesia in Southeast Asia; Syria and Yemen in the Near East; and Malawi and Burundi in Africa, to mention just a few — where per capita income is also exceedingly low.

In some cases a nation's poverty may be attributable to adverse climatic conditions, as in desert areas; sometimes to overpopulation, as in India; again, to soil conditions unfavorable to agricultural development, as in the arid steppe of East Jordan; still others lack mineral and water-power resources. The term *underdeveloped* implies that natural resources are very limited or that the human and natural resources of a country have not been adequately utilized.

It is impossible to say just how many people in the world have incomes that permit them to maintain a decent scale of living. But on the basis of studies that have been made, two thirds of the world's population subsists on less than one sixth of the world's income. One and one-half billion

Illus. 29-1. The term "underdeveloped" implies that natural resources are very limited or that human and natural resources of a country have not been adequately utilized.

POPULATION OF THE LESS DEVELOPED COUNTRIES OF THE NONCOMMUNIST WORLD

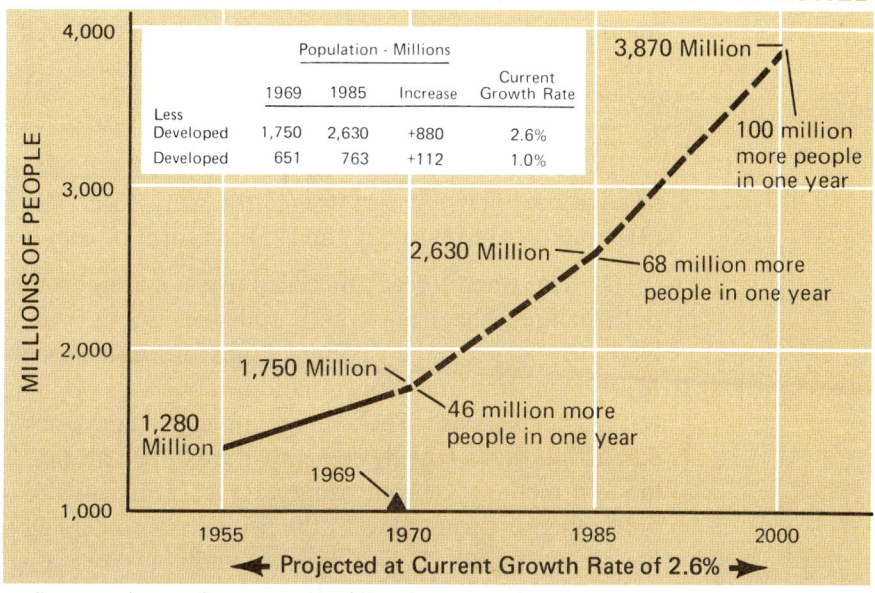

	Population - Millions			Current Growth Rate
	1969	1985	Increase	
Less Developed	1,750	2,630	+880	2.6%
Developed	651	763	+112	1.0%

- 1955: 1,280 Million
- 1969: 1,750 Million — 46 million more people in one year
- 1985: 2,630 Million — 68 million more people in one year
- 2000: 3,870 Million — 100 million more people in one year

← Projected at Current Growth Rate of 2.6% →

Figure 29-1.

SOURCE: Agency for International Development.

The world population explosion threatens the underdeveloped nations with prospects of intensified poverty.

people in a hundred developing lands are affected by every kind of deprivation that leaves them ill-fed, ill-clothed, ill-housed, and illiterate.

The world *population explosion*, that is, a rapidly rising birthrate coupled with medical advances which have increased life expectancy, threatens the underdeveloped nations with prospects of intensified poverty. Since the less-developed nations tend to have the greatest rate of population growth, and since they are least able to provide high scales of living, their peoples have become increasingly restless and tense.

THE UNDERDEVELOPED NATIONS ARE IN FERMENT

For a long time the people in the developing regions of the world have been discontented. But it seems that since World War II they have become determined to do something about trying to raise their scales of living. Former colonial possessions of European powers in many cases have declared their independence, which has been duly recognized. But these newly formed nations have not been able to increase the incomes of the people to a satisfactory level, and discord follows. Moreover, the people of nations long established — such as those in South America —

have lived for long decades in poverty. They, too, have become conscious of the injustices that may exist in a nation comprised of very poor and very rich families; and they, too, are trying to find a way by which the economic condition of the "little man" may be improved.

WHAT IS NECESSARY FOR A NATION TO ACHIEVE ECONOMIC DEVELOPMENT?

There are five factors that are essential in the economic development of a nation. These factors are (1) the work force; (2) material resources; (3) capital; (4) technology; and (5) the form of economic order.

(1) The work force. In order for a nation to develop its economic potentialities, there must be a sufficient number of workers of various kinds to carry on the different kinds of work that must be performed. Most of the underdeveloped nations have large populations in proportion to their land areas. The average life expectancy, however, is short compared with that in the more highly developed nations. But with the use of modern methods of combating germ-carrying insects, and other ways of preventing or curing disease, the people are now living longer. The longer life span, combined with their fecundity, is resulting in a tremendous boom in population. Since job opportunities are lacking, most of those who are able to work find it impossible to become fully employed. Moreover, in many cases it has long been the custom for the family unit to seek self-sufficiency — thus sacrificing the efficiency of specialization and the roundabout process in production.

In parts of tropical Africa, for instance, where so many new nations have been formed in recent years, the productivity of an agricultural worker is low. It takes, on an average, six persons — men, women, and children — to raise enough food to supply their own needs and those of one additional non-food-growing adult. Contrast this with the productivity of the agricultural workers in this country where 5.4 percent of the workers supply a vast excess beyond the needs of a population of over 197 million. One very important psychological factor helps to explain this situation — the African has long-established attitudes toward work. Certain types of work are definitely regarded as unworthy of a male, and to participate in such forms of labor is to lose prestige in the community. Men have long been accustomed to a great deal of leisure, and among a people where money is not yet a dominant value the laborer is not likely to be highly productive.

(2) Material resources. Some of the less-developed countries have limited quantities of varieties of natural resources; but others are extremely fortunate in this respect. Perhaps the growing importance of Africa in world affairs is the result of the vast resources of minerals, timber, and water power of that continent. There are important sources of beryllium in Southern Rhodesia; chrome in Katanga; cobalt in Nyasaland; diamonds and manganese in Ghana; platinum in the Republic of South Africa; and tin in Nigeria. In other less fortunate areas, needed resources must be purchased if the nation is to develop its industrial potentials.

(3) Capital. It is impossible for a country to achieve a high level of development without proper tools and machines. The accumulation of capital goods is made possible by diverting labor from the production of

STRATEGIC IMPORTS ARE ESSENTIAL TO OUR INDUSTRY

Mineral	Import %
NICKEL	92%
TIN	100%
COBALT	90%
PLATINUM	95%
BERYLLIUM	96%
MANGANESE	98%
INDUSTRIAL DIAMONDS	100%
NATURAL RUBBER	100%
CHROME	90%
ANTIMONY	90%
FLUORSPAR	71%
BAUXITE	90%

Imports / U.S. Production

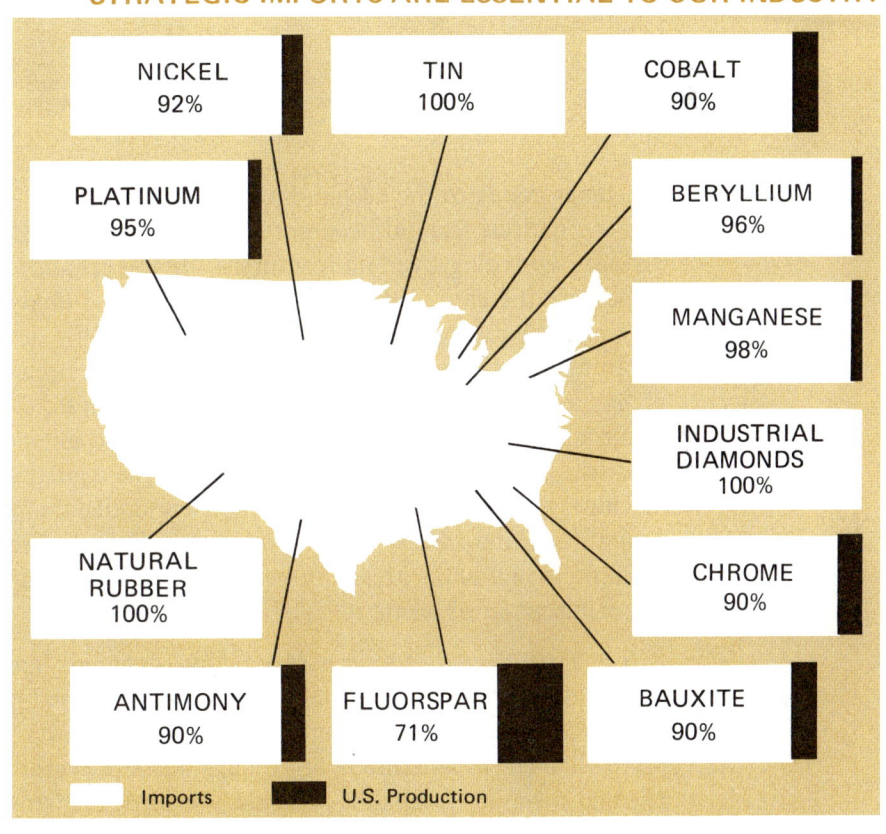

Figure 29-2.

Source: Department of State.

There are important sources of beryllium in Southern Rhodesia; chrome in Kantanga; cobalt in Nyasaland; diamonds and manganese in Ghana; platinum in the Republic of South Africa; and tin in Nigeria.

Illus. 29-2. It is impossible for a country to achieve a high level of development without proper tools and machines.

consumer goods to the accumulation of capital goods. In the case of the western nations, capital accumulation and maintenance has been a long process, extending over the centuries. If the less-developed nations are to acquire the capital they need for any marked increase in production, they must acquire much of it from the more highly developed nations.

In many of these areas capital had previously been supplied by enterprisers in the nations which had established colonies. But the tremendous upsurge in nationalism in these newly proclaimed independent nations has made the present leaders eager to undertake the regulation of the economic machinery — and reluctant to see industry under the control of "foreign capital." Enterprisers, on the other hand, have been understandably hesitant to invest in areas where political unrest might easily result in the confiscation of property.

(4) Technology. Modern production demands much technical skill and "know-how," which is lacking in underdeveloped nations. Any large construction job, such as building a dam or a power plant, or building roads through mountainous or swampy terrain, requires the use of complicated machinery capable of doing the work of many humans. Transportation has been revolutionized by the use of trucks, trains, and airplanes. Helicopters capable of carrying a small house have been devised. Building construction in any of our large cities utilizes cranes and concrete mixers, and various other types of machinery, whereas in Hong Kong,

UNITED STATES OVERSEAS LOANS AND GRANTS, BY TYPE AND AREA, FISCAL YEARS 1962–68[1]

(Millions of dollars)

Type of program and fiscal period	Total	Near East and South Asia	Latin America	Vietnam	East Asia	Africa	Europe	Other and non-regional
Economic loans and grants to less developed countries, by program:[2]								
Net obligations and loan authorizations:								
1962–67 average	4,538	1,576	1,163	347	446	397	167	442
1968	4,445	1,279	1,362	444	468	337	21	534
Repayments and interest:								
1962–67 average	678	245	273	11	53	27	60	8
1968	976	348	393	4	64	48	113	7
Agency for International Development:								
Net obligations and loan authorizations:								
1962–67 average	2,297	764	557	278	226	209	2	261
1968	1,891	440	496	304	230	116	*	304
Repayments and interest:								
1962–67 average	196	108	20	11	21	16	17	3
1968	270	148	50	3	26	25	18	1

[1]Some data are preliminary.

[2]Countries have been classified "less developed" on the basis of the standard list of less developed countries used by the Development Assistance Committee of the Organization for Economic Cooperation and Development. On this basis, "less developed" countries include all countries receiving U.S. loans or grants except the following which are considered "developed:" Japan, Australia, New Zealand, Republic of South Africa, Canada, and all of Europe except Malta, Spain, and Yugoslavia.

SOURCE: Agency for International Development.

If the less-developed nations are to acquire the capital they need for any marked increase in production, they must acquire much of it from the more highly developed nations.

barefoot workers carry buckets of cement as they climb up bamboo scaffolding so that an apartment house may rise slowly on the hillside. But the tools and machinery of technology also require persons skilled in their operations and in their maintenance.

Commercial farming in modern nations, where much use is made of tractors and other improved farm machinery, is a far cry from farming in parts of Southeast Asia where the carabao still pulls a crude wooden plow.

(5) The form of economic and political order. Modern production requires cooperation by means of specialization in production. This procedure results in a growing interdependence among the people. Therefore, the goods produced by an individual or a group must become available for use by others. Whatever one individual contributes to production must be paid for in terms of money, which can be used to buy what others produce. It is easy to see, therefore, why a system of social and political order is necessary.

In the developing countries only two classes exist — the rich and the poor. There is no large middle class as there is in the United States, Canada, England, and other nations that have made great economic progress. If the wealth is controlled by a few families, a disproportionate amount of the productive energies of the people will be utilized to provide the luxuries for this group. In the case of the developed nations, the wide dispersion of wealth and income results in a market for a greater variety of goods and services.

WHAT ARE THE CONDITIONS IN THE UNDERDEVELOPED NATIONS?

The relatively large populations in the less-developed countries would be able to supply an adequate work force, provided there were sufficient jobs available and the workers had the proper training and attitudes. In many parts of the world, manual labor is regarded as degrading. Some of the countries have excellent supplies of raw materials and are blessed with many natural resources, but the processes for utilizing these resources are not available. In other cases, resources have suffered a reduction in value, as, for instance, the supplies of natural rubber in Malaysia, which are not so valuable as they once were since man has discovered the secret of making synthetic rubber. If these populations are to achieve any degree of rapid progress in production, they must obtain capital goods from other countries. Technicians must be sent who will teach the young in these areas to operate machines and to master the techniques of modern management. A certain stability must be established in their social, economic, and political orders.

OUR INTEREST IN THE PROBLEMS OF THE UNDERDEVELOPED NATIONS

Why should you or any student be interested in the economic problems of Thailand, Afghanistan, or Yemen, or any of the other economically underdeveloped countries where the majority of the people are poor and restless? It might seem that there are enough problems of our own to keep us busy.

True, there are many economic problems — both personal and national. At the same time, if the situation is examined carefully, the problems which at first appear to be purely domestic are related to the problems

Ch. 29   OUR INTEREST IN THE UNDERDEVELOPED NATIONS

VOLUNTARY CONTRIBUTIONS TO MULTILATERAL ORGANIZATIONS
Proposed Fy 1971 Programs — $ millions

- UN Development Program $100.0
- UN Children's Fund $13.0
- UN Population Program $7.5 [1]
- Int'l Atomic Energy Agency Operational Program $1.55
- World Meteorological Org. Voluntary Program $1.5
- FAO, World Food Program $1.5
- Special Contributions to Vietnam $0.95
- Other Technical Assistance $0.62 [2]
- UNRWA $13.3
- UN Force in Cyprus $6.0
- Arab Refugee Vocational Training (UNRWA) $1.0
- Indus Basin
  - Loans $7.96
  - Grants $5.85

Total Fy 1971 Programs $160.7 Million

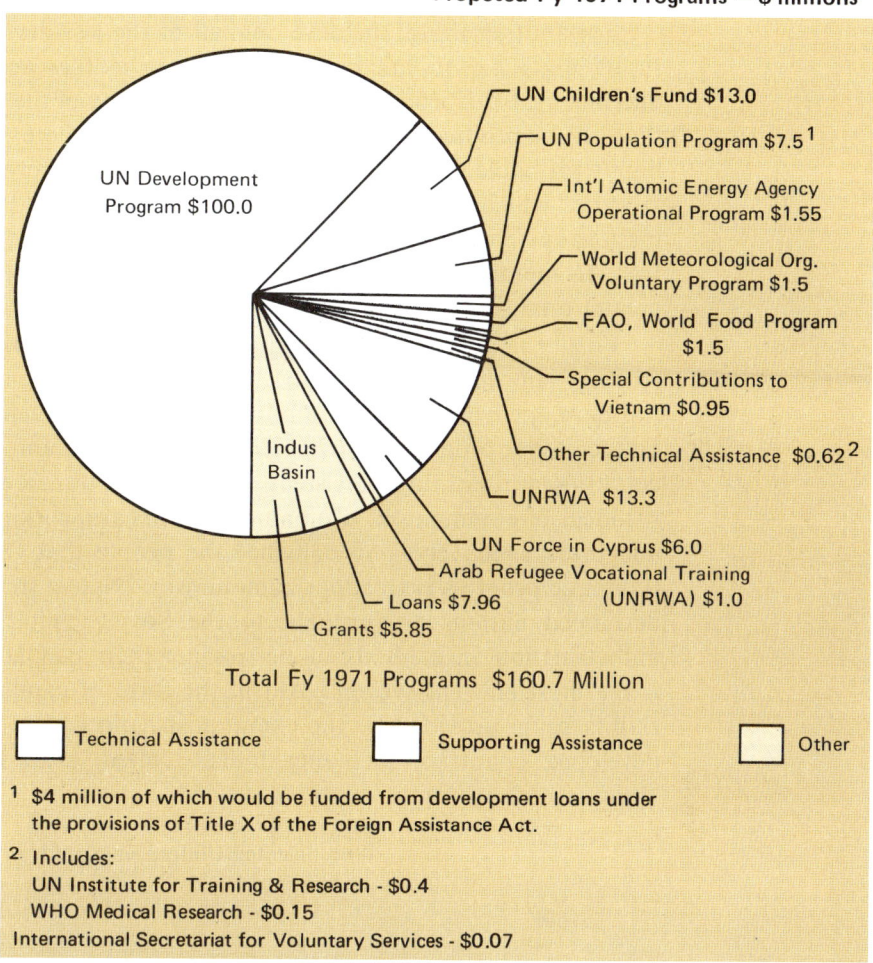

☐ Technical Assistance   ☐ Supporting Assistance   ☐ Other

[1] $4 million of which would be funded from development loans under the provisions of Title X of the Foreign Assistance Act.

[2] Includes:
UN Institute for Training & Research - $0.4
WHO Medical Research - $0.15
International Secretariat for Voluntary Services - $0.07

Figure 29-3.

SOURCE: Agency for International Development.

Interest should be taken in the problems of the underdeveloped nations.

of other nations. It will be discovered, too, that other people, both in the advanced and in the underdeveloped nations, have problems the solution of which may definitely affect our lives.

So it may be concluded that there are three very good reasons why an interest should be taken in the problems of other peoples around the globe who are trying to achieve a better life. For one thing, if it is known how poor and poverty-stricken most of the people in the developing nations are, one cannot help feeling sympathetic toward them. Individual humanitarian impulses make it impossible to ignore their misery while others are enjoying the benefits of their own good fortune.

For another thing, the development of the less-developed nations can result in great economic benefit to us. For as they acquire more wealth and income from production, they can buy many of the goods and services that can be produced in excess of what is needed here at home. It is also highly probable that these nations would be able to produce certain commodities which could be enjoyed and added to our standard of living: mahogany from Africa, silk from Thailand, tin from Bolivia, oil from Iran, to mention just a few articles that are needed or could be used in greater quantities.

Finally — and perhaps most people would say this is the most urgent reason — in their eagerness to improve their economic condition, the less-developed nations may adopt communism as their form of political and economic order. The Soviet Union, Red China, and other communistic countries are working persistently to sell the underdeveloped countries the ideas of communism. Communist agents are working continuously — and often effectively — to convince the people that their only hope for economic progress is to adopt communism. Native students from underdeveloped nations are brought to the Soviet Union for training and indoctrination in methods of persuading their people that communism is the most efficient system. Aid in the form of capital and engineering skill is being provided by the communist nations to a number of underdeveloped countries, including India, United Arab Republic (Egypt),

GROWTH IN SOVIET TOTAL TRADE*
With Selected Underdeveloped Non-Communist Nations

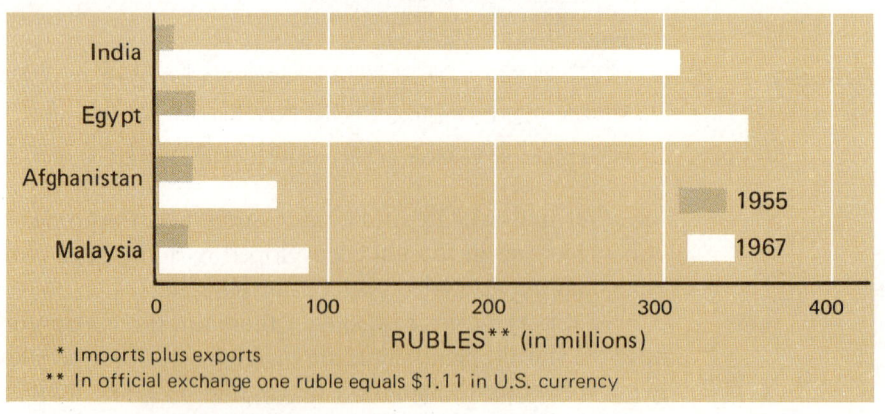

* Imports plus exports
** In official exchange one ruble equals $1.11 in U.S. currency

Figure 29-4.

SOURCE: *UN Monthly Bulletin of Statistics.*

Afghanistan, and others. It seems evident that the Soviet Union and China are spending considerable sums of money and much effort to win the South American countries to their political and economic ideas. "What good is freedom if you are hungry?" is an expression commonly heard in these nations.

Close to one third of the people in the world live under communist government. Of the remaining two thirds, more than half live in nations and regions that are considered poorly developed. If these people adopt communism, then the free governments in the rest of the world will be endangered.

WHAT CAN BE DONE TO HELP UNDERDEVELOPED COUNTRIES?

It has already been indicated in a general way what must be done if the economically backward nations are to become more productive and if the people are to achieve a higher level of living. But how shall it be done?

Temporary relief and aid programs. A basic food supply is a prime necessity for life; thus, people who are presently faced with starvation — however caused — cannot wait until a future food supply can be produced. To breach this gap between existing food shortages and minimal food needs, the people of the United States have initiated and are operating two major programs. One, *Food for Freedom*, is a governmental program that operates under Public Laws 83-480 and 88-638. Under this program, food produced in the United States is made available to certain countries whose current food supplies are inadequate. Each year, food valued at over $1.3 billion is donated or sold on liberal credit terms by our government to the less-developed nations. The second program, *CARE* (Cooperative for American Relief Everywhere), is operated by a private charitable organization that collects donations and then sends food packages to people in the critical food shortage areas. In addition, food is also made available to less-developed nations for distribution through orphanages and other local groups. CARE also sends gift packages that contain critically needed seeds, hand tools, school supplies, and other essentials to underprivileged peoples. The latter is a first step toward making local areas economically self-sufficient.

Health service is also a vital need that is in short supply in underdeveloped countries. *HOPE* (Health Opportunity for People Everywhere), operated by the People-to-People Health Foundation, is one of the many such private organizations in the health services field. Under the HOPE program, a hospital ship equipped with medical supplies and trained

Illus. 29-3. CARE is operated by a private charitable organization that collects donations and sends food packages to people in the critical food shortage areas.

personnel brings medical and surgical services to health-deficient areas. It also helps, during its visit, to train, retrain, and upgrade native or local medical personnel so that they may better serve their own countrymen.

Loans and grants for production purposes. The most direct way of helping the underdeveloped nations is to lend or give them the money or capital needed to enable them to increase production. During the second World War and since that time financial aid has been extended to many nations all over the world. Much of what was loaned is used to buy capital goods in this country, and thus has desirable effects on production and employment in this country. The total amount of these loans and grants from the United States runs into many billions of dollars.

It is generally agreed that our aid to the developing nations should be in the form of long-term loans. Then when, and if, the nations develop, they can repay the loans. This has been the idea behind the efforts of the International Monetary Fund, the World Bank, and the International Development Association. The money for such loans, however, must be

Ch. 29   OUR INTEREST IN THE UNDERDEVELOPED NATIONS 485

Illus. 29-4. Under the HOPE program, a hospital ship equipped with medical supplies and trained personnel brings medical and surgical services to health-deficient areas.

HOPE

obtained from the people of this country or from banks. After the loans are made, if the recipients of the loans are unable to meet their obligations, interest on the total amount must be paid by the American taxpayer.

The World Bank and IDA have been of great help in many productive projects undertaken in the nations under discussion. By 1969, these agencies had made over 636 loans in 86 countries or territories. Electric-power and irrigation projects, the building of roads, ports, mining, and agriculture are some of the projects supported. India, Iraq, Chile, Costa Rica, and the Philippines have been among the recipients of such help. In late 1965 the United Nations — with major financial contributions from the United States — instituted the United Nations Development Programme as another weapon in the battle against world poverty.

Increasing international trade. If the underdeveloped nations are to buy and sell goods from and to other nations, the restrictions on international trade must not be prohibitive. This means that the United States and the other free nations must not impose tariffs on the import of goods that will prevent the export of goods from those nations to which loans have been made. If the free western nations are unwilling to accept the goods, export and import trade ties with the USSR would undoubtedly be increased by the developing nations.

Increasing literacy, education, and technology in the less-developed nations. The great majority of the people in many of the underdeveloped nations cannot read and write. If the people in a nation are to achieve and maintain freedom for themselves, the form of government must be democratic. That means that they must be able to read and write and to be informed as to the nature and source of the problems in the economy in which they live. Unfortunately, however, literacy in a people is not accomplished overnight. And, as it has been said, these people also lack the skills that are necessary for the use of modern methods of production. Obviously, therefore, efforts should be made to raise the educational level of the people. The establishment of the Peace Corps is an effort in this direction. In 1961, Congress passed this measure and allotted $40 million for the first year's work. Since then thousands of volunteers have been trained and have rendered personal service in many types of educative work within the developing nations.

Any specific proposal as to what should be done to aid the underdeveloped nations usually becomes a political issue, discussed vehemently, while the problem remains before us.

Increasing the stability and progress of our own economy. If the ups and downs of business in this country can be controlled and our economy can be kept expanding, any burden resulting from aid to other countries will be relatively lighter. This is most important. For, although America has a vital interest in the progress of the underdeveloped countries, it cannot afford to weaken its national economic strength. Fortunately there is evidence to support the belief that progress has been made in the discovery of ways and means for stabilizing our economy and promoting its growth — and in this way our prestige may be increased throughout the world.

SUMMARY

There is great variation as to the extent to which the nations of the earth have achieved economic development. One measure of the degree of development of a nation is the amount of per capita income in the nation. According to this criterion, the United States, Canada, and some of the Western European nations are highly developed. Others are only partially developed. Still others, constituting most of the world's population, are underdeveloped.

The developing nations are restless. They are in ferment and determined to achieve a higher scale of living, although they may not have any definite idea as to how they can go about doing it.

The requisites for economic development are an adequate work force, sufficient available material resources, capital, technology, and a form of economic order that is conducive to stability and progress. The underdeveloped nations are lacking in most — or all, in some cases — of these requisites. They have sufficient populations to provide workers, but they lack a work force that is skilled in the methods of modern production. They lack tools and equipment and a sufficient variety of natural resources. Their forms of political and economic order are not suitable to economic production and progress in the modern world. For one thing, the ownership of wealth is highly concentrated, so that there is an absence of a middle class, which constitutes the majority of the population in our country.

For humanitarian reasons we should be interested in the condition of the peoples in the less-developed countries. Moreover, their development would likely be profitable to us. But the danger in the situation is that in their search for a better economic life the people in these nations are likely to accept communism as the best and quickest solution to their problem unless they can be convinced that a free way of life offers them hope.

It would appear that the free and developed nations have an obligation to lend assistance to the economically backward nations. This can be done in either or both of two ways: by extending grants of money and capital goods, or by making long-term loans which can be repaid after the nations have achieved some measure of development. The obligation to do these things rests on the free nations of Western Europe and North America.

Our wealth and productive capacity will enable us to carry our fair share of the burden of financial aid to the developing nations, provided we can maintain a stable and growing economy. But it should not be forgotten that the economic health of the United States is basic to maintaining an effective program of aid to the underdeveloped nations.

NEW TERMS

CARE
Food for Freedom
HOPE

population explosion
underdeveloped (nation)

QUESTIONS ON THE CHAPTER

1. What statistical evidence is there to illustrate the extent to which some peoples live in poverty in underdeveloped nations?
2. What post-World War II "ferment" has brought new problems in less-developed areas of the world?
3. What work-force problems face some underdeveloped nations?
4. What problems of developing nations revolve around their lack of capital?
5. How does distribution of wealth in underdeveloped nations create problems?

6. Are there reasons why we should be concerned with the problems of less-developed nations? Discuss.
7. What can we do to help prevent the spread of communism?

APPLYING YOUR ECONOMIC UNDERSTANDING

1. It has been said that the underdeveloped nations may have strategic materials vital to our economy. What evidence supports the statement that such materials are strategic?
2. What are some of the forces that have aroused a desire for change and economic progress in the people in the developing nations?
3. Certain underdeveloped nations believe that the development of steel makes a nation economically developed. Is this a logical conclusion? Why or why not?
4. Select an economically less-developed country such as Bolivia, Burma, Indonesia, or Afghanistan. Determine its major resources and industries. On the basis of research, what steps would you advocate for its economic advancement?
5. Why do the new nations of Africa place a high priority on assistance for the improvement of their educational systems as a basis for their economic development?
6. Some owners of private capital seek places for the investment of their capital. Why are they hesitant about making such investments in an area such as Southeast Asia, which then necessitates direct action in such areas by financing or aid through an outside government?

CHALLENGES TO ECONOMIC COMPETENCE

1. Prepare a bar graph showing the status of five developing nations in terms of their average per capita income for the previous year.
2. Make a scrapbook on "Underdeveloped Nations" showing phases of their economic status as they are depicted in current newspaper clippings and articles.
3. Invite a nearby university student from a less-developed country to present the economic needs of his or her nation at a school assembly. Moderate the discussion following the presentation.
4. Write a synopsis of the work of one of the following agencies in aiding the underdeveloped nations: (a) OAS; (b) SEATO; (c) Peace Corps; (d) IBRD; (e) IDA; (f) HOPE; (g) CARE.

Unit 9

Personal and Domestic Economic Problems

Chapter 30 Your Work
Chapter 31 Planning and Spending
Chapter 32 Private Insurance and Social Security
Chapter 33 Saving and Investing
Chapter 34 Domestic Economic Problems

THURSTONE EMPLOYMENT TESTS
By L. L. Thurstone
Department of Psychology, Carnegie Institute of Technology

EXAMINATION IN CLERICAL WORK: FORM A

Fill the following blanks, giving your r...
or turn over the booklet until you are t...

Name... First name... Initial or middle nam...
Address...
Date... 19...
For what position are you applying?...

What grade did you reach in public school?...
What courses have you had in business school?...

Courses...

How old were you when you left business schoo...

Are you now employed?... If not, ...
Name of firm where last (or now) employed...
Address of firm...
Kind of work done...
Why did you leave?...
Name of firm where employed just previously...
Address of firm...
Kind of work done...
Why did you leave?...

How long have you worked at:
Stenography?... Dictaphone?...
Filing?...

	Test	Error Score
	1	
	2	
	3	

- Finishing Time
- Starting Time
- Total Time
- Total Error Score
- Combined Score
- Speed Rating
- Accuracy Rating
- Combined Rating

Cincinnati Bell
- LOCAL TELEPHONE SERVICE ... 6 90
- LONG DISTANCE CALLS
- TAXES ... 60
- ADDITIONAL LOCAL CALLS ... 75
- OTHER CHARGES AND...
- DIRECTORY...

Thomas R. Bosley
275 Ritchie Avenue
Cincinnati, Ohio 45241
TELEPHONE 562-645...
DATE OF BI... Nov 23

DATE	CODE	LONG DISTANCE CALLS	AM
9 03	1	Olean NY 716 372-5379	
		US Tax .06 Total Excl Tax	

The Newport National Bank
NEWPORT, KY.

FOR DEPOSIT TO THE ACCOUNT OF
ACCOUNT NUMBER
NAME
ADDRESS
DATE ___ 19___

CHECKS AND OTHER ITEMS ARE RECEIVED FOR DEPOSIT SUBJECT TO THE TERMS AND CONDITIONS OF THIS BANK'S COLLECTION AGREEMENT.

	DOLLARS	CENTS
CURRENCY		
SILVER		
CHECKS AS FOLLOWS, PROPERLY ENDORSED		
TOTAL DEPOSIT		

UNITED ACCIDENT POLICY
Association Casualty
... Surety Company
New York, N.Y.

CLERICAL
INVENTORY CONTROL...

INSURANCE

CLERK-TYPIST

CLERK - TYPIST

Comptometer Operator

COOK

COUNTER WORK—ASSISTANT MANAGER

Keypunch Operator

Permanent Pigments

KEY PUNCH OPERATOR

KEYPUNCH OPERATOR

LADIES—OVER 18

$ NURSE
JR'S OFFICE
LPN
LPNS
TOR'S OFFICE

Increase Your Income
Teach and sell make-up.
Call 671-0336
VIVIANE WOODWARD COSMETICS
Subsidiary of General Foods.

TRADE MARK — CANNON — MADE IN U.S.A.

Good Housekeeping

MAJOR
Certificate
of
Contract

BLUE SHIELD

NUMBER
26-01622

Loan No...
Mortgage FROM
TO

CERTIFICATE FOR
SHARES OF
ISSUED TO
DATED

CITIZENS NATION...
Baltimore, Maryl...
Ray M. Armstrong
121 Oxford Road
Baltimore, Maryla...

FORM W-4 (Rev. Jan. 1967) EMPLOYEE'S WITHHOLDING EXEMPTION CERTIFICATE
U.S. Treasury Department — Internal Revenue Service

Social Security No. ___ City ___ State ___ Zip ___
Type or print full name
Home address

EMPLOYEE: File this form with your employer. Otherwise, he must withhold U.S. income tax from your wages with-out exemption.
EMPLOYER: Keep this certificate with your records. If the employee is believed to have claimed too many exemptions, the District Director should be so advised.

HOW TO CLAIM YOUR WITHHOLDING EXEMPTIONS

1. IF SINGLE (or if married and wish withholding as single person), write "1". If you claim no exemptions, write "0".
2. IF MARRIED, one exemption each is allowable for husband and wife if not claimed on another certificate.
   (a) If you claim both of these exemptions, write "2"; (b) If you claim one of these exemptions, write "1"; (c) If you claim neither of these exemptions (applicable only to you and your wife but not to dependents) write "0".
3. Exemptions for age and blindness (applicable only to you and your wife at the end of the year, and you claim this exemption, write "1"; if both will be 65 years of age or older at the end of the year, and you claim both of these exemptions, write "2".
   (b) If you or your wife are blind, and you claim this exemption, write "1"; If both are blind, write "2".
4. If you claim exemptions for one or more dependents, write the number of such exemptions. (Do not claim exemption for a dependent unless you are qualified under instruction 4 on other side.)
5. If you claim additional withholding allowances for itemized deductions fill out and attach Schedule A (Form W-4), and enter the number of allowances claimed (if claimed file new Form W-4 each year) here.
6. Add the exemptions and allowances (if any) which you have claimed above and write total ___ $
7. Additional withholding per pay period under agreement with employer. (See Instruction 1.) ___ $

I CERTIFY that the number of withholding exemptions claimed on this certificate does not exceed the number to which I am entitled.
___ 19___ (Signed) ___
(Date)

(REV. P-RT)

	CHECKS	CHECKS	DEPOSITS			
		15.95			April 23	
			20.50	2	April 24	382.16
	6.22		160.00	3	April 26	359.64
	18.95					249.58
	24.33			4	April 27	173.14
	12.85		160.00		April 29	333.14
				1	April 30	328.89
					April 30	327.64

CC — Certified Check
CM — Credit Memo
DM — Debit Memo
EC — Error Corrected
LS — List of Checks
NC — Check Not Counted
OD — Overdrawn
RT — Returned Item
SC — Service Charge

Chapter 30

Your Work

What occupation should you choose?
Are employment, earnings, and education interrelated?
How can you qualify for the type of work you want to do?
What agencies might help you to decide what work you should do?
Why is it important to you and to society that you find the right job?

Sometimes economics is defined as the "science of wealth-getting and wealth-using." Throughout this book the discussion has been concerned largely with our national and international problems related to wealth-getting and wealth-using. In this, the final section of the book, some matters will be considered that are of immediate personal concern to you.

For most of us, wealth-getting means earning a living — and earning a living means finding a job for which we will be paid. Moreover, all of us would like to experience some degree of success in our chosen work. As the term is used, success means the attainment of some sought end. Each one of us, then, must answer the question: What work can I do that will prove interesting to me, that will challenge my abilities, that will enable me to earn a livelihood, and that will contribute to human welfare? Let us consider this important problem of selecting a vocation.

ARE EMPLOYMENT, EARNINGS, AND EDUCATION INTERRELATED?

Some young people quit school because of a false belief that taking a job will free them from rules, discipline, and authority. But acceptance of a job merely substitutes new obligations and responsibilities. As an employee, one's actions must be centered around and controlled by the business in which one is employed. Other young people, as school dropouts, may be misled by the lure of immediate paydays. In most cases, such reasoning deprives them of a more complete education and a larger total of lifetime earnings.

A recent study conducted by the U.S. Department of Commerce indicated that the median income of women college graduates was 71 percent more than that of women who did not complete high school. Women high school graduates had median earnings that were 24 percent more than that of women who had but 1 to 3 years of high school. The median earnings of male college graduates was 61 percent more than that of males who did not complete high school. Median earnings of male high school graduates were 13 percent higher than that of males who had but 1 to 3 years of high school. These and other comparisons are shown in the accompanying graph.

MEDIAN MONEY INCOME IN 1968
(Year-round workers 25 years old and over)

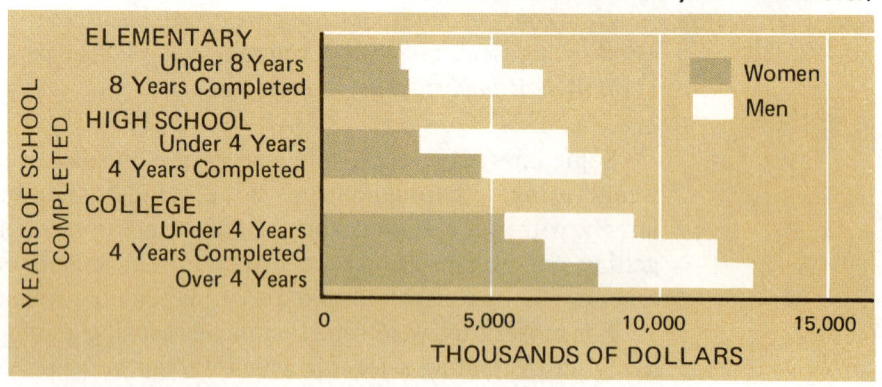

YEARS OF SCHOOL COMPLETED
- ELEMENTARY
  - Under 8 Years
  - 8 Years Completed
- HIGH SCHOOL
  - Under 4 Years
  - 4 Years Completed
- COLLEGE
  - Under 4 Years
  - 4 Years Completed
  - Over 4 Years

THOUSANDS OF DOLLARS: 0, 5,000, 10,000, 15,000

Women / Men

Figure 30-1.

SOURCE: U.S. Department of Commerce, Bureau of the Census.

To be able to get a job is only an initial step. Holding a job against better educated competitors becomes more important for personal welfare; but it also becomes more difficult to accomplish. In our rapidly changing society one cannot afford to terminate his education until sufficient training for his occupation has been acquired. Changes in the number of workers in several occupational groups from 1968 to 1980 favor workers prepared for state and local government, trade, manufacturing, and the service areas. These statistics also indicate that opportunities will be greater in those vocations that require longer periods of educational training.

JOB OPPORTUNITY TRENDS FOR THE '70s

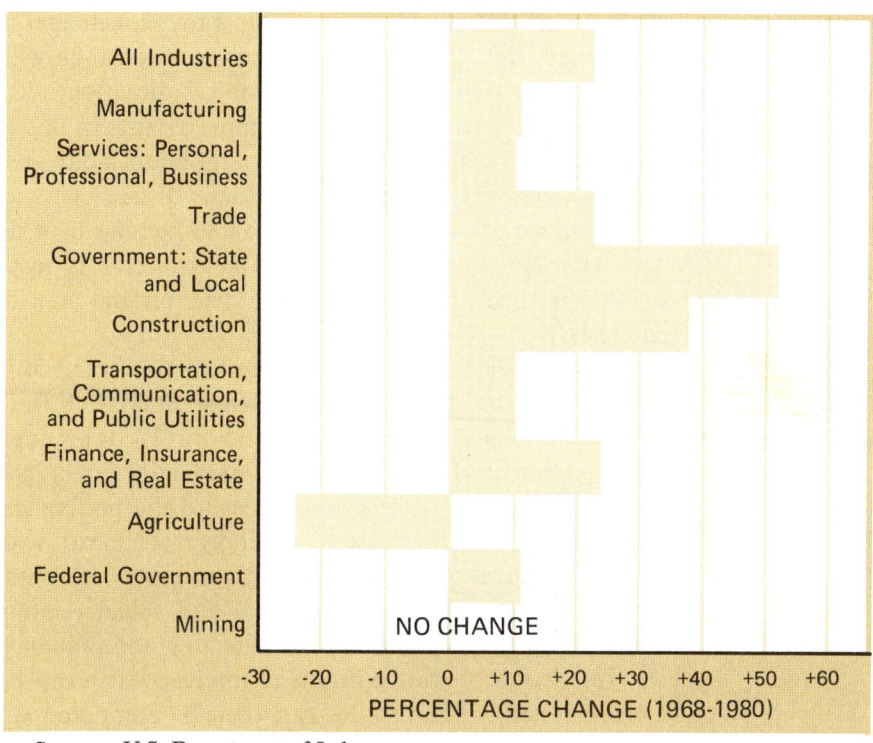

Figure 30-2.

SOURCE: U.S. Department of Labor.

WHAT KIND OF WORK CAN YOU DO WELL?

In which one of the 36,000 different kinds of jobs to be found in industry, business, and government will you find the answer to the question above? If one is to find satisfaction in his chosen vocation, he must be capable of doing the work; and he must feel that the job demands the exercise of his abilities. Some jobs demand a great deal of intellectual ability and long periods of university training, as in the professions of law, medicine, engineering, and teaching. Others may require one or more years of college education. High school graduation is becoming a minimum requirement for applicants seeking jobs as clerks or typists. And there are still jobs available for those who do not complete high school.

WHAT ARE THE AIMS OF VOCATIONAL COUNSELING?

Counseling, together with its testing procedures, may help you to find answers to four basic questions that relate to constructive thinking about choosing a vocation.

(1) Will the vocation satisfy your interests? What is an interest? A baby seems interested in a rattle; a child in a toy; a teen-ager in a new recording; and an adult in his job. An *interest* is an attitude which predisposes an individual to regard favorably an object, situation, idea, or person. It is undoubtedly true that much unhappiness exists in this world because men and women are employed seven or eight hours a day at work in which they are not interested or which they actually dislike. How can you be assured that you are selecting as a life work something in which you will be interested? No one can give you that assurance. It is possible, however, that an interest test might help you to discover the area of your vocational interests.

Tests that have been widely used in this connection are: (a) Kuder Preference New Occupational Interest Survey (Form DD); (b) Kuder Preference General Interest Survey (Form E); (c) Kuder Preference Occupational Survey (Form D); and (d) the Kuder Preference Personal Interest Survey (Form A). These tests measure the preference interests of individuals relative to activities — outdoor, mechanical, scientific, artistic, and others; relative to particular occupations — accountant, dentist, truck driver, etc.; or relative to personal and social relationships — avoiding conflict, working with ideas, and directing and influencing others.

Test scores provide patterns of interest which can be profiled for each person tested. The profiles can then be compared with occupations in which similar patterns of interest predominate. Form DD, which is the most recent in the Kuder series, provides individual preference comparisons with the preferences of people in over 100 representative occupational groups. It also provides for preference comparisons with interests of persons enrolled in more than 30 college major programs.

(2) Is your general ability adequate? Although intelligence is not the sole basis for the selection of an occupation, an individual who is realistic about making his choice would do well to utilize the vocational counseling services available in his school. Although the counselor will not reveal the actual grade made on an intelligence test, he will indicate whether or not you apparently possess the ability needed for certain kinds of specialized training, and whether you might profit from college or graduate school attendance. If one seems to be limited in general scholastic ability and has high ambitions, he should realize that in order to attain the success he craves he will have to work that much harder. There is no substitute for hard work.

Although no one will assert that tests of intelligence or achievement are completely accurate and trustworthy, they have been used long enough to establish acceptance as indicators of ability. The types of tests might include: (a) Ohio State University Psychological Test; (b) Thurstone Test of Mental Alertness; (c) Iowa Tests of Educational Development; and (d) College Entrance Board Examinations. Test scores for (a) and (b) are used as a basis for comparing college entrants relative to general intelligence; test scores for (c) and (d) are used to indicate how well one has achieved academically in comparison with others who may be applying for college admission. The student should realize that tests of intelligence or scholastic ability should be taken seriously, and one should try to perform at his very best when taking such tests. The work you want to do may require advanced training. In these days of crowded classrooms, admission to college is frequently influenced by the scores on such tests.

(3) Do you have special vocational aptitudes? An *aptitude* is a special capacity to learn a specific skill. Some jobs call for special skills — a newspaper reporter should have some verbal facility; a radio or a television repairman must have some mechanical aptitude; work as an inspector on an assembly line demands speed of visual perception. Each of us has a different combination of aptitudes. There are those with musical aptitude who will profit from instruction in that art; those with mathematical aptitude find quantitative relations are easily understood; some have artistic aptitudes, some have mechanical aptitudes. A few individuals are thrice-blessed — they seem to be highly endowed; and for them the choice of a vocation can be very difficult, for there are so many things they could learn to do well.

Many high schools today administer a battery of tests to determine the student's specialized capacity. Among those most frequently used are the Differential Aptitude Test (DAT), Flanagan Aptitude Classification Test (FACT), Flanagan Industrial Tests, and others. The tests may include measurements of (1) verbal reasoning, (2) numerical ability, (3) abstract reasoning, (4) space relations, (5) mechanical reasoning, (6) clerical speed and accuracy, and (7) language usage. The student's profile on these tests shows how far above or below average he falls on each of the subtests. It is the total picture that is important, not a single score. If a student scores highest on clerical speed, that does not automatically indicate that the student will do well as an office worker with an insurance firm. Such a job might demand, in addition, language facility and numerical ability. The scores that a student achieves on these tests are used by his counselor to supplement what is known about his intelligence and his academic performance — the grades he has achieved in various subjects. By now you must be convinced that vocational counseling is not an easy job!

The United States Employment Service uses a somewhat different battery of tests. It includes some tests which are definitely planned to measure certain specific skills. There are 15 subtests to differentiate ten aptitudes which in varying combinations may predict occupational success. For instance, one pattern which is designated "NSM" includes numerical ability, spacial ability, and manual dexterity. An individual with this pattern, and other relevant characteristics, might be advised to train for plumbing or metal structural work.

If one has been thoroughly tested and has been exposed to counseling advice, he might now be able to think more constructively with regard to a choice of occupation that will challenge his abilities.

(4) How is personality related to your vocation? The personality of an individual is very important in helping one to secure a job. It is even more important in helping him to keep a job!

Personality may be defined in either of two ways: (a) in the popular sense and (b) in the scientific sense, as psychologists think of it.

(a) According to the common or popular idea, personality is the total impression that one makes upon other people. The way we look, act, talk, and give physical evidences of the way we feel — all these matters cause people to react or to feel as they do toward us. If they are friendly toward us, or if they admire us for any reason, they do so because we behave in such a way as to cause them to have these attitudes toward us.

People judge and classify us according to our personalities. Since we know this, each of us makes some effort to create a favorable impression on others. On many occasions we make a special effort to "put our best foot forward." As a rule we want people to like, respect, and admire us. Therefore, we speak, dress, work, play, and act in such a manner that others may see in us the qualities that they like, respect, and admire.

(b) The scientist does not think of personality as the impression we create on others. He would define it as the sum total of everything that we are — our mental, temperamental, and emotional makeup, as well as our physical characteristics. This is a more fundamental idea of personality than the popular version. It is more important, for sooner or later others will find us out and we will be judged by what we are — not by what we pretend to be. Therefore, if we want people to think we are honest, we must be honest. If we want others to think we are capable and dependable, we must be capable and dependable.

As you review the accompanying list of specific personality traits, how would you rate yourself on the answers to the questions? No one would

SPECIFIC PERSONALITY TRAITS

Ambition	Do you really want to succeed, so that you are willing to work (not merely to wish for success)?
Industriousness	Do you work steadily and persistently?
Patience	Can you work without becoming irritable?
Dependability	Can people depend on you to keep your word and to do the work you are supposed to do?
Self-confidence	Can you work without fear of failure?
Memory	Do you have a good memory for faces, names, and facts?
Health	Do you feel and look well?
Sensitiveness	Can you take criticism without becoming discouraged?
Cheerfulness	Are you optimistic and enthusiastic?
Speech	Can you express your ideas well and in a pleasant voice?
Adaptability	Can you readily adjust to situations and people?
Tactfulness	Do you manage to say the right thing in the right way and without giving offense?
Friendliness	Do you make friends easily?
Honesty	Are you really what you pretend to be? Are you truthful?
Appearance	Do you walk and stand erect and dress neatly and appropriately?
Habits of economy	Especially, do you use your time to the best advantage?
Right thinking	Is your mind reserved for wholesome, worthwhile thoughts?

score one hundred percent on all of them. But the higher your average score for all the traits, the more effective your personality is likely to be.

Tests have been devised to measure *personality traits*. Two such tests that relate to personality measurement are the Thurstone Temperament Schedule and the Survey of Interpersonal Values. Scores on the former measure the degree to which a person is active, vigorous, impulsive, dominant, sociable, etc. Scores on the latter indicate the value that a person places on his relationships with others and the strengths of his motivational

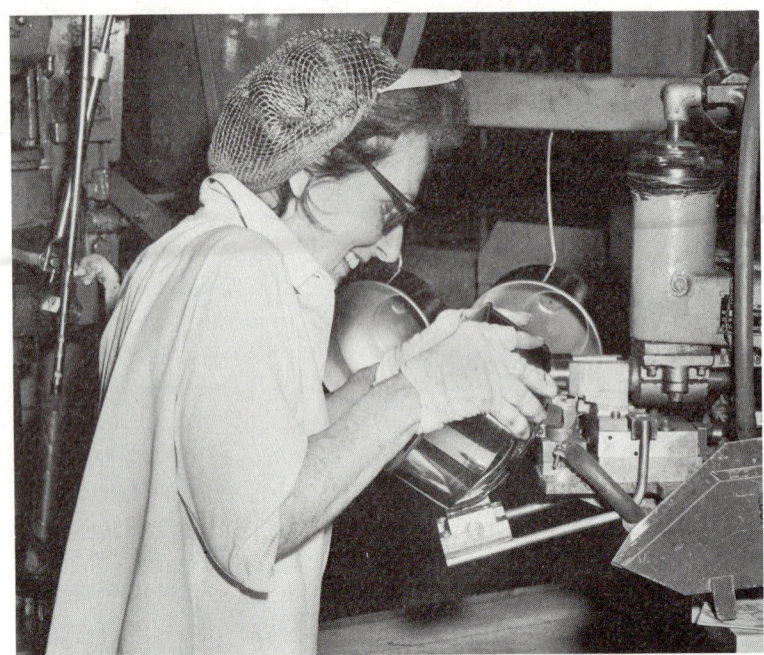

Illus. 30-1. If we want others to think we are capable and dependable, we must be capable and dependable.

The West Bend Company

pattern. However, if you do not wish to take such tests or are unable to do so, you should study the traits listed on page 497.

If you do not have as effective a personality as you would like, can you do anything about it? The answer is definitely "Yes." If you have the necessary general intelligence and aptitudes for a job, you can develop the qualities needed for success in that job. Some years ago the psychologist Dr. L. M. Terman stated that — given a minimum of intelligence — the qualities needed for success are (1) interest and effort, (2) self-confidence, and (3) strength of character. If you have these, you will in all likelihood have an effective personality.

WHAT IS THE BEST JOB FOR YOU?

Having given the matter of interest, ability, aptitude, and personality some careful consideration, the next step is to discover the kind of job in which you could succeed after you have acquired the necessary knowledge and skill.

What are the major occupational families? Varied attempts have been made to classify occupations into broad areas. One convenient way to classify the *occupational families* is as follows:

Ch. 30 YOUR WORK

Agriculture
Communication
Construction
Domestic service
Manufacturing
Mining
Office service

Personal services
Professions
Protective service
Public service
Trade
Transportation

In each of these occupational families there are many members, or particular kinds of jobs. Assume that you would like to earn your living in the occupational family of "Professions." One branch of this family is named "Economics." In this family branch, according to your interest and ability, you would have vocational choice from 16 general areas. Should your interest be even more specialized, there are 57 area subdivisions from which to choose. Some examples of the variety of demand for economists' services are indicated in the classification chart on page 500.

In some of the occupational families there are skilled and unskilled workers, supervisors and administrators, salesmen, and so on. To consider the occupational family first may give you some idea as to the nature of the work and perhaps enable you to sense the general atmosphere in which particular jobs are carried on.

Where can one find information about specific jobs? No matter how you go about it, making an intelligent choice of an occupation is likely to take time and much effort. And learning about the different jobs for which one may be well suited is not the least of the total undertaking. The United States Employment Service has prepared a descriptive list of many thousands of different kinds of jobs called *The Dictionary of Occupational Titles*. This book is an invaluable source of information and is extremely readable. Some of the suggestions listed below might be of some help to you in finding out more about specific jobs:

Conferring with a vocational counselor.
Reading books on vocational guidance.
Watching moving pictures dealing with different kinds of work.
Studying exhibits of workmanship.
Visiting school museums.
Listening to talks on certain kinds of occupations.
Visiting different kinds of business and industry.
Doing part-time work.
Working on occupational study committees.
Talking with people in different occupations about their work.

SPECIALIZATION FIELDS IN ECONOMICS

1. **GENERAL ECONOMIC THEORY**
   a) Methodology
   b) General Equilibrium (including general welfare economics)
   c) Microeconomic Theory
   d) Macroeconomic Theory

2. **ECONOMIC HISTORY; HISTORY OF THOUGHT**
   a) Economic History
   b) History of Thought

3. **ECONOMIC DEVELOPMENT AND PLANNING**
   a) National
   b) Regional
   c) Section, specify
   d) Project

4. **ECONOMIC STATISTICS**
   a) Statistical Methods
   b) Econometrics
   c) Social Accounting
   d) Input-Output Analysis

5. **ECONOMIC SYSTEMS; COOPERATION**
   a) Economic Systems
   b) Cooperation

6. **MONEY, CREDIT, AND BANKING**
   a) Monetary Theory and Policy
   b) Commercial Banking and Other Short-term Credit
   c) Consumer Finance and Mortgage Credit

7. **PUBLIC FINANCE; FISCAL POLICY**
   a) Central Government Finance; Fiscal Policy
   b) State and Local Finance

8. **INTERNATIONAL ECONOMICS**
   a) Trade; Commercial Policy
   b) Foreign Exchange; International Finance
   c) Imperialism; Colonialism

9. **BUSINESS FINANCE: INVESTMENT AND SECURITY MARKETS**
   a) Business Finance
   b) Investment and Security Markets
   c) Insurance (private)

10. **BUSINESS ADMINISTRATION; MARKETING AND ACCOUNTING**
    a) Business Organization
    b) Managerial Economics and Industrial Management
    c) Marketing and Advertising
    d) Accounting

11. **INDUSTRIAL ORGANIZATION; GOVERNMENT AND BUSINESS; INDUSTRY STUDIES**
    a) Industrial Organization and Market Structure; Business, Price, and Related Policies
    b) Policies Concerning Competition and Monopoly; Government Ownership and Operation; Wartime Operations and Control
    c) Public Utilities; Communications
    d) Studies of Manufacturing, Construction, and Service Industries
    e) Transportation

12. **AGRICULTURAL ECONOMICS**
    a) Production Economics
    b) Farm Management
    c) Agricultural Finance and Marketing
    d) Processing of Agricultural Products

13. **LAND ECONOMICS; ECONOMIC GEOGRAPHY; HOUSING**
    a) Forestry
    b) Fisheries
    c) Natural Resources; Mining
    d) Economic Geography
    e) Housing

14. **LABOR ECONOMICS**
    a) Labor Market Analysis
    b) Wages, Hours, Conditions of Employment
    c) Trade Unions; Collective Bargaining; Labor Management Relations
    d) Public Policy; Role of Government
    e) Manpower Planning
    f) Investment in Education

15. **POPULATION: WELFARE PROGRAMS: STANDARDS OF LIVING**
    a) Population; Migration
    b) Welfare Programs and Social Security (public)
    c) Consumer Economics; Level and Standards of Living

16. **EDUCATIONAL ADMINISTRATION**
    a) Curriculum Development
    b) General Administration
    c) Teaching Technique

SOURCE: American Economic Association.

WHAT PREPARATION DO YOU NEED FOR YOUR JOB?

In every occupation there are many more mediocre workers than experts. But only the experts achieve outstanding success and recognition. If you know of an exception to this rule, you should realize that it is an exception. In planning your career, you should not expect success to come by way of an exception to the ordinary course of events.

Provided you have at least average general intelligence, you should not neglect such studies as mathematics, social science, language arts, and science, regardless of your occupational choice. There are two reasons for this. One is that general education will probably help to make more meaningful the special training for your job, even though such training may not appear to be directly related to these subjects. The other reason is that you will also be a citizen and a member of society and that such general education will help to make life meaningful and enjoyable.

If the occupation of your choice demands special training, how and where you will obtain it will depend largely (1) on the definite standards that have been set up, as in the case of the education of physicians and lawyers and (2) on the usual training practices and facilities that exist for job training, as in the case of barbers or of workers in many industries where training on the job is the rule.

Individuals and agencies that may be able to help you to decide how and where to obtain appropriate training are vocational counselors, your state department of education, and the central offices of labor unions if the job is one that is likely to be unionized.

Illus. 30-2. **Never in our economic history have job training and placement opportunities been greater.**

American Oil Company

Never in our economic history have job training and placement opportunities been greater. Many of the opportunities provide income payments concurrently with job experiences. Recently created agencies are the Youth Opportunity Centers of the Neighborhood Youth Corps and the Job Corps; both are sponsored under the Economic Opportunity Act. State vocational agencies conduct programs in Occupational Training and Retraining in Redevelopment areas as well as in Manpower Development and Training. At local levels Community Work Training, Apprenticeship Training, and Vocational and Technical Education programs are operative.

NOTICE

The Carpenters Joint Apprenticeship Committee Has Openings for Apprentice Carpenters.

APPLICATIONS WILL BE ACCEPTED UNTIL 4:00 P.M. MAY 29, 1970.

Please call Cecil Stephens, Secretary – JATC for an appointment at 833-4941.

To be Considered, All Applicants Must Have the Following Qualifications: Must Live Within Jurisdiction of Local Union No. 1883 At Least One Year, American Citizen or in the Process of Becoming a Citizen, High School Graduate or GED Certificate, At Least 17 years of Age and Not Over 27; Applicants with Honorable Discharge from Military Service May Be Accepted Between the Ages of 17 Through 32 Years. Must Provide Birth Certificate.

SOURCE: *Macomb Daily Journal.*

At local levels Community Work Training, Apprenticeship Training, and Technical Education programs are operative.

HOW DOES ONE LOCATE HIS FIRST PERMANENT JOB?

After one knows exactly what he wants to do and is prepared to do it, it may be necessary to spend some time locating the particular job he wants. Just how you will go about finding your job will depend, of course, on the nature of the work and the local situation, since most persons find their first jobs close to home.

Depending on the nature of the job for which you are looking, one of the following persons, methods, or agencies might be of help: vocational counselors; classified directories; want ads; public employment agencies; private employment agencies; city chambers of commerce; friends who are employed; direct application to an employer; and announcements of civil service examinations, which are posted in post offices.

CAN YOU EARN A LIVELIHOOD AT THE JOB?

Here again one's standard of living and scales of value must be taken into consideration. Individuals recognize that the wages or salary that one receives is just one of the satisfactions of the job. An elementary schoolteacher may not earn as much as a truck driver. But the teacher has greater security during the day's work; her hours are more pleasant; and she has the pleasure of aiding in the development of young minds. Similarly, physical production workers, such as electricians, carpenters, or plumbers, may receive more dollars in their paychecks than do office workers. However, the office workers may enjoy fringe benefits in the form of recreational lounges, subsidized lunches, avocational club activities, or training programs which have money value. The dollar costs, in these examples, are assumed by the employer rather than by the employees.

One need not be considered mercenary because he hopes to earn good wages. But in choosing a vocation one must consider the financial limitations of certain occupations. A typist doesn't earn as much as a stenographer; a proofreader doesn't earn as much as an editor. But in the occupations that offer less pay, less skill is usually demanded. Consequently, any person who wants to be assured a good income should consider a vocation which offers some opportunities for advancement.

WILL THE JOB CONTRIBUTE TO HUMAN WELFARE?

Most young people are idealistic as to the type of work they want to do. Our study of economics up to this point has emphasized that all productive work is important. Our cooperative attempts to supply mankind's needs have emphasized that thousands of types of services and goods are essential. The man who, working on an assembly line, fastens countless bolts on the wheels of scores of cars daily is contributing to the welfare and security of American families. If the work is honest and productive, it will contribute to the sum total of human happiness. It is for this reason that the Peace Corps, VISTA, and HOPE, as typical occupational opportunities, appeal to those who are idealistic and who find happiness in self-directed working situations.

SUMMARY

Employment, earnings, and education are interrelated in the achievement of vocational success. Success means the attainment of an aim or goal. To achieve success in a job, it is necessary that the individual have the required qualifications for the work.

Personal qualifications for a job are of four kinds: (1) interests, (2) ability, (3) aptitudes, and (4) the right kind of personality.

Interest in an occupation is shown by the pleasure and satisfaction that one derives from performing the work involved in the job.

Ability implies knowledge or skills that have been acquired and can be put to use.

Aptitude refers to one's capacity to learn or to acquire knowledge or skills of certain types. Of the tens of thousands of different jobs, many call for the same fundamental aptitudes. So we conclude that, if one can do one kind of work, he probably can learn to do quite a number of other kinds of work that require the same kinds of aptitudes.

Personality includes an individual's capacities, abilities, desires, attitudes, likes and dislikes, ambitions, weaknesses, and temperament, as well as his physique and sense of values.

One can improve his personality. But it is important to understand that personality is what one really is, and not what he may pretend to be or what others think he is.

A logically planned procedure for making an occupational choice involves (1) the discovery of one's real occupational interests, (2) an understanding of his aptitudes as well as his limitations, (3) the development of the ability required for the work, and (4) information as to where the job is to be found.

NEW TERMS

aptitude
Dictionary of Occupational Titles
interest

occupational families
personality
personality traits

QUESTIONS ON THE CHAPTER

1. What four general objectives should successful work help you to attain?
2. What specific evidence can be cited to show that one's earning capacity is related to educational achievement?
3. What role can modern tests of intelligence, aptitude, and achievement play in assisting you to attain your occupational goals?
4. What is an "interest"? How does it differ from an "aptitude"?
5. What distinction is made between the popular and the scientific viewpoints of personality?

6. What ways are there for improving one's personality?
7. What are the specific personality traits that are mentioned in the text?
8. What is an occupational family? Is a knowledge of the occupational families of any value in helping one to decide what job he should select? Explain.
9. Of what importance to you is *The Dictionary of Occupational Titles* (DOT)?
10. How can one learn more about the different kinds of jobs?
11. Does general education have any relation to success in a job? Discuss.
12. Of what value is specialized education? What kinds of specialized education can you mention?
13. How can one go about getting a job?
14. What are some of the nonmonetary benefits that one may find in particular jobs?

APPLYING YOUR ECONOMIC UNDERSTANDING

1. (a) What types or forms of student vocational interest inventories are used in your school? (b) What interest areas do they analyze?
2. Various studies have shown that more persons are fired from positions because they lacked the ability to get along with fellow employees than because they lacked job skills. Discuss this statement.
3. What sources of information do you believe will be most helpful to you in the choice of the type of work which you plan to follow upon the completion of schooling?
4. More employers are placing greater emphasis on the breadth of the general education background of their prospective key employees. What reasons may be responsible for this trend?
5. Labor unions are concerned with the replacement of many union members by fewer persons who are trained technicians. They are also advocating that their members register for technical training programs. Why?
6. (a) What are the available sources and agencies in your community for the securing of a job? (b) How do these sources differ?
7. Why will a combination of your interest in a particular kind of work and your ability to do that work — after you have secured the necessary training — make you a more effective contributor to the nation's economy?
8. Discuss the reasons why service with the Peace Corps, VISTA, or HOPE is idealistic rather than materialistic.
9. Secure a copy of a large city newspaper. Analyze the section listing jobs and positions available and the wages and salaries offered. Discuss the wide differences as to the rates of pay offered.

CHALLENGES TO ECONOMIC COMPETENCE

1. Read several articles on Career Days and offer your help to the school guidance counselor in planning a career day for your school.
2. Develop a bulletin board display on the theme "Preparing for Tomorrow's Job Today."
3. Prepare a booklet using clippings to show the kinds of employment changes which automation creates.
4. Invite a speaker from your state's employment service to present to the class information about the work of that agency. Moderate the question-and-answer period which follows the presentation.
5. Make a study of the kinds of scholarships and grants which industry and business make to persons seeking higher education. Report your findings to the class.
6. Prepare a synopsis of an article which discusses one of the following topics: (a) Nuclear Energy and Tomorrow's Jobs, (b) The Potential Job Areas for the 1970's, (c) The Costs of Job Training Programs.

Chapter 31

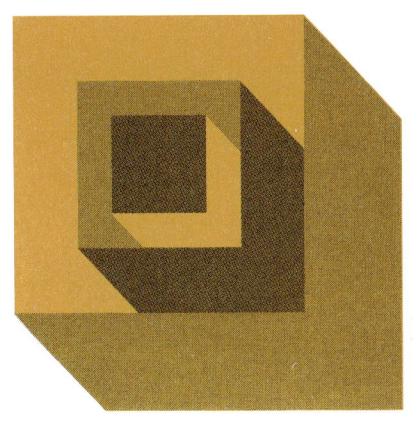

Planning and Spending

What general rules can help one to use his income wisely?
Does budgeting help one to use his income economically?
What public and private agencies aid or protect consumers?
Can the consumer protect himself against unwise spending?

Individuals and nations are seldom satisfied with their incomes. As was emphasized previously, the amount of goods and services available to individuals in a nation is dependent upon income. For the size of your income determines the amount you can spend and the amount you can save. This is true regardless of whether your income is in the form of an allowance, wages, salary, rent, interest, dividends, or profit. But the size of the income is not the only thing that counts in determining how much enjoyment you get from the use of your money. Of equal importance is the good sense you exercise in using the income you have. This implies economizing or avoiding waste or loss of one's money. To get the greatest possible satisfaction from the use of our incomes — now and in the future — one must plan his expenditures carefully, spend his money wisely, and invest his savings judiciously. This chapter will be concerned only with the first two aspects of wealth-using: planning and spending.

The word economics is derived from two Greek words meaning "management of a household." And the principles that apply to the careful management of income are equally pertinent to an individual, a family, or a nation.

THERE ARE SOME GENERAL RULES FOR USING MONEY WISELY

Certain principles for income management will aid one in the use of his income.

Estimating the amount of income. Decide what your income in the near and the more remote future will probably be. In estimating your income, try to be realistic, not overly optimistic, nor unduly pessimistic. Unless the individual lives beyond his means, the amount of income must cover all expenditures. As someone has said, "He who does not stretch himself according to the coverlet finds his feet uncovered." And he who does not first determine the probable amount of his income before he plans his expenditures is likely to find himself financially embarrassed.

Setting financial goals. How much do you plan to save each month? Should every individual and family have a definite goal for investments? A high school student might be saving toward a college education. A young couple might plan to buy a house. An older couple might be making investments that will make retirement easier. The attainment of such goals requires planning and effort. They will, however, serve as continuing incentives to practice economy in the use of money. Saving can soon become a well-established habit.

Planning expenditures. It is impossible to lay down rules as to exactly how much of your income you should spend and how much you should save. Likewise, it is impossible to say just what you should buy and how much, for individuals and families with the same incomes have different needs, responsibilities, and tastes. But the very fact that one considers his varied needs in advance, and undertakes to divide his income accordingly, enables him to balance his expenditures. *Personal distribution of income* concerns the categories for which individuals and families spend their incomes; it also concerns the amounts spent in each category.

A very helpful classification of personal income distribution has been prepared by the United States Department of Agriculture, as follows:

(1) Food
(2) Housing
    Rent
    Taxes — property
    Fire insurance, etc.
(3) Operating
    Fuel
    Light and power
    Telephone
    Laundry done out
    Rent of safety-deposit box
    Fare on city bus, etc.
(4) Furnishings and Equipment
    Furniture
    Bedding
    Stoves
(5) Clothing
(6) Health
(7) Developmental
    Formal education
    Reading matter
    Public welfare
    Recreation
    Vacation and trips
    Vocation
(8) Personal
    Candy, tobacco, beauty parlor
    Barbershop, cosmetics
(9) Automobile
(10) Savings
    Emergency fund
    Savings account
    Insurance, life
    Payments on house
    Investments
(11) Other Items
    Personal taxes
    Gifts

Engel's laws. About a hundred years ago a Prussian statistician, Ernst Engel, made a study of the expenditures of working-class families in Europe. From his study he arrived at certain conclusions, which have come to be known as *Engel's laws*. These laws, or generalizations, may be stated briefly as follows:

1. As income increases, the relative amount or percentage of income spent for food tends to decrease.
2. The relative amount spent for clothing tends to remain about the same, regardless of the amount of income.
3. The relative amount spent for housing tends to remain about the same, regardless of the amount of income.
4. The relative amount of income used for miscellaneous purposes (including savings) increases as the amount of income increases.

Studies made by the Bureau of Labor Statistics confirm Engel's law as to expenditures for food. But in America, at least up to a certain point, we tend to spend a larger percentage for clothing as our incomes get larger. The Bureau's studies also show that the percentage of income spent for housing in this country, as income increases, tends to decrease, which is contrary to Engel's conclusion. Finally, the studies with respect to miscellaneous expenditures agree with Engel.

KEEP RECORDS OF YOUR INCOME AND EXPENDITURES

If one is to handle his money systematically and with the highest degree of efficiency, he must prepare a budget and "keep books" or financial records.

Budgeting is essential. A *budget* is a statement of expected income and a plan for expenditures over a future period of time. The period of time may be a week, a month, or a year.

In the case of an individual who is not in business and who does not have a great deal of money to manage, the preparation of a budget is a simple matter. Making up the family budget, however, is more difficult. In deciding the kinds and amounts of expenditures, it is often well to call a family council and talk things over so that the budget will be in harmony with the family's objectives, needs, and wants.

A family budget should be prepared each year. The average family's objectives in order of decreased dollars of expenditure would include: (1) food, (2) housing and household expense, (3) transportation, (4) clothing, accessories, and jewelry, (5) medical care, (6) recreation, (7) personal business, (8) personal care, and (9) miscellaneous. How family income is to be secured — sources of income — would also be listed.

Budgets should be flexible. Family budgetary expenses and income are estimated. The actual expenditures and incomes will generally be larger or smaller than anticipated. Accidents or serious illness may mean that the family plans for purchasing a new car must be postponed. In your own budget an excessive amount spent for clothing might make serious inroads on the amount allotted to a vacation trip. Similarly, an unexpected wage increase or an unanticipated plant shutdown might significantly change the actual income available for total spending. Such unforeseen developments may require a considerable adjustment in the budget.

Cash record. A *cash record* for expenditures is simply an itemized account of the receipt of income and the way in which it is spent. Record forms with columns provided for classes of expenditures are available for purchase. The totals of the columns in such a record form make it possible to compare monthly and yearly expenditures with the budget estimates. Such records are very helpful in preparing income tax reports.

Household inventory. In addition to the cash record, many families keep a household inventory. The *household inventory* is a list of household articles, giving the cost and date of purchase. It is especially useful in estimating the amount of insurance needed and in making loss adjustment with the insurance company in case of fire.

Balance sheet. It is worthwhile for families to make an annual balance sheet. A *balance sheet* is a statement containing a list of all *assets* (classes of things owned listed at their present values), *liabilities* (debts), and *present worth* (the difference between the total value of the assets and the total amount of the liabilities).

HOW CAN ONE GET THE BEST VALUE FOR HIS MONEY?

As a rule this is the question that people are trying to answer when they go shopping. Even the careful and intelligent buyer is often at a loss to know how and where he can get the best value for his money. A few of the things that you might do are discussed below.

Buy at the right place. Generally speaking, it is safer to buy at a store with a good reputation than to buy from a dealer whose reputation is unknown. If the reputations of two or more stores are equally good, one must be guided entirely by his judgment as to the quality of the goods and the services provided by each store. For example, in the case of buying groceries, one may be puzzled as to whether to buy from a good chain store and pay cash and carry his purchases or to buy from an independent grocer who will charge and deliver the purchases. The chain store will probably sell at lower prices; but the buyer may be willing to pay more in order to obtain the extra services provided by the independent. In such a case the customer must decide what it is that he wants for his money: more goods and less service, or fewer goods and more service.

One should shop around as much as possible, without wasting too much time. To the extent that people seek the best value for their money, shopping by consumers stimulates competition on the part of merchants and as a result tends to bring about reasonable prices.

Buy at the right time. The time at which some goods are bought is sometimes an important matter to consider. For example, the supply of fresh fruits and vegetables is seasonal. If one cares to vary his eating habits somewhat, he may increase his purchases of this class of food when there are abundant supplies on the market and thus save money.

Style goods cost more at the beginning of the season than later. Therefore, those consumers who are not highly style-conscious can usually save money by not rushing to the stores to buy when style goods first appear. Likewise, one can save substantial amounts by buying particular lines of articles when stores conduct their seasonal sales of certain kinds of goods. Such goods include linens, men's and women's clothing, and furniture.

Buy the right amount. Frequently it is possible to buy a larger number of units of a good at a lower price per unit than if only one or a few units were purchased. For example, it may be possible to buy 10 pounds of sugar at a lower price per pound than if only one pound were bought. On the other hand, such matters as the possibility of spoilage, storage facilities, and the amount of money one has at the time are also matters that must be considered.

Buy the best article for your money. "But," you may ask, "which is the best article?" Here, again, is a question that is not easy to answer.

CAN WE BELIEVE ADVERTISERS' CLAIMS?

Often it is difficult to know which brand of an article is the best. For example, suppose you are buying tooth powder or toothpaste. The manufacturer of each brand either asserts or attempts to lead you to believe that his product is the best. On the television and radio he pleads with you day after day to buy his brand. The advantages of a given product may be presented in song with the hope that the rhythm will make it impossible for you to forget the name which is also spelled out for you.

In most cases merchants and manufacturers believe that the products they sell are good values for the prices they ask. To keep one's self-respect, one must believe in himself and in the worth of what he is doing for a living. This is as true of people who sell goods as it is of those who engage in other kinds of economic activity.

Illus. 31-1. In most cases merchants and manufacturers believe that the products they sell are good values for the prices they ask.

Ethan Allen

DOES ADVERTISING HELP OR HINDER THE CONSUMER?

A few advertisements are definitely untruthful. Some advertisements are deliberately designed to mislead consumers. In the majority of cases, however, the worst that can be said is that the advertisements do not mention the defects or possible shortcomings of the articles. If one buys an article that possesses all the good qualities claimed for it by the seller but which also has an undesirable feature not mentioned in the advertisement, he may be inclined to feel that the advertisement was untruthful.

Advertisements may announce new products that have been produced and put on the market. They may give the names and locations of dealers who sell certain articles. They may explain certain qualities of new goods. They may explain how products can be used. They may also provide the public with other information that would aid the consumer in making up his mind as to whether a certain article would be worth its cost to him. Such advertising is educational.

How can undesirable advertising be prevented? Many people become quite disgusted with some of the methods and claims used by certain advertisers. They may believe "there ought to be a law" imposing very strict controls over the practices employed in advertising goods. But it has always been permissible for a seller to "talk up" or to "puff" his merchandise. Advertising and salesmanship are intended to set forth the good points of an article and induce people to buy it.

But just where puffing ends and misrepresentation begins is sometimes a difficult question to decide. For example, suppose an automobile salesman asserts, "This is the best car on the market within its price range." It may be, and, again, it may not be. But if the salesman honestly thinks so, should it be against the law for him to say that it is? Even if a reliable comparison with other cars could be made as to materials, gas and oil consumption, speed, ease in handling, safety, and resale value, there would still remain the important matter of appearance and style. And individuals differ as to what they want in color and design of an automobile.

Thus, as we can see, it is not easy to say just what limits should be put on advertising statements. Of course, statements and claims that are not true when tested by expert knowledge should not be permitted.

Labels help the consumer make choices. Three kinds of labels may be used on consumers' goods. A *brand label* uses an emblem, picture, or name by which consumers may identify the product of a particular producer. A *descriptive label* sets forth the characteristics of the contents of the package, such as the size and variety of the fruit, the style of pack, or the nature of the material in the article. A *grade label* indicates a definite standard of quality.

Brand labeling enables one to obtain an article of the quality standard adopted by a certain producer, at least so long as he continues to observe that standard. But it does not tell the buyer anything definite about the quality of the article. Purely descriptive labeling merely tells one what the physical or chemical contents of an article are. It does not attempt to indicate whether the article is superior, good, or poor in quality.

Grade labeling, on the other hand, enables one to buy an article on the basis of his experience and regardless of the name of the maker. For example, when raw milk is graded according to the standards established by the United States Public Health Service, it is Grade A, Grade B, or Grade C; and milk sold by different dairymen according to these grades is about the same.

Not all products can be labeled according to grades. In all cases, however, informative labeling can be used by sellers. And if consumers

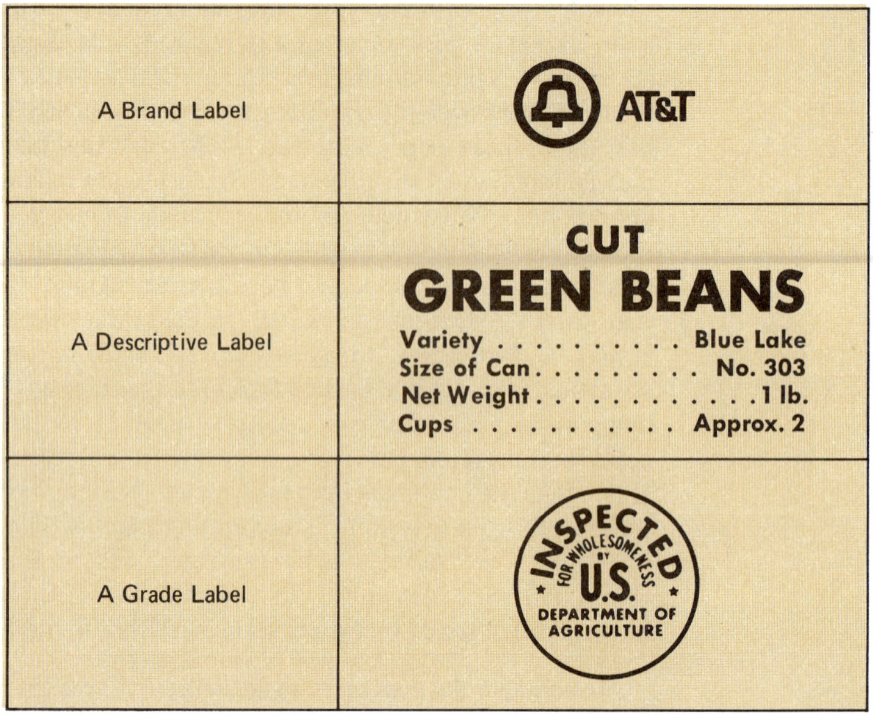

A Brand Label	⊕ AT&T
A Descriptive Label	**CUT GREEN BEANS** Variety .... Blue Lake Size of Can .... No. 303 Net Weight .... 1 lb. Cups .... Approx. 2
A Grade Label	INSPECTED FOR WHOLESOMENESS BY U.S. DEPARTMENT OF AGRICULTURE

Figure 31-1.

Three kinds of labels may be used on consumer's goods.

demanded it, manufacturers would provide them with the information they need in order to buy goods intelligently and with confidence. As a result producers would be compelled to compete more keenly for sales, which would tend to keep prices lower.

Other considerations in buying. Trademarks are sometimes helpful in buying. But it is only after one has discovered a good trademarked article that the trademark is of any aid.

It is probably safer to buy guaranteed articles than those that are not guaranteed. Reputable merchants stand ready to exchange goods or to refund the purchase price of articles that prove to be unsatisfactory.

Generally speaking, goods of high quality cost more than do goods of low quality. On the other hand, experiments and investigations have revealed that in some cases articles selling at a much lower price are better than others that sell at higher prices. This is sometimes true in the case of highly advertised brands. For example, studies that have been made lead investigators to assert that this is often true in the case of many brands of toothpastes and tooth powders, soaps, cosmetics, breakfast foods, radios, as well as other highly advertised goods. Hence, the buyer cannot always depend on price and advertising to indicate quality.

After all, experience, if properly used, is the best teacher of the art of buying goods. But one can profit by experience most quickly if he follows the suggestions for buying that have been outlined.

Since individual and national welfare is dependent upon the goods and services used, both public and private agencies have developed in order to aid and protect the consumer in the utilization of his income.

PRIVATE CONSUMER AGENCIES AID AND PROTECT CONSUMERS

A number of nongovernment organizations, some of which are discussed below, provide aid for consumers.

Private consumer research agencies. Two rather widely known private research agencies are maintained for the purpose of providing subscribers with information that will aid them in selecting reliable merchandise. These agencies are the Consumers Union, Inc., New York City, and Consumers' Research, Inc., Washington, New Jersey. The declared aim of these agencies is to provide advice for consumers.

These organizations conduct experiments with or make analyses of certain classes of branded merchandise, and they issue reports to their subscribers as to their opinion of the qualities and value of the merchandise they have examined. For example, the different brands of soap, razor blades, radios, and many other nationally advertised products may be ranked as "best buys," "acceptable," "not acceptable," "recommended," "intermediate," or "not recommended." Subscribers pay a fee and receive a number of reports throughout the year.

Magazines and newspapers. Some magazines and newspapers show considerable interest in the quality of articles they advertise. Some of them maintain testing bureaus and laboratories in which certain articles offered by manufacturers and merchants are examined. For example, *Good Housekeeping*, *Parents' Magazine*, and the *Progressive Farmer* investigate the quality of goods that are to be advertised in their publications.

Trade associations. A *trade association* is made up of businessmen and concerns engaged in a similar kind of business. For example, both can manufacturers and dry goods retailers have national associations. The general objective of a trade association is to promote the type of business in which the members are engaged and to provide information that will enable members to conduct their individual businesses more successfully.

Formerly, trade associations devoted all their attention to the problems of production, labor relations, price control, and legislation. Now some of them maintain laboratories and bureaus for the purpose of setting up certain standards that will be of value to their members. When members follow such standards, it is sometimes possible to reduce production costs, some of the saving of which may be passed on to consumers. Some associations issue seals that may be placed on the products sold by members; these aid the consumer when he is interested in buying such products. The National Canners Association sets up certain standards as to the size of cans, quality of contents, and methods of describing the contents. Members are not required to observe the standards, but are encouraged to do so.

American Standards Association. The membership of this association is composed of manufacturers, trade associations, and private testing and standardizing organizations. The general aim of the Association is the encouragement of the development and use of standards of various kinds for manufactured goods. The Association publishes a yearbook and also a monthly bulletin. To the extent that the work of the Association promotes standardization and decreases production and marketing costs, it may be of benefit to consumers.

Professional organizations. A considerable number of associations or organizations are composed of professional workers, such as physicians, dentists, dietitians, and home economics teachers. The activities of these associations are directed to the education and protection of consumers.

(a) American Medical Association. The *Journal* of this association is intended for members, but it often contains information of value to consumers. The Association also publishes a magazine, *Today's Health*, which is devoted to the promotion of health education, and other publications, including the book *New and Nonofficial Remedies*. It maintains councils on pharmacy, on chemistry, on therapy, and on foods and nutrition. The councils on pharmacy, on chemistry, and on foods and nutrition have issued seals to manufacturers whose products measured up to the standards of the Association.

(b) American Dental Association. This association maintains the Council on Dental Therapeutics, which publishes a list of dentifrices that have met the standards of the Association.

(c) American Home Economics Association. This organization is mainly concerned with the education and protection of consumers. It provides buying guides for certain kinds of food, clothing, and house furnishings.

It publishes a monthly magazine and issues bulletins from time to time. It is also concerned with the passage of legislation for the protection of consumers.

Better business bureaus. Most large cities have an organization called a *better business bureau*. The bureau is financed by local business concerns, including retail stores, banks, and other kinds of business and industrial establishments. Better business bureaus undertake to:

1. Encourage truthfulness and accuracy in advertising.
2. Expose fraudulent schemes for imposing on the public. Examples of such schemes include continuous "going-out-of-business" sales; the use of "bait" displays to attract customers into a store when duplications of the bait merchandise are not in stock; advertising articles as genuine, when the articles sold are not genuine; and "gyp" door-to-door sales schemes.
3. Prevent or do away with unfair methods of competition between merchants.
4. Provide an easy and fair method of settling disputes between business concerns and their customers.

The bureaus depend largely upon publicity to accomplish their purposes, although they sometimes resort to prosecution of individuals and concerns in court. Any customer or businessman who has been mistreated by a seller or competitor should report the matter to the local bureau.

GOVERNMENT AGENCIES AID AND PROTECT CONSUMERS

Protection of its citizens has long been a recognized function or duty of government. Our Federal Constitution also asserts that one of the purposes of the government is to "promote the general welfare." There is no clearly defined line as to how far government may or should go in protecting the people or in promoting their welfare. At one time, for example, insofar as the purchase of goods by consumers was concerned, local, state, and the federal governments for the most part followed the policy of *caveat emptor*, which is Latin for "let the buyer beware." According to this idea, buyers of goods were supposed to be able to take care of their own interests in business dealings. If they did not use care and if sellers took advantage of them, little could be done about it at law, except in very extreme cases. Today, the situation is quite different.

Local, state, and the federal governments are now doing a great deal to protect consumers. In most cases local and state governments cooperate in the enforcement of these laws. Common examples of laws of this kind are those that provide for the inspection of weights and measures, the inspection of food products offered for sale to the public, and the inspection of public eating places. Local and state governments usually give particular attention to the conditions under which milk and meats are prepared and sold.

THE FEDERAL GOVERNMENT PROTECTS CONSUMERS

The federal government has little control over business that originates and is carried on entirely within a state. Such business or trade is *intrastate*. But the federal government does have power to regulate *interstate* business, that is, business carried on between individuals located in different states. For example, the federal government has no control over the slaughter and sale of meat in a city if the meat is not shipped out of the state; the federal government has control over automobile manufacturing and has established built-in safety requirements for automobiles since the latter are involved in interstate travel.

In general, the government aids and protects consumers in three ways: (1) by the passage of certain laws that must be obeyed by those engaged in interstate trade; (2) by distributing information as to quality standards, and other matters; and (3) by working out standards for labeling goods.

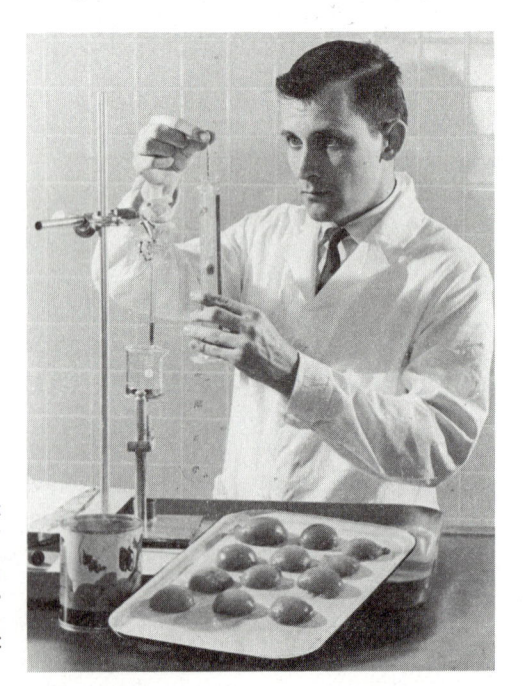

Illus. 31-2. In general, the government aids and protects consumers in three ways: (1) the passage of certain laws that must be obeyed by those engaged in interstate trade; (2) by distributing information as to quality standards, and other matters; and (3) by working out standards for labeling goods.

Food and Drug Administration

Bureau of Standards. This bureau was established to carry on research that would be helpful to manufacturers and to make other scientific investigations. It tests goods that are purchased by the government. State and local governments may also use the Bureau for testing supplies and materials that they consider buying. The work of the Bureau serves consumers in two ways: (1) it helps manufacturers to buy materials according to certain standards, a practice that tends to reduce manufacturing costs; and (2) it supplies manufacturers and others with a list of producers who have adopted the Bureau's standards, a factor that also may reduce production cost. Manufacturers may submit their products for testing. If their products measure up to the standards, they may state in their advertisements that their goods meet the minimum standards set up by the Bureau; but they must guarantee their goods as to quality.

United States Public Health Service. This organization operates under the Department of Health, Education, and Welfare. It inspects oyster beds, packing plants, and water carried on trains and vessels operating within the United States, attempts to control and prevent contagious diseases, and renders other services in the interest of public health.

Federal Trade Commission. The Commission has many duties. Under the Wheeler-Lea Act (1938) it can, in some instances, stop the sale of dangerous articles immediately.

The Commission tries to prevent such practices as misbranding articles, selling rebuilt products as new, imitating standard containers and trademarks, giving products misleading names, selling below cost in order to put competitors out of business, and other dishonest practices.

Federal Food and Drug Administration. This agency is under the Department of Health, Education, and Welfare. It administers the Food, Drug, and Cosmetic Act (1938), which took the place of the original Federal Pure Food and Drug Act (1906), and other laws intended to safeguard the health of the people. It prohibits in interstate commerce shipments of adulterated and misbranded food and drugs. Habit-forming drugs must carry the label "Warning — May Be Habit-Forming." Goods produced under unsanitary conditions may not be shipped. Some types of coloring matter and preserving materials are not permitted to be used. Those materials that are used must be indicated on the label. The package label for cigarettes states, "Warning: The Surgeon General Has Determined That Cigarette Smoking Is Dangerous to Your Health." New drug products sold in interstate trade must have the approval of the administration. All patent medicines must bear a label giving a statement of all active ingredients and the quantity of each.

United States Department of Agriculture. Under the law the Department provides inspectors who inspect all meats sold in interstate trade. The purposes of this inspection are: (1) prevention of the sale of meat derived from diseased animals; (2) enforcement of sanitary standards in slaughterhouses; (3) prevention of the use of unhealthful meat preservatives; and (4) provision for the proper labeling of all meats sold in interstate trade. All meat that is found to be wholesome and that passes inspection must be stamped "Inspected and Passed, U. S." before it may be sold.

The Department of Agriculture has also worked out standards for grading meats. These grades for beef are: prime, choice, good, commercial, utility, cutter, and canner. Meat-packers who wish to grade and sell their meat according to these standards must pay the cost of inspection by government inspectors.

United States Postal Service. Using the mails to promote fraudulent schemes and to obtain money dishonestly is against the law. The Service will prosecute those who thus use the mails, although, of course, someone must first make a complaint.

ARE MORE LAWS NEEDED TO PROTECT CONSUMERS?

A great part of the explanation for dishonest methods in marketing and selling is to be found in the consumer himself. Unless buyers prefer

---

How Consumers Can Protect Themselves

1. Try to learn how to judge the quality of goods.
2. Read labels carefully. Do not overlook the fine print.
3. Find out more about existing laws for the protection of consumers, including local, state, and federal laws.
4. Report all violations of consumer-protection laws to the proper authorities. As a rule, in the case of food, drugs, and cosmetics, report violations to the Food and Drug Administration, Washington, D. C.
5. Insist that consumer law enforcement agencies — local, state, and federal — be given enough funds to enable them to carry on their work efficiently. Providing such funds is the responsibility of city assemblies or councils, state legislatures, and Congress.

Ch. 31 PLANNING AND SPENDING

to live in a regimented society where everyone is told just what he can do and what he cannot do, they should not ask for laws to protect themselves against their own folly, stupidity, carelessness, and lack of initiative. Possibly some new laws are needed. But, instead of additional laws, what is needed more is the enforcement of the existing laws. The law enforcement agencies should have enough funds to enable them to operate efficiently. The public should cooperate with the government by reporting all cases of shady practices by any sellers of merchandise.

SUMMARY

Our incomes are limited. Therefore, if we are to derive the greatest amount of total satisfaction from their use, it will be necessary for us to plan our expenditures carefully and spend our money wisely. Although individuals enjoy the privilege of making their decisions as to what, where, when, and how much they will spend, agencies have developed in this country to help the consumer get the most value for his money.

To economize in the use of income means to think ahead and to plan how we will spend or save our money. The general rules or principles to be observed in using income wisely are: (1) estimate the amount of probable income; (2) set up financial goals; (3) plan expenditures and savings; (4) keep financial records; and (5) try to get your money's worth.

A budget is a statement of estimated income and a plan for spending and saving. Budgets are guides for spending and saving. In every case they must be somewhat flexible because they cannot always be adhered to exactly. Personal distribution of income concerns the categories and dollar expenditures by individuals and families for economic goods and services. This may be useful in budget making; but few budgeted expenditures can be the same as the average for all individuals and families with equal incomes.

A cash record may be used for receipts of income and expenditures for different classes of goods and services. A household inventory is a list of household items, including the cost and date of purchase. A balance sheet is a statement of assets, liabilities, and present worth.

Some things that you can do to get the most for your money are: (1) buy at the right place; (2) buy at the right time; (3) buy the right amount; and (4) buy the best article for your money.

Consumers often need some form of protection from those who would take advantage of them. Advertising is helpful, if it does not misrepresent goods, to the extent it lets consumers know that sellers have goods for sale.

Brand labeling helps to identify a manufacturer's product. Descriptive labeling tells something about the nature and uses of an article. Grade labeling indicates the quality of an article.

Nongovernment consumer agencies to aid and protect consumers include (1) private consumer research agencies, (2) magazines and newspapers, (3) trade associations, (4) the American Standards Association, (5) professional organizations, and (6) better business bureaus.

NEW TERMS

assets
balance sheet
better business bureau
brand label
budget
cash record
caveat emptor
descriptive label
Engel's laws
grade label
household inventory

interstate
intrastate
liabilities
personal distribution of income
present worth
trade association

QUESTIONS ON THE CHAPTER

1. What rules will be helpful to you in making wise use of your money?
2. Why is it impossible for any rule to tell you just what you must do with your money? Should the rules be discarded? Discuss.
3. How would you outline a way of classifying expenditures?
4. What are Engel's laws? Are they valid in the United States today?
5. What is meant by relative expenditures?
6. Why is budgeting essential?
7. What is a cash record, and how is it used?
8. How can a household inventory be useful?
9. What is a balance sheet? How is it used?
10. What are the meanings of "assets," "liabilities," and "present worth"?
11. What is meant by buying at the right place? Buying at the right time? Buying the right amount? Buying the best article for your money?
12. In what ways can advertising help consumers? Give examples.
13. In what ways can advertising prove harmful to consumers? Give examples.
14. How easy is it to prevent undesirable advertising? Discuss.
15. Should sellers be allowed to "puff" their merchandise? Why or why not?
16. What is the difference between grade labeling and other kinds of labeling?
17. Do investigations show that "you get what you pay for"? Discuss.
18. What are the objectives of better business bureaus? How are these bureaus financed?
19. How do the following agencies help consumers: the United States Bureau of Standards; the United States Public Health Service; the Federal Trade Commission; the Federal Food and Drug Administration; the United States Department of Agriculture; the United States Postal Service?

APPLYING YOUR ECONOMIC UNDERSTANDING

1. Newspapers have carried stories about persons who were found in an undernourished condition or were found dead in extremely poor living conditions despite money they had hidden around them or that they had in savings and investments. How do such cases relate to economizing?
2. A number of families do not keep a budget but have a checking account and pay most bills by check. Is this similar to budgeting? Why or why not?
3. Although personal disposable income for each year of a three-year period increased, the percentage spent for clothing decreased by about .1 percent from the preceding year in each of those years. (a) How does this relate to Engel's law? (b) What may have been some reasons for the decreased percentage spent for clothing although the incomes rose?
4. If a family spends $360 a year for various insurance premiums which are paid annually, how would this be shown in a monthly budget? Discuss the reasoning behind your answer.
5. Since a budget is an estimate of receipts and expenditures, under what circumstances might it be necessary or advisable to deviate from a budget? Illustrate your answer.
6. Various studies indicate that women are responsible for the major portion of consumer expenditures. How does this affect the family financial responsibility placed upon wives?
7. Count the total number of columns in your local newspaper which are used for consumer advertising. Discuss how it relates to the saying "In America the consumer is king!"
8. (a) Which of the nongovernment consumer agencies are available in your community for the aid and protection of consumers? (b) What services, if any, does your local chamber of commerce provide in this area?
9. Review several issues of a consumer research agency publication. (a) Is the higher priced article always judged the best buy? (b) Is the lowest priced article always the best buy? (c) What specific data support your answers?
10. Select five processed food items that you particularly enjoy. (a) What ingredients does each food item contain? (b) What was your source of information about the ingredients used?
11. The label on an advertised product commonly used as a tonic lists the ingredients. (a) Would most users know what these ingredients are or what each specifically does? (b) What assurance does the user have that it will not be harmful to his or her health?

CHALLENGES TO ECONOMIC COMPETENCE

1. Arrange to have a teacher of home economics demonstrate budget making to the class. Lead the summary discussion following the demonstration.

2. Prepare a bulletin board display on the topic "Family Budgets." Use various budget forms as its main theme.
3. Arrange a bulletin board display on the theme "Protection for the Consumer."
4. Prepare a written report on one of the following: (a) The Value of a Household Inventory, (b) Agencies Which Help the Home Budgeter, (c) How Consumers Spend Their Incomes, (d) Travel You Can Afford, (e) Services of the Federal Food and Drug Administration, (f) Our State and Consumer Protection, (g) Guidelines for Wise Buying, (h) Salesclerks Can Be Helpful, (i) Let's Improve Our Advertising.
5. Ask the librarian to aid you in the selection of a book which discusses the advertising industry. Review the book and prepare an oral report on it for class presentation.

Chapter 32

Private Insurance and Social Security

What types of private insurance may be purchased?
What is social insurance or social security?
How can one make more nearly certain that he will have some income in the future?

The American economic system provides two major satisfactions: (1) it makes possible the production of an increasing amount of goods and national income for one's enjoyment, and (2) at the same time, it enables one to enjoy that degree of personal freedom which is essential to the feeling of worth and dignity as an individual. As previously stated, the American social and economic system is based on a philosophy that emphasizes the importance of the individual. This system encourages the development and exercise of personal initiative and industry.

There is one major economic problem, however, that confronts each individual, and for most persons it is a difficult problem to solve. That is the problem of economic security. Regardless of how much income one has at present, he would like the assurance of at least sufficient income in the future to provide for his basic wants. How can one arrange his financial affairs so that he may gain such assurance? One way — that of a planned program of investments — will be discussed in the following chapter. Another way is through an insurance program, which may be provided by private companies, by government, or by a combination of the two. It should be understood, however, that the costs are paid for by the individuals and groups who are insured.

PRIVATE INSURANCE

The principle underlying insurance is the sharing of efforts to minimize financial risks. Whether one is thinking in terms of health insurance, life insurance, accident insurance, or property insurance, the basic assumption is the same: A certain number of persons in a group are likely to suffer a loss of some particular kind during a given period of time — some will become ill, some will die, some will be involved in accidents, or some will suffer loss of or damage to their houses by fire.

The primary functions of insurance companies are (1) to provide protection against various kinds of risks, and (2) to collect, in the form of premiums, funds that will be used to reimburse those who suffer financial loss.

Statistics are collected which permit the making of an intelligent estimate as to the likelihood of a certain type of loss occurring in a given number of cases. The statistics may indicate that a certain number of residences in every one hundred thousand will be destroyed by fire this year. A particular individual does not know whether his home will be one that will be razed by fire or not. In order to protect himself against the possible loss, he may be willing to pay into a fund an annual amount called a *premium*. Thousands of other homeowners are willing to do likewise, so the fund is large enough to indemnify those individuals whose homes are destroyed.

TYPES OF INSURANCE POLICIES

An *insurance policy* is a contract whereby an insurance company agrees to indemnify the policyholder in case of loss due to the occurrence of some contingency. The terms named in the agreement specify the amount of premium that must be paid. There are many types of insurance policies available. Each of these policies possesses advantages and disadvantages for particular individuals. A family generally considers it desirable to carry health and accident insurance, as well as life insurance, for one or more members of the family, but particularly for the breadwinner. If one owns property in the form of a house or a car, he is certain to feel a need for protection against loss. The risks that one encounters daily are almost endless — and so, it would seem, are the types of insurance that one might possibly purchase.

Health and accident insurance. The purpose of insurance of this type is to reduce the risk of unexpected expenses due to illness or injury. The usual types of health insurance policies include (1) major medical expense, (2) general medical expense, (3) surgical expense, (4) hospitalization expense, and (5) loss of income. Policies covering such risks are sold by private companies and by nonprofit or mutual insurance organizations.

Property insurance. Certain kinds of risks result from the ownership of property. To lessen the amount of such risks, one may buy insurance policies covering losses due to fire, theft, weather conditions such as lightning, hurricanes, and other dangers. Automobiles should be protected against loss by fire, theft, or involvement in an accident. In the case of accident involvement, one may insure the occupants of the car against loss of life or limb. Or one may carry insurance to protect the other persons or property that might be involved in case of a collision. The cost of such insurance varies with the nature of the property and the amount of protection purchased. Automobile insurance premiums are also influenced by the age, sex, and residence of the insured. Rates are higher in areas that have a high rate of traffic accidents.

Annuities. An *annuity* is the payment and the receipt by a beneficiary of a fixed amount of money at uniform intervals of time, say a month or a year. A person may purchase an annuity to guarantee himself a given annual income for life after he retires. An *immediate annuity* can be purchased by giving an insurance company a certain sum of money, and the annuity payments will begin immediately. For example, a man might pay an insurance company $20,000, and, depending on his age, he might

Illus. 32-1. An annuity is the payment and the receipt by a beneficiary of a fixed amount of money at uniform intervals of time, say a month or a year.

Social Security Administration

receive an annuity of $1,200 a year. Or one might buy a *deferred annuity* contract while he is still quite young, so that when he reaches retirement age, he will have a stated amount of annual income. The cost of the installments on a deferred annuity will depend on age and sex and, of course, on the annual income selected. A *nonrefund annuity* provides the individual with an income as long as he lives; a *refund annuity* provides an adjustment for the named beneficiary in case the individual dies before he has collected as much as was paid into the annuity.

Life insurance. *Life insurance* is protection against economic loss to one's dependents or to his estate as a result of death. Some kinds of life insurance also make it easy for one to build up an estate that he can use later in life. For these reasons some kinds of life insurance may be regarded as a form of saving or investment.

Kinds of life insurance policies. One of the most common life insurance policies is known as a *straight life* or *whole life policy*, for which premiums must be paid as long as the policyholder lives. This kind of life insurance is less expensive than most other forms of policies.

Three other types of policies are limited-payment life, endowment, and term insurance plans. Under the *limited-payment plan* the insured person pays his regular premiums for a certain number of years, probably fifteen or twenty. At the expiration of the stated period of time, the payment of premiums is discontinued. Upon the death of the insured person, the

ANNUAL PREMIUM RATES FOR $1,000 FOR EACH OF FOUR TYPES OF LIFE INSURANCE POLICIES*

Taken at Age	Straight Life	Limited-Payment Life (Paid Up at Age 65)	Endowment (at Age 65)	Five-Year Term (Renewable and Convertible)
15	$13.75	$14.65	$16.50	$ 6.45
16	14.10	15.05	17.00	6.50
17	14.50	15.50	17.50	6.60
18	14.85	15.95	18.00	6.65
19	15.25	16.40	18.60	6.75
20	15.70	16.90	19.15	6.80
25	18.00	19.80	22.55	7.30
30	20.95	23.55	26.95	8.05
40	29.25	35.45	41.15	11.30
50	43.10	62.25	73.00	19.70

*Rates shown are approximate premium rates for life insurance protection. Rates of "participating" policies would be slightly higher, but the cost would be lowered by annual dividends. "Nonparticipating" policy premium rates would be somewhat lower than those shown, and no dividends would be paid.

SOURCE: Institute of Life Insurance

company pays to his beneficiary the amount of the insurance policy. Under the *endowment plan* the insured person pays a stated premium for a given number of years. If he is living at the end of that time, he receives the amount of the policy. If he should die, the amount of the policy is paid to his beneficiary. *Term insurance* is offered at low rates. It provides the greatest amount of insurance protection for a limited time period.

Planning your life insurance protection. One's life insurance protection is a very personal and individual matter. The amount and the kind of insurance that are appropriate for a young man or woman who has just graduated from school and secured a job may not be suitable for a more mature person who is married and perhaps has one or more children. Moreover, the amount of life insurance one should undertake to carry depends largely on the amount of his income.

The principal life insurance needs of a person who has dependents relate to such things as: (1) cash for doctor bills, hospital bills, funeral expenses, and any debts he may owe; (2) cash for a period of adjustment by his dependents — such as finding a home, training for a job, or looking for work; (3) cash income for children until they are old enough to take a regular job; (4) cash for the college education of one's children; (5) income for any dependent who is unable to work because of age or infirmity; and (6) income when the policyholder reaches retirement age.

There are many other types of policies available so that the particular needs of any individual or family are likely to be met. In order to decide what type of insurance you should carry, you should consult at length with a well-qualified and reliable insurance agent.

SOCIAL INSURANCE

During most of our American history, individuals were almost entirely dependent on one of two sources of income, their own efforts and charity. More recently, the people through government have undertaken to provide themselves with a certain degree of social or economic security. In addition to the federal social security and "Medicare" programs, these efforts have taken the form of laws relating to workmen's compensation for injuries arising from employment, unemployment insurance, veterans' programs, and others.

THE SOCIAL SECURITY ACT

The *Social Security Act*, which was passed in 1935, provided for the establishment of the Social Security Administration. The law has been amended numerous times and it provides for several security programs, social insurance, health and hospital insurance (Medicare), public assistance to the needy, and children's services. The Department of Health, Education, and Welfare is responsible for the overall administration of the amended Act's various provisions.

Old-Age, Survivors, and Disability Insurance (OASDI). Most jobs are covered by this provision of the law. If you work for an employer and your job is covered by the law, you pay a social security tax and your employer contributes a like amount. If you are self-employed and your work is covered by the law, you alone pay the tax, which is three fourths as much as the total tax that would be paid by both an employee and an employer on the same amount of earnings. Whether you are an employee or are self-employed, upon reaching the required age, you can retire and draw whatever social security benefits to which you may be entitled.

Persons covered by OASDI. More than 90 percent of those gainfully employed have applied for an account number and are covered by the social security law. These include most employees and most persons who are self-employed.

Self-employed farmers and agricultural employees are also covered. A state government can bring members of a state or local retirement

Illus. 32-2. Upon reaching the required age, you can retire and draw whatever social security benefits to which you may be entitled.

Continental Bank

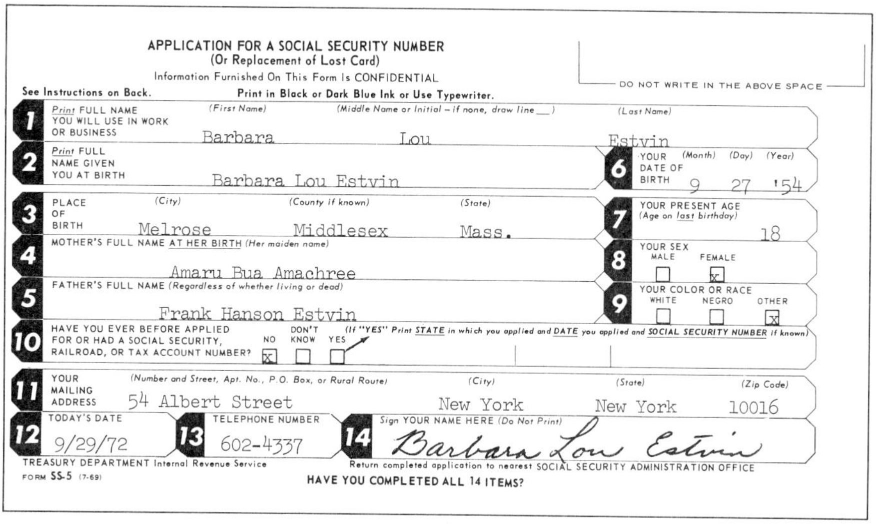

APPLICATION FOR A SOCIAL SECURITY NUMBER
(Or Replacement of Lost Card)
Information Furnished On This Form Is CONFIDENTIAL

DO NOT WRITE IN THE ABOVE SPACE

See Instructions on Back. Print in Black or Dark Blue Ink or Use Typewriter.

1 Print FULL NAME YOU WILL USE IN WORK OR BUSINESS (First Name) Barbara (Middle Name or Initial – if none, draw line ___) Lou (Last Name) Estvin

2 Print FULL NAME GIVEN YOU AT BIRTH Barbara Lou Estvin

6 YOUR DATE OF BIRTH (Month) 9 (Day) 27 (Year) '54

3 PLACE OF BIRTH (City) Melrose (County if known) Middlesex (State) Mass.

7 YOUR PRESENT AGE (Age on last birthday) 18

4 MOTHER'S FULL NAME AT HER BIRTH (Her maiden name) Amaru Bua Amachree

8 YOUR SEX MALE ☐ FEMALE ☒

5 FATHER'S FULL NAME (Regardless of whether living or dead) Frank Hanson Estvin

9 YOUR COLOR OR RACE WHITE ☐ NEGRO ☐ OTHER ☒

10 HAVE YOU EVER BEFORE APPLIED FOR OR HAD A SOCIAL SECURITY, RAILROAD, OR TAX ACCOUNT NUMBER? NO ☒ DON'T KNOW ☐ YES ☐ (If "YES" Print STATE in which you applied and DATE you applied and SOCIAL SECURITY NUMBER if known)

11 YOUR MAILING ADDRESS (Number and Street, Apt. No., P.O. Box, or Rural Route) 54 Albert Street (City) New York (State) New York (Zip Code) 10016

12 TODAY'S DATE 9/29/72

13 TELEPHONE NUMBER 602-4337

14 Sign YOUR NAME HERE (Do Not Print) Barbara Lou Estvin

TREASURY DEPARTMENT Internal Revenue Service
FORM SS-5 (7-69)

Return completed application to nearest SOCIAL SECURITY ADMINISTRATION OFFICE

HAVE YOU COMPLETED ALL 14 ITEMS?

Figure 32-1.

More than 90 percent of those gainfully employed have applied for an account number and are covered by social security law.

system (except policemen and firemen who are under a state or local retirement system) under its old-age and survivors insurance agreement if a majority of the persons in the system so desire. Under certain conditions, ministers and members of religious orders may come under the social security law. Household workers, fishermen, and those on active duty in the Armed Forces are covered. U. S. citizens who work in the United States for foreign governments and international organizations are also covered.

Amount of benefits. The exact amount of one's old-age and survivors or disability insurance benefits payable on his account cannot be determined until a claim for payment is made. The reason is that the benefits must be figured from the record of his earnings up to the year in which he retires, dies, or is disabled. The examples in the table on page 532 indicate the payments under given conditions.[1]

Retired workers who earn incomes. After retirement those who are covered by social security and are under 72 years of age may receive full social security benefits so long as they do not earn more than $1,680 from any kind of employment or self-employment. If they earn over $1,680, their social security benefits are reduced as their earnings go up.

[1]Consult local social security office for current rates and benefits.

Eligibility for OASDI benefits. The law requires that persons born in 1929 or later must earn 40 quarters of coverage to qualify for retirement benefits. Quarters of coverage means that the year is divided into four parts or quarters each of which consists of three calendar months. Credit for each calendar quarter is earned when social security taxes are paid on an insured employee's earnings of $50 or more during the quarter. Self-employed persons may receive credit for four quarters of coverage when social security taxes are paid on a net profit of $400 or more during the calendar year. Special rules apply to self-employed farmers.

Eligibility for disability benefits usually requires that the insured worker must accumulate credit for five years out of ten years prior to the disability. Special regulations apply to those disabled due to blindness.

To secure more specific information concerning an individual's eligibility, one should consult his local social security officer or refer to the agency's various publications.

EXAMPLES OF MONTHLY OASDI CASH PAYMENTS

Average yearly earnings after 1950[1]	$923 or less	$1800	$3000	$4200	$5400	$6600	$7800	$9000
Retired worker — 65 or older Disabled worker — under 65	70.40	111.90	145.60	177.70	208.80	240.30	275.80	295.40
Wife 65 or older	35.20	56.00	72.80	88.90	104.40	120.20	137.90	147.70
Retired worker at 62	56.40	89.60	116.50	142.20	167.10	192.30	220.70	236.40
Wife at 62, no child	26.40	42.00	54.60	66.70	78.30	90.20	103.50	110.80
Widow at 62 or older	70.40	92.40	120.20	146.70	172.30	198.30	227.60	243.80
Widow at 60, no child	61.10	80.10	104.20	127.20	149.40	171.90	197.30	211.30
Disabled widow at 50, no child	42.80	56.10	73.00	89.00	104.50	120.30	138.10	147.70
Wife under 65 and one child	35.20	56.10	77.30	131.40	181.10	195.00	202.20	221.60
Widow under 62 and one child	105.60	168.00	218.40	266.60	313.20	360.60	413.80	443.20
Widow under 62 and two children	105.60	168.00	222.70	308.90	389.90	435.30	477.90	517.00
One child of retired or disabled worker	35.20	56.00	72.90	88.90	104.40	120.20	138.00	147.70
One surviving child	70.40	84.00	109.20	133.30	156.60	180.30	206.90	221.60
Maximum family payment	105.60	167.90	222.70	308.90	389.90	435.20	482.70	517.00
Lump-sum death payment	192.00	255.00	255.00	255.00	255.00	255.00	255.00	255.00

[1]Generally, average earnings are figured over the period from 1950 until the worker reaches retirement age, becomes disabled, or dies. Up to 5 years of low earnings or no earnings can be excluded. The maximum earnings creditable for social security are $3,600 for 1951–54; $4,200 for 1955–58; $4,800 for 1959–65; $6,600 for 1966–67; and $7,800 for 1968–71. The maximum creditable in 1972 and after is $9,000, but average earnings cannot reach this amount until later. Because of this, the benefits shown in the last column on the right generally will not be payable until later. When a person is entitled to more than one benefit, the amount actually payable is limited to the larger of the benefits.

Illus. 32-3. To secure more specific information one should consult his local social security officer or refer to the agency's various publications.

Health insurance for the aged. Many people have insisted that there should be a compulsory national system for the prepayment of the costs of medical care, which would be financed by contributions from both employers and employees. Some persons think this public program for health insurance should cover all the people. They claim that millions of people in the United States do not have adequate medical care and that a national system of health insurance under the Social Security Act, commonly called *Medicare*, would make an all-important contribution to the nation's health, with resulting long-range benefits to productivity and income. Others oppose the proposal for any further additions to a national system of compulsory health insurance which would cover all persons. They assert that our present medical and hospital services and facilities are inadequate and overburdened; thus, the adoption of an all-inclusive health insurance program would result in a deterioration of present health and hospital services. Still others say that a national health insurance program would result in the socialization of the medical profession, which they consider undesirable.

Two new programs to provide health protection for the elderly were included in the 1965 amendments to the Social Security Act. Most Americans aged 65 and over became eligible beginning July, 1966, for hospital insurance and, at their option, voluntary medical insurance. The costs for hospital insurance for those not covered under social security are paid from

Illus. 32-4. Most Americans aged 65 and over became eligible beginning July, 1966, for hospital insurance and, at their option, voluntary medical insurance.

general revenue. For persons covered under social security, the costs are paid from a Hospital Insurance Trust Fund. In 1966 workers, employers, and self-employed persons began to pay health insurance taxes into the fund. The costs for medical insurance are payable at a rate of $5.60 monthly by the insured; the federal government contributes a like amount from general revenue.

Hospital insurance partially covers: (a) payment for 90 days of hospital treatment; (b) 20 days of prepaid care and up to 80 days of additional partial-payment care in nursing homes or other centers following a period of hospitalization; (c) up to 100 home-health visits by nurses or health workers; and (d) a portion of limited out-patient diagnostic testing costs. Medical insurance provides 80 percent of the reasonable payments toward physicians' and surgeons' services, home-health services up to 100 visits per year, and certain other medical and health services. The insured must pay a basic $50 deductible in each calendar year before drawing medical insurance benefits.

OASDI and Medicare tax rates. The various tax rates on earnings up to the maximum of $9,000 are shown in the table on page 535.

Employers deduct the tax from the wages or salaries of their employees, and contribute an equal amount. Self-employed persons must report their earnings and pay their taxes each year when they file their individual income tax returns. Social security and Medicare funds held by the Treasury are invested in interest-bearing government securities.

Public assistance. Under this phase of the social security program four classes of persons may be eligible: (1) needy old persons — old-age assistance and medical assistance for the aged; (2) the blind; (3) dependent children; and (4) all permanently and totally disabled persons. To receive assistance, the persons aided must be needy according to the definition of need used in the state assistance program.

SCHEDULE OF SOCIAL SECURITY TAXES INCLUDING MEDICARE

(Based upon first $7,800 of wages or salaries for 1971 and $9,000 thereafter.)

	Employee and Employer (Each)				Self-Employed Worker			
Calendar Year	For Retirement, Survivors, and Disability Insurance	For Hospital Insurance	Total Tax Rate	Maximum Dollar Tax	For Retirement, Survivors, and Disability Insurance	For Hospital Insurance	Total Tax Rate	Maximum Dollar Tax
1971	4.6 %	.6 %	5.2 %	$405.60	6.9%	.6 %	7.5 %	$585.00
1972	4.6 %	.6 %	5.2 %	468.00	6.9%	.6 %	7.5 %	675.00
1973–75	5.0 %	.65%	5.65%	508.50	7.0%	.65%	7.65%	688.50
1976–79	5.15%	.7 %	5.85%	526.50	7.0%	.7 %	7.7 %	693.00
1980–86	5.15%	.8 %	5.95%	535.50	7.0%	.8 %	7.8 %	702.00
1987 and thereafter	5.15%	.9 %	6.05%	544.50	7.0%	.9 %	7.9 %	711.00

The Social Security Act permits each of the states to decide whether it wants to take part in the assistance program. If a state so desires, its assistance program must be approved by federal authorities. Each of the states has such a program. The federal grant of money to a state meets half of the cost of administering the program and part of the cost of aid to the four classes of persons who may be eligible.

The amount of the federal grant to a state is determined by what the state spends. The states carry on the public assistance programs under their own laws. As might be expected, there is variation among state programs.

Services for maternal and child health and child welfare. Under the program for services for maternal and child health and welfare, no money is paid by the federal government directly to a mother or child. Grants of funds are made from the federal government to the states on condition that the states will add to this amount. Most of the money is used to pay doctors, dentists, nurses, medical and social workers, and other professional persons who work to give children a fair start in life.

Congress appropriates money for maternal and child health services, for services for crippled children, and for the support of child welfare services. The grants to the states are administered by the Children's Bureau of the Social Security Administration.

The social security law emphasizes the encouragement of services for children living in rural localities and other areas having special needs. Each state's share of federal funds depends partly on the relative number of rural children and the financial needs of the state. Only by supplying part of the money needed can a state take full advantage of the opportunity to secure federal funds.

Plans for state programs include local health departments, child-health conferences, provisions for public health nurses, locating crippled children, planning medical aid to children, and aid of several kinds to children whose need is brought to the attention of the local welfare agency.

OTHER PROGRAMS RELATE TO SOCIAL SECURITY

There are other federal and state social security programs that are important to certain groups.

War on poverty. In October, 1964, the federal government officially launched a *war on poverty* which has directly or indirectly affected more than 3.8 million Americans. Federal spending for economic opportunity programs during the 1968 fiscal year exceeded one billion dollars. The separate programs are administered through the Office of Economic Opportunity (OEO). Some of the program's initiators have as their objective the aiding, in one way or another, of some 35 million Americans — about one sixth of the total population.

The major projects in the war on poverty include: Community Action Program; Job Corps; Project Headstart; VISTA (Volunteers in Service to America); Neighborhood Youth Corps; Work Experience; College Work Study; Adult Basic Education; and Aid to Migrants. In some of these programs the emphasis is placed on providing increased economic opportunity for adolescents. Encouraging the "dropout" to resume education, providing job and vocational training or retraining, developing paid work experiences, and creating a desire in youth to serve others are some of the "war's" objectives.

Unemployment insurance. There are two reasons for *unemployment insurance*. In the first place, when business recessions occur, employees, often through no fault of their own, become unemployed. As a result, widespread privation may occur. In the second place, when recessions come, industry and business lose profits because of a decrease in demand for goods due to the fact that many persons have less money to spend.

Also men and women may lose their jobs by the introduction of labor-saving devices. If the employee who thus loses his job is a highly specialized worker, he may find it difficult to find employment, even in good times. If he is getting along in years — 40-50 years of age — or if times are not good, he will probably find it necessary to take work for which he is not suited and at a lower wage than he had been receiving.

The object of the unemployment insurance provision of the Social Security Act was to encourage the states to set up unemployment systems of their own, not to provide federal unemployment insurance. In order to induce the states to provide insurance against unemployment, the law specified that employers of 1 or more persons must pay a tax of 3.2 percent of their payrolls (at present, on wages up to $4,200 a year) to the United States Treasury, unless the state had an unemployment system that was acceptable to the Social Security Administration. If the system was acceptable, the employer might pay an unemployment tax of 2.7 percent to the state fund and the remaining 0.5 percent to the Federal Treasury.

In recent years, the states have reduced the unemployment insurance taxes of employers whose workers have little unemployment. In some states an employer may be excused from making any contribution at all. However, the state tax that would otherwise have been collected is paid by employers to the Treasury and goes into the general federal revenues.

Unemployment benefits in the different states vary greatly. The average weekly benefit in 1970 was $48.15. The maximum number of weeks for which compensation is paid varies among the states.

As a rule, an unemployed worker is entitled to benefits if he complies with the following requirements: (1) he must register and enter his claim with a public employment office; (2) he must have been employed in a job covered by the state law; (3) he must have earned a minimum number of "wage credits" in covered jobs before he lost his job; (4) he must be able and willing to work if a suitable job is offered to him. If he is unemployed because of a labor dispute, if he quit his job without good cause, or if he refuses to accept suitable work, he becomes disqualified for unemployment insurance benefits.

Workmen's compensation. Under laws in various states, employers of more than a certain number of persons are liable for most job-connected accidents to their workers. Injured workmen are entitled to compensation for injuries resulting from accidents that incapacitate them. In some states all employers contribute to a state insurance fund, from which benefits are paid to workers who, while on their jobs, suffer accidental injuries that prevent them from working. In other states employers are allowed to carry private insurance for the protection of their employees.

Here, again, there is great variety as to the nature of the laws of the states and as to the benefits that injured workers receive under the laws. In some states the amount of compensation is perhaps adequate, while in others, it is very small.

Social insurance for railroad workers. Those who work for interstate railroads have protection under the social security programs provided by the two federal laws, the Railroad Retirement Act and the Railroad Unemployment Insurance Act. The first of these acts provides benefits for retired workers, and the second, benefits for employees who have been out of employment for a certain number of days.

Veterans' programs for social security. The federal government maintains a variety of payments and services for men and women who have served in the armed forces or to their survivors. In some cases benefits are payable to the families of living veterans.

Retirement systems of public employees. All three levels of government — federal, state, and local — maintain retirement systems covering some or all of their employees. Many of these also provide disability benefits. Some provide annuities for the survivors of employees.

EMPLOYEE SUPPLEMENTAL COMPENSATION IN THE PRIVATE NONFARM ECONOMY: 1968

(Based on a sample survey. Covers employees in private nonfarm establishments having 1 or more paid workers.)

Compensation Practice	All Industries, All Employees Per-cent[1]	All Industries, All Employees Dol-lars[2]	Manufacturing Office Per-cent[1]	Manufacturing Office Dol-lars[2]	Manufacturing Nonoffice Per-cent[1]	Manufacturing Nonoffice Dol-lars[2]	Nonmanufacturing Office Per-cent[1]	Nonmanufacturing Office Dol-lars[2]	Nonmanufacturing Nonoffice Per-cent[1]	Nonmanufacturing Nonoffice Dol-lars[2]
Total compensation..	100.0	$3.89	100.0	$5.82	100.0	$3.69	100.0	$4.67	100.0	$3.15
Pay for leave time.........	5.9	.24	7.8	.46	6.2	.23	6.8	.32	4.3	.13
Vacations...............	3.1	.12	4.0	.24	3.6	.13	3.3	.16	2.2	.07
Holidays...............	2.0	.08	2.5	.15	2.1	.08	2.2	.10	1.3	.04
Sick, civic personal......	.07	.04	1.2	.07	0.4	.02	1.2	.06	0.5	.01
Nonproduction bonuses and severance...............	1.1	.04	2.1	.13	0.6	.03	1.8	.09	0.5	.02
Supplements[3].............	10.3	.40	10.5	.61	11.6	.43	8.9	.42	10.2	.32
Social security[4].........	3.3	.13	2.8	.16	3.5	.13	3.1	.14	3.7	.12
Unemployment insurance.	0.8	.03	0.6	.03	0.9	.03	0.6	.03	1.0	.03
Workmen's compensation.	0.9	.03	0.3	.02	1.0	.04	0.3	.01	1.4	.05
Life, accident, and health insurance...............	2.2	.09	2.4	.14	3.1	.12	1.7	.08	1.8	.06
Private pension plans.....	2.7	.11	3.9	.23	2.6	.10	3.1	.15	2.0	.06
Other...................	0.3	.01	0.5	.03	0.2	(z)	0.2	.01	0.2	.01

(z) Less than $0.005.
[1] Of total compensation.
[2] Per hour of working time.
[3] Employer expenditures.
[4] Includes railroad retirement.

SOURCE: Dept. of Labor, Bureau of Labor Statistics, *Employee Compensation in the Private Nonfarm Economy, 1968.*

HEALTH, INSURANCE, WELFARE, AND RETIREMENT PLANS UNDER COLLECTIVE BARGAINING AGREEMENTS

In recent decades many employers and labor organizations have agreed to establish insurance and pension plans. These programs vary greatly in scope and detail. In some cases the plan includes provisions for life insurance, sickness and accident insurance, hospitalization and surgical insurance, and retirement benefits or pensions. In most cases the benefits under these programs are more liberal than most people would have thought possible a few years ago. In nearly all instances these plans are financed entirely by the employer. In addition, some employers provide "supplementary unemployment benefits" programs. The table at the bottom of page 538 illustrates some of the varieties and amounts of compensation which supplement actual wages.

SUMMARY

The United States is the richest nation in the world. This, of course, does not mean that all the individuals and families are rich. There is a wide range in the levels of income of individuals and families, which results from the legal and economic institutions that we support and which we believe are essential to the maintenance of a free society. By giving proper thought to the matter, however, it is possible for us to eliminate poverty and privation for all who are willing to work but require job training or other opportunity.

Individuals who attempt to provide for the economic security of themselves and their dependents may plan a program of private insurance. Besides insurance against loss of property, private insurance companies provide a great many policies that are intended to insure individuals against financial loss due to death or inability to work. Life insurance is intended to insure against financial loss due to death. An endowment policy is payable to the person insured if he is still living when the policy matures. An annuity policy provides for an income immediately or at some designated time, depending upon the type of policy purchased.

Social insurance performs two functions: (1) it helps to insure individuals and families against want and privation; and (2) it provides a source of spending which aids business.

The Social Security Administration undertakes the major responsibility for the operation or support of four programs: old-age, survivors, and disability insurance; Medicare; public assistance; and services for maternal and child health and child welfare. Some of these programs are national and uniform in scope and administration; others are designed for a degree of cooperation between the federal and state governments, and provide for a great deal of freedom on the part of the states with respect to the programs.

The "war on poverty" program is designed to provide economic opportunities for all people in the nation; its programs are directed by the Office of Economic Opportunity (OEO).

There are other federal and state programs for social security. Among these are plans for unemployment insurance, workmen's compensation, social insurance for railroad workers, veterans' programs, and retirement systems for public employees.

Besides these government-sponsored efforts toward social security, there are health, insurance, welfare, and retirement plans that are the result of collective bargaining between labor unions and employers.

NEW TERMS

annuity
deferred annuity
endowment plan
immediate annuity
insurance policy
life insurance
limited-payment plan
Medicare

nonrefund annuity
premium
refund annuity
Social Security Act
straight life *or* whole life policy
term insurance
unemployment insurance
war on poverty

QUESTIONS ON THE CHAPTER

1. What great advantages are derived from our economic system?
2. What are two private means of gaining economic security?
3. How would you explain the principle underlying insurance?
4. What are the types of health and accident insurance?
5. How are age, sex, and place of residence of the insured related to automobile insurance rates?
6. What is the difference between an immediate annuity and a deferred annuity?
7. What two objectives may be sought through life insurance?
8. What are the advantages of (a) straight life insurance, (b) endowment insurance, and (c) limited-payment insurance?
9. What is the Social Security Act, and when was it passed? Explain its basic provisions.
10. Should we have a compulsory health insurance program for all persons?
11. What are the main provisions of the Medicare program?
12. What are the objectives of the "war on poverty"?
13. How important to individuals, their families, and society is regular employment?
14. Does government have a responsibility for providing employment opportunities? Discuss.
15. What is workmen's compensation?

Ch. 32 PRIVATE INSURANCE AND SOCIAL SECURITY

16. What is the meaning of (a) social insurance for railroad workers, (b) veterans' programs for social security, and (c) retirement systems for public employees?

17. What has been the relation of collective bargaining to economic security programs?

APPLYING YOUR ECONOMIC UNDERSTANDING

1. John Smith, age 25, has a newborn son and wishes to make certain that this son will have the funds to attend college when he reaches the age of 18. What specific life insurance plan might achieve this aim? Why?

2. Mr. and Mrs. White purchased a new home. They paid $4,000 in cash and mortgaged the home for the balance of $12,000. Would an insurance program be important to the Whites? What type of program would you suggest in this situation and why?

3. The Roe family consists of a husband, wife, and three children. Mr. Roe wishes to provide his family with income until the children are of age and also to provide a lifetime income for his wife. Since his income is not large, he needs a low-cost type of insurance. What type of insurance would be helpful for this family?

4. At present, over 90 percent of our people are covered directly or indirectly by social security programs of government. (a) What are some of the groups which are not covered? (b) Should these groups be brought into the social security program? (c) Why or why not? (d) Should the federal social security law be changed, and if so, why?

5. For the average worker in a plant employing over 100 persons, by what types of social insurance are the worker and his family covered? For each type of social insurance discuss the portion of its cost which the worker pays, and the portion which the employer pays.

6. When social security legislation was being discussed, some insurance companies believed that the competition would force them out of business. However, private insurance has increased and employer pension and welfare plans exceed those of social security. How do you account for this development?

7. A new development in welfare and pension funds is the creation of funds which have been organized by labor unions for their members. What are some of the problems which have resulted from this program?

8. Why is there general agreement that government should provide opportunities for employment?

CHALLENGES TO ECONOMIC COMPETENCE

1. Arrange for a panel discussion on the topic "Private and Social Insurance." This panel should include a representative from Social Security, a representative of your local insurance underwriters association, a personnel representative of a large local business or industry, and a person to represent the general public.
2. Form a committee to prepare a bulletin board display on "Forms of Insurance and Personal Security."
3. Study the data on the income and expenditures of the federal social security program and present your findings to the class.
4. Prepare a written report on one of the following topics: (a) Our State's Unemployment Insurance Program, (b) The Growth of Social Security Insurance, (c) Private Pension Plans of Today, (d) The Why and The How of Health Insurance, (e) The Family Income Plan of Insurance.
5. Prepare and present to your school library: (a) a compilation of materials concerning the "war on poverty", and (b) a collection of materials which relate to all aspects of the social security program. Publications from OASDI and OEO might be used as the basic resource references for your projects.
6. Organize a group of students to prepare and to present a sociodrama which portrays the importance of financial security for a typical family.

Chapter 33

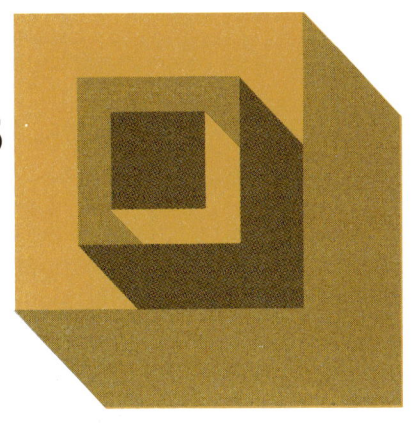

Saving and Investing

Are investment decisions important?
What are the advantages of buying government bonds?
Why are credit unions growing rapidly?
Why should one plan an investment program?

The American people as a whole have never been considered extremely thrifty. Nevertheless, in a recent year their personal savings in the aggregate amounted to more than $42 billion, or somewhat more than six percent of the total amount of disposable personal income in the nation. This huge sum is partly the result of small savings by many people. As it was noted previously, if these savings are turned into investments, it means a decided increase in national prosperity.

For many persons saving is difficult. And deciding what is the best thing to do with one's savings is also a problem. One would like to think that his hard-earned money is safe, but he would also like his savings to bring him some added income. One can achieve relative safety for his savings by putting the money in a bank, by buying high-grade bonds, or by buying private insurance. If one can afford to take the risk, he may find it desirable to buy corporation stock because the rate of earnings may possibly be higher than that from bonds. If possible, it might be desirable for one to diversify his investments and not "put all his eggs in one basket."

INVESTING IS MAKING MONEY WORK FOR YOU

There are two ways by which money can be made to work for the owner and thus to earn an income for him. One way is for the owner to set up in business for himself or to buy stock in a corporation. If the business is successful, the investor is entitled to all or a part of the profits. His profit is his reward for risking his capital funds. But the reward may be negative, that is, it may be a loss instead of a gain.

The other way to make money work for you is by lending your money or allowing some business concern to use it in return for a promise to repay the loan at some future time and in the meantime to pay interest on the amount at regular intervals or at the time the principal is repaid. One can become an investor of this kind by depositing his savings in a savings deposit account in a commercial bank, a building and loan association, or a savings bank, or by buying bonds or lending money to some other kind of borrower. Let us consider several kinds of financial institutions that one may use for the purpose of investing his savings.

Commercial banks. The services of commercial banks include savings accounts on which interest is paid. The interest rate on savings or time deposit accounts varies from 4½ to 7½ percent, which may be compounded on a daily, quarterly, or some other basis. As discussed in Chapter 21, the bank may require as much as 30 days' notice before a savings or time deposit is withdrawn, but such notice is seldom if ever enforced.

Savings banks. The main purposes of some banks are (a) to accept deposits and (b) to lend these deposits on long-time terms to reliable borrowers at a higher rate of interest than the banks pay depositors. Such institutions are called savings banks. Savings banks are intended to provide a safe place for the investment of the savings of wage earners and others whose savings are not large. The amount of deposits on which interest will be paid is limited.

When money is deposited in a savings bank, the bank has a right to demand notice before allowing the money to be withdrawn. The reason for this rule is that the bank lends to responsible persons or businesses the deposits that it receives and thus may require time to accumulate enough cash with which to pay a depositor. If the amount of the withdrawal is not large, the depositor usually may withdraw part or all of his deposit at any time. Checks may not be written against deposits in savings banks.

Savings banks provide a comparatively safe place in which a person can keep his savings and, at the same time, receive a modest income from the investment that was made by using his savings. These banks also provide a valuable service to society by collecting the savings of many thousands of small investors and by making the funds thus assembled available for use by city, county, state, and federal governments, as well as by sound and conservative business concerns.

Stock savings banks. A *stock savings bank* is organized and conducted for profit by the owners of its capital stock. The greater number of stock savings banks are located in the midwestern states.

The bank is under the regulation of the state in which it has been chartered. In order to help protect depositors by discouraging the managers of banks from taking too much risk in making investments, the state usually issues a list of the kinds of borrowers to whom the funds of a bank may be lent. A part of the profits is usually retained as reserves in the bank, and the remainder is paid to the stockholders.

Mutual savings banks. The depositors are the owners of a *mutual savings bank*. In effect they simply pool their savings, which are invested by a board of trustees and a hired manager. Depositors are not paid a fixed rate of interest on their deposits. Whatever earnings are made from the investments belong to the depositors and are divided among them in proportion to the amount and the time of their deposits. As in the case of stock savings banks, the investments of mutual savings banks are usually regulated by state laws. A considerable number of mutual banks are located in the New England and the Middle Atlantic states.

United States Treasury and savings bonds. In 1935 the United States Treasury began the practice of selling bonds of comparatively small denominations to individuals. These bonds are usually referred to as *savings bonds*. There are now two series of these bonds, "E" and "H."

The seven denominations of "E" bonds which an individual may buy have maturity values as follows: $25, $50, $75, $100, $200, $500, and $1,000. The price of each denomination is respectively, $18.75, $37.50, $56.25, $75, $150, $375, and $750. The maturity date is 5 years, 10 months after issue. The interest rate is 5 percent, compounded semiannually, if the bond is held to maturity. There is a lower rate if the bond is redeemed — cashed — before maturity. A savings bond may be redeemed through a commercial bank any time after two months from date of purchase without previous notice, but it cannot be sold to someone else.

The maximum amount of "E" savings bonds that a person may purchase in one year is limited to a total purchase price of $5,000. If the owner of a savings bond does not wish to cash any bond at maturity, he may hold it and receive interest on it at a rate of 5 percent, compounded semiannually.

"H" bonds are sold at their redemption values of $500, $1,000, and $5,000. Interest is paid semiannually by check on a graduated scale, and increases until the maturity of the bond. An average rate of 4.29 percent is paid the first year; thereafter 5.10 percent to maturity. "H" bonds mature in 10 years and they are not negotiable. The maximum amount that may be purchased, individually or jointly, is limited to $5,000 per calendar year.

Savings and loan associations. The objects of this type of financial organization are: (a) the encouragement of thrift, and (b) assisting present and future homeowners. The names by which these associations are known vary in different parts of the country. They may be referred to as building and loan associations, savings and loan associations, or cooperative banks. There is considerable variation in the ways in which savings and loan associations are organized and operate. Some are organized under state charters, and others, under federal charters.

The encouragement of thrift. Some savings and loan associations are cooperative institutions; that is, they are owned by the members, who are entitled to receive any interest or profit that is earned on their deposits. Funds are received by these associations from members whose deposits increase their shareholdings. Other associations are organized in the manner of stockholder corporations; California, Ohio, and Texas are states which permit this form of *guaranteed stock association*.

Savings and loan institutions are not authorized to handle demand-deposit or checking accounts. Thus, savings and loan deposits are similar to time deposits. Savings accounts in the savings and loan associations are usually insured up to a maximum of $20,000 a person under a special federal savings and loan insurance plan similar to that for insuring bank deposits.

Assisting present and future homeowners. Most of the loans that are made by savings and loan associations are on residential properties and are secured by mortgages. In some cases the amount of the loan may amount to as much as 80 percent of the value of the property. Other loans are made to enable the homeowner to repair, improve, or enlarge his residence. The latter are short-term loans, secured by liens; the former are long-term loans for periods of time extending to thirty years.

Repayment of the loan is generally set at a fixed dollar amount on a monthly basis. Part of the repayment is used to pay interest on the remaining debt and the balance is used to reduce the amount of the debt itself.

Investment trusts. In an *investment trust*, or mutual fund, the funds are invested in a diversified group of stocks and bonds of other corporations. The trust company obtains its funds by selling shares in the company. The funds thus obtained are invested by the company in the securities of corporations that are considered to be financially sound and well managed.

Ch. 33 SAVING AND INVESTING 547

Illus. 33-1. Most of the loans that are made by savings and loan associations are on residential properties and are secured by mortgages.

American Telephone and Telegraph Co.

Since about 1940, the number of individuals and families who hold investment trust shares has increased very greatly. Like any outlet for investment funds, investment trusts vary as to the quality of managerial ability.

Insurance companies. Insurance companies also help the investor by selling annuity policies which enable one to build up a fund from which he will receive regular income some time in the future. These policies were discussed in Chapter 32. One may also purchase the stock of some insurance companies; by such ownership one shares in its profits or its losses.

Because of the nature of their business, insurance companies have large sums to invest. Many real estate developments, large buildings, and shopping centers are financed with money lent by insurance companies.

Credit unions. One of the fastest growing institutions in the country to help individuals save is the credit union. There are more than 11 million members in the federally chartered credit unions. These members own in excess of $7 billion of deposits. Credit unions are owned by their members. They have three purposes: to help their members save; to enable members to borrow money for good purposes at a low interest rate; and to educate members in money management. Usually members buy shares in the credit union for from $5 to $10; each additional deposit they make increases their shareholdings. Credit unions are really cooperative small-loan banks that lend amounts to their members at reasonable rates of interest, usually 1 percent per month on the unpaid balance (which would be a true interest rate of 12 percent annually instead of the 30 to 40 percent true interest rate usually charged by small-loan companies). Federal and state laws vary as to the maximum amount that may be loaned by a credit union.

Credit unions are organized like a club. The union is for a particular group, as those working for the same employer or the members of a church. Members ordinarily receive dividends amounting to 4 to 5 percent on the value of the shares they own. A number of credit unions provide some form of deposit insurance to protect their depositors. Some credit unions also provide credit life insurance to protect the borrower in the event of death or disability.

INVESTING IN REAL ESTATE

Probably most families would consider investing in a house the most important type of investment they could make. The Federal Housing Administration (FHA) increases the sources of mortgage funds for prospective buyers through a mortgage guarantee and insurance program which protects the lenders of mortgage funds. Under the program the family purchase of a home is possible with a small down payment and a long-term mortgage. A well-constructed house in a good location and kept in repair is not likely to decrease — it may increase — in value. On the other hand, if the neighborhood becomes less desirable for a homesite because of changes in population and business locations, the value of the property may decrease.

In deciding whether to buy or rent a home, one should consider a number of factors. The factors include pride of ownership, quality of construction, size, location, repairs, taxes, insurance, possible increase in value, interest that might be obtained on the money used for the investment, and other matters.

Investments may be made in residential and business real estate for the purpose of deriving income from the investment or for speculative purposes. Such investments, however, usually require a considerable down payment of, say $5,000 to $10,000. Rental property of this kind requires that the owner bear the cost of upkeep and insurance. In some cases the value of the investment may increase greatly, but the possibility of a decrease in value may also be present.

Obviously, if one contemplates an investment in real estate, he must give careful study to a number of factors. Otherwise, he may lose part of his investment.

INVESTING IN CORPORATION SECURITIES — STOCKS AND BONDS

Some of the stocks and bonds of American corporations offer attractive opportunities for investment. There are more than 20 million persons who hold securities that are traded on the 16 stock exchanges in this country. Some persons own only a few shares of stock, while a few own thousands of shares. Some of the stocks pay good dividends, but some stocks do not pay anything.

There are two classes of persons who buy corporation securities — speculators and investors. The speculators are interested primarily in making a quick profit as a result of changes in the market prices of the stocks or bonds they buy. The investors are looking for a higher *rate of return* than they could probably get from safer types of investments; and yet, as a general rule, they buy only the stock of the companies that they regard as being financially sound and likely to be able to pay dividends. The investor may also buy the stock of corporations that seem to have growth possibilities.

Whether one should buy corporation securities and how he can tell which securities are reasonably safe investments are questions that puzzle the wisest investors — and speculators.

STOCK YIELDS ON COMMON STOCKS

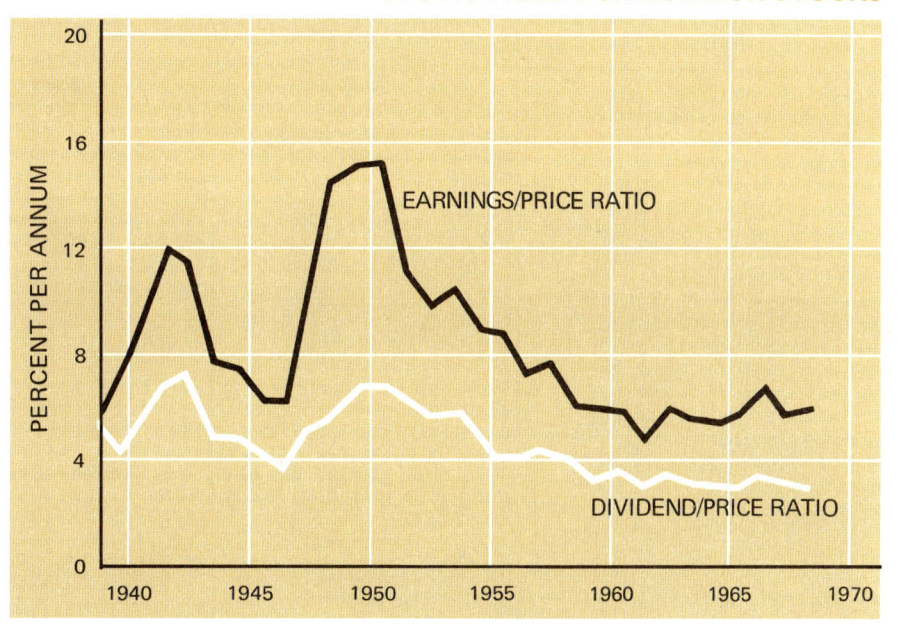

Figure 33-1.

SOURCE: *Historical Chart Book 1969*, Board of Governors of the Federal Reserve System.

Stocks versus bonds. The bonds of the strongest and soundest corporations are generally regarded as safe investments, although possibly not as safe as some other investments — United States savings bonds, for example. The rate of return on such securities is about the same as, or a little more than, that on savings bonds. Hence, as to the rate of return on his investment, the small investor has little to gain by buying corporate bonds as compared to buying savings bonds — provided, of course, the savings bonds are held to maturity.

The possible advantages of buying stocks are (1) the rate of return at the time of purchase is likely to be higher than that on bonds, and (2) the profits and dividends may become larger in the future, so that both the value of the investment and the amount of dividends may increase. As Figure 33-1 on page 549 on stock yields indicates, a rise in earnings relative to the price of stocks may result in a larger dividend income or yield relative to price for the stockholder. Conversely, decreased earnings on stocks may result in decreased dividends or smaller returns to the stockholder for his dollars of investment.

Investors sometimes buy corporation stocks rather than bonds in attempting to hedge against inflation. They feel that if inflation occurs, the market prices of many stocks will rise, while the price or value of bonds may remain the same or possibly fall. During 1969 and 1970,

COMPARISON OF STOCKS AND BONDS

	Stocks	Bonds
1.	Stocks represent ownership. The stockholder is a part owner of the corporation.	Bonds represent creditorship. The bondholder is a creditor of the corporation.
2.	Stocks have no fixed rate of dividend that must be paid. Even preferred dividends must be declared by the board of directors.	Bond interest must be paid whether any profit is earned or not.
3.	Stockholders elect the directors, who control the corporation.	Bondholders ordinarily have no voice in management.
4.	Stocks have no maturity date for payment. Ordinarily the corporation does not repay the stockholder.	Bonds have a maturity date, at which time the bondholder is repaid the amount of his loan.
5.	All business corporations have shares of stock, which are held by stockholders.	Corporations do not have to issue bonds.
6.	Stockholders have a claim against the property and income of the corporation *after* creditors have been paid.	Bondholders have a claim against the property and income of the corporation *before* the stockholders may claim anything.

despite increasing inflation, the market price of stocks did not rise as anticipated. There was a sharp decline in stock prices. Thus, investing in stocks is not always an assured hedge against inflation.

If one decides to buy corporation securities, he can make arrangements to make his purchases through a broker who is a member of a stock exchange.

Stock exchanges. A *stock exchange* is an organization of individuals that is formed for the purpose of trading in corporation securities. Because corporations play so important a part in the ownership of productive enterprises, there must be some means by which stocks and bonds may be bought and sold readily. The stock exchanges exist to perform this important function. The most important of the security exchanges in the United States are the New York Stock Exchange and the American Stock Exchange.

The federal government exercises control over stock exchanges by means of the Securities and Exchange Commission, which is composed of five members appointed by the President and approved by the Senate. Exchanges must be licensed before beginning operation. Corporations whose securities are listed on a stock exchange must file with the Commission complete statements showing the organization and the financial condition of the concerns. Prospective buyers of stocks and bonds can therefore obtain information concerning the companies in whose securities they may be interested.

The Board of Governors of the Federal Reserve System has the power to fix the margins required on securities purchased through stockbrokers. Margin, as we saw in Chapter 16, is the amount of money that the buyer must deposit with the stockbroker when he buys stocks or bonds. If the buyer makes his purchase on margin, he borrows from his broker the remainder of the amount he needs. In the event that the price of the security he buys rises, the buyer can sell the security at a profit. But if the price falls, the broker would be compelled to sell the stock unless the buyer deposited more money. In case the broker was compelled to sell the security, the buyer would lose part or all the money that he had invested in the stock or bonds.

INVESTMENT PLANNING

Just as one by careful planning may spend his money wisely, so, too, by exercising caution he may invest his savings judiciously. The establishment and carrying out of a successful investment program require that the individual give careful attention to a number of matters. First, on the basis of probable facts, he should estimate what the amount of his savings will be over some extended period. Second, he should consider the possible needs of himself and his dependents for cash in that same length of time. Third, he should examine the various opportunities there are for using his savings to the best advantage. In making his decisions he should be guided by facts and competent advisers, and not by wishful thinking and mere rumor as to what constitutes a good investment.

SUMMARY

Investors, as a rule, are influenced by two considerations: safety and income. Conservative investors are concerned primarily with the safety of their investments, while those who are less conservative and more venturesome give greater attention to the possibility of income from their investments.

There are no specific rules that will enable one to know for a certainty just how he should invest his savings. But by knowing something about the different kinds of investment opportunities and by following a few general rules, he can pursue an investment policy that will help in solving the problem of what to do with his savings.

The most important kinds of savings institutions are commercial banks, savings banks, the United States Treasury, savings and loan associations, investment trusts, insurance companies, and credit unions.

Bonds of the government and of large business concerns and savings deposits provide comparatively safe ways for investing one's savings. Often investments in common stocks yield a higher income than do those in bonds and savings accounts, but the risk is greater. The rate of return is the ratio between the amount of income and the cost of the investment.

In making an investment one should be guided by actual information and the advice of those who have demonstrated ability to select sound and profitable investments.

NEW TERMS

guaranteed stock association
investment trust
mutual savings bank
rate of return

savings bonds
stock exchange
stock savings bank

QUESTIONS ON THE CHAPTER

1. What are the individual and social results of saving?
2. What two broad objectives do we seek in selecting an outlet for our savings?

3. What do you understand by "investing"? What are two ways of investing?
4. What are time deposits? How is interest paid on them?
5. What are the main purposes of savings banks?
6. What social service do savings banks perform?
7. How would you compare stock savings banks and mutual savings banks?
8. What is an "E" bond? An "H" bond?
9. On what does the cash value of an "E" bond depend? An "H" bond?
10. What are the objectives of savings and loan associations?
11. What is the object of an investment trust?
12. How does a credit union operate?
13. In periods of rising prices, why do investors sometimes buy corporation stocks in preference to bonds?
14. What points of comparison can be made between the features of stocks and bonds?
15. What is a stock exchange?
16. What is meant by "margin" in connection with buying and selling securities on a stock exchange?
17. What is required for successful investment planning?

APPLYING YOUR ECONOMIC UNDERSTANDING

1. Name some of the agencies in your community in which the individual can place his savings where they will be loaned out for him.
2. One of the insurance firms used by college professors puts half of its savings in bonds at fixed rates of interest. The other half is used to buy stocks in certain corporations. Why may this plan have an advantage for the professors when they retire?
3. Check the rate of interest paid by your nearest commercial bank with the interest rate of a local building and loan association. (a) Which pays the higher rate? (b) What factors might account for the difference?
4. Do your local savings institutions provide insurance on deposits? What are the maximum amounts of insurance protection provided?
5. Would you advise younger persons to hold, as owners, the same kinds of stocks as people who are retired and are dependent upon their investment earnings? Explain the reason for your answer.
6. Explain why a series "E" bond cannot be indorsed and used to pay for a purchase made by its owner.
7. A daughter requested permission from her parents to transfer her money from a savings account into a credit union. Her mother consented, but her father suggested that she first find out when the bank entered interest credits to her account. Why did the father not give his immediate consent?

8. Many reputable brokerage firms will advise customers not to purchase stocks until they have first built up some savings and insurance. Discuss why these brokers will forego a commission on a possible present-day purchase.
9. Mr. Wilson brought an "H" bond to his local bank with the intention of using it as security for a personal loan. As a loan officer of the bank, what suggestions or advice might you give to Mr. Wilson?

CHALLENGES TO ECONOMIC COMPETENCE

1. Prepare a bulletin board display focused on the idea "Saving In Our Community and What It Does." Use photographs taken in your community as its major visual presentation.
2. Prepare a notebook on "The Methods of Investing."
3. Invite a representative of a stock brokerage firm to present information about the buying and selling of stocks and bonds. Moderate the question-and-answer period and then summarize the main points for the class.
4. Prepare a written report on one of the following topics: (a) How to Read the Newspaper's Stock Market Report, (b) How Savings and Loan Associations Invest Their Funds, (c) Protecting the Investor During Inflation, (d) The Art of Saving and Investing.
5. Review the booklet, *You and the Investment World*, which is available from the School Relations Department of the New York Stock Exchange. In a written report, summarize the highlights of the booklet and compare them with the discussion presented in this chapter of your textbook.

Chapter 34

Domestic Economic Problems

Are there difficulties in analyzing domestic economic problems?
What is the nature of the rural farm flight problem?
Is city blight and plight related to farm flight?
What economic challenge confronts a more youthful population?

You will recall that Chapter 1 discussed economic wants which arise from needs. One's organic needs are usually satisfied by the use of material or economic goods. Of equal importance are one's personality or psychological needs. The satisfaction of the latter is often as necessary to one's happiness as is the satisfaction of organic needs. Thomas Jefferson recognized this relationship of happiness to the basic economic problem. In 1788 he wrote, "It is neither wealth nor splendor, but tranquillity and occupation, which give happiness."

In Jefferson's day, the environment — basically agricultural — provided a family and community life that was relatively free from or unaffected by disturbing emotions. Similarly, occupation — either in the form of work or the employment of one's resources — supplied man with the material economic goods that satisfied his organic needs. When the social and economic system provides for both types of needs, happiness prevails and problems are minimal. Whenever these organic and personality needs cannot be satisfied, problem situations develop.

SOME DIFFICULTIES IN SELECTING AND ANALYZING PROBLEMS

Today most persons would agree that many pressing domestic economic problems exist. However, one would find less agreement on the number of problems or the priority importance of each problem. Moreover, any major problem is frequently a combination of a number of interrelated problems. Problem solutions demand making difficult choices from alternative types of action possibilities. Thus, selecting one choice may merely create or substitute a new problem for the original one. Recognizing these difficulties, this concluding chapter will review two typical domestic problems. These problems involve environmental differences. One concerns the rural family and community confronted by farm flight. The other contrasts the problem of the city family and community affected by blight.

A RURAL PROBLEM: FARM FLIGHT

Agricultural production is largely performed in the nation's rural environment. Since 1950 the farm population has decreased from 15.2 percent of total population to 5.1 percent in 1969. In numbers of persons, farm population has decreased during the same period by over 12 million to a present total of 10 million. In addition, farm employment has dropped from 9.9 million workers in 1950 to 4.6 million in 1969; this indicates a loss of 5.3 million farm workers in less than two decades. All of these shifts indicate *farm flight* — the rapid departure from agricultural life and the rural area.

An understanding of the farm flight problem can be achieved by a study of two features of the problem. These features are:

1. Some causal factors of farm flight.
2. Some interrelated aspects of farm flight.

The problem will indicate a basic economic problem — satisfying wants for agricultural products by the most efficient use of resources. In solving the problem, society achieved the goals of growth of farm production and stability of farm prices. Achievement of these goals between 1950 and 1970 sacrificed the goals of economic security and full employment in agriculture for more than half of the farm population.

(1) Some causal factors of farm flight. Among the causes of the farm exodus are: (a) the pressure of inflation on farm costs, and (b) inflation's impact on the distribution of farm income.

The pressure of inflation on farm costs. The disposable income for the farm sector is not the income from farm sales. From farm sales' revenue the farm producers must deduct various costs incurred during the production process. As the accompanying table indicates, total gross income from farming increased from $32.3 billion in 1950 to $54.6 billion in 1969. This was an increase in gross income of $22.3 billion. The table also indicates that production expenses increased from $19.4 billion to $38.6

INCOME FROM AGRICULTURE, 1950-69

| Year or quarter | Personal income received by total farm population ||| Income received from farming ||||| Net income per farm, including net inventory change ||
| | From all sources | From farm sources[1] | From nonfarm sources[2] | Realized gross || Production expenses | Net to farm operators || ||
				Total[3]	Cash receipts from marketings		Excluding net inventory change	Including net inventory change[4]	Current prices	1957-59 prices[5]
	Billions of dollars									Dollars	
1950	20.4	14.1	6.3	32.3	28.5	19.4	12.9	13.7	2,421	2,815
1951	22.7	16.2	6.5	37.1	32.9	22.3	14.8	16.0	2,946	3,134
1952	22.1	15.4	6.7	36.8	32.5	22.6	14.1	15.1	2,896	3,048
1953	19.8	13.4	6.4	35.0	31.0	21.3	13.7	13.1	2,626	2,794
1954	18.4	12.5	5.9	33.6	29.8	21.6	12.0	12.5	2,606	2,772
1955	17.6	11.4	6.2	33.1	29.5	21.9	11.2	11.5	2,463	2,593
1956	17.8	11.2	6.6	34.3	30.4	22.4	11.9	11.4	2,535	2,641
1957	17.7	11.0	6.6	34.0	29.7	23.3	10.7	11.3	2,590	2,616
1958	19.5	12.8	6.7	37.9	33.5	25.2	12.7	13.5	3,189	3,189
1959	18.1	11.0	7.0	37.5	33.5	26.1	11.4	11.5	2,795	2,767
1960	18.7	11.5	7.2	38.1	34.2	26.4	11.7	12.1	3,049	2,989
1961	19.7	12.2	7.5	39.8	35.1	27.1	12.6	13.0	3,399	3,332
1962	20.4	12.3	8.2	41.3	36.4	28.6	12.6	13.2	3,586	3,482
1963	20.6	12.1	8.5	42.3	37.4	29.7	12.6	13.2	3,708	3,565
1964	20.6	11.3	9.3	42.6	37.2	29.5	13.1	12.3	3,564	3,394
1965	23.6	13.5	10.0	44.9	39.3	30.9	14.0	15.0	4,487	4,193
1966	24.9	14.4	10.5	49.7	43.3	33.4	16.3	16.3	5,019	4,563
1967	23.9	13.0	10.9	49.0	42.7	34.8	14.2	14.7	4,683	4,144
1968	24.9	13.1	11.8	51.1	44.4	36.3	14.8	14.7	4,805	4,107
1969	27.1	14.5	12.6	54.6	47.4	38.6	16.0	16.2	5,468	4,446

[1]Net income to farm operators including net inventory change, less net income of nonresident operators, plus wages and salaries and other labor income of farm resident workers, less contributions of farm resident operators and workers to social insurance.
[2]Consists of income received by farm residents from nonfarm sources, such as wages and salaries from nonfarm employment, nonfarm business and professional income, rents from nonfarm real estate, dividends, interest, royalties, unemployment compensation, and social security payments.
[3]Cash receipts from marketings, government payments, and nonmoney income furnished by farms.
[4]Includes net change in inventory of crops and livestock valued at the average price for the year.
[5]Income in current prices divided by the index of prices paid by farmers for family living items on a 1957-59 base.
SOURCE: Department of Agriculture.

billion during the same time span. This was an increase of $19.2 billion. More significantly, gross farm income increased by only 69 percent while production expenses had increased by 99 percent. The increase in production expense effectively wiped out most of the additional income for the farm sector from increased gross receipts.

Using the index (1957-1959 = 100) other data reveals that interest costs to farmers increased by 266 percent, tax costs increased by 141 percent, and farm wage rates increased by 101 percent between 1950 and 1969. Similarly, costs of fertilizers, farm chemicals, farm machinery, and other farm capital were rising with the inflationary trend. However, during those same years prices received by farmers increased by less than 7 percent. Thus, farm inflationary costs benefited the suppliers of farm capital and services. The total population benefited as consumers of farm products. During the same periods consumer prices had risen 43.9 percent for all commodities, while farm product prices were held to the 7 percent increase.

The rise in farm costs forced the more efficient farmers to increase their use of the more efficient land and capital inputs as a replacement for the more costly and less efficient labor resources. The less efficient farmers were forced out of farm production; some of their land and capital resources were acquired by the fewer farm producers who remained in production. Other capital and land formerly used in farm production as resources was abandoned.

Inflation's impact on the distribution of farm income. Based on the index (1957–1959 = 100) gross weekly earnings in nonfarm private industries rose 116 percent between 1950 and 1969. During the same period farm wage rates increased by 101 percent. To double farm wage income in 1969 while maintaining the same number of workers as were employed in 1950 would have required drastic price increases for agricultural products. Since the market would not sustain such additional wage cost increases within the agricultural product price structure, it became necessary to remove from farm employment over one half of the farm labor force. This reduction of the number of farm workers permitted the total dollars of farm wages to be distributed to the decreased number who remained in the farm labor force. Thus, the redistribution had the effect of doubling the wages of those remaining in the farm labor force. It also had the effect of wiping out farm wage income for the more than 5 million persons who lost their farm jobs.

The farm unemployed now faced two types of income problems. The first was a decrease in their income which would decrease their personal living. The second was the rising cost of living despite decreased income for spending. Even for farm labor that retained its income, the situation became serious. The latter's income was not rising fast enough to keep pace with the inflation in prices of consumer products as a whole. During the 19 years from 1950 to 1969, the personal income of the total farm population from farm sources had increased only by 3 percent.

Farm unemployment rose while rural nonfarm job opportunities increased too slowly to absorb the jobless. The contributing role of farm flight to the rural problem became self-evident. New sources of income for unemployed farm labor had to be found off the farms and outside of the rural areas.

(2) Some interrelated aspects of farm flight. The exodus of farm population had its effect on the incomes of rural businesses. These businesses had been dependent on farm family consumption spending. Faced with rising business costs, decreased business volume, and falling business incomes, increasing numbers of rural merchants, doctors, lawyers, dentists, and service suppliers began to close up.

A failure to shift inefficient or underemployed farm labor resources from farm production would have been uneconomic. The shift did force the release of labor toward its economic use in more productive ways. The abandonment of assets of the unemployed, their homes, and the rural towns would also be uneconomic. Equally uneconomic would be any farm or rural population migration into already crowded cities. This mass influx would add to the strains on already overtaxed public services, housing, and other phases of city life.

Fortunately, three forces were becoming operative on the rural scene. These forces were: (a) farm sector response, (b) private nonfarm response, and (c) governmental response.

Farm sector response. Farm producers who desired to succeed in farming had to adapt to changing economic conditions. Part-time farming and subsistence farming were rapidly replaced by commercial or business operation farming. The fear of debt held by the older farm generation began to disappear as young scientifically trained producers took over farm operations. The wise use of credit and credit agencies as a source of capital funds and the leasing of land and equipment rather than tying up funds in outright ownership became sound business practice for the new farm generation.

By increasing the size of farms and through the more intensive use of capital, farm production in crop yields rose. Livestock production was increased as capital intensive applications minimized land resource use for the raising of livestock. Affiliations with farm producer and distributive cooperatives achieved economies of costs in production and in marketing. Average assets per farm began to exceed $100,000. Output per man hour on the farm quadrupled from 1950 to 1970. The anemia of farming was being supplanted by the vitality of agribusiness. More importantly, the economic health of the farm sector began to halt farm flight as it stabilized farm population.

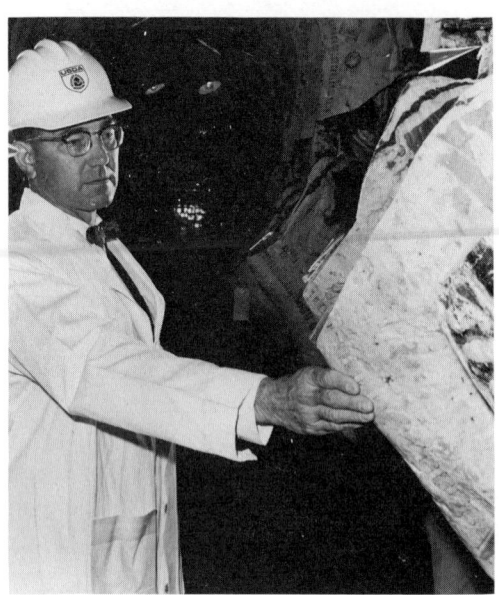

Illus. 34-1. Livestock production was increased as capital intensive applications minimized land resource use for the raising of livestock.

Public Health Service

Private nonfarm response. Economic efficiency in private production requires the use of the lowest cost resource inputs of land, labor, and capital. Land released from agriculture lowered rural land costs relative to rising land costs in the cities. Labor released from agriculture provided a lower cost labor pool relative to the higher cost labor within cities. Taxes on corporate capital and earnings tended to be lower in rural areas relative to taxes levied in cities. Thus, the desire for efficiency ushered in an era of industrial decentralization in the 1960's.

Numerous producers of both capital goods and consumer items moved or expanded their operations into the rural and partly rural areas. Small cities, small towns, and former cornfields along the Mississippi and Ohio river systems were transformed by the construction and operation of blast furnaces, steel mills, and metal working plants. Other plants were expanded in the areas of the Great Lakes and the Upper Southeast to meet growing industrial needs for chemicals, drugs, and capital machinery. Similarly, increased quantities of consumer goods for use within the home, in home yards and gardens, and in recreational activities were flowing from newly located rural plants.

Some of the farmland was converted into resorts and recreational areas. Former farms were converted into small private and public college campuses. Other services in rural areas, such as motels, restaurants, service stations, drive-ins, and shopping centers were established to serve the needs

Ch. 34   DOMESTIC ECONOMIC PROBLEMS   561

Illus. 34-2. Similarly, increased quantities of consumer goods were flowing from newly located rural areas.

Armstrong Cork Company

of an increased population of travellers on the expanded interstate highways. Consequently, all of these economic action responses added to rural incomes. Each response gave new life and added to the economic health and growth of the rural sector.

Governmental response. The federal government has been aware of farm flight since the 1920's. As discussed in Chapter 15, one response was the support of farm prices. Another response was the farmland retirement program which was designed to replace income that would no longer be received from farm production. However, other types of indirect and planned responses were also undertaken.

During the 1940's, the United States was involved in war and cold war. Faced with the need for movement of defense forces overland within the nation and the possible need for evacuation of civilians from threatened cities, the federal government planned a system of defense highways. Other needs required an improved and expanded network of highways to link together the major cities of the nation. These necessities led to the planning of 42,500 miles of interstate and defense highways. The major acquisition and construction costs were to be paid from federal funds. These factors resulted in the creation of the Interstate Highway System. By 1970, over 30,000 miles of roadway had been constructed and opened for use. Although the system was not directly planned to solve the rural problem or farm flight, it did benefit indirectly the rural sector of the nation.

Most of the system's roadway had to be located in rural areas. Payments for acquisitions of right-of-ways were thus made to the farmer and rural landowners; the payments provided the rural sellers with immediate capital funds for investment as sources of income. Construction required the employment of a labor force. Thus, numbers of rural unemployed were enabled to secure jobs and job incomes. The influx of nonrural construction workers necessitated spending of income in the rural areas as payments for food, lodging, and other consumption goods and services. The construction process frequently required local purchases of sand, gravel, cement, fuel for equipment, and other items. Such purchases further increased total rural income.

Much of the income was short-run; it would cease within the brief time period needed for the completion of each section of the highway. However, as each section was completed, new sources of long-run income would be provided. Some of the long-run income would be derived from the use of local resources that would be continuously needed to service and maintain the local highway sections. Other long-run income would arise from the external economies that resulted from the use of the highways which were a form of social overhead capital.

Social overhead capital refers to an economic good whose costs are charged to or borne by the whole society. *External economies* are savings or reductions in costs that result from economic behavior outside of a firm. Society's funds rather than the internal or private funds of a firm provided the highway system. A firm may use the highway system, an external resource; its use may reduce its private production costs. The firm's savings or reduction of costs resulted from the behavior of society. Society's investment in the Interstate Highway System encouraged producers to avail themselves of the external economies of lowered land transportation costs. These economies contributed to the decentralization of industries and the movement to new highway sites in rural areas.

Planned governmental response calls for direct forms of action in the rural sector. This sector contains a third of the nation's population. Within the sector is half of the nation's poor. The rural area also contains the major portion of the nation's substandard housing. Since 1950 some 25 million persons have migrated from the sector into the cities and suburbs. Present estimates indicate that 50 to 80 million acres of cropland now in use are in excess of that needed for agricultural production. By 1980, the number of farms is expected to decrease from the 3 million existing in 1970 to about 2 million. Thus, planned governmental response must be related to all of these factors.

Federal executive planning in 1970 proposed a return to the use of market forces in farm pricing; the existing price support programs would not be retained. It is assumed that market pricing would restore price

Ch. 34 DOMESTIC ECONOMIC PROBLEMS

Illus. 34-3. The Interstate Highway System encouraged producers to avail themselves of the external economies of lowered land transportation costs.

Dept. of Business and Economic Development, State of Illinois

flexibility. This should enable farmers to hold and expand their domestic and foreign sales. The new governmental support would be a price floor rather than a price ceiling. The price floor would be used to prevent excessive price fluctuations and to ensure some base for farm credit. Less dependency would be placed on limiting individual crop production; crop control regulation would be removed. All of these proposals are directed toward promoting a healthy farm sector. A more prosperous farm sector would maintain and add to rural economic growth through expanded farm purchases of local goods and services.

The proposed plan recognizes that its adoption poses problems for segments of the farm population that would be adversely affected. Additional farm producers who could not compete would be forced to leave agriculture. Farm incomes would decrease for farm producers who refused to give up less efficient or inefficient farm operations. The adoption would reduce the existing farm labor force by eliminating underemployed farm labor. These newly created problems of lost incomes would be incentives to further farm flight. As solutions, the proposed plan advocates an income substitution by means of a system of direct income payments. These payments would arise from cropland retirement and family assistance plans.

Small operators, displaced by market price flexibility, would be paid to retire their croplands for long-term time periods. The land would be converted to wildlife and recreational use. Additional income would be derived from jobs created by the conversion and its utilization.

The President also proposed to Congress that a Family Assistance Plan (FAP) be established. As an example of its operation, each family of four would be provided income necessary to reach a minimum of $1,600. Under the federal food stamp proposal an additional $850 in food stamps would be made available to the family. Incentives would encourage the family to seek job incomes. Families that earned job incomes would continue to receive some FAP assistance until family income reached $3,920.

The trend of migration from the rural sector has moved downward. The elimination of some of the causes of flight has contributed to the lessened migration. The responses of farmers, nonfarm producers, and government have and will continue to influence the trend. Improvements in economic life for rural Americans may be an indicator of a more balanced economic growth rate for the future.

A CITY PROBLEM: URBAN BLIGHT

Cities are confronted with numerous and varied problems. In viewing urban blight, as one of these problems, major attention will be focused on a single form of blight. This *urban blight* is in the form of substandard housing which is frequently concentrated within one section or several scattered sections of a city. The blighted area is within the city, but in ways it may be isolated from total city life; the area is often an island or pocket of poverty. The process to be used in analyzing this blight will be limited to two major features. These are:

1. Some causal factors of urban blight.
2. Some interrelated aspects of urban blight.

(1) Some causal factors of urban blight. The factors or pressures which contribute to urban blight include: (a) population density, (b) socio-economic cultural change, (c) inflation, and (d) static forces. Frequently each factor is interrelated with the other factors.

Population density. Population density increases when births and immigration exceed deaths and outward migration for any regional grouping of people. An increased density requires a proportional increase in the number of housing units, facilities, and services if the level of living is to be maintained. Within the blighted areas, a reverse process takes place. The number of housing units decreases. The remaining units are forced to accommodate additional dwellers which the original units were not designed to service.

Increased population density also creates pressures on public services. When public services are not expanded as rapidly as the population increases, crowded and less efficient schools, understaffed health and medical facilities, inadequate police and fire protection, together with lessened sanitation and garbage removal services add to the plight of population in the blighted area.

Socioeconomic cultural change. A city's middle-income class includes homeowners and renters. If owners, they are largely motivated to personally keep their property repaired and renovated. As owners, they are strong supporters of private property rights and property protection. Renters in this income class are usually equally concerned about their living environment. Their loyalty is to the cause of maintaining a "nice" or "good" neighborhood; their values are opposed to the defacing or destruction of their neighborhood. This class, as a whole, is strongly motivated to support education which it believes is the key to the unlocking of economic opportunities in the forms of better jobs and higher incomes. Children within this group, desirous of both parental and class approval, tend to adopt a similar system of values and drives.

The hope of economic betterment, although often unattained, was the magnet that drew the migration of large numbers of the no-income and low-income masses into the cities. The size of the city offered the possibility of more job vacancies; its diversity offered the possibility of a wide variety of jobs which might be performed by the uneducated, the unskilled, or the non-English speaking job applicant.

Many of the parent migrants had never completed an elementary education; necessity had forced many to drop out at elementary grade levels to seek work and supplement family income. Many youth migrants were educationally deprived; their former school districts often lacked the local tax base required to maintain adequate schools. Other youth migrants came from areas where a foreign language was the dominant one; the foreign language became an educational barrier in the city school system where the English language was both dominant and basic to educational success. In other ways the low-income group differed from the middle-income group which added to the socioeconomic cultural differences.

When two different cultures conflict, a merger of the two is time-consuming and difficult. A more rapid solution is through the process of conflict avoidance. Many of the city middle-income class used the latter solution. By leaving the city and migrating to the surburbs, the pressures of increased population density could be left behind. This type of escape was not available to the low-income group on whom the pressures increased with each new addition of low-income migrants. Overcrowding led to a more rapid depreciation of the housing, to strains on the plumbing, and to greater property damage through wear and tear. Blight and its spread was underway.

Inflation. Basic costs of government increase as services are expanded to meet increased population needs; costs are further increased by demands for added or improved services for an increased population. When inflation increases those costs, taxes must be proportionately increased; the increased taxes become increased costs to property owners. Inflation also adds to the costs of the property owner who must provide heating, cleaning, janitorial services, painting, repairing, and renovating. The pressures of increased taxes and housing costs induced many city homeowners to sell their properties and migrate to the suburbs. The same pressures increased rents for the middle-income renters; many tenants sought relief by moving to the suburbs.

Since the low-income family lacked funds and credit to buy the available housing, landlord investors became the purchasers. The units designed for single-family occupancy required rental payments that were too high for a single low-income family to pay. The solution was the sharing of a single unit by a number of families who then shared the unit's rent. Other rental units were subdivided into multiple-dwelling units which provided less space at lowered rents. Landlords were also induced to lessen services, delay repairs, and halt renovations to reduce costs. Consequently, cost-push inflation further contributed to housing blight.

Static forces. Blight is progressive unless it is halted or reversed. Blight also limits or reverses economic growth. Property owners and prospective owners in blighted areas have a direct concern in halting or reversing blight. The promotion of property improvement, a form of economic growth, is in their economic interest. However, static forces hold back or prevent the change that will result in improvement.

The supply and availability of construction labor determines labor costs for repairs, renovation, or new construction. Practices of construction labor unions may restrict the number of apprentices and master craftsmen. Labor union craft rules may prevent the use of less costly new construction technology or new substitute types of materials. Where such labor practices exist, they contribute to static forces which can perpetuate blight.

City governments are also a source of static forces. Zoning laws may prevent the construction of a multiple dwelling as a replacement for a blighted single-dwelling unit. Long-entrenched building codes may require current continued use of more costly older construction processes and older, less efficient types of materials. Permits, licenses, fees, bureaucracy, and red tape may serve to further discourage blighted property owners from making property improvements and repairs. The retention of rent control laws, enacted in past years, may limit the property owners' current income from which the costs for blight elimination must be paid.

Certain types of capital fund loan policy and insurance practices may be static forces. The policies of financial institutions may limit or prohibit the lending of funds which are to be used for property improvement or construction in blighted areas. Similarly, insurance companies may consider a blighted area as one of high risk. Consequently, a property owner who desires to share the risk through insurance may find the insurance either too costly or unobtainable.

The culture habits of renters may also be involved as static forces. When household foods are not properly stored in adequate ways, the food attracts flies, ants, and roaches. Larger vermin, such as mice and rats, are equally attracted. The latter may gnaw through floors, woodwork, and walls to obtain the exposed food. While food is being prepared or eaten, scraps and crumbs may fall on the floor or in furniture and bedding. If the renters' culture pattern does not include habits of proper food storage and cleanliness, the blight and plight become increasingly serious. Numerous other examples of the role of culture habits as static forces become obvious to residents of and visitors to blighted housing units.

(2) Some interrelated aspects of urban blight. The harmful effects of urban blight are numerous and varied. Escape from its effects is not limited to the middle economic class whose economic means enable it to migrate and reestablish itself in the suburbs. Fathers and heads of families frequently sought escape by desertion, commonly known as the poor man's divorce. Others sought escape through addiction to alcohol and drugs. The latter subjected small businessmen in the area to greater incidences of shoplifting, petty extortion, armed robbery, and burglary. Law-abiding families, locked in the area by low incomes and poverty, were also forced to bear the incidence of an increased crime rate. Thus, blight is not limited to the visible ugliness of decayed buildings.

Action was needed to counteract the effects of blight. The counteractions included three types: (a) consumer response, (b) private producer response, and (c) governmental response.

Consumer response. Renters are consumers of the use and services which rental housing provides. Previously, residents had isolated themselves from neighbors as self-defense against overcrowding. Since isolation did not bring a solution to the effects of blight, new tactics were needed. Renters began to form coalitions by showing others how improvement and development through the process of group action would benefit each individual as well as the whole community.

Renter coalitions began to withhold payments of rent. This action began to force landlords to obey city codes which required certain minimum standards of services to protect the health and safety of the residents. Greater use was made of the court system and governmental agencies to solve the plight of the residents. More persons became active as group participants in health, education, welfare, community planning, and work opportunity agencies. The support of youth was enlisted in projects such as Neighborhood Youth Corps and Youth Against Crime.

Private producer response. Labor organizations began to reexamine their past practices. Joint Apprenticeship Programs to train youth for building trades jobs were organized. Building Service Unions instituted job-training and job-upgrading programs for building superintendents and building service workers. Unions imposed restrictions on new types of building materials and new technological construction procedures were loosened or removed. Construction firms using newer technology, such as prefabricated building components or complete housing units, and producers of new-type building materials began to gain acceptance as participants in the war against blight. Private financial institutions and insurance companies reversed restrictive policies and became active participants in urban redevelopment. These positive responses were economic stimulants that encouraged landlords to become more active in repairing and renovating their blighted properties.

Governmental response. At the federal level, the Housing Act of 1949 set as its goal "a decent home . . . for every American family." To achieve this goal, the Act of 1968 proposed the construction and rehabilitation of 26 million houses by 1980. Six million homes were to be allocated for low- and moderate-income families. Neither the costs of meeting the goal nor decisions for funding the costs were established in the Act. Moreover, the goal will fall short of the increased demand for housing due to the rising family formations in this decade. Until housing funds are actually allocated, the decent home for every American family is a goal rather than a reality.

Housing distinctions should be made between housing for low-income groups and housing for the rest of the population. The method of subsidization — use of governmental allocated funds — is firmly entrenched for low-income housing. For the larger component of nonsubsidized housing, no single method of solution seems appropriate. Government's role in this component will be directed toward the improvement of private market mechanisms. The capital funds market, the labor market, and the construction materials market are involved as three key elements.

Housing contractors rarely own the total funds that are necessary to complete their construction projects. Few families have the cash funds to purchase housing outright. Both groups require credit; they need to borrow funds. However, housing loans are generally tied to long-term credit instruments with fixed interest rates. In inflationary periods, interest rates tend to rise; in these periods, lenders prefer to invest their capital funds in short-run, liquid, and flexible interest rate ventures. Consequently, tight money and high interest rates act as barriers to housing construction and home purchases.

To partially offset these barriers, government has provided some relief through its agencies of the Farmers Home Administration, the Federal Home Loan Bank Board, the Federal Housing Administration, the Government National Mortgage Association, the Veterans Administration, and the Department of Housing and Urban Development. Under federal executive consideration is the concept of a new type of mortgage. The interest rate of this mortgage would vary as market rates changed; the time period of repayment would be readjusted as the interest rate changed.

In an effort to increase the availability and supply of the construction work force, an executive order of 1969 established a federal Construction Industry Collective Bargaining Commission. The Commissioners' duties will include seeking solutions to train and develop construction manpower, to increase productivity and mobility of the construction labor force, to counteract instability and seasonality of construction employment, and to assist in the settlement of construction labor disputes. Another effort is through the Philadelphia Plan. This is an experimental program which is designed to increase opportunities for members of minority groups in those construction craft unions that are involved in federal construction projects.

Operation Breakthrough is sponsored by the Department of Housing and Urban Development (HUD). It will support projects that utilize new production techniques which tend to increase construction efficiency and productivity. HUD will encourage private industries that engage in volume production and mass marketing of construction materials, housing components, and complete housing units. Another function of HUD will be directed toward the change of zoning and building regulations which hamper housing improvement and redevelopment.

Although the problem of urban blight has not been solved, the causes of the problem are slowly being removed. Additionally, positive responses, presently underway, are in the direction of a future solution. Further progress toward a solution will require a continuance of social concern as well as increased expenditure of society's resources.

THE PROBLEM OF ECONOMIC CHANGE AND ITS CHALLENGE

As long as human life survives, man's expectation for economic progress will be continuous. Progress is change; change requires the acceptance of challenge and action directed toward problem solutions. As in the past, these actions will decide whether the use of present and future tools of economic analysis will be directed toward a continuance of the nation as a mixed economy.

The goal of progress may be universal; but men hold diverse views concerning the forms of progress and the speed of progress achievement. Decisions as to change and the rapidity of change are effected through a market economy, governmental action, or the interaction of both. Thus, the implementation of the decisions will determine the nature of the future economic system. Countless statistics indicate the economic progress that has been made by the generations of the present and past. It is the new and younger generation of the present and future that is confronted by the challenge of exceeding this past progress for the tomorrow.

SUMMARY

Problems arise whenever organic and personality needs cannot be satisfied. There is major agreement on the existence of pressing domestic economic problems. However, there is less agreement on the number of problems or the priority of their importance.

Problem analysis usually indicates that a number of interrelated problems are combined within a single problem. Alternative actions may be used to reach a problem solution; the selected solution may create or substitute a new problem as a replacement for the original one.

A study of farm flight reveals causal factors that include the pressure of inflation on farm costs and inflation's impact on distribution of farm income. Among the interrelated aspects of farm flight are the responses of the farm sector, the private nonfarm sector, and the governmental sector. One response of government has been its indirect action of creating social overhead capital. Thus, the Interstate

Highway System provided private production with external economies that encouraged economic growth in rural areas. Other governmental planned or direct responses have been forms of subsidization. The adopted solutions have achieved some progress in halting rural farm flight.

The problem of urban blight reveals that its causes include: (a) population density, (b) socioeconomic cultural change, (c) inflation, and (d) static forces. Responses to achieve solutions have been made by separate and interrelated actions of consumers, private producers, and government. Although governmental goals for decent housing have been enacted, the allocation of funds to reach the housing goal has not been made. Major roles in solving urban housing problems have been assigned to the Construction Industry Collective Bargaining Commission and the Department of Housing and Urban Development. Further progress toward solutions for urban blight will require continued social concern and increased allocations of society's resources.

Economic progress involves change. Change creates problems which call for for solutions. Man, in the past, has made great strides in advancing economic progress. During the period of that achievement, a mixed economic system prevailed in which private enterprise was predominant. Now a new and younger population is confronted with the challenge of exceeding that past progress.

NEW TERMS

external economies
farm flight

social overhead capital
urban blight

QUESTIONS ON THE CHAPTER

1. In seeking solutions to economic problems, why is it sometimes frustrating to have to make the necessary choices among alternative means?
2. What have been the dimensions of the flight from agriculture in recent decades?
3. What caused the flight from agriculture in recent decades?
4. What was the response of agriculture to the economic problems it faced?
5. As the farming economy was being reorganized, how did the private nonfarm sector and government help to ease the problem?
6. What is meant by "external economies"?
7. What was suggested by the President in the early 1970's that would affect low-income farm families?
8. What factors have contributed to urban blight?
9. What are some of the interrelated side effects or by-products of urban blight?
10. What are some of the ways in which consumers and private producers have responded to improve urban living conditions?
11. Why must the government play an important role in solving the problem of urban blight?

APPLYING YOUR ECONOMIC UNDERSTANDING

1. Americans annually consume beverages in millions of gallons. Many of these beverages require containers of metal or glass. How do these facts relate to organic and personality needs? In what way may they relate to a major problem of environmental pollution?
2. A boycott is applied against retailers who sell California table grapes. What groups might be affected by this boycott? How might the priority of its importance differ for each group?
3. A foreign tanker strikes a reef and its oil cargo washes up on the shores of the English Channel. A control valve on an American offshore well bursts and oil washes up on the Mississippi coast. How do both incidents relate to a common problem? Are both incidents examples of domestic economic problems? Why or why not?
4. Is the discussion of the rural problem in this chapter largely macroeconomic or microeconomic? Was economic analysis used in reporting the problem? What evidence can you cite concerning the use of income and price analysis?
5. A new city airport whose construction costs were paid from federal, state, and local governmental funds is put into operation. Are social overhead capital and external economies related to this situation? Explain.
6. There is a seventh-grade class of students in an English-oriented public school. This class is increased in size to accommodate six additional students limited to a foreign language background. Discuss some of the economic effects of the change caused by the increase.
7. A building and loan association adopts the new type of mortgage proposed by the administration in Washington, D.C. The mortgage will call for fixed payments of $120 monthly for a period of thirty years. If mortgage interest rates rise, will the date for final payment be prior to or later than thirty years? Why?

CHALLENGES TO ECONOMIC COMPETENCE

1. Select a major basic economic problem such as inflation. Break the problem down into headings of its related problems. Then prepare a bulletin board display which uses clippings that relate to each heading.
2. Poll the class to determine the major domestic economic problem that exists in your state. Invite an official from the appropriate state agency to present information to the class about the selected problem. Moderate the question-and-answer period and then summarize the main points for the class.
3. Secure and study data concerning the problem of public transportation in your city or state. Present your findings to the class.

Appendixes

Part A Bibliography: Text and Other References for Advanced Reading and Study
Part B Glossary

APPENDIX A — BIBLIOGRAPHY

PART I

Following are some suggested references for additional reading and study. Since many of them are revised periodically, no particular editions are cited. Therefore, in requesting these publications from your library or ordering them from the publishers, you should specify the latest available editions. Numbers in parentheses refer to the list of publishers starting on page 578.

General references for all units

Basic Economics, by Thomas J. Hailstones. (36)
Contemporary Economic Problems and Issues, by Thomas J. Hailstones and Bernard L. Martin. (36)
Dictionary of Economics and Business, by Erwin Esser Nemmers. (23)
Economic Analysis and Policy: Background Readings for Current Issues, by Myron L. Joseph, Norton C. Seeber, and George Leland Bach. (32)
Economic Issues: Readings and Cases, edited by Campbell R. McConnell. (25)
Economics, An Analysis of Principles and Policies, by Thomas J. Hailstones and Michael J. Brennan, Jr. (36)
Economics in Action, Readings in Current Economic Issues, edited by Shelly M. Mark. (44)
Readings in Economics, edited by Thomas J. Hailstones. (36)
Readings in Economics, edited by Heinz Hohler. (20)
Readings in Economics, edited by Paul A. Samuelson and Felicity Skidmore. (25)
The Economic System, by Roger Weiss. (34)
What Everyone Should Know About the American Economy and Its Problems. (7)
World Almanac. (30)

Individual unit references

Unit I

Adjusting to Automation, Publication No. 144. (5)
Automation: The Impact of Technological Change, by Yale Brozen. (4)
Economics in Brief, by Carl G. Uhr. (34)
How the American Economy is Organized, A Primer of Economics, by Clark C. Bloom. (40)
Manpower Report of the President. (43)
The American Business System in Transition, by Morton S. Baratz. (38)
The Making of Economic Society, by Robert L. Heilbroner. (32)
To Tell the Truth to All the World. (3)
What are Economic Problems? by Lewis E. Wagner. (37)

Unit II

A Primer on Food, Agriculture, and Public Policy, by Earl O. Heady. (34)
Business Enterprise in the American Economy, by Laurence de Rycke and Alvin H. Thompson. (26)
Farms and Farmers in an Urban Age, by Edward Higbee. (39)

Introduction to Business, by R. E. Glos and Harold A. Baker. (36)
Market for Millions. (6)
What Everyone Should Know About Financial Statements. (7)

Unit III

Agricultural Policy in an Affluent Society, by Vernon W. Ruttan, Arley D. Waldo, and James P. Houck. (45)
Agriculture and the Public Interest — Toward a New Farm Program Based upon Abundance, by Leon H. Keyserling. (15)
American Capitalism: An Introduction. (26)
Do You Know Your Economic ABC's? Patents, Spur to American Progress. (43)
Government and Business, by Ronald A. Anderson. (36)
The Consumer Price Index. (42)

Unit IV

Annual Digest of State and Federal Labor Legislation. (42)
Collective Bargaining in Public Employment, by Michael H. Moskow, J. Joseph Loewenberg, and Edward Clifford Koziara. (34)
Do You Know Your Economic ABC's? Profits and the American Economy. (43)
Employment and Earnings and Monthly Report on the Labor Force. (43)
Fringe Benefits: Wage or Social Obligations? (28)
Labor Looks at Automation, Publication No. 21. (5)
Prices, Profits, and Wages, A Study in Economic Principles and Human Well-Being, The American Competitive Enterprise Economy, Pamphlet No. VIII. (11)
Profits at Work, "Everyday Economics No. 6." (40)
The Wage-Price Guideposts, by John Sheahan. (9)
Unions, Management and the Public: Readings and Text, edited by E. Wight Bakke, Clark Kerr, and Charles W. Arond. (18)
Union Powers and Union Functions: Toward a Better Balance. (13)

Unit V

A Primer on Money. (43)
A Primer on Money, Banking, and Gold, by Peter Bernstein. (34)
A Primer on Money Supplement: Money Facts, 169 Questions and Answers on Money. (43)
Federal Reserve Bulletin. (8)
Money and Banking, by Eugene S. Klise. (36)
The Federal Reserve System: Purposes and Functions. (8)
Understanding Money and Banking. (40)

Unit VI

Comments on the President's Economic Report. (2)
Do You Know Your Economic ABC's? A Simplified Explanation of GNP and How it Mirrors our Economy. (43)
Economic Report of the President and *The Annual Report of the Council of Economic Advisers.* (43)
Income, Employment, and Prices, A Primer of Economics No. 4, by Lewis E. Wagner. (37)
National Economic Planning: What Purpose Does it Serve? What's in it for Free Enterprise? (10)

The Federal Budget, Its Impact on the Economy. (14)
Understanding Economic Growth, by Marion Daugherty. (35)
Understanding Macroeconomics, by Robert L. Heilbroner. (32)

Unit VII

A Primer on Government Spending, by Robert L. Heilbroner and Peter L. Bernstein. (34)
Can We Save Our Cities? (33)
Economics of the Community, by Myles Boylan. (35)
Financing State and Local Governments, by James A. Maxwell. (9)
Governmental Finances. (41)
On Taxes and Inflation, by Amotz Morag. (34)
The Challenge of Megalopolis, by Wolf Von Eckardt. (24)
The Federal Deficit, Fiscal Imprudence or Policy Weapon? edited by William Hamovitch. (16)
The Politics and Economics of State-Local Finance, by L. L. Ecker-Racz. (32)
The Two Faces of Debt. (17)
The Taxes We Pay, Public Affairs Pamphlet No. 289, by Maxwell S. Stewart. (33)

Unit VIII

A Primer on International Trade, by Jan Pen. (34)
Capitalism, Communism, Socialism, by Meno Lovenstein. (35)
Comparative Economic Systems, by Martin C. Schnitzer and James Nordyke. (36)
Do You Know Your Economic ABC's? U.S. Balance of Payments. (43)
East-West Trade: A Common Policy for the West. (13)
Economic Systems in Action, by Alfred Oxenfeldt and Vsevold Holubnychy. (20)
Poor Lands, Rich Lands, The Widening Gap, by L. J. Zimmerman. (34)
The U.S.A. in the World Economy, by David Steinberg. (26)
Today's Isms: Communism, Fascism, Capitalism, Socialism, by William Ebenstein. (32)
Trade Policy in the 70's, by Gordon L. Weil. (39)

Unit IX

A Primer on the Economics of Poverty, by David Hamilton. (34)
College Educated Workers, 1968-80, Bulletin 1676. (43)
Consumer Behavior, by James F. Engel, David T. Kollat, and Roger D. Blackwell. (20)
Consumer Buying Prospects. (12)
Economics and the Consumer. (22)
Handbook for Young Workers — Labor Laws, Training Opportunities, Sources of Help. (42)
Health Insurance Under Social Security — Your Medicare Handbook. (43)
Inequality and Poverty, edited by Edward C. Budd. (45)
Life Insurance Fact Book. (21)
Men Behind the Ticker Tape. (29)
Personal Finance, by Maurice A. Unger and Harold A. Wolf. (1)
Poverty in Affluence, The Social, Political, and Economic Dimensions of Poverty in the United States, by Robert E. Will and Harold G. Vatter. (18)
Progress or Poverty — The U.S. at the Crossroads, by Leon H. Keyserling. (15)
The Consumer in American Society: Personal and Family Finance, by Arch W. Troelstrup. (25)
The Other America: Poverty in the United States, by Michael Harrington. (31)
The Search for Economic Security. (21)

The Stock Market, by Edwin A. Roberts, Jr. (27)
You and the Investment World. (29)
You, Your Bank, & Your Mortgage. (19)

Publishers

(1) Allyn and Bacon, Inc.
470 Atlantic Ave.
Boston, Massachusetts 02210

(2) American Bankers Association
90 Park Avenue
New York, New York 10016

(3) American Economic Foundation
51 East 42nd Street
New York, New York 10017

(4) American Enterprise Institute for Public Policy Research
1200 17th Street, N.W.
Washington, D.C. 20036

(5) American Federation of Labor and Congress of Industrial Organizations
815 Sixteenth Street, N.W.
Washington, D.C. 20006

(6) American Stock Exchange
86 Trinity Place
New York, New York 10006

(7) Channing L. Bete Co., Inc.
Greenfield, Massachusetts 01300

(8) Board of Governors of the Federal Reserve System
20th St. & Constitution Ave., N.W.
Washington, D.C. 20551

(9) Brookings Institution
1775 Massachusetts Avenue, N.W.
Washington, D.C. 20036

(10) Center for Information on America
Washington, Connecticut 06793

(11) Chamber of Commerce of the United States
1615 H Street, N.W.
Washington, D.C. 20006

(12) Commercial Credit Co.
300 St. Paul Place
Baltimore, Maryland 21202

(13) Committee for Economic Development
477 Madison Avenue
New York, New York 10022

(14) Conference Board, Inc.
845 Third Avenue
New York, New York 10022

(15) Conference on Economic Progress
1001 Connecticut Avenue, N.W.
Washington, D.C. 20036

(16) D. C. Heath and Co.
125 Spring Street
Lexington, Massachusetts 02173

(17) Federal Reserve Bank of Chicago
P.O. Box 834
Chicago, Illinois 60690

(18) Harcourt Brace Jovanovich, Inc.
757 Third Avenue
New York, New York 10017

(19) Harris Trust and Savings Bank
111 W. Monroe Street
Chicago, Illinois 60690

(20) Holt, Rinehart & Winston, Inc.
383 Madison Avenue
New York, New York 10017

(21) Institute of Life Insurance and Health Insurance Institute
277 Park Avenue
New York, New York 10017

(22) Joint Council on Economic Education
1212 Avenue of the Americas
New York, New York 10036

(23) Littlefield, Adams & Company
87 Adams Dr.
Totowa, New Jersey 07512

(24) The Macmillan Company
866 Third Avenue
New York, New York 10022

(25) McGraw-Hill Inc.
1221 Avenue of the Americas
New York, New York 10020

(26) McGraw-Hill Book Company
Webster Division
1221 Avenue of the Americas
New York, New York 10020

BIBLIOGRAPHY

(27) National Observer
11501 Columbia Pike
Silver Springs, Maryland 20904

(28) New York State School of Industrial and Labor Relations
Distribution Center
Cornell University
Ithaca, New York 14850

(29) New York Stock Exchange
School and College Relations
11 Wall Street
New York, New York 10005

(30) Newspaper Enterprise Association, Inc.
The World Almanac Division
230 Park Avenue
New York, New York 10017

(31) Penguin Books, Inc.
7110 Ambassador Road
Baltimore, Maryland 21207

(32) Prentice-Hall, Inc.
Englewood Cliffs, New Jersey 07632

(33) Public Affairs Committee, Inc.
381 Park Avenue South
New York, New York 10016

(34) Random House
201 East 50th Street
New York, New York 10022

(35) Scott, Foresman and Company
1900 E. Lake Avenue
Glenview, Illinois 60025

(36) South-Western Publishing Co.
5101 Madison Road
Cincinnati, Ohio 45227

(37) Bureau of Business and Economic Research
State University of Iowa
Iowa City, Iowa 52200

(38) Thomas Y. Crowell Company
201 Park Avenue South
New York, New York 10003

(39) Twentieth Century Fund
41 East 70th Street
New York, New York 10021

(40) University of Chicago Press
5801 Ellis Avenue
Chicago, Illinois 60637

(41) Bureau of the Census
U.S. Department of Commerce
Suitland, Maryland 20233

(42) Bureau of Labor Statistics
U.S. Department of Labor
14th St. & Constitution Ave., N.W.
Washington, D.C. 20210

(43) U.S. Government Printing Office
Superintendent of Documents
Washington, D.C. 20402

(44) Wadsworth Publishing Co., Inc.
Belmont, California 94002

(45) W. W. Norton & Company, Inc.
55 Fifth Avenue
New York, New York 10003

PART II

Some nonprofit, professional, government, and business organizations that issue pamphlets, reports, or periodicals that are very helpful and interesting in the study and teaching of economics.

Air Transport Association of America
1000 Connecticut Avenue, N.W.
Washington, D.C. 20036

American Council on Education
One Dupont Circle
Washington, D.C. 20036

American Federation of Labor & Congress of Industrial Organizations
815 Sixteenth Street, N.W.
Washington, D.C. 20006

American Forest Institute
1816 N Street, N.W.
Washington, D.C. 20036

American Institute of Cooperation
1200 17th St., N.W.
Washington, D.C. 20036

American Institute for Economic Research
Great Barrington, Massachusetts 01230

Arabian American Oil Company
505 Park Avenue
New York, New York 10022

Association of American Railroads
American Railroad Building
1920 L St., N.W.
Washington, D.C. 20036

Association of Better Business Bureaus
One Greenwich Plaza
Greenwich, Conn. 06830

Board of Governors of the Federal Reserve System
20th St. & Constitution Ave., N.W.
Washington, D.C. 20551

British Information Service
845 Third Avenue
New York, New York 10022

Brookings Institution
1775 Massachusetts Avenue, N.W.
Washington, D.C. 20036

Bureau of the Census
U.S. Department of Commerce
Suitland, Maryland 20233

The Calvin K. Kazanjian Economics Foundation, Inc.
P.O. Box 431
Westport, Connecticut 06880

Center for the Study of Democratic Institutions
Box 4068
Santa Barbara, California 93103

Center for Information on America
Washington, Connecticut 06793

Chamber of Commerce of the United States
1615 H Street, N.W.
Washington, D.C. 20006

Chase Manhattan Bank
1 Chase Manhattan Plaza
New York, New York 10015

Committee for Economic Development
477 Madison Ave.
New York, New York 10022

Conference Board, Inc.
845 Third Avenue
New York, New York 10022

Conference on Economic Progress
1001 Connecticut Avenue, N.W.
Washington, D.C. 20036

Consumer's Research, Inc.
Consumer's Rd.
Washington, New Jersey 07882

Consumers Union of U.S.
256 Washington Street
Mount Vernon, New York 10553

Cooperative League of the U.S.A.
59 E. Van Buren Street
Chicago, Illinois 60605

Council for the Advancement of Secondary Education
1201 Sixteenth Street, N.W.
Washington, D.C. 20036

CUNA International
P.O. Box 431
Madison, Wisconsin 53701

Curriculum Resources, Inc.
1515 W. Lake Street
Minneapolis, Minnesota 55408

E. I. DuPont de Nemours & Company
Wilmington, Delaware 19898

European Community Information Service
808 Farragut Building
Washington, D.C. 20006

Federal Reserve Bank of (Boston, New York, Philadelphia, Richmond, Atlanta, Cleveland, Chicago, St. Louis, Minneapolis, Denver, Dallas, San Francisco)

First National City Bank of New York
New York, New York

Fund for the Republic
Box 4068
Santa Barbara, California 93102

Household Finance Corporation
Prudential Plaza
Chicago, Illinois 60601

Institute of Life Insurance
277 Park Avenue
New York, New York 10017

BIBLIOGRAPHY

International Bank for Reconstruction and Development
1818 H Street, N.W.
Washington, D.C. 20433

Joint Council on Economic Education
1212 Avenue of the Americas
New York, New York 10036

Joint Economic Council, Council of Economic Advisers
Washington, D.C. 20506

National Association of Manufacturers
277 Park Avenue
New York, New York 10017

National Council for the Social Studies
1201 16th Street, N.W.
Washington, D.C. 20036

National Education Association
1201 16th Street, N.W.
Washington, D.C. 20036

National Planning Association
1606 New Hampshire Avenue, N.W.
Washington, D.C. 20009

National Tax Association
100 East Broad St.
Columbus, Ohio 43215

New York Stock Exchange
11 Wall Street
New York, New York 10005

Organization of American States
17th and Constitution Avenue, N.W.
Washington, D.C. 20006

Organization for Economic Cooperation & Development
1346 Connecticut Avenue, N.W.
Washington, D.C. 20036

Public Affairs Committee
381 Park Avenue South
New York, New York 10016

Standard Oil Company (N.J.)
500 N. Broad Street
Elizabeth, New Jersey 07208

Tax Foundation
50 Rockefeller Plaza
New York, New York 10020

The Greater Hartford Council on Economic Education
Hartford, Connecticut

Twentieth Century Fund
41 East 70th Street
New York, New York 10021

United Nations (Information Division)
Foot of E. 42 Street
New York, New York 10017

United States Steel Corporation
71 Broadway
New York, New York 10006

U.S. Department of Agriculture
14th St. & Independence Ave., S.W.
Washington, D.C. 20250

U.S. Department of Commerce
14th St. between Constitution Avenue and E Street, N.W.
Washington, D.C. 20230

U.S. Department of Health, Education, and Welfare
330 Independence Ave., S.W.
Washington, D.C. 20201

U.S. Department of Labor
14th St. and Constitution Avenue, N.W.
Washington, D.C. 20210

U.S. Department of State
2201 C Street, N.W.
Washington, D.C. 20520

U.S. Department of Treasury
15th St. and Pennsylvania Avenue, N.W.
Washington, D.C. 20220

PART III
PERIODICAL PUBLICATIONS

American Federationist
Americas
Banking: Journal of the American Bankers Association
Business Week
Changing Times
Economic Indicators
Economic World
Federal Reserve Bulletin
Fortune
Monthly Labor Review
Newsweek
The Nation's Business
The National Observer
The Reporter
Time
U.S. News and World Report
Wall Street Journal

APPENDIX B — GLOSSARY

Economic terms that are listed at the end of each chapter are defined briefly in this glossary. For other terms that are not included here, refer to the index which follows.

A

Ability-to-pay theory. A theory of taxation advocating that individuals pay taxes according to their ability to pay.

Acceleration principle. The principle that a change in the demand for finished goods or services tends to give rise to a relatively greater demand for producers' goods to make the finished goods.

Acceptability. That quality of money that makes individuals and business concerns willing to accept the money in exchange for what they wish to sell.

Acceptor. The person on whom a draft is drawn and who agrees to pay it.

Administered price. A price that is set by the producer and maintained for a time at the desired level by adjusting supply.

Advance. A loan made by a federal reserve bank to a member bank and secured by government obligations.

AFL-CIO. The federation created by the merger, in 1955, of the American Federation of Labor and the Congress of Industrial Organizations.

Agency-shop contracts. Forms of union security contracts under which all employees in the bargaining unit must pay regular dues and fees, but are not required to join the union.

Agents (marketing). Middlemen, such as brokers or commission men who buy and sell for others.

Aggregate demand. The total demand for goods and services by consumers, producers, government, and foreign purchasers.

Agricultural credit. Credit used by farmers for the purchase of agricultural land, the erection of farm buildings, the purchase of livestock, and the marketing of crops.

Amalgamation (consolidation). The combining of two or more corporations into a new single corporation.

American capitalism. The form of our economic system based largely upon free enterprise and private property.

Annual improvement factor. A provision in some collective bargaining agreements calling for an annual wage increase based on the assumption that the productivity of workers will constantly increase due to improved methods of production.

Annuity. A contract that calls for the periodic payment of a certain sum of money by the insured person to the insurance company for a stated number of years. At the end of that time the insurance company will pay the person a fixed income for his lifetime or for a designated number of years.

Antiprotectionists. Those who oppose a protective tariff.

Applied economics. The use of economic principles in the solution of everyday economic problems.

Apprentice. One who is under contract to work for another in order to learn a trade.

Aptitude. The ability of an individual to learn to perform a certain activity or a number of related activities.

Articles of copartnership. A written agreement setting forth the terms of a partnership agreement.

Articles of incorporation. A paper, including the name, the purpose, and the location as well as any other items that are considered necessary, which is drawn up for the formation of a corporation.

Assets. Owned things of value; property.

Automatic stabilizers. Counter-cycle factors which automatically come into operation when the business cycle rises or falls.

Automation. The automatic control of a manufacturing process.

B

Balance of international payments. A statement showing international transactions that give rise to money payments between countries.

Balance sheet. A statement of assets, liabilities, and present worth.

Bank (commercial) credit. Refers to loans made by banks to proprietors and business concerns for relatively short periods of time, say from thirty to ninety days.

Bank draft. An order by one bank on another bank directing the latter to pay a certain sum of money to the order of the person named in the draft.

Barter. The exchange of one commodity for another without the use of money.

Base date. The period upon which a price index number of any given year is calculated.

Benefit theory. A theory of taxation advocating that one pay taxes in proportion to the benefits he receives from government.

Better business bureau. An organization in most large cities to protect consumers against unfair business practices.

Bimetallism. The use of two metals at a fixed ratio of value as a monetary standard.

Blacklists. Lists of unacceptable workers.

Board of directors. A group elected by the stockholders to manage a corporation.

Bonds (corporation). Certificates issued to show the debt to be repaid and the security pledged for its repayment.

Book value. The worth — according to accounting records — of stock shares based upon the assets remaining after all debts have been deducted.

Borrowing (business). The securing of capital or capital funds with a promise to repay at some future date and usually with interest.

Boycott. Refraining by concerted action from having dealings with another person or group; a refusal by workers to use materials made by a concern.

Brand label. A label used to identify the product of a particular producer.

Brassage. Charge made by the government to cover the cost of coinage.

Broker. A middleman who brings prospective buyers and sellers together.

Budget. A statement of expected income and a plan for expenditures over a future period of time.

Business corporations. Chartered enterprises that are organized to make profits.

Business cycles. Periods of time that include the characteristic alternating phases of good and bad times in business.

Business-service cooperatives. Enterprises organized under cooperative principles which produce services for the owner-members.

Business unit (firm). The factors of production organized under one management.

Bylaws. A formal list of rules, stating the procedures to be followed in conducting the affairs of a corporation.

C

Canons (principles) of taxation. Adam Smith's standards of justice, certainty, convenience, and economy.

Capacity. In connection with the credit rating of an individual, capacity relates to his ability to pay his debts out of his current income.

Capital. Things that are intended to be used in the production of goods or services. Also used to refer to the amount of property, such as land, houses, or stocks and bonds, that a person owns.

Capital formation. The accumulation of funds or producers' good for use in future production.

Capital funds. The value of invested capital expressed in money amounts.

Capital (producers') goods. Anything, made by man, intended to be used in the production of goods or services; producers' goods.

Capitalism. An economic order or theory wherein the private ownership of capital and the existence of the profit motive in production are recognized as being fundamental.

Capitalizing income. Finding the principal that will produce a certain amount of income at a certain percentage or interest rate.

Capital resources. Producers' goods available for use in production in any economic society.

Capital stock. Shares of ownership that a corporation has a right to issue.

CARE. A private charitable organization that makes food and other necessities directly available to needy persons abroad.

Carrying charge. A charge on an installment purchase to cover interest and costs of handling.

Cartel. A combination by business concerns in different countries to control the prices and production of commodities.

Cash dividends. Dividends that are paid in the form of cash.

Cashier's check. A check drawn by a bank upon its own funds.

Cash record. A record of cash receipts and expenditures.

Cash sale. A sale of goods on a commodity exchange for immediate delivery.

Caveat emptor. Let the buyer beware.

Certificate of incorporation (charter). A written instrument issued by the state or the federal government, creating a corporation and defining the rights and the powers of the corporation.

Certified check. A depositor's check, the payment of which is in effect guaranteed by the bank on which it is drawn.

Changes in demand. At a given price the quantity of a good that will be bought either increases or decreases.

Character. In connection with the credit rating of an individual, character refers to an individual's willingness to pay his obligations.

Charge account. A common form of consumer credit whereby one obtains the goods at the time of purchase but pays for them at a later date, usually during the first part of the following month.

Charter (certificate of incorporation). A written instrument issued by the state or the federal government,

GLOSSARY

creating a corporation and defining the rights and the powers of the corporation.

Check. A depositor's written order on a bank, directing the bank to pay a sum of money to a designated person or "bearer."

Checkoff. An agreement under which the employer deducts union dues from the employees' pay and turns the money over to the union.

Child labor. This term is usually defined as the gainful employment of persons at ages below those permitted by law.

Circulating capital. Production goods that are quickly used up.

Civilian labor force. The labor force exclusive of persons in the military services.

Civil Rights Act of 1964. An act of Congress forbidding, among other things, discrimination in employment on the basis of race, religion, color, sex, or national origin.

Clearinghouse. A room or a building set aside for the purpose of collecting and clearing checks among banks.

Closed shop. An enterprise in which employment is limited to members of a union who must be members before employment.

Cognizability. The quality of money that makes it possible to recognize it easily.

Collateral (surety). Stocks, bonds, or other personal property deposited to secure a loan.

Collective bargaining. Fixing of terms of employment by representatives of the employers and of the employees.

Comaker (surety). One who indorses a borrower's promissory note, thereby promising to repay the loan himself if the borrower fails to do so.

Commercial bank. A financial institution, the main functions of which are: (1) to receive deposits of money and credit and (2) to lend money or credit to individuals and business firms.

Commercial (bank) credit. Loans made by banks to proprietors and business concerns for relatively short periods of time.

Commercial draft. A written order by one party directing another party to pay a sum of money to a third party.

Commercial (contract) rent. Rent that is paid according to agreement.

Commission merchants. Agents who receive goods on consignment for sale to consumers or others.

Committee on Political Education. An AFL-CIO organization that has been active in making campaign contributions and in "getting out the vote" for candidates favorable to labor.

Commodity Exchange Authority. A federal agency the function of which is to regulate future trading in wheat, rice, corn, barley, rye, flaxseed, sorghum, mill feeds, cotton, butter, eggs, Irish potatoes, and wool tops.

Common stock. A certificate showing ownership and its rights in a corporation.

Communism. A doctrine that advocates the public ownership of all capital goods and that usually claims that violent means are justified in overthrowing capitalism.

Communist Manifesto. A document by Karl Marx and Friedrich Engels, published in 1848, which serves as the basis for communist doctrine.

Community of interest. The condition that exists when two or more concerns refrain from competing with each other. Results when managers in different companies prevent their companies from competing.

Company union. An organization of employees in an establishment, unaffiliated with any other labor group.

Compensated dollar. A dollar the purchasing power of which would remain fixed by changing the gold content of the dollar.

Compensation of employees. The total amount of wages and salaries paid to employees, including contributions by employers to the social security program.

Competition. An economic institution that involves economic rivalry.

Competitive profits. Profits earned by a business that competes with other businesses in the sale of its products.

Compulsory arbitration. Arbitration by a government agency that has the right to enforce its decisions in labor disputes.

Concentration (marketing). Movement of goods toward a common center.

Conciliation (mediation). Settling a labor dispute by discussion between the employer and the union with the assistance of a third party.

Conglomerate. A business combination which includes firms engaged in unrelated kinds of production.

Conservation. Action to use economically some or all forms of natural resources.

Consolidation (amalgamation). A combination of two or more corporations involving the dissolution of the former businesses and the formation of an entirely new corporation.

Constant dollars. The purchasing power of the dollar in some base year.

Consumer (personal) credit. Credit that is used for the purpose of obtaining goods or funds for the satisfaction of personal wants.

Consumer finance companies. Types of small loan companies, specializing in consumers' loans.

Consumer Price Index. An index of consumer prices published by the Bureau of Labor Statistics.

Consumers' cooperatives. Cooperatives organized for the purpose of purchasing commodities or services for its members.

Consumers' goods. Economic goods that are used directly in the satisfaction of wants.

Consumers' loans. Loans made to consumers in amounts up to some relatively low maximum figure, such as $600. (Small or remedial loans)

Consumption. The utilization of the utilities of a good or service.

Consumption tax. A tax on expenditures for consumption goods and services.

Contract. An agreement between two or more individuals or groups that is enforceable by law.

Contraction. Phase of the business cycle following the peak.

Contract (commercial) rent. Rent that is paid according to agreement.

Contractual interest. Interest paid according to agreement.

Convertible preferred stock. A form of stock which can be exchanged at a fixed ratio for shares of common stock.

Cooperatives. Group-owned and operated enterprises which produce goods and services for their owner-members.

Cooperative societies. Cooperative organizations designed to provide services for their members, such as buying or selling goods.

Co-prosperity. A pre-World War II plan for the unification of Asia and its supposed economic betterment under Japanese domination.

Copyright. The exclusive right that is granted by the federal government to an author or an artist to produce and sell works of literature or art that he has created.

Corporate profits. The net amount of income earned by corporations before the payment of corporate taxes or the payment of dividends to stockholders.

Corporation. "A corporation is an artificial being, invisible, intangible, and existing only in the contemplation of the law," authorized by a charter that gives continuous existence to an enterprise without reference to the lives of the persons connected with the enterprise.

Correspondent banks. Banks in which another bank keeps deposits.

Cost-of-living (escalator) wage clauses. Clauses that require specified wage adjustments to be made according to changes in the cost of living as indicated by the Consumer Price Index issued by the Bureau of Labor Statistics.

Cost-of-service principle. The principle which holds that public utility rates should be fixed slightly above the cost of rendering the service.

Cost-push inflation. A rise in prices caused by raising wages in major industries more rapidly than the labor productivity increases.

Craft guilds. Medieval organizations of workers.

Craft union. A union of workers with the same or similar skills (carpenters, for example).

Credit. The ability to obtain goods or services in exchange for a promise to make payment later.

Credit card. A credit device used to authorize a person to charge hotel bills, meals, car rental, gasoline, airplane fare, and other expenses and purchases.

Credit instrument. A written instrument used in creating or in transferring credit, such as a promissory note or a commercial draft.

Creditor nation. A nation to which other nations owe more money than it owes to them.

Credit union. A cooperative association intended to promote saving among its members and to provide them with loans when needed.

Cumulative preferred stock. Stock on which the stated amount of dividend must be paid before dividends are paid to the common stockholders, the amount accumulating each year until paid.

Currency. Coins and paper money that are issued by the government and put into circulation by banks.

Current dollars. The present value of the dollar.

Customs duties. Taxes levied on goods that are transported from one country or political jurisdiction to another.

D

Debenture bonds. Bonds secured only by a general claim against the assets of the corporation.

Deductions (tax). Nontaxable amounts of income allowed for such payments as contributions to educational institutions, certain taxes, and interest paid on borrowed funds.

Deferred annuity. A purchased insurance contract that provides a stated amount of income to be paid in the future.

Deficit. Debt; the amount of money spent in excess of income.

GLOSSARY

Degressive tax. A tax for which the rate increases but at a slower rate than the increase in the amount of income or the value of the property to be taxed.

Demand. The number of units of a good that buyers stand ready to buy in a market at a particular time at different prices.

Demand curve. A graphic representation of a demand schedule.

Demand deposit. A deposit in a checking account that may be withdrawn at any time without previous notice.

Demand for loanable funds. The total amount of purchasing power that borrowers will take at specific prices (interest rates) at a given time.

Demand schedule. A table indicating the amounts that buyers would buy at various prices in a given market at a given time.

Deposit currency. The bank credit that circulates in the form of bank checks, which are payable on demand and in cash by the banks on which the checks are drawn.

Depositor. One who has funds in a bank.

Deposits. The amount that a bank owes the depositors which may be withdrawn in cash or transferred by check.

Depression. A stage of the business cycle during which business is bad and incomes and employment are low.

Derivative deposit. A deposit resulting from a bank loan. The deposit is derived from money held by the bank in the form of primary deposits.

Derived demand. The demand for productive resources that comes about because there is a demand for the things that the productive resources can produce.

Descriptive label. A label that sets forth the characteristics of the contents of the package.

Devaluation (money). Reducing the weight or value of the unit of standard money.

Dictatorship of the proletariat. Absolute government control by dictators who profess to represent workers only.

Dictionary of Occupational Titles. A descriptive listing of the many different kinds of jobs.

Direct (tax). A tax paid directly to the government by the persons upon whom it has been imposed.

Discount. A loan made by a federal reserve bank to a member bank which pledges commercial paper as collateral.

Discretionary fiscal action. Economic policy involving spending or taxing by government to control the business cycle.

Dispersion (marketing). Movement of goods from a common center.

Disposable personal income. The total amount received by consumers, less the total amount of their income, property and social security taxes, and any other compulsory deductions.

Distribution. The sharing of income in a society and an indication of how wealth is allocated.

Dividends. Shares of the profits of a corporation paid to stockholders.

Divisibility. The quality of money that makes it possible to calculate values in terms of fractions of the unit and also in terms of multiples of the unit.

Division of labor (specialization). Specialization of effort in production.

Dollar glut. The possession of dollars by foreigners in excess of their needs for purchasing American products.

Dollar shortages. Other nations want to buy a great many goods from the United States, but they have few dollars with which to pay for our goods.

Domestic (inland) bill. A commercial draft drawn on another person or business concern in the same state.

Domestic system. Production of goods in homes instead of in factories. This system prevailed in the period preceding the Industrial Revolution.

Draft. A written commercial instrument ordering a payment of money.

Drawer. A person who draws a draft.

Dumping. Practice of selling goods in another country at a price that is below the cost of producing the goods, the objective being to get rid of a surplus or to destroy an industry or business in a foreign country.

Durability. The enduring quality of money or the quality that makes it easy to replace without expense.

Durable consumers' goods. Consumers' goods that may be used over and over again for a considerable period of time.

Duty. A tax imposed on articles imported from another country.

Dynamics. Forces that bring about change.

E

Ecology. A branch of biology that studies organisms and their environment.

Economic freedom. The right to go into business for yourself, to own property, and to enter into binding agreements to buy or sell goods and services, and to compete for the sale or purchase of goods and services.

Economic goods. Material goods that require effort to produce. (The term is sometimes used to include services.)

Economic indicators. Statistics and charts showing changes in employment, production, expenditures, and income in phases of the economy and in the gross national product.

Economic law. An economic theory adopted and accepted as an economic truth or fact.

Economic problem. The selection of the process by which society can best satisfy its unlimited wants within the limits of relatively scarce productive resources.

Economic (pure) profit. The amount remaining to the owner of a business after an allowance has been made for the use of his own services, his land, and his capital.

Economic rent (for land). The annual value of the income from a plot of land in excess of the cost of producing the income.

Economics. That branch of social science that is concerned with man's efforts to produce and to use material and immaterial things to satisfy wants.

Economic theory. A conclusion reached by applying scientific reasoning to economic data.

Economic value. A characteristic of something that has utility, is relatively scarce, and the worth of which can be measured in some way.

Economic wants. Needs or desires for an economic good or service.

Economy. A system of producing, distributing, and consuming wealth.

EEC. The European Economic Community, established in 1958, or "common market," an organization pledged to remove certain trade restrictions and to promote the economic development of its six West European member nations.

EFTA. The European Free Trade Association, composed of several West European nations outside of the "common market," which seeks to abolish tariffs within its organization.

Elastic (demand). Demand is elastic when a change in price results in a considerable change in the quantity of a good that people will buy.

Elasticity of demand. The extent to which changes in price affect the quantity of a good that is consumed.

Employment Act of 1946. An act of Congress declaring governmental policy in favor of high levels of employment and economic activity.

Endowment plan. An insurance policy on which the insured person pays a stated premium for a given number of years. At the end of that time he receives the amount of the policy.

Engel's laws. Statements of relationships that tend to exist between the size of personal and family incomes and the percentages that people spend for various classes of goods.

Enterprise. Responsible for the initiation, organization, and operation of productive establishments and for the assumption of the risks of failure of productive establishments.

Entrepreneurial risks. Risks assumed by an enterpriser.

Entrepreneurs (enterprisers). Those who assume the risks of a business.

Equilibrium price. The price at which the quantities of a good demanded and supplied in the market are brought into balance.

Escalator (cost-of-living) wage clauses. Clauses in a collective bargaining agreement requiring that specified wage adjustments be made according to changes in the cost of living as indicated by the Consumer Price Index.

Estate tax. A "death tax" that is levied on an estate before the property passes to the heirs.

Excess-profits tax. Business tax levied when net income is above a specified rate.

Excess reserves. A bank's reserves over and above the amount of required legal reserves.

Exchange. A function of an economy in which a good or service is given up for something else of value.

Exchange control. A governmental action restricting international payments or regulating exchange rates.

Exchange value. Value based upon a comparison of marginal utilities of the goods or services involved.

Excises. Taxes imposed on goods at the time of their sale.

Exemption (tax). A specific amount of one's income on which one does not have to pay any tax, such as an amount for each dependent of the taxpayer, in addition to an amount allowed for himself.

Expansion. A stage of the business cycle in which business is making marked improvement.

Export. Any transaction the result of which calls for the payment of money or credit by a foreign individual or concern to a domestic producer; a good or service sold abroad.

Export-Import Bank. A federal agency established in 1934 to assist in the financing of exports and imports using borrowed Treasury funds.

External economies. Savings or reductions in costs that result from economic behavior outside of a firm.

F

Factory (industrial) stage. The era of production using extensive capital equipment and the factory system of organization.

Fair Labor Standards Act. The federal law, dealing with wages and hours, that applies to employees who in

GLOSSARY

any way have anything to do with goods or services that move in interstate commerce. (Wage and Hour Law)

Farmers' cooperatives. Cooperatives organized for the purpose of marketing or processing farmers' products.

Farm flight. The rapid departure of population from agricultural life and the rural area.

Fascism. A doctrine that, from an economic standpoint, permits the right of private productive property, but makes individuals and classes absolutely subordinate to the state; politically, a dictatorship.

Favorable balance of trade. The condition that exists when the value of a country's exports exceeds the value of its imports.

Federal Mediation and Conciliation Service. An organization that is designed to mediate all kinds of labor disputes except those in the railroad and airline industries.

Federal utility commissions. Several federal commissions having the purpose of regulating utilities that are engaged in interstate business.

Fees. Charges for a government service that is of special benefit to the person receiving the service.

Fiat money. Money that circulates by reason of the order of the government.

Final products. Goods and services purchased and in the hands of consumers. In terms of value, the value of the raw material plus the value added by expenditures at each stage of production.

Firm (business unit). The factors of production organized under one management.

Fiscal agent. A financial agent that holds and pays out government money.

Fiscal policy. The use of the powers of taxation and spending by the federal government for the purpose of increasing or decreasing production, income, and employment in the economy.

Fixed capital. Specialized capital; machinery, structures, equipment, etc.

Fixed costs. Costs that do not vary greatly with the volume of production.

Food for Freedom. A federal program appropriating funds to purchase surplus grains and foodstuffs to be sent as aid to nations that have critical food shortages.

Foreign bill. A commercial draft drawn in one state or country on a person or business in another state or country.

Foreign exchange. The currency of countries other than one's own; dollars are foreign exchange to other countries.

Form utility. The shape or structure of materials that make the materials more usable.

Franchise. A government permit that gives the owner at least a partial monopoly.

Free capital. A capital good capable of being used for various purposes.

Free coinage. The right of anyone to have bullion coined by the government.

Free competition. Competition involving a great number of both producers and consumers of a product, and where it is easy for producers to enter or to leave a field of production.

Freedom of enterprise. An economic institution which permits private owners to gather, coordinate, and use productive resources to create economic goods.

Free goods. Material goods that are supplied free by nature.

Free trade. Absence of restrictions on foreign trade.

Future or **future sale.** A contract to sell a security or a commodity, which the seller does not own at the time, that calls for delivery at some future date.

G

GATT. The General Agreement on Tariffs and Trade was adopted by numerous nations to provide for discussions related to the reduction of restrictions on international trade.

General partners. Members of a partnership who share equally in management, profits, and liability.

General partnerships. Partnerships in which the members share equally in management and liability.

General sales tax. A tax on most consumer goods collected at the time of the sale of the goods.

General welfare clause. The clause in Article I of the Constitution which states that Congress shall have the power "To lay and collect taxes, duties, imposts, and excises, to pay the debts and provide for the common defense and the general welfare of the United States."

Gift tax. A tax on gifts designed to make it impossible for an estate to escape taxation because it is given to heirs before the death of the owner.

Gold-coin standard. This standard means that: A unit of gold is the measure of value for goods, services, and other money; the government will coin an unlimited amount of gold bullion; all other money can be exchanged for gold at its face value; gold is legal tender; people are free to own and use gold as they do any other commodity.

Gold export point. The rate of exchange that causes gold to move out of a country.

Gold-par rate of exchange. The rate of exchange for the monetary units of two countries expressed in terms of the gold contents of such units.

Good. Anything that people desire; material things or services.

Gosplan. The national planning board of the USSR.

Government (public-owned) corporations. Corporations that are organized for purposes of government; those that are owned by the government.

Grade label. A label that indicates a definite standard of quality.

Greenback. A United States note used as money. It was first issued during the Civil War.

Gresham's law. The tendency for an inferior money to drive a superior money out of circulation.

Grievance procedure. An arrangement between a company and a union whereby day-to-day complaints arising in industrial relations can be settled by negotiation.

Gross interest. The net interest on a loan plus any charge that may be added to compensate the lender for his risks and expenses incurred in making the loan.

Gross national product. The total of all the goods and services produced during the year and valued at current prices.

Gross profit. The difference between the amount that is paid for goods and the amount that is received when the goods are sold.

Guaranteed annual wage (GAW). The employer agrees to pay his employees a specified wage for a certain number of weeks even if the workers are laid off because of lack of work.

Guaranteed stock association. A type of saving and loan enterprise which is chartered as a profit-making corporation.

Guideposts. Standards suggested by government to help business and organized labor to make price and wage decisions that will not be inflationary.

H

Head (poll) tax. Tax levied on an individual without reference to benefits received by him or his ability to pay.

Hidden taxes. Commodity taxes that are apparently paid by the manufacturer but are actually paid by consumers in the form of higher prices.

Holding company. A corporation that holds stock in another company or companies for the purpose of control.

Home market. A market for commodities in the same country in which the commodities are produced.

Homogeneity. A characteristic of anything having all units alike.

HOPE. A private charitable organization that provides health, medical, and surgical services to less-developed nations.

Horizontal combination. The organization formed when two or more concerns engaged in the same kind of business combine.

Household inventory. A list of household articles at their present value.

I

Immediate annuity. A purchased insurance contract in which payments begin immediately after the purchase.

Imports. Any transactions that call for the payment of money or credit to a foreign individual or concern by a domestic producer; goods or services purchased from foreigners.

Imputed interest. That part of one's income that arises from the use of his capital in his own business.

Imputed wages. The estimated value placed upon the labor of self-employed persons when no cash payment for wages is made.

Income. Benefits received, or which may be claimed, the value of which is usually stated in terms of money; wealth received during a period of time.

Income effect. An explanation of the downward slope of the demand curve. When the price of a good decreases, the buyer feels that he has more purchasing power from his income and reacts by buying more of the good.

Income taxes. Taxes on net income.

Independent union. A union not affiliated with any federation.

Indirect (tax). A tax, the expense of which is borne by one person, but the final cost of which is passed on to another.

Individualism. The theory that self-reliance and individual effort should be the most important factors in providing for one's needs.

Individual (sole) proprietorship. A business enterprise owned by a single individual.

Indorsement. Transferring a negotiable instrument to another by writing one's name on the back of the instrument.

Industrial banks. Types of small loan companies, specializing in consumer's loans.

Industrial Revolution. Change in the methods of production through the rapid introduction of power and machinery during the latter part of the eighteenth century and the first part of the nineteenth century.

Industrial (factory) stage. The era of production using extensive capital equipment and the factory system of organization.

GLOSSARY

Industrial union. A labor union that endeavors to organize all the workers in an industry, as a coal miners' union.

Inelastic (demand). Demand is inelastic when a change in price has little or no effect on the quantity bought.

Infant industries. Industries in the first period of life.

Inflation. A general decrease in the purchasing power of the monetary unit.

Inheritance tax. A tax that is levied on the share of an estate received by an heir.

Injunction. A court order restraining an individual or a group from the performance of a certain act.

Inland (domestic) bill. A commercial draft drawn on another person or business concern in the same state.

Innovations. As an economic force: introduction of new products, new types of industry, and new methods of production.

Installment credit. A form of personal or consumer credit used to obtain goods for consumption by making a series of payments over a period of time rather than an earlier single payment.

Institutions (economic). The well established and accepted relationships which are essential to and support an economic system.

Insurance policy. A written agreement or contract between an insurance company and the insured party.

Interest. Compensation that goes to the owner of capital. Also an attitude which predisposes an individual to regard favorably an object, practice, or situation.

Interest rate. The price paid for the loan of funds.

International Bank for Reconstruction and Development (IBRD). A financial institution designed to encourage international lending by nations and private business.

International cartel. A combination or arrangement between two or more business concerns located in different countries for the purpose of conducting their affairs in such a way as to make profit.

International Monetary Fund (IMF). A fund set up by 111 nations to aid international trade and finance.

Interstate. The term applied to business that is carried on between firms located in different states.

Intrastate. The term applied to business that originates and is carried on entirely within a state.

Investment banks. Institutions that supply long-term credit and commonly serve as a medium for distributing securities to the general public.

Investment credit. Long-term credit for the purchase of land and capital goods.

Investment trust. A financial organization that sells shares of the trust and invests the funds thus obtained in the stocks and bonds of a group or other companies.

Invisible (export or import) items. Securities or services sold to foreigners or purchased abroad from foreigners; not material goods.

ITO. The International Trade Organization was a proposal to form an international organization the purpose of which was to study and try to discover ways for reducing or removing tariffs and other trade barriers that interefere with trade between nations.

J

Joint costs. Costs that are common to the production of two or more goods.

Journeyman. A worker who has learned a handicraft or trade. Formerly, a man hired to work by the day. A medieval guild worker.

L

Labor force. All persons sixteen years of age or older who are working or looking for work.

Labor-Management Relations Act of 1947. A law the general intent of which is to limit some of the rights enjoyed by labor organizations under the Norris-LaGuardia and the National Labor Relations Act.

Labor-Management Reporting and Disclosure Act of 1959. Federal law pertaining to unions and management. (Landrum-Griffin Act)

Labor resources. The quantity and quality of human effort available for productive services in a society.

Labor's League for Political Education. An AFL organization that was active in making campaign contributions and in "getting out the vote" for candidates favorable to labor.

Laissez faire. The policy of allowing business to control itself without interefernce by government.

Land. Natural resources from which all of the goods that we use originate.

Landrum-Griffin Act. Federal law pertaining to unions and management. (Labor-Management Reporting and Disclosure Act)

Law of comparative advantage or cost. The tendency for a region to devote its resources to the production of those commodities or services in which it has the greatest advantage or the least comparative disadvantage.

Law of demand. In a given market at a given time, the quantity of a good that people will buy tends to vary inversely with the price of the good.

Law of diminishing marginal utility. The tendency for the utility of a given unit of stock of goods to decrease when the supply increases.

Law of diminishing returns. The tendency for a factor of production ultimately to yield a less-than-proportional increase in output when successive units of the factor are added to fixed quantities of the other factors.

Law of supply. In a given market at a given time, the quantity of a good that will be offered for sale tends to vary directly with the price of the good.

Law of supply and demand. In a competitive market, given sufficient time for adjustments to take place, the quantity of a good that buyers want and the quantity that sellers will offer for sale are brought into balance at some price that will just clear the market.

Legal reserve. The reserve that members of the Federal Reserve System are required to keep on deposit with the federal reserve banks of which they are members, which is equal to a certain percentage of their deposits.

Lend-lease program. A program for supplying goods to our allies in World War II and having indefinite terms for repayment.

Liabilities. Responsibilities for the payment of debts.

License. Written permission from government allowing an individual or concern to perform certain acts or to carry on a business.

Life insurance. The pooling or shifting of probable risks of loss of life among a group.

Limited partners. Persons whose liability is fixed in accordance with agreements between members of the enterprise.

Limited partnership associations. Partnerships in which the liability of all partners is limited under state laws.

Limited partnerships. Partnerships in which the liability of one or more partners is limited with limited partners taking no part in management of the firm.

Limited-payment plan. An insurance policy under which the insured person pays regular premiums for a certain number of years. At the expiration of the stated period of time, the payment of premiums is discontinued. Upon the death of the insured person, the company pays to his beneficiary the amount of the policy.

Limiting output. A means used by workers to force employers to agree to conditions demanded by the workers.

Liquidation. Termination of a business involving the sale of its assets.

Liquidity. The quality or characteristic of an asset that makes it possible easily to convert the asset into cash.

Liquidity preference. The preference of people to keep their savings in the form of cash for current purchases, for precaution against need, and for possible speculation in the future.

Lockout. The closing of an establishment by an employer in response to the demands of employees for more wages or a change in working conditions.

Long run. A production period long enough for an industry to make the adjustments which result in normal price.

M

Macroeconomics. A study of the aggregates or totals of production, income, employment, and price levels.

Maintenance-of-membership clause. A clause in some union contracts which means that each union member must keep up his membership or be discharged.

Managed currency. Broadly speaking, a currency that is changed in order to offset changes in the price level. This term also refers to the proposal to abolish a metallic standard by the use of paper money. It may also include a fluctuating standard.

Margin (buying on). Amount of money that the buyer of stocks or bonds must deposit with the stockbroker.

Marginal land. Land the produce of which pays only for the cost of utilizing the land. (No-rent land)

Marginal producers. Producers whose income from the sale of goods produced equals only the cost of production.

Marginal productivity. The amount or value added to the total product by the use of one more unit of a factor of production while the quantities of the other factors remain unchanged.

Marginal productivity theory of wages. Under conditions of pure competition, employers tend to hire additional workers up to the point where the amount of wages becomes equal to the value of the product that would be lost by the employer if one less worker were employed.

Marginal utility. The utility of one of the units of a given stock of goods when the units are alike in every respect; or the utility of an additional unit.

Marketing. Broadly speaking, all business activities related to the buying and selling of goods.

Marketing cooperatives. Businesses organized and operated under cooperative principles which provide marketing services for the member-owners.

Marketing function. An activity classified under one of the following headings: (1) selling and buying, (2) standardization and grading, (3) financing, (4) transportation, (5) storage, and (6) risk bearing.

Market ratio. The rate at which two commodities are exchanged for each other in the market; for example,

GLOSSARY

silver and gold, at one time, exchanged at the rate of 16 to 1.

Master workman. A worker approved by the guild who could set up his own shop, make and sell goods of a certain kind, train apprentices, and hire journeymen.

Mediation (conciliation). A means for bringing a voluntary, negotiated end to a labor dispute. A third party assists the company and union to reach an agreement.

Medicare. A system of hospital and medical insurance sponsored by the federal government.

Member banks. National or state banks that are members of the Federal Reserve System.

Mercantilism. The theory or practice of the mercantile system.

Merchant. One who aims to make a profit by buying and selling goods.

Merchant guilds. Medieval organizations of merchants.

Merger. A combination of corporations involving the dissolution of one of them and the sale of its assets to a second corporation.

Microeconomics. A study of a specific small segment of economics, such as market pricing.

Middlemen. Persons who engage in marketing activities.

Mint ratio. Values fixed by the government when two or more metals are used as the monetary standard — for example, silver and gold, 16 to 1.

Mixed economic system. One that uses a combination of capitalism and socialism or some other composite variation.

Monetary policy. The use of devices to control the supply of money and credit in the economy.

Money. The medium of exchange used by an organized group of people.

Money income. The amount of money that one receives during a given period of time.

Money (nominal) wages. The amount of money paid for given amounts of work.

Monopolistic competition. A market situation in which there is a number of sellers of products that are not identical but that are close substitutes.

Monopoly. Control by an individual, a business concern, a group, or government that makes it possible to control production and fix prices of one or more articles or services.

Monopoly profits. Those profits that are received by a concern that controls the supply and prices of the goods or the services that it sells.

Monopsony. A market situation in which there is only one buyer of a good.

Moral suasion. The making of suggestions by federal reserve banks to member banks to encourage or discourage loans to customers.

Mortgage. A conditional conveyance of property as a pledge for the payment of a debt or the performance of some other obligation.

Mortgage bonds. Long-term promissory notes secured by a mortgage or a lien on specific property.

Multiple bank credit contraction. The process whereby the commercial banking system as a whole can reduce total deposits by several times the amount of any deposits permanently withdrawn from the banking system.

Multiple bank credit expansion. The process whereby the commercial banking system as a whole can lend several times the amount of any new deposits it acquires.

Multiplier principle. The operation of economic forces that cause the ultimate increase in income resulting from an additional amount of spending to be several times the original amount spent.

Mutual savings bank. A savings bank owned by its depositors.

N

National income. The total income paid to the owners of the factors of production for a given period of time.

Nationalism. Exalting one's own people and institutions.

National Labor Relations Board. A governmental agency that administers an act which is designed to insure to workers the right to organize and to bargain collectively with their employers (National Labor Relations Act).

National wealth. The sum of all the valuable material things owned by private individuals and concerns and the different units of government.

Natural monopoly. An industry in which competition is not feasible.

Natural resources. Total wealth supplied by nature. Includes mineral deposits, timber, soil fertility, fish, and all wildlife.

Nazism. The economic and political order (the fundamentals of fascism) adopted in Germany prior to World War II.

Need. A state of tension or stress within an individual.

Negotiable bill of lading. A receipt for a shipment whose ownership can be transferred by indorsement.

Net exports. Our exports less our imports.

Net income. The amount of income after certain deductions have been allowed.

Net (pure) interest. The net return for the use of capital.

Net national product. The amount of gross national product remaining after deducting the amount of depreciation involved in producing the GNP.

Net profit. The amount remaining after the total amount of all expenses has been deducted from the gross profit.

Nominal (money) wages. The amount of money paid for given amounts of work.

Noncumulative preferred stock. Preferred stock on which dividends are lost if they are not declared and paid in the year in which they are supposed to be earned.

Nondurable consumers' goods. Consumers' goods that are used up quickly.

Noneconomic wants. Desires for nonmonetary things which one believes will give him pleasure or satisfaction.

Nonparticipating preferred stock. Preferred stock that does not entitle the holder to more than a stated amount of profits.

Nonprofit corporations. Corporations designed for social, charitable, and educational purposes.

Nonrefund annuity. Provides income to the recipient only, with no residual payments to a third party.

No-par-value stock. Stock that has no money value stated in the stock certificate.

Normal price. Long-run price; price that tends to exist under pure competition.

Norris-LaGuardia Act. An act of Congress (1932) which, among other things, makes yellow-dog contracts unenforceable in federal courts.

O

OAS (Organization of American States). A treaty (1948) agreement among North and South American nations to provide for their common security and to promote their economic interests.

Occupational families. Classifications of job opportunities into broad areas.

Officers (corporation). Persons who are elected by a board of directors and are given the responsibility of carrying on the business.

Oligopoly. Relatively few sellers of a product, resulting in some control over production and prices.

Open-market operations. The buying and selling of bonds and certain kinds of commercial credit instruments.

Opportunity cost. The amount of payment which is necessary to attract a given amount of a factor of production from an alternative use.

Organic needs. Those needs which relate to physical health and well-being.

Organization for Economic Cooperation and Development. A federal agency which serves in a consultative way on economic foreign affairs.

Organized commodity exchange. A place where standardized commodities are bought and sold.

Ownership (possession) utility. Utility possessed by a good based on the right to use it.

P

Parity prices. Prices fixed for certain commodities in order to keep the purchasing power of such prices at a par with prices of the same commodities at some previous time.

Participating preferred stock. Preferred stock that entitles the holder to share profits with the holders of common stock, usually after a stipulated amount has been paid to the holders of the common stock.

Partnership. A form of business in which two or more persons combine their resources and undertake a venture for profit.

Par-value stock. Stock that has a money value stated in the certificate.

Patent. Exclusive right conferred by government to make and to sell an article that one has invented.

Patronage refunds. Savings, derived from the operation of a cooperative enterprise, which the members share proportionately.

Peak. The highest level of economic activity in the business cycle.

Personal consumption expenditures. All expenditures at market value for goods and services purchased by individuals, families, and nonprofit institutions.

Personal (consumer) credit. Credit that is used for the purpose of obtaining goods or funds for the satisfaction of personal wants.

Personal distribution of income. The major consumer spending categories; the amounts spent in categories by individuals and families.

Personal income. The aggregate income of all persons in the country from all sources; also the dollars received by each individual from one's contribution to production.

Personality. The sum total of everything that one is.

Personality needs. Social needs that cannot be satisfied by the consumption of material goods.

Personality traits. The particular characteristics of personality.

Place utility. The capacity of a good to satisfy a want by being at the place where it is wanted.

Political Action Committee. A CIO organization that was active in making campaign contributions and in "getting out the vote" for candidates favorable to labor.

Political freedom. The right to be equal to others before the law; to run for public office; to vote in the election

GLOSSARY

of public officers; to speak and write our opinions as to what is needed in government, as well as on other matters; to criticize government and public officials, and so on.

Poll (head) tax. Tax levied on an individual without reference to benefits received by him or to his ability to pay.

Pool. An agreement between producers to divide the business and profits within a given territory.

Population explosion. A rapid increase in world population which raises problems of balancing people's needs with the world's resources.

Portability. That quality of money that makes it possible to carry it around without too much inconvenience.

Possession (ownership) utility. The utility that a good possesses because it is possible to use the good.

Preferential shop arrangement. An arrangement whereby the employer agrees to give preference in hiring to workers who are members of a union.

Preferred stock. Stock that entitles the holder to preferential treatment with respect to dividends or the distribution of assets, or both.

Premium. In insurance, the payment made by a policyholder to a group fund for protection against risk or loss.

Present worth. The difference between the total value of the assets and the total amount of the liabilities.

Price. The exchange value of a commodity or a service stated in terms of money.

Price index number. A measure of the average price at one date as compared with the average price at another date.

Price level. The average price of a number of goods and services.

Primary deposit. Results when one deposits currency or checks in a bank.

Principles (canons) of taxation. Adam Smith's standards of justice, certainty, convenience, and economy.

Private corporations. Corporations that are subject to control by the members as stockholders and that are not owned by the government.

Private monopolies. Monopolies held by a private concern or an individual.

Private property. The right to the exclusive control, within limits, of a good.

Private wealth. Material economic goods that are owned by individuals and private business.

Producers' (capital) goods. Anything, made by man, that is intended to be used in the production of goods or services.

Product differentiation. Giving an article a distinct name, appearance, or slightly unique quality.

Production. The creation of utility, or want-satisfying power, in goods or services.

Production cooperatives. Group-owned and operated enterprises which use cooperative principles to produce various kinds of economic goods.

Production possibility curve. A graphic figure showing possible outputs of product related to various combinations of productive resources.

Productivity. Refers to the amount of output of goods that results from the use of a unit of a factor of production.

Profit motive. The production of an article because the producer is interested in making a profit from the sale of the article.

Progressive tax. A tax the rate for which increases as the tax base increases.

Promissory note. An unconditional promise in writing made by one person to another to pay on demand or at a definite time a certain sum in money.

Proportional tax. A tax the rate for which remains constant as the tax base increases.

Proprietors' income. The amount earned by sole proprietors, partnerships, and self-employed persons.

Prosperity. A stage of the business cycle during which business conditions are good and incomes and employment are high.

Protectionists. Those who favor a protective tariff.

Proxy. A signed statement by a stockholder giving another the power to cast the stockholder's vote at a stockholders' meeting.

Public (government-owned) corporations. Corporations that are organized for purposes of government; those that are owned by the government.

Public domain. All land owned by the government.

Public monopolies. Monopolies belonging to government.

Public utilities. Business concerns that produce services that are essential to modern living conditions, prices of which are regulated by government rather than by competition. Public utilities enjoy a certain degree of monopoly owing to the fact that they are granted a franchise from the government.

Public wealth. Material economic goods owned by government.

Purchasing cooperatives. Group-owned enterprises which are primarily operated to purchase farm supplies for members.

Purchasing-power parity theory. Rate of international exchange that is determined by the value or purchasing power of the money in the respective countries.

Pure competition. A market situation where there are so many sellers and buyers of a good that no one seller or buyer can influence the price.

Pure (net) interest. The net return for the use of capital.

Pure monopoly. A market situation in which there is one seller of a good.

Pure (economic) profit. Profit remaining after allowances have been made for implicit rent, wages, and interest.

Pyramiding control. Control of producing companies by means of a holding company.

Q

Quantity theory of money. The theory that the amount of money in circulation and its velocity are the most important factors in the determination of prices.

R

Rate discrimination. Act of a public utility in charging more for one service than another.

Rate of exchange. The conversion value of the money of one country to that of the money of another country.

Rate of return (on investment). The ratio of investment income received relative to the total amount of money invested as capital funds.

Rates. The term applied to revenues that are derived from businesses operated by the government, such as waterworks.

Real income. The actual goods received during a given period of time or the amounts of actual goods that could be bought with the money received during a period of time.

Real wages. The amount of goods and services that money wages will provide.

Receipts (government). Money and credit received from both taxes and loans from the people.

Reciprocal Trade Agreements Act. An act permitting arrangements between the President and representatives of other nations whereby the President without Congressional approval may raise or lower tariffs by as much as 50 percent.

Refund annuity. An adjustment may be paid to a third party when the insured dies before he has collected the amount paid into the annuity.

Refunding (debt). Borrowing in order to repay bonds or other obligations that are currently due.

Regressive tax. A tax the rate for which decreases as the tax base increases.

Reinvestment. The use of profit derived from production as additional capital or capital funds for use in the enterprise.

Remedial loans. Loans made to consumers in amounts up to some relatively low maximum, such as $600. (Small or consumers' loans)

Rent. Compensation to the owner of land.

Rental income of persons. The measure of the rental income received by property owners, including the estimated rental value of nonfarm residential and business property.

Retailer. One who sells to consumers.

Revenues. Funds that the government collects but does not have to repay.

Revenue sharing. A plan whereby the federal government would turn over to state and local governments a portion of the revenues collected by the federal government.

Right-to-work laws. State laws that do not allow unions to require union membership of a person in order to secure or to maintain employment.

S

Sabotage. The damaging of machinery or goods by workers because of resentment against an employer. Any kind of restriction of output has on occasion been called sabotage.

Savings and loan associations. Savings institutions designed to aid home building.

Savings banks. Financial institutions that accept deposits, which ordinarily are left with the bank for a considerable length of time.

Savings bonds. Usually refers to "E" and "H" bonds issued by the United States Treasury.

Savings certificates of deposit. A means of saving whereby the depositor places a specified minimum amount with a bank for an extended period of time and receives a higher rate of interest than that which is paid on regular time deposits.

Scabs. Workers who refuse to go out on strike.

Scale of living. The way people actually live.

Scientific method. A process of study which involves the collection, validation, and organization of data to reach a factual conclusion.

Secondary boycott. The boycott that occurs when a labor union prohibits its members from using goods of another employer.

Secret partner. A partner who is unknown to the public.

Seigniorage. A charge for coinage that yields a profit to the government.

Selective controls. Measures used during periods of national emergency by federal reserve banks to influence the demand for loans for the purpose of buying goods.

GLOSSARY

Seniority rating. A system of layoffs, rehirings, and promotions according to length of service with the company.

Severance taxes. Taxes on natural resources that are removed and sold.

Shifting a tax. Transferring the burden of a tax from one group of persons to another.

Shortage. A condition of supply existing when, at the prevailing price, buyers are attempting to buy more of a good than sellers are offering for sale.

Silent partner. A partner who takes no part in the management of the firm.

Single-tax proposal. A proposed tax under which all rent would be appropriated for purposes of government and which, it is claimed, would render other taxes unnecessary.

Slowdowns. Workers give the appearance of working while in agreement to reduce output.

Small loans. Loans made to consumers in amounts up to some relatively low maximum figure, such as $600. (Consumers' or remedial loans)

Socialism. The doctrine that advocates the public ownership of productive capital.

Social overhead capital. An economic good whose costs are charged to or borne by the whole society.

Social Security Act. The federal law that provides for unemployment compensation for certain classes of workers; old-age and survivors' benefits for workers covered by the law; aid for the needy, aged, blind, and disabled; aid for children who lack parental support; maternal and child health services; medical care for crippled children; Medicare; and certain kinds of welfare work in communities.

Soil bank. Refers to a government program, adopted in 1956, that offers payments to farmers who agree to withdraw land from cultivation.

Sole (individual) proprietorship. A business enterprise owned by a single individual.

Special assessments. Payments made by the owner of land to the government for improvements made by the government.

Specialization (division of labor). A division of labor in the economy; production of a specific or limited nature.

Specialized capital. Capital goods that can be used in but one or a few ways.

Speculation. Buying goods or property with the expectation of selling at a profit as a result of a change in the market price.

Speculative profits. Profits that are made as a result of a change in price after one has bought something.

Stability of value. To be used successfully as money, the value of the thing must not fluctuate too much.

Standard of living. The way one would like to live as compared with the scale of living.

Standard wage rates. Fixed wage rates for particular types of work.

Statics. Forces that tend toward equilibrium and resist change or growth.

Stock. A share of ownership in a corporation which includes certain rights relative to entrepreneurship.

Stock certificate. An instrument certifying to the ownership of stock in a corporation.

Stock dividends. Additional shares of stock given to stockholders in payment of a dividend.

Stock exchange. A place and organization for the buying and selling of corporation stocks and bonds.

Stockholders. Those persons who share in the ownership of a business organized as a corporation.

Stock savings bank. A savings bank organized and conducted for profit by its stockholders.

Straight (whole) life policy. An insurance policy for which premiums must be paid as long as the policyholder lives.

Strike. The voluntary cessation of work by employees in order to enforce their demands on the employer.

Strikebreakers. Those employed to take the place of striking workers.

Submarginal land. Land that produces an income less than the cost of the labor and capital used on it.

Submarginal producers. Producers whose cost of production exceeds the income received from the sale of the goods produced.

Subsidiary companies. Business corporations whose stock is held or owned by another company or by a holding company.

Subsidies. Financial gifts to encourage production.

Substitution effect. An explanation for the downward slope of the demand curve. More of good "A" will be purchased if its price falls because it will be substituted for another good, the price of which has not fallen.

Supplementary unemployment benefits. Plans that provide for employer-financed funds out of which benefits received from state unemployment compensation are supplemented according to a negotiated formula.

Supply. The number of units of a good that sellers stand ready to offer for sale in a market at a particular time at different prices.

Supply of loanable funds. The amount of funds that people and business concerns will lend at specific rates of interest at a certain time.

Supply schedule. A tabular representation of supply.

Supramarginal land. Land that yields rent.

Supramarginal producers. Those producers whose cost of production is less than they receive from the sale of their products.

Supreme Soviet. The Council or legislative body of the Union of the Soviet Socialist Republics.

Surety (comaker). One who indorses a borrower's promissory note, thereby promising to repay the loan himself if the borrower fails to do so.

Surplus (corporate). The excess value of the assets over the amount of the liabilities and the issued capital stock; accumulated profits belong to the stockholders.

Surplus (supply). A condition of supply existing when, at the prevailing price, sellers are offering for sale more of a good than buyers are willing to buy.

Sympathetic strike. A strike that is called in order to help another group of workers, even though the strikers do not have any grievance of their own.

T

Taft-Hartley Act. The Labor-Management Relations Act, usually called the Taft-Hartley Act after Senator Robert A. Taft and Representative Fred A. Hartley, sponsors of the act.

Tariff Commission. A federal agency which was intended to provide for scientific tariffs that would equalize the cost of production at home and abroad.

Tariffs. Taxes, usually on imports.

Tax. A compulsory charge upon individuals or property, usually in the form of money, for the support of government.

Taxable income. The amount of income determined by subtracting certain allowable deductions and credits from the gross income.

Tax evasion. Deliberately failing to declare all taxable income or property for tax purposes or claiming deductions, expenses, or exemptions with the intent to defraud the government.

Technological unemployment. Unemployment caused by the introduction of laborsaving machinery.

Technology. A branch of knowledge in which art, skill, or science is used to promote economic production.

Term insurance. Insurance that runs for a stated period of time.

Time deposits. Deposits left with banks in savings accounts on which the banks will pay interest.

Time utility. The power of a good to satisfy a want because it is available when it is wanted.

Totalitarianism. An economic system in which private enterprise may exist but all production and distribution are under centralized or dictatorial control.

Trade acceptance. A commercial draft drawn by the seller upon the buyer at the time of the sale of goods.

Trade agreement. An agreement, usually written, that sets forth the terms under which union workers are to be employed, including wages, hours, working conditions, order in which employees may be discharged, and so on.

Trade association. An organization of individuals and concerns engaged in similar kinds of business for the purpose of promoting the interest of the members.

Transfer payments. Money payments by government or business for which no services are currently rendered.

Trough. The lowest point of a depression.

Trust. An arrangement whereby the stockholders in competing corporations surrender their stock to a group of trustees, receiving in exchange trust certificates.

U

Underdeveloped. A less-developed or developing condition of a nation whose resources are inadequate or are not effectively used for production.

Unearned income. The value of land, which arises because of economic rent.

Unemployment insurance. Insurance of employees against loss of pay due to unemployment, the cost of the insurance being provided by taxation.

Unfavorable balance of trade. The condition that exists if the value of imports exceeds the value of exports.

Union federation. An organization composed of national unions of different kinds.

Union label. A label testifying that a product was made by union labor.

Union-management cooperation. A program by which unions agree to cooperate with management in reducing production costs, and union members and management work together in a spirit of cooperation, friendship, and fairness toward each other.

Union security. A term applied to any of several contractual devices used by a union to acquire a stronger position within a firm, such as the union shop and maintenance-of-membership.

Union-shop agreement. An agreement whereby the employer is free to hire anyone he chooses provided the employee agrees to become a union member within a specified time.

Urban blight. A city section affected by decay, deterioration, or poverty; such as an area of substandard housing.

Utility. The quality of a good that enables the good to satisfy a want.

GLOSSARY

V

Value-of-service principle. Principle for determining public utility rates on the basis of what the service is worth to the user.

Variable costs. Costs that change in total amount as production changes.

Velocity of money. The rate at which money changes hands.

Vertical combination. A company engaged in the production of a finished article and which controls other companies or plants, each of which completes certain stages in the production of the article.

Visible (export and import) item. A commodity export or import.

Voluntary arbitration. The method of settlement when both sides agree to submit their difficulties to an individual or a group and to abide by the decision.

W

Wage and Hour Law, 1938. The law, also known as the Fair Labor Standards Act, that applies to employees who in any way have anything to do with goods or services that move in interstate commerce.

Wage rates. The prices for labor per hour, per week, per month, or for some other unit of time; or the price for pieces of work.

Wages. The amount paid for labor.

Wages of management. The value of the labor of a self-employed worker in performing managerial functions himself rather than hiring someone else to do this for him.

Wagner Act. The National Labor Relations Act.

Walsh-Healey Act. The federal law which requires that persons working on government contracts in excess of $10,000 be paid no less than the prevailing wages in the community and that no males below 16 years of age or females below 18 years of age be employed on such contracts.

Want. A desire for something that we feel will give us pleasure or satisfaction.

War on poverty. The concerted federal programs which are intended to lessen chronic unemployment and raise low levels of living.

Watered stock. Stock that has been issued in exchange for property of less value than the par or the declared value of the stock.

Wealth. Material economic goods subject to ownership.

Weighted index number. For prices, an arithmetical average that takes into consideration the different quantities of goods that are normally purchased. Thus, some prices are made to "weigh" more heavily in the average.

Whole (straight) life policy. A life insurance contract which calls for premium payments throughout the insured's lifetime.

Wholesalers. Persons who sell to retailers or other middlemen.

Working reserve. The amount of money that a bank must keep on hand with which to pay the checks that will likely be drawn on it.

World Bank (IBRD). An international financial institution designed to encourage international lending by private individuals and businesses for developmental and trade purposes.

Y

Yellow-dog contracts. Wage contracts by which the employee agrees not to belong to a labor union.

Index

A

Ability-to-pay theory, 405
Acceleration principle, 374; cumulative effects of the, on the production of capital goods, 373
Acceptability of money, 300
Acceptor, 322
Accident insurance, 526
Administered price, 173
Advance, 310
Advertising, does, help or hinder consumer? 512; preventing undesirable, 513
Advertising claims, 511
AFL-CIO, 282; structural organization, 279
Agency shop contracts, 283
Agents, 89
Aggregate demand, 367; control of, 369; increases and decreases in, 370
Agricultural Adjustment Act, 189
Agricultural credit, 317
Agricultural Marketing Act, 189
Agriculture, income from, 557
Air Quality Act of 1967, 27
Air resources, 25
Alliance for Progress, 433, 446
All-Union Communist Party, 463
Allowable tax deductions, 412
Amalgamation, 138
American capitalism, 45
American Dental Association, 516
American Home Economics Association, 516
American Medical Association, 516
American Standards Association, 516
American Stock Exchange, 551
AMTRAK, 188
Annual improvement factor, 237
Annuities, 527; deferred, 528; defined, 527; immediate, 527; nonrefund, 528; refund, 528
Antiprotectionists, 424
Applied economics, 4
Apprentice, 31
Aptitude, 495
Arbitration, compulsory, 289; voluntary, 288
Articles of copartnership, 101
Articles of incorporation, 110
Assessments, special, 397, 409
Assets, 510
Automatic stabilizers, 377
Automation, 55, 226; effect of, on demand for labor, 226

B

Balance of international payments, 440
Balance of trade, favorable, 441; unfavorable, 441
Balance sheet, 510
Bank credit, 317; control of amount of, by Federal Reserve System, 339; extensions of, 260
Bank deposit, 328
Bank draft, 320
Bank loans, extensions of credit, 329
Bank reserves and monetary policy, 375
Banks, clear and collect checks, 330; commercial, 328, 544; correspondent, 332; create deposit currency, 333; federal reserve, 337; importance of, 343; industrial, 255; investment, 327; keep reserves, 332; kinds of, 327; member, 336; mutual savings, 545; organization and operation of, 330; savings, 327, 544; savings and loan associations, 328, 546; stock savings, 545
Bank's statement of condition, 335
Bargaining, collective, 275
Barter, 29
Base date, 198
Bears, 91
Benefit theory, 405
Better business bureau, 517
Bill of lading, negotiable, 439
Bimetallic standard, 302
Bimetallism, 302

Blacklists, 287
Board of directors of a corporation, 110
Board of Governors of Federal Reserve system, 336, 337, 551
Bonds, 114; comparison of stocks and, 550; debenture, 114; investing in, 550; mortgage, 114; Series E and H, 545; United States Treasury and savings, 545
Book value of share of stock, 115
Borrowing, by businessmen, 257; by consumers, 255; by corporation, 114; by governments, 257; for productive purposes, 256; for speculation, 258; government, 398
Boycott, 284; secondary, 284
Brand label, 513
Brand labeling, 513
Brassage, 302
Broker, 89
Budgeting is essential, 509
Budgets, 509; flexibility of, 510
Bulls, 91
Bureau of Labor Statistics, 509
Bureau of Standards, 72, 519
Business, organizing and managing, 95
Business associations, employers and, 287
Business corporation, comparison to a cooperative association, 123
Business corporations, 120
Business cycle, phases of, 366
Business cycles, 366; and economic growth, 365; contraction phase of, 366; definition of, 366; expansion phase of, 366; peak of, 366; theories as to the causes of, 367; trough of, 367
Business firm, 96
Businessmen, borrowing by, 257
Business ownership, kinds of, 96
Business risks, kinds of, 95
Business-service cooperatives, 125
Business taxes, 411
Business unit, 96

601

Buying, 84, 510
Buying and selling between nations, 419
Bylaws of a corporation, 110

C

Canons of taxation, 407
Capacity, 316
Capital, 8, 316, 477; circulating, 64, 65; classified according to durability, 65; classified according to use, 65; fixed, 64, 65; free, 64, 65; interest for, 253; sources of, for corporations, 113; specialized, 64, 65
Capital formation, 8; in corporations, 113
Capital funds, 8
Capital goods, 63, 64; cumulative effects of the acceleration principle on the production of, 373
Capital resource employment, 145
Capital resources, 7
Capital stock, 114, 115
Capitalism, definition of, 34; *laissez-faire*, 44; nature of, 34; political freedom is essential to, 42
Capitalizing income, 262
Capitation taxes, 396, 413
CARE, 483
Carrying charge, 319; cost of, 319
Cartel, 141; international, 430
Cash dividends, 112
Cashier's check, 321
Cash record, 510
Cash sale, 90
Caveat emptor, 517
Centralized control, the problem of, 139
Certificate, stock, 113
Certificate of incorporation, 110
Certified check, 321
Changes in demand, 158
Character, 316
Charge account, advantages of, 317; definition of, 317; disadvantages of, 318
Charter, 110
Check, 320; cashier's, 321; certified, 321; illustration of, 321
Checkoff, 283
Checks, banks clear and collect, 330
Chicago Board of Trade, 91
Child labor, 232
Children's Bureau of Social Security Administration, 535

Children's Bureau of the Department of Labor, 234
Child welfare, 535
Circulating capital, 64, 65
City problem, urban blight as a, 564
Civil Aeronautics Board, 184
Civilian labor force, 228
Civil Rights Act of 1964, 235
Clearinghouse, 330
Closed shop, 283
Cognizability of money, 301
Coins, minor, 309; nonsilver, 308; silver, 308
Collateral, 255
Collective bargaining, 275, 283; health, insurance, welfare, and retirement plans under, 539; in government employment, 291
Comaker, 255
Commercial banks, 544; definition of, 328
Commercial credit, 317
Commercial draft, 322
Commercial rent, 243; demand and supply determine, 246
Commission merchants, 89
Committee for Economic Development (CED), 193
Committee on Political Education (COPE), 282
Commodity Exchange Authority, 91
Commodity exchanges, organized, 90; regulated by governments, 91
Common stock, 117
Communism, 462; growth of, 465
Communist Manifesto, 462
Community of interest, 141
Company union, 287
Comparative advantage, law of, 420
Comparative cost, law of, 420
Compensated dollar, 206
Compensation of employees, 355
Competition, 36; free, 170; pure, 154
Competitive prices, graphic illustration of, 163; how demand and supply result in, 162
Competitive profits, 266
Compulsory arbitration, 289
Concentration, 82
Conciliation, 288
Condition, bank's statement of, 335
Conglomerate, 137
Conservation, 22

Consolidation, 138
Constant dollars, 360
Construction Industry Collective Bargaining Commission, 569
Consumer agencies, private, aid and protect consumers, 515
Consumer cooperatives, 125
Consumer credit, 317
Consumer finance companies, 255
Consumer Price Index, 199
Consumers, are more laws needed to protect?, 520; borrowing by, 255; government agencies protect, 517; marketing from producers to, 79; private consumer agencies aid and protect, 515
Consumers' goods, 64, 65; durable, 64, 66; nondurable, 64, 66; prices apportion, 152
Consumers' loans, 255
Consumer spending, cumulative effect of the multiplier principle on, 371
Consumers' Research, Inc., 515
Consumers Union, Inc., 515
Consumption, 13; personal, 134
Consumption taxes, 395, 410
Contract, definition of, 35
Contraction, 366
Contract rent, 243
Contractual interest, 254
Convertible preferred stock, 118
Cooperative association, comparison of a business corporation and a, 123
Cooperative business, 97
Cooperatives, 121; based on the Rochdale principles, 122; business-service, 125; consumers', 125; farmers', 124; marketing, 125; production, 125; purchasing, 125; types of in the United States, 124
Cooperative societies, 121
Co-prosperity, 467
Copyright, 172
Corporate profits, 355
Corporation, 109; chartered by government, 110; controlled by board of directors, 110; definition of, 109; gifts to, 114
Corporations, 97, 109; advantages of, 118; assets of, owned by the, 113; business, 120; bylaws of, 110; capital in, 118; classification of, 120; continuous existence of, 118; definition of, 97; disadvantages of, 119; governmental control of, 120;

Index

limitations of credit in, 120; limited liability of, 118; non-profit, 120; organization of manufacturing, 112; private, 120; public, 120; taxes imposed on, 120; transfer of investment in, 119
Corporation securities, investing in, 549
Correspondent banks, 332
Cost of living, 200
Cost-of-living clauses, 237
Cost-of-service principle, 185
Cost-push inflation, 207
Costs, equalization of, 427
Council of Economic Advisors, 208
Craft guilds, 31
Craft union, 277
Credit, advantages of, 323; agricultural, 317; bank, 317; bank loans are extensions of, 329; commercial, 317; consumer, 317; definition of, 315; disadvantages of, 323; installment, 317; investment, 317; is based on confidence, 316; kinds of, 316; money as a basis of, 300; personal, 317
Credit card, 322
Credit instrument, 320
Credit instruments, drawn on banks, 320; kinds of, 320
Creditor nation, 440
Credit ratings, 316
Credit union, 125
Credit unions, 255, 547
Cropland Adjustment Program, 192
Cumulative preferred stock, 118
Currency, 298; deposit, 333; devaluating, 444; managed, 205
Current dollars, 360
Customs duties, 396, 419

D

Debenture bonds, 114
Deductions, allowable tax, 412
Deferred annuity, 528
Deficit financing, 377
Deficit of a corporation, 112
Degressive tax, 406
Demand, 154; affects wages, 235; aggregate, 367; and supply determine commercial rent, 246; and supply determine interest rates, 254; changes in, 158; derived, 225; elastic, 157; elasticity of, 157; for labor, 225; for labor, effect of automation on, 226; for land, 245; inelastic, 157; law of, 155
Demand and supply, law of, 162
Demand curve, 155; explanation for the downward slope of, 155
Demand deposit, 331
Demand for loanable funds, 255
Demand schedule, 154
Department of Agriculture, 72, 184, 520
Department of Commerce, 200
Department of Health, Education, and Welfare, 27, 519, 530
Department of Housing and Urban Development (HUD), 569, 570
Department of Justice, 184
Deposit currency, 333
Depositor, 320
Deposits, 331; demand, 331; derivative, 328; F.D.I.C. insures, 343; primary, 328; time, 331
Depression, 367
Derivative deposit, 328
Derived demand, 225
Descriptive label, 513
Devaluating currency, 444
Devaluation, 306, 444; effects of, 306
Dictatorship of the proletariat, 463
Dictionary of Occupational Titles, 499
Differential Aptitude Test, 495
Diminishing returns, law of, 219
Directors, 110
Direct taxes, 408
Discount, 310
Discretionary fiscal action, 377
Dispersion, 82
Disposable income, 216, 356
Disposable personal income (DPI), 216, 356, 357
Distribution, 12
Dividends, 112; cash, 112; stock, 112
Divisibility of money, 301
Division of labor, 46
Dollar glut, 445
Dollar shortages, 444
Domestic bill, 322
Domestic economic problems, some difficulty in selecting and analyzing, 555
Domestic system, 31
Draft, 439; bank, 320; commercial, 322
Drawer, 322
Dumping, 426
Durability of money, 301
Durable consumers' goods, 66
Duties, 419; customs, 396
Dynamics, definition of, 28

E

"E" bonds, 545
Earth's resources, 24
Ecology, 21
Economic change, the problem of, and its challenge, 570
Economic development, essential factors in achieving, 476
Economic evolution and development, 29
Economic freedom, 43
Economic goods, 63, 64; classes of, 63; material, 63
Economic growth, business cycles and, 365
Economic indicators, 377; illustrations of, 378
Economic law, 16
Economic motives, 137
Economic order, form of, 479
Economic problem, and our economic resources, 6; and our economic wants, 4; defined, 4; involves economic activities, 11; raises some major questions, 9; some difficulties in selecting and analyzing domestic, 555; the basic, affects our lives, 4
Economic profit, 266
Economic rent, 243
Economic resources, our, and the economic problem, 6
Economics, applied, 4; definition of, 4; how to study, 15; importance of, 17; meaning of, 4; specialization fields in, 500
Economic society, nature of our, 27
Economic systems, of other nations, 453; the changing nature of, 453
Economic theory, 16
Economic value, 151
Economic wants, 6; our, and the economic problem, 4
Economy, definition of, 27; increasing stability and progress of our, to help underdeveloped nations, 486; of USSR, 464
Elastic demand, 157
Elasticity of demand, 157

Index

Employees, retirement systems of public, 538
Employers, and business associations, 287; labor unions and, 274; ways, oppose labor unions, 287
Employment, capital resource, 145; collective bargaining in government, 291; control of ups and downs in, 374; labor resource, 142; land resource, 143; of men, regulation of, 234; of women, regulation of, 234
Employment Act of 1946, 374
Endowment plan of life insurance, 529
Engel's laws, 509
Enterprise, 71; freedom of, 35; government, 97
Enterprisers, profits for, 265
Entrepreneurial risks, 266
Entrepreneurs, 71, 213
Equilibrium price, 162
Escalator wage clauses, 237
Estate tax, 396, 413
European Economic Community (EEC), 431
European Free Trade Association, 432
Evolution and development, economic, 29
Excess-profits tax, 270, 411
Excess reserves, 334
Exchange, 13; foreign, 439; official rate of, 442; organized commodity, 90; stock, 551
Exchange controls, 441; forms of, 442; nature of, 441
Exchange rates, 441; determination of, 442; purchasing-power parity, 443
Exchange value, 151
Excises, 395
Exemption, tax, 412
Expansion, 366
Expenditures, keeping records of, 509; planning, 508
Export-Import Bank (E-IB), 446
Exports, 422; definition of, 440; payments for, 438; U.S. merchandise by continent, 423; value of, 422
External economies, defined, 562

F

Factors of production, 213
Factory stage, 33
Fair Labor Standards Act of 1938, 232, 234
Family Assistance Plan, 564
Farm costs, pressure of inflation on, 556
Farmers' cooperative, 124
Farmers Home Administration, 569
Farm flight, a rural problem, 556; defined, 556; farm sector response to, 559; governmental response to, 561; private nonfarm response to, 560; some causal factors of, 556; some interrelated aspects of, 559
Farm income, inflation's impact on the distribution of, 558
Farm prices, federal government influences, 188
Farm problem, 193
Fascism, 467
Favorable balance of trade, 441
Federal Advisory Council, 336
Federal Bureau of Investigation (FBI), 389
Federal Communications Commission, 184
Federal debt, size of the, 399
Federal Deposit Insurance Corporation, 343
Federal Farm Board, 189
Federal Food and Drug Administration, 519
Federal government, administrative budget totals and public debt, 394; services and expenditures of, 392
Federal Home Loan Board, 569
Federal Housing Administration, 548, 569
Federal Mediation and Conciliation Service, 288
Federal Open Market Committee, 336
Federal Power Commission, 184
Federal Pure Food and Drug Act, 519
Federal Reserve Act, 337
Federal reserve banks, 337
Federal reserve currency, 310
Federal Reserve System, 336; Board of Governors of, 337; clearinghouse for member banks, 341; control of amount of bank credit, by 339; fiscal agent for the United States government, 341; functions of, 337; management of, 337; organization of, 337
Federal Trade Commission, 184, 519
Federal utility commissions, 184
Federations, union, 280
Fees, 397, 409
Fiat money, 307; our experience with, 307
Final products, 351
Finance companies, consumer, 255
Financial goals, setting, 508
Financing, 85
Firm, 96
Fiscal agent, 341
Fiscal policy, 376; discretionary, 377; does it work? 377; in practice, 379
Fixed capital, 64, 65
Fixed costs, 173
Flow of income and expenditures, 357
Food and Agriculture Act, 192
Food, Drug, and Cosmetic Act, 519
Food for Freedom, 483
Forced saving, 9
Foreign bill, 322
Foreign exchange, 439; where you can purchase, 437
Form utility, 69
Franchise, 171
Free capital, 64, 65
Free coinage, 302
Free competition, 170
Freedom, economic, 43; of enterprise, 35; political, 42
Free enterprise, and role of profits, 270; charges of socialists against, 454; our defense of, 456; political freedom is essential to, 42
Free goods, 63, 64
Free trade, 423
Fringe benefits, 277, 283
Future, 90
Future sale, 90

G

General agreement on tariffs and trade (GATT), 431
General partners, 101
General partnerships, 101
General property tax, 395, 409
General sales tax, 395
General welfare clause, 392
Gifts, to government, 398
Gift tax, 396
Goals, setting financial, 508
Gold bullion, 304, 308
Gold certificates, 308

Index

Gold-coin standard, 304, 305
Gold export point, 442
Gold-par rate of exchange, 441
Gold Reserve Act, 305
Gold standard, 441
Goods, capital, 63, 64; consumers', 64, 65; consumers' durable, 66; definition of a, 62; durable consumers', 64; economic, 63, 64; free, 63, 64; intangible, 64; material, 63, 64; nondurable consumers', 64, 66; nonmaterial, 64; producers', 63, 64; tangible, 64
Gosplan, 465
Government, aids production, 72; borrowing by, 257; federal, services and expenditures of, 392; functions of, 385; how, gets the money it spends, 393; increasing control of prices by, 181; local, services and expenditures of, 388; modern, provides many services, 386; -owned corporations, 120; regulates business, 44; state, services and expenditures of, 389; three-level form, 388
Government agencies, aids and protects consumers, 517
Government borrowing, 398; dangers of, 398; reasons for, 398
Government employment, collective bargaining in, 291
Government enterprise, 97
Government National Mortgage Association, 569
Government purchases of goods and services, 353
Government revenue, 428
Government spending and public policy, 401
Grade label, 513
Grade labeling, 513
Grading, 84
Greenbacks, 309
Gresham's law, 303; operation of, 303
Grievance procedure, 277
Gross interest, 254
Gross national product (GNP), 350, 357; and income, 350; and income distribution of, 354; components of the, 351; how is measured, 350; in current and constant dollars, 360
Gross private domestic investment, 352
Gross profit, 266

Gross-receipts tax, 396
Guaranteed annual wage agreement (GAW), 236
Guaranteed Stock Association, 546
Guideposts, 208
Guilds, craft, 31; merchant, 31

H

Handicrafts, the development of, 31
Head tax, 397, 413
Health, insurance, welfare, and retirement plans under collective bargaining agreements, 539
Health and accident insurance, 526
Health insurance for aged, 533
Hidden taxes, 408
Holding companies, 140
Home market, 425
Homeowners, assisting present and future, 546
Homogeneity of money, 301
HOPE, 483
Horizontal combination, 137
Hospital Insurance Trust Fund, 534
Household inventory, 510
Housing Act, 568
Human welfare, job contributes to, 503

I

Immediate annuity, 527
Imperfect competition, 268
Imports, 422; definition of, 440; importance of our, 422; payment for, 439; U.S. merchandise by continent, 423; why, are often discouraged, 423
Imputed interest, 254
Imputed wages, 223
Income, 67; control of ups and downs in, 374; disposable, 216, 356; disposable personal, 216, 356; distribution of in the United States, 214; distribution of family, 214; does marginal productivity determine? 220; estimating the amount of, 508; fluctuations in production and, may be cumulative, 371; from agriculture, 557; is limited by productivity, 218; money, 68; national, 214, 354, 357; net, 396; of the farm population, 190; per capita disposable personal, 216, 356; personal, 214, 355; taxable, 412; unearned, 249; ways of studying, 68
Income effect, 155
Income of unincorporated marketing enterprises, table of the, 81
Income taxes, 396; arguments for and against, 412; methods of collecting personal, 412; negative, 413; personal, 411
Independent union, 282
Index numbers, price changes are measured by, 197; weighted, 199
Indirect taxes, 408
Individualism, doctrine of, 34
Individual proprietorship, 97
Indorsement, 322
Industrial banks, 255
Industrial jurisprudence, 277
Industrial Revolution, 34
Industrial stage, 33
Industrial union, 278
Industry, infant, 426; the age of modern, 33
Inelastic demand, 157
Infant industries, 426
Inflation, control of, by banks and government, 207; control of, by business and labor, 208; cost-push, 207; definition of, 206; general causes of, 207; impact of, on the distribution of farm income, 558; impact of, on urban blight, 566; pressure of, on farm costs, 556
Inheritance tax, 396, 413
Injunction, 288
Inland bill, 322
Innovations, 370
Installment buying, advantages of, 320; disadvantages of, 320
Installment credit, 317
Installment plan, 319
Installment purchases, differences between account and, 319
Institutions, economic, 34
Insurance, health and accident, 526; life, 528; old-age and survivors, 530; private, 525; property, 527; social, 529; unemployment, 536
Insurance companies, 547; functions of, 526
Insurance policies, 526; types of, 526
Insurance protection, planning life, 529

Intangible goods, 64
Interest, 494; attitude of society toward, 253; contractual, 254; definition of, 254; for capital, 253; gross, 254; how it allocates resources, 261; imputed, 254; net, 254; pure, 254
Interest rates, 254; demand and supply affect, 261; demand and supply determine, 254
International Bank for Reconstruction and Development (IBRD), 447
International cartel, 430
International Development Association, 484
International Monetary Fund (IMF), 447, 484
International trade, future, of our, and finance, 448; increasing, 485; problems of, 444
International Trade Organization (ITO), 431
Interstate business, 518
Interstate Commerce Act, 178
Interstate Commerce Commission, 184, 187
Interstate trade, 518
Intrastate, 518
Inventions, 33
Inventory, household, 510
Investing, saving and, 543
Investment banks, 327
Investment credit, 317
Investment planning, 551
Investments, in real estate, 548
Investment trust, 546
Invisible exports, 440
Invisible imports, 440

J

Job, best for you, 498; information about specific, 499; locating first permanent, 502; preparation for your, 501; security of, 277
Joint costs, 186
Journeyman, 31
Just price, 181

K

Kuder Preference tests, 494

L

Label, brand, 513; descriptive, 513; grade, 513

Labor, cannot be separated from the person, 229; characteristics of, 228; child, 232; demand for, 225; division of, 46; effect of automation on the demand for, 226; is perishable, 228; organized, and politics, 282; protection of, 427; supply of, 228; supply of, does not change quickly, 229; supply of, laws affect, 231; wages for, 223
Labor disputes, methods for settling, 288
Labor force, 228; civilian, 228
Labor-Management Relations Act, 289
Labor Management Reporting and Disclosure Act, 290
Labor resource employment, 142
Labor resources, 7
Labor's League for Political Education, 282
Labor supply, standards of living and, 230
Labor unions, 274; craft, 277; general aims of, 275; government of, 278; independent, 282; industrial, 278; methods used by, 283; organization of, 278; reasons for two types of, 278; specific aims of, 275; types of, 277; ways employers have opposed, 287
Laissez-faire capitalism, 44
Land, 6, 64; definition of, 63; demand for, 245; marginal, 243; rent for, 241; submarginal, 243; supply of is limited, 246; supramarginal, 243
Land erosion, 247
Land resource employment, 142
Landrum-Griffin Act, 290
Law of comparative advantage, 420
Law of comparative cost, 420
Law of demand, 155
Law of demand and supply, 162
Law of diminishing marginal utility, 156
Law of diminishing returns, 219; affects rent, 244
Law of supply, 159
Laws, right-to-work, 284
Legal reserve, 332
Legal tender, 305
Lend-lease program, 445
Liabilities, 510
Licenses, 397, 409; import, 442
Life insurance, 528; endowment plan, 529; kinds of, 528; limited-payment plan, 528; straight, 528; term, 529; whole, 528
Life insurance protection planning, 529
Limited partners, 101
Limited partnership association, 102
Limited partnerships, 101
Limited-payment plan insurance, 528
Limiting output, 284
Liquidation, 117
Liquidity, 119
Liquidity preference, 259
Livelihood, earning a, 503
Loanable funds, demand for, 255; government policy affects the supply of, 260; sources of the supply of, 259; supply of, 259
Loans, consumers', 255; remedial, 255; small, 255
Local governments, services and expenditures of, 388
Lockout, 287
Long run, 170

M

Macroeconomics, 68
Maintenance-of-membership clause, 283
Managed currency, 205
Margin, 551; buying on, 258, 551
Marginal land, 243
Marginal producers, 161
Marginal productivity, 219, 224; does, determine incomes?, 220; importance of, 219; limits wages, 224; proportions of the factors of production affect, 220; theory of wages, 224
Marginal utility, 156; law of diminishing, 156
Market, home, 425
Market-directed price system, preserving freedom in a, 164
Marketing, 80; definition of, 80; economics in, benefit consumers, 89; from producers to consumers, 79; functions of, 83; involves a twofold flow of products, 81; phase of production, 81; roles of middlemen in, 87
Marketing agencies, miscellaneous, 89
Marketing cooperatives, 125

Index

Marketing enterprises, table of the income of unincorporated, 81
Marketing function, 83
Market ratio, 303
Market speculation, case for and against, 91
Marshall Plan, 446
Marx, Karl, 462
Marxian socialism, 464
Master workman, 31
Material goods, 63, 64
Material resources, 476
Median income, 214
Mediation, 288
Medicare, 533
Medium of exchange, money as a, 298, 300
Member banks, 336
Men, employment of, regulation of, 234
Mercantilism, 32; being revived? 44; the era of, 32
Merchandise, puffing, 513
Merchant, 87; commission, 89
Merchant guilds, 31
Merger, 137
Microeconomics, 68
Middlemen, 81; roles of, in marketing, 87
Military necessity, 425, 469
Minor coins, 309
Mint ratio, 303
Mixed economic system, 45
Modern industry, the age of, 33
Monetary policy, 375; bank reserves and, 375; does it work? 377; in practice, 379
Money, as a basis for credit, 300; as a measure of value, 298; as a medium of exchange, 298, 300; as a standard of deferred payment, 300; as a store of value, 299; as wealth, 67; causes of changes in value of, 204; currency and coin outstanding and in circulation, 311; definition of, 297; fiat, 307; functions of, 298; general rules for using wisely, 507; Germany's experience with printing press, 308; getting best value for, 510; in circulation, 311; kinds of our, 308; only the government coins and prints, 301; qualities of, 300; quantity theory of, 205; stabilization of, 205; things that have been used for, 298; velocity of, 204

Money income, 68
Money metals, gold and silver are favorite, 301
Money wages, 223
Monopolistic competition, 176; prices determined by, 175
Monopoly, and prices, 169; definition of, 171; laws necessary to control, 177; natural, 182; origin of private, 171; private, 171; provides a means of setting prices, 171; public, 171; pure, 268
Monopoly price, as related to cost of production, 173; factors affecting, 175
Monopoly profits, 266
Monopsony, 170
Moral suasion, 376; and selective controls, 376
Mortgage, 321
Mortgage bonds, 114
Multiple bank credit contraction, 335
Multiple bank credit expansion, 334
Multiplier principle, cumulative effect of the, on consumer spending, 371
Mutual funds, 546
Mutual savings banks, 545

N

National Aeronautics and Space Administration, 73
National Bank Act, 309
National bank notes, 309
National income, 68, 214, 354, 357; measures of our, 349; sharing the, 213
Nationalism, 425
National Labor Relations Act, 287, 289
National Labor Relations Board, 184, 289, 290
National Mediation Board, 184, 288
National production, measures of our, 349
National Rail Passenger Corporation, 188
National wealth, 67
Nations, creditor, 440; underdeveloped, 473, 474
Natural monopoly, 182; government regulates the prices of some, 182
Natural resources, 6, 21; conservation of our, 22; limited, of some nations, 421; of nations, 421
Nazism, 467
Needs, definition of, 4; organic, 5; personality, 5; physical, 5; psychological, 5; social, 5
Negotiable bill of lading, 439
Net exports of goods and services, 353
Net income, 396
Net interest, 254, 355
Net national product (NNP), 354, 357
Net profit, 266
New Economic Policy (NEP), 466
New York Stock Exchange, 551
Nominal wages, 223
Noncumulative preferred stock, 118
Nondurable consumers' goods, 66
Noneconomic wants, 6
Nonmaterial goods, 64
Nonparticipating preferred stock, 118
Nonprofit corporations, 120
Nonrefund annuity, 528
Nonsilver coins, 308
No-par-value stock, 116
Normal price, 170
Norris-LaGuardia Act, 288, 290

O

Occupational families, major, 498
Occupation groups, 47
Office of Economic Opportunity (OEO), 536
Officers, of a corporation, 111
Official rate of exchange, 442
Old-age, survivors, and disability insurance (OASDI), 530; amount of benefits, 531; fully insured, 532; persons covered by, 530; retired workers who earn incomes, 531
Oligopoly, 176
Open-market operations, 340
Operation Breakthrough, 569
Opportunity cost, 72
Organic needs, 5
Organization for Economic Cooperation and Development (OECD), 446
Organization for European Economic Cooperation (OEEC), 446
Organization of American States (OAS), 433

Organized commodity exchange, 90
Output, limitation of, 284
Overinvestment, 367
Overproduction, 367
Ownership, business, kinds of, 96
Ownership utility, 70

P

Parity price, 189
Participating preferred stock, 117
Partners, general, 101; limited, 101; secret, 102; silent, 102
Partnership agreements, 101
Partnerships, 97, 101; advantages of, 102; danger of disagreement in, 103; difficulty of transferring a partnership interest in, 103; disadvantages of, 102; division of profits of, 103; general, 101; greater capital in, 102; greater efficiency in, 102; kinds of, 101; limited, 101; limited possibilities of, 103; lower income tax liability in, 102; unlimited liability of, 103
Par-value stock, 115
Patent, 172
Patronage refunds, 123
Payments, between nations, 437
Peace Corps, 486
Peak, 366
Personal consumption, 134
Personal consumption expenditures, 351, 357
Personal credit, 317
Personal income (PI), 214, 355, 357; disposable, 355; distribution of, 508; taxes, 411; taxes, methods of collecting, 412
Personality, 496; needs, 5; relation of, to your vocation, 496; traits, 496; traits, specific, 497
Personal motives, 136
Philadelphia Plan, 569
Physical needs, 5
Picketing, 284
Place utility, 69
Political Action Committee, 282
Political freedom, 42; essential to capitalism or free enterprise, 42; increased by acceptance of capitalism, 44
Political order, form of, 479
Politics, and the tariff, 428; organized labor and, 282
Poll tax, 397, 413
Pool, 139
Population change, 131

Population density, relation of, to urban blight, 564
Population explosion, 475
Portability of money, 300
Possession utility, 70
Postwar loans and grants by the United States, 446
Preferential shop arrangement, 283
Preferred stock, 117; cumulative, 118; convertible, 118; non-cumulative, 118; nonparticipating, 118; participating, 117
Premium, insurance, 526
Present worth, 510
Price, 152; administered, 173; monopoly, factors affecting, 175; regulation, by government of some natural monopolies, 182
Price changes, effects of, on amount of investment, 201; effects of, on governmental expenditures, 201; effects of, on profits, 203; effects of, on value of debt payments, 201; effects of, on value of fixed incomes, 201; effects of, on value of investments, 203; effects of, on value of wages, 202; measured by index numbers, 197
Price index numbers, 198; how to calculate, 198
Price level, 198; effects of changes in the, 200, 202
Prices, actions of government affect all, 194; and the value of money, 197; apportion consumers' goods, 152; causes of changes in, and the value of money, 205; changes in, cause changes in rent, 247; determine production, 152; farm, federal government influence, 188; government control of, 181; increasing control by government, 181; influence the use of the factors of production, 152; just, 181; monopoly, cost of production's relation to, 173; monopoly and, 169; normal, 170; parity, 189; stabilization of, 205; ways of determining, 153
Price system, the market-directed, helps to preserve freedom, 164
Pricing, productive-resource, 216
Primary deposit, 328
Principles of diminishing returns, 219

Principles of taxation, 407
Printing-press money, Germany's experience with, 308
Private consumer research agencies, 515
Private corporations, 120
Private insurance, 525
Private monopolies, 171; origin of, 171
Private property, 35
Private security measures, 525
Private wealth, 66
Producer motives, 135
Producers, marginal, 161; submarginal, 161; supramarginal, 161
Producers' goods, 63, 64
Product differentiation, 176
Production, 11, 68; control of ups and downs in, 374; creation of utility, 70; factors of, 213; factors of, affect marginal productivity, 220; fluctuations in, and income may be cumulative, 371; government aids, 72; marketing is a phase of, 81; prices determine, 152; prices influence the use of the factors of, 152; problems of modern, 131; resource problems of modern, 142; the for whom of, 11; the how of, 10; the what and the how many of, 9
Production cooperatives, 125
Production methods, results of change in, 73
Production possibility curve, 15
Production problems, personal consumption change and, 134; population change and, 131
Productive purposes, borrowing for, 256
Productive-resource pricing, importance of, in our economy, 216
Productivity, 219; income is limited by, 218; marginal, 219
Professional organizations, 516
Profit, competitive, 266; economic, 266; for enterprisers, 265; from increased production, 138; gross, 266; meaning of, 266; monopoly, 266; necessary in our society, 269; net, 266; pure, 266; reward for initiative and risk-bearing, 265; should be limited by law? 270; sources of, 267; speculative,

Index

266; wages of management are not pure, 266
Profit motive, 36
Programs, resource conservation, 26
Progressive tax, 405
Promissory note, 321; illustration of a, 322
Promoters' profits, 137
Property, private, 35
Property insurance, 527
Property tax, general, 395, 409
Proportional tax, 405
Proprietorship, sole or individual, 97
Proprietors' income, 355
Prosperity, 366
Protection, arguments for and against tariffs, 424; of labor, 427
Protectionists, 424
Proxy, 141
Psychological needs, 5
Public assistance, 534
Public corporations, 120
Public debt, 399
Public domain, 397
Public employees, retirement systems of, 538
Public monopolies, 171
Public utilities, 183; principles in regulating, 184; regulated by state and federal commissions, 183
Public wealth, 67
Puffing merchandise, 513
Purchasing cooperatives, 125
Purchasing power, relative, 442
Purchasing-power parity of exchange rates, 443
Purchasing-power parity theory, 444
Pure competition, 154; determining prices by, 164; results in normal price, 170
Pure interest, 254
Pure monopoly, 170, 268
Pure profit, 266; calculation of, 267
Pyramiding control, 140

Q

Quantity theory of money, 205

R

Railpax, 188
Railroad rates, 185; how fixed, 187
Railroad service, 185
Railroad workers, social insurance for, 537
Rate discrimination, 184
Rate of exchange, 438; gold-par, 441; official, 442; purchasing-power parity, 443
Rate of return on investment, 549
Rates, 397; interest, 254
Real estate, investments in, 548
Real income, 68
Real wages, 223
Receipts, 393
Reciprocal Trade Agreements Act, 429
Refund annuity, 528
Refunding the debt, 399
Regional trade associations, 433
Regressive tax, 406
Reinvestment, 114
Remedial loans, 255
Rent, 242; agricultural problems connected with, 246; allocates scarce resources economically, 250; changes in prices cause changes in, 247; city slum problem connected with, 248; commercial, 243; contract, 243; demand and supply determine commercial, 246; economic, 243; for land, 241; land erosion reduces, 247; landowners earn, 249; law of diminishing returns affects, 244
Rental income of persons, 355
Research agencies, private consumer, 515
Reserves, banks must keep, 332; excess, 334; legal, 332; working, 332
Resource conservation programs, 26
Resources, air, 25; capital, 7; earth's 24; labor, 7; material, 476; natural, 6, 21; natural conservation of our, 22; of nations of world, 421; water, 24
Retailer, 88
Retail stores, important kinds of, 88
Retirement systems of public employees, 538
Revenue, 393; governmental, 428; merits of different means of obtaining, 409
Revenue Act of 1964, 408
Revenue sharing, 391; concept of, 390
Right-to-work laws, 284
Risk, business, 95; entrepreneurial, 266
Risk bearing, 86; profit reward for, 265
Rochdale pioneers, 122; principles of, 122
Rural development, early stages of, 29
Rural problem, farm flight as a, 556

S

Sabotage, 286
Sale, cash, 90; future, 90
Sales tax, general, 395
Savings, and investing, 543; of business firms, 260; of individuals and families, 259
Savings and loan associations, 328, 546
Savings banks, 327, 544; mutual, 545; stock, 545
Savings bonds, 545; E and H types, 545
Savings certificates of deposit, 332
Scabs, 284
Scale of living, 230
Scientific method, of formulating a theory, 16
Secondary boycott, 284
Secret partner, 102
Securities and Exchange Commission, 184, 551
Seigniorage, 302
Selective controls, 376; and moral suasion, 376
Self-employed persons covered by OASDI, 530; contribution rates, 535
Selling, 83; buying and, between nations, 419
Seniority, rating, 277
Severance taxes, 411
Shares, of stock, 115
Sherman Antitrust Act, 178
Shifting a tax, 408
Shop, closed, 283
Shortage, 164
Silent partner, 102
Silver bullion, 308
Silver certificates, 308
Silver coins, 308
Single-tax proposal, 249
Slowdowns, 286
Small business, competitive threat to survival of, 104; opportunity areas in, 104; problem of

survival of, 103; requisites for survival of, 105
Small Business Act of 1953, 105
Small Business Administration, 105
Small loans, 255
Social insurance, 529; for railroad workers, 537
Socialism, definition of, 454; experience of Great Britain with, 461; Marxism, 464; nature of, in the USSR, 463; policy of, 461; program of, 460; variations of, 454
Socialists, charges of, against free enterprise, 454
Socialist Party of the United States, 461
Social needs, 5
Social overhead capital, defined, 562
Social security, tax rates, 535; veterans' programs for, 538
Social security account number, employees' application for, 531
Social Security Act, 529, 533, 536
Social Security Administration, 529, 537
Socioeconomic cultural change, urban blight and, 565
Soil bank, 192
Soil Bank Act of 1956, 192
Soil Conservation Act, 191
Soil Conservation Service, 248
Sole proprietorships, 97; advantages of, 97; burden of losses in, 100; disadvantages of, 99; ease of beginning, 98; ease of dissolution of, 99; freedom from special property and income taxes, 99; length of existence in, 101; liability for debts of the business in, 100; limited capital in, 99; limited managerial ability in, 100; personal relations of employer and employees in, 98; pride of ownership in, 98
Special assessments, 397, 409
Specialization, according to tasks, 48; advantages of, 48; by geographic regions, 48; by stages of production, 47; by trade or profession, 47; definition of, 46; disadvantages of, 50; forms of, 47; the nature of, 45; the role of, in our economy, 53
Specialized capital, 64, 65
Speculation, borrowing for, 258; defined, 258; market, 91
Speculative profits, 266
Stability of value of money, 301
Stabilizers, automatic, 377
Standardization, 84
Standard of living, 230; and the labor supply, 230
Standard wages rates, 275
State governments, services and expenditures of, 389
Statics, definition of, 29
Stock, book value of, 115; capital, 114, 115; classification of, 117; common, 117; cumulative preferred, 118; convertible preferred, 118; definition of, 115; investing in, 549; noncumulative preferred, 118; nonparticipating preferred, 118; no-par-value, 116; participating preferred, 117; par-value, 115; preferred, 117; shares of, 115; versus bonds, 550; watered, 141
Stock certificate, 113; illustration of a, 113
Stock dividends, 112
Stock exchange, 551
Stockholders, 110
Stock savings bank, 545
Storage, 85
Straight life insurance, 528
Strike, 284; slowdown, 286; sympathetic, 284
Strikebreakers, 284
Submarginal land, 243
Submarginal producers, 161
Subsidiary companies, 140
Subsidy, 114
Substitution effect, 155
Supplementary unemployment benefit (SUB), 237
Supply, 159; affects wages, 235; demand and, determine commercial rent, 246; demand and, determine interest rates, 254; law of, 159; of labor, 228; of labor, laws affect, 231; of land is limited, 246
Supply curve, 160
Supply of loanable funds, 259; government policy affects, 260; sources of the, 259
Supply schedule, 159
Supramarginal land, 243
Supramarginal producers, 161
Supreme Soviet, 464
Surety, 255
Surplus, 112, 164
Sympathetic strike, 284

T

Taft-Hartley Act, 283, 284, 286, 289, 290
Tangible goods, 64
Tariff Commission, 429
Tariff restrictions, 429
Tariffs, 396, 423; politics and, 428
Tax, 395; business, 411; capitation, 396, 413; consumption, 395, 410; degressive, 406; direct, 408; estate, 396, 413; excess-profits, 270, 411; excise, 395; general property, 395, 409; general sales, 395; gift, 396; gross-receipts, 396; head, 397, 413; hidden, 408; income, 396; indirect, 408; inheritance, 396, 413; personal income, 411; poll, 397, 413; progressive, 405; proportional, 405; regressive, 406; severance, 411; shifting a, 408
Taxable income, 412
Taxation, ability-to-pay theory of, 405; benefit theory of, 405; canons of, 407; equity in, 404; justice in, 404; principles of, 407; Smith's four canons of, 407
Taxes, for controlling business cycle, 408; for paying necessary expenses of government, 407; purposes for which levied, 407; under OASDI, 535
Tax evasion, 409
Tax rates, social security, 535
Tax structure, improvement of, 413
Tax system, our, 404
Technological revolution, the age of, 55
Technological unemployment, 73
Technology, 55, 478
Term insurance, 529
Thrift, the encouragement of, 546
Time deposit, 331
Time utility, 70
Tobacco Acreage-Poundage Act, 192
Totalitarianism, 467; economy under, 467; political features of, 467
Trade, favorable balance of, 441; free, 423; international, increasing, 485; international problems of, 444; unfavorable balance of, 441; with other people, 420

Index

Trade acceptance, 322
Trade agreement, 283
Trade associations, 515; regional, 433
Transfer payments, 357
Transportation, 85
Treasury notes of 1890, 310
Trough, 367
Trusts, 139

U

Underdeveloped nations, 473; conditions in the, 480; how we can help, 483; in ferment, 475; literacy, education, and technology in, 486; loans and grants to, for production purposes, 484; our interest in, 473, 483; our interest in the problems of, 473, 480
Underinvestment, 367
Unearned income, 249
Unemployment, technological, 73
Unemployment insurance, 536
Unfavorable balance of trade, 441
Union federations, 280
Union labels, 284
Union-management cooperation, 291
Union membership in the United States, 281
Union of Soviet Socialist Republics (USSR), constitution of the, 464; government of the, 463
Union recognition, 283
Unions, credit, 255, 547
Union security, 283
Union-shop agreement, 283
United States Department of Agriculture, 508, 520
United States Employment Service, 496
United States Maritime Commission, 184
United States notes, 309
United States Patent Office, 172
United States Postal Service, 520
United States Public Health Service, 513, 519
United States Treasury and savings bonds, 545
Unit of value, 299
Urban blight, a city problem, 564; consumer response to, 568; defined, 564; governmental response to, 568; inflation and, 566; population density and, 564; private producer response to, 568; socioeconomic cultural change and, 565; some causal factors of, 564; some interrelated aspects of, 567; static forces and, 566
Urban economic life, 31
Utilities, public, principles in regulating, 184
Utility, 68, 151; form, 69; marginal, 156; ownership, 70; place, 69; possession, 70; production as the creation of, 70; time, 70
Utility commissions, federal, 184

V

Value, 151; economic, 151; exchange, 151
Value of money, 204
Value-of-service principle, 185
Variable costs, 173
Velocity of money, 204
Vertical combination, 137
Veterans Administration, 569
Veterans' programs for social security, 538
Visible exports, 440
Visible imports, 440
Vocational counseling, aims of, 493
Voluntary arbitration, 288

W

Wage and Hour Law, 234
Wage rates, 223; standard, 275
Wages, definition of, 223; how demand and supply affect, 235; imputed, 223; marginal productivity limits, 224; money, 223; nominal, 223; of management are not pure profits, 266; other factors affecting, 236; raising and maintaining, 276; real, 223
Wages and Hours Administration, 184
Wages of management, 224
Wagner Act, 289
Walsh-Healey Act of 1936, 234
Wants, definition of, 5; economic, 6; noneconomic, 6; satisfying, in different societies, 14
War, threat of, 401
War on poverty, 536
Watered stock, 141
Water resources, 24
Wealth, 66; national, 67; private, 66; public, 67
Weather Bureau, 72
Weighted index numbers, 199
Wheeler-Lea Act, 519
Whole life insurance policy, 528
Wholesalers, 88
Women, regulation of the employment of, 234
Work force, 476
Working conditions, improvement of, 276
Working reserve, 332
Workmen's compensation, 537
World bank, 448, 484

Y

Yellow-dog contract, 287